THE AUSTRIANS

THE
AUSTRIANS

A THOUSAND-YEAR ODYSSEY

Gordon Brook-Shepherd

CARROLL & GRAF PUBLISHERS, INC.
NEW YORK

First Carroll & Graf edition 1997
First paperback edition 1998

Carroll & Graf Publishers, Inc.
19 West 21st Street
New York, NY 10010

Library of Congress Cataloging-in-Publication Data is available.
ISBN: 0-7867-0520-5

Manufactured in the United States of America

To the memory of 'Nata',
Princess Natalie Hohenlohe-Schillingsfürst

A true Austrian and a much-loved family friend

CONTENTS

viii CONTENTS

ILLUSTRATIONS

The victory that launched a dynasty. On 26 August 1278, Count Rudolph Habsburg destroys King Ottokar of Bohemia, his rival for the crown of the Holy Roman Empire, at the battle of the Marchfeld near Vienna. (*Bildarchiv der Österreichischen Nationalbibliothek*)

The siege of Vienna, 1683. The Austrian relief forces, headed by King Sobieski of Poland, rout the 200,000-strong Turkish army camped at the gates of the beleaguered capital. (*Mary Evans Picture Library*)

Prince Eugen of Savoy (1663–1736), the French-born servant of the Habsburgs whose military and political deeds first made Austria into a European power. (*Mary Evans Picture Library*)

Maria Theresa (1717–1780), the only woman to reign over the Habsburg empire. (*AKG, London*)

The rulers of the rival German dynasties, the Hohenzollern King Frederick II of Prussia and the Emperor Joseph II of Austria, at Mährisch-Neustadt in 1770. (*Bildarchiv der Österreichischen Nationalbibliothek*)

Napoleon, scourge of the old European order. (*AKG, London*)

Wolfgang Amadeus Mozart (1756–1791). (*Bildarchiv der Österreichischen Nationalbibliothek*)

Franz Schubert (1797–1828). (*Österreichisches Bundeskanzleramt*)

Prince Clement Metternich (1773–1859), for nearly forty years Foreign Minister of the Monarchy. (*AKG, London*)

Prince Felix Schwarzenberg (1800–1852). A proud faith in Austria, bad in himself. (*Bildarchiv der Österreichischen Nationalbibliothek*)

Königgrätz, 3 July 1866. The battle at which the disciplined Prussians defeated the poorly-led and badly-equipped Austrians and sealed the supremacy of the Hohenzollerns over the Habsburgs in the German world. (*Bildarchiv der Österreichischen Nationalbibliothek*)

Prince Otto Bismark (1815–1898), Germany's 'Iron Chancellor' from 1871 to 1890 and the greatest European statesman of his time. (*AKG, London*)

Foreign Minister 1916–1918. (*Bildarchiv der Österreichischen Nationalbibliothek*)

The toll of war: Austro-Hungarian troops after the bloody battle for the key Galician fortress of Przemyśl, 3 June 1915. (*Österreichisches Bundeskanzleramt*)

14 August 1918. The Emperor Charles arrives for his last meeting with Emperor William II, held at the Prussian Army Headquarters in Spa, Belgium. (*Bildarchiv der Österreichischen Nationalbibliothek*)

Cheers, and drizzle, outside the Vienna Parliament as the First Austrian Republic is proclaimed, 12 November 1918. (*Österreichisches Bundeskanzleramt*)

Karl Renner, the Socialist Chancellor of the post-war Republic, signs the dictated peace of St Germain, 10 September 1919. (*Österreichisches Bundeskanzleramt*)

15 July 1927: left-wing mobs set fire to the Ministry of Justice in Vienna. (*Bildarchiv der Österreichischen Nationalbibliothek*)

February 1934: a victim of the Austrian civil war. (*Österreichisches Bundeskanzleramt*)

Ignaz Seipel (1876–1932), the prelate-statesman who dominated the Republic's right-wing rule in the 1920s. (*Österreichisches Bundeskanzleramt*)

Engelbert Dollfuss (1892–1934), the heartbeat of a new Austrian patriotism which Hitler silenced. (*Österreichisches Bundeskanzleramt*)

Kurt Schuschnigg (1897–1977), the Austrian Chancellor who yielded to Hitler because he 'could not shed German blood'. (*Bildarchiv der Österreichischen Nationalbibliothek*)

Wilhelm Miklas, the right-wing Austrian President who held out against Hitler to the bitter end. (*Österreichisches Bundeskanzleramt*)

14 March 1938: Hitler enters a half-passive, half-enthusiastic Vienna after the bloodless *Anschluss*. (*Österreichisches Institut für Zeitgeschichte*)

12 March 1938: the mayfly Austrian pro-Nazi Cabinet of Seyss-Inquart. (*Österreichisches Institut für Zeitgeschichte*)

Rampant anti-Semitism moves in at Hitler's heels: in Vienna, a portly Austrian Nazi supervises the daubing of 'Jew' on one of the capital's many closed-down Jewish shops. (*Österreichisches Institut für Zeitgeschichte*)

The grim entrance gates to Mauthausen concentration camp. More than 35,000 prisoners perished here. (*Österreichisches Bundeskanzleramt*)

April 1945. Red Army troops storm the outskirts of Vienna. (*Österreichisches Bundeskanzleramt*)

MAPS

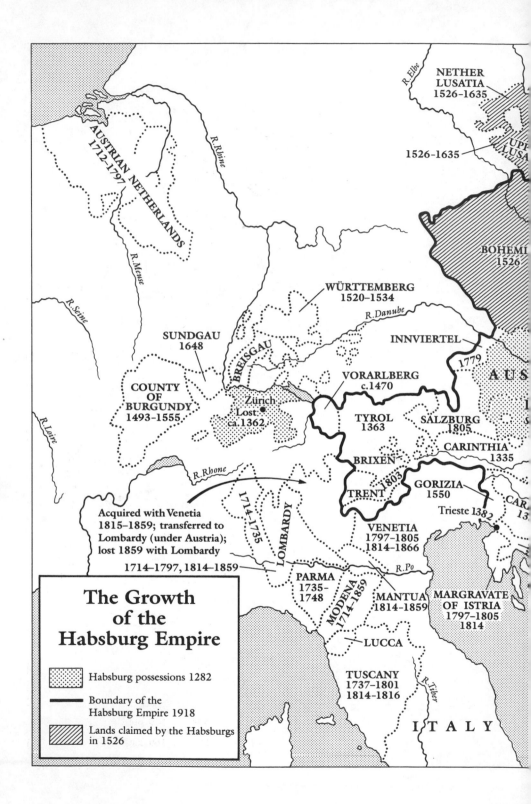

The Growth of the Habsburg Empire

NETHER LUSATIA
1526–1635

1526–1635

UPP
LUSA

AUSTRIAN NETHERLANDS
1712–1797

R.Elbe

R.Rhine

BOHEMI
1526

R.Meuse

R.Seine

WÜRTTEMBERG
1520–1534

R.Danube

INNVIERTEL

SUNDGAU
1648

BREISGAU

1779

AUS

VORARLBERG
c.1470

COUNTY
OF
BURGUNDY
1493–1555

Zürich
Lost
ca.1362

TYROL
1363

SALZBURG
1805

CARINTHIA
1335

R.Loire

BRIXEN

1803

GORIZIA
1550

CAR
13

R.Rhone

TRENT

Trieste 1382

Acquired with Venetia
1815–1859; transferred to
Lombardy (under Austria);
lost 1859 with Lombardy

1714–1735

LOMBARDY

VENETIA
1797–1805
1814–1866

1714–1797, 1814–1859

R.Po

PARMA
1735–
1748

MODENA
1714–1859

MANTUA
1814–1859

MARGRAVATE
OF ISTRIA
1797–1805
1814

**The Growth
of the
Habsburg Empire**

LUCCA

TUSCANY
1737–1801
1814–1816

R.Tiber

Habsburg possessions 1282

Boundary of the
Habsburg Empire 1918

Lands claimed by the Habsburgs
in 1526

ITALY

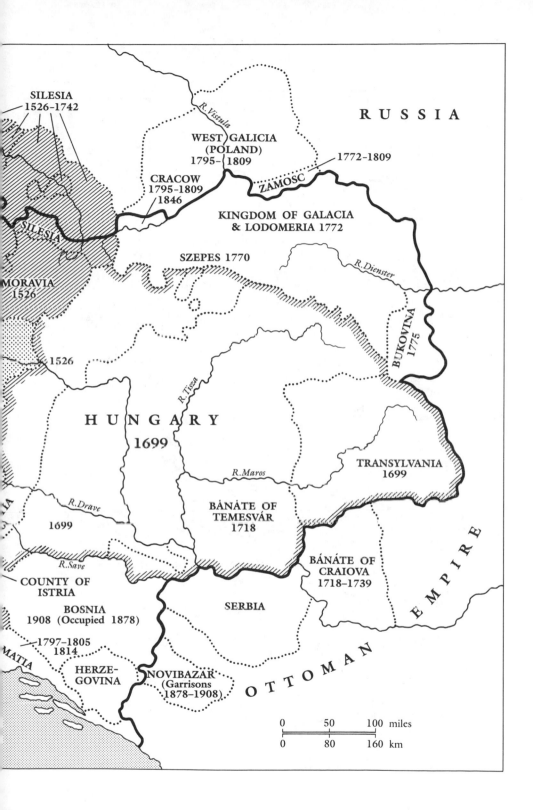

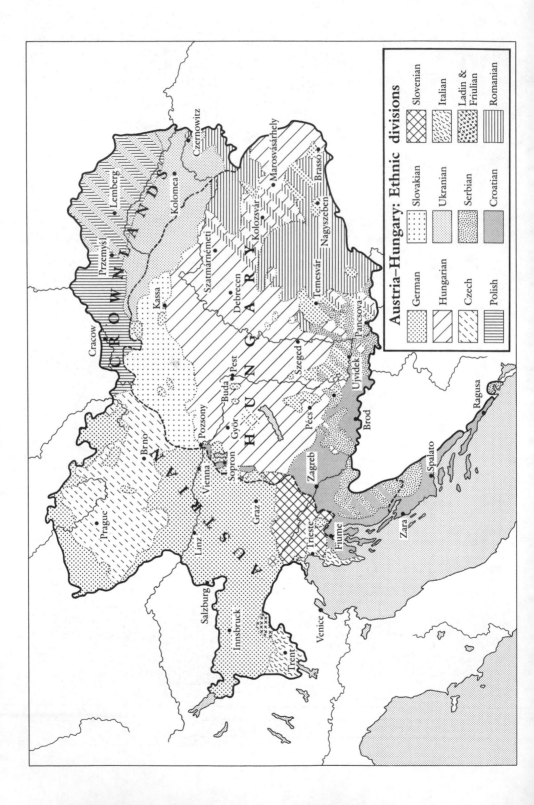

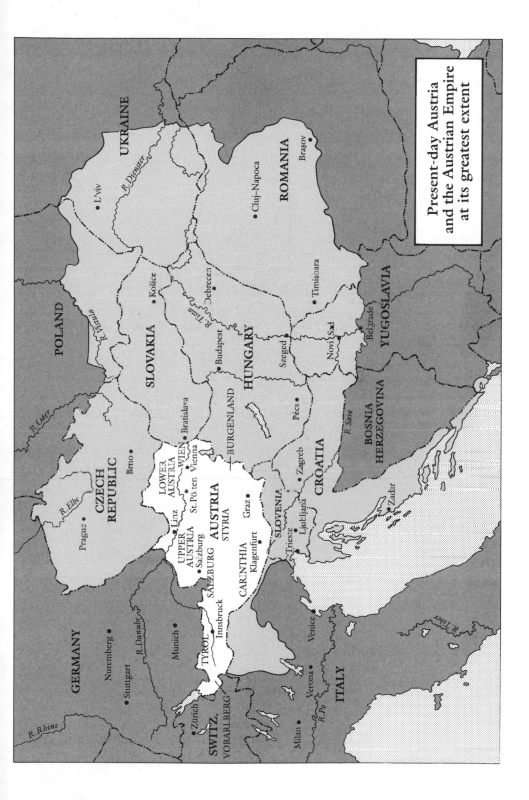

Present-day Austria
and the Austrian Empire
at its greatest extent

FOREWORD

1996, THE YEAR IN WHICH the Austrians celebrated a thousand years
of their recorded existence, seemed a good time to try to sum up their
struggle to find their own role in the world. So far as I am concerned,
this will be a signing-off as well as a summing-up. Half of my sixteen
books have concerned their Habsburg dynasty, the Danube Basin over
which it ruled, the Great War which consumed it, and the Austrian
Republics which succeeded it. If I put pen to paper again (and that is
still the antiquated way I work), it will not be on this subject, on which
I have said all I can.

This book is not, however, an exercise in repetition. To begin with,
it is the first attempt to tell the millennium story of this fascinating (but
often maddening) people right down to the present day, always in
terms of their unceasing search for their own identity. Their quest for
nationhood has been blocked on the one hand by their multi-national
training and traditions, and on the other by the fateful Germanic tie
that runs throughout their history. The quest starts afresh now that they
are part of a united Europe alongside Germany, with their Danubian
neighbours eventually to join in as partners.

The book has a unique feature in that it combines half a century of
academic research on the subject with a similar span of personal experience of the country and its people. First as a General Staff officer on
the post-war Allied Commission in Vienna, then as a foreign corres-
pondent and, in recent years, as the writer and presenter of various
television documentaries on the Monarchy, I have been in continuous
contact with Austria and its joys and problems ever since 1945. So
much so that the original concept of the work, as agreed with the
publisher, was that this fifty-year period should be cast in auto-
biographical form.

The idea was abandoned at my own suggestion, and this for a variety
of reasons. To begin with, though I was a lieutenant-colonel at a

precocious age in Vienna, this was a rank at which one could observe and execute policy, but not shape it. Even less did that apply to the twelve succeeding years (1948–60), when I ran the Central and South-East European Bureau of the *Daily Telegraph*, again based in Vienna. I witnessed many of the seminal events of those years – notably the struggle of Tito's Yugoslavia with the Kremlin, and the Hungarian revolution – and was able to indulge in some fascinating 'extra-mural' activities in the region. But, for the most part, one was on the outside looking in. Too many memoir-writers from the media have tried to inflate their own importance by pretending that, for them, it was the other way round. I wanted to avoid that distortion.

I mention all this because I fear that the reader may well find it irksome that there are so many references in the latter part of the book to my key sources being also my personal friends. I can assure him that this number could, without difficulty, have been trebled. So far as possible, I have confined such references to footnotes linked to direct quotation of original material. Thus, as regards the Monarchy, I have drawn on a friendship of some thirty years with that wonderful royal figure, the former Empress Zita of Austria-Hungary (who only died in 1989, aged nearly ninety-seven), and her eldest son Archduke Otto Habsburg, thankfully still alive and thriving today as the senior member of the Strasbourg European Parliament. Between them, they provided not only a wealth of their own reminiscences but the fullest access ever given to any outside eye to the Habsburg family papers, one of the richest of Europe's unpublished royal archives.

I got to know well most of the leading figures of the First Austrian Republic (1918–38), including the ill-fated Chancellor Kurt Schuschnigg, while researching my book *The Anschluss* and a biography of Engelbert Dollfuss. During the Second World War I had been in touch – though intermittently and at far remove – with developments in Austria while serving with Military Intelligence in London. For obvious reasons, my contacts with the leaders of the Second post-war Republic have been the most extensive. I even had the privilege of being '*per du*', i.e. on the closest friendship terms, with both the great right-wing Chancellor Leopold Figl and his equally formidable socialist rival and successor Bruno Kreisky. (This caused much raising of eyebrows in both camps: the Austrians of the day were not used to their great ideological gap being bridged by anyone.)

I have had dozens of friendly helpers in the preparation of the present work. I would like to single out, on the diplomatic front, the Austrian Foreign Minister, Dr Alois Mock; his genial Secretary-General, Dr Wolfgang Schallenberg; and three successive Austrian envoys to London, Ambassadors Thomas, Magrutsch and Hennig. Dr Bernard Stillfried has been of great assistance in the cultural field, and Dr Manfried Rauchensteiner, Director of the Military History Museum in Vienna, equally valuable on matters of military history. Fritz Molden and Carl Szokoll were among those who, from their own vivid experiences, provided insights into Austria's brave but blighted wartime resistance movements. The Governor of Styria, Dr Josef Krainer (whose father I well remember, holding that same post before him), gave a frank picture of Nazi and post-Nazi life in one of Austria's key provinces. I owe special thanks to Sektionschef Dr Neumayr and his charming deputy, Dr Ingeborg Schweikert, in the Federal Chancellory for organising my recent researches in Vienna.

In London, I have profited from the encyclopaedic knowledge of an old friend, Hans-Heinrich Coudenhove, who pointed out several errors of spelling, time and place in the first draft. This agreeably continued a family tradition: it was his father, Gerolf, who translated two of my earliest books into German, placidly amending the text as he went. Both of my admirable editors, Richard Johnson and Robert Lacey, also gave close attention to the final draft, which was somewhat late in arriving and considerably over-length when it did. I am sure there are still some slips which have eluded all of us. This, after all, is an immensely complex picture: a thousand years of European history passed through the prism of the Austrian experience.

I am aware of inconsistencies as between the English and German spelling of names. They are deliberate in the sense that the form chosen is the one with which I am comfortable. I feel equally at home with Franz Josef or Francis Joseph, but could never think of Karl Lueger, for example, as 'Charles', or Georg von Schönerer as 'George'. The word 'England' is used because that was how Great Britain was generally referred to, especially on the Continent, at that time (though 'British' was sometimes used as an adjective). As for our sovereigns, Victoria and Edward VII were almost always spoken of as Queen and King of England – and thought of themselves as such.

Finally, I would like to give yet another vote of thanks to my longtime secretary Susan Small, who has once again turned an untidy manuscript into a perfect typescript – this time working from her new home in South Africa. Chapter after chapter has winged its way safely, if not speedily, from the Chilterns to Cape Town and back. Only after the last one had returned did it occur to me that we might have used fax.

GORDON BROOK-SHEPHERD
Turville Park
Oxon

Foreword to the Paperback Edition

It is pleasant to be able to report that in the short space of time between the appearance of the hardback and paperback editions of this book, Austria has been able to smooth away one awkward trace of its past. The present republic inherited, along with its post-1918 constitutional laws, the demand that any member of the former Habsburg dynasty who wished to return to the country should renounce not only all dynastic claims, but even the membership of his own family.

The head of the house, Archduke Otto, once described this to me as 'a madness that could only have come from the brain of some indescribable small-minded fanatic'. None the less, he felt obliged to agree to it thirty years ago in order to take up his seat in the European Parliament, where he is now the senior member. However, two of his brothers, the Archdukes Felix and Karl Ludwig, now aged seventy-nine and seventy-seven respectively, refused to accept this condition. Both remained in exile until March 1996, when Felix descended unannounced on Vienna and publicly levelled a legal pistol at the government's head. As Austria had the previous year joined the European Union, he argued that it was now obliged to accept the ruling of freedom of movement for all EU citizens. An embarrassed government took no action against him, said it would urgently ponder the matter, and rapidly dropped the embarrassing clause altogether. It is said to be privately relieved that Brussels legislation has enabled the present-day republic to come to terms at last with its illustrious past.

GORDON BROOK-SHEPHERD
June 1996

PROLOGUE

===

A Styrian Painting

EARLY IN THE EIGHTEENTH CENTURY, an unknown artist living in the Habsburg duchy of Styria painted his 'Short Description of the Peoples of Europe, together with their Characteristics' (to put his flowery German title into English). Across the top of the panel are stretched the beautifully coloured portraits of the ten figures he has chosen. These range from 'Spanier' on the left to 'Tirk oder Griech' on the far right, a reminder that, in those days, the Ottoman empire still sprawled somnolently over what became modern Greece. Each is shown in miniature full-length, wearing full national costumes which light up the contrasts in the continent they depict. There is everything from silk turbans to cockaded helmets and plumed soft hats among the headgear. Outer garments vary from brocaded cloaks, with swords or sabres, sticking out behind, to rather foppish 'redingotes', with not a weapon in sight. One feature is unvaried. Each personage is male, affirming that, in the Europe of the day, only a man could appear as the representative of his people. The portraits are only the beginning of the story.

Running downwards from the shoes or riding boots of each figure is a table listing seventeen characteristics of the nation to which he belongs. 'Temperament' is the first of these. A rather bizarre entry 'Way of Death', the last. Though not as sure with his pen as he is with his brush, the artist makes some telling points. Thus, the 'Engerländer' is declared to be 'Changeable like the Moon' as regards his 'Worship of God' and 'Now this one, now that' when it comes to describing his sovereign; fair comment on the upheavals which had shaken the crown and the religious faith of England during the previous two centuries. The great maritime people are duly entered as 'Sea Heroes' under 'Special Art of War' and, accordingly, have 'In Water' as their most likely ending.

Quirks abound. It is not at all clear, for example, why only the Swiss should be singled out as 'Cruel' under the 'Character' column, nor why the Poles should be accused of 'Believing anybody' when it comes to religion. But the oddest (and most significant) thing of all to modern eyes about this 'Table of Peoples', as it became known, was something which evidently appeared perfectly natural to the artist. Though he was a subject of the Austrian Monarchy – living indeed in one of the oldest hereditary lands of the 'Casa Austria' – there is no mention of Austrians among the ten nations of his Europe. They are simply subsumed under one composite heading, 'The Germans'.

That he was thinking, even vaguely, of his own people is shown by the way he enters 'Emperor' under the column 'Ruled by Whom?' In the early eighteenth century, only the German-speaking Austrians had their 'Kaiser'; the sovereigns whose courts spread across the rest of the Teutonic world were then an assortment of scores of kings and prince-lings. Yet this image of separate identity lurks only at the back of his mind. In the forefront is the Germanic imprint. This ethnic blur, this lack of national profile or focus was to have debilitating and, ultimately, disastrous consequences for the Austrian people in the two centuries which lay ahead. It was rooted in some nine centuries of tangled history which had gone before.

PART ONE

THE PATH TO EMPIRE

I

A Germanic Cradle

IT WAS A COLOURLESS BEGINNING for a people destined to know such splendour and high drama. Their territory, which was eventually to be called 'Austria', started life as the military colony of a foreign kingdom, the 'Eastern March' of the great Frankish ruler Charlemagne. Having conquered most of western Christendom in fifty-three campaigns waged during the last quarter of the eighth century, he had been duly crowned as its emperor by Pope Leo XII in Rome on Christmas Day of 800 A.D.

According to some chronicles, Charlemagne felt misgivings at having the golden crown of a revived Roman empire placed on his head. He was a German king whose base lay north of the Alps. Now he was donning the mantle of the Caesars, whose power had centred always on the Mediterranean. History was to bear out those misgivings with a vengeance. His immediate concern, however, was to protect those conquests which had now been sanctified, and one of the most dangerous threats was posed by the formidable Avars to the east. There thus arose, in 803, the 'Avarian Mark', to give the future Austria another of its earliest names. This was a belt of land stretching along the middle Danube from the River Enns to the outskirts of the city which was to become 'Wienne'. German Franks were already settled there, along with the flotsam of other tribes left behind by the ebb and flow of those great migrations which followed the collapse of Roman power. Now its inhabitants had imposed upon them a task they were to be called on to fulfil down the ages: the defence of Western Europe against whatever threatened it from the East. They were not chosen because of who they were but because of where they were. The Austrians of the future thus entered history not as a tribal (let alone national) entity, but as a geographical concept.

Though their task stayed the same, their imperial taskmasters changed. The Carolingian empire, already partitioned soon after the great man's death in 814, was finally extinguished in 888. Western Europe was again plunged into chaos and the invaders again stormed in through the breaches: the Saracens into Rome; the Vikings along the Atlantic; the Magyars, a new menace, from the steppes. Yet, once more, the hour produced its man, this time the Saxon king Otto the Great. He first subdued his rivals in the German lands and was crowned King of Germany on Charlemagne's throne at Aachen in 936. In 955 he inflicted a massive defeat on the Magyars at Lechfeld, thus securing his eastern frontier. In 961, on a second expedition to restore order south of the Alps, he assumed the kingship of Lombardy and, a year later, was crowned Emperor of Rome by Pope John XII. That fateful link between German military might and a nebulous Roman splendour, first forged by Charlemagne, was now strengthened. The kings of Germany became, nominally, the secular lords of the world. The task was to prove both exhausting and unreal.

Like Charlemagne before him, Otto's immediate task was to cushion his borders with military security belts. So, as regards the middle Danube, the old 'Carolingian Mark' now re-emerged as the 'Ottonian Mark', but with a difference. The territory now acquired a profile of its own, even if this was only in a state of feudal subjection to yet another German prince. In 976 the Mark was bestowed by the Emperor on the capable house of Babenberg who ruled over it in unbroken succession for the next 270 years – first as margraves and finally as dukes. (Like their Habsburg successors, they were never crowned as its kings.)

Some fuzzy outlines of an Austrian identity now began to emerge. In 996, for example, only twenty years after the Babenbergs took over, the name *'Ostarrîchi'* appears for the first time in writing to describe the lands over which they ruled.* On 1 November of that year, the third of the Ottonian emperors made a gift to the bishopric of Freising of a property in Neuhofen an der Ybbs. The Latin parchment describes the village as lying in the *'regione vulgari vocabulo ostarrîchi'*, or 'the area commonly known as Austria' ('Oesterreich').

Two things need to be stressed about this birth certificate. The first is that it still describes not a distinctive people, but the inhabitants of a strategic area. Throughout the early middle ages this mark of the

---

* There are some Austrian scholars who place it even earlier. The word 'Ostmark', on the other hand, was an invention of nineteenth-century German nationalists.

Babenbergs continued to be called in Latin '*provincia orientalis*', '*terra orientalis*' or even, sometimes, simply '*oriens*'. Given the position it occupied at the crossroads of Europe, where trade routes, valleys and rivers converged, geopolitics was always to control its fate. But something else, apart from the strong Germanic birthmark, was in this people's cradle, namely the dynastic tie. To add to the confusion as to what the infant should be called, it was also, in the early days, known as the '*Marchio Liutpold*', after its first ruler, the Margrave Leopold.

Under Leopold's successors (he died in 994 of a poisoned arrow mysteriously directed at him at a tournament in Würzburg) the Margravate was steadily extended. By the middle of the twelfth century, the Babenberg realm stretched eastwards to the River Leitha, later to become a fixed border with the Magyars; northwards to the River Thaya, to form a frontier line with Bohemia; and westwards towards Salzburg. 1156 marked a milestone in its history and, therefore, in the history of the Austrians. On 17 September of that year the German Emperor Frederick I raised the Margravate to the dignity of a Duchy with far-reaching independence from the empire. These new Dukes of Austria were exempted from all duties except attendance at the Imperial Diets. Their military obligations were confined to following their emperor only in campaigns directed against their own neighbours, i.e. to protect themselves.

That same year, the Babenbergs moved their residence to Vienna, the old Roman town of Vindobona; hugely extended, it now became an important economic and cultural centre. It is also at this time that the black single-headed eagle appears as their coat of arms, the first of many eagles of varying designs under which Austrians were to serve. In 1192 the sister duchy of Styria, home of our eighteenth-century painter, was added to the Babenberg realm. It was becoming a small unofficial Monarchy, and fifty years later there was talk of turning these 'Dukes of Austria and Styria' into proper kings; indeed, Duke Frederick II was said to have already received his royal ring from the German emperor of the day. But in 1246 that same Duke Frederick fell on the battlefield of Ebenfurth, fighting against the Hungarians, and with him died the last of his line in male descent.* The time of the Babenbergs in Austria was over.

* Duke Frederick wore on the field the red-white-red band of colours which became the emblem of Austria. Legend – but legend only! – ascribes the origin of these colours to the bloody wound stripe which stained the white cloak of his predecessor Duke Leopold V, a wound received while fighting in the Holy Land as a Crusader in 1190.

Nothing illustrates the vulnerability of Vienna as a crossroads capital more than the thirty years of chaos which now followed. The last Babenberg duke had fallen on the eastern Magyar frontier of his realm. The man who came to claim his possessions was a Slav, marching in from the north. And the man who, in turn, wrested the Austrian lands from him came from the west, with a hereditary power-base far away in what is now German Switzerland.

The Slav claimant was the Przemysl Crown Prince, later King Ottokar II of Bohemia. He settled in Vienna in December 1251, declared himself to be Duke of both Austria and Styria, and tried to buttress his claim the following April by taking for his wife Margaret, sister of the last Babenberg, despite the fact that she was twenty-six years older than himself. The wider world of German princes was plunged into equal confusion at the time; their Roman empire had fallen into desuetude following the death in 1250 of its last great emperor, Frederick II, who had anyway been declared deposed by the Vatican five years before. How was the void to be filled and how was Ottokar to be displaced?

In 1273 the Imperial electors met to choose, not a new emperor, but simply a German king. Their choice fell on the fifty-five-year-old Swabian Swiss Count Rudolph IV of Habsburg. He was selected not because he was the most powerful candidate in the field, but because, on the contrary, his 'Hausmacht', or feudal power-base,* was modest and so, presumably, would be any of his short-term family ambitions. Few calculations have proven more erroneous. The compromise candidate was to demonstrate the force of the French saying: 'Rien ne dure comme le provisoire'. When, five years later, on 26 August 1278, Rudolph triumphed over King Ottokar on the plains of the Marchfeld east of Vienna, he took up a dominion over the Danube Basin which the Habsburg eagle was to maintain for six and a half centuries.**

First the Carolingians, then the Babenbergs and now the Habsburgs: this was the third Germanic ruling house to be set in place, without their asking, over the people of 'Ostarrîchi'. As the centuries rolled on, this Habsburg sovereignty must have seemed eternal. It brought to its

* His *Stammschloss* or ancestral castle was Habichtsburg near the upper Rhine in Aargau, from which castle the family took its name.
** However, Rudolph's death in 1291 put an end, for the time being, to the dignity of German kingship. His successor was Albrecht of Nassau, and after him the electors chose kings from Luxembourg, Bavaria and Bohemia before the Habsburgs returned in 1438. From then on, with one trifling break, they had an unbroken run of 360 years.

Austrian subjects, as prime servants of the dynasty, an ever-increasing share of power, privilege and prosperity. The cost was the stunting of their own sense of identity.

This is perhaps the moment to move the slide-rule sideways across Western Europe to show how that sense of national consciousness had already developed among peoples like the English and the French. Only then can we realise how heavily such feelings lay smothered for the Austrians under their heavy dynastic cloaks.

It was as far back as 731–2 that the Venerable Bede, working in his Northumbrian monastery of St Paul at Jarrow, compiled his *Ecclesiastical History of Britain, and especially of the race of the English*. His purpose was to describe the conversion to Christianity of the Anglo-Saxon tribes; and it needed five tomes of the *Historia Ecclesiastica* to take the story from the Roman raids of Julius Caesar in 55–54 B.C. down to the enthronement of Saint Augustine as the first Archbishop of Canterbury six centuries later. The 'Anguls' were a German tribe who, together with Saxons and Jutes, had migrated to Britain in the fifth century, displacing the Celts (the original 'Briten') and establishing a patchwork of seven kingdoms in their place. The Venerable Bede had been right to concentrate on 'the race of the English', for they became the nexus of the nation. When Egbert of Wessex finally succeeded, in the ninth century, to unite all the kingdoms into one, he named it Anglia, or England. The English thus started out in life bearing the name of their country.

This was nearly two centuries before those territories along the middle Danube were first described in writing as '*Ostarrîchi*'. Moreover – and a consideration even more important than the calendar – these earliest of English kings fought in person for their people, as Alfred the Great did successfully against the Danes in the ninth century and Harold, unsuccessfully, against the Normans in 1066. Even more remarkably, the Danish raider Canute, who in 1016 absorbed England temporarily into his Scandinavian empire, 'went native' himself and became completely anglicised. Other foreign kings alternated with the native ones on England's throne. For at least a century the Normans ruled as French monarchs, but those foreigners who came after them, like the German Hanoverians, the Dutch (William of Orange) and the Germans again (Saxe-Coburg-Gotha), all felt themselves as consorts or kings of England. Indeed, the last of them to have had not one drop of anything but German blood in his veins, Edward VII, was as English a king as any Tudor had been. Yet even in his day, when the Habsburg

Monarchy was nearing the end of its enormous run, there was still no place in its emperor's eyes for an Austrian nation.

The contrast is even stronger when we look at France. When the Carolingian empire was peacefully split up (by the agreement of Verdun in August 843), the eastern Frankish kingdom became the nucleus of what would one day become Germany. But though the Franks were a Germanic tribe, the name did not stay in the east. Instead, it was the western part of the kingdom, soon to be known as France, which took over this corporate identity. The French people, unlike the English, with their chopping and changing, had only French monarchs on their throne for the next eight centuries. The Capetians, who took over from the last of the Carolingians in 987 and ruled until the line died out in 1328; the Valois, who succeeded them down to 1589; and finally the Bourbons, who reigned from then until being literally cut off by the Revolution in 1793: all were pure French royal houses, national dynasties linked indissolubly for good or bad with their subjects.

More was to come, for when, in 1337, Edward III of England laid claim to the throne of France, the two nationalistic whetstones of medieval Europe proceeded to sharpen themselves further against each other. The so-called Hundred Years' War, which dragged on until 1453, was a patriotic as well as a dynastic war in which English and French kings did battle at the head of English and French armies. Indeed, on at least two occasions during the enormous conflict, English kings challenged their French counterparts to settle the whole dispute by single combat. The synthesis between ruler and ruled became complete. In the village square of Crécy in northern France where, on 26 August 1346, King Edward III of England and his son, Edward the Black Prince, defeated Philip IV of France, a memorial commemorates the French who fell on that day (they included 1500 knights). It is inscribed simply: '*Morts pour la Patrie*'.

Shakespeare, who worked from the accounts of chroniclers, has immortalised the patriotic fervour among the English invaders. Thus, most famously, Henry V, later in that long war, at the siege of Harfleur in 1415:

> Once more unto the breach, dear friends, once more;
> Or close the wall up with our English dead!
> . . . And you, good yeomen,
> Whose limbs were made in England, show us here

The mettle of your pasture . . .
   The game's afoot:
Follow your spirit; and, upon this charge
Cry 'God for Harry, England and St George!'

This language was not the product of poetic licence. Despite the
burden of war taxes, a succession of English Parliaments backed the
war. The armies raised by those taxes were truly national armies, in
which the ordinary yeomen with their long bows did as much, if not
more, damage than the noble knights in armour.

By contrast, all was feudal squabble and confusion in the Habsburg
lands at the time, where the dynasty was struggling with both the Wittelsbachs and the Luxembourgers for possession of Carinthia and Tyrol.
King John of Bohemia, seeing the German princes in such disarray,
was, for his part, plotting to mount an electoral coup and install his
own son as German king-emperor. The plot came to nothing with
Ottokar's death – ironically on that same field of Crécy, where he was
fighting as an ally of the French king.

Indeed, it was not until after the Hundred Years' War was over that
the first Habsburg appeared on the scene who tried to stamp a specifically Austrian character on his realm. This was Duke Rudolph IV,
known as 'Rudolph the Founder', whose brief reign (1358–65) is in
such contrast to everything which had preceded it, and most of what
followed it, that it appears like something out of a time warp, a manifestation coming out of nowhere and leading, in the end, to nothing.
True, in this fourteenth century the first troubadours had appeared who
praised the beauty of Austria as 'the fairest land on earth'; also the
first forerunner of a specifically Austrian history, the *Chronicle of the
Ninety-Five Estates* compiled by the Augustinian monk Leopold Stain-
reuter. But the very title he gave to his work marks the conceptual
gulf separating it from that plain popular approach adopted by another
monk-chronicler in north-east England six hundred years before. Nothing in fact prepares us for the words with which the remarkable Duke
Rudolph, on 12 March 1365, in the last year of his short life, founded
his university in Vienna. Translated from the medieval German (not
Latin!) the dedication reads: 'For the special honour and enhancement
of our land Austria and of our city, Vienna'. At least one Habsburg
duke had fused his dynasty with his subjects, even if the deed was done
only on parchment and not on the battlefield.

Not that Rudolph's university, once it got established after his death, did much to sharpen any sense of a specifically Austrian identity. It was divided up into so-called 'Nations', of which the 'Austrian Nation' held pride of place. But this phrase – ironically appearing for the first time – did not signify a distinctive ethnic group. On the contrary, it referred to an assortment of students coming from the Austrian lands but also from Aquilea, Italy and other territories south of the Alps. Most of the Germans, together with English, Irish, Scottish, Danish and Swedish students, were lumped together in the 'Saxon Nation'.

Such groupings were typical of other medieval European universities, yet they had a special symbolism for Vienna. A similar sense of diffusion began to spread among the Austrian people themselves as their dynasty now began to grow enormously in its dominion, power and dignity. Each stage of this growth except the first took the Austrian subjects a step further away from any nationalism of their own. The exception came in 1453 when, through the so-called 'Great Patent of Freedom' (*Privilegium Maius*), the earlier efforts of Rudolph the Founder to have Austria established as a separate entity from the German Reich were confirmed. This could have marked the starting-point for the development of a distinct Austrian nation-state along the lines already firmly set in France and England; indeed it probably would have done, had the Austrians been ruled by any other royal house. The Habsburgs, now masters of a virtually independent Austria, were also kings of Germany again. They soon dubbed themselves sovereigns of one of the most bizarre political freaks of all time: the so-called 'Holy Roman Empire of the German Nation'. The title was only used in those parts of the realm where German was spoken, yet its very introduction presaged that clash between the national and the international which was to dog the dynasty until the end.

The Holy Roman Empire had been famously dismissed as being 'neither holy, Roman, nor an empire'.* But to tack on to it 'German Nation' centuries before any such thing as a German nation existed was to wrap one mental fog over another. Yet this was the amorphous, almost nonsensical concept which the Austrians, as loyal subjects of their dynasty, were called upon to follow and promote, for the Habsburgs remained the sovereigns of this fantasy empire right down to the begin-

* The remark is attributed originally to the fifteenth-century Hungarian King Mathias Corvinus, though it was to be poached by political wags down the centuries, including Voltaire.

ning of the nineteenth century. It was the Habsburg Frederick III who in his capacity as German king-emperor had confirmed the 'Great Patent' for his own patrimony, declaring all the hereditary lands of the family to be an indivisible entail. Yet to suggest, as many Austrian historians have done in their search for national roots, that this made the fat, lazy and rather engaging Frederick an early species of Austrian patriot is to put modern words into late-medieval mouths. He was, in the first place, engaged in the traditional pursuit of all his fellow German princes: the strengthening of their own '*Hausmacht*' or hereditary territorial base.

Much has been made of the fact that in Frederick III's long reign (fifty-three years, from 1440 to 1493) the initials AEIOU are to be found for the first time carved in the portals or archways of castles, cathedrals and public buildings throughout his Austrian lands. It is assumed that the 'A' stands for Austria, and the commonest rendering of the cypher is the Latin '*Austria erit in orbe ultima*' or 'Austria will survive all others on earth'. Did Frederick mean the country and its people, or the '*Casa Austria*', his dynasty? Did he mean either? Nothing is more typical of this so-called birthmark of Austrian nationhood than that it should have been given down the centuries no fewer than three hundred different interpretations, mostly couched in German or Latin. Some of these readings are pompous, some trivial, and the supposed messages they convey vary hugely. Yet the cypher itself has never been broken and it was never spelt out. The suggestion may sound sacrilegious, but perhaps it never had any precise meaning in the first place. Personal emblems such as this were fairly common whims among the princes of the day. It is conceivable that Frederick – or some unknown stonemason whose idea captured his sovereign's fancy – simply liked the sight of all five vowels in the alphabet carved side by side.

One thing is beyond dispute. If that Latin solution given above be true, then Frederick's successors did indeed scheme long and hard so that their Austria, and their dynasty, might become truly universal. The process by which the Habsburgs promoted themselves during the space of less than fifty years from a secondary European royal house into a world-wide power without drawing a sword in battle is a dizzy one. It is best, therefore, told at a dizzy pace. The Emperor Maximilian I, who ruled from 1493 to 1519, had married Maria, daughter and heiress of Duke Charles the Bold of Burgundy. At the Duke's death in 1478, all the Burgundian possessions, which included the Netherlands, passed into Habsburg hands. Maximilian's only son married in 1496 Princess

Joanna of Spain, and their son Charles rounded off the link by marrying the other Iberian heiress, Isabella of Portugal. This son was the enigmatic Charles V who, when he succeeded his father in 1519, truly ruled over an empire on which the sun never set, stretching as it did from the Danube Basin across Western Europe and then over the Atlantic Ocean to the new Spanish possessions of South America. This huge extension and diffusion of power only widened the gap which separated the Habsburg dynasty from its Austrian people in the feudal heartlands of the empire. In the thirty-eight years of his reign, Charles twice crossed the Channel to visit England, where he was known, quite simply, as 'Charles of Europe'. He constantly travelled in Italy, France, the Netherlands, Germany and, of course, Spain. But he never visited Prague or Budapest, and was only once in Vienna.

His heritage was indeed almost too vast to contemplate and certainly too unwieldy to administer from one centre. Before withdrawing from the world to die as a monk in 1558, Charles divided up his empire, keeping the Spanish and Burgundian possessions for himself (with the imperial title during his lifetime) but handing over all the Austrian territories, the historic '*Hausmacht*' of the Habsburgs, to his younger brother Ferdinand, who duly succeeded him as emperor.

Ferdinand soon became the beneficiary of another astounding matrimonial coup planned long ago by his wily grandfather. Maximilian, that indefatigable matchmaker, had married him off in infancy to Anne, daughter of the powerful King Wladislaw of the Polish Jagellons, who at that time ruled over both Bohemia and Hungary. To double-tie the knot, the Jagellons' own son Louis had married Ferdinand's sister Maria. The crucial provision in this second marriage was that if Louis were to die without male issue, Anne and her husband would inherit all his possessions. In 1516 Louis succeeded his father as King of Bohemia and of Hungary. Ten years later he died defending the latter kingdom against the Turks, who crushed the Magyar forces in the great battle of Mohács. He left no son behind; Ferdinand accordingly claimed both crowns.

There were two psychological effects in all this for the Austrian subjects of the Habsburgs. Hitherto they had lived in a basically Teutonic world, for the three royal houses which had provided their rulers had all been German. Now the Austrian inheritance comprised, among other newcomers, Slavs in the lands of the Bohemian Crown (which included Moravia), and more Slavs (notably the Croats) alongside the Magyars in the lands of the Hungarian Crown. The Archduke of Austria had become king over all. Though it took the Habsburgs some time to make their dual kingship fully effective (central and eastern Hungary, including Budapest, were not recaptured from the Turks until 1699, for example), the 'Casa Austria' was transformed irrevocably into a multi-national concept. Moreover, this transformation had been entirely a dynastic affair, in which the people had played no role. These vast new possessions had not been fought for with kings riding at the head of national armies, but simply accumulated at the altar. As the oft-quoted tag went, with its echoes of envy and admiration: *'Bella gerant alii, tu felix Austria nube'* ('Let others wage war; you, happy Austria, marry'). What was to prove less happy for the Austrians were the long-term consequences of a ruling house gobbling up territory in isolation from its subjects.

If we again move the slide-rule across Western Europe to find a contemporary sixteenth-century contrast, staring us in the face is the indomitable figure of Queen Elizabeth I of England. In 1588 she stood on Tilbury docks to address her fleet mustered to do battle with the great Spanish Armada despatched by Philip II (son of that fleeting world emperor Charles V) to conquer England. This time the words are those of the sovereign, not the poet:

> I have but the body of a weak and feeble woman, but I have
> the heart and stomach of a King, and a King of England too . . .

This was a world away from the wedding-ring empire of the Habsburgs. Indeed, Elizabeth, Virgin Queen or not, never married.

II

Through the Crucible

'THE HOLY ROMAN EMPIRE of the German Nation' was soon to be torn apart by the conflict implicit in its name. The great religious conflagrations of the sixteenth and seventeenth centuries left scars on the empire's Austrian subjects which were still to be felt in the twentieth. They were however covered up, if only partly, by the spectacular Christian triumph which followed over the alien Moslem faith advancing under green Turkish banners from the east.

So long as Martin Luther, the Saxon peasant turned Augustinian monk and preacher, confined his attacks on Rome to the notorious corruption of the Catholic Church (notably the large-scale sale of papal indulgences against sin) he remained an overdue reformer playing a potentially constructive role. But it was another story after 1520, when he publicly burned the papal bull excommunicating him for heresy and founded his own Protestant movement. That defiance, which placed him in open competition with the Vatican for the souls of men, not only destroyed for ever the unity of Christian faith; it also extinguished any spiritual meaning that was left in the Holy Roman Empire of the Habsburgs.

In the process, Luther had helped immeasurably to strengthen Germanic, as opposed to Latin, consciousness and culture. For him and his followers, the German people were now leading the world to salvation. Moreover, the banners of their march were to be inscribed in their native tongue. Through his own renderings of the Bible from Greek and Hebrew into German translations which, thanks to the invention of printing, could now be circulated freely throughout the continent, he created a Germanic sense of mission and intellectual authority ('*Germania docet*') which, in years to come, was to weigh heavily on the Austrian, as well as the German, consciousness. While trying to

14

consolidate, he split the German nation in two. Some of its rulers, like Frederick the Wise, who gave Luther shelter in his Saxon kingdom, moved over to the new faith, and in 1526 a League of Protestant States was set up at Torgau to counter the League of Catholic States which had been founded at Ratisbon two years earlier.

In one of his famous three treatises of 1520, the year of rupture, Luther had appealed 'To the Christian Nobility of the German Nation' to join him to a man in his work of reformation. In the end, he caused Lutheran armies to fight Imperial Catholic armies in the German lands. The division seemed to be set in concrete for all time by the pact reached between the two warring camps at the so-called Peace of Augsburg in 1555, nine years after Luther's death. According to the famous tenet laid down there of '*Cuius regio, eius religio*', the subjects of any king or princeling in the empire (and there were over three hundred of them) had to follow the religious faith adopted by their ruler. Not that this restraint on basic individual freedom would have bothered Luther, who had pointedly distanced himself from the great peasant revolts of 1524–25. Indeed, in one of his less admirable treatises, he had called for ruthless suppression by the nobles. This creed of Germanic authoritarianism and submission to the powers that be was enshrined in his treatise 'Of Temporal Power'. It was not the only unsavoury message Luther sent out down the centuries. He was also a rabid anti-Semite.

The Peace of Augsburg proved only a temporary truce in Europe's battle of the faiths and it was a Habsburg emperor who broke it, literally with a vengeance. Ferdinand II, who came to the throne in 1619, was an uncomfortable novelty – the first ruler of the empire to have been educated at a college of the Jesuits, who were dedicated to wiping out the stain of Protestantism from the earth. Before ascending to the throne, their royal pupil and follower had served notice of his religious mission by launching all-out war against the Protestants in his hereditary Austrian lands. Here, Lutheranism had made astonishingly large inroads. According to later estimates, no less than nine-tenths of the population, including most of the nobility, had turned to Protestantism by the time of Luther's death. The reasons, as the peasant revolts had indicated, were as much economic as spiritual. It was a time of food shortage, over-population and labour exploitation. The cities had succumbed as massively as the countryside to the new faith. In Graz, capital of Styria, for example, the number of Catholics taking Mass had shrunk by the mid-sixteenth century to a paltry two hundred.

For the Habsburgs, who had been Dukes of Styria since the founding of their dynasty, the great counter-reformation now began at home, with very little charity to accompany it. Protestant churches were destroyed by the hundreds; Protestant books burnt by the tens of thousands. In 1585 a new university was founded in Graz and placed in the Jesuits' hands. The Lutherans of Austria were at last confronted with something they had hitherto been spared: an implacable and internationally organised intellectual foe already numbering over 10,000 dedicated priests. The spectre of the 'Schwarzen', the black Catholic reactionaries, had arisen. It was to haunt even the Austrian politics of today.

Once on the throne, Ferdinand extended this domestic backyard offensive throughout his non-Germanic domains. This was to have disastrous consequences when applied to the Slavs of Bohemia who, nearly two hundred years before, in tumult provoked by the great martyr John Hus, had shown what passion they could put into a religious battle. It was in Prague where, in another and greater conflict of faiths, those passions now boiled over again. This time they brought disastrous results not just for Austria but for the entire continent. The Bohemian Protestants, led by the nobleman Count Henry Matthias Thurn, came out in open rebellion against the Emperor's persecution of their faith. To his decree forbidding them even to hold assemblies, they responded on 23 May 1618 by pitching the Emperor's two Catholic Regents out of his Hradshin Palace windows into the ditch below, where they made a soft but humiliating landing. Drastic though such defiance was, nobody on either side of the brawl could have imagined its consequences. The so-called 'Defenestration of Prague' touched off Europe's religious war of the Thirty Years.

The twists and turns of this drawn-out conflict, the dragging-in of one European state after another, the interplay of their religious engagement with down-to-earth power politics and the plain grab for land, land, ever more land – these only concern us in outline. More to the point is the effect of all these convulsions on any emerging Austrian consciousness. Here something significant did take place, and as with the legacy of Martin Luther himself, it was to feel its way down the generations, the grip tightening almost into a stranglehold over the Austrians as they entered the twentieth century. For this sixteenth-century struggle for the souls of the people living in the Habsburg heartland (the old 'Mark' along the middle Danube, Styria, Carinthia and Tyrol) took on the form of a struggle for their loyalty. Faced with a Catholic counter-reformation, directed by Jesuits, for the restored glory of Rome, the patriotic Austrian drum begins erratically to beat. Protestant writers who, along with Protestant priests and nobles, had now fled these heartlands in their thousands, wrote in exile of the 'beloved fatherland Austria' they had left behind. Even Count Adam Herberstorff, the Emperor's principal henchman in the purge of his domestic 'heretics',* was not above resorting to patriotism as well as the gallows. He would appeal to Lutheran leaders contemplating emigration not to desert 'their Austria', for they would surely find no other country to match it abroad. However, there was a psychological side-effect even here. It was to Germany, home of Lutheranism, that most of the Austrian Protestant exiles had fled, seeing in it their cultural and spiritual home. It was to the north that many of their descendants went on looking for inspiration.

It was to the north that the Bohemians also looked for allies in their rebellion against Ferdinand's Jesuitical onslaught, and they found a resplendent figurehead in the person of Frederick V, the Protestant Elector of the Rhine-Pfalz Palatinate. They offered him their crown, thus, in effect, deposing their own Emperor as King of Bohemia. The young and inexperienced Frederick was rash enough to accept, and thus – of all countries – England became the first outside power to be sucked into this confessional vortex. Frederick had married the lovely Princess Elisabeth, daughter of England's King James I, whose subjects were already submerging under that wave of Puritanism which was to carry his son Charles I to the scaffold. The Puritans wanted nothing better in 1620 than to do battle with their fellow-minded German prince against the reactionary Catholic demons of Austria and Spain. But when battle was joined, on the White Hill just west of Prague on 8 November of that year, Frederick's forces were totally crushed. Unheroically, he made no attempt to reorganise his supporters but simply fled the field and abandoned the cause, leaving Bohemia's Protestants to the untender mercies of an exultant and unforgiving Emperor.

Ferdinand now embarked on a campaign of extirpation, directed not just against the rebellious Protestant leaders but against the entire nation, a campaign which, in its systematic and sustained ferocity, was

* Herberstorff was typical of many who swung between the rival creeds at the time. His parents were both staunch Lutherans, and he had himself been educated at Lutheran schools and universities. When he embraced 'the old faith' instead, it was with all the virulence of an opportunistic fanatic.

to be unique in the history of the Habsburgs' Austrian domains. Those of the Czech nobility who had not perished on the White Hill were nearly all driven into exile and their properties confiscated. It was reckoned that only eight of the great Bohemian families survived the tempest,* and with no middle class of substance to take their place, the Czech nation was left rudderless. For his part, Ferdinand proceeded not only to Catholicise Bohemia, but to Germanise it at the same time. Here is the relevance of this conflict to our Austrian theme.

All manner of European Catholic freebooters and adventurers got their hands on the spoils of the confiscated Bohemian estates, and some two-thirds of all land in the country changed hands in the process. The newcomers included Irish, French, Italians and Spaniards; but it was Germans, among them many from the German-speaking Austrian lands, who predominated, as they did in the new bureaucracy which was introduced to administer Bohemia, and in the universities which set the cultural tone. German was made the language of government and instruction. Czech was left to the peasants. Ferdinand thus turned Bohemia into a German colony, almost as completely as Cromwell was soon to turn Ireland into an English colony (though there, of course, the triumph of the faiths was reversed). In both cases, violent trouble was stored up for the future.

The war itself spluttered on in a series of violent and often unconnected campaigns which spread the length and breadth of the continent. King Christian of Denmark, encouraged by England, marched south to aid the beleaguered Protestants. As a good Lutheran, his heart may well have been in the cause; but his eyes were equally firmly fixed on the rich pickings to be won from the bishoprics of northern Germany. His challenge was dismissed in one crushing defeat at the hands of Catholic forces on the battlefield of Lutter in Thuringia on 27 August 1626. Five years later, another Scandinavian monarch brought an army south, a truly great leader who made not only King Christian but all the other princes of Europe look pygmies in comparison. This was Gustavus Adolphus of Sweden, who entered the fray financed by France, whose wily Chief Minister Cardinal Richelieu was seeking any instrument to reduce the growing power of Austria.

Like the Dane, Gustavus Adolphus was also after territory, in his

---

* Lobkowitz, Czernin, Kinsky, Kolowrat, Kaunitz, Schlick, Waldstein and Sternberg (the last three being Czech despite the German name of their ancestral home).

case a slice of the Baltic coast to promote his commerce and protect his modest kingdom of a mere one and a half millions against Poland and Russia. Unlike King Christian, however, he proved a great soldier as well as a great statesman. Within eighteen months his troops in their distinctive yellow and blue uniforms had swept right down across Europe, entering the Bavarian capital, Munich, in triumph.* The Swedes carried on the fight even after the death of their warrior-king on the battlefield of Lützen on 16 November 1632. Indeed, three years later Sweden became officially allied to Catholic France, opposed by an equally mixed coalition of faiths: Catholic Austria and Catholic Spain fighting alongside Lutheran Germany and the Protestant Dutch Republic. Spain's futile attempt to lead the coalition resulted, among other things, in the revolt of the Portuguese against Madrid and the establishment of the independent Portuguese kingdom of the Braganzas. As can be seen, for the nations of Europe, the Thirty Years' War had become an arena for power politics, and not a crusade of the soul.

If we were to select one individual to personify not only the ruthless self-seeking spirit of the conflict but also its hopelessly muddled end, that could only be Prince Albert Wenceslas Wallenstein, the Bohemian noble who led a private army into battle in the Emperor's name. Like the Emperor's domestic henchman Count Herberstorff, Wallenstein had been educated at Protestant schools and universities; like him, he converted to Catholicism and espoused the Habsburg cause because he sniffed the scent of power as well as incense. However, his achievements, both on and off the battlefield, eclipsed anything the Styrian count had accomplished. Wallenstein was indeed one of the greatest freebooters of all time. Made Governor of Bohemia as a reward for his military prowess (it was he who had helped to crush the Danish threat and who had then defeated Gustavus Adolphus at Lützen), he proceeded, in effect, to pillage his own country. Given the right to mint, he debased the coinage and, with the profits, bought up no fewer than sixty of the confiscated Protestant estates. Weary of war and laden with possessions, he finally sought to play the great statesman and organise not only a personal army but also a personal peace of his own with the Swedes. This was his undoing, for the emperor now proscribed him as a traitor.

---

* To this day, a wayside cross three miles outside the Tyrolean ski resort of Kitzbühel bears the legend: *'Bis Hierher und nicht weiter kamen die Swedischen Reiter'* ('This far, and no further, came the Swedish horsemen').

The manner of his murder, at camp in Eger in 1634, typified the free-for-all enterprise of war in which he had himself over-indulged. The captain who drove the halberd into Wallenstein's body was an Englishman acting on the orders of a Scots colonel. The colonel, in turn, was under an Irish general. It was a strange chain of command for a Habsburg execution.

Fourteen years after Wallenstein's violent death, the settlement which he had sought to bring about by personal intrigue was reached at last by state diplomacy. The Peace of Westphalia (so-called because the negotiators had argued for nearly four years at the Westphalian towns of Münster and Osnabrück) gave something to both rival camps, reflecting the military deadlock between them. Sweden got her hold on the Baltic and western Pomerania; Bavaria was rewarded with the Upper Rhine Palatinate; France secured the provinces of Upper and Lower Alsace – a hostage to much future history. As for the Austrian Habsburgs who had started the conflagration, they were at least confirmed in their possession of both Bohemia and Hungary. One price they paid was the loss of some 40,000 of their Protestant subjects who left for Germany.

If the dynasty had consolidated its hold on the hereditary lands, that 'Holy Roman Empire of the German Nation' over which it was still the titular ruler had become even more of a nonsense after the Westphalian Peace. The 'German Nation' itself, which had never properly existed, was now a mosaic of over 350 separate states, divided again, roughly in two clusters of north and south, by the same faiths for which they had drawn the sword a century before. Yet this was the creation which had a century and a half of zombie-like existence still ahead of it.

One event did, however, bring the spirit of this zombie twitching into life, and that was the defence of all Christian Europe against the Turk. As we have seen, the first great Turkish incursion had brought about the crushing defeat of the Magyars, on the battlefield of Mohács in 1526, and with it the Turkish occupations for a century and a half of most of Hungary. But Budapest was not the only Western capital which Suleiman the Magnificent had coveted. Three years later his armies were battering away at the inner defence ramparts of Vienna, only for this vastly superior besieging force to be withdrawn – abruptly and with no clear reason – in October 1529. The empire had sent token reinforcements, a few hundred cavalry from the Rhineland, to help ward off this first invasion. But both the degree of danger and the scale of outside help were magnified many times over when the Turks, whose janissaries had never ceased to harass the Austrian frontier districts, struck again at Vienna in 1683.

This time the Grand Vizier, Kara Mustapha, had thrown up a circle of some 200,000 men,* lodged in 25,000 tents, all around the capital. The garrison had the advantage of a newly-constructed defensive system, a massive stone girdle of walls, ramparts and ditches which had only been completed a few years before. But they were outnumbered by nearly ten to one when the siege began on 12 July; by the beginning of September, battle casualties and disease had reduced those capable of bearing arms by half. Though the defence force consisted mainly of imperial troops, it was a very Viennese affair. The town commander, Count Starhemberg, was at his post to lead the resistance, together with the Mayor, Andreas von Liebenburg, and the bishop of the regional diocese, Count Kolonitz. (The Emperor Leopold had prudently withdrawn to Linz just before the Turkish tents went up.) There was thus a spirit of citizen solidarity about the ordeal which did much to bolster the special character of the Viennese in years to come. But in 1683 it was touch and go whether the green crescent of Islam would not be hoisted over their great cathedral of Saint Stephen. Turkish troops had already breached the defensive walls and were fighting their way into the city when, on 12 September, the great Christian relief army reached the ridge of the Kahlenberg Hills above the capital. At 4 a.m. Mass was read by the Papal legate, Marco d'Aviano, to the assembled officers. Twelve hours later it was all over. The rescue army, after fighting its way down the vineyards and the villages into the north-west approaches to the capital, met the main mass of Kara Mustapha's forces head on and broke them. The retreat turned into a rout as the Turks fled eastwards, never to return. The Viennese now gorged themselves on plunder. Apart from the sacks of beans on which they later founded their coffee houses, the Grand Vizier had abandoned some 30,000 cattle and pack animals and vast stores. One macabre find in his luxurious living tent was a pet ostrich which he had decapitated rather than leave behind for infidel hands.

The relief army contained contingents from several states of the

---

* This excluded the enormous train of camp followers – everything from tradesmen and gypsies to singers, clowns and jugglers to entertain the troops. Prostitutes also abounded, with the Grand Vizier himself setting the example of sexual indulgence. His travelling harem numbered 1500 women, with seven hundred black eunuchs as guards.

Emperor's 'German Nation', to which frantic appeals for help had been
sent – Saxony, Bavaria, Franconia and Swabia. But the most powerful
component was a force of some 20,000 Polish cavalrymen who had
ridden down across the Carpathians to take part in the rescue. At their
head was their monarch, King John III Sobieski, who, as the only
sovereign on the field, had assumed command of the entire operation
once the various columns had assembled. He was not the only non-
German to lead the repulse of the Turks from Central Europe. The man
who first wrested all of Hungary back for the Habsburgs and then
cleared Turkish forces from the rest of the Danube Basin* was born in
Paris and hailed from a cadet branch of the house of Savoy. Prince
Franz Eugen had fought as a volunteer in the battle of September
1683, and three months later was given command of an Austrian cavalry
regiment by a grateful emperor. It proved a good investment for the
dynasty. The newly promoted colonel, who was then twenty years old,
became a general at twenty-two and a field marshal at thirty. He was
to fight seventeen campaigns, spread across eight European theatres of
war, in the cause of three successive Habsburg emperors, Leopold I,
Joseph I and Charles VI, and to serve also as their political counsellor.
Yet this legendary 'noble knight', who was revered as an Austrian hero,
could hardly speak German, let alone write it. And though his finest
residence, the ill-fated Belvedere Palace,** was built in Vienna (with a
splendid view up to those Kahlenberg Hills), its first owner never
thought or felt as a Viennese. Indeed there is only one way in which
he might be said to be typical of the capital's inhabitants: they were
already on their way to becoming one of Europe's most intricately
intertwined breed of races. Prince Eugen, with his 256 traceable ancestors
(ranging from Spanish to Bulgarian and from Czech to Italian) was the
noble apotheosis of such mixed blood. All of Europe was in his veins.

What impact could all these mighty military happenings have had on
the Austrians as a people? Though the Viennese could burst with pride

* Notably by conquering Belgrade in 1717. The resulting Peace of Passarowitz, signed
in July of the following year, gave northern Serbia, the adjoining region of Banat and
Wallachia to the Habsburgs, so that the Austrian monarchy, at its territorial zenith,
stretched from the mountains of Transylvania to Ostend.
** It was from the Belvedere that, in April 1770, the Archduchess Maria Antoinette
left for Paris to become the bride of Louis XVI with whom she was to die at the
guillotine. It was also from here that in June 1914 the Archduke Francis Ferdinand left
on the visit to Sarajevo which was to bring about his assassination and spark off the
Great War.

(it had, after all, been *their* siege), the final repulse of the Turks had not been a national victory but the very opposite: a crusading campaign of Western Christendom, commanded by a foreigner and waged for the greater glory of an increasingly multi-national dynasty. There was nothing to strengthen even a Germanic, let alone a specifically Austrian identity here, except perhaps on the cultural side. (This did not stop Adolf Hitler, two centuries after Prince Eugen's death, placing him in the Valhalla of German heroes. In the Third Reich, both a battleship and a crack armoured division were named after him, while his regiment had carried his name in the Austrian army until the collapse of the Monarchy in 1918.)

The campaigns against the Turks had underlined something else which was also more dynastic than national. The function of the old 'Eastern March', with the Austrians serving primarily as a military buffer, was revived and, indeed, institutionalised. Alongside certain quaint results of the siege (such as the birth of the Viennese coffee house) and the marvellous cultural flowering of the baroque, came the strategic creation of the so-called 'Military Frontier' along the border regions of the Habsburg lands. This was a chain of special districts stretching along the eastern fringe of the Austrian Monarchy all the way from the Adriatic coast up and around to the Carpathians. Within these districts, every able-bodied man was liable for military service, and those not called up took turns on picket duties along the frontier with the Ottoman empire. The regular units were based, like fire services, on individual villages, and this enabled the entire carpet of defence units to be moved backwards or forwards as the strategic situation demanded. The German language was introduced into the schools of those districts, since the local boys, of whatever race or creed, had the linguistic need for service in the imperial colours.* And though these so-called '*Grenzer*' or Frontiersmen became a special breed, they were very much the emperor's men. They were commanded by officers drawn from all parts of the Monarchy and constituted a permanent cordon of civilian and military servants of the dynasty.

This concept of an institutionalised public service dated back in embryonic form to the Emperor Maximilian. It was both sharpened and

---

* The problem can be appreciated by looking at the population breakdown of the Hungarian Military Frontier towards the end of the eighteenth century. This contained no Magyars(!); only 20,000 German speakers, but 360,000 Croats, 240,000 Serbs and 80,000 Roumanians.

broadened under the great Empress Maria Theresa, who came to the throne in 1740, four years after Prince Eugen had left the scene. She created what in a democratic system would have been a state bureaucracy, answerable to the government of the day, but which, in the Habsburg context, constituted one vast flock of dynastic administrators, all answerable only to a Monarchy which held itself to be self-perpetuating.

Indeed, the very issue of its self-perpetuation led to the first armed conflict of her reign. Forty years before, Europe had been plunged into war over who was to succeed Charles II, the last of the Spanish Habsburgs, a human wreck who had died in November 1700 without siring an heir: was it to be Philip of France or Charles of Austria, both of whom were named in his will? For thirteen years the major powers, including England, had done battle in this War of the Spanish Succession. Now, fighting broke out again over Habsburg family title and Habsburg family lands. Though closer to home, this War of the Austrian Succession must have seemed even more confusing to the Austrians. To begin with – and this was the key to the dispute – their dynasty altered its ancient rules of inheritance and ended up by changing even its name. Maria Theresa had been the only child of the Emperor Charles VI and, according to the ancient Salic law, could not succeed him as a daughter. He therefore promulgated in 1713 a radical new family statute, known as the Pragmatic Sanction, which provided for her to accede to his crown and to all his possessions.

But the Habsburg Monarchy, though a purely family affair to its members, was also a major player in European power politics, and such a transformation in its structure had to be sold abroad. Each country had its price for acceptance, as Charles discovered to his cost over a series of complex negotiations which dragged on almost until his death. England, for example, secured trading concessions in the Indian Ocean, where a rival company based in Ostend was operating; France secured the reversion of Lorraine. Finally, in 1738, after a manic imbroglio which also involved the Polish succession (Europe seemed to have nothing on its hands at the time but dynastic squabbles), the continuing dispute between Paris and Vienna was settled by the marriage of Maria Theresa to France's Duke of Lorraine. When the Austrian heiress duly succeeded to her throne two years later therefore, the dynasty became – and remained – that of Habsburg-Lorraine.

There is no need to recount here how the young and inexperienced empress survived the onslaught on her inheritance which was now lavished by those same powers who had promised to respect it; but survive, at the end, she did, though at the heavy cost of yielding up Silesia to Frederick II of Prussia.* It was he who had struck the first blow by invading the province without provocation or warning only three months after her accession. The defeat of a wobbly Austrian army by the highly drilled Prussian infantry on the field of Mollwitz was a foretaste of the far more momentous victory scored by Prussia over the forces of the Habsburg Monarchy at Königgrätz in the century to come. But what needs stressing for our purposes is that all Maria Theresa's struggles in this and subsequent wars did not create any concept of the French, the English or even the Prussians as being *the* enemy of the Austrian people. Her famous 'reversal of alliances', when she abandoned her partnership with England and switched to one with France to form a new anti-Prussian coalition, anyway complicated the question of allegiances.

The Austrians were not, as it happened, to find their foe of the emotional knee-jerk, their 'national enemy', until the Italians came to fulfil that role two hundred years later. Maria Theresa came to be revered as their *Landesmutter*, or 'mother of the people', and if the Austrians fought with any enthusiasm in her battle to keep her dynastic possessions, this was not conventional patriotism but rather the fidelity of gamekeepers and estate workers, all banded together to save the family castle under siege. Not for nothing is the first of her great conflicts known as 'The War of the Austrian Succession'. What the struggle with Prussia did bring about was an exacerbation of the great energy-draining religious conflict which had already split the Monarchy since Luther's time. At one point in the conflict, the Protestant Hohenzollern King of Prussia occupied Prague, subduing the Jesuits. But in 1743 Maria Theresa came back in triumph, the crown of Bohemia was placed on her head and the Catholic supremacy restored with more anti-Protestant edicts than ever.**

Nor was the deepening conflict between north and south confined

---

* The crisis had even cost the dynasty a temporary loss of the Holy Roman Crown itself. In the hope of placating King Charles of Bavaria, who was also contesting Maria Theresa's succession, she transferred the Imperial title to him. It was soon regained.
** In 1752, for example, she declared any follower of the Protestant faith to be the equivalent of a traitor or rebel, and liable to execution. Frederick of Prussia was, of course, urging the Protestants of Bohemia to try to stir up trouble for the Empress.

to religion. The centralised bureaucracy which Maria Theresa now set up (its chief architect was Count Frederick Haugwitz, a general from Lutheran Saxony) embraced Slav Bohemia and Magyar Hungary as well as the feudal Austrian lands. It was a multi-national concept of administration which for the first time had emerged as the Monarchy's best chance of survival. Unfortunately, opposing it from now on stood a violent, uncompromising and ambitious newcomer on Europe's royal scene. Brandenburg-Prussia had only been raised to the dignity of a kingdom in 1700 (by Leopold I, the Habsburg Holy Roman Emperor of the day; who else?). Yet the parvenu soon turned challenger. Hohenzollern Prussia became the herald of a purely German patriotism, anti-Slav from the outset and eventually anti-anything which stood outside the sacred Teutonic bloc. It was from this dual opposition, nationalist as well as religious, each spawning rival outpourings in literature and art, that there arose that spiritual tug-of-war which almost destroyed the Austrians in the twentieth century.

But did this momentous reign of such a great sovereign, with all its switchbacks of tragedy and triumphs, leave behind it no impulse, no mark which was specifically Austrian? The answer is yes, and the symbol of it looks at us today in the western suburbs of Vienna: Schönbrunn Palace. Maria Theresa did not build the palace (work started under the Emperor Leopold in 1696 and was completed by 1711, more than thirty years before her accession); but after she moved in, in 1740, she made it her own. For the rest of her life and reign it was her summer home as well as her centre of government. All sixteen of her children were raised there. One of many incidents which emphasised the domesticity of the place happened on that evening of 12 February 1768 when she burst into her box at the palace's theatre in the middle of a performance and stopped the actors dead in their tracks by shouting to one and all: 'Children, "Poldi" [Leopold] has just had a boy!' She was announcing the arrival of a new grandson; and as the 'Mother of the People' she tended to address her subjects in intimate surroundings as 'children'.

The very existence of that theatre, and indeed the design of the whole palace, points us to another specific: Austrian baroque. The first baroque palaces of Vienna, for example those of Lobkowitz, Starhemberg, Harrach in the city centre, were designed in the late seventeenth century by architects from Italy, from where the original inspiration for baroque in most of its forms had come. But Fischer von Erlach, whose basic design for Schönbrunn survived many changes,* was born in Graz. Like that other great architect of Austrian baroque, Johann Lukas von Hildebrandt (who, in the same period, had built the great Belvedere Palace for Prince Eugen), Fischer von Erlach could, and did, evolve a specifically Austrian style. But what was this style, and how could it be said to represent anything by now characteristic of the people?

Here we come across something not unexpected but nonetheless intriguing. Austrian baroque is not native, but rather a unique blend of foreign styles. It does not spring from Austrian roots, but from a mix of other roots. Antiquity, Renaissance, Oriental and, of course, Italian and French influences are combined in Schönbrunn: on the front façade, for example, are tall Ionic pilasters placed between each of the thirty-seven window sections (some of these oblong, some arched, some square, some pedimented, but all topped with Roman-style statuary). The theme of classic austerity combined with eighteenth-century voluptuousness is repeated in the showpiece of the interior: the Great Gallery, where plain fluted columns support the extravagances of the curving painted ceilings. And in the lovely Blue Room – the very place where, one day, Maria Theresa's dynasty was to bow itself out of power for ever – the Far East is recalled by oval and rectangular Chinese motifs set in the walls.

The baroque theatre itself – one of the finest in existence – is also symbolic of Austrian style in Maria Theresa's age, for this was very much a culture of the theatre. By this is meant not merely the stage of actors and singers, flourishing though this was. More all-pervasive was the calculated high drama of church festivals and religious services, feasts for the eyes, nose and ears which spread, like the distinctive yellow of Schönbrunn, to the thousands of baroque abbeys and churches built throughout the Monarchy. Vienna's Corpus Christi Day processions became the apotheosis of this cultural propaganda: gigantic theatrical shows, with the cream of religious and lay society as their star attractions. The aim was to dazzle and to glorify, and the chief object of veneration, alongside the deity, was the monarch. The Holy Trinity found its secular counterpart in Austria, Hungary and Bohemia, the three great jewels of the Habsburg crown. Thus the exuberance of the baroque age – an

* His first plan, for five ornamental terraces leading to a magnificent building stretching all along the crest of a ridge, was abandoned because it would have cost too much. The three domes of his original design for the more modest project were torn down by the architect Nicolaus Pacassi in favour of a flat roof.

exuberance felt with special zest in a Vienna delivered from the night-mare of Turkish occupation – was itself channelled to the greater glory of the dynasty. The Austrians were gradually being enfolded by that family allegiance immortalised by the comment of their Emperor Francis II on hearing one of his subjects being praised for patriotism: 'Is he a patriot for me?'

A prodigious thinker was on hand to encapsulate all this in philos-ophy: Gottfried Wilhelm Leibniz. In his principal work, *Theodizee*, he proclaimed the world of the eighteenth century to be the creation of God and its governance the best of all systems for humankind. The Habsburg Monarchy was a great favourite of this prolific polymath. (Leibniz's tracts and letters, nearly 100,000 in number, covered mathe-matics, physics and linguistics as well as politics and religion.) For in the Monarchy, and the Holy Roman Empire whose crown it also bore, Leibniz saw the perfect living fusion of all the faiths, creeds, races and social systems of Christian Europe. This has led him to be hailed by some historians as the Austrian thinker *par excellence*. One caveat needs to be entered, however. Leibniz was no Austrian. He was a German, the founder and first president of the Academy of Sciences in Berlin.

A lack of state patriotism, as much of Europe was coming to under-stand that concept, was not the only shackle on the Austrian spirit as it entered the modern age. The other was its very limited and muddled concepts of constitutional and individual liberty. Maria Theresa's son and successor, Joseph II, had indeed carried out many radical reforms during the ten years (1780–90) of his reign. His 'Toleration Patent', while leaving Catholicism as the dominant religion of the Monarchy, did allow the other main faiths to build their own churches and schools; some seven hundred monasteries, on the other hand, were dissolved. Marriage was made a purely civil contract; a new penal code abolished both the death penalty and torture to extract confessions, and the long-suffering peasantry were at least granted major freedoms.* There was even a system of poor-law relief which could be claimed by anyone resident for ten years in their local parish.

All this certainly entitles Maria Theresa's son to his niche among the icons of 'benevolent despots'. Yet two reservations must be made, as

---

* Barbarous punishments continued to be meted out, however, sometimes ordered by Joseph II in person; and when in 1784 a revolt of the Wallachian peasants of Transylvania was put down, the fate of the ringleaders was appalling. Hora, the chief of the rebels, was broken on the wheel and 150 of his followers publicly impaled.

concerns the impact of his reforms on his Austrian subjects. The first is that many of his measures were either cancelled or watered down by his brother and successor, Leopold II, who hailed from the cadet family line established in Tuscany. The second is a dual one. On the one hand, much of Joseph's benevolence had a hard pragmatic aim: in casting off many of the feudal chains which shackled his peasantry, for example, he sought to make them a more productive source of labour and income. On the other hand, he remained very much the despot. Indeed, the Monarchy's secret police force, which was to play such a dark role in Austrian life under his successors, was in fact his creation. It was the great reformer who, in 1782, converted the court's crude surveillance network into a permanent and separate service. Its chief, Count Anton Pergen, enlisted a horde of informers to spy on the army and the bureaucracy. The Count reported directly to the Emperor.

Foreigners and political suspects were added as targets in later years, when Count Pergen's secret police began its transformation into an instrument of suppression. The immediate aims of its founder were to ensure that the soulless administrative machine he had created to govern 'the state' (by which, of course, was meant the dynasty in its governmental garb) should run smoothly to discharge the decrees he had laid down. These were almost mind-boggling in their volume and scope. By the end of his brief ten-year reign there were over 6000 new imperial edicts, the majority prescribed by the ruler himself. His roving commissioners were charged to investigate everything in the districts they visited, from whether the houses had numbers to whether the local clergy were respected; from what was being done for blind, deaf and crippled children to whether the sale of contraceptive methods was permitted. His own detailed decisions included adding a zebra to the Schönbrunn Zoo; banning corsets for girls in mixed schools so as to reduce any distracting enhancement of their bodies; the rationing of candles; the re-use of coffins; and forbidding the peasantry to bake gingerbread because of its bad effect on their stomachs.

His object was to make his subjects happy, as well as efficient – and both by decree. But the result was to implant on the people a nervous reverence for 'Obrigkeit' or state authority. This became a graver matter when that state authority, which Joseph II endowed with omnipotence as well as omniscience, passed into less scrupulous hands. It was also, however benign the initial aim, the birth for the Austrians of the 'informer society'. Servants were to inform on their masters; clerks on their departmental chiefs; priests on their bishops; subalterns on their colonels; and coachmen on everyone. The legacy of this needs no underlining.

There was a reaction even in Joseph's time: the growth of Masonic societies and other secret organisations, such as the 'Illuminati'.* The emperor trod warily against them for a while, if only because his own father had been a Grand Master. However, towards the end of his reign, his patience snapped with these mysterious radicals about whom Count Pergen was constantly reporting. In December 1785 he issued a special decree to try and bring the Masons to heel. Vienna's eight lodges were cut down to two. Provincial capitals were to be restricted to one lodge only and lists of members throughout the Monarchy were to be submitted to the police.

The most famous Masonic sympathiser of the day was, of course, Wolfgang Amadeus Mozart, who flaunted the symbolism of Free-masonry for all time in his last operatic masterpiece, Die Zauberflöte. It was altogether not surprising that Joseph II felt a little unsure about the greatest composer of his reign (and some would claim, of any reign). His well-known comment after hearing Die Entführung aus dem Serail for the first time: 'Too beautiful for our ears and much too many notes, dear Mozart,'** sums up the contrast between the Germanic imperial bureaucrat (who preferred the plainer operatic fare of the German-born Christoph Gluck) and this unpredictable, irrepressible genius who belonged nowhere, yet everywhere. It was just as well for the Emperor's temper that he died the year before Die Zauberflöte was created.

The century towards which the Habsburgs were now moving was to see the gradual triumph of two concepts: democracy and nationalism. Each was in itself a threat to the survival of the dynasty. When the two joined hands, any hope of stability inside the Monarchy was doomed. Before describing its slow death, we need to see how the Austrians themselves were equipped to face this dual challenge to their future.

The empire that Joseph II left behind had enjoyed a taste of individual liberty, and the taste lingered on even after the cup had been drawn away

---

* Founded by a German professor, Adam Weishaupt, of Ingolstadt University. Its members included many Austrian nobles and intellectuals. It had its lodges and grades of office, like the Masons, and some of its ceremonies denounced religion as a fraud and rulers as usurpers.

** Less often quoted is Mozart's remarkably robust reply: 'Just so many, Your Majesty, as are needed!'

by his successor. But the Monarchy and, above all, its Austro-German administrators, remained a hopeless misfit for the modern age which was almost upon them. Its social structure resembled a rigid pyramid at whose apex stood a family of semi-deities (the Habsburg emperor and his clan of archdukes); a thick wedge of nobility underneath; a class of non-noble bureaucrats, university graduates and professional men (defined officially in the 1780 census as '*Honoratior*') below them; a relatively small group of '*burghers*' in the towns; and finally, in the countryside which represented most of the Monarchy's wealth, the peasantry who generated that wealth.

But this was not, as in some other European countries at the time, a flexible pyramid which could adjust readily to pressures for change. The ruling dynasty, for example, drew a firm and very thick line between itself and all but a handful of even the high nobility.* This '*Hochadel*', in turn, kept itself leagues apart from the great mass of society below. Nobles occupied the top posts in the army, in diplomacy, in domestic administration and largely even in the Church; their birth guaranteed initial recruitment, and special channels of privilege their promotion. Their wealth came from their entailed estates, some of them the size of English counties. A few hundred of these families owned, between them, almost half the land in the empire. The lesser nobility, especially in Hungary, stood closer to the ordinary people and, therefore, were a potential force for change. But essentially the nobles high and low were hereditary stewards of the Habsburg estate. Parliament, or any other such people's forum, did not, of course, exist. Royal power was exercised in each land, through a governor. He was a noble and so were the leaders of the so-called '*Diets*' which met under him. Such a pyramid was almost impossible to reshape. It was easier to topple it altogether.

When one looks back from the viewpoint of nationalism at the Habsburg Monarchy as it entered the nineteenth century, the prospect appears positively nightmarish. Only the oldest hereditary territories of Lower and Upper Austria were ethnically compact: their combined population of some 180,000 was solidly German, or German-speaking, if we can already think of 'Austria'. Elsewhere, even in the other Austrian lands of Styria, Carinthia or the Tirol, Slovenes and Italians loom large

---

* Only twenty-one families in the monarchy (fifteen princely and six headed by counts) enjoyed the privilege of automatic access to the court and the right to marry into the imperial family. A whole chapter would be needed to describe the intrigues surrounding the selection process.

on the census rolls, whereas in provinces like Carniola or Gorizia the German element is simply swamped.

The mixture in the two main kingdoms of the Monarchy was just as jumbled. Bohemia, for example, returned about 1.5 million Czechs to a million Germans in the 1780 census while the lands of the Hungarian crown showed some 3.3 million Magyars heavily outnumbered in total by Slovaks, Croats, Romanians, Serbs, Ruthenes, Germans and Slovenes – to name only the main groups. Nor were these races distributed in tidy packages; there were ethnic overspills and left-overs from earlier treaties or battles or waves of migration left stranded in all directions. Again, the near-hopelessness of finding any tidy solution stands out – even before nationalist agitation complicated the task a hundredfold. Like the social pyramid, this map was easier to destroy altogether than to reshape.

The very proclamation by which Joseph II had assumed the succession sets out the grandiose complexity of the Habsburg inheritance at the end of the eighteenth century, a complexity which was ultimately to become fatal in the twentieth. It begins:

> We, Joseph II, by God's Grace the elected Roman Emperor . . .
> King in Germany, of Jerusalem, Hungary, Bohemia, Dalmatia,
> Croatia, Slavonia, Galizia and Lodomeria, Archduke of Austria;
> Duke of Burgundy, of Lorraine, of Styria, of Carinthia and
> of Krainia; Grand Duke of Tuscany, Prince of Transylvania;
> Margrave of Moravia; Duke of Brabant, of Limburg, of Luxem-
> burg and Geldern, of Württemberg, of Upper and Lower Silesia,
> of Milan, of Mantua, of Parma, Placenza, Quastalla, Auschwitz
> and Zator, of Calabria, of Bar, of Montferrat and Teschen;
> Prince of Swabia and of Charlesville; Princely Count of Habs-
> burg, of Flanders, of Tyrol, of Hennegau, of Kyburg, of Gorizia
> and Gradiska; Margrave of the Holy Roman Empire, of Burgau;
> of Upper and Lower Lusatia; of Pont à Mousson and Nimenü;
> Count of Namur, of Vaudemont, of Blankenburg, of Zutphen,
> of Saarwerden, of Salm and of Falkenstein; Lord of the
> Windisch Mark and Melcheln . . .

Some of these titles, like that to Jerusalem, rested on little more than a religious quirk; some, like that of Burgundy, were in name only. Others, like the Italian possessions, were first to be augmented by victories in war and diplomacy, only to be stripped away, one by one, by the forces of liberal nationalism. Both processes were now precipitated by the approaching storm of the French Revolution, and the giant who rode it, Napoleon Bonaparte.

III

Winds of Change

JOSEPH THE REFORMER may have been spared having to endure the undisguised Freemasonry of Mozart's *Zauberflöte*; but the Emperor had lived long enough to learn of the storming of the Bastille in Paris in 1789, and to take in something of its message. The conservative Catholic Habsburgs were the arch-enemies of the Revolution. This was rubbed home soon enough for Joseph's brother and short-lived successor Leopold II, who was crowned Roman Emperor at Frankfurt on 6 October 1790. The coronation was something of an act of defiance. Two months previously, the Constituent Assembly in Paris had abolished all feudal rights, including those of the German princes in Alsace and Lorraine. By this decree, Revolutionary France declared war on the monarchical system of the entire continent and, as regards the Habsburg Monarchy, had sought to extinguish even the dynasty's proper name. As Roman Emperor and, more practically, as King of Germany, Leopold protested; a circular letter issued by his Chancellor, Kaunitz, called on all Europe's sovereigns to unite against the common menace. The immediate result was the alliance of 1792 between Austria and Prussia – the two German states henceforth destined to be both rivals and partners in the European power game.

A year later, the revolutionaries struck a savage personal blow at the Habsburg family. The Archduchess Maria Antoinette had married the future Louis XVI in 1770, entering history as the feckless and extravagant Queen Marie Antoinette. In 1793, with France declared a republic, the National Convention then in power ordered her execution, following that of her husband.

After Napoleon's rise to power, the Habsburgs felt something far more than a family bereavement. His military genius soon threatened the very existence of their Monarchy. To begin with, he faced them as a mere general, commander-in-chief of the French Army of Italy, where the Habsburgs held possessions stretching from Trieste down to Tuscany. In the spring of 1796 he drove them out of Milan; the following year he took the great fortress of Mantua, beating back in succession the four relief armies sent over the Alps to save the garrison. Napoleon then marched north on Vienna itself and was within sixty miles of the capital when the Monarchy (now ruled by Francis I) sued for an armistice. At the Peace of Campo Formio in October 1797 Austria ceded to France its provinces in the south Netherlands (Belgium) and acknowledged the new Cisalpine Republic of Lombardy which Napoleon had set up as an outpost of French power. It was a humiliating trade-off.

When Napoleon struck next at Austria, three years later, it was as First Consul of the Republic and virtual master of France. The battlefield was again Italy, where he flung himself at the Austrian forces who were besieging Genoa. Despite the fact that he had hauled across the Alps only fifteen guns to the enemy's two hundred, he won a crushing victory at Marengo on 4 June 1800. Once again, the Emperor Francis had to sue for peace, and at Lunéville in February of the following year Austria was obliged to recognise the Rhine, along with the Alps and the Pyrenees, as France's 'natural frontiers' and also acknowledge all the client-republics which Napoleon had established beyond those frontiers.

In his final metamorphosis Napoleon confronted the Habsburgs as a self-styled, self-crowned emperor. It was his police chief Joseph Fouché (later to be created Duke of Otranto by his grateful master) who seems to have suggested to Bonaparte in the spring of 1804 that he should transform his office of Life Consul into an imperial throne. Fouché had recently uncovered an English-financed plot to assassinate the Consul; if Napoleon substituted a hereditary empire for the consulate and sired a son, then, Fouché argued, the succession could be assured whatever happened. The police chief and others who floated the idea were conjuring up a dream which was already stirring in the Consul's mind. Napoleon could only imagine himself, not as the successor of Louis XVI, whom he despised, but of Charlemagne, the master of Western Europe a thousand years before, whom he venerated. The French empire was duly proclaimed in May 1804 and, on 2 December, the coronation followed in the Cathedral of Notre Dame. Pope Pius VII had been summoned up from Rome to direct the ceremony but, just as he was lowering the imperial crown, Napoleon seized it from his hands and crowned himself.

The challenge to the Habsburg title was inescapable. Europe had room for only one latter-day Charlemagne. On 10 August 1804, Francis prudently bowed before fate by styling himself 'Hereditary Emperor of Austria', thus securing for his dynasty an imperial bolt-hole from which not even Bonaparte could dislodge him. For some months he went on issuing documents in the old style of 'Roman Emperor Elect' alongside his new designation. But Napoleon swiftly killed off the charade, beginning, as usual, on the battlefield. On 2 December 1805, in what became recognised as the most brilliant of all his victories, he crushed the combined Austrian and Russian armies at Austerlitz, killing and wounding 15,000 of the allied army and taking 20,000 prisoner.* The Peace of Pressburg, which followed on 26 December, was equally crushing. Austria now lost not only that portion of the Venetian Republic Napoleon had given her eight years before, but also suffered terrible amputations in the historic lands. Tyrol and Vorarlberg were ceded to Bavaria, while Napoleon's other allies, Baden and Württemberg, took what was left of the Habsburgs' German possessions. (As usual, Napoleon offered an ironic sweetener. At Campo Formio, it had been a portion of Venice; now, he condescended to hand Salzburg to the Monarchy.)

The Peace of Pressburg had driven Austria's presence out of western Germany. The following summer, Napoleon filled the political vacuum he had created. On 17 July 1806, Bavaria, Württemberg and Baden led the procession of sixteen German states who assembled at Paris to constitute the so-called Confederation of the Rhine. In return for substantial bribes from their new master (Bavaria and Württemberg were made into kingdoms; Baden was turned into a grand duchy), the sixteen princes repudiated the laws of the Roman empire and on 1 August Napoleon, now installed as the 'Protector' of the Confederation, pronounced the old Roman empire to be defunct. The legal death certificate still had to be written out, and there was only one person who could discharge this formality: the Emperor Francis II** himself. On 6 August 1806, he declared the thousand-year-old empire of Charlemagne, whose elective crown his dynasty had borne, virtually without interruption, since 1438, to be dissolved. The creation of the new Rhenish Confederation, his proclamation rang, 'had made it totally

---

* On 9 August of that year Austria, Russia and England had formed up in a new coalition to defeat Napoleon, who, during the autumn, had advanced swiftly down the Danube towards Vienna, sweeping Austrian forces out of his path.
** This was his title as Holy Roman Emperor; as Emperor of Austria he was Francis I.

impossible for us to discharge any longer our imperial office'. All the principalities and estates were discharged of their loyalties and, in an empty gesture, commended to the care of the newly declared 'Hereditary Empire of Austria'. This was a pathetic touch, as though the proprietor of an old-established but now bankrupt family business were touting for clients under different management. Even the brass plate was redesigned accordingly. To try and retain some link with the pre-Napoleonic past, Francis declared that the Holy Roman symbol of the double-headed eagle and the traditional colours of the German Empire, black and gold, would both be carried by Habsburg Austria.

Napoleon also turned to the past in a search for ready-made lineage. This Corsican adventurer, nicknamed (out of his hearing) '*le petit tondu*' because of his inelegant close-cropped hair, was now an emperor himself and was soon scanning the courts of Europe for a suitable imperial bride. To begin with, it was by now clear that his existing wife, Josephine de Beauharnais, whom he had married in 1796, would not bear him the son he required to succeed him as emperor. Furthermore, political profit could only derive from a match with one of the great continental dynasties arrayed in shifting coalitions against him.

He first favoured a Russian grand duchess, and put out feelers in St Petersburg for the hand of Anna, the fifteen-year-old youngest sister of Tsar Alexander. However, it was Austria which finally carried the day, despite the fact that in 1809 Napoleon, on the warpath again, had once more marched down the Danube and entered Vienna as a conqueror. This time, the Austrian armies (each commanded by brothers of the Emperor Francis, the Archdukes Charles, John and Joseph) had put up a much stiffer resistance than that offered four years previously. Indeed, on the Danube meadows of Aspern, just outside the capital, the Archduke Charles had scored one of the few battlefield victories ever registered against Napoleon. But the end was familiar. The French forces regrouped to crush their opponents; the Emperor Francis again fled (this time to western Hungary); on 13 May 1809, Napoleon again slept in Schönbrunn Palace; and it was there on 14 October 1809 that Austria had to sign yet another hard Napoleonic peace.* Francis was

---

* By this so-called Peace of Schönbrunn, the Monarchy gave up its share of Poland, parts of Carinthia, Carniola and Croatia; what was left of its Adriatic possessions and even some of its Germanic territories along the Bavarian borders. The Emperor, at one blow, lost some 3.25 million of his subjects.

lucky to escape with his crown; at one point Napoleon had seemed determined to depose him.

Yet only six months later, on 11 March 1810, the Archduchess Maria Louisa, eighteen-year-old daughter of the Austrian Emperor, was married by proxy to Napoleon in the chapel of the Vienna Hofburg. The man who stood in for the bridegroom at the ceremony was none other than the Archduke Charles who had fought him so valiantly on the Danube plains. All the church bells in the capital pealed in salute and the Viennese cheered vociferously in the streets when the new Empress of France set out to join her husband. Having first seen his sister and brother-in-law killed by the French Revolution, the Emperor Francis had now acquired a French son-in-law in the person of the all-conquering heir to that revolution. Two points need noting: first, the predominance of dynasty in all this and, second, the absence of any patriotic anti-French sentiment among the Austrian people. The two factors are not, of course, unrelated.

Once again, in tracing the Austrian people's faltering consciousness of themselves down the centuries, it is worth contrasting the mood created by the Napoleonic wars in other European countries, above all in England. The populace of London would have rioted against any English princess rash enough to contemplate marriage with Bonaparte. As 'Boney', he had become a new symbol of the age-old rivalry between the two nations, a symbol so potent and so rooted in popular feeling that, all over Britain, mothers would warn their wayward children that, like some Gallic Saint Nicholas, this ogre would come for them in person if they did not mend their ways. The anti-invasion Martello towers which went up along the coasts reflected the official panic that 'Boney' was coming anyway. Not surprisingly, the crucial sea-battle of Trafalgar on 21 October 1805, which had virtually banished the threat of that invasion, entered the psyche of the island people. So much so that, nearly two centuries later, when the search was on for a new British *national* holiday, 'Trafalgar Day' was one suggestion. The idea was dropped, mainly because of its chauvinistic tone, unwelcome in the drive for pan-European harmony with which the twentieth century ended. When the nineteenth century began, however, that was precisely the right note to strike. The homage paid by the dynasty to the Habsburg archduke who had inflicted a temporary setback on Napoleon at Aspern was a puny thing compared with the giant column raised, with public support, in the heart of London to the victor of Trafalgar. Admiral

Nelson's famous signal to his fleet before that battle: 'England expects that every man will do his duty' echoed down the ages. Throughout Europe – the Habsburg Monarchy included – the French Revolution and the great legal reforms of Napoleon which followed had sown seeds of liberalism which were eventually to germinate and burst up through the hard crust of autocracy. But among the Austrian people, the struggle against France produced no comparable patriotic surge despite the fact that Napoleon had twice entered their capital as a conqueror. More and yet also less than that: such outbursts of 'Austrian' patriotism which were registered during the Napoleonic era were, for the most part, not national at all. They were provincial at one end of the scale, and Germanic at the other. Andreas Hofer, the innkeeper from the Passeirer valley who led the revolt of his Tyrolean followers against the French in 1809, is the supreme example of regional resistance. Indeed, with his famous victory over the forces of General Lefèbre on the Isel, he joins the Archduke Charles and his officers in that tiny group of Austrian commanders who got the better of Napoleon's troops. But the Tyrol had always been a special island in the Teutonic ocean. Hofer's shabby fate (executed in Mantua a year later on charges of treason) only strengthened the Tyroleans' fierce provincial pride.

Those who fought at the time with their pens for a so-called Austrian identity were, with the exception of the archivist Johann von Hormayr (himself a Tyrolean), largely Germans. The most influential of this group was Friedrick von Gentz, a Prussian who had entered the service of the Habsburgs in 1802. He, and colleagues like Friedrich Schlegel, produced a stream of manifestos and newspaper articles to mobilise popular resistance against Napoleon. But their leaflets were usually addressed to 'The Germans' or 'The German Nation'; where Vienna was singled out for mention, it was as 'a precious part of Germany'. The fact that the great age of German literature was now flowering, headed by the prolific genius of Goethe, made this subsummation all the easier to apply to the Austrians, and all the easier for them to live with.

It was Goethe himself who, in his *Dichtung und Wahrheit*, described how the walls of the Electoral Hall in Frankfurt had been covered with the portraits of one Holy Roman Emperor after another until, towards the end of the eighteenth century, there was room for only one more. That place had been filled in 1792 by the Emperor Francis, who in 1806 was indeed to prove the last of the line. And yet, during that tense summer of 1809, with its seesaw military struggles around Vienna, the question had been mooted in the Habsburg camp as to whether the Holy Roman Empire might, after all, be revived as Austria's best hope of mobilising continental resistance to Napoleon. The idea was to be raised again in 1815, this time by the German princes, panicking at the news that Bonaparte had returned from exile in Elba to challenge his enemies again. Was there any flicker of life under the Roman empire's shroud?

When the records of the defunct body were examined, more than 20,000 unresolved cases were found in the archives of one of its judicial organs, the so-called Aulic Council in Vienna. Among the disputes which had been settled was one which had taken most of the fifteenth and part of the sixteenth centuries to resolve, doubtless to the delight and profit of the generations of lawyers involved. Such absurdities seemed to belong only to an empire of the clouds. Yet, in its late medieval form, when the Habsburgs began their long tenure as Holy Roman emperors, the classical concept of the empire – embodying the union in peace of Western Christendom – had not yet been shattered by the great religious wars. Nationalism had not yet put down wide roots, so the idea of a supreme European power, set above all peoples of the continent, was still feasible. Nor was that power only spiritual. The emperor alone could create kingdoms and make monarchs out of princes, and from the Divine Right of emperors emanated the Divine Right of kings. (Even Frederick I, as we have seen, had to seek his Prussian crown from this fount of all sovereignty.) The great orders of chivalry which had no country could only be based on pope and emperor, reflecting the conviction that Europe was something more than the sum of its separate parts.

It was the upsurge of nationalism which eroded this concept of universality: first through the absorption of the Holy Roman Empire into the German empire; then through the Thirty Years of religious conflict which cracked the empire's sacramental base and increased Europe's centripetal tendencies; and finally through the great liberal-national movements of the nineteenth century. It was now that the Habsburgs, though no longer wearing the Holy Roman crown, fought their long losing battle for the supra-nationalism which that crown had represented. Their Austrian subjects were to be caught slap in the middle of this tug-of-war between the old and the new.

For a while, however, something perversely between the two emerged, the so-called Concert of Europe. Appropriately, the setting was Vienna. It had been from the Austrian capital that, in 1791, the appeal had gone out to all the European powers to unite against the French revolutionary menace. After the defeat of Napoleon, the giant thrown up by that revolution, it was in Vienna that the great Congress of powers gathered to trace not only the new frontiers of Europe, but the path which the continent was now to tread between them.

At the centre of this Vienna stage, both as impresario and as leading actor, stood the figure of Metternich. He so dominates the Austrian scene from the year of triumph in 1815 to the year of tumult in 1848 that the whole period is called – somewhat generously perhaps – the Age of Metternich. Here again, we meet that ever-recurring paradox in the story of Austria, namely that those who shaped its fate were so often foreigners. Clement Wenceslas Lothar von Metternich-Winneburg-Beilstein, to give him his full name, came from an ancient Rhenish family. Though (thanks to an ancestor fighting on the winning side in the Battle of the White Hill in 1620) they had acquired a property at Konigswart in Bohemia, it was Rhinelanders that they remained. Here they were based on a village near Coblenz which carried their first name, with the properties from which they drew their other titles strung along the Moselle valley down to Trier. The spirit of the region was fiercely parochial. It was at the same time European, for the Rhine had been for centuries the borderland between Latin and Germanic cultures. Such was the non-national ethos which Metternich carried with him to Austria itself, the borderland between Germans and Slavs.

For nearly twenty years before the Congress of Vienna opened, the young Metternich had been moving steadily in from the wings of the Habsburg scene. His father, Count Francis, had entered the diplomatic service of the Monarchy in 1773, the year of Clement's birth, and on 9 October 1790 the seventeen-year-old boy was first presented to the dynasty he was later to serve through so many decades. The occasion was the coronation of Leopold II as Holy Roman Emperor, and the Metternichs certainly arrived in style. No fewer than ninety-eight coaches were needed to convey the family and their retinue into town, a display of ostentation which widened the eyes even of the crowned sovereigns in attendance. They were all back in Frankfurt again less than two years later when, after Leopold's sudden death in March 1792, his twenty-four-year-old son Francis became the new ruler of the Austrian Monarchy and the twentieth (and last) Habsburg to wear the crown of Charlemagne. It was this Francis whom Metternich was to serve, first as ambassador, then as Foreign Minister and finally as Chancellor down to that worthy Emperor's death in 1835. He had been at his Emperor's side on the battlefield of Wagram in the disastrous summer of 1809 and again four years later, to witness the triumph of the allied armies against Napoleon in the great 'Battle of Nations' at Leipzig. In between it was he who had helped negotiate the marriage of the Archduchess Marie Louise to Bonaparte (an intrigue after his own heart, for it was partly conducted by overtures at masked balls where the amorous Metternich was just as much at home as at his office desk). It was Metternich who, as Foreign Minister, had courted the Emperor's new son-in-law, even to the point of persuading him into a short-lived Austro–French alliance. It was Metternich who, when Napoleon's star began at last to fade, laboured in vain to persuade him to settle for sovereignty over France alone. Now, after Bonaparte's final defeat at Waterloo and exile to remote St Helena, it was Metternich who sought to salvage the best for the Habsburgs out of the debris of his conquests.

In this initial aim he served his master well, for Austria came out best of all in the Second Treaty of Paris, signed after more than four months of haggling between the victorious allies on 20 November 1815.* The Habsburg Monarchy (or 'Austrian Empire' as it had been styled for the past decade) regained Lombardy, Salzburg and the Tyrol and expanded down the Adriatic into Venetia, Istria and Dalmatia. This was handsome compensation for accepting the loss of Belgium and parts of Galicia. History was to show that this straggling empire – which of course included all the hereditary Austrian lands as well as the kingdoms of Hungary and Bohemia – was over-extended. Events were also to prove that it was politically as well as geographically mis-shapen; the trans-alpine Italian possessions, in particular, were to prove hostages to a nationalist fortune. But on the map, and for the moment, it looked brilliant. Austria was astride the Mediterranean as well as the Danube, and president to boot of the re-established Germanic Confederation. The Emperor had more prestige than ever, as well as more than four million new subjects. Francis had raised his Chancellor to the dignity of prince after the Battle of Leipzig, at which Metternich had been a mere spectator. The promotion would have been more appropriate now,

---

* The so-called First Peace of Paris had been concluded in 1814, after Napoleon's abdication; most of the territorial provisions had been agreed by the Final Act of the Treaty of Vienna, signed on 19 June 1815. This was, in fact, the day after Waterloo, though news of the great allied victory had not yet reached the Austrian capital.

after his exertions over fourteen months at the salons and the green baize tables, an exhausting diplomatic campaign in which he had always been the leader.*

But Metternich was aware of one reality above all others: this giant patchwork of kingdoms and peoples now ruled over by Vienna could only survive if nothing stirred to unstitch it. At home, that meant stamping down on anything which revived the liberal spirit of Bonaparte the reformer. Abroad, it meant creating a European framework of conservatism which would prevent the return of republican France as the conqueror. Essential to that second aim was continuity, and the keys to such continuity were the dynasties. Both principles had been enshrined in Paris itself where the Bourbons, in the person of Louis XVIII, had been restored to power. Moreover, as Napoleon was now deemed to have assaulted dynasties rather than countries, something very rare in the history of peacemaking could be observed in Vienna: France, purged of her guilt by becoming royalist again, gradually asserted herself at the Congress as a full and equal participating member. This feat was due in no small measure to the talents of her chief negotiator, Prince Maurice de Talleyrand-Périgord.

Talleyrand was a survivor supreme even in this age of opportunists: an excommunicated priest and a married Catholic bishop, he had prospered in turn under the Revolution, Napoleon, and the restored monarchy. He now promoted the Bourbon cause by exploiting differences between the other peacemaking powers, notably Russia and Prussia, but it was his call for legitimacy which set the seal of agreement between them. The Wettin dynasty was restored in a truncated Saxony, for example, despite the fact that King Frederick Augustus had deserted the allied camp to join Napoleon. Indeed, in his so-called Holy Alliance, the Russian Emperor, Tsar Alexander I, had sought to elevate the dynastic principle into a mystical instrument of European power politics. This unstable sovereign, whose flights of fancy verged on plain dottiness, persuaded the Emperor Francis and King Frederick William of Prussia to sign with him, on 15 October 1815, a personal pact based upon 'the sublime truths which the Holy Religion of our Saviour teaches'. The three sovereigns vowed to aid each other 'on all occasions and in all

* The famous jibe of the Prince de Ligne at Vienna: 'Le congrès danse, mais il ne marche pas,' was more witty than fair. Ballrooms and salons were the scenes of much private business as well as pleasure. Moreover, there were months when all the protagonists, and especially Metternich, needed to gain time – which often meant wasting it.

places', declaring themselves as 'delegated by Providence to govern three branches of the One family, namely Austria, Prussia and Russia'. Inasmuch as the three rulers involved were respectively Catholic, Protestant and Orthodox, this could be regarded as an early example of the Christian ecumenical movement. It was little else, for it had neither military nor political clauses. Britain, using constitutional arguments as her pretext, declined the open invitation to sign up. Her Foreign Secretary, Lord Castlereagh, who at Vienna had secured for his country Malta, the Cape of Good Hope, Mauritius and Ceylon, went so far as to dismiss the Tsar's High Altar diplomacy as 'nonsense'. But he did not dispute its underlying premiss: namely, that Europe after 1815 should unite and hold fast around the rock of hereditary kingship, which had survived all the batterings of the French Revolution and the conquests of Napoleon.

To this end, he gladly signed on 20 November 1815 (the same day as the final Treaty of Paris was concluded) a renewal of the wartime Quadruple Alliance against Napoleon. The four allies – Austria, Prussia, Russia and Britain – specifically pledged themselves to join action if, among other ghosts from the past, the spectre of revolution should ever arise again in France. That was indeed a novelty among treaty clauses. Even more remarkable was Clause VI of the new pact under which, at Castlereagh's suggestion, the four powers agreed that their foreign ministers should meet whenever events in Europe gave ground for common concern. This was the birth of the so-called 'Congress System' which was to convene repeatedly during the early years of the 'Metternich era'* – always to try and stop the hands of Europe's political clocks from moving forward. The rights and freedoms of the British under their Parliament remained unaffected. Castlereagh had signed up for continental stability, not for ideology. But the Austrians, still nearly a century away from even a foretaste of parliamentary democracy, continued to be smothered under the dynastic purple. Indeed, for the burgeoning liberals inside the Monarchy, the Congress System soon emerged as an instrument of domestic repression.

In August 1815, Baron von Hagen, the relatively moderate chief of police in Vienna, was replaced by the much tougher Count Josef Sedlnitzky; the strings of censorship were immediately pulled much

---

* For example, at Aix-la-Chapelle in 1818; at Karlsbad in 1819; at Vienna and Troppau in 1820; at Laibach in 1821 and at Verona in 1822.

tighter, in an attempt to choke at birth any expressions of free-thinking. For Metternich – who now acquired a second police service, answerable directly to him – there was little to choose between liberalism and Jacobinism, except that the German variety might well prove more dangerous because, being Teutonic, it would be more dogged. On 18 October 1817, his suspicions of the universities as seedbeds of trouble seemed dramatically confirmed when a few hundred students from Jena, Kiel, Vienna and Berlin gathered at the Castle of Wartburg in the Grand Duchy of Weimar for a joint demonstration. Nominally, they were there to mark the three hundredth anniversary of the Reformation (Luther had been given sanctuary at Wartburg) and also to honour the great victory over Napoleon at Leipzig four years before. But there were splutterings of political protest amidst the celebrations. Slogans were shouted denouncing tyranny, and one student had even brought along a copy of the Final Treaty of Vienna to be tossed into the bonfire.

For Metternich, this was as heinous as burning the Bible itself. More-over, though his agents had kept him fully informed about the growth of the *Burschenschaften* or student societies in German-language universi-ties, the mere fact that something like the Wartburg gathering had been organised between them, without his knowledge, was alarming. It was true that the societies were, so far, non-violent (except among them-selves, when it came to duelling). It was also clear that when they sang the praises of a German 'Fatherland' they had no idea what precisely this meant – a fuzziness which applied particularly to the Austrians. Nonetheless, liberalism and nationalism, that combination which Met-ternich rightly dreaded for the Monarchy, seemed to have touched fingers at Wartburg, and he determined to marshal all the resources of the Concert of Europe against them.

The eventual outcome was the Austro–Prussian Congress of Karls-bad,* held in August 1819 for the specific purpose of tightening control over both university teaching and the freedom of the printed word. The Karlsbad decrees, which were essentially of Metternich's own drafting, gave every German state the right to suppress any publication of more than twenty pages printed anywhere in the Confederation. A central commission was set up at Mainz to monitor the political tenor of lectures

---

* Russia, whom Metternich suspected of fomenting the student troubles, did not attend. The Tsar's dissent marked a significant fracture in the Congress System.

at every university and to keep a general look-out for any sign of
'revolutionary activity'. Inside the Habsburg Monarchy, Metternich
and Sedlnitzky set the pace by monitoring even the books which the
professors took out from libraries and by forbidding foreigners to be
employed anywhere as teachers, even as private tutors. The staff of state
schools were henceforth to be vetted for political reliability and had
to serve a three-year probation period before their appointments were
confirmed. All this fell far short of a reign of terror, especially as administered inside the Monarchy with the endemic slackness of the Austrians.
It signified not the regime's strength, but the built-in weakness of any
static political structure. Metternich may have already felt the shiver in
his bones. If a fairly harmless gathering of a few hundred students
in Weimar could produce such a panic, what might happen one day in
Vienna? He was to discover the answer nearly thirty years later.

Meanwhile, in the interval, it is instructive to look at how the Austrians themselves, and especially the Viennese, fared in this atmosphere
of repression. Another typical paradox: they actually blossomed. This
they achieved by sailing just close enough to the wind to avoid trouble
with the printed word, and for the rest, by taking refuge in a cosy world
of non-politics, which was largely of their own making. The 'Age of
Biedermeier'* was the obverse of the Age of Metternich, but part of
the self-same coin. It was a conscious flight from reality, a mass
manoeuvre in which the Austrians were to specialise from now on. Yet
at its core was a great truth: that human and cultural values have a
permanence which no government can destroy.

Biedermeier was essentially a domestic culture. Its credo was happy
middle-class family life, screened off from the challenges of ideology
and nationalism, and savouring the arts where it was both safe and
agreeable to do so. That place was the home, so it is not surprising that
the hallmark of Biedermeier should have been its furniture. This was
geometric rather than comfortable and, as with Austrian baroque, a
blend of other people's styles, with a dash of Viennese added, to give
the end product the semblance of being native. In this case, the main
influence was not Italian, as in the century before, but French: Biedermeier stiff chairs and sofas, with their light inlaid woods, were a blend

---

* The name came originally from a comic character, 'Papa Biedermeier', created by the
German poet Ludwig Eichrocht and intended to symbolise bourgeois bad taste. It came
to represent, throughout Germany and Scandinavia as well as Austria, what the middle
classes considered to be their best taste.

of Empire and Directoire styles (themselves, of course, a mixture of classical and modern).

Of greater significance were some of the items themselves. There was, for example, always a desk in Biedermeier drawing-rooms; letter-writing (to relatives and friends, though definitely not to newspapers or political figures) was part of the lifestyle. Another regular feature was the piano, for dutiful daytime practice by the daughters of the house and, in the evenings, for 'house music', with other family members or friends making up trios or quartets. It is here that Biedermeier joined hands with that greater artistic world which, despite Police Chief Sedlnitzky's constraints, was flourishing outside these domestic salons. Franz Schubert was a true son of Vienna and the native symbol of the Romantic movement which was engulfing Europe. Many of his six hundred songs,* his fifteen string quartets and (difficult though some of them were) even his twenty-two piano sonatas would have featured in Biedermeier '*Hausmusik*'. The symphonies, operas and choral works which he also poured out until his early death in 1828 needed, of course, a larger stage. This even the Vienna of Metternich's censors could provide, and there was room on it not just for composers. It was also the age of another Franz, the dramatist Grillparzer, as native to the scene as Schubert, and the greatest poet his people were ever to produce.

With Grillparzer, we can indeed begin to speak of an Austrian literature, famed not just wherever German was spoken, but throughout the cultural world. Yet, in the Vienna of his day, the laurels did not always settle comfortably on his brow. The success of his very first play, *Die Ahnfrau* ('The Ancestress'), which appeared in 1817, secured him the post of Archive Director at the Court Theatre, an appointment he hung on to until his retirement in 1856. However, he narrowly escaped dismissal on at least one occasion when a lament he wrote on the tragedy of ancient Rome was deemed by Sedlnitzky's 'thought police' to be a barbed parallel with the fragile state of the Habsburg Monarchy. Even his most famous play, *König Ottokars Glück und Ende*, dealing with the rise and fall (at Archduke Rudolph's hands) of the thirteenth-century Bohemian ruler, had problems reaching the stage. The fact that all his works – with themes of history, myth or fantasy – were produced at the Burgtheater was due not least to its director at the time, the very

* It was characteristic both of the composer and of the Vienna in which he lived that the loveliest of all of these did not concern nature, romance or tragedy. It was (at least in the author's subjective judgement!) '*An die Musik*', an ode to his own art.

talented and open-minded Joseph Schreyvogel. Grillparzer's works were
the Austrian answer to plays like *Don Carlos*, *William Tell* or *Wallenstein*,
written a generation earlier by the great German dramatist Friedrich
Schiller – all of them with an anti-Habsburg message. Thus, for a while,
there was balance in the poetic scales of the two Germanic cultures. The
playwright Ferdinand Raimund* helped to weight the Austrian pan
with his popular comedies. His contribution, though not so resplendent
as Grillparzer's, was more typically Viennese: he sought to present fairy
tales as the answer to the conundrum of life but ended up, in 1836, by
taking his own.

All this was an implicit challenge to an authoritarian regime which
was more bigoted than brutal. But explicit challenges also grew, even
though the appeal to patriotic resistance was, as so often, obscured by
being wrapped up in the Germanic equation. Nonetheless, these open
challenges to the system were important in that they were often presented by members of the Austrian aristocracy, whose vested interests
the system was dedicated to preserving. These high-born mavericks
numbered a Colloredo-Mansfeld and a Montecuccoli among their ranks,
but the most energetic among them was Count Anton Auersperg. In
his own identity, he spoke out for a 'German-Austrian Monarchy',
purged of all Jesuitical elements (a foretaste here of the anti-Catholic
pan-Germanism which was to stalk the Vienna political scene later in
the century). Meanwhile, under the pseudonym 'Anastasius Grün', the
count published verse which, if not of immortal quality, was at least
distinguished by its liberal and patriotic tones in an age which sought
to quash both.

But the real damage to the system came from outside. As Metternich
had always realised, unrest could only be contained inside the Monarchy
if it was suppressed in continental Europe as a whole. But on this
broader screen, the rents soon appeared in his Congress fabric. If, in
the 1820s, insurrections had been successfully put down in Spain, Piedmont and Naples, the revolutions of 1830 carried all before them. After
Greece finally secured her freedom from the Ottoman empire in 1829
(a romantic victory for nationalism, symbolised by Lord Byron's death
in the rebel cause), the Belgians rose up against the Dutch, with whom
they had been united in the peace settlements of 1815. Nine years
later, they were confirmed as an independent kingdom. But it was the

---

* A theatre named after him still flourishes in Vienna today.

lightning midsummer revolution in Paris which delivered the heaviest blow to the Europe of Metternich. In protest against reactionary ordinances issued by the blinkered and archaic King Charles X (successor of the relatively sensible Louis XVIII), the Parisians took to the barricades, a potent army of frustrated republicans and latter-day Bonapartists. Within three days, 27–29 July 1830, they had driven the last, and probably the least distinguished, of all the Bourbons from his throne, and seized power.

From the strictly dynastic point of view, no formal damage had been done in all this. Prince Otto of Bavaria was made ruler of the new kingdom of Greece. The crown of Belgium was bestowed, by Anglo–French agreement, on Leopold of Saxe-Coburg-Gotha, that remarkable German 'stud farm' which was soon to provide Victorian England with its Consort. Even in France no republic was, as yet, proclaimed. Instead, Louis Philippe,* head of the House of Orléans, was put on the throne to inaugurate a spell of bourgeois monarchy. The fateful writing on the wall for Metternich and his system of perpetual, divinely sanctioned rule was the fact that this change from Bourbon to Orléanist had come not from God, but from the mob.

Austrian historians have tended to mark the death of the Emperor Francis on 2 March 1835, rather than the upheavals of 1830, as the beginning of the end of the Metternich era. This is true only in the sense that a partnership between sovereign and Chancellor which Vienna – and Europe – had come to take for granted for the past twenty years was now broken. The rupture was made far worse by the fact that Ferdinand, the old Emperor's son and successor, was an amiable ninny who would have been dubbed a village idiot had he been born a peasant.** This meant that the Austrian empire had become a Monarchy without a proper monarch and even without a proper Regency, for Metternich had to struggle to maintain his influence in the cumbrous State Council set up with the Archduke Ludwig in the chair to rule in the Emperor's name. All this weakened centralist power and prestige. Though the centre itself – now an overcrowded city of some 400,000 inhabitants – seemed to be waltzing on unconcernedly with Biedermeier self-absorption, unrest was stirring elsewhere

---

* His credentials were impeccable for the occasion. He was the son of 'Philippe Egalité', who had supported the French Revolution.
** Indeed, the populace dubbed him 'Nandl der Trottel', or 'Ferdy the Dotty', which showed affection if not respect.

in the Monarchy, especially in Hungary. Here the system was being threatened by the mild liberalism of that far-sighted reformist magnate Count István Széchényi,* and, to a far greater degree, by the extremist ideas of a Magyar-Slovak squire, Lajos Kossuth, of whom the Monarchy and the world were about to hear much more. He was to combine liberalism with nationalism into a doctrine of revolution which went straight back in spirit to the barricades of Paris. Metternich's Vienna had to wait awhile for these germs to infect its escapist atmosphere of contentment. In the end, the carriers turned out to be the young men whom the Chancellor had singled out as his main adversaries ever since the 'Festival of Wartburg': Austria's university students. In 1817, their challenge had been well-organised but trivial; in 1848, it was chaotic but lethal.

The impetus, as usual, came from outside and, yet again, it was tumult in Paris which touched off the continental slide into violence. The Habsburg Monarchy, it is true, was already trembling at its extremities. Two years before, a bloody peasant revolt in Galicia had cost the lives of several hundred landlords before the small Austrian garrison could put it down, with the help of Russian and Prussian contingents. The following year, 1847, the Emperor's Italian provinces – the poisoned chalice of the 1815 awards – again erupted, with street riots in Milan, Pavia and Padua and unrest even in the normally passive Venice. The calls for liberalism and nationalism were intertwining tighter than ever. The first cause had been boosted by the elevation of Cardinal Mastai-Ferrari, Bishop of Imola, to the Papacy: as 'Pio Nono', or Pius IX, he became the apostle of enlightenment within the Church and therefore the symbol of reform outside it. The second cause, that of Italian nationalism, was being nursed by the ambitious King Charles Albert of Piedmont, whose anti-Austrian designs had only been camouflaged by his marriage to a daughter of the House of Habsburg. The commander of the imperial garrison in Lombardy-Venetia, General Josef Radetzky (another name that was about to be on everyone's lips), was soon struggling to keep order with his scattered and overstretched forces.

As for the Austrian heart of the Monarchy, food shortages – brought about by bad cereal harvests three years in succession – seemed more of a problem to the regime than political agitation as 1848 dawned.

---

* The idea of throwing a chain bridge across the Danube had been one of his brain-children. Even more startling was his proposal that the nobles – hitherto exempt from all forms of taxation – should also pay toll charges at the bridge.

Vienna, already suffering from overcrowding, was among the worst-hit of the cities, as thousands of unemployed and undernourished workers from the Czech lands poured into the capital with their families in search of jobs and a square meal. Some of the outer suburbs were little better than starving slums, yet in the relatively prosperous centre of the capital the candles blazed unconcernedly from the chandeliers. *Fasching*, the traditional winter carnival season, had got off to a brilliant start, with Franz Liszt at his piano and Jenny Lind in full concert voice. The festivities were at their height when, on 29 February, the news arrived from Paris that Louis Philippe had abdicated. Once again, it had been the work of the street mobs. But in contrast to 1830, when that bourgeois monarch from the House of Orléans had been summoned to replace the House of Bourbon, this time the throne itself was toppled and a republic declared. Would Metternich be toppled as well?

The Chancellor was said to have fainted clean away when, at five o'clock on that Tuesday afternoon, the news was brought to him by his friend and financial guru, the Jewish banker Salomon Rothschild.* But Metternich recovered his composure as soon as his consciousness and immediately launched a diplomatic campaign among his Congress partners to ward off this renewed blast of French radicalism. Despite the predictable run on the banks and general financial panic (with some shopkeepers refusing to accept any paper money), the city itself remained calm. Count Sedlnitzky — still in office as chief of police — assured his master that the capital was in no danger. As for the students, its eventual conquerors, they continued, in true Viennese style, to dance and drink away at the carnival, right down to its last waltz. Ash Wednesday did not fall until 8 March that year, and it was only on the following day that the student societies turned grudgingly aside from their frolics to hold their first joint discussion about the Paris revolution, now ten days old.

Metternich might indeed have got away with it — at least for a while — had it not been for Lajos Kossuth, the only man along the Danube's banks who seemed to sense exactly what the news from France could signify. On 3 March, in a speech to the Lower House of the Hungarian Diet at Pozsony, he turned a debate on the financial crisis into a motion

---

* Salomon had been settled in Vienna since 1820. His four brothers, James, Charles, Nathan and Amschel, were based in Paris, Naples, London and Frankfurt respectively. They had set up between them Europe's fastest and most reliable courier service, from which Metternich regularly profited.

for 'responsible and independent' government in Hungary. Though couched in correct terms (his motion was carried in the form of an 'Address to the Crown'), it was in essence a declaration of war on Vienna, on Metternich's system and on the dynasty itself. This was the message which helped to seal Metternich's fate.

The focus of action was the Landhaus in the Herrengasse of the Inner City where, on Monday 13 March, the provincial leaders of Lower Austria were to convene in session. Petitions reflecting the growing unrest against the regime poured in throughout the weekend, including one from the Vienna students which demanded not only greater freedom in the universities but more democracy in the state. By now, reports of Kossuth's speech (though not, as yet, the full text) had reached Vienna, putting fresh fire into the bellies of all liberal reformers, both inside and outside the lecture halls.* On the Sunday, the university dons belatedly stirred themselves. Two of their number, Professors Hye and Endlicher, carried a new student petition to the Hofburg itself, where they had a long talk with Archduke Ludwig, on behalf of the State Council, and even a short audience with the dim-witted Emperor Ferdinand. On the surface, everything was still manageable; Sedlnitzky continued to exude confidence on the security front. But Archduke Ludwig was less certain, and contemplated declaring martial law. Metternich backed his police chief and was all for 'Wait and see'.

Everything shattered around the regime's ears in precisely twelve hours on the following day. At nine o'clock in the morning the students massed outside the Lower Austrian Landhaus. Their ranks were swelled by a typically Viennese crowd of '*Adabeis*',** and a few hundred workers from those slum-like suburbs, real trouble-makers, who had come to hurl stones in any cause which sounded promising. The crowd forced its way past the heavy gates in the courtyard of the building where, among other instant orators, a young doctor named Adolf Fischhof reissued the call for sweeping reforms. This was cheered loudly enough, but it was Kossuth's words which turned the cheers into hysteria. German translations of his Pozsony speech had been hurriedly printed in

---

* The non-academic agitators petitioning the Estates included the Viennese comedy playwright Edward Bauernfeld (in whose name a special prize was founded) and a lawyer with political ambitions, Alexander von Bach. He later turned conservative and became Imperial Minister of Interior.

** '*Auch dabeis*', or 'also-theres': people who, whether personally involved or not, do not wish to miss anything interesting.

Vienna over the weekend, and a bundle of them was now brought down to the Landhaus. As the leaflets were being handed out, a Tyrolean student called Patz had the brilliant idea of declaiming the text in a stentorian voice.

That did it. The crowd erupted. Some of them forced their way into the Landhaus and began to wreck furniture. More to the point, others moved the few hundred yards down the Herrengasse to the Hofburg Palace, where a deputation presented the latest demands of the people. Half-measures had been dropped. They now called for a proper constitution, and for Metternich's head.

Controlled military action combined with a couple of judiciously phrased statements issued by anyone in power except Metternich might at least have won time. Instead, one afternoon of almost indescribable muddle, confusion, weakness and divided counsel proved enough to push him and his system over the brink and into oblivion by nightfall.

There were 14,000 troops in the Vienna garrison, including three infantry and two cavalry regiments, but their unimaginative commander, the Archduke Albrecht, had left most of them in barracks well outside the Inner City limits. At lunchtime some did begin to arrive, to reinforce the palace and Chancellery guards; Archduke Ludwig, who was young Albrecht's uncle, had issued the orders at Metternich's suggestion. However, they proved quite incapable of restoring order. A panic move by one patrol which, instead of firing warning shots in the air, loosed a volley straight into the crowd, killing four and wounding many more, precipitated the final crisis. A new issue arose: who should take control of the streets after the failure of the Emperor's troops, now anyway reviled as murderers?

Metternich, still immaculately attired and outwardly confident, had his own solution. General Alfred Windisch-Graetz,* a fellow prince of the empire and a fellow landowner in Bohemia, happened to be in Vienna on a private visit and was to dine with Metternich that evening. Why, the Chancellor suggested, should his dinner guest not simply change into his uniform and take over on the spot from the discredited Albrecht? A man who had distinguished himself as a youthful officer at the great victory over Napoleon at Leipzig and who was now Military Governor of Bohemia should surely have no problem in putting this undisciplined mob of Viennese rowdies in their place. Windisch-Graetz was all for it.

---

* He was later promoted to field marshal.

But other people in the capital had other ideas; impracticable though these were, the frenzied scene that day was not set for imperial commanders. The Bürgermaster of Vienna, Ignaz von Czapka, had spoken up for his terrified citizens, urging that his own Military Civic Guard* should take over from the garrison forces. Another, and more alarming, proposal to reach Archduke Ludwig and his State Councillors came from the Rector of the University. His solution was that his students should be issued arms with which to form their own Academia Legion.

All the while, reports of arson and looting poured in (Metternich's own residence in the Rennweg barely escaped destruction), and shooting could clearly be heard in the Hofburg, coming from all directions. The antechambers of the great palace were swarming with demonstrators and would-be mediators. One of the latter, a wine merchant called Scherzer,** calmly gave the State Council two hours to withdraw the army, sack the Chancellor or face the consequences. (Other demands for Metternich's resignation had already been delivered at his office in the nearby Ballhausplatz.) Grillparzer was among the fascinated onlookers as this page of history was turned. It seemed to him, as he wrote afterwards, that almost anyone could simply walk into the Hofburg that afternoon, bang on the table and hurl abuse at the presiding Archduke.

When Metternich and Windisch-Graetz returned to the palace at six o'clock after their meal ('dinner' was often consumed at what would now be teatime), the mood of the State Council still seemed to favour traditional solutions, and the General even went to his Vienna residence to put on his uniform. But when Metternich returned an hour later, Archduke Ludwig had been persuaded – by the Chancellor's own rivals in the Council as much as by the increasing ugliness of the situation – to change course completely. It had been agreed that units of the Civic Guard and the armed students should both be deployed to take over, post by post, from the garrison troops, and that eventually a full-scale National Guard would replace the army in the capital.

That left only the resignation question to be resolved. Metternich demurred for an hour and a half, irritating the Council with a long

* This still consisted, in theory, of two infantry regiments with supporting troops under the Mayor's personal command. Ever since the Napoleonic era, however, when it had served as a standby garrison, it had been a purely token force which turned out only on ceremonial occasions. 13 March 1848 scarcely fitted that bill.
** Literally 'joker', though not on this occasion.

lecture on the instability of Europe and the need for him to remain in office to deal with it. Finally the Archduke John, Ludwig's uncle and a long-time critic of the Chancellor, took out his watch and bluntly informed Prince Metternich that he had only another thirty minutes to take his decision. Nothing had been heard from the Emperor Ferdinand in all this; but he was present, and it was the dim-witted monarch who suddenly spoke up to end the argument. 'I'm the sovereign and I'm the one to decide,' he declared with unwonted force. 'Tell the people I agree to everything.' That was tantamount to a royal dismissal.

It only remained for Metternich to bow out in proper ceremonial fashion. In 1835, he had promised the dying Emperor Francis that he would always stand by his inadequate successor. The Chancellor now demanded of all the archdukes present that they individually release him from that oath. They all complied; one of their number was the seventeen-year-old Francis Joseph, who already had some inkling of what might well be lying in store for him.

And that was that. The statesman who had ridden the coach of Europe for nearly four decades, trampling over everything in his path, had been toppled from his box by the equivalent of a student rag turned sour.* His exit was pathetic. Persuaded that he and his family were in danger of their lives, they fled at first to Feldsberg, a Liechtenstein property on the Moravian border. Then, supplied with false passports (and some cash for the journey from Rothschild), came a nine-week odyssey across Germany and Holland to England. It was three years before Metternich was to return from exile, and then only as a powerless oracle from the past.

General Windisch-Graetz, who had returned to the Hofburg in full fig that fateful evening only to be told that he was no longer needed, had better fortune. He was soon in uniform again, and with devastating effect.

---

* 'At times I ruled over Europe, but never over Austria,' was Metternich's own verdict on his fate.

PART TWO

FRANCIS JOSEPH: THE PATH TO 'KAKANIA'

I

A False Dawn

THE GREAT WAVE OF REVOLUTION loomed up only after Metternich's departure; it came from Germany and surged like a tidal bore down the Danube. Yet in little more than a year its force was spent and only froth, mixed with some blood, was left on the banks. Indeed, it actually set in place a rock which was to symbolise the tenacity of the dynastic principle it had sought to weaken. This rock was the enormous sixty-eight-year reign of the Emperor Francis Joseph, who came closer than any of his illustrious house before him to achieving the nimbus of a demi-god, an aura which clung to him right down to his death, well into the twentieth century. Both the revolution and that monarchical phenomenon which it launched have a bearing on our underlying theme, the suppressed development of an Austrian consciousness.

Let us stay, for the moment, with the House of Habsburg which now, as for centuries past, both asserted and negated the Austrian identity. There were times in the fifteen months of chaos which followed Metternich's fall when its fortunes looked precarious. To begin with, as one result of the April uprising,* the wretched Ferdinand lost all that mechanism of Regency rule which had kept his empire going since his accession. His Privy Chancellery was abolished; so too was the ruling State Conference, whose well-intentioned President, Archduke Ludwig, now retired from public life. In place of this came a 'Responsible Ministry', composed largely of earnest bureaucrats who had only one factor in common: no experience whatever of responsibility. The most liberal of these, Baron Franz von Pillersdorf, eventually produced the constitution which had been promised as part of the April compromise.

---

* Among the others were a general amnesty for all political offenders and the legal abolition of the so-called 'robot' system of compulsory peasant labour for landlords.

The mere word was anathema to any Habsburg, conveying as it did the dilution of divine right, which was tantamount to denying it altogether.

Pillersdorf had, it is true, made some genuflections towards the dynasty in his first draft. The emperor could nominate an unspecified number of life members to the Senate, or Upper House, of the proposed two-chamber Parliament. He could suspend or dissolve it, though not indefinitely. Finally, he was allowed to veto any of the laws it might pass.

The concept of power-sharing between the crown and a Constituent Assembly had at least been aired in Vienna. Events on 15 May 1848 showed where, for the moment, that power still lay in the capital. Students, workers and National Guardsmen packed the streets and laid siege to the Hofburg, demanding the scrapping of Pillersdorf's proposals, which had already been watered down, in favour of more radical reforms. The call now was for a single-chamber Parliament directly elected by popular franchise. The Emperor and his 'Responsible Ministry' took fright and caved in to the demands; posters to that effect were pasted up in the city the following day. Mob pressure had swept away, on paper, the Emperor's crucial powers. It also removed him from his capital. Persuaded by the ladies of his court that all their lives were again in danger, Ferdinand and his wife set out as though for a normal carriage ride in Vienna but made instead for Innsbruck, where he arrived after a thirty-six-hour drive on the evening of the seventeenth. Other members of the family joined them later. Once again the dynasty had sought refuge in the Tyrol from the violence of the capital.

The single-chamber Parliament, or Reichstag, opened its formal proceedings in Vienna later that summer, with the Emperor and his court still lurking in internal exile at Innsbruck. Theoretically, the chance was now given for the peoples of the Habsburg Monarchy (excepting the Magyars who, as usual, were going their own way) to transform themselves into a democratic federation of equal nations united under a constitutional ruler. Merely to state that proposition is to underline the impossibility of achieving it in practice in 1848, given the historic rifts between the races and the calibre of the deputies assembled to try and mend those rifts in the common cause of liberalism. Of the 303 members, 160 were Austrians (i.e. German-speaking subjects of the Emperor) and the remainder Slavs, Roumanians or Italians. Their individual backgrounds were as varied as the racial mix,* but one almost universal factor soon emerged: their inability to think beyond their own racial horizons.

The Austrians were, as ever, in a daze as to what those horizons were. The best of the few capable brains they had were anyway absent, sitting in the all-German revolutionary Parliament which was in simultaneous session at the Paulskirche in Frankfurt. The two assemblies were living examples of the tug-of-war between the Germanic and the Habsburg destinies of the Austrians. Those elected to the Vienna Assembly tried to play the role of impartial reconcilers; they dispersed themselves to sit among the other racial groupings, who, to a man, had taken their places in nationalist blocks. But it was not long before the would-be reconcilers and the Slavs (in particular the Bohemian Czechs) were abusing each other inside the Assembly building and even assaulting each other outside.

The Czechs had sent their best team to Vienna, headed by the great historian František Palacky. On 11 April he had caused something of a sensation by refusing an invitation to the Frankfurt Parliament on the grounds that he was not a German but a subject of the Austrian empire. Austria, he had declared, should have close political and economic links with any German state but should always remain separate: a union of equal peoples under the Habsburg sceptre. 'I am not a German,' he wrote at the time, 'I am a Bohemian of Slavonic stock.' It was something of an irony that this clearest of all clarion calls for the independent role of the Monarchy in Europe – later labelled 'Austro-Slavism' – should have come from a Czech. In a verdict that he made famous (though did not actually invent) Palacky had also bestowed on that Monarchy its historic claim to live: 'Truly, had not Austria already existed, it would have been necessary to create her, in the interests of Europe and of humanity itself.'

The trouble with this soothing message was that what Palacky really had at the back of his mind might rather be termed 'Slavo-Austrianism', namely a bid to transform the Monarchy from an empire resting upon its German-speaking subjects to one resting on Bohemians, Moravians, Slovenes and the like. And quite apart from all the ethnic, linguistic and

* The biggest single group were the ninety-four peasant deputies. They were followed by seventy-four officials of various sorts; forty-eight lawyers; forty-six nobles; twenty-two doctors; twenty priests; eighteen industrialists; thirteen professors; nine merchants; nine journalists and the rest 'miscellaneous'.

cultural impulses behind this Slavonic programme, there was also a down-to-earth human one: the grasp for what, in modern parlance, would be called 'more jobs for the boys'. The Danube Basin was not to change in that respect in the upheavals of 1918, nor in those at the end of the century.

The Habsburg dynasty, and the mass of its Austrian subjects, had always felt in the past and would continue in the future to feel too Germanic in their souls to embrace Palacky's pan-Slav vision. In any case, it was not the spiritual struggle but the physical one which was now to decide the outcome. On 16 June the rebel regime in Prague surrendered, after a brief bombardment, to the forces of General Windisch-Graetz, who promptly dissolved the Bohemian Diet and declared martial law. (In doing so, he had overridden, with contempt, attempts at mediation launched by the weak-kneed 'Responsible Ministry' in Vienna.) At the same time, down in northern Italy, another imperial commander, General Josef Radetzky, was also ignoring cease-fire instructions from Austria to intensify his campaign against the nationalist forces led by King Charles Albert of Piedmont-Sardinia. Throughout the summer he dislodged the Piedmontese from town after town and by the beginning of August, after a decisive victory at Custozza, he had driven them clean out of Lombardy. The crown of Milan, like the crown of Bohemia, had been preserved for the Monarchy by generals disobeying its orders. Whatever the authorities thought at the time, the muses of Vienna lavished durable praise on the victor of Lombardy. His earlier triumph at Santa Lucia in June inspired Grillparzer to write the ode with the well-known line: 'In your camp stands Austria'. It was to become the slogan behind all future appeals for dynastic loyalty in the multi-national imperial army. The final triumph in July moved Johann Strauss the elder* to compose an even more famous tribute which was to outlast the Monarchy itself: the 'Radetzky March', to this day still among the half-dozen finest military marches ever written for any army in the world.

More to the point, in 1848 the Austrian success in Lombardy had put some stuffing back into the Habsburg camp. On 12 August, three weeks after Custozza, the Emperor Ferdinand and his court came back to Vienna. Though careful to emphasise in public that he had returned as a constitutional monarch, he secretly authorised Windisch-Graetz to

* Father of the famous 'Waltz King', who bore the same Christian name.

assume both supreme military command and overall civil powers 'in case of emergency'. As far as Vienna was concerned, that emergency lay just around the corner.

Throughout August and September rioting had broken out in the capital, largely by workers protesting against the savage effects of rising prices combined with cuts in pay rates. Yet, once again, it was events in Hungary which set the torch to a blaze.

On 6 October a regiment sent to reinforce the troops* fighting against Kossuth's nationalistic forces mutinied and refused to entrain army reinforcements sent down to restore order, touching off a minia-ture battle. There were casualties on all sides, including among the crowd which had surrounded the railway station. At this, the mob again took brief but vicious control of the Vienna streets. In the ensuing mayhem the luckless Minister of War, Count Theodor Latour, was dragged from his desk, lynched, and his naked and mutilated body hung from a lamp-post. Viennese demonstrators normally confined them-selves to hurling abuse or, at worst, stones. This act of bestiality was doubly alarming because it was so uncharacteristic. Was the imperial city about to erupt in a Balkans-style bloodbath?

The Emperor was not allowed to find out. The following morning, he and his family, following a contingency plan prepared long before by Windisch-Graetz, took to their heels again. This time their desti-nation was Olmütz in Moravia, and they travelled not as frightened passengers in a stage-coach, but as a miniature court under strong military escort.

As for Windisch-Graetz, his hour had come at last. Formally invested with plenipotentiary powers, he now marched on a Vienna in which the Reichstag was crumbling and on which the members of the 'Responsible Ministry' were turning their backs, many of them heading for Olmütz. That ministerial corpse dangling from the lamp-post had sobered every-one up. The students attempted to take the reins again by forming an emergency 'Central Committee' to administer the capital. But the days of Vienna's revolution were numbered, and its last phase – the second fortnight of October – was marked by a familiar mixture of farce, tragedy and muddle. A trickle of volunteers from the provinces got through the cordon of imperial troops to join the 'Central Committee's' garrison.

* Their leader was a Croat, General Josip Jellacic, who was serving the Emperor's cause – albeit somewhat erratically – by striving to free Croatia from the threat of Magyar domination.

A few soldiers of fortune turned up.* But the only serious hope of reinforcement lay with Kossuth's Hungarian forces which were now advancing towards Vienna. A detachment of their cavalry reached the suburbs on the morning of 30 October, the day after the capital had surrendered to Windisch-Graetz after a week of street fighting. The token rescue bid did more harm than good by sparking off one final, and futile, burst of resistance. At a cost of some 2000 dead, the uprising in Vienna (and in the western half of the Monarchy) was over. Nor were the burghers too aghast at the wave of arrests, followed by twenty-five executions among the ringleaders, which followed. Most of the good bourgeois had been frightened out of their skins by these storms of domestic violence which had battered at the walls of their cosy Biedermeier world. The next so-called 'revolution' in Vienna – itself a mild affair compared with that of 1848 – lay a good seventy years in the future.

The time had now come to settle an issue which had been troubling the ruling house and its advisers ever since the death of Francis I in 1835. 'Nandl', his good-hearted but dim-witted and epileptic son, had reigned in name for more than a decade, but only through the instrument of the Regency Council. Once that device had been exploded by the revolution, and the revolution had itself petered out, stability in a chaotic world could only be sought through the throne itself. It was an embarrassing business. After much humming and ha-ing by the court doctors, Ferdinand had been allowed to take a wife in 1831. The unfortunate bride was Princess Marie Anne of Savoy, a stoic royal lady whose role has generally been underestimated in the events of 1848. One whose role has often been overestimated was her sister-in-law the Archduchess Sophie, wife of the Emperor's brother Francis Charles. As it was clear that, though married, the wretched Ferdinand would never father a child, the line of direct descent rested upon Sophie's fecundity. After a series of miscarriages, this Bavarian princess (who had all the vitality of the Wittelsbachs but without any of their loopiness) was to oblige handsomely. On 18 August 1830 she bore her husband a son, Francis Joseph, and followed up with two more – Maximilian coming into the world on 6 July 1832, and Charles Louis on 30 July a year later.

---

* Among them the Pole Josef Bem, who was to play a heroic role in the last phase of the revolution still rampant in neighbouring Hungary.

It makes a stirring story to present the Archduchess as the power not only behind the palace but also behind the revolution – conspiring against Metternich to place her family on the throne. But the facts – notably her own diaries and letters – do not support that scenario. Both she and her husband, who served on the State Council,* were close friends and devotees of Metternich, and the mere idea of liberalism was as abhorrent to them both as to the great Chancellor. Nor is it correct to present the dynastic changes now put into place as springing directly from the crisis of 1848. As far back as November 1847, Ferdinand's wife had argued with Metternich that not only her husband but also her brother-in-law should renounce the throne in favour of his first-born, the Archduke Francis Joseph, then only seventeen years old. The boy's mother seems to have taken no part in these initial discussions, and may well have been unaware of them for some months. After Metternich's fall, it was Windisch-Graetz who called the tune, on this as on other matters. Twice in that tumultuous summer of 1848 he was approached by the Empress to make the change (most insistently on Francis Joseph's eighteenth birthday); twice he put her off, though he approved of the arrangement. Finally, with the court in exile at Olmütz, Windisch-Graetz gave the word. Not without some difficulty, both Ferdinand and his brother were persuaded to renounce the throne, and on 2 December 1848, at a brief ceremony in the Archbishop's palace, the young Francis Joseph entered on his massive inheritance. Ferdinand accepted his fate with affecting grace and simplicity. He stroked the head of the boy-emperor who knelt before him, saying to the youth: 'God bless you. Be good. God will protect you. I don't mind.' With that, 'Nandl' bowed out of history. He died in Prague in 1875, an almost-forgotten Habsburg.

There had been much talk at the court as to how the new ruler should sign himself. Both he and his parents were all for a simple 'Francis II', in honour of the grandfather who was venerated by the people as well as by the family. Their ministers persuaded them to opt for the double name instead: it was, they argued, so much more suggestive of the new era which was supposed to be dawning. The double name was indeed a novelty for a Habsburg sovereign; moreover, the addition of 'Joseph' would surely carry a refreshing whiff of Enlightenment into the sultry

---

* He actually took over the chair from his uncle, the Archduke Ludwig, in the final days of the 1848 crisis.

political climate of the day. It was to prove, in the end, a bogus prospectus. To begin with, however, ideas were bandied about which would have taken the breath of the Great Reformer himself.

The Reichstag had been moved from the unstable capital to Kremsier, another Moravian refuge. It was in the Archbishop's castle there that, on 4 January 1849, the Deputies resumed the task broken off in Vienna the previous autumn – the quest for a New Jerusalem, a liberal constitution for an ancient Monarchy. Sub-committees had been labouring for weeks over the text but the opening words of their draft: 'All sovereignty derives from the people,' show how overblown was their concept in any Habsburg context. Even more outrageous to conservative minds were clauses which abolished all titles of nobility and removed the Roman Catholic Church from its centuries-old position as the religion of the state. It was one thing to declare everyone equal before the law and to re-assert the rights of a free press, free speech and free assembly (which the Kremsier hopefuls also propounded); these phrases were by now too familiar to shock and too general to alarm. But a simultaneous bid to displace both the aristocracy from their pedestals and the prelates from their altars (and this in a prince-archbishop's residence) was begging for trouble.

Indeed, the court and its imperial ministry were only waiting for some military success in Hungary (where the battle against Kossuth's rebel army was still raging) to ring down the curtain on the Kremsier ideologues. The government which had meanwhile been formed at Olmütz during the autumn was a powerful one. It was headed by the forty-eight-year-old Prince Felix Schwarzenberg, brother-in-law of Field Marshal Windisch-Graetz, who had proposed him for the job. He was to prove a fateful choice. Like the Field Marshal, Schwarzenberg could boast of a lineage as ancient as that of the dynasty itself. But, until this moment, he could boast of little else. He had drifted between the army, diplomacy, and his vast Bohemian estates all his life, as mood and opportunity took him. At times he had served his Emperor well; at times he had caused acute embarrassment.* His hallmark (apart from exceptional good looks, which often led him into trouble) was an arrogance breathtaking even by the haughty standards of his class. He despised the people

---

* Notably by his notorious love affair with Jane Ellenborough, wife of England's Lord Privy Seal, conducted when he was serving as Austrian envoy in London. The scandal ended in divorce. Schwarzenberg's 'punishment' took the form of a transfer to Paris, a more tolerant capital, to which the infatuated Lady Jane followed him.

because they had no blue blood, and his fellow nobles because they had no brains. Writing to his brother-in-law in January 1849 about the perennial problem of devising a new constitution, he pooh-poohed the idea of giving it a specifically aristocratic colouring because 'I do not know of more than a dozen men of our class in the entire Monarchy who could in the present circumstances serve usefully in an Upper Chamber.'

The team which Schwarzenberg had gathered around him at Olmütz suggested that he really believed what he said. Only one, Count Philipp Stadion, who took the key post of Minister of Interior, came from the higher aristocracy. Alexander von Bach (Justice) was the same ambitious lawyer who, the year before, had been in the camp of the Vienna rebels. He was to rise to great things in the decade ahead. The others were bureaucrats or professional men who had climbed the social ladder on personal merit to the lowest rung of baronial nobility (to be duly despised by those who had done nothing whatever towards earning their own inherited titles). Most of these 'Freiherrs von' were unremarkable and sank with little trace. One, however, Karl von Brück, who looked after Commerce and Communications, was outstanding. As a future Minister of Finance, he was to become the economic guru of the age, urging the fusion of the Habsburg Monarchy and the German Confederation into a single customs union seventy millions strong. Like Metternich, he was a Rhinelander – yet another example of a foreigner moulding Austrian affairs.

The dynastic question had been settled very satisfactorily in the last month of the old year. Schwarzenberg's first task in 1849 was to sort out the constitutional muddle; that meant bringing the big top down on the political circus at Kremsier. When 'presenting' his new government to the Assembly the previous November, he had shamelessly lied to its gratified delegates by pledging to 'take the lead' in installing liberal and popular institutions. But on 28 February, when Windisch-Graetz, still struggling in Hungary, won a useful if indecisive victory against Kossuth's army at Kápolna, Schwarzenberg felt strong enough to strike on the home front. He despatched Stadion to Kremsier to inform an astonished Assembly that, as the new Emperor was going to proclaim his own constitution, their labours were at an end. Notices were posted up the following morning, announcing the Reichstag's dissolution. The date they carried showed they had been printed three days before. Hard on the heels of the proclamation, Bach's policemen arrived in Kremsier with orders to arrest the most radical of the delegates. Some fled as far afield as America.* A new age of absolutism had dawned.

It was exemplified in the new constitution which Stadion announced (there was no question of consultation). The earnest planners of Kremsier, while pronouncing that all power derived from the people, had in fact tried to divide that power between crown and Parliament. The monarch was left with complete control over foreign policy, but on domestic issues Parliament would ultimately have the last word. As to the future shape of the multi-national empire, all its people were declared equal, with the inviolable right to run their own administration and, above all, to cultivate their own language. It was thus basically only a blueprint for cultural co-existence, and an incomplete one at that, for Hungary had been virtually ignored by the Czech and German delegates who did most of the arguing.

If the Kremsier draft had represented a vision dreamt up for the Austrian half of the Monarchy, Stadion's replacement spelled out the reality of power. Though, under his plan, the sovereign took an oath on the constitution, he was to dominate its proceedings at home as well as abroad. He had the power of veto on any legislation; he could appoint and dismiss Ministers and officials at will; he could dissolve Parliament whenever he chose and even, in times of emergency, rule by decree. The by now familiar guarantees of civil, linguistic, legal and religious rights for all citizens were again paraded. Behind this liberal screen, however, stood the substance of almost unfettered monarchical power. In contrast to the Kremsier draft, Stadion's system was strongly centralist. Even Hungary (divided into three Crownlands) was to be absorbed into one legal system and one Parliament, and the monarch was to be crowned once only, as Emperor of Austria. To treat the Hungarians, with their own thousand-year-old elective Crown of St Stephen, and the 'sacred lands' attached to it, in this cavalier fashion was as unrealistic as to ignore them altogether.

This the Magyars were still busily demonstrating. Indeed, as the fighting against Kossuth's revolutionary army dragged on throughout the winter of 1848–49, it became clear even to the haughty Schwarzenberg that his own, and Habsburg, pride would have to be swallowed

---

* Count Stadion, a decent man, had understandable qualms of conscience over the betrayal of the Kremsier conference. He had tipped off its leading reformists that they were now facing prison, thus allowing those who wanted to flee the time to do so before the constables from Olmütz arrived.

by a summons for outside aid. The rescuer, fortunately, was already standing on the doorstep. Ever since Francis Joseph mounted the throne, Tsar Nicholas had been assuring his young fellow-emperor that he was ready to help suppress the Magyar revolution – which might well threaten his own realm if the ferment crossed over their common border.* A powerful army stood ready to advance from Galicia. Vienna only had to ask it to march. On 1 May the request to St Petersburg was finally sent.

It was not until six weeks later, in mid-June 1849, that the Russian forces, over 100,000 strong, crossed into Hungary to join the 175,000 Austrian troops already engaged against Kossuth. Even Magyar tenacity and ingenuity had to yield to the massive weight of these combined armies. By the middle of August, Kossuth himself had fled to Turkey, burying St Stephen's Crown under a mulberry bush outside Orsava before leaving Hungarian soil. (It was recovered and taken to Vienna three years later, after a Hungarian émigré had been bribed to reveal the secret of its hiding place.)

Schwarzenberg now talked his hesitant young Emperor into ordering draconian reprisals. General Haynau, the newly-appointed Austrian commander in Hungary, proved a moderate soldier but an outstanding butcher of psychopathic proportions. In all, his courts martial passed some five hundred death sentences on all those deemed to have played any prominent role in the insurrection. Of these, only 114 were actually carried out, the most notable victims being Count Ludwig Batthyány and thirteen Hungarian generals who had formerly served in the imperial army. Most of those who escaped death joined some 2000 others sentenced to long terms of imprisonment. The young Emperor's reign had started with an absolutist regime draped in liberal verbiage being proclaimed from the Austrian half of his realm, and a bloodbath carried out in the Hungarian half.

It is time to take a closer look at this teenage sovereign whose reign was to stretch well into the twentieth century. In appearance he certainly personified the image which the court had tried to present to the people when placing him on the throne: that of a vibrant young monarch untainted by the upheavals of the past and undaunted by the challenges of the future. Contemporary portraits show a handsome and pleasing

---

* The fact that Polish generals like Joseph Bem and Henrik Dembinski were playing such a leading role in Kossuth's campaigns only increased the Tsar's concern.

countenance: fair-haired, blue-eyed, with a noble brow and hardly a trace of that ugly Habsburg lower jaw which had disfigured the faces of so many of his ancestors. He was slim of figure, and an elegant dancer as well as a good horseman. All in all, it seemed, here was an emperor for a new age which would combine tradition with progress.

That these young limbs were already politically arthritic was something his subjects could not have guessed and were slow to learn. Indeed, Francis Joseph would have needed phenomenal qualities of statesmanship and imagination for it to have been otherwise. As it was, he possessed only a well-stocked mind but with no pretensions of intellect and no feeling at all for the arts – not even for music, that staple diet of the Viennese spirit. He did not lack confidence, nor a willingness to lead. Indeed, at the beginning of his reign he acted, on both the political and military fronts, with great self-assurance (though very mixed success). Later, lethargy took over from enthusiasm and his whole approach to his task was transformed. He started off believing that he could do great things on the European stage to extend his heritage. He ended up glumly convinced that the only way he could save what remained of that heritage was to do nothing.

At his accession, two lessons stared him in the face, and he never forgot to learn and follow both of them. On the one hand, as it was his ancient dynasty which had triumphed over all this new-fangled liberalism, so, henceforth, unswerving loyalty to the crown must remain the watchword of all government, and the credo of all his peoples. On the other hand, as military force had cleared the steps of his throne, and kept them clear in all the tumult of revolution, so the army must remain the foundation of his own power and, beyond that, the cement of his multi-national empire. Like many an archduke, he had become a colonel virtually in his cradle. Where Francis Joseph differed from the rest was that he wore a uniform of sorts throughout almost every hour of his long life. He put on regimental dress whenever at work inside or outside his palaces, and traditional green loden hunting garb – itself recognised as an unofficial uniform – when at his beloved summer villa at Bad Ischl. One suspects he would have gladly donned a military nightgown in bed, had such a thing existed. The rare photographs of him in normal civilian clothes (as, for example, in 1904 when visiting the Riviera) are so unfamiliar as to make one wonder, at first sight, whether this can be the same man.

Eventually his character, like his limbs, became set in military cloth. This brought with it, on the positive side, diligence, a sense of responsibility and a striving for impartiality. On the negative side came the worship of the rulebook and an increasing inability to think, let alone act, outside it. Needless to say, it was a rulebook written in golden Habsburg letters. This was to prove crucial for the fortunes of his Austrian subjects. Though he spoke good Hungarian, and some Czech and Serbo-Croat, German was his native tongue and the language spoken in the family. It was natural he should have leant, first and foremost, on the German speakers of his realm. That the privilege was double-edged would not have occurred to him.

Two things happened in the first years of his reign to strengthen the image, particularly in Austrian eyes, of Francis Joseph as the very incarnation of their being. Both events were unplanned and unexpected, yet providence could not have arranged them better. The first was an assassination attempt; the second a lightning betrothal and marriage to the most beautiful princess of Europe.

The would-be assassin was a Hungarian tailor's apprentice called Johann Libényi who, on 18 February 1853, jumped at the Emperor as he was strolling with his adjutant on the Vienna Bastei, and tried to drive a dagger through his neck. The sovereign, as ever, was wearing uniform (this time that of a Ulan cavalry regiment), and the stiff collar reduced the damage to a nasty but relatively minor wound. The motive for the attack became clear when Libényi yelled 'Eljen Kossuth' ('Long live Kossuth') as he was being carried away. Vienna reacted as though Kossuth's vanquished revolutionaries were again marching on the capital. The city gates were closed; the railway stations occupied; extra artillery was brought in. That evening a sumptuous 'Te Deum' was celebrated in the cathedral and the Emperor's already legendary mother, the Archduchess Sophie, was cheered to the echo by a vast crowd when she arrived at the head of a court phalanx. It was an anti-Magyar, pro-Habsburg demonstration and the young Emperor, in bed with a fever, was its beneficiary.*

Even more stirring (and even more Austrian in its slightly sugary character) was the romance which followed that same summer. This might have been taken straight out of one of those operettas which

---

* The Viennese even erected a church, the neo-Gothic Votivkirche, in gratitude for the sovereign's survival.

were soon to flourish on the Viennese stage. The setting itself was operatic: the yellow-washed imperial villa at Bad Ischl in the heart of the Salzammergut's mountains and lakes. So was the original plot devised by the Archduchess Sophie, which was to marry Francis Joseph to Princess Helene of Bavaria, the elder daughter of her sister Louise and of the unconventional Duke Max. But emperors, who are expected to be married long before they step on their thrones, are quite unlike crown princes, in that they can brush aside arranged matches and choose for themselves. This was precisely what happened when the Bavarian royal family arrived at Ischl on 16 August 1853, ostensibly to celebrate the young Emperor's twenty-third birthday two days later. The intended bride of nineteen years, known as 'Nene', was of course on parade when the two families gathered at the villa for tea. But so was her sister Elisabeth, or 'Sissi', not yet sixteen years old, and for Francis Joseph it was an imperial *coup de foudre* the moment he set eyes on this younger cousin of his. She must indeed have presented a lethal combination of attractions to any impressionable suitor: sensual, dark-haired beauty still only half-conscious of itself and wrapped around with a kittenish innocence.

The revised libretto moved on at the gallop. The next morning, the young Emperor appeared in his mother's bedroom to declare his passion for the sixteen-year-old in preference to the older sister. The following evening, at a ball in the villa, he displayed it for all ninety guests to see by dancing the midnight cotillon with Sissi, and even handing her the entire bundle of flower-sprays which, by rights, ought to have been distributed among his other dance partners. These were more than impulsive gestures. In the protocol of the time, they amounted to a formal declaration. The next day, his twenty-third birthday, everything was settled between the two agitated mothers, and on 19 August the engagement was announced. The citizens of Bad Ischl expressed the dutiful delirium of a nation by tracing out in torches that night the giant letters FJ and E on the peak of the Siriuskogel, their local mountain. Like the setting, the occasion was, above all, an Austrian one. The identification of the dynasty with its German-speaking subjects had moved still closer. The wedding, in the chapel of the Hofburg on 24 April of the following year, sealed this emotional fusion. It is almost superfluous to note that the bridegroom went to the altar in army uniform, this time that of a field marshal.

II

Cutting the Knot

THE ARCHDUCHESS SOPHIE had nursed political as well as family motives by marrying her son to a Bavarian princess. Prussia was already the most powerful of the thirty-eight kingdoms and principalities which made up the German Confederation of states; but the Hohenzollerns were as fiercely Protestant as the Habsburgs were devoutly Catholic. Bavaria, on the other hand, shared both a common creed and a common border with Austria and, north of that border, Munich was second only in importance to Berlin. So the altar might once again help Habsburg fortunes by linking all Germans, Austrians and non-Austrians, of the Catholic south, leading perhaps to supremacy throughout the German-speaking world.

This was indeed the great issue of the time. It had surfaced during the 1848 Revolution, when the Austrian delegates to the first Parliament at Frankfurt had come under heavy fire. The attacks ranged from sneers that they were only 'half-Germans' to the charge that any north German union with the Habsburg Monarchy would mean swamping the Protestant Teutonic world with Catholics and Slavs – unwelcome in equal measure.

On the other hand, the Habsburg dynasty possessed an almost mystic and still unchallenged prestige in the German world. Its sovereigns had, after all, worn the crown of Charlemagne as Holy Roman Emperors for nearly four centuries. The Hohenzollerns, as we have seen, had sought formal acceptance of their own kingship from that fount of sovereignty. Such prestige could wane and damage itself (as it did). But the Monarchy which carried it could never be eclipsed spiritually on the German stage by Prussia or any other power. In the end, it would have to be swept right off that stage by force. Murmurings to this effect had already been heard in the Paulskirche at Frankfurt. Yet that drastic solution could only come when Prussia, Austria's only serious rival, had accumulated enough strength – as well as confidence and leadership – to tackle it.

How low that confidence stood in Berlin to begin with was shown by the refusal of King Frederick William IV of Prussia to accept the crown of Germany which the Frankfurt Assembly had naively offered him on 3 April 1849. The reason he gave was that this 'crown of mud' had been proffered by revolutionary delegates (who in truth had no standing whatever in the matter) and not by the hereditary princes. But underlying this ideological repugnance was his awe of the Habsburgs, for him the only sovereigns who could aspire to such heights. Ironically, three months before, the befuddled Assembly had offered that same German crown to Francis Joseph. He might have taken it, if the desperate struggle for mastery in his Hungarian lands had not made him so vulnerable.

The dynasty's pre-eminence was nonetheless personified in the Paulskirche itself: on 29 June 1848 this first all-German Parliament had chosen as its President, or Imperial Regent, the same Archduke John who as a young man had helped to organise the Tyroleans' heroic resistance against Napoleon. How the *'Casa Austria'* should be fitted into this liberal world which the delegates imagined had come to stay became one of their main philosophical preoccupations. Should there be a 'Greater Germany', a union of all the Germanic states under Austrian leadership? Or should the 'Small German' solution prevail, which would exclude Austria altogether, and leave everything that remained under Prussian dominance?

The Frankfurt delegates debated for months on end but could find no academic answer to the riddle (most perplexed of all were the 115 Austrian delegates in their midst). There was of course no academic answer; the solution could only come through a real-life test of strength between Berlin and Vienna. King Frederick William was the first to throw down the gauntlet by announcing his own 'Small German' solution. After reconquering his capital and then stamping out the revolution throughout Saxony, Hanover and Baden, he launched, on 20 March 1850, a North German federation under Prussian leadership.

This may have been more modest than any imperial pretensions on Prussia's part, but it was a solid challenge which Schwarzenberg, now the real power behind the throne in Vienna,* could not ignore. Indeed, it dramatically opposed his own vision for the future, which was far more ambitious than anything contemplated in Berlin. As befitted this supremely arrogant aristocrat and the dynasty which he served, Schwarzenberg put forward the 'Greater Austrian' solution, the so-called 'Empire of Seventy Millions'. This envisaged nothing less than the fusion of the entire Habsburg Monarchy – Slavs, Magyars, Roumanians, Italians and all the rest included – with the German Confederation. Economically, they were to be bound together in one customs union. Militarily, German armies would be available to protect the Monarchy's vulnerable borders. Politically, Austrian leadership was to be ensured through a majority of supportive rulers in a seven-member supreme Directory. Though some Austrians took it seriously at the time (as did some Austrian historians afterwards), it was in fact a hare-brained scheme which could never have functioned had it ever got off the drawing board.

The important thing, however, was that there was somebody in Vienna who actually believed in the vision and was prepared to fight for it. Throughout 1850, Austria and Prussia snarled and intrigued against each other to realise their rival schemes. By the autumn their armies were also snarling at each other, and continental Europe was bracing itself for war. Then, in November, King Frederick William – fearful of his modest military strength at the time and unable to secure Russian support – backed down before an Austrian ultimatum. By the so-called Punctuation of Olmütz (the two sides met there in the aptly-named, if unglamorous, setting of the Hotel 'Zur Krone') Prussia dropped her plan for a separate North German League. She agreed instead to join the post-Napoleonic confederation of thirty-five German princes and four free cities which Austria now revived and whose ruling Diet she could control. This Habsburg triumph was as illusory as it was spectacular. Austria had only bought time; the inevitable passage of arms was only postponed. Indeed, Nemesis was already in attendance when the reconstituted Diet of 1815 assembled at Frankfurt in place of the defunct Parliament. The Prussian delegate was Otto von Bismarck, then only a cocky young Junker diplomat, but destined eventually to

---

* The once-mighty Windisch-Graetz had disappeared from the political scene in April 1849. He was dismissed, partly for his military failure in the field against Kossuth's army, but also because he had developed alarming political ambitions, demanding a veto over anything the Emperor or his Ministers decided. The dismissal came direct from the teenage sovereign.

become the master of continental Europe, and the arbiter of Austria's fate.

On 5 April 1852, barely fifteen months after his humiliation of Prussia, Schwarzenberg suddenly died. The handsome prince – as accomplished at dalliance as at diplomacy – departed in style. He was carried off by a heart attack while changing for a ball at which he was hoping to dance with his latest conquest, the attractive Polish wife of an army officer. She was not the only lady of Viennese society to mourn him, but he left far more behind him than a string of well-born mistresses. There was, to begin with, the new system of government he had inspired – one which doused the last embers of liberalism which had flickered under Stadion's formula of 1849. The 'Silvester Patent' of 1851 (so-called because it was formally proclaimed by the Emperor on the last day of the year) amounted to untrammelled absolutism. The concept of a parliamentary constitution, of the people having any share in the exercise of legislation, was not only sidestepped; it was formally denounced. All power was now passed back to the crown which, though operating through a Ministerial Council, in fact ruled by decree. Press freedoms were abolished; so was trial by jury and even the old promises of 'free national development' for the peoples of the empire.

For Schwarzenberg, and for his sovereign, who had been an eager partner in the process, absolutism at home was the necessary counterpart to displaying a similar virility in tackling the Prussians abroad. This was one of several occasions when Austria's foreign policy fashioned her domestic affairs. The culmination was to come sixteen years later, when the Monarchy's most catastrophic defeat on the battlefield led directly to the most drastic transformation of its internal structure. Constitutions were picked up by the Emperor and cast aside like so many cloaks chosen against the prevailing climate. More durable in its effect among his countrymen was the memory of Schwarzenberg's passionate faith in Austria. Its last herald was to be the Archduke Francis Ferdinand, he whose death at Sarajevo presaged the death of the Monarchy itself.

With Schwarzenberg gone, the Emperor, still only twenty-two years old, took the remarkably bold decision to strike out on his own. He appointed no new President of the Ministerial Council, announcing on 14 April 1852 that he would henceforth chair its meetings himself. He thus became, in effect, the leader of his government as well as the sovereign of his empire, with all the threads of policy gathered in his young hands. 'Now,' he commented to the humbled Windisch-Graetz, 'my name will be under every order, so any criticism will amount to treason.' The trouble with this lofty assumption of supreme power was that henceforth failure and success alike could be laid only at the Hofburg's gates, and before the decade was out the Monarchy had committed a big blunder in diplomacy and suffered a heavy defeat on the battlefield. The inexperienced autocrat was personally implicated in both.

The blunder was over the Crimean War of 1853–56. In July 1853 the Tsar Nicholas – ignoring pleas from Francis Joseph to hold his hand – marched into the Balkan principalities of Moldavia and Wallachia, then part of the Turkish empire. Turkey had no option but to declare war on Russia; England and France, both determined to stem any Russian thrust towards Constantinople, followed suit six months later. Prussia opted for strict neutrality, and kept to it throughout the long and bloody conflict which followed. Francis Joseph, on the other hand, now indulged in an imperial display of that 'half-and-halfness' which Grillparzer had identified as the Austrians' national affliction. He mobilised heavily against Russia (three army corps in Hungary in 1853 and four more in Galicia the following year) yet rejected the advice of his own Ministers* to declare war outright. As a result, Austria came away empty-handed at the peace conference in Paris in March 1856 which followed the war. Worse than that, she had emerged isolated. Her Emperor, in trying to manoeuvre between the powers, had succeeded in offending all of them: Turkey, France and England because he had not joined their alliance, and Russia because he had pinned down large numbers of her troops along the Danube and coveted the principalities for himself. For the Tsar, Francis Joseph's behaviour had been a slap in the face: this was indeed shabby repayment for rescuing Hungary for him in 1849 and backing him in the stand-off with Prussia a year later. But then, as the Habsburgs cheerfully admitted, gratitude was never among their strongest points.

The military defeat of 1859 was even more of a personal setback for the young Austrian Emperor. Again, the setting was the provinces of northern Italy, that fateful legacy the Monarchy had inherited in 1815; again, it was the tiny kingdom of Piedmont-Sardinia which led this second round in the struggle of Italian nationalism against Austrian

---

* Notably Count Charles Buol Schauenstein, a career diplomat who had the invidious task of serving as Foreign Minister at the time.

rule; again, a Napoleon stalked the battlefield – this time Louis Napoleon, nephew of the 'Grand Corsair', who in 1851 had staged a coup d'état in Paris and declared himself the new Emperor of the French. The scores of the Crimean conflict were now settled on both sides of the account, when, in April 1859, Vienna rashly sent an ultimatum to Piedmont to demobilise her forces, and then invaded the kingdom. Prussia kept out of the war despite the strongest pressure from Austria; Piedmont, on the other hand, could look to England for sympathy and to her new ally, France, for military help. Louis Napoleon, who had in fact planned the whole imbroglio in advance with the Piedmontese Prime Minister, Cavour, was prompt to respond. French reinforcements were sent across the Alps for the Piedmontese army, and on 24 June came the decisive clash. The battle of Solferino was not a crushing defeat for the Austrian army, who indeed had scored an initial success. But as it was their troops who were ordered to leave the field after heavy casualties all round, it was a defeat all the same. The real loser was Francis Joseph who, after dithering between offensive and defensive strategies, finally issued the command to withdraw. Seven days before, he had taken over personal command of his two army corps engaged. 'I now know how it feels to be a beaten general,' he wrote in chastened mood to his 'Sissi', adding, 'This tragedy will have serious consequences.'

These were rapidly spelt out in the preliminary peace settlement at Villafranca on 12 July.* Though Louis Napoleon allowed the Habsburg Monarchy to linger on in Venetia, the key province of Lombardy was lost. Among the face-saving concessions Francis Joseph secured for himself was the right to go on conferring the Lombard Order of the Iron Crown so long as he lived. It was a pathetic display of dynastic vanity, and totally at odds with the sense of humiliation which ran throughout the empire. It was here, at home, that those 'serious consequences' of which the Emperor had written were manifested. The anti-Habsburg reformists in Hungary, whose zeal had been suppressed but not extinguished ten years before, took new heart. The demand for total separation from Vienna was heard loudly again in Budapest, though in Ferenc Deak, who had succeeded Kossuth as the leader of Hungarian nationalism, the Magyars now had a true statesman as opposed to a romantic firebrand in charge.

In the Emperor's own Austrian provinces there was, of course, no

* Finalised at Zürich on 10 November, with terms even less favourable to Austria.

such unrest. But much bitterness and anger were felt, for the Italians were by now established as *the* national enemy. Francis Joseph did not help his cause by shutting himself up with his family in his castle at Laxenburg, near Vienna, for weeks after his return from the front. When he reappeared in public on 12 September to attend a parade, there were as many boos as cheers to be heard from the crowd. The nimbus of the young Emperor had been temporarily dimmed. Yet it had been at its height only the year before. On 21 August 1858, after bearing him two daughters, his wife had at last presented the Monarchy with its eagerly-awaited heir, the ill-fated Archduke Rudolph. The nimbus was to shine again later in the reign, though with the softer, almost sombre glow bestowed by nothing more than the passing of years. For the time being, however, the Monarchy had no choice but once more to respond to events abroad by changes at home. An erratic retreat from the central-ised absolutism of Schwarzenberg now began. The reasoning was both absurd and compelling: times were bad, so, therefore, must be the prevailing system.

The first variant, whose guidelines had been drawn up with the Emperor's full participation, was an elaborate camouflage laid over imperial power. By the 'October Diploma' (so-called because the new order was proclaimed on 20 October 1860) a façade of popular rep-resentation was erected throughout the empire. The old Parliament was resurrected and given, on paper, the power to reject or approve taxation, and to 'cooperate' on framing legislation. The Emperor's personal con-trol over his army and foreign policy remained, however, beyond the law. The old conservatism also remained in force in the provinces; here, Diets were to be set up, giving some measure of decentralisation, but the method of election guaranteed that these would be in the hands of the feudal nobility. The idea that local landowners could serve as the guardians of liberalism was one of the many absurdities of the October system, which had satisfied nobody. In just over four months it was replaced by a far more ambitious experiment in representative govern-ment. This again had a foreign policy dimension as part of an attempt to revive Schwarzenberg's 'Empire of Seventy Millions' under Habsburg leadership. The Austrian empire numbered some forty millions at the time. For its bid to have any chance of acceptance among the thirty million Germans to the north, the Emperor would need to have dusted off the constitutional cloak which he had locked in the wardrobe since 1849.

The so-called 'February Patent' of 1861 established a two-chamber Parliament whose solid-looking foundations covered the empire as a whole. Its Upper House may have been simply the old order lined up on benches: the adult archdukes, large landowners, ecclesiastical magnates plus an assortment of life members nominated by the crown. But the Lower House of 323 delegates* and the reconstituted Diets in the provinces did allow the election, for the first time on a regularised basis, of the bourgeoisie. The feudal element still had more than its fair share of seats in the Diets, but they were outnumbered by the burgeoning middle classes of the empire, predominantly the German-speaking elements of the towns and cities which the dynasty, now as ever, looked to for its main support. As the Diets were called upon, by a Byzantine system, to elect the central Parliament in Vienna, the advance of the bourgeoisie marched strongly on the capital. With them, the Jews appeared for the first time on the central political stage of the empire, a stage which they had so far influenced only from the wings, where the big bankers stood.

Nationalism, embracing and inspiring reform, was the loud cry of the day: in Germany, in Italy (where its patron was Louis Napoleon), and, just as strident, in Hungary. The challenge from Budapest was in some ways the gravest of the three for Vienna, yet the Austrians became so mesmerised by the all-German vision beyond their borders that they took their eyes off this Magyar drive for separatism which was eating away the heart of their empire. The Hungarian nationalists had rejected every constitutional reshuffle proclaimed from Vienna because they all overrode Kossuth's basic demand of 1848 for an independent Hungarian legislature. This was especially true of the strongly centralised February Patent. Accordingly, they had refused to send to its central Parliament any of the eighty-five delegates allotted to Hungary. That may well have been the largest entitlement given to any people in the empire; but it still left them permanently outvoted in the total assembly. The Magyars wanted to vote for themselves and by themselves in a capital of their own. The problem was how to reconcile what amounted

---

* The breakdown was eighty-five from Hungary; fifty-four from Bohemia; thirty-eight from Galicia; twenty-six from Transylvania; twenty-two from Moravia; eighteen from Lower Austria; thirteen from Styria; ten each from Upper Austria and Tyrol; nine from Croatia; six each from Carniola and Silesia; five each from Dalmatia, Carinthia and the Bukovina; three from Salzburg; and two each from Trieste, Vorarlberg, Istria and Gorizia.

to separatism with a continued existence under the Habsburg sceptre. Deak, unlike Kossuth, accepted that Hungary could only play a role in Europe as part of the multi-national Austrian empire, itself the most venerable among the Great Powers. Neither he nor Francis Joseph could have expected that the answer to this conundrum, and several others, was about to come, not from Vienna or Budapest, but from Berlin.

On 23 September 1862, Otto von Bismarck was recalled from the political sidelines of a diplomatic career* to become Chancellor and, a fortnight later, also Foreign Minister of Prussia. At the top of his agenda was to cut the Gordian knot of history and sentiment which bound Austrians and Germans together in such a muddled but seemingly inextricable fashion. His instrument was the same that Alexander the Great had used to sever the Gordian knot of legend: the sword. He had made no secret of his aim, even while serving as a young diplomat at Frankfurt. His dispatch to Berlin of 15 February 1854 contained the vivid warning against 'chaining the trim seaworthy frigate of Prussia to the ancient worm-eaten galleon of Austria'. More ominous, as well as more famous, was his prophecy that the great issues of the time could only be solved 'by blood and iron'. Part of Bismarck's technique was to speak with such unvarnished bluntness that his interlocutors would hesitate to take him in full earnest. It was an excellent method, for where it failed as blackmail, it worked as deception. Bismarck really did mean what he said, and that applied in the first instance to the Habsburg Monarchy.

In the historic showdown which was now approaching, the Austrians of that Monarchy were at a hopeless disadvantage. They had no minister of any substance to put in the field; even less did they have anyone, like Metternich or Schwarzenberg of old, who could control their sovereign. In Bismarck, Prussia now possessed not only the greatest diplomatist of the age but also the most powerful influence over the monarch he served. The new Chancellor faced arguments, delays and setbacks; but essentially Prussian foreign policy now became Bismarck's own. The second crushing advantage which he possessed was the united nationalist spirit of the Prussian people which bore both him and the crown along. How different that clear, sharp light was from the mental fog in which

---

* After eight years (1851–59) as Prussian delegate to the Frankfurt Diet, he had served successively as his country's ambassador to St Petersburg and Paris.

the Austrians still lived is best illustrated by an *obiter dictum* pronounced by their own sovereign in the very year which had brought Bismarck to power. During the 1862 Congress of the International Lawyers' Association in Vienna, Francis Joseph declared: 'I am first and foremost an Austrian, but I am also a German prince.'

The Emperor was thinking dynastically, harking back to the days when his ancestors were 'Holy Roman Emperors of the German nation'. It appeared an exercise in pure nostalgia; yet, in startling (and totally deceptive) fashion, this glorious past seemed for a moment to come alive again the following year. The idea to call together a Congress of German princes at Frankfurt – with the Austrian Emperor inevitably presiding – started in paradoxical fashion. Its originator seems to have been Julius Fröbel, a leader of the 1848 rebellion in Vienna, who had returned from emigration in America. The idea took wings when it was picked up and presented to Francis Joseph by his brother-in-law, Prince Thurn and Taxis. The sovereign declared himself delighted with the scheme and, to the dismay of his Ministers, promptly made it his own. It was, he told his mother, 'the last chance to unify Germany'. By that, of course, he meant unification under Austrian leadership, though this was to be very cautiously expressed. The final plan he presented at Frankfurt on 16 August 1863 – two days before his thirty-third birthday – called for a Directory under his chairmanship with limited powers to control the affairs of the new all-German Federation. A new popular Assembly, to be elected by the various state parliaments, was given even fewer teeth to bite with.

Perhaps because of its moderation, the plan caught the imagination of the majority of the German princes present, and even impressed the rest of Europe. Louis Napoleon felt that this might at last mean the emergence of that unified German-Austria which he so feared. Queen Victoria of England, whom Francis Joseph called on in her husband's native Coburg soon after the Congress, addressed the Emperor as though he were already the arbiter of the German world. Would he promise, she nervously enquired, to do nothing which might damage the position of the Prussian Crown Prince Frederick (the husband of her own eldest daughter Vicky)? What the Queen of England, and everyone else, seemed to have overlooked in the flush of the moment was that it was Austria who, now more than ever, would need protection from a vengeful Prussia. Thanks to Bismarck, who had fought and won a herculean struggle with his sovereign over the issue, King William had not gone to Frankfurt.* The Prussian veto rendered everything that was decided there a dead letter in advance. Nonetheless, the Habsburg Monarchy had achieved a moral victory by presiding over a congress of thirty German princes, and that only spurred Bismarck on to settle accounts with her once and for all, and the sooner the better. His chance emerged only three months later. On 15 November 1863 King Frederick of Denmark died, leaving the succession to the two Danish-ruled provinces of Schleswig-Holstein in an unholy political and genea-logical muddle. According to Bismarck, its intricacies were understood by only three people in Europe – of whom he, naturally, was one. The details of the confusion do not concern us here, only the fact that out of it Bismarck conjured up the permanent destruction of Austria as a German power.

First, Berlin and Vienna made common cause in challenging Den-mark's right to retain Schleswig-Holstein in the face of the rival claims which had now surfaced. Their combined armies had little difficulty in driving the Danes out of the provinces which, after renewed fighting, were finally surrendered to the two German powers on 30 October 1864. To begin with, they shared the spoils in joint rule. Then, by the Treaty of Gastein of 14 August 1865, they divided the spoils between them: hence-forth, Prussia was to govern Schleswig, while Holstein fell to Austria. Finally, they quarrelled over the spoils. Bismarck frankly admitted later that the quarrel was of his making because it would lead to that other war he had been obsessed with for more than ten years, the war against Austria. He had prepared for it step by step by ensuring that, when the showdown came, the Habsburg empire would be fighting alone.

The goodwill of the Tsar – who was anyway still smarting under Austria's ungrateful behaviour during the Crimean War – was bought by Bismarck's refusal to back the Polish rebellion of 1863 against Russia. (Austria, on the other hand, had joined with France and England in a joint attempt to secure a degree of autonomy for Poland.) French neutrality was secured by little more than buttering up Louis Napoleon and promising him that after Austria's defeat she would have

---

* The struggle took place at the Austrian spa of Bad Gadstein, where King William was taking the cure that summer. First, Francis Joseph came in person to plead with the Prussian King to attend. Then a formal invitation was sent in the name of twenty German princes. Only by threatening to resign did Bismarck hold the King back. Afterwards, on regaining his room in the hotel, the Chancellor had to smash his water-jug to relieve the strain he had gone through.

to surrender Venice, her last remaining Italian province, to King Victor Emmanuel. Bismarck's master-stroke was the treaty he then signed on 8 April 1866 with the new Italian kingdom. Prussia promised nothing at all, beyond repeating the pledge over Venice. Italy, on the other hand, agreed to put all her forces in the field to assist Prussia in a war against Austria. This most extraordinary of pacts was to last for three months only. That was all Bismarck needed.

On 5 May, Prussia put her army on a war footing, and Austria, already mobilised in Italy, ordered general mobilisation on her northern front. This 'provocation' played into Bismarck's hands, and on 15 June he persuaded King William to order the attack against Hanover, Saxony and Hesse-Cassel, three of Austria's main allies in the dispute. From then on, it was all over in seven weeks, an object lesson to Europe as to what a combination of better logistics, more modern weapons and superior generalship could achieve. Prussia had five railway lines into the campaign area to Austria's one. She had the latest needle-firing rifle to Austria's old muzzle-loader. Above all, in von Moltke, she had a commander who completely overshadowed his opponent, General Benedek. This worthy but unimaginative soldier had been unwisely transferred from the Italian front, which he knew inside out, to Bohemia, where he was, in his own words, 'a donkey'.*

The issue was decided on 3 July 1866 outside the town of Königgrätz. It was as though the imaginary encounter between the 'trim seaworthy frigate' of Bismarck's Prussia and the 'worm-eaten galleon' of Austria had taken place not on the high seas but here, in real earnest, on the eastern bank of the Elbe. Benedek's cavalry fought well, and the Austrian artillery, as always, was formidable. But in infantry, the decisive arm, the Austrians proved sadly lacking. Benedek himself squandered what chances he had by dithering between advance and retreat, and the Austrian cause was not helped by the insubordination of two of his corps commanders, the Counts Thun and Festetics. This pair of arrogant noblemen ignored orders to defend the army's northern flank and attacked instead, in a costly but futile attempt to put victory laurels on their own brows. It was Moltke who claimed those laurels as the Austrian forces suddenly disintegrated during the afternoon and began streaming back across the river in a retreat which came perilously close

---

* It was generally accepted that the commander Francis Joseph should have chosen against Prussia was the very able Archduke Albrecht, who instead was wasting his talents on the Italian front.

to a rout. Even Moltke, who collapsed with a nervous fever that night, was taken aback by the enormity of his triumph. Not surprisingly, when the grim battlefield count was taken the following day, the Austrians were found to have lost some 13,000 dead, with about the same number taken prisoner and another 17,000 wounded. Moltke's casualties totalled 9172, of whom only 1935 had been killed. The scale of Prussia's victory in the battle for supremacy in Germany was measured in those contrasting blood tallies.

It remained to transfer the victory won on the battlefield to the parallel field of diplomacy. It was here that Bismarck began to show his true greatness. Hitherto, the Junker from Schönhausen had distinguished himself as a brilliant speaker, a passionate Prussian patriot, a devoted king's man, and an ingenious diplomat. The moderation which he now displayed in the hour of triumph invested him with the mantle of Europe's foremost statesman, a mantle he was to wear for almost twenty-five years.

Though Austria had to be driven out of Germany proper, Bismarck was determined to preserve the Habsburg empire as a future partner and ally, for Prussia could never develop her strength in Europe against the long-term enmity of Vienna. Accordingly, in the preliminary peace signed at the Dietrichstein family castle of Nikolsburg in Moravia on 6 August (and finalised at Prague three weeks later), the Austrian empire was confirmed in all its territories – excepting only Venice, whose cession to Italy had long been accepted by Francis Joseph. His real loss was political, not territorial, and was set out in the next clause. This laid down that Germany would now be reorganised 'without the participation of the Austrian empire'. Prussia would henceforth head a new federation of north German states. As for the kingdoms and principalities of the Catholic south, they were to be left separate and independent for the moment; but should they ever create their own federation in the future, this would be allowed to join up with the northern union. Bismarck had thus laid down a formal marker for the next stage in Prussia's expansion, which was to come only five years later with the creation of his own German empire.*

* Among the minor provisions of the peace, Austria ceded her share of Schleswig-Holstein and paid an indemnity of 20 million thalers (less than half Prussia's original demand). Bismarck had a ding-dong battle with his sovereign to dissuade King William from annexing territory from Saxony, Austria's closest ally in the conflict. Francis Joseph, for once fanatically loyal, had threatened to renew fighting if Prussia pressed the issue.

The days of the Habsburgs as German emperors were over for good. True, it was only fictional power, the shroud of Charlemagne, which had been surrendered; yet the loss smarted, for that fiction had been part of the dynasty's glory. As in 1859, defeat on the battlefield had taken the shine off Francis Joseph's crown. Again, the cheers were muted and mixed with boos when he appeared in public. On this occasion there were even mutterings that his lovely wife (then at the height of her popularity, especially in Hungary, where she was spending much of her time) might replace him for a while as Regent. This was idle chatter, yet his emotional dependence on her was never stronger than now. The letters he sent to her in Budapest during these weeks of crisis were signed 'Your poor little one'.

As well as seeking safety, Elisabeth was indulging what became a lifelong love affair with the Magyars by leaving the Emperor alone for so long in Vienna and even taking their three children with her to Budapest. (Her excuse to him for lingering there, that she found the climate in Vienna too unhealthy, was patently threadbare: the Hungarian capital in midsummer could be even hotter.) But she had also started to indulge in politics. In letter after letter to her husband, she pleaded with him to put Count Julius Andrassy, one of the leaders of Hungarian nationalism and a close friend of hers, in place of Count Alexander Mensdorff, the cavalry officer who was doing his best as Imperial Foreign Minister. Andrassy was to be denied that office for another five years, but there was no holding back the Magyar cause which he and Ferenc Deak were pressing. The defeat at Königgrätz was momentous not only in setting the future course of German history. It was decisive also in transforming the entire structure of the Austrian empire, and in turning the Habsburg Monarchy into the most artificial political creation of the century.

A whole new official language had to be evolved to describe it. Eventually, everything pertaining to Hungary alone was labelled 'K' (for *Königlich* or royal). The same label could not be applied to matters affecting Austria alone, so, to avoid confusion, these were called 'K.K.' (for *Kaiserlich-Königlich* or imperial-royal). Similar distinctions separated pure Hungarian from pure Austrian regiments in the army. Yet those organs, like the Army High Command, which represented the Habsburg empire as a whole, had to be distinguished from all the rest.

This was done by inserting a 'u' (for '*und*' or 'and') between the two 'Ks'. Such were the birthmarks of that weird realm which the satirists were later to dub 'Kakania'.

III

The Destroyers

HOW SHOULD FRANCIS JOSEPH and his Austrian-Germans have responded to the humiliation of 1866? The question is better put: what *could* the Emperor have done? Many historians, Austrians and non-Austrians, have reproached him for not reacting by promptly converting his empire into a genuine federation of nation-states. In this way, the argument goes, the Habsburg lands, shut out from Greater Germany, could have been rejuvenated to stand on their own as a stable and united empire. Yet this comes close to armchair theorising, made worse when conditioned by nostalgia or ideology – neither of them the best counsellors for the historian. The down-to-earth truth is that, though countless theoretical solutions for reshaping the imperial orb were put forward throughout the nineteenth and early twentieth centuries, none of them looked convincing on paper, let alone feasible in practice. This does not mean that reform should not have been attempted; simply that it would have been appallingly difficult to realise.

Bismarck's Germany could form an empire built on kingdoms, because each of those kingdoms was German in population and German in its deep and distinctive dynastic roots. The unification of Italy could, and did, proceed along similar national-linguistic lines. But, as we have seen, the lands of the Habsburgs lay sprawled across the most complex racial jigsaw to be found anywhere in Europe. Indeed, it was not even a proper jigsaw, in that the different ethnic pieces could never be neatly fitted into one another. Only in the west was the pattern solidly German: in the ancient heartlands of Upper and Lower Austria astride the Danube, in Salzburg and the Tyrol, and, except for their Slav fringes, also in Carinthia and Styria. Everywhere else, the people of the Monarchy had been sprinkled over the centuries all across each other's back gardens: Magyars among Roumanians; Ukrainians among Poles; Croats and Italians among Slovenes; and strong clusters of Germans all the way from Bohemia to Transylvania. One Balkan legend used to say that God, when creating the world, carried in a sack the stones he needed to fashion its mountains and valleys. Weakened by wear, the sack burst open one day, loosing a wild cascade of rocks on the earth. The legend, which was recounted to explain the ethnic muddle of tiny Montenegro, could illustrate just as aptly the entire Austrian empire. Apart from conquests in battle and acquisitions at the altar, the Monarchy was made up of places where nomads had halted in the Dark Ages, or colonies of artists and merchants had been set up in medieval times. It was a slow-growing muddle created out of strife and coincidence.

Nor did history help, for Hungary was not the only land to look back to an ancient kingdom founded on a racial mix. If the Magyars venerated their 'lands of St Stephen', the Czechs cherished memories of the 'lands of St Wenceslas' which had once embraced the crowns of Poland, Hungary and even, for twenty-two years in the fourteenth century, of Germany itself. We have noted how, in the fifteenth and sixteenth centuries, the great Jagellon dynasty had established Polish rule among the neighbouring races. Even the so-called 'non-historic' (and looked down upon as such) peoples of the Monarchy had once enjoyed their own age of glory, if one went back far enough. Croatia, for example, under its mighty King Tomislav, had been a multi-racial kingdom extending to the Adriatic as long ago as 924, more than three hundred years before the Habsburgs appeared on the European scene. In fact, all the great ethnic conflicts which plagued the Habsburg Monarchy, and survived it – from that of the Sudeten Germans in Bohemia down to the 'South Slav problem' itself – had deep and tangled roots in the past.

Nothing better illustrates the difficulties which faced Francis Joseph, who was now obliged to contemplate remedial action of some sort on the domestic front, than the ideas tossed into the political void created by the disaster of Königgrätz. The Czechs, for example, summoned a 'Federalists' Conference' in Vienna, at which they proposed a division of the Monarchy into five equal units: 'Old Austria', 'Inner Austria', Galicia, the Bohemian lands, and, inevitably, Hungary-Croatia. This so-called 'Pentarchy', like so many would-be solutions, was far too neat to work. The Croats wanted, if possible, to split off again from Hungary; the Slovenes, who had not even been invited to the conference, responded huffily by calling for a 'Greater Slovenia' of their own.

Francis Joseph can therefore hardly be reproached for not producing out of the hat a workable new master-plan for his empire now that it found itself cast out of the German world. He can, however, be blamed for choosing the worst possible solution (if federalism was ever to have a chance); and, moreover, choosing it for the wrong reason. He simply refused to accept that his defeat at Bismarck's hands was final, and that the Monarchy therefore had no choice but to make its own multi-national way in the world. On the contrary, on 30 October 1866, only two months after the Peace of Prague, he imported Baron Frederick Ferdinand von Beust, a former Prime Minister of Saxony, to serve as the Monarchy's new Foreign Minister. Beust was a long-standing enemy of Bismarck's, and his appointed task now was to prepare the ground for an Austrian counter-offensive against Prussia. His first port of call was Budapest. It was through a settlement with the Magyars, and with them only, that the Emperor's hands were to be freed for a renewed challenge to Berlin. That challenge was never mounted.* Yet in the effort to prepare for it, a Saxon Protestant and two sensibly passionate Magyars, Andrassy and Deak, gave the Habsburg Monarchy the shape it was to retain until the chaotic final weeks of its life. (Non-Austrians deciding Austria's fate yet again.)

The negotiations had to clear many legal and political hurdles, but even had they wished it otherwise they were condemned to agree, and agree swiftly, given the climate of the time. That first reconnaissance visit of Beust to Budapest had been on 20 December 1866. On 18 February 1867, Andrassy was entrusted with the formation of a 'respon-sible' Hungarian government, whose members descended on Vienna with their programme. The moderate Magyar nationalists now in the saddle had long ago made it clear that, unlike Kossuth, they were pre-pared for Hungary to continue in the so-called Personal Union under the crown as part of the Monarchy, provided their claims for virtual autonomy within that common realm were met.** Before the end of May, this circle had been squared with the acceptance of 'Law XII of 1867' by the Hungarian Diet. It was a somewhat pedestrian label

* The plan was to build a new anti-Prussian front based on the south German kingdoms and any other state which stood in fear of Berlin. Bismarck had got in first by courting their sympathies and allowing them time to think.
** From exile, Kossuth managed to get a Cassandra-like pamphlet circulated in Hungary just before the negotiations were concluded. This accused Deak of betraying the Magyar faith by accepting anything short of complete independence from Vienna.

for this momentous pact which abolished the Austrian Empire as such and replaced it with a new constitutional entity, the so-called Dual Monarchy.

Henceforth, only foreign affairs, defence and the joint budget remained as common to both Budapest and Vienna. The Emperor retained virtually complete control over the first two sectors, which had been his fundamental condition throughout the negotiations. Finance was, however, among the matters upon which the new 'joint delegations' (sixty from each side) were to decide. As if this were not giving enough future hostages to fortune, it was laid down that the whole complex of proportional taxation and tariffs should be renegotiated every ten years. A major battle between Vienna and Budapest was thus guaranteed for each of the five decades which lay ahead of the Dual Monarchy's life.

Law XII entered into force on 28 July 1867, when Francis Joseph gave it his royal sanction. Henceforth, the only curbs on Hungarian domestic self-rule were the rights which the Emperor retained to appoint and dismiss his own Hungarian Prime Minister and to convoke, suspend or dissolve the Hungarian Parliament. The Magyar nationalists were prepared to accept these curbs, for they had already secured something far more precious to them than any political trappings. On 8 June, seven weeks before Francis Joseph signed away his control over the Hungarians as Emperor, he had confirmed, as their King, all their historic claims to the 'Lands of St Stephen'. By his coronation at the Gothic cathedral of Mathias Corvinus – a radiant Elisabeth at his side – he had sworn 'not to reduce but as far as possible increase' the kingdom's ancient territories. The ritual provided for a theatrical enactment of this pledge which every king of Hungary was called upon to make. After the cathedral ceremony, the newly-crowned successor to St Stephen rode up the 'Diszter', or coronation mound, in the nearby palace square and swung the great sword of state to all four corners of the compass, signalling defiance against all and any challenges to the integrity of the kingdom. To an outsider this might smack of mumbo-jumbo.* To the Magyars, it was a plain reaffirmation of their own special identity as a people and as a nation.

---

* A cloud of legend surrounded the actual regalia. The crown itself was popularly believed to be the same one which Pope Sylvester had bestowed on Stephen for his coronation as Hungary's first king in 1000 A.D. In fact, at most the four open arches are from the original. The story that 'St Stephen's sword' was once swung by Attila the Hun is even more fanciful.

The defenders of the new dualism between Vienna and Budapest (whither Bismarck sardonically suggested that Francis Joseph should now transfer his imperial capital) have pleaded that, at least, it gave the new Austria-Hungary a basic stability which was to endure for half a century. The 1867 Compromise is thus presented as a practical, even inevitable, division of power between the two strongest and most populous races of the empire; compared with it, no other rearrangement of the racial jigsaw looked as simple. The huge problems which stood in the way of any root-and-branch restructuring of the Monarchy have been acknowledged above. There was indeed another complication. No emperor could have embarked on a programme of genuine federalism unless he were strong and confident; those, however, were the very conditions under which the risks would have seemed not worth running. As it was, constitutional change was only wrung from the crown when the dynasty was weakened, and this applied above all to the settlement with Hungary.

Yet this reform of 1867 was unique and fateful in that it stood in the way of any future reform. Even had a magic formula of federation been produced afterwards, it could never have been launched, given that millions of Roumanians, Croats, Serbs, Slovaks and Ruthenes were locked by the King-Emperor's oath into the Hungary of St Stephen. In chess, the end does not come when the king is captured, or his crown toppled. It comes when he is unable to move to any other square on the board. That was the position of Francis Joseph after 1867, and he had checkmated himself.

The immediate effects are seen when we look at the repercussions on what might now be loosely described as 'the Austrian half' of his empire. The 1867 Compromise had been a straight pact between the Emperor and the Hungarian magnates. His other subjects had not even been consulted, let alone involved. Yet they now had to be given some political profile of their own. The solution devised dealt a further lasting blow to the Austrians' struggle to emerge as a people in their own right, with their own national conscience.

As regards the dynasty, Francis Joseph announced his own changes to meet the new situation. On 14 November 1868 he informed Beust, his Chancellor,* that he would henceforth be styled in the short version

---

* The title had been conferred to put Beust on an equal standing with Bismarck, in preparation for the renewed political battle against Prussia which never came. Beust eventually reverted to being only Foreign Minister of the Dual Monarchy, a post which he held until 1871.

'Emperor of Austria and Apostolic King of Hungary'. As for his realm, that would now be called either 'the Austro-Hungarian Empire' or 'the Austro-Hungarian Monarchy' (eventually it became known simply as 'Austria-Hungary'). But whereas everyone knew what King of Hungary meant, Apostolic or otherwise, nobody had any clear notion about the Austria over which he was calling himself emperor, though he had never been crowned as such. A notion had to be devised, but it remained far from clear.

The peoples of the western half of the Monarchy were now bundled together in a new constitution based on the old 'February Patent' of 1861. There was again a centralised Parliament composed of delegates from the various national Diets, who would, as before, spend most of their time arguing over which language was to be used in which law court or primary school.

New laws were passed which promised, and actually delivered, a real measure of individual liberty: freedom of the press, the right to civil marriage, and so on. The German-speaking delegates from the towns and cities were still preponderant, with the Czechs as their main challengers. But these German-speaking subjects of the Emperor were not helped along their twisted path towards becoming plain and simple Austrians. Instead, yet another psychological obstacle was erected. The best description that the new constitution-makers could devise for this western half of the Dual Monarchy was 'the lands and kingdoms represented in the Imperial Parliament'. As for a geographical label, this was taken from a muddy little stream, the Leitha, which trickles away south of Vienna along the border with Hungary. Everything to the east became known as 'Transleithania' and everything to the west 'Cisleithania'.* It is hard to imagine anyone composing a national anthem for that. Yet this artificial concoction was supposed to represent the homeland of the Austrians, and it was not until the middle of the Great War, when Cisleithania and the entire Monarchy were moving towards extinction, that the plain and simple name of 'Austria' was adopted at long last.

The defeat at Königgrätz had been received by the Viennese with a typical mixture of bitterness and shoulder-shrugging. A huge outdoor summer carnival had been planned for the day on which the news from

---

* Apart from the hereditary Austrian lands, this now included Bohemia, Moravia, Galicia, the Bukovina and part of Silesia.

the battlefield reached the capital. It went ahead, and 2000 revellers ate, drank and danced away in the Prater that evening as though they were celebrating a victory. The dynasty flew some token black banners of its own, though they were not displayed for long. Thus, all the archdukes who were honorary colonels-in-chief of Prussian regiments ostentatiously resigned their commands. All reappeared in the army lists one year later.

Yet no amount of bowing before the storm could soften its impact. Bismarck had not only shifted the centre of gravity of the Habsburg Monarchy. He had forced the Austrians to decide where they stood in this absurd wonderland of 'Cisleithania'. We have seen already how blind loyalty to the dynasty always stood in conflict with their own development as a people, and how Catholics had been pitted against Protestants. Now, political divisions were added to these personal and religious ones. Henceforth, the riddle as to whether a 'homo austriacus' really existed, or whether he was simply another species of south German, was to be carried over into party votes and, ultimately, into the plebiscites of Schuschnigg and Hitler.

To begin with, a sharp polarisation of sentiment took place. On the one hand, many Austrians perversely became more Germanic the moment they were excluded from Germany. In 1868, two years after Königgrätz, the 'Deutscher Volksverein', or 'German People's Union', was founded in Vienna, and the same year saw a magnificent gathering in the Prater of the 'Third Assembly of German Marksmen'. Bismarck's crushing defeat of France in 1870, followed by his proclamation of the German empire, were widely greeted in Austria as though they had been triumphs for the Austrians themselves. Many of the new streets in the rapidly expanding capital were called after German philosophers such as Hegel, Fichte and Schelling. It was a rarity for any student union at schools and universities throughout 'Cisleithania' to choose a simple patriotic name like 'Austria' (causing even that self-declared 'German prince', the Emperor Francis Joseph, to mumble about treason*). Instead, most of the student associations became hotbeds of German nationalism: the 'Tauriskia' in Klagenfurt; the 'Orion' in Graz; the 'Quercus' in Prague and the 'Teutonia' in Brünn were typical examples.

All the while, organisations like the German 'Turnverein', or 'League

---

* He had every reason: anti-Habsburg, pro-Bismarck mania grew so wild in Graz that in November 1887 a bust of the Emperor was actually removed by unknown hands from the assembly hall.

of Gymnasts', which had been founded in Coburg in 1860, were finding growing swarms of followers in the Monarchy. These were the role-models for what were later styled the 'pure Aryans': racialistic, anti-Semitic, combining a cult of mass-organised physical fitness with the spiritual worship of Germania. (Their veneration of the 'thousand-year empire' of the old German nation had its thunderous echo in the new version proclaimed in the century to come by Hitler.) For thousands of young Austrians of 'Cisleithania', Bismarck's Protestant, anti-Slav Germany and not the Catholic, multi-national empire of the Habsburgs was their spiritual home. A demagogue soon emerged who declared it to be their political home as well.

Georg von Schönerer, the son of an ennobled Viennese engineer, was twenty-two years old when Bismarck staged Austria's shotgun divorce from Prussia. The event did not drive him immediately into either unconditional surrender to Germany or fanatical anti-Semitism, the two qualities which stamped his later life. As a young German Liberal Deputy to Parliament in the early 1870s, he had actually won praise from the largely Jewish-controlled press of Vienna for sponsoring a series of social reforms to improve the condition of peasants, craftsmen and factory workers alike. Moreover, his first great stride down the pan-German path, the so-called 'Linz Programme' of 1882, was taken arm-in-arm with two Jews: Viktor Adler, later to become the founder of Austrian socialism, and Heinrich Friedjung, the greatest Austrian historian of the age. The transformations to the Monarchy's structure proposed by this incongruous trio were radical enough.* Nonetheless, the new German state they envisaged for the Austrians was still to exist as a separate entity under the Habsburgs, albeit in the closest possible relationship with Germany, who would become its protector. But the extremist devil in Schönerer's soul soon emerged, on both the racial and the political fronts. These, for the first time, he fused together, a fateful development in the Austrian story.

The milestones in his march towards nationalist extremism included his call for the 'evangelisation of the German Ostmark people' (thus adding religion to the racial and political mix); his creation of a new Germanic calendar in which June became 'Heumond' or 'Hay Month'

---

* The programme for the so-called 'German People's Party' (which was never launched) would have redrawn Cisleithania along the lines of the old historic units – i.e. the hereditary Habsburg possession and the Bohemian lands, with German as the sole official language. Nothing about this was very new.

and Christmas re-emerged as 'Julfest' or 'Yulefeast'; and even the introduction of the harsh heathen greeting '*Heil*' in place of the gentle
Catholic '*Grüss Gott*' of the southern Germans. Though Hitler was to
develop this last idea with dramatic effect (and also proposals floated by
the Schönerer clique for 'punishment camps'), none of these extravagant
proposals took off at the time. Indeed, in terms of political representation, Schönerer's followers remained a tiny minority. His own party,
the 'German National Union', began with only three members in Parliament, and never emerged as a significant faction. In the everyday world,
many an Austrian student who had shouted pan-German slogans at
university found his vehemence softened after twelve months of compulsory service in the Emperor's multi-racial army which remained, right
to the bitter end, the core of the Monarchy.

Yet the importance of Schönerer is not to be sought in the Parliamentary voting lobbies or the university lecture halls of his day. Any political
system is like a military parade ground; it must have a right marker
from which the others measure their distance. Austria now had this
marker in the person of Georg von Schönerer, who was to end his
career by calling upon his fellow-Austrians to break altogether with
Catholic Rome and unite both their souls and their country with Protestant
Germany. He was the first of this new breed of party politicians to
declare that Austria could only find her true destiny and identity by
destroying herself. The message was taken up fifty years later by the
Nazis of the First Austrian Republic.

Those were not the only seeds that Schönerer, among others, helped
to sow for the future. His anti-Semitism also fell on alarmingly fertile
ground, especially in Vienna. Already by 1878 he was declaring in
Parliament that anti-Semitism was 'the greatest national achievement of
the century'. By the 1880s (despite the partnership with two outstanding
Jewish intellectuals in his 'Linz Programme') he had fixed on that anti-
Semitism as the ultimate lodestar of his personal and political life. His
followers composed anti-Jewish songs and distributed anti-Jewish
posters. Some fanatics even wore on their watch chains silver images of
Jews with the hangman's noose around their necks. Others smoked
pipes whose bowls were carved with the heads of Galician Jews, a breed
whose features were a real-life caricature of the race.

The mere fact that Schönerer's admirers – among them many solid
burghers – could indulge in such obscenities shows how deep and wide
the anti-Semitic roots were planted in Austria, above all in Vienna. It

is time to take a look at these roots, for they are very much entangled with the struggle for Austrian self-expression. Any nation, like any individual, is liable to seek a scapegoat when it lacks confidence in itself or when it is, quite simply, going through hard times. With the Austrians, those problems had arisen more than with most European peoples. With more vehemence than most, the scapegoat they picked on was the Jew in their midst.

Vienna led the way. The first public demonstrations against the Jews of the capital were chronicled as far back as 1303. Savage pogroms took place throughout the hereditary Austrian lands after the Black Death had swept up the Danube in 1348. (This was a classic case of mass feelings being vented somehow against inexplicable tragedy; on a petty personal scale it was repeated three centuries later, when a Spanish-born Empress expelled the Jews from Vienna because she blamed them for her miscarriage.) A succession of persecutions followed the Black Death pogroms, accompanied by a steady flow of anti-Jewish laws. Some of these were vivid omens of the future: an order of the great Emperor Charles V, for example, that Jews should wear cloth flaps of yellow would skip three centuries to re-emerge as the yellow star of Hitler's racial laws.

By the eighteenth century the Jews of Vienna, who had been so numerous in medieval times,* had shrunk to a few hundred, though the annexation of Galicia-Bukovina added a massive 200,000 of them to the total in the Monarchy as a whole. They were forced to live in ghettos (the one in Vienna was not finally done away with until 1848), made to pay special taxes, and generally sealed off from the Christian population, into which they were forbidden to marry. Their permitted occupations were similarly restricted. Medicine was the only profession open to them, and even as doctors they were not allowed to treat Christian patients. What did lie open to them was to make the best of their financial wits. These they put to use as humble tradesmen at the bottom end of the scale up to estate managers in the households of idle noblemen contemptuous of 'business' at the top end.

At the end of the century the Jews of the Monarchy profited, like Joseph II's other subjects, from the humane and commonsense measures of the Great Reformer. The 'Jew badge', the infamous yellow cloth patch, was abolished wherever it was still enforced; the special taxes

---

* Austria had even been dubbed 'Judaeis Apta', or 'The Land of Judah'.

were rescinded; and in Joseph's so-called Toleration Patents of 1782*
the Jews were promoted to what might be described as fully-fledged
second-class citizens. They were now allowed to send their children to
state schools or build schools of their own; they could become appren-
ticed to Christian masters in all the arts and crafts; careers in commerce,
industry and banking were formally opened up to them. Here, as elsewhere, the worthy Emperor's aim was basically pragmatic: to make the
Jews, in his words, 'more useful to the state'.

There was even a provision for the mounting social aspirations of
ambitious and successful Jews who now began that quest for 'status'
which has endured into modern times. Important Jewish merchants,
Joseph decreed, could 'dress like gentlemen', a provision which included
the jealously guarded right to wear swords. The nobility were taken
aback, just as the Christian Churches had been appalled at the privilege
granted to their ancient 'Israelite enemies'. This reaction was particularly
strong among the Catholics of the Austrian lands. Both these elements
– snobbish disdain of the pushy and vulgar newcomer and a broad-based
Christian enmity to his advancement – played a role in the social and
political developments ahead.

Significantly, the Jews, or at least their rabbis, were themselves nervous about setting foot in what had for so long been forbidden territory.
The prospect of being conscripted into the imperial army seemed particularly disturbing to the pious. How, they agonised, could an orthodox
Jew hold on to his beliefs if secular schools pulled him away from the
Talmud and service under the Habsburg colours turned him into the
soldier of a Catholic monarch? Once again, the problem of identity had
surfaced, this time among those in the Monarchy whose identity had been
preserved for centuries by persecution. For thousands of Austrian Jews,
the solution was sought in changing that identity. The search for assimi-
lation, going hand-in-hand with the search for acceptance, now began,
and intensified as the range of opportunity widened in the years ahead.

More doors were, of course, opened to them in the nineteenth century, especially after the liberal reforms which followed the revolution.
All civic inequalities had been abolished by the constitutional laws of
1867, and the advance of Jews into the professions followed apace.
Fifteen years later, more than 60 per cent of all doctors in the capital

* These were first introduced for Lower Austria and later promulgated for the other
crown lands, even, in the last months of his reign, to the huge 200,000-strong Jewish
population of Galicia.

were Jews, with no restrictions on their practice. Five years after that, well over half of all lawyers registered in the capital (394 out of 681) were Jewish, and nearly all of Vienna's most important newspapers were largely owned and staffed by Jews.* In an age without radio or television, this gave them a powerful lever over public opinion which, to put it mildly, was not always exercised to the benefit of the Monarchy. (The pan-German ideology of the famous Moritz Benedikt, a Bismarck worshipper whose long reign as editor of the *Neue Freie Presse* started in 1881, was the outstanding example.)

But it was the Jews in the rapidly-expanding finance world of the capital who prospered most – and who attracted the most envy, a quality with which the Viennese have always been liberally endowed. The giants among these Jewish financiers – notably the Rothschilds – had long been established as a European force; in Vienna, as we have seen, Salomon Rothschild had acted for years as Metternich's banker and close confidant. Indeed, Vienna's great private bank, the Creditanstalt, which went on to finance countless enterprises in the Monarchy, had been founded back in 1855, with help from the Rothschild clan.** Salomon had worked for the most part in secret. Now, in the boom years which followed the humiliation of Königgrätz, hundreds of little Salomons appeared, all operating in public on the Vienna scene. No fewer than 443 banks were among the joint-stock companies founded over five short years in the late 1860s and early 1870s. Most were in Jewish hands, as was the Vienna stock exchange. They presided over, and profited from, a frantic spiral of speculation.

The bubble had to burst one day, and it chose the worst possible time to do so. In May 1873 a World Exhibition was staged in the Vienna Prater. It was billed as the first ever to be held 'on German soil', and the real Germans were well represented. The pavilion of the newly-created German empire was the mightiest of all those erected in the exhibition grounds, where hundreds of old trees and dozens of even older inns had been levelled to produce an artificial carpet of flower beds and gravel paths. The aged Emperor William and his Chancellor

* This reflected a steady rise in the overall number of Jews in the capital – from some 40,000 in 1870 to 72,000 in 1880, and over 118,000 in 1890. Most of the newcomers had streamed in from Galicia on the newly-built railways.
** Though not from Salomon himself. He had fled Vienna in 1848, a target of popular anger, and never returned. He died in the year the Creditanstalt was founded, to be succeeded in Paris by his son Anselm.

Bismarck turned up in person (the destroyer of Austria being greeted with rapturous applause by the Viennese crowds). The Shah of Persia, Nasr Eddin, led the notables from Asia, and his exotic behaviour made him an even greater popular success. One of Vienna's smaller suburban palaces, Hetzendorf, had been given over entirely to his harem, and when he rode out from it he was mounted on a grey horse with a red-painted tail, and wearing an astrakhan hat embellished with a huge diamond pin. But it was not the Shah, but Austria's flourishing economy, the rebirth of the Monarchy, which was supposed to be on show here, to the rest of Europe and to the world. On 9 May, after Francis Joseph had formally opened the Exhibition, the Austrian boom burst apart for all the world to see. On that 'Black Friday' the over-inflated Vienna stock market collapsed. Thousands of investors, including many small-time speculators, were ruined before the day was out. One after the other, eight banks were declared bankrupt and forty more went into liquidation. They took with them scores of industrial enterprises throughout the Monarchy. Even some railway lines were left unfinished.

The Jews were blamed for it all, the old familiar scapegoats being sought out for another unimaginable Vienna catastrophe.* However exaggerated this reaction may have been, the memory of 'Black Friday' was burnt into the popular mind as a brand-mark of Austrian anti-Semitism. Its corrosive effects were to last down the century, and beyond.

---

* Another smear earlier in the century was that the 1848 Revolution had itself been engineered by 'Jewish liberals'. Though false, this charge was more understandable in that three of the four orators who sparked off the first demonstrations on 13 March were Jews, while Jewish university students took a full part in the upheavals which followed.

IV

The Believers

IT WOULD OF COURSE BE FALSE to paint the Monarchy in general, and its capital in particular, in nothing but pan-German and anti-Semitic colours at this time. The tens of thousands of imperial bureaucrats and army officers (which Jews could now become, up to the rank of colonel) felt themselves in Cisleithania to be 'Austrians', even if this meant, more and more, being primarily the privileged servants of the dynasty. '*Schwarz-gelb*', black and yellow, the colours of the Habsburgs, was their badge. Though this was not a mark of Austrian patriotism in the strict sense of the word (indeed, as we have seen, it militated steadily against that patriotism), at least it was anti-Prussian.

Moreover, there were to be found in all walks of life men who still believed ardently in Schwarzenberg's dream of an 'Austrian mission'. In the newspaper world, for example, the pan-German Jewish editor of the *Neue Freie Presse* found a doughty, if under-financed, opponent in Dr Friedrich Funder, the long-time publisher of the Catholic and monarchist *Reichspost*.* In Parliament, the Austrian flag-bearer was, above all, Karl Lueger, a lawyer of lowly Viennese origins (his father was a concierge and his mother ran a tobacco stall) who had the most extraordinary career of any political figure in the Monarchy. Lueger was the opportunist *par excellence*. He started off in public office in 1875 as a Municipal Councillor of Vienna, where he soon changed from being a Liberal to a Democrat. This gave him a better platform from which to launch violent attacks against corruption and the vested interests of industry and commerce, all protected by their financial providers, the

---

* This remarkable man survived the Monarchy, the First World War, the First Austrian Republic, and the beginning of Hitler's Third Reich to edit another Vienna Catholic journal, *Die Furche*, in the Second Austrian Republic. He died, his faith and traditionalist sympathies undimmed, in 1953.

banks. Inevitably, the Jews of Vienna became a regular target of his tirades, yet this was an anti-Semitism which came more from the head than the heart. Lueger, a 'humble son of Vienna' in his origins, presented himself as the champion of all the small men of the capital, who felt they were missing out on their share of Austrian prosperity (rapidly regained after the 'Black Friday' débâcle). The fact that he deliberately, and successfully, exploited anti-Semitism as the emotional wrapping for his programme is another sign of how widespread anti-Jewish feeling was among the ordinary people of the capital.

He continued his tirades in Parliament, to which he was elected in 1885; here a second transformation took place. Originally sympathetic to the German nationals of Schönerer's camp, he broke with them completely to found his own Christian Social Party in time for the 1891 elections, at which he won fourteen seats, half of them in Vienna. Despite his extraordinary mixture of partners,* Lueger's Christian Socials were all agreed on two main principles. The first was the need for action to better the lot of their 'little men'. Here the rhetoric had been turned into reality. A series of measures limiting working hours for men, women and children (with Sunday as a compulsory rest day) and introducing accident and sickness insurance into the factories and mines gave Austria, in theory at least, one of the most advanced social-industrial systems to be found anywhere in Europe. Their second guiding star was a stubborn and by now somewhat unfashionable belief in a 'Greater Austria' and in the Habsburg dynasty as its anointed champion. Inevitably, there were furious exchanges in Parliament between Lueger and Schönerer over this, with most of the other deputies stranded emotionally somewhere in between. It was this passionate loyalty to Austria's Catholic dynasty which had persuaded Pope Leo XIII to give Lueger his blessing, despite complaints to the Vatican over his rabid anti-Semitism.

This had, in fact, already been toned down once Lueger became an established party leader. Having served its purpose as an electoral slogan, it eventually faded even further after he had entered upon his final political incarnation as Mayor of Vienna. To hold this office was the ultimate ambition of the Vienna concierge's son; it was not achieved without a struggle against unexpected opposition. From 1895 onwards

---

* His co-founders were the 'progressive' aristocrat Prince Alois Liechtenstein; a university official, Dr Albert Gessmann; a mechanic, Ernest Schneider; and a workman, Leopold Kunschak. The spiritual founder of the new party was Karl von Vogelsang, originally a Prussian Protestant.

he was repeatedly elected Mayor, yet the Emperor, persuaded that Lueger was nothing better than a dangerous demagogue, refused to confirm the appointment. Finally, in 1897, after Lueger's Christian Social voters had carried the day convincingly yet again, Francis Joseph agreed to meet the demagogue face-to-face. He soon recognised in the handsome bearded orator precisely the 'black-yellow' populist whom the dynasty needed in its capital. Lueger was duly installed in the huge neo-Gothic Rathaus, where he was to remain until his death in 1910.

Karl Lueger's achievements as Mayor – whether in the construction of public buildings or in the development of the capital's exemplary tramways – have left their mark on the Vienna of today. His political legacy also survived him, though in more distorted form. The Christian Social Party survived the Monarchy to become the dominant political force for much of the First Republic's life. It tried to repeat the blend of populism (based on the peasantry rather than the workers) with pronounced Catholicism; it even tried to hold up the grail of monarchist tradition in the face of all the republican storms. Yet one reason why it then drifted into dictatorship must be sought in the Vienna of its cradle.* Like the Austrian Social Democratic party which Viktor Adler created almost single-handedly in 1889, the Christian Socials never knew the tolerance and the decencies of democratic Parliamentary life, with its respect for opposition as well as government. The Reichsrat of Schönerer, Lueger, Adler and the rest was essentially a public arena for the racial battles of the Monarchy; it saw much brawling, hurling of ink-pots and banging of desks, but hardly any rational debate. This remained of little more importance than the antics of a circus so long as the Emperor stood over it, aloof and near-omnipotent. It became another matter when the dynasty vanished, and real power and responsibility suddenly

---

* There was present in the launching of the movement a dangerous element of hero-worship and a cult of unswerving obedience to the leader. The Christian Social 'battle song', which reverberated through the streets of Vienna, was a hymn of quasi-religious dedication to Lueger. Its first verse translates:

> Let us praise the hero, who leads us in the fight,
> Joyfully show him praise and thanks which are his due.
> Let us also raise our hands for him in prayer,
> May God make us victorious, wherever his banner flies.

The words could have been written for that devout and well-intentioned Austrian dictator of the First Republic, Engelbert Dollfuss. With God stripped out, they could even have been sung by the worshippers of Hitler.

passed into the hands of deputies who had no experience of either.

Lueger and Schönerer are, in their different ways, such seminal figures in the politics of nineteenth-century Austria that they project themselves, almost automatically, into the twentieth. It is time to return to the 1880s and to others who still believed in those days in the 'Austrian mission'. We can find them at the very top of the imperial pyramid, in the person of Crown Prince Rudolph himself and his followers.

The boy whose birth on 21 August 1858 had set cannon firing and church bells ringing throughout the Monarchy had grown up into a restless, haunted young man. He was possessed of good looks and a lively intelligence, yet both were to be ravaged by a dissolute lifestyle, excessive even by the over-indulgent standards of most Habsburg arch-dukes. The restlessness might well have come from his mother, who took to wandering all over Europe, ranging from Ireland (rain and fox-hunting) to Corfu (sunshine and poetry), while her hapless husband laboured over his state papers and poured out his love and longing for her in a stream of childishly touching letters. Rudolph had clearly also inherited from the Empress something of that mental instability which ran like a febrile streak in the Wittelsbach line. But in his belief in Austria, and his consequential fear of Bismarck's Germany, he harked back to a very sane and sensible Wittelsbach, his grandmother, the Archduchess Sophie. Behind her on the family tree stood the doughty image of another anti-Prussian woman, the great Empress Maria Theresa.

As heir to the throne, Rudolph was unable to come out in public with feelings which ran counter to the allegiance of that self-styled 'German Prince', Francis Joseph. Moreover, as his distrustful father shut his son off from any part in state affairs, Rudolph was unable to operate through the government or the bureaucracy. He was thus driven into the political underworld. Two newspaper editors who shared his anti-Bismarck passion – Moriz Szeps of the *Neues Wiener Tagblatt* and Max Falk of the Budapest journal *Pester Lloyd* – gave him space for his unsigned leader articles calling for a liberal reform of the empire. Even these bold spirits found some of his outpourings too dangerous to print, and he occasionally had to resort to what would later be called '*samizdats*' – pamphlets of outright rebellion printed under a *nom de plume* abroad and then smuggled back into the Monarchy.

Germany, in Rudolph's eyes, was not only incapable of understanding his concept of a genuinely democratic and multi-racial Monarchy.

Through her strident nationalism, her autocracy and her hostility towards all Slavs, she was working all the time against it. In this case, he concluded, might not the Monarchy be better off without Germany altogether, seeking her partners instead among the Western democracies who would instinctively favour reform? Such thoughts were heresy against the creed of Teutonic solidarity; yet, for the true Austrian believer, they spelt the only salvation. Indeed, Charles, the last of all the Habsburg rulers, was actually to go down this path when the Monarchy was in its death-throes. It may have been heresy but it was not fantasy.

In the last ten years of his life, Rudolph saw only frustration and seeming defeat for his ideas, beginning with the signing of the Austro–German alliance. This had always been in Bismarck's scheme of things. Military partnership between the two German powers was in the long run just as vital for him as the confrontation to settle the issue of supremacy between them. The Russian war of 1878 against Turkey* alerted both Vienna and Berlin to the dangers they both faced from St Petersburg; the outcome was the defensive treaty of 7 October 1879. This provided that if either party were attacked by Russia, or by a combination of opponents which included Russia, the other signatory would come to its partner's aid with all the forces at its disposal. Thus the first stone was laid in that fateful construction of rival alliances which would eventually divide the six European powers, three by three, against each other: Germany, Austria-Hungary and Italy in one camp, faced by a looser grouping of Russia, France and England in the other.

By the treaty, Bismarck had done, on the military front, what he had sworn to avoid on the political front, namely, to shackle the 'trim seaworthy frigate' of his state to the 'worm-eaten galleon' of the Habsburgs. He was not to know that when the great storm raged over Europe half a century ahead, it was the galleon which would bring the frigate down with it. For everyone involved (and it was Julius Andrassy, co-architect of the 1867 Settlement, and now Austro-Hungarian Foreign Minister, who signed for the Emperor) all this lay far over the foreseeable horizon. To the 'Greater Austrians' in Vienna, this new alliance seemed to cut off the Dual Monarchy from both France in the

---

* As one of the consequences of the peace which concluded it (at a Congress of the Powers in Berlin in June 1878), Austria was allowed to occupy indefinitely the provinces of Bosnia-Herzegovina. Thirty years later she was to cause a major European crisis by unilaterally declaring their annexation.

west and Russia in the north.* It thus marked a formal subjugation, without escape routes, to the victors of Königgrätz. The reception accorded to Bismarck's seventieth birthday on 1 April 1885 seemed only to ram home the point. It was widely celebrated in the Monarchy as though he had been its hero, not its conqueror.

A greater personal blow to Rudolph even than the 1879 Treaty was the tragically early death, on 15 June 1888, of King Frederick III of Germany. This kindly and modest man, together with his English-born wife (Victoria, eldest daughter of the Queen of England) was, in his eyes – and in the eyes of many other European observers – the only reassuring figure on the Berlin stage. When cancer of the throat cut short his reign, after only ninety days, the crown passed to a vain, unstable braggart, William II, only twenty-nine years old but already fretting for power. He was the very incarnation of that titanic burst of energy which, within twenty years, had made Germany just as supreme on the military and industrial fronts as Bismarck had made her in the diplomatic field. Henceforth, the Hohenzollern crown would no longer contain that explosive force, but project it.

The closer Rudolph moved towards his own violent end, the more open and outspoken became his attacks on the policies of his father. In April 1888 a pamphlet attributed to him and published in Paris under the pen-name 'Julius Felix' flatly accused the Emperor of acting as Bismarck's accomplice in the destruction of Austria. The pamphlet, which took the form of a letter addressed to the Emperor, called on him to abandon both the German link and the Monarchy's Balkan entanglements: 'Shake it all off, Your Majesty, while there is still time.' As for Crown Prince William, who was soon to ascend the German throne, this was the man, warned 'Julius Felix', whose intemperate ambition would one day bring about the ruin of Europe, and with it drown both the Austrian and German empires in a 'sea of blood'.** Six months later, in October 1888, William visited Vienna for the first time as

* The so-called *'Dreikaiserbund'* between the emperors of Austria-Hungary, Germany and Russia, binding them to benevolent neutrality in case any one of them should be engaged in war, finally lapsed, after periodic renewals, in 1887. The same year, Bismarck concluded his private 'Re-insurance Treaty' with St Petersburg, leaving Austria out in the cold.

** This prediction exactly matched the fears of another impatient heir to an empire, Queen Victoria's eldest son, the Prince of Wales. Prince Edward and Archduke Rudolph had become personal friends – not least because their opinions, like their situations, ran parallel.

Emperor and promptly confirmed the worst fears of the Monarchy's true believers. With a bumptious tactlessness which was to become his imperial hallmark, he attacked his hosts for everything from having too sloppy an army to being too friendly to the Slavs and too gentle with the press. As for any ideas about turning the empire into a federation, that, he warned, would create doubts in Berlin about the Monarchy's credentials as an ally, something he would have to think about when the 1879 pact came round for the second of its five-year renewals. Even the sheer rudeness of such behaviour paled beside the megalomania it revealed. The tragedy was that there were many Austrians who were prepared to swallow it, and quite a few of Schönerer's persuasion who were glad to applaud it.

Rudolph's state of mind can be measured by the last desperate patriotic shout uttered in his name. In mid-January 1889, a fortnight before his death, an article which set out the 'Ten Commandments for an Austrian' appeared in *Schwarzgelb*, a new Monarchist periodical. Commandment number one called on his fellow-countrymen to believe in nothing but imperial Austria, 'ancient, united and undivided'. So nobody should be left in doubt as to the real enemy, number four called on Austrians to stop idolising Prussia and the Germany which it dominated. Number five was even more precise: it told them not to fear either Bismarck or Moltke,* both of them 'tired and weak old men' who were 'close to their graves'.

Rudolph was far closer to his own. On the morning of 30 January 1889, his dead body was found next to the corpse of the seventeen-year-old Baroness Marie Vetsera, in the bedroom of a snowbound shooting lodge at Mayerling. The first rumour was that the girl had poisoned her royal lover with cyanide. The truth, soon established by the police, was less comfortable for the Catholic dynasty. The Crown Prince had first killed the girl, then turned his revolver on himself. Quite why this pathetic teenager had to die is one of Mayerling's many enduring mysteries. A suicide pact it obviously was. A tragedy of deep but hopeless love between them it certainly was not. Marie was clearly besotted with Rudolph, though in all probability it was the aphrodisiac of his rank and reputation to which she had succumbed. Her family stood on the lowest rung of the aristocratic ladder and had seemingly beggared themselves to get there. For a pretty girl of such *parvenu* background,

---

* General Helmuth von Moltke, the German Chief of Staff.

an affair with any archduke would have been a thrilling prospect. To go to bed with the heir to the throne was the peak of romance; to go to her death with him was to scale an even higher pinnacle.

Rudolph, for his part, seems simply to have gathered Marie up as the last and most docile of a long succession of mistresses who had been strung like gaudy beads through his life. Only one of these seemed to have touched his heart: Mizzi Caspar, a black-haired, plump-faced girl from Graz who was taken up – and indeed publicly taken out – by the Archduke from 1886 onwards. She was evidently a good listener as well as a lusty bedmate. To her he poured out his family woes, talked of shooting himself and even, in 1888, suggested that they commit suicide together in the so-called 'Temple of Hussars' in the Vienna woods. Mizzi laughed at the idea; no Mayerling for her. (As it was, Rudolph spent his last night in the capital at the house he had helped her buy, and he was to leave her all his spare cash. She repaid him by never revealing anything of their relationship.) Marie Vetsera was in a different category. She worshipped Rudolph, without thought of reward, and he reacted accordingly. He took her with him into death as a Pharaoh would choose a burial treasure to accompany him into eternity. We shall never know for certain what his motives for his own death were on that 29 January, since by the beginning of 1889 his mind was no longer lucid.

Rudolph had long shown signs of manic depression, and Mizzi Caspar was not the only one to whom he had spoken of death and suicide. Moreover, the last three years of his life had been devastated by the remorseless advance of venereal disease. It was believed to be gonorrhoea, for which no cure was then known; instead he was given morphine, and became addicted to that. Next to women, his favourite pleasure (in true Austrian style) had always been shooting, but in February 1888 an eye complaint, surely a side-effect of his illness, had put paid to that. What was there left to make life worthwhile? He knew by now that he would never live to be emperor, nor sire a male heir.

He could find neither joy nor solace in his family, and certainly no tie strong enough to hold him back. In 1881, aged twenty-three, he had been married to Princess Stephanie, daughter of the repellent King Leopold II of the Belgians. But though she made a dynastically suitable match, there was nothing about this plain and gauche sixteen-year-old which could satisfy the sexual demon in her husband. Dull though she was born, and spiteful though she became, she did not deserve what was inflicted on her: her husband's own disease, which he infected her with soon after catching it himself.

As for his parents, the Empress Elisabeth, frigid and unstable herself, was the opposite of an understanding and warm-hearted mother. The Emperor he never seems to have known as a father, or even as a human being. Rudolph left behind farewell letters or messages to his wife, his mother, his sister Marie Valerie, the banker Baron Hirsch, who had financed his indulgences, Mizzi, the most expensive of those indulgences, and even to his valet Loschek, who had hammered down the bedroom door on that dreadful night. To his father he sent not one word of farewell. His emperor was for him not just a stranger, but the supreme traitor.

Here we come back to the political context of Rudolph's suicide. Much rumour swirled around at the time over his strong Hungarian connections. Budapest, as we have seen, provided one of the strongest outlets for airing his liberal and federalist views. This was something of an irony in view of Hungary's drive towards separatism and its social and political system dominated by the conservative magnates. Indeed, the Dual Monarchy itself (which Rudolph came to question) stood in direct contradiction to the multi-national empire under the centralised control of Vienna for which he had always hoped. Nonetheless, he was bound always to pay it lip service, and there was much talk of him following his father by taking the coronation oath in Budapest. He was seriously considering this in the early 1880s, with the curious round-about reasoning that he might be able to introduce liberalism into Hungary through a royal back door. This was a naive thought indeed.

But whatever unorthodox company he sometimes kept in Hungary (where he bought himself a shooting estate), to suggest that he chose death to avoid being unmasked as patron of a coup d'état against the Emperor is to misread the world of Francis Joseph. Nobody – and least of all a crown prince – would have ever dreamt of trying to overturn that granite Titan. If a single political impulse existed behind the suicide, it is surely to be sought in the cry of despair which resounds in those 'Ten Commandments', and in the bombastic antics of the newly-crowned William II which prompted their publication. The behaviour of the German Emperor on his first visit to Vienna had been enough to drive any patriotic Austrian to the bottle, and a mental wreck like Rudolph to his revolver. Whatever the background, with his passing the Monarchy had lost the most august of its true believers. It would go too far to say that it had also lost its potential saviour. Many of his ideas were fanciful and capricious. His intelligence, even before it became deformed by sickness, was lively rather than profound. The mould of his character was not that from which a wise monarch could have been formed. His faith was his one positive legacy.*

On the negative side, he helped to augment an ugly upsurge of that anti-Semitism which was to darken the final decades of the Monarchy's life. This was hardly surprising, given the company he kept. Both of his principal champions in the press world, Moriz Szeps in Vienna and Max Falk in Budapest, were Jews; so was his main source of money, the banker Baron Moritz Hirsch; so was the industrialist Emil Kuranda (a *mari complaisant* whose wife, also Jewish, he bedded); so were most of his literary friends, like Friedrich Kraus and Joseph Weilen. It was no wonder that his enemies – above all Schönerer – inveighed against the 'Jewish clique' which surrounded the heir to the throne.

The year before his suicide, the Archduke had himself become embroiled in a political storm over Schönerer's anti-Semitism. The issue that touched it off was one to which Rudolph was particularly sensitive: the succession to the throne in Berlin. In March 1888, several Vienna papers rushed out special editions with black borders announcing the death of William I. They were, in fact, only a day ahead of events, and there is no reason to suppose that their editors acted on anything but over-hasty despatches from Berlin. Schönerer promptly blew up these premature reports to represent a calculated insult to German honour by the Jews who dominated the Vienna press.** Moreover, on this occasion, he matched words with deeds: that same evening, accompanied by a gang of his thugs, he invaded the premises of the *Neues Wiener Tagblatt* and beat up the journalists on duty. That was too much to swallow, even for a divided Parliament and the 'German Prince' who sat on the throne. His heir led the clamour for action. As a result, Schönerer's mandate as Deputy was removed, and with it his immunity

---

* The poet Robert Hamerling, in an ode on Rudolph's death, beautifully encapsulates its aura of mystery. The last lines translate:

> And he stays silent if you ask him more
> For silence is the great right of the dead.

** The fact that the Vienna stock market rose sharply when the death was confirmed produced another ugly rumour that Jewish speculators had profited from the earlier inaccurate reports.

from prosecution. The courts duly sentenced him to four months' imprisonment, and the Emperor obliged by revoking his patent of nobility.* The streets of the capital erupted in pro- and anti-Schönerer demonstrations. These were made all the wilder because the sentencing came just before the unveiling in Vienna of a new statue to the memory of that doughty anti-Prussian champion, the Empress Maria Theresa.

The mêlée now became confused almost beyond description, lighting up, once again, the dark muddle of the Austrian soul. To the shouts of 'Long live Schönerer' and 'Down with the Jews' were added the rival musical strains of the Austrian anthem '*Gott erhalte*' and the song which symbolised the Germanic creed, '*Die Wacht am Rhein*'. The pan-Austrian camp had itself been publicly split by the anti-Semitic factor. Thus Karl Lueger and his followers, though worshipping at the shrine of Maria Theresa and all she had stood for, nonetheless joined wholeheartedly in the anti-Jewish howls. Rudolph's carriage was among those which got stuck among the hysterically divided mob on the day the statue to his great ancestor was unveiled, and he was forced to make his way back to the Hofburg on foot. It was an apt symbol of his political frustration.

Despite this gulf between them over racial intolerance, Lueger the Christian Social leader and Rudolph the Crown Prince both go down in history as heralds of the Austrian cause. Who else can be found, at that high level? We can identify a third prominent believer among the ranks of the Emperor's prime ministers, though in this case faith was grounded less on passion than on genial calculation. Count Edward Taaffe headed the imperial government from 1879 until 1893. It was not only the length of his tenure, unparalleled since the Metternich era, which was exceptional; so too was the degree of stability, prosperity and superficial harmony which the fourteen-year 'Taaffe era' brought to the Monarchy. The Count (of Irish descent, though the Taaffes had been settled in Moravia since the days of Wallenstein) was not merely '*Schwarz-gelb*', or a Habsburg man, in general. He was passionately loyal in particular to Francis Joseph, who had been a childhood playmate, and called himself, first and foremost, 'the Emperor's Minister'. What was unique was the way he served that master.

Taaffe was appointed after a complicated deadlock had been broken allowing the Czech delegates, who had been boycotting Parliament, to

* This was restored in 1917, as a gesture to wartime solidarity with Germany by the last Habsburg ruler, the young Emperor Charles.

stop sulking in Prague and resume their seats. The experience confirmed the new Prime Minister in his belief that there was no point in trying to govern through a normal regime of party majorities. Instead, he manufactured a right-wing government bloc supporting the so-called 'Iron Ring' made up of German Clericals who represented the peasantry; the feudal landowners, who represented themselves; and the Slavs of the empire represented by the Czechs and the powerful faction of Poles known as the Polish Club. The coalition remained solid, despite its artificial construction, and gave Taaffe a steady, if small, majority of votes over the more divided factions on the left. He was thus able to rule, to all intents and purposes, constitutionally through Parliament, though he had, in fact, serenely bypassed it with his mathematical calibrations. Taaffe now applied the same technique to the national problems of the Monarchy as a whole.

There is a type of rotation clock, made in Taaffe's day, which later became known as an 'Atmos' to the specialists in the antique trade. In it, the movement is propelled by the action of two solid balls whose weight is finely balanced so that they swing in a wide arc, first to one side and then to the other, but always checking before they complete the circle and then returning smoothly to the central point of control. The Count may even have had such a clock to gaze and reflect upon; at all events, he now tried to govern the eleven main peoples of the Habsburg empire on the Atmos principle. He would incline to one side where expedient, then to the other. He would share out favours, mainly in respect of cultural and language concessions, to this race and then to that. He would avoid at all costs giving any one people virtually everything they demanded. That would have completed the circle, thus breaking the circuit and stopping the clock altogether. Instead, every part of the Monarchy's internal mechanism had to be given enough of a push to keep it in motion with the rest, while still thrusting for something more.

Taaffe once summed up this technique as 'preserving all the nationalities of the Monarchy in a state of balanced and well-modulated discontent'. He was thus an Austrian believer not only in his unqualified loyalty to the dynasty, but because he thought he had discovered the ideal way of preserving it. His German liberal opponents (who had been sidelined by the Count's pro-Slav policy of balance) derided his policy as one of 'Fortwursteln', a delicious Viennese phrase which is inadequately translated as 'muddling along somehow'. Taaffe was happy to accept this, even to quote it with approval, for what his critics were attacking was, in fact, a main trait in the Austrian character. All the Count did was to institutionalise it. The experiment, like the Atmos clock, did not run for ever. Yet while it ran, there was an illusion of perpetual motion which was both soothing and stimulating to a Monarchy already haunted by *Angst* about its future.

Austria (that is to say the non-Magyar lands of Cisleithania) prospered economically and bloomed culturally in the Taaffe era. By 1890 its population had risen to almost twenty-four million, compared with twenty-two million ten years before. Industry had made huge strides, after the temporary check of the 1873 'Black Friday', so that it was no longer an overwhelmingly agrarian economy. More than 60 per cent of the population still worked on the land and two-thirds of them still lived in the countryside. But mining and manufacturing were absorbing a steadily growing proportion of the workforce: the 1890 breakdown showed nearly 300,000 employed in the textile industry, nearly 100,000 in metal production, 72,000 in stone and glass work and 33,000 even in the new branch of chemicals.

In the hereditary lands, the showpiece was the great Alpine Montan works of Styria, founded in 1881 to develop the iron resources of the province (and still operating at the end of the twentieth century). The other main centre of expansion was Bohemia, where the great landlords, overcoming their feudal distaste for 'trade', had plunged into lucrative commercial ventures on their estates. By the end of the 1880s, eighty out of the 120 sugar beet refineries of Bohemia were in the magnates' hands, as were nearly half of the nine hundred breweries and three-quarters of the four hundred distilleries. Despite this, and their steady income from timber, many estates contrived to be heavily mortgaged; but that was the fault of extravagance and mismanagement.

The capital reflected and basked in this general prosperity. Greater Vienna had grown by the Taaffe era into a major European metropolis with over 1,300,000 inhabitants (already over-heavy by comparison with the other major cities, and destined one day to become overwhelmingly so). Architecturally, it had also blossomed into its full nineteenth-century form. The famous Ringstrasse, built in the 1860s on the site of the levelled fortifications to encircle the old Inner City, now had all its jewels set in position: the Opera House, the Burgtheater, the two great museums of art and nature, the Ministries of War and Justice and the neo-Gothic Town Hall. The men who had built and embellished it reflected, now as in the days of baroque, the pull of Vienna as a cosmopolitan magnet. Native talent was, of course, represented. Van der Nüll and Siccardsburg, the much-hounded creators of the Opera House, were Austrians, as was Ferstel, the young architect of the Votiv Church. Hans Gasser, who created one of the city's loveliest statues, the 'Danube Maiden' in the Stadtpark, was a Tyrolean. But among the other builders and sculptors who also left their mark were men from Swabia, Copenhagen, Switzerland, Erfurt, Speyer and Westphalia. The most prolific was the Dane, Hansen, who seemed to shake his new palaces out along the Ring as though they fell straight out of his coat-sleeves.

Architecturally, this Vienna never rivalled Paris in beauty, London in dignity, or Bismarckian Berlin in sheer massivity. Politically, it was but one of the six great power capitals of Europe, and by no means the most influential among them. But musically, it had become, in this last quarter of the nineteenth century, the unchallenged centre of the Western world. Its classical giants were Johannes Brahms, who settled in Vienna in 1863; Gustav Mahler, whose ten symphonies (and even more exhausting labours as director of the Opera House) stretched into the next century; Anton Bruckner, who wrote all nine of his in the nineteenth; and Hugo Wolf, whose three hundred songs included many of the finest written before or since.

Among the popular music composers of the age it is, of course, the Strauss family and above all the figure of Johann Strauss the younger which stands out from a gathering crowd. Contrary to the accepted beliefs, the music of the 'Waltz King' is not all champagne bubbles. True, that 'one eye weeping' (to go with the 'one eye laughing') which makes up so much of the Viennese spirit is hard to find in his music; but it is there all the same, and sometimes in very revealing fashion. In 1889 he wrote his 'Emperor Waltz', as Francis Joseph was entering the fifth decade of his reign. Majesty was to be expected in such a piece, with a touch of awe. Yet the slow introduction vibrates with something else: foreboding. And the key melody of his greatest operetta, *Die Fledermaus* ('The Bat'), exudes another half-suppressed mood of the time which went with that foreboding, namely resignation. 'Happy is he who forgets that which can't be changed' goes the refrain.* The lines sum

---

* Or, in the rhyming original:

> *Glücklich ist, wer vergisst*
> *Was nicht mehr zu ändern ist.*

up that acceptance of an uncertain fate, combined with a determination to have fun in the meantime, with which the Austrians approached the new century. Perhaps that was one reason – apart, of course, from its lovely melodies and its personification of the rich opulence of the age – why this composition was recognised in its time as a classic which stood uniquely above the ordinary run of operetta. In 1897, no less a person than Gustav Mahler admitted *Die Fledermaus* to the repertoire of the Court Opera.*

Everything we have been describing, from the growth in population and urban development, the surge in factory and mining output and the expansion of trade to the building of railways, the founding of banks and the introduction of broad social legislation – these all had one common denominator for the governments of the age: the need for a larger and more complex structure of administration, and the consequent requirement of more state employees to operate it. As regards the Habsburg Monarchy, whose affairs were complicated enough from the start by its racial diversity, this meant recruiting more imperial bureaucrats not just by the hundreds, but, eventually, by the tens of thousands. The pool of officialdom became a great lake. Even the flowering of the arts helped to feed it. The curators and cleaners of the new museums, the singers and musicians of the opera and the actors and scene-changers of the Burgtheater: all, from the highest to the humblest, could qualify as established government employees, with the coveted status, lifelong security and retirement pensions which that embraced. This brings us right back to Taaffe and his 'Atmos clock' approach to government.

With the Magyars and their subordinate peoples locked away in the Hungarian kingdom of 1867, the main problem which the Austrian half of the Dual Monarchy had to face over the last fifty years of its life was how to accommodate Slav pressures for more privileges and rights. This came at first mainly from the north Slavs and, in particular, from the Czechs of Bohemia; and what much of that pressure boiled down to at bottom was, quite simply, the demand for more jobs. To put the issue in these unromantic materialistic terms is not to deny the steady growth of a nationalist Czech spirit throughout the period – especially after 1874, when the more radical movement of the Young Czechs under Karl Skladovsky was established. It is not to overlook either the

---

* Not unlike perhaps the admission to twentieth-century classical concerts of compositions such as *Rhapsody in Blue* by the popular songwriter George Gershwin.

burgeoning of Czech culture. By 1881, they had their own university and their own national theatre in Prague; while in the field of music, where composers like Dvořák and Smetana were achieving world fame. Nonetheless, something needs asserting here which will be reasserted later, when describing the Monarchy's death-throes. What these nationalist leaders, and also the peoples for whom they spoke, wanted was not independence from the empire, nor even a plain extension of that dualist rule set up between Vienna and Budapest. The Magyars were seen as being incontestably a special case, and not only in their own eyes.* What the other races sought was a bigger piece of the imperial cake, for, as all but a few fanatics appreciated, only the empire could provide a cake of such size and richness for everyone to nibble at. Taaffe's great balancing act consisted of measuring out its crumbs and slices so that nobody became satiated and nobody went famished.

Language was the key. It controlled the development of national consciousness in general and access to the imperial bureaucracy in particular. It was therefore logical that Taaffe should reward the Czechs for entering his 'Iron Ring' with their fifty-four Parliamentary delegates with a series of language and cultural concessions for Bohemia and Moravia. The most important, enacted on 18 April 1880, put Czech and German on an equal footing in all official dealings, oral or written, with members of the public, including judicial proceedings. This was the so-called 'outer service' of administration, and gave the aspiring Czech professionals – especially the lawyers – a basic foothold on the bottom rung of the bureaucratic ladder. To climb further up, they had to secure similar equality in the 'inner service', i.e. the language in which officials throughout the Monarchy corresponded with each other. This, as regards Cisleithania, remained exclusively German. To share the top rung with the Austrians, and if possible knock most of them off it, was now the aim of every ambitious, educated Czech. Predictably, those whose privileged preserves were threatened protested immediately, and were eventually to erupt into violence.

It would take too long to detail how, throughout the 1880s, Taaffe kept these restless Austrians under some sort of control while conducting his balancing act among the Poles, Slovenes, Ruthenians and the other peoples under Vienna's control. The Czech issue was the crucial one,

---

* The closest the Czechs came to aiming at the Hungarian model was their unavailing pressure for recognition of the so-called '*Böhmisches Staatsrecht*', i.e. the formal acceptance of the 'Lands of the Bohemian Crown' as a constitutional unit of the Monarchy.

so much so that it was finally not only to bring him down, but to topple one of his successors as well. In 1890, he brought the Austrians and the Czechs together in Vienna to try and settle their smouldering dispute over the administration of Bohemia. Agreement was reached on dividing up the districts of mixed-language provinces on national lines and on establishing linguistic qualifications for Supreme Court judges – an indication of how far up the ladder the Czechs were climbing. Henceforth, twenty-six of the Supreme Court's forty-one members had to be bilingual, while the other fifteen needed to know only German. Peace seemed about to break out until the radical Young Czechs, who had not been invited to the talks, denounced the concessions as not going far enough. Moreover, their stand clearly reflected the popular mood at home, for in the elections of March 1891 they were returned with thirty-seven mandates, reducing the more moderate 'Old Czechs' who had negotiated the deal to twelve. The 1890 compromise remained a dead letter.

In 1893 Taaffe made his final, and fatal, attempt to secure the support of Czechs both Young and Old by electoral reforms throughout Cisleithania. In October of that year a bill was presented which, in effect, extended the right to vote to every male taxpayer over the age of twenty-five who could read and write in his own language. The measure, which had been prepared in the deepest secrecy, had the full backing of the Emperor; Francis Joseph was now persuaded that the 'little men' among his subjects would show more gratitude and loyalty towards the dynasty than the increasingly troublesome bourgeois liberals. There was something in that argument, but the venture itself was a disaster. This time, only the Young Czechs declared their support. All the other main factions recoiled before the prospect of a mass electorate which, in various ways, would reduce their own power and privilege, with prosperous peasants and skilled workers everywhere taking over from the middle and landowning classes. The bill was decisively rejected, and on 10 November Taaffe, whose 'Iron Ring' seemed now to be permanently corroded, was relieved of office. The fourteen-year lull in the Monarchy's life was ended. Ructions lay ahead, nearly all of them in the linguistic minefield.

In the first of these crises, the humble Slovenes, one of the 'non-historic' peoples, took centre stage. For years, they too had been pressing for more school teaching in their own tongue, and their campaign now focused on the little town of Cilli in southern Styria. This was a German enclave in a predominantly Slovene countryside, and the German-speaking inhabitants, fanatical as always wherever in the Monarchy they lived on Slav fringes, were fiercely resisting the demand for parallel language instruction in the local grammar schools. At that time, a shaky coalition government was in office to replace Taaffe, headed by Prince Alfred Windisch-Graetz, grandson of the maverick soldier of 1848 fame. When in 1895 its Finance Minister, Ernst von Plener, rashly sanctioned the budget for dual language teaching in Cilli, his party colleagues denounced him, the coalition broke apart, and the government fell. This quarrel over a village school was ludicrous in its impact yet, given the underlying issue, logical as well.

For the second, and far more serious, explosion, the scene moved back to the main battlefield of Bohemia. Count Casimir Badeni, the Polish noble whom the Emperor eventually appointed as his prime minister, inherited a Czech–German quarrel which had only been sharpened by the clownish crisis over Cilli. Moreover, in 1897, during the run-up to the tricky decennial renewal of the 1867 Compromise with Hungary, he sought to guard his rear by making sure of the Young Czech votes. So far from guarding his rear, the over-ambitious bribe which he offered them plunged Cisleithania into tumult and ejected him from office.

By his enactments of 5 April 1896, the Czech language in Bohemia and Moravia would have virtually leapfrogged over the German. First, the use of Czech in the 'outer service' was widely extended. Far more important were the changes proposed to the 'inner service'; henceforth, any case had to be discussed, orally or in writing, in the language in which it had been initiated. The impact of this on the relentless scramble for official posts would have been enormous, with the German-speakers, relatively few of whom knew Czech, the losers all the way down the line. They erupted in fury, not just in Bohemia but also in Vienna, Salzburg and (with memories of Cilli still fresh) inevitably in Graz. Rioting on a scale not seen since 1848 broke out in the streets and continued throughout the year. Finally, on 28 November, with the capital almost paralysed by pan-German agitation, the Emperor yielded to the storm and dismissed the author of the 'Badeni riots'.

It was, of course, Schönerer's finest hour, not least because sympathy demonstrations had been staged throughout Germany itself. Here lies the significance of the affair for our consideration of the Austrians' awareness of their own identity. This crisis, the last the Monarchy was to go through in the nineteenth century, was not one where Austrians had fought for their existence as a nation against external threat, but one where they had battled for their personal and public standing inside a multi-national empire. The issue was not one of patriotism, but of patronage. The broader background to the conflict – Germandom versus Slavdom – was equally inhibiting to the growth of any truly Austrian spirit.

PART THREE

THE ROAD TO WAR

I

Fin de Siècle

THERE WAS A SPATE OF DYING as the Austrians and their dynasty, now over six hundred years old, moved across the threshold of the twentieth century. It was as though many whose names had given a glitter to the nineteenth were hurrying to leave it while there was still time and the memory was still bright. In the musical world alone, this *'Grosses Sterben'*, as they called it in Vienna, had swept away von Suppé in 1895, Bruckner in 1896, Brahms in 1897 and Johann Strauss in 1899. Millöcker, his lesser colleague in the world of light opera, left it to the very last day of the century to follow them.

The most illustrious death of these closing years was neither peaceful nor natural: the assassination of the Empress Elisabeth in Geneva on 10 September 1898. There was a gruesome symmetry between murderer and victim. The Empress's life had long since become a random affair, a sequence of restless travels, strung together by whim and pointing to no goal. The assassin, Luigi Lucheni, a twenty-six-year-old Italian labourer and self-styled 'individual anarchist', had himself been wandering from country to country before landing up by chance in Geneva and deciding to kill anyone famous enough to get his name in the history books. He had at first thought that the Duke of Orléans, who was expected in the city, would suit his purpose. When the Duke failed to show up, he hit upon the Austrian Empress as a substitute, only after reading the programme of her visit in the local paper. Even the stiletto which he drove into her heart as she was boarding the lake steamer outside the Beau Rivage hotel was a makeshift weapon he had cobbled together himself. It was indeed a random end to her random existence.

An even greater irony attended her funeral a week later in the gloomy mausoleum of the Habsburgs, the Church of the Capuchins in Vienna. On the first day, the coffin which tens of thousands filed past had borne the simple inscription 'Elisabeth, Empress of Austria'. Immediately, the Hungarian mourners complained: what about our crown, which she had also worn? The protests became so emphatic that the words 'and Queen of Hungary' were hastily added on that same evening. This, in turn, prompted a formal request from Prague to have the title 'Queen of Bohemia' engraved as well. The pressures crowding on the dynasty for nationalist status had made themselves felt even in its crypt. All in all, it was a gloomy monarch who, on 2 December of this terrible year, saw in the fiftieth anniversary of his accession.

The importance, as opposed to the symbolism, of Elisabeth's death can be measured only by its effect on her husband. A series of public humiliations, culminating in Königgrätz, and family tragedies, the most spectacular of which was Rudolph's suicide, had smothered ordinary human feeling in the Emperor. But, as in most such cases, there is usually one final blow which snuffs the spark out for good. This, for Francis Joseph, was the death of his wife, whom he had continued to adore despite her virtual abandonment of him, both as a husband and as a sovereign. Indeed, for years almost his only normal contact with the outside world had been his daily chats with *Die Gnädige Frau*', the Burgtheater actress Katharina Schratt. This extraordinary link had been forged out of his need for someone to talk to and her talent for diverting and soothing companionship. It had been encouraged by the Empress, as a sop to a guilty conscience over her incessant absences from his side. She knew it was a staid if affectionate affair of *café au lait* in the mornings, and not of champagne drunk out of slippers at night. Now, to cap everything, even this friendship underwent a strain, just when, in the aftermath of his wife's death, the Emperor needed it most. A coolness between them had arisen in 1899, when he studiously held aloof from a quarrel over the renewal of Katharina's Burgtheater contract; his aim, of course, had only been to avoid embarrassing her by a public intervention.* Brooding afterwards as to how, with his wife gone, they too were drifting apart, he wrote to her: 'You yourself wanted to bring this about . . . I feel endlessly sad in my hopeless loneliness; my age is making itself more and more felt, especially recently, and I am very tired.' Yet this weary and disillusioned old sovereign had nonetheless leapt into action, like a veteran soldier ignoring all his battle wounds,

---

* The actress had shown even less commonsense by taking offence at not being made a member of the prestigious 'Elisabeth Order', established for ladies of impeccable lineage and solid Catholic probity.

to face the threat which suddenly arose over the succession to the crown itself.

Archduke Francis Ferdinand was the eldest son of the Emperor's oldest surviving brother, Charles Louis, who, technically, had become the heir to the throne after the suicide of Crown Prince Rudolph. Charles Louis had never shown either inclination or aptitude for the succession, and had anyway died in 1896, from which date his first-born became the clear successor. By now, Francis Ferdinand was thirty-three years old. As a child he had been brooding and introspective, a puzzle to his happy parents and his siblings. As a man, he was prickly, quick-tempered, assertive in his opinions, impatient of opposition, highly intelligent but totally lacking in that redeeming Austrian quality of charm. More to the point, the heir to the throne was also still, as the century ended, lacking a wife. The only possible candidates were presumed to be Catholic princesses and, as he wrote to a woman friend at the time (with characteristic vehemence), these were all 'chicks' ('*Piperl*') of seventeen and eighteen, one uglier than the other!

In fact, by the time he wrote those lines, the Archduke had already found the woman with whom he was determined to share his life. She was a mature twenty-seven by the time he first fell in love with her and, though no classical beauty, she was a strikingly handsome and wholesome woman, with a serenity well calculated to offset his explosive temperament. The only problem with this paragon was that Sophie Chotek was a 'mere' countess. The Choteks of Chotkova and Wognin had been Bohemian barons since 1556; Counts of Bohemia since 1723, and Counts of the Empire since 1745. Yet even this illustrious Czech ancestry left them outside that small, august circle of families deemed worthy of marriage to a Habsburg, and to be outside the circle was to be beyond the pale.* The matter was not helped by the fact that, throughout the secret courtship, Sophie had been a lady-in-waiting to the Archduchess Isabella, an immensely built and immensely ambitious woman who wanted the heir-apparent for her son-in-law.**

The scandal finally erupted in midsummer of 1899, by which time Sophie was thirty-one and her royal suitor thirty-five. The Emperor did

---

* The original list, published on 7 October 1825, was headed by fourteen 'princely houses domiciled in the Monarchy'.

** Born a Princess of Cröy, Isabella had married, in 1878, the richest of all the Habsburgs, Archduke Frederick, by whom she produced six daughters in a row. It was the eldest of these, Maria Christina, a teenage 'chick', that she hoped to turn into a future empress.

not need the fulminations at court of the Archduchess Isabella and her circle to know where his duty to the dynasty lay. Other archdukes had disgraced the family by marrying 'beneath them', and more shocks were to come. Yet Francis Ferdinand was no ordinary case; he could, at any time, succeed his aged uncle as Emperor of Austria-Hungary; an empress *née* Chotek was inconceivable at the Hofburg. For months, uncle and nephew, Emperor and heir-apparent, were locked in rigid combat like those stags in the rutting season which they both stalked with such passion. The Archduke began by demanding everything: the bride and the throne. This was clearly too much. Within a maelstrom of intrigue, courtiers, ministers and constitutional experts worked well into the new century to produce the inescapable compromise.

This was formalised at noon on Thursday 28 June 1900 in the secret council chamber of the Hofburg, the same room at the heart of Habsburg history where, fifty-two years before, the young Francis Joseph had read out his own speech from the throne. He now stepped on the dais again, flanked by all fifteen adult archdukes of the family, to read out the terms of this unique dynastic bargain. Consent was given to the marriage but, in view of the bride's 'noble but unequal birth', the union could only be morganatic. Neither she nor (more importantly) her children could be accorded any of the royal rights of a marriage between equals. Francis Ferdinand then signed the declaration of renunciation, together with its accompanying deeds in German and Hungarian, affixed his personal seal and, within thirty minutes, the council chamber was empty again.

Three days later, the 'unequal' couple were married, well away from Vienna, at the Habsburg castle of Reichstadt in northern Bohemia. The Emperor did not attend, neither did any one of those fifteen uncles, brothers and cousins of the bridegroom who had witnessed his oath in the Hofburg. Francis Ferdinand was the only archduke at his wedding. Some consolation was provided by a telegram, sent on the Emperor's authority, which raised Countess Sophie to the hereditary title of Princess Hohenberg (the name recalled a south German possession of the Habsburgs in medieval times). For the bride to be brought this close to the golden circle of the dynasty, yet still denied admission, launched a battle of protocol between nephew and uncle which was to last until the beaming newly-weds of Reichstadt met their death side by side at Sarajevo.

This family conflict soon merged into a battle for political influence between Emperor and heir-apparent; how could it be otherwise, in a capital where the reigning house was itself synonymous with power? The glove was thrown down by the Archduke less than a year after his controversial marriage. The dispute was over nothing less than the issue of 'Germandom', which lay at the heart of the Austrian dilemma. As we have seen, Schönerer had brought religion into his campaign for the absorption of the Dual Monarchy into the German empire: it was the triumph of Protestantism over Catholicism he championed, as well as the final victory of Berlin over Vienna. Hence the '*Los-von-Rom*', or 'Away from Rome' movement which he preached alongside his anti-Slav and anti-Habsburg campaigns. In his first entry on to the political arena, the Archduke took Schönerer on face-to-face. On 8 April 1901, without consulting the Emperor, he announced that he had agreed to become patron of the League of Catholic Schools. This, in itself, was a declaration of war on anyone who sought to weaken the dynasty by challenging its apostolic title. The rebuttal was spelt out in his speech of acceptance. 'Away from Rome', the heir-apparent declared, was the same thing as 'away from Austria', and he would fight both trends 'in word and deed'.

The speech caused an outcry in both halves of the Monarchy. In Cisleithania, many liberals joined the rabid pan-Germans in protest. In Hungary, which had a large Protestant flock, the reaction was even stronger. Partly to try to smooth these ruffled Magyar feathers, and partly to give vent to his own irritation at not having been consulted by his nephew in the matter, the Emperor sent him a written rebuke. Such 'demonstrative behaviour', he told the Archduke, had been 'precipitate to a high degree'. The reprimand was underlined by a formal decree forbidding any member of the imperial house to accept the patronage of any type of league or corporation without the previous consent of the sovereign.

Thus we see another heir to the throne emerging as an Austrian 'believer' – and this time one in full possession of his faculties, and with a serenely happy family life to underpin his political energies. Facing him was the same august figure consigned to immobility both by his character and his policies: Francis Joseph, in his own words Emperor of Austria 'but also a German prince'; Francis Joseph, King of Hungary and creator of the Dual Monarchy whose very structure blocked further reform.

The two heirs tried to chip away at this imperial monolith in different

ways and from different angles, if only because their own approach to
the Monarchy's problems contrasted so sharply. Francis Ferdinand, who
came to the succession after the Bismarckian era had closed, did not
have the same fear of Germany as Rudolph, and certainly did not share
in that neurotic anti-William complex which had ended by helping to
push his cousin to suicide. Indeed, Francis Ferdinand eventually stood
on close personal terms with the German Emperor, largely because
William was shrewd enough to pay court to Sophie, treating her, whenever they met, as a fully royal consort. The Archduke's attack on the
'Away from Rome' movement was directed at the treachery of his own
countrymen, and not at any attempt of Berlin to suborn them. Moreover, unlike Rudolph, who was an out-and-out liberal in ideology,
Francis Ferdinand, like William II, was an arch-conservative.

When it came to Hungary, however, and that second great identity
problem for the Austrians, the neurosis went the other way round.
Rudolph, like his mother, was totally at ease with the Hungarians,
whose rackety, feckless way of life appealed to the sensual vagabond in
him. Francis Ferdinand, on the other hand, both hated and despised
them as a people. He was barely polite to them in public, and fulminated
against them in private ('moustachioed gypsies' was one of his more
printable descriptions of the Magyars). This was partly a personal aver-
sion, but also largely a political one. Dualism, which Rudolph came
very late in the day to question, and then only with reluctance, was
something Francis Ferdinand identified from the start as the root of the
Monarchy's constitutional problems. Moreover, it was a root which,
once the throne was his, he was determined to pull up, by force if
necessary. Quite how this was to be achieved without toppling the entire
spider-rooted Habsburg tree was never made clear; his death anyway
spared him the challenge. But we know that one early favourite notion
of his had been to remove the Croats from the control of Budapest and
lump them, together with the Bosnians, into a third South Slav kingdom, with Dalmatia and Trieste tacked on. Yet eventually he seemed
to have abandoned this so-called 'Trialist Solution' (not least because
the Croats were developing chauvinistic ideas of their own), and was
always casting around for other magic formulae.

One that seriously took his eye had been dreamt up by a Roumanian
professor, Aurel Popovici, who proposed taking the entire racial jigsaw
of Austria-Hungary apart and reassembling it in sixteen new units, to
be based as closely as possible on race. One look at the rearranged

pattern should have convinced the Archduke that, like so many armchair solutions put forward before and since, Popovici's blueprint could never have left the drawing board. He had done as good a job as possible in tidying the jumble up along ethnic lines, which could be done by simply drawing new dotted lines around racial patterns on the map.* The problem was reconciling the revision with past history and current chauvinistic politics, which came together most powerfully in the case of the Magyars. The Monarchy had too much of both crammed into it – and too little space to play with – to accommodate Popovici's ideas. This was why American liberals, who were soon to enter the European stage, were quite incapable of understanding the Austro-Hungarian dilemma. Their country had hardly any history to contend with, and almost limitless space at its disposal.

By proposing that both Transylvania and Croatia (both of them 'lands of St Stephen') should be prised away from Magyar control, Popovici clearly struck his loudest chord with Francis Ferdinand. 'Cutting the Hungarians down to size' – which was the Archduke's emphatically vague objective – may have been too formidable a task if it meant carving up their territories. But there was one practical issue on which the Archduke could stand and fight them, and that was on the crucial military field. The use of the German language, that familiar touchstone of privilege and status, was, once again, the problem here. As a young colonel sent by the Emperor in April 1890 to command the 9th Regiment of Hungarian Hussars at Ödenburg, Francis Ferdinand had been enraged by his officers' refusal to speak anything but Hungarian. This was in flagrant breach of a key clause in the Dual Monarchy's regulations, which laid it down that German was to be the language of command and service throughout the regular armed forces of the empire, including its Hungarian units.** The Archduke complained bitterly to Vienna that, even in front of him, the officers would only speak Hungarian: 'In short, not a word of that German language so detested by the Hussars.'

* His new units were: German-Austria; German-Bohemia; German-Moravia and German-Silesia ('German' meaning in all cases, of course, German-speaking). Then came Czech-Bohemia; Czech-Moravia; Magyar-Hungary (by itself!); Transylvania; Croatia-Slavonia; Polish West Galicia; Ruthenian East Galicia; Slovakia; Krain; the Vojvodina; Trente; the Szeklerland; Trieste; and Dalmatia with Bosnia-Herzegovina.
** As a sop to Hungarian chauvinism, second-line forces (known in Austria as the *Landwehr* and in Hungary as the *Honvédség*) were created in which the indigenous language of command could be used.

It was an educational experience for Francis Ferdinand. To the end of his life and military career (and he was to finish up as Inspector-General of all the Monarchy's armed forces) he fought the Hungarians' persistent attempts to have their oath of loyalty taken to the Hungarian constitution, and Magyar as the language of command in the place of German, in their own units within the imperial army. He well knew that what was at stake was nothing less than the cohesion, and even the existence, of the Monarchy itself.* The message to Marshal Radetzky on the Italian battlefield half a century before, 'In your camp stands Austria,' held good more than ever in an age of increasing nationalism. The imperial army was the cement-mixer, as well as the actual cement, for the multi-racial Monarchy. It still worked in peacetime, and before long was to work in battle: not many recruits emerged from their two years' compulsory service without feeling that they were something more than just a Pole, a Slovene, a Roumanian or a Croat. On this, whatever else they differed about, all in Cisleithania agreed: the liberals as well as the pan-Germans; Jews as well as non-Jews; Catholics and Protestants; Rudolph and Francis Ferdinand as well as the Emperor. Even in practical terms – let alone ideological ones – if this army had to stay united, it had to operate in one language, and that had to be the language of the dynasty.

A ruling house divided at the summit by the rivalry between Schönbrunn and Belvedere; a Dual Monarchy split by squabbles between its twin capitals over military command; a multi-national empire seemingly incapable of adapting to a nationalist age; an autocracy resisting the pressures for democratic reform – all this would seem to paint a picture of complete stagnation. But nothing on the Austrian scene is ever as straightforward as that. Vienna at the turn of the century was no exception, above all on the cultural scene. If it was a time of dying, this *fin de siècle* was also an age of rebirth, a sunburst of new art forms and new intellectual challenges which lit up the whole of the Western world.

Sigmund Freud, in his major work *The Interpretation of Dreams*, published in 1899, developed a new theory of human behaviour and a new treatment – psychoanalysis – of mental problems, both of which went far outside the field of medicine in their impact on the century to come. Hard on his heels came Ludwig Wittgenstein, another of Vienna's

---

* In Vienna, the threat was taken seriously enough for 'Plan U' (for '*Ungarn*') to be drawn up by the General Staff. This provided for the occupation of Budapest by Austrian regiments marching in from the south and west.

scintillating band of Jewish intellectuals; his attempts to redefine the relationship between language and philosophy also reshaped the thinking of anyone capable of understanding them. These were men who deliberately broke new ground, as though the Habsburg Monarchy were an intellectual graveyard from which they were determined to escape. This search for new forms and new horizons comes out just as strongly among the artistic pioneers of the age.

Thus, in music we have Arnold Schönberg (also Jewish), who at the turn of the century introduced a new concept of composition to a sceptical Vienna: the atonal chromatic scale to replace the traditional harmony based on keys which had been handed down by all the great composers.* In architecture, men like Adolf Loos were leading a parallel onslaught on the past. For Loos, the highly decorative style of nineteenth-century Viennese buildings and furniture was little better than refined barbarism. Indeed, he went further and proscribed any decoration for decoration's sake. Design should instead be functional, and that meant simple, with no external embellishment. Like Schönberg and Freud, Loos had injected a stream of fresh thinking into the Western mind.

In painting, the arbiter of that decorative style Loos so abhorred was Professor Hans Makart, who presided over Vienna's Imperial Academy. In 1897 there came the inevitable rebellion from within this cathedral of tradition: the artist Gustav Klimt led a band of nineteen other students to walk out and form their own modernistic movement, the 'Secession'.** Klimt certainly did not share the horror of decoration and worship of the plain line which were the hallmarks of Adolf Loos. On the contrary, some of his greatest paintings were iridescent with gold and silver ornamentation. Yet there was a certain symbiosis about the building constructed just off the Ringstrasse to house the works of the Secessionist artists. Despite its famous 'golden cabbage' cupola, the basic lines are severely rectangular, not arched, reflecting the reformist teaching of Otto Wagner, the architect who had deserted the Imperial Academy to join Klimt. Moreover, the money for the building was provided by the Wittgenstein family, who were as rich as they were gifted.

---

* Some, like Wagner, had given hints of an earlier breakaway, while Schönberg's work was to be continued by his two most famous pupils, Alban Berg and Anton Webern.
** Like Biedermeier, this so-called 'Viennese' art form came to Austria from the north. Secessionist movements had been founded in 1892 in Munich, in 1893 in Dresden and in 1896 in Karlsruhe.

In literature, the most remarkable of many great names of *fin de siècle* Vienna was Karl Kraus, again a Jew and again a seeker for a new purity, in his case a new honesty and precision of language.* It was hardly surprising that Kraus should have found his niche – and lasting fame – as a satirist, for the targets were spread all around him. His fortnightly periodical *Die Fackel* ('The Torch'), which he started writing for in 1888, and composed single-handed from 1911 onwards, lambasted everything from corruption and hypocrisy to the superficiality and sensuality which he saw around him in the Vienna of his day. Franz Lehar, whose operettas, most famously *Die Lustige Witwe* ('The Merry Widow'), put a sugary sentimental gloss over all these delinquencies, was a special victim of Krausian venom. On the other hand, though an anti-feminist, Kraus stoutly defended the thousands of prostitutes in the capital; for him, they were the ultimate victims of the prevailing decadence.

Like Musil, Kraus produced one monumental masterpiece on the end of the Habsburg era. *Die Letzten Tagen der Menschheit* ('The Last Days of Mankind') is a so-called play which is, in fact, virtually unperformable (its list of characters alone covers no fewer than thirteen pages); for all this, it remains the greatest satire ever written on the First World War – or indeed on any other war. It displays historical perception along with a sardonic perception of human frailty. For all his scorn about the dynasty, Francis Ferdinand is grudgingly recognised as the one man who, by his belief in the crown, might have saved it; German militarism is pilloried as the force which eventually dragged Austria down. A certain ambivalence runs through the seven hundred pages, expressed in frequent conversations between 'The Grumbler' and 'The Optimist'. Even for the unyielding Kraus there were, at least in retrospect, always two ways of looking at things.

So, what *was* the real temper of Vienna as this 'City of Lights' entered on its last years as an imperial capital? The answer – as so often in its past – seems to have been a mood of foreboding held at arm's length

---

* An even greater literary figure was Robert Musil, the inventor of the 'Kakania' label for the Habsburg Monarchy. The word in German carries the sub-meaning of 'Excrementia', but its direct reference is to the assortment of *'Kaiserlich und Königlich'* titles given to the different imperial and royal, as well as pure Austrian and pure Hungarian, aspects of the Dual Monarchy. However, Musil, though twenty at the end of the century, belongs as a writer to the post-imperial age. His masterpiece, *Der Mann ohne Eigenschaften* ('The Man Without Qualities'), a massive novel about the declining years of the empire, was written in the 1930s.

by frivolity, of self-doubt deadened by self-indulgence. And the contemporary writer who best expressed all this is one who stands well below the giants of the period though a considerable figure in his own right, Arthur Schnitzler. Here is yet another Viennese Jew whose plays centre on what, in his eyes, were the two characteristic evils of the time: anti-Semitism and sexuality. Schnitzler was unique as an Austrian writer in that he came from a medical family and had himself qualified as a doctor. When he turned from medicine to drama he brought to his work a clinical approach: his business was no longer to heal but simply to analyse. Thus, he found Austrian anti-Semitism revealing because it reflected the incurable malaise of a whole people. Equally incurable was the unbridled sexuality of the day, which reflected the malaise of the individual. And, for him, both excesses represented a crisis of identity. *Professor Bernhardi* is the most powerful of his plays on the Jewish problem. *Reigen*, or *La Ronde*, won international fame as the classic portrayal of loveless sex permeating a whole society: its ten characters, who covered Vienna's social stratum, from aristocrat down to street-walker, all link up with each other, like some daisychain of desire, in their meaningless search for self-gratification.

Like Kraus and Musil (though in less explicit fashion), Schnitzler placed the dynasty at the centre of all this malaise. Yet the world of 'Kakania' found its literary champions at the turn of the century, most notably in the young poet Hugo von Hofmannstal. For him, the cure for the social malaise was not to deride the dynasty but to free it from Teutonism, and reburnish all its old Austrian values. This he was to do most notably in his libretto for *Der Rosenkavalier*, the loveliest of all the operas of Richard Strauss,* which is a glowing panegyric to the old order.

Indeed, whether attacked or defended (and nobody ever dreamt of abolishing it), the dynasty in general and Francis Joseph in particular were the rocks around which all this froth and ferment simply swirled. By now in his seventies, the Emperor had ruled for longer than most of his fifty million subjects had lived. None of them – not even the restless Czechs and Magyars – could imagine a world without him, or even a morning which would not begin without him rising from his iron army bed at 4 a.m. and beginning that daily routine – set like

---

* The German composer and conductor and, of course, unrelated to the Vienna waltz family.

tramlines over the decades – of giving his audiences and signing his mound of papers. Not everyone who crossed themselves at the mere thought of their Emperor's passing felt affection, as opposed to awe, towards him. Many were not even loyalists at heart, as opposed to being monarchists out of habit and careerism. But they all felt in their bones that, whatever doubts they had about the world of Francis Joseph, whatever came after him would be far worse – a premonition that most of the twentieth century was to fulfil along the Danube's banks. Thus the Emperor became both the talisman and the metronome of his empire.

And, indeed, for the first years of the new century, that empire did not look such a bad place to live in after all. To begin with, this Indian summer of the Monarchy saw an upsurge of economic vitality which almost matched what was happening in the cultural field. The over-dependence on agriculture, and the overpopulation of the countryside which went with it, was giving way, especially in the Austrian half of the empire, to a far better balance between investment and labour. The output from mines and new factories almost doubled in the first decade of the century. As for agriculture, despite the drift to the towns, production figures for all the main crops had risen sharply, thanks to improved farming methods and the re-use of fallow land.

All sectors had benefited from the new prosperity, with the average increase in income exceeding any rise in the cost of living. Even the state coffers, normally down to their last crown, had filled up. In 1907 the Austrian budget recorded the greatest surplus in its history though, perversely, a bad harvest that year had forced the government to import food. No aspect of this expansion matched the titanic economic upsurge going on in neighbouring Germany, to which tens of thousands of Austrian workers had emigrated. Yet, by Austrian standards, overall domestic prosperity was greater than anything that could be re-membered. The picture sometimes painted of the Dual Monarchy limping along on crutches towards its inevitable doom is a totally misleading one.

There was even some belated rejuvenation on the constitutional front – albeit on the basis of pragmatic calculation rather than idealism. In 1905 the famous 'Moravian Compromise' was concluded, which resolved the deadly quarrel over language, at least in this segment of the Slav lands. The province was divided up into districts, in each of which Czech or German was to be used as the official language, depending on the ethnic majority in the region. Moreover, henceforth every voter to the Provincial Assembly could cast his vote personally as a member of his race wherever he lived. It was unrealistic to hail this as a model solution for the Monarchy as a whole, where reform was blocked even more by conflicting historical claims than by the racial tangle. Unlike the Bohemians, the Moravians had no crown of St Wenceslas to revere. Strictly speaking they had no homeland, and this made them naturally passive subjects for such a laboratory experiment. Nonetheless, it had been proven, at least in one corner of the empire, that cat and dog, Slav and German, could be made to lie down peaceably together.

At the same time, even more startling reforms appeared to be launched in the empire as a whole. On 3 November 1905, the Emperor suddenly announced to his ministers that he had decided to introduce 'general suffrage' in both halves of the Monarchy. The issue had been debated for years in both Vienna and Budapest; what drove Francis Joseph into action now was the pledge just made by his fellow-autocrat Tsar Nicholas to convoke a Duma, or representative parliament, in Russia. It was not until May 1907 – after long arguments over new constituencies and national mandates – that Vienna's new Parliament finally convened. Of course it did not represent democratic rule in any accepted sense of the words. The Emperor was still supreme. He and his ministers could still pass any measure they chose, whatever the deputies thought or said, through the notorious Paragraph Fourteen of the old constitution which sanctioned any 'emergency measure' deemed necessary by the crown. For all that, Austria now had a parliamentary body in which the citizenry as a whole were represented – either through a complex of small racial blocs or through the two major political parties, Catholic Christian Socials and Social Democrats, each of whom now took on a stronger profile. At least the Austrian half of the Monarchy had been dragged by one foot into the twentieth century.* That this had been done by imperial decree, in order to fight liberalism with populism (and thus protect the dynasty), is another matter.

Finally, the dynasty itself, in the person of the old Emperor, enjoyed an apotheosis of its own during these sunset years. 1908 saw the sixtieth anniversary of Francis Joseph's accession, celebrated in a frenzy of

* Not surprisingly, after much debate the Hungarian half failed to follow suit. Its magnates clung to what they imagined was the shelter of the nineteenth century which, in political and social terms, resembled the eighteenth.

monarchist fervour, which was the nearest the Austrians could get to the glow of patriotism. Fireworks and mountaintop bonfires blazed throughout the land. Every mayor produced his loyal address, every barrack square its special parade. In Vienna, on 21 May, more than 80,000 schoolchildren marched through the courtyard of Schönbrunn Palace, and the old monarch was duly moved by the sight. But what may well have brought him even deeper satisfaction was a ceremony which had unfolded inside that palace a few days before. On 8 May, all the kings and princes still ruling or residing in Germany came to Schönbrunn to pay collective homage to the most illustrious of them all. Heading the group was William II. It was as though they were acknowledging that, despite the transfer of economic, political and military supremacy from Vienna to Berlin, the German world still had only one real emperor.

The moment seemed to set the Habsburg dynasty on new foundations. Yet, only five months later, that same Emperor lit the slow fuse which was to blow Europe apart, destroying his own house, and those of the Hohenzollerns and Romanovs, in the explosion.

The victory that launched a dynasty. On 26 August 1278, Count Rudolph Habsburg destroys King Ottokar of Bohemia, his rival for the crown of the Holy Roman Empire, at the battle of the Marchfeld near Vienna.

The siege of Vienna, 1683. The Austrian relief forces, headed by King Sobieski of Poland, rout the 200,000-strong Turkish army camped at the gates of the beleaguered capital.

EUGENE-FRANÇOIS. PRINCE
DE SAVOYE.
Generalissime des Armées de l'Empereur
N: L: 18. Octobre 1663.

Prince Eugen of Savoy (1663–1736), the
French-born servant of the Habsburgs whose
military and political deeds first made Austria
into a European power.

Maria Theresa (1717–1780), the only woman to
reign over the Habsburg empire. She had to battle
abroad, with mixed fortunes, over her accession.
At home, she ruled with motherly absolutism.

The rulers of the rival German dynasties, the Hohenzollern King Frederick II of Prussia and the
Emperor Joseph II of Austria (Maria Theresa's son and successor), in a friendly-looking promenade
at Mährisch-Neustadt in 1770. Both were regarded as enlightened despots, Joseph the more
enlightened of the pair.

Napoleon, scourge of the old European order, crowned himself Emperor of the new French empire on 2 December 1804.

BELOW LEFT:
Wolfgang Amadeus Mozart (1756–1791). 'Too many notes, Herr Mozart' (Joseph II). 'Not one more than is needed, Your Majesty.'

BELOW RIGHT:
Franz Schubert (1797–1828) the genius who characterized the Viennese spirit: 'One eye laughing, one eye weeping.'

Prince Clement Metternich (1773–1859), for nearly forty years Foreign Minister of the Monarchy. 'At times I ruled over Europe, but never over Austria.'

Prince Felix Schwarzenberg (1800–1852). A proud faith in Austria, bad in himself.

Königgrätz, 3 July 1866. The battle at which the disciplined Prussians (left) defeated the poorly-led and badly-equipped Austrians and sealed the supremacy of the Hohenzollerns over the Habsburgs in the German world.

ABOVE: Prince Otto Bismarck (1815–1898), Germany's 'Iron Chancellor' from 1871 to 1890 and the greatest European statesman of his time. Unfortunately for the Habsburgs, he was also the greatest antagonist of the Monarchy.

RIGHT: Archduke Rudolph and Princess Stephanie of Belgium, 1881. A disastrous marriage of dynastic convenience: the plain, shy bride could never contain the sensual excesses of her husband.

II : Fin de Siècle Vienna

LEFT: Karl Lueger (1844–1910),
right-wing Christian-Socialist leader and
Vienna's most famous Mayor. Champion
of the 'little man' and of Habsburg
Austria.

BELOW: Georg von Schönerer
(1842–1921), the anti-Austria Austrian
who argued that the Monarchy should be
absorbed into Germany. Anti-Semitism
was his only link with Lueger.

ABOVE: Viktor Adler (1852–1918), founder of the Austrian Social-Democratic Party. He died on the day the Austrian Republic was founded.

LEFT: Otto Bauer (1882–1939), the fiery ideologue of the Austrian Socialists, but a revolutionary in words only.

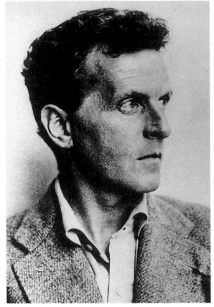

Four Austrians who broke the mould of Western culture (clockwise from top left)

Psychoanalysis
Sigmund Freud (1856–1939) with his daughter Anna. The meaning of dreams.

Philosophy
Ludwig Wittgenstein (1889–1951). The meaning of language.

Music
Arnold Schönberg (1874–1951). The high priest of atonality.

Architecture
Adolf Loos (1870–1933). Austerity and functionalism.

Schönbrunn Palace, 8 May 1908. In the sixtieth anniversary year of his accession, all the German rulers, headed by Emperor William II, pay homage to Francis Joseph – the most illustrious, though no longer the most powerful, of them all.

The diligent metronome of the empire: Francis Joseph at his plain work-desk, 1913.

The ill-fated young Archduke Charles, who succeeded his great-uncle Francis Joseph on 21 November 1916 to become the last of the Habsburg emperors, at his wedding to Princess Zita of Bourbon-Parma on 21 October 1911.

BELOW LEFT:
Count Leopold Berchtold (1863–1942), Austrian Foreign Minister in the crisis of 1914, and largely responsible for the catastrophe which followed.

BELOW RIGHT:
Count Stefan Tisza (1861–1918), Hungarian Prime Minister and the only voice in the Monarchy to warn of the dangers of war.

28 June 1914. Archduke Francis Ferdinand and his wife Sophie leave the train at Sarajevo. They had barely two hours to live.

ABOVE: Prince Sixtus of Bourbon-Parma (1886–1934), brother of the Empress Zita and indefatigable searcher for peace – on France's terms.

RIGHT: Count Ottokar Czernin (1872–1932), Austria's gifted but unstable Foreign Minister 1916–1918. Resigned in the public scandal he had engineered over the Sixtus secret peace affair.

The toll of war: Austro-Hungarian troops after the bloody battle for the key Galician fortress of Przemyśl, 3 June 1915.

14 August 1918. The Emperor Charles arrives for his last meeting with Emperor William II, held at the Prussian Army Headquarters in Spa, Belgium.

II

Balkan Storm Signals

ON 5 OCTOBER 1908, in the autumn of his jubilee year, the Emperor Francis Joseph announced that he had 'extended our sovereign rights to Bosnia and Herzegovina, which would henceforth fall under the hereditary provisions of the House of Habsburg'. The two South Slav provinces bordered on the expansionist kingdom of Serbia, which coveted them for itself. Always an unruly and troublesome neighbour, Serbia was turned by that unilateral declaration into the Monarchy's most implacable enemy, all its energies dedicated to vengeance. The scene was thus set for that 'final battle between Germandom and Slavdom' which William II had predicted with such relish. The Austrians had staged the prelude to world war.

There were pretexts, even pressing reasons, for their action. Tension had been mounting throughout the year between Vienna and the crumbling Ottoman empire (to whom the provinces still technically belonged, as part of 'Turkey in Europe'), and a fresh crisis arose in July after the reformist 'Young Turks' took control in Constantinople. On the twenty-fifth of that month, they forced the now powerless Sultan Abdul Hamid to convene a parliament in his capital to which all the territories of his empire, including Bosnia-Herzegovina, were required to send delegates.

For almost exactly forty years, the two provinces had been 'occupied and administered' by Austria, as part of the general agreement reached at the Congress of Berlin in 1878 to settle the Russo–Turkish conflict.* The idea of annexation had been mooted by the Austrians at St Petersburg as early as 1897, and the European powers tacitly accepted that occupation would amount one day to an agreed formula of

* Touched off, ironically, by a revolt against Turkish misrule in Bosnia-Herzegovina.

possession. For Vienna, that day had now arrived. So, by happy chance, had the solution. On the very eve of the Turkish revolution, the Austrian Foreign Minister, Baron Alois Aehrenthal, had received a letter from his Russian counterpart, Alexander Izvolski, offering a far-reaching bargain: Russia would support an Austrian annexation of the disputed provinces if Vienna, in return, would back Russian claims for increased access to the Black Sea Straits.

It was no coincidence that the project should be so ambitious, and so personal. Both men were seeking political triumphs to offset their social complexes. Aehrenthal's case had about it a whiff of Viennese anti-Semitism. He was reputed to be the grandson of one Lexa, a rich Jewish grain merchant of Prague, ennobled under an aptly chosen title (Aehrenthal means 'corn valley'). Though his grandmother, his mother and his own wife all came from the higher aristocracies of the Monarchy,* this only made the Foreign Minister's paternal line of descent look even shabbier. In any case, in the ossified social codex of the day, the minor title of 'Freiherr von', bestowed less than a century before, scarcely counted as nobility. Aehrenthal, who looked the very picture of the languidly arrogant Austrian aristocrat, was determined to climb higher. The ladder started at his office desk.

Alexander Izvolski was even more desperate for self-advancement. He was a lowly-born Kalmuck from the Mongol tribes who had had the good fortune to be serving as the Russian Minister in Copenhagen when the immensely influential King Edward VII visited the Danish capital in 1904 to stay with his wife's family. The ugly but highly intelligent envoy impressed the British monarch, who urged his nephew Tsar Nicholas II to make better use of him. Such august patronage helped to elevate Izvolski at one bound into one of the key political posts of the continent. Once installed in 1906 as Foreign Minister at St Petersburg, he resolved to make his mark in history and, at the same time, repay the confidence of his royal master. That, he knew, could best be done by achieving the age-old Russian dream of securing a permanently open window on the Mediterranean through the Black Sea Straits.

Such were the two men – so contrasting in appearance but so similar in their motivation – who now plunged all Europe into crisis. Aehrenthal got approval for his annexation plan at a Joint Council of

* Respectively a Wilczek, a Thun and a Széchényi.

Austrian and Hungarian Ministers held on 19 August, the day after the seventy-eighth birthday of the Emperor. On 15 September, the two conspirators met in secret at Buchlau Castle in Moravia to put the final touches to their plan. The venue itself had an ominous symbolism, as though the finger of tragedy were pointing forwards.* There was fatal confusion – or deception – on the day itself. Izvolski departed on a leisurely tour of western capitals in the belief that the bargain would be implemented in due course and at a time to be coordinated in advance between the two empires. Aehrenthal launched his part of the deal only three weeks later after it had been prematurely leaked by his embassy in Paris. Vienna then added insult to injury by refusing to back Izvolski's parallel campaign over the Straits. There was indeed no honour between this pair of political plunderers.

After six months of European crisis, with Austrian troops threatening to march on Belgrade, the Monarchy emerged unscathed with its spoils and Aehrenthal was duly made a count. Russia had finally backed down from her menacing but dithering support of Serbia; Turkey was bought off with a bribe of 2.5 million Turkish pounds. Yet Vienna's victory was not merely hollow; it was poisoned. To all the European powers, the annexation appeared as an act of irresponsible folly. If the Habsburg Monarchy had a mission in their eyes, it was to keep the lid on the Balkan cauldron, not to stir the pot. Moreover, the precipitate way in which Austria had acted ran counter not only to diplomatic usage but also to dynastic decencies (in those days much the same thing). Francis Joseph's autograph letters to his fellow monarchs announcing his intentions over Bosnia-Herzegovina had been despatched only days before his unilateral proclamation. Through a muddle, the imperial round-robin message was not handed to Edward VII until the annexation had been announced.** Neither the King nor his Foreign Office ever put the same trust in Vienna again.

The reaction in Berlin was more ambivalent, despite the fact that the affair heralded a new era in the saga of Austro–German relations. The German Emperor was even more offended than the King of England

---

* Buchlau belonged to Count Leopold Berchtold, at the time Austrian ambassador to St Petersburg but soon to succeed Aehrenthal in the Monarchy's years of crisis.
** King Edward, who had paid the last of his periodic visits to Francis Joseph at Bad Ischl on 12–13 August 1908, simply could not believe reports of the impending annexation. His fellow-sovereign, he reasoned, would surely have warned him personally in advance.

about being given such short notice, and being informed in such peremptory fashion.* The indignation coupled with astonishment felt in Potsdam was understandable. However senior the House of Habsburg remained as a dynasty, the Dual Monarchy had been, since Bismarck's day, very much the junior partner politically in the forty-year-old alliance between the two empires. It was in that capacity that she had been dragged to the Algeciras Conference of 1906, there to support the German challenge to French dominance in Morocco, a challenge led by William II in person, with typical theatrical overkill. Again displaying his boundless lack of tact, the German Emperor had gone out of his way to underline Austria's subordinate status by praising her, after the Algeciras settlement, as Germany's 'brilliant second on the duelling ground'. Now, however, two years later, that second had taken the pistols from the alliance box and, without even asking, had fired them off himself.

Yet there was also a certain sense of relief in Berlin that Germany's only reliable ally, so long suspect for feeble indecision, had demonstrated such confidence and panache. Even if this was a somewhat forced display of virility for such an ancient performer, it was far preferable to impotence. So William swallowed his indignation and Germany promptly reasserted herself as the leading anti-Slav champion among the Central Powers. Indeed, it was German pressure on Russia, transmitted downwards from St Petersburg to Belgrade, which finally led Serbia, on 31 March 1909, to recognise the annexation and even to pledge 'good neighbourly relations' with Austria.

That promise, made through gritted teeth, was, of course, bogus; indeed, it was in the Slav world that the most calamitous effects of the Buchlau pact were felt. Just as Aehrenthal, the winner from that pact, had received plaudits and a nine-pointed coronet as reward, so Izvolski, the loser, was eventually demoted in 1910, albeit to the agreeable post of ambassador in Paris.** His successor at the Foreign Office, Serge Sazanov, continued Izvolski's programme of establishing long-term Russian influence in south-east Europe by organising four of its states (Serbia, Bulgaria, Greece and Montenegro) into the so-called 'Balkan

* Due to the fact that key ministers and officials were away from Berlin on holiday, the Kaiser, like Edward VII, only learnt the news as it was happening.
** From here, he worked with demonic fury to get his revenge on Austria by fomenting Franco–Russian feeling against the Central Powers. 'C'est ma guerre,' he cried, with outstretched arms, in August 1914.

League'. A miniature power bloc of assorted hotheads was thus created under Russian patronage, with blatant anti-Turkish and anti-Austrian aspirations. They were soon to explode in violence.

Inasmuch as the League had any political and spiritual centre, this was Belgrade – always dreaming of 'Greater Serbia' with its opening onto the Adriatic, and now resolved to realise that dream by propaganda, terrorism or open war. Bosnia was the prime target of these ambitions, and the annexation crisis had spawned a clutch of irredentist groups with Sarajevo firmly in their sights. The 'Narodna Odbrana' or 'National Defence' was the principal official movement, supposedly dedicated to purely 'cultural activities'. In its shadow, the 'Cerna Ruka', or 'Black Hand', was set up on 11 May 1911, a secret society more concerned with bombs and assassinations than with pamphleteering. This was no coffee-house gathering of wild-eyed students but a group of elite extremists – mainly army officers, but including senior civil servants, lawyers and academics. Beneath all the *Grand Guignol* pantomime of their rituals stood a dedication to Article One of their statutes, which called for 'the union of all Serbs'. It was linked with the government, in certain if undefinable fashion, through the person of its leader, Colonel Dragutin Dimitrievic, Head of Army Military Intelligence and a well-known hatchet man.*

Finally, as the extension of all this irredentism to within Bosnia itself came the 'Mlada Bosna' ('Young Bosnia'), an indigenous group of terrorists made up of Bosnian Serbs who, since 1908, had become subjects of the empire they were pledged to overthrow. The annexation had thus bred treason within the Monarchy as well as all-round pan-Slav pressure from without.

The heaviest price Austria had to pay was geopolitical. We have seen how the Habsburgs began their rule as dukes straddling the middle Danube's banks. By war and marriage, they had extended their dominion down that great river. But once they moved far from the Danube Basin, that dominion weakened. The disastrous struggle for the Italian possessions, the poisoned chalice of the nineteenth century, had already demonstrated that. Now, in the twentieth century, came the even more exhausting distraction, which they had themselves

---

* It was he who had organised the slaughter and bestial mutilation of King Alexander and Queen Draga in their Belgrade palace on the night of 10–11 June 1903. The murders marked the end of the Obrenović dynasty and their replacement by their old rivals, the House of Karageorgević.

contrived, of the Balkans. This ran counter to the ideological, as well as the geographical, structure of the Monarchy. The Habsburg dynasty was multi-national or it was nothing. After 1908, it got sucked more and more into the purely racial conflict of Teutons versus Slavs. It could, therefore, no longer be true even to itself, let alone to the expectations of the outside world.

The Balkan League was a seed bed of violence, and it duly produced the Balkan wars, despite Sazanov's last-minute attempts to dissuade his protégés from taking the law into their own hands. The tiny mountain kingdom of Montenegro, home of that extraordinary political brigand King Nikita,* led his partners into war against Turkey on the very day − 8 October 1912 − he received a joint warning from St Petersburg and Vienna. Sazanov had created a band of demons he could no longer control. Nor, indeed, could they control themselves. Within a fortnight, the 700,000 men of the four Balkan armies had toppled the obese Turkish giant and, swarming ahead like killer ants, had devoured almost all of Turkey-in-Europe. The Bulgarians marched right down to the forts which defended Constantinople itself; the Greeks took Salonica; the Serbs seized the upper Vardar valley and set up a common frontier with their closest ally, Montenegro.**

But it was the former Turkish province of Albania which brought the Balkan turmoil close to a European war. The two million Albanians declared their independence once the Turkish garrison had been routed and, on 28 November 1912, hoisted their ancient flag, the black double-headed eagle of Scanderberg. Serbia and her Montenegrin surrogate coveted the territory for themselves because of its precious coastline, and occupied the northern half. Austria backed Albanian independence precisely in order to bar Serbia's path to the sea. Russia supported her small Slav brother and, as a result, the Habsburg and Romanov empires began mobilising against each other. Great-power diplomacy stirred into action to prevent escalation of the Balkan squabble, and London was chosen as the venue. In December 1912, the envoys to Britain of

* Nikita had achieved a diplomatic influence in Europe out of all proportion to his puny strength by arranging brilliant matches for his ten children − seven of whom were beautiful and stately daughters. He became father-in-law to the King of Italy, two Russian grand dukes, a German princess and members of both the rival royal houses of Serbia.
** These two peoples were to stick together through thick and thin. When, at the end of the century, the multi-racial state of Yugoslavia fell apart, only Serbia and Montenegro remained as a rump.

all five continental powers – Germany, Austria, Italy, France and Russia – assembled in St James's Palace with Sir Edward Grey, the British Foreign Secretary, in the chair.

This 'Ambassadors' Conference' was the last tranquil image to be reflected in an old world mirror which was about to be shattered for ever. The members gathered informally at around four o'clock on weekday afternoons, breaking off for tea, and then ending their business in plenty of time for dinner. Grey called them 'a committee of friends'. They were, in fact, closer than that. At one meeting, the ambassadors' talk drifted from the tedious Balkan imbroglio to their own family trees. Three of them – Count Alexander Benckendorff of Russia, Count Albert Mensdorff-Pouilly of Austria and Prince Karl Max Lichnowsky of Germany – established to their amused delight that they were all cousins. Their Italian colleague, Imperiali, though unrelated, was also a count, while their chairman came from a long line of Northumbrian baronets and earls. (Paul Cambon, the famous French diplomatist, was the only one of the sextet not to have an ancient title.) Surely, the unspoken assumption must have been, men such as these, whose common backgrounds criss-crossed all political divides, could sort out any problem which troubled their European order?

They did not, in fact, achieve very much. Their official task, which was to broker a peace deal between Turkey and the triumphant Balkan League, was concluded by the Treaty of London, signed on 30 May 1913. Yet everything was nullified when the fighting erupted again exactly one month later. Bulgaria, which had done very well out of the First Balkan War, rashly started the Second by attacking Serbia on 30 June in a squabble over Macedonia. Within five weeks, the Bulgarian army was crushed by a combined onslaught from all her neighbours; Romania joined in for the first time and even Turkey re-entered the fray to regain part of Thrace. The peace that ended this conflict was concluded in August 1913 at Bucharest, a thousand miles away from Grey's 'committee of friends' in London, who simply sat and watched.

What that committee had achieved was agreement that an Albanian state of some sort should be established, though its actual boundaries were left undetermined. The process of fixing those frontiers dragged on for ten months, with the fiery King Nikita, whose troops had occupied Scutari, snapping his fingers at all six great powers assembled in St James's Palace. Their combined fleets gathered in the Adriatic, and at one point they even contemplated a joint land action, with a British infantry brigade sailing across from Malta. In the end, like the Sultan of Turkey, King Nikita was bought off. In April 1913 the London Conference offered him a 'loan' of £1,200,000 to evacuate the town, and he reluctantly complied a month later. That summer, the Ambassadors' Conference faded away, with Albania's frontiers still undecided. There were no final speeches or photographs. The six of them, having set up three boundary commissions, simply agreed there was no further point in their meeting.

The Balkan crisis was thus handed back to the chancellories of Europe to settle, and it was now that the ominous overture to the catastrophe of 1914 was fully played out. Austria's 'mission', Austria's impulsiveness, Austria's ambivalent relationship with Germany – all played their part in what became a near-miss to a European war. As we have seen, the annexation of 1908 meant that henceforth the Monarchy would have to keep one eye permanently glued on Belgrade and the challenge of 'Greater Serbia'. Now, only five years later, that challenge had suddenly become reality on the ground, not rhetoric in the air. Serbia had snatched the greatest share of the Turkish spoils. She had almost doubled her territory and increased her population by some 50 per cent to nearly 4.5 million. Together with her satellite partner Montenegro, she partly enclosed the new Habsburg provinces of Bosnia-Herzegovina. Exhausted though she was for the moment, this physical expansion brought with it for Serbia a new self-confidence as the first power in the Balkans. The Monarchy had to respond if the standing of the dynasty were to be preserved and the integrity of the two provinces – the only territories to be added to the crown during the whole of Francis Joseph's reign – was to be guaranteed. The heyday of the war party, the 'hawks' of Vienna, had come.

Foremost among them was the Chief of the General Staff, Conrad von Hötzendorf, who can be added to our list of Habsburg 'believers' though, unfortunately, he was one of those Austrians obsessed with the anti-Slav crusade of the German Emperor rather than the racial even-handedness of his own monarch. Conrad owed his appointment in 1906 to the patronage of that most august of the 'believers', Archduke Francis Ferdinand. The General shared the strange, stormy and self-willed character of the heir-apparent. He also shared the same all-consuming devotion to a woman who was technically 'out of bounds'. In Conrad's case this was a young, dark-haired beauty, nearly thirty years his junior, called Gina von Reininghaus. Though she was the wife of an ennobled Styrian brewer and the mother of his six children, the General laid siege to her with a passionate letter written every day of his life from 1907 onwards.*

Conrad, like the Archduke, was seized with fury at the muddle and lethargy crippling the Monarchy's armed forces which, in a few short years, he had managed to drag into the twentieth century. By the time of the Balkan Wars, both the telephone and the automobile had been put into general military usage, machine guns had been introduced, a small air force created and up-to-date fighting manuals issued to all ranks. It was no wonder that Conrad was being hailed as the greatest Austrian soldier since Radetzky. It was even less surprising that he should be itching to unleash this cherished modernised army of his on what he regarded as its most venomous foe, the Serbs. Already in 1908, Conrad had urged a preventive war against Serbia to settle the annexation crisis once and for all, and it was largely due to Francis Ferdinand's moderating influence that the Emperor held back from general mobilisation.**

Now, in the mayhem of the Balkan Wars, Conrad tried again. As a precaution, the Monarchy had anyway mobilised its four army corps which faced Serbia in the south and also, as an added safeguard in case Russia should make any move to help the Serbs, its three army corps stationed in the north-eastern province of Galicia. Within forty-eight hours of being reappointed as Chief of Staff on 12 December 1908,*** Conrad started bombarding both Schönbrunn and the Belvedere with memoranda urging a 'final settlement' with the Serbs while the opportunity was still there. Though the Archduke was glad to have Conrad back in the saddle, he was determined not to let him charge. His own reasoning was hard-headedly pragmatic. Any war, he argued, could only shake the already wobbly structure of the Monarchy. As for an invasion of Serbia, even if Austria got away with it unscathed, what would it bring for the crown? 'Just one more pile of thieves, murderers and

---

* He finally won his battle in 1915, when the lady steeled herself to get a divorce and married him.

** What Conrad did push through, in December of that year, was the so-called 'Brown Mobilisation' of Austrian forces in the south. This was a show of strength involving a reinforcement by twenty-nine infantry battalions and one cavalry squadron.

*** He had resigned in a huff the year before after a long squabble with Aehrenthal, and had been reinstated after pressure on the Emperor from Francis Ferdinand. The Archduke's sole motive was to get the best soldier back in charge in case the conflict escalated.

rascals, plus a few plum trees!' The heir-apparent may have had an arrogant contempt for the Serbs (as indeed he had, *inter alia*, for Italians and Magyars), but he had no desire to prise open the Pandora's Box of a Teutonic crusade against them.

Someone who, to everyone's surprise, was prepared to take that risk was the Emperor's new Foreign Minister, Count Leopold Berchtold, who had succeeded Aehrenthal, mortally stricken with leukaemia, in February 1912. The Archduke's hand had been at work also in this appointment, though it was to prove, in the end, a dreadful mistake. Berchtold's experience of major diplomacy had been his spell as ambassador to St Petersburg, which was considered a prime qualification. His only true expertise was in horse-breeding; as a statesman, he was to prove woefully deficient for the Monarchy and for Europe. It was 1913 which primed him for the calamitous blunders which lay ahead. After initially restraining the messianic fervour of Conrad, he ended up as little more than the General's political mouthpiece over the Serbian question. Even worse, before the year was out he scored a single-handed diplomatic triumph over Belgrade which fired his modest intellect with illusions of grandeur. Here we are brought back to that key factor in the Monarchy's fortunes, the relationship with Germany.

Germany had complemented her ally's drive southwards by over-arching it. Their different projects for railway construction illustrated this. Austria, as far back as 1900, planned to build a line linking Vienna with Sarajevo, which would have given some substance to Francis Joseph's proclamation eight years later that the provinces of Bosnia-Herzegovina were integral parts of the Habsburg inheritance.* Building had even begun, though the track petered out in Styria, to where it still runs today, in very leisurely fashion. Berlin's plans were far more ambitious, envisaging a German railway running all the way from Turkey to Baghdad. The strategic interests of France and England, as well as Russia, were brought into play here. Like the Austrians, they had stopped well short of the Taurus mountains. Talks between the four interested powers over the control and financing of the project continued, however, and an agreement in principle was actually arrived at on 15 June 1914 – two weeks before an event which was to tear everything up on the European agenda.

* As it was, after the annexation the two provinces remained neither one thing nor the other. Their ambivalent status was expressed by the fact that they were administered by Leon von Bilinski, the Finance Minister of the Dual Monarchy: 'Kakania' at its best!

That Germany wanted to bring the expiring Ottoman empire, and indeed the wider Moslem world, into her sphere of influence was self-evident in all this (indeed, her Kaiser had openly said as much). That she was prepared to launch a world war for this, or any other ambition is, on the other hand, far from proven. Prince Bernard von Bülow, who was Germany's Chancellor at the time of the annexation crisis, had summed up his policy thus: 'I would never abandon Austria; but I did not intend to allow her to involve us in a European war.' Though Bülow was the most silver-tongued of all German apologists, Berlin's major role in brokering a settlement in 1908 bears out his words on this occasion. Bülow had resigned, heaped with praise and honours, on 26 June 1909,* and his successor was a horse of very different colours.

Theobald von Bethmann-Hollweg, whom the Kaiser now chose for his Chancellor, was a long-standing personal friend (William II had shot his first roebuck at the Bethmann-Hollweg family estate of Hohenfinow). Though well-versed, as Minister of Interior, in domestic policy, he had absolutely no experience of foreign affairs – a deficiency which the Kaiser had airily discounted because, in his view, he himself could look after all that. So instead of an experienced, smooth, if somewhat slippery practitioner, Germany acquired a diligent, well-meaning, but nervous novice at the diplomatic game. As such, he was far more under the influence of his royal master than Bülow had ever been, as well as lacking either the personality or the strength of will to stand up, when required, to the Prussian military camp.**

All this was to play its fateful role in the years ahead. But the point to note here is that during the protracted crisis of the Balkan Wars (which could have given Germany the ideal pretext to start a wider conflagration), both Bethmann and his imperial master were content to follow the line which Bülow had drawn in 1908. Throughout the summer of 1913, Germany's pledges of general support for Austria were accompanied by very specific warnings to Vienna not to go too far against Serbia. One such personal injunction, sent by Bethmann to Berchtold on 6 July 1913, stated bluntly that any attempt to solve the Serbian problem by force of arms would mean a European war and,

* The ostensible reason was the blocking of his new Finance Bill, but after ten wearying years in office – the most exhausting aspect of which had been coping with his imperial master – Bülow was anyway quite relieved to go.

** It was the German High Command which brought about his resignation on 14 July 1917.

for that reason, Austria must 'insistently be warned against the idea of wanting to gobble up Serbia'. Berlin can be cleared of war-mongering, at least for this phase of the mounting Balkan crisis.

Despite all this, in October 1913 Austria suddenly lashed out on her own, thus repeating the pattern of 1908. The Albanian boundary commissions, which Grey's ambassadorial conference had set up before melting away, proved incapable of drawing up agreed frontiers. Fighting broke out and the Serbian army reoccupied Albanian soil. The gauntlet of 'Greater Serbia' was again thrown down, and Vienna had to decide whether or not to pick it up and, if it were picked up, how to handle it. The matter was debated at great length at two Ministerial Councils, one held on 3 October and the other ten days later. There were some uncanny parallels with those more agitated arguments over a far more serious crisis which was to unfold in Vienna nine months later. General Conrad pressed for all-out military action against the Serbs, that 'final reckoning' he had called for in 1908 and was to go on demanding. But a new and powerful voice was now heard in the council chamber to oppose him. This was that of Count Stefan Tisza, who had become Prime Minister of Hungary only four months before. He was to represent, from now on, the main if not the only force of moderation in the councils of the Dual Monarchy. The Albanian crisis, he argued, should be settled by diplomacy and not by war. The use of force would unite Europe against the Monarchy as well as depleting its coffers and shaking up its ethnic composition in dangerous fashion. This was the language of that rarest of phenomena, a minister who was also a statesman.

Berchtold dithered and wavered between the two arguments, knowing that the Emperor was dubious about the wisdom of war and that the heir-apparent was dead against it. Above all, he was unsure of Germany's attitude. So, on 14 October he contented himself with a message to Belgrade simply urging withdrawal. The mildness of this step, which did not contain even the suggestion of armed action, looked all the more extraordinary in view of the fact that the Serb army had just burnt down several Albanian villages and massacred many of the inhabitants. Then, on 15 October Berchtold asked for, and received, assurances of Germany's 'moral support' in the affair. It was enough to galvanise the ditherer into action. On the night of 17–18 October, without consulting or informing Berlin further, he despatched a note to Belgrade demanding the withdrawal of her forces from Albania within eight days, failing which Austria would be forced to take 'appropriate action'. As with a later, and more momentous, demand to Serbia, this was coyly described as a 'note with a time limit', rather than an ultimatum.

Everyone, in Europe as in Belgrade, knew what the note meant, and everyone was jolted out of the illusion that the Albanian problem would eventually dissolve itself while the outside world looked on. Russia remained militarily motionless while, on the diplomatic front, the other European powers joined forces in urging Serbia to respect the will of the London Conference. Nicholas Pašić, the Serbian Prime Minister, had no option but to give in. His troops pulled out of Albania; Berchtold had his hour of triumph; Conrad snorted in despair; all Europe breathed a sigh of relief. It was a deceptive triumph for the peacemakers, and a very short-lived one.

III

Austria's Armageddon

SPECULATION IN THE CHANCELLORIES of Europe had long been centred not on whether a general war might break out, but on when. The rival networks of military alliances,* which had spread across the continent like iron cobwebs, as good as guaranteed that once any local conflict brought in any one of the great powers, it would soon involve them all. There was even less doubt as to where the fight would begin. The Balkans, in ferment ever since the annexation crisis of 1908, had displaced colonial rivalries, and even naval rivalries, as the most dangerous field of confrontation. Despite all this, the exact scenario which started the tragedy was predicted by no one – except, half in earnest, by the principal victim.

The murder by a young Bosnian-Serb fanatic of Francis Ferdinand and his wife Sophie in Sarajevo on 28 June 1914 plunged the whole of Europe into shock. Messages of condolence poured into Vienna from palaces and presidential offices throughout the world. The message of sympathy sent by Tsar Nicholas II was as warm as any: despite the political rivalry between Habsburgs and Romanovs, assassination was a personal threat which menaced both dynasties in common. Even the King of England, who was far remoter from the scene than the Tsar, responded by immediately ordering a week's full court mourning and, far more unusually, by calling the next day at the Austrian Embassy to offer his condolences to Count Mensdorff, a distant relative, in person.**

---

* The oldest, the Dual Alliance of 1879 between Germany and Austria-Hungary, had become a Triple Alliance by the accession of Italy (a very dubious partner) in 1882. Against this central military bloc, the flanking powers – France, Russia and England – had formed up in the so-called Triple Entente which, as the name implies, fell short of all-out commitment.
** King George and Queen Mary had a private reason for sorrow over the Archduke's death. Only seven months before, in November 1913, Francis Ferdinand had notched

As we have seen, little love had been lost between the Emperor and his difficult nephew whom, without meaning it, he had in fact sent to his doom. On 17 August 1913 the Archduke had been appointed by his uncle Inspector-General of the Monarchy's armed forces – the most important post he was to hold. One of his first decisions, taken together with General Conrad, was to hold the main summer manoeuvres of the following year in Bosnia. He was thus obliged, morally and officially, to attend them. Whatever prompted his uncanny premonitions that he would never return from the visit alive we shall never know. But they were so strong that on the eve of his departure he had instructed his flabbergasted nephew, Archduke Charles, who was next in line, where to find his political testament after his death. The die was only cast over the Sarajevo journey on 4 June 1914, when Francis Ferdinand had his last audience with the Emperor. The old monarch not only did nothing to dissuade the Archduke from going; he made his departure almost certain by agreeing that Duchess Sophie could accompany him, more or less as an equal.* That was an irresistible lure for the husband who had been battling like a tiger in the hostile protocol jungle of Vienna to have his morganatic wife accepted in court society.

Now, after a series of flukes, blunders and muddles that would take up several pages to recount, both were dead, killed at point-blank range by the revolver of the nineteen-year-old Bosnian revolutionary Gavrilo Princip. The process by which those two pistol shots went on to kill eight million more, destroying three continental empires and the old European order in the process, does not concern us here, even in general outline. What needs to be singled out are the three aspects relevant to our theme: what it reveals of the Austrian character, of the Habsburg dilemma and, above all, of Austria's relationship with Germany. Always a determinant factor, this now became dominant. It was also, for that matter, dominant in the catastrophe itself.

The outrage of Sarajevo introduced what was, even by turbulent Balkan standards, an unprecedented atmosphere of crisis. It was, after all, not just the Inspector-General of the Dual Monarchy but the heir to the throne itself who had been assassinated. Moreover, his murderer

---

up a great protocol triumph by being invited to Windsor Castle with Sophie for a pheasant shoot. (Renowned sportsman though he was, he found England's equally renowned high pheasants hard to cope with at first.)

* She was still obliged, however, to travel separately and by a different route, via Budapest.

had killed in the name of Greater Serbia, the Slav vision which, since 1908, had become the gravest of all the threats to the Monarchy's existence. The complicity of Belgrade was suspected from the start, and though guilt could never be placed directly at the door of Pašić and his government, it was soon established that it lay at the threshold. It was the 'Black Hand' which had issued Princip and his fellow-conspirators with their bombs and pistols, and trained them in their use. Retribution of some sort had to be exacted from Serbia; but when should the Monarchy strike, and how far should it go?

As with all things Austrian, there was ambivalence. In this, the Emperor and his advisers reflected a general conflict of moods. On the one hand, there was determination that an insult should be avenged. More than that: the feeling was widespread that if Vienna failed to respond energetically, the Dual Monarchy could never hold its head up again. Abroad, and above all in Berlin, it would be seen as incapable of discharging its role as an effective multi-national power. At home, the ethnic ambitions and rivalries which made that role so hard to sustain would only sharpen if it became clear that the Monarchy was afraid to protect its southern provinces by standing up to the Serbs. On the other hand, the very thought of war made even resolute souls uneasy and scared the wits out of the nervous. Implicit in all those *fin de siècle* moods described above – the resignation, the cynicism, and the frantic plunge into the pleasures of the moment – was the presentiment that the Monarchy's days were numbered. In that case, the final count would be on some as yet unknown battlefield. As the Sarajevo crisis mounted, the old Emperor let slip a remark which summed all this up: 'If the Monarchy must die,' he is quoted as saying, 'then it must at least die with honour.'

It is worth pointing out straight away that Francis Joseph did precious little himself to prevent that death. He had, of course, returned to his capital from Bad Ischl to attend the funeral of the murdered couple (a ceremony at which court protocol had its final posthumous dig at the morganatic wife), but he was the only crowned head who stood at the bier. It was initially taken for granted that the usual gathering of royal mourners would attend. This meant, above all, the German Emperor, whose imminent arrival had even been announced. He was, after all, a personal friend of the dead man, whose last act on the political stage had been to receive William II at Konopischt on 12–13 June for a thorough but very pacific review of the Balkan scene. A royal reunion would have brought not only all the other German princes to Vienna, but also high representatives of the Triple Entente powers, perhaps even including Tsar Nicholas, who had sent his own message of condolence to Francis Joseph. Such a gathering could only have produced a mood of polite stock-taking between the rival alliances. Slanging-matches do not go with funerals.

Sadly, the opportunity was missed, with security problems being given as the reason. This was at best a pretext. After Tsar Alexander II had been blown to pieces by a bomb in the streets of his own capital, fear of assassination had not stopped England's Prince of Wales from joining other foreign royal mourners at the funeral. Vienna in 1914 was a far safer place than St Petersburg in 1881. The real reason why no foreign potentates came was simply that Francis Joseph had declared himself unwilling to face all the ceremonial involved. It is true that he had only recovered a few weeks before from one of his periodical bronchial attacks; yet he was not a sick man – only a weary one, aching to get back to the peace and quiet of his beloved Bad Ischl where he had spent the last sixty summers of his life. It was there he duly returned on 7 July, three days after the sparse fifteen-minute official ceremony in the Hofburg.* It was there he stayed, not coming back to his capital until the end of the month only after the 'iron dice of war'** had started rolling. As we shall see, this did nothing to hold them back.

Neither for the Emperor nor for his Ministers was the Archduke's funeral the main preoccupation during that first week of July. The most pressing question was how revenge on Serbia was to be exacted, and that depended, above all, on how Berlin would react. The first Balkan crisis of 1908 had been entirely of Austria's making, a surprise even for her closest ally. Yet that ally had soon rallied to her side by persuading Russia to resist provocation. At the end of the second protracted crisis of the Balkan Wars, Berchtold had sought Germany's 'moral support' before launching his ultimatum on Serbia. This third crisis (destined to be the final and fatal one) was, as everyone in Vienna sensed from the start, set in a different dimension of danger to everything that had gone

---

* What the dead couple would have regarded as their true funeral was held at Artstetten, the Archduke's castle near Melk Abbey on the Danube, the following day, 4 July. Indeed, everything had been prepared for it long in advance, the twin sarcophagi in the crypt being equal in every respect. In the Hofburg Chapel, Sophie's casket had been smaller than that of her husband, and its stand set some eighteen inches lower.
** A graphic phrase of Bethmann-Hollweg's – worthy, unlike his policies, of Bismarck himself.

before. It was no longer a question of formally annexing two occupied provinces and getting away with the *fait accompli*, nor of simply rattling the sabre over Albania. This time the sabre would have to be drawn, and that meant that something more than moral support was needed from Berlin. There was a double irony developing here. Bismarck had striven to separate the 'trim seaworthy frigate' of Prussian Germany for ever from the 'worm-eaten galleon' of the Austrian empire. Yet now the galleon, heading towards the rocks, was dragging the frigate after it.

A change needs to be noted which had taken place at the galleon's helm. Conrad, as ever, was for decisive action, but he had now been joined from the start by Berchtold. The ditherer of 1913 had become the swashbuckler of 1914, even though the pair of them were too frightened to fight alone. Before the old Emperor left again for his Salzkammergut mountains, they had mapped out their course with him. It was to be a dual approach, the one reinforcing the other. At Berchtold's request, Francis Joseph penned a personal letter to William II in which he blamed Serbia outright for the Sarajevo outrage and called for her elimination 'as a power factor in the Balkans'. All European monarchs, he continued, were menaced so long as 'this focus of criminal agitation continues unpunished'. These were strong words, and there is no evidence that the old monarch, whose mind was perfectly lucid, needed any encouragement to use them.

At the same time, Berchtold forwarded to Vienna a general memorandum on the Balkan situation drawn up earlier in June along mild and peaceful lines which Gavrilo Princip had just rendered somewhat obsolete. By an extraordinary exercise in bureaucratic ambivalence, it was decided to despatch the pacific document unaltered, though with a postscript which flatly contradicted both its tenor and its contents. The 'terrible events of Sarajevo', the postscript pointed out, had now given proof of the 'unbridgeable antagonism' between Serbia and the Monarchy, which the latter would have to dispose of 'with a firm hand'. To lend extra weight to this diplomatic barrage, the memorandum, with postscript and imperial letter, were not despatched by normal courier to Berlin. Instead they were sent by hand of Berchtold's *Chef de Cabinet*, Count Alexander Hoyos, who was also told to drum up all the support he could while in the German capital.*

* Hoyos and his colleague at the Ballhausplatz, Count Alexander Forgach, a senior departmental chief, were both dedicated 'hawks', and their influence on Berchtold behind the scenes is easy to underestimate.

The decision now rested with Berlin, or rather with the imperial palace at Potsdam. Though the German generals played a major role in the last phase of the crisis (and gradually took over completely once the fighting began), it was the Emperor and Supreme War Lord William II who was in undisputed command throughout the fateful month which followed. That is why German policy zig-zagged and even somersaulted during these weeks. Its fulcrum was the Emperor's own temperament, as erratic as it was impulsive, as touchy as it was theatrical. Once this is accepted, theories that Germany was planning all along to use the Balkans as the pretext for world war (even selecting June 1914 as the starting date!*) fall to the ground.

The evidence to the contrary begins in Vienna only forty-eight hours after the assassination, and four days before Hoyos set out for Berlin with his august pleas for help. On 30 June, the German ambassador to Vienna, Count Heinrich Leonard von Tschirschky und Bögendorff (to give him his resounding title in full) sent a telegram to his Chancellor which, as he well knew, would be copied to their Emperor. Tschirschky was no ordinary envoy. He had served as Secretary of State at the Foreign Office before being appointed by Bülow to the key embassy in Vienna in 1907. He was on excellent personal terms with his sovereign (Bülow once described him as 'the Kaiser's travelling companion') and had received special praise from William II for his handling of the annexation crisis. By 1914, therefore, this senior and eminently trusted diplomatist had been at his post for seven years. Had there been any scheme in Berlin either to instigate an Austro–Serb crisis in the Balkans that summer, or even to exploit any trouble brewing up in order to provoke general war, Tschirschky would have been in on the secret, since he was the man who would have to play Germany's card on the spot in the capital of her main ally. But what, in fact, does this first substantive telegram of his say about the crisis?

First, the envoy reports on a talk with Berchtold in which the Foreign Minister informed him that the threads of the Sarajevo conspiracy almost certainly 'ran together in Belgrade'. The ambassador goes on to report other talks with senior figures in Vienna who had frequently expressed

* Every General Staff of the great powers had its best and its worst time for any major action plotted out in advance, and in each capital there were arguments among the professionals. In Berlin, for example, Grand Admiral Tirpitz, who towered above all his colleagues, urged that if Germany were to engage in war, she should wait until at least 1920, when his navy would be ready.

to him the wish for 'a final and fundamental settlement with the Serbs'.
But then Tschirschky comments: 'I take the opportunity of every such
occasion to advise quietly, but with great emphasis and gravity, against
too hasty steps.' Austria, he concludes, must weigh carefully the results
of any unconsidered action and keep the interests of her allies, and of
the whole of Europe, in mind. So much for any theory of pre-prepared
conspiracy.

But if Tschirschky imagined that his soothing peacemaking tone
would find favour with his imperial 'travelling companion', both he and
the German Foreign Office (which had also been urging 'great prudence'
on Austria) were in for a rude shock. In one of those famous 'marginal
comments' which he scribbled on all major despatches,* the Kaiser blew
this pacific approach clean out of the water. Who, he demanded, had
authorised the ambassador to act in this fashion? Then comes the
imperial edict: 'Let Tschirschky be good enough to drop this nonsense.
The Serbs must be disposed of, and that promptly.'

And from that moment on – until the Kaiser was seized by a different
brainstorm one month later – the 'nonsense' was dropped. Tschirschky
became instantly converted from a dove to a hawk, though in the last
phase of the catastrophe, the bewildered man was ordered to stick his
dove's feathers on again. There was no question of him protesting, of
following his own convictions, let alone resigning. A vain and arrogant
man in the eyes of his colleagues, he was an out-and-out careerist whose
ambitions, like those of Aehrenthal, masked a sense of insecurity. In
Tschirschky's case, this centred on his wife who, though extremely
wealthy, was the daughter of a Budapest industrialist of reputedly Jewish
origin. The tentacles of anti-Semitism reached everywhere.

The Kaiser was attending the regatta and naval review at Kiel (a
fixture on his calendar) when the news from Sarajevo reached him. He
immediately cancelled the event, ordered all vessels present to lower
their flags to half-mast, and hurried back to Potsdam, from where he
launched Germany's tough line. It was just as well that he was back in
his palace so promptly, for all the other main seats of power in the
capital were empty at the end of June, a circumstance which hardly
supports the conspiracy theory. The Chancellor had to be summoned

---

* These have great historical importance. First, they reveal the explosive and unpredictable temperament of the sovereign who, until the war started, ran German policy on all
fronts. Second, unlike all the apologia presented in post-war memoirs, they reflect the
unvarnished mood of the moment.

back from his estate at Hohenfinow; General von Moltke, the Chief of Staff, was taking the waters at Carlsbad, while Admiral Alfred von Tirpitz, the Navy Minister, whose influence was even greater, was similarly engaged at the Swiss spa of Tarasp. The Foreign Office was also without its leader, Gottlieb von Jagow, who had been appointed Secretary of State the previous year. He was most inconvenienced of all by the crisis, for he was actually away on his honeymoon. In his absence it was the Under-Secretary of State, Alfred Zimmermann, who had been peddling the same line of prudence and restraint in Berlin which Tschirschky had been putting forward in Vienna. The news that Count Hoyos was on his way to Berlin, bearing a personal letter from Francis Joseph, presented the Kaiser with the perfect setting to move from the margins to centre stage. This he now did, with fateful results.

The setting for the issue of Germany's famous 'blank cheque' of unqualified support for Austria in the crisis was discreet and decorous. The Kaiser issued no dramatic public pronouncements, as was his normal style.* Indeed, over lunch at the palace with the Austrian ambassador Count Szögyeny-Marich (who had handed over the document from Vienna), he began on a cautious note. Pointing to 'possible serious European complications' over the crisis, he said he could give no definite answer before consulting his Chancellor. (Bethmann-Hollweg was only now on his way back to Berlin!) The veteran Austrian envoy, who had been at his post ever since 1892, and was on the point of retiring, wanted something better than that out of the last and most critical assignment of his career. So, after the meal, he pressed the Emperor again.

It was now that William II issued his blank cheque of unlimited credit to Austria – subject, he still stressed, to the counter-signature of his Chancellor. Francis Joseph could rely 'in this case, as in all others, upon Germany's full support'. Action against Serbia should not be delayed. As for a possible widening of the conflict, he personally did not believe that Russia was ready for war, and felt it would 'think twice' before intervening. However, should a war between Austria-Hungary and Russia prove unavoidable, the Austrians could rest assured that

---

* The most theatrical example had been his improvised speech on the quayside of Bremerhaven on 27 June 1900, to his troops embarking for the Far East as part of the European military expedition to put down the so-called 'Boxer Rebellion' in Peking. He compared them to the conquering Huns of Attila a thousand years before, and enjoined them 'to imprint the German name on China for a thousand years to come'.

Germany, 'their old faithful ally', would be at their side. It was this additional pledge of support, even if the crisis were to escalate, which did the damage. As the Kaiser again made quite clear at meetings with his military advisors at Potsdam, which began that same afternoon, he did not expect any widening of the conflict.* Apart from the unpreparedness of both France and Russia, there was for him a dynastic dimension to the Sarajevo outrage: 'The Tsar would not take the part of regicides.' And so, at 9.15 the following morning, the Kaiser left his capital to resume his annual cruise in northern waters, believing he had ensured that the Serbs would be 'taught their lesson'. What he had in fact done was to hand over the fate of Europe to the eighty-four-year-old Austrian Emperor in Bad Ischl, which, in effect, handed it to a band of ministerial hawks in Vienna.

It was symbolic of this *ad hoc* transfer of power that the first formal top-level discussion of the crisis was held in the capital on the very day that Francis Joseph started on his way back to his summer villa. When the Joint Ministerial Council of the Dual Monarchy met on 7 July, its members had before them not only Ambassador Szögyeny's telegram with the Kaiser's 'blank cheque', but also a verbal report to back it all up from Count Hoyos, who had returned to Vienna that morning.

Hesitation and 'half-and-halfness' were, as we have seen, natural characteristics of the Austrian temperament. In this respect, the Emperor's black Habsburg eagle, whose twin heads gazed steadfastly in opposite directions, was an excellent symbol for his subjects. But the desire to play safe often conceals a suppressed urge to lash out and give proof of virility. This, with one distinguished exception, was what surfaced around the council table now. Berchtold, who had called the meeting, pointed to the all-round pledges of Germany's unconditional support (Bethmann-Hollweg having now backed up his Emperor). In view of this, he urged 'a timely settlement of accounts with Serbia', even if this meant war with Russia. Count Stürgkh, the Austrian Prime Minister, shared his view, adding that 'action shall and must be taken'. The Monarchy's Joint Ministers for War and Finance, Krobatin and Bilinski, both fell into line.

Only one voice spoke out in opposition, but it was a powerful voice, belonging to the strongest personality around the table and the one

---

* Tirpitz and Moltke both placidly continued with their cures in Switzerland and Bohemia respectively, and were represented by deputies.

far-seeing minister in the Dual Monarchy. Count Stefan Tisza was no amateur in the Berchtold mould. He was then serving, for the second time, as Hungarian Prime Minister, and was the son of Koloman Tisza, the Liberal leader who had held the same office before him from 1875 to 1890. Like all Hungarian nobles, he swore by the ancient crown of St Stephen and the lands it had bequeathed. However, unlike many of his fellows, he saw the Dual Monarchy in its existing form, with the Habsburg dynasty on the throne, as the best, safest guarantors of this sacred Magyar inheritance.

Vision is what distinguishes the statesman from the run-of-the-mill politician and, from the moment of the Sarajevo outrage, Tisza spotted the dangers that military escalation would bring to the Monarchy's delicate ethnic balance. Above all, any attempt to dismember Serbia might well bring more Serbs into the Hungarian kingdom, which had enough racial problems on its hands already, notably with its Roumanian and Croat subjects. That was why he had argued, before the assassinations, for a policy of diplomatic containment to control Greater Serbia, above all by persuading Bulgaria to join the Central Powers' alliance. The memorandum just delivered in Berlin had been largely based on his concept. That was why, on 1 July, immediately after the assassinations, he had sent a personal memorandum to Francis Joseph arguing against war – at least until the right 'diplomatic constellation' had been set up.*

No one at the council table on 7 July was therefore surprised to hear Tisza expand on these views: he would never agree, he declared, to a surprise attack on Serbia without preliminary diplomatic preparation. Yes, demands for satisfaction should be presented in Belgrade, followed, if need be, by an ultimatum; but these demands, though stiff, should not be 'impossible of fulfilment'. Above all, there must be no thought of destroying Serbia. This would not only bring Russia into the conflict but would destabilise the Monarchy itself if more South Slav territory were to be absorbed.** Berchtold had no option but to record Tisza's opposition to a solution by military aggression (especially as the Hungarian leader was about to repeat it in another memorandum to the

---

* It is worth adding that, as a devout Calvinist, Tisza also had a deep moral abhorrence for war.

** Tisza was particularly appalled by a crass and totally unauthorised suggestion Hoyos had made in conversation with Bethmann-Hollweg that Serbia should eventually be divided between Roumania and Bulgaria.

absent Emperor); yet, in the minutes, the Foreign Minister managed
to stiffen up the reference to those crucial demands to be presented in
Belgrade. These were now to be 'so far-reaching . . . as would render
their rejection probable, in order to clear the way for a radical solution
by way of military operations'.

During the next fortnight, Berchtold and his principal lieutenants
laboured away at drafting an ultimatum which would make rejection
by Belgrade not only probable but certain, and thus render inevitable
an Austrian–Serbian war. The official detailed to compose the document was Alexander von Musulin, who was of Croatian origin and
well-versed in Balkan affairs. Even more to the point, he was considered
to be the deftest draughtsman in the Ministry. In his apologia published
after the war he insisted that every clause in the note was carefully drawn
up in a form considered acceptable to Belgrade, and that Vienna was
searching only for a diplomatic solution. This was deception (or self-
deception) of the highest order. The Ballhausplatz archives show that
when Baron Vladimir Giesl, the Austrian Minister to Belgrade, was
briefed by Berchtold before returning to his post, he was told that
however the Serbs responded, relations with the Monarchy must be
broken off, so that war could follow. Those flat instructions were issued
on 7 July, soon after the Joint Council meeting at which Tisza's opposition to war had still not been overcome.

It took another week before, on 14 July, Berchtold persuaded the
Hungarian Prime Minister to agree that Serbia should be sent an ultimatum with a short time-limit.* Tisza had been won over, or worn
down, on four counts: by the relentless pressure from Berlin to see her
Austrian ally act with speed and vigour; by the foolishly intransigent
tone coming out of Belgrade; by the arguments of military expediency
being canvassed by Conrad; and, finally, by the reluctant conclusion
that the Monarchy was facing a challenge which could not be ignored
if the dynasty were to remain strong at home and respected abroad. He
made one condition: that, before the ultimatum was delivered, another
Joint Ministerial Council should formally declare that in the event of
war, Austria would seek no acquisition of Serbian territory. Five days
later, on 19 July, this council was duly convened (for greater secrecy,

* The day before, Berchtold's legal counsellor, Dr Friedrich von Wiesner, who had been
sent on a forty-eight-hour fact-finding mission to Belgrade, had reported from there that
the Serbian government had at least 'tolerated' the pan-Serb societies responsible for all
the trouble.

in Berchtold's Vienna residence), and Tisza's condition of 'no conquest' was entered in the minutes, though with so many reservations as to render it almost meaningless.

The main business of this gathering was to agree the final terms of the Belgrade ultimatum. These had been ready in rough outline for a week, but each of Musulin's drafts and redrafts had been honed and rehoned by Count Forgach and then by Berchtold himself to give it an ever sharper point. As a result, the note which Baron Giesl handed over in Belgrade at 6 p.m. on Thursday 23 July* was like a dagger at the heart of Serbia's continued existence as an independent state. Crucial in this respect were clauses five and six of the detailed ten-point demand. These called respectively for the 'collaboration' of Austro-Hungarian officials in the suppression of subversive movements and – even more drastically – for the actual participation of Austrian representatives in judicial proceedings against 'accessories to the 28 June plot'. That demand was tantamount to turning the kingdom of Serbia into an Austrian colony. It was the clause of which Berchtold and his advisers were particularly proud and on which – rightly as it turned out – they placed their greatest hopes of rejection.

Berchtold and his military *alter ego*, General Conrad, seem to have been driven at this point by a manic sense of destiny, as though it was, at last, they, and not the Germans, who were fulfilling the anti-Slav mission of the Teutonic race. This mood had reached such a pitch that the Austrian Foreign Minister now began to sidestep both his monarch and his allies. The absence of Francis Joseph from his capital for the past fortnight had already served Berchtold's cause by allowing him to play his own cards in Vienna, free from any imperial restraint. As the old Emperor hated the telephone, contact had been maintained mainly by Berchtold making the seven-hour rail journey to Bad Ischl to secure approval for measures the government had already decided.** Francis Joseph, who had ruled for more than sixty years, surmounting in the

---

* Delivery had been postponed until President Poincaré of France was on his way home by ship from his two-day official visit to St Petersburg. Berchtold did not want to allow his rival allies the chance of discussing the ultimatum and coordinating their reaction on the spot.
** Apart from isolating the Emperor, the repeated train journeys made it difficult for Berchtold to stay abreast of things. On one occasion he had to be pulled off the train at Lambach to deal with an urgent plea from St Petersburg that the 'time limit' for the ultimatum should be extended.

process dozens of major crises through holding audiences, found nothing unusual about this disastrous arrangement. Its climax began now when, on 20 July, the ultimatum was despatched abroad without even being shown – let alone approved – by the Emperor in its final form. For once, even he got irritated, and on that same day telegraphed to ask his Foreign Minister what was going on. Berchtold hastily despatched a copy by courier to Bad Ischl, where he arrived himself the following morning to seek approval. This was duly given, without any changes to the text.

It was, of course, already too late for changes. The text of the ultimatum (again coyly described as a 'note with a time limit') was now in the hands not just of Baron Giesl in Belgrade but also of Austria's ambassadors to all the great powers. These were instructed to communicate it to their governments on the morning of Friday 24 July, the day after its presentation in Vienna.

From this moment on, the Sarajevo crisis began its swift and inexorable march towards a European war. Though it was generally expected that the Austrians would make severe demands on Belgrade, the actual text of the ultimatum caused tremors of concern and even shock. The Germans had known its broad outline for more than a week, and had been pressing hard ever since for the full details. When Germany did get them, a little in advance of the other powers,* both Jagow at the Foreign Office and Chancellor Bethmann-Hollweg (away at Hohenfinow again) declared that it went too far, and reproached Berchtold for revealing it only at the last minute. The Emperor William was even more irritated, though for a different reason: cruising on the *Hohenzollern*, the first information he received was from a German news agency report monitored on the yacht.

In London, the first sight of the text on the morning of the twenty-fourth produced from Sir Edward Grey the oft-quoted comment that it was 'the most formidable document' he had ever seen 'addressed by one state to another that was independent'. Grey was the most respected and, after the limited success of his 1913 Ambassadors' Conference, the most influential Foreign Minister in Europe. Yet, though the ultimatum shook him, he failed to grasp and tackle in time the threat which it posed. His top official, Sir Eyre Crowe, a man of outstanding vision,

---

* As a special concession to his insistent allies, Berchtold had finally agreed to show the ultimatum in Berlin on the afternoon of Tuesday 22 July.

did urge immediate action in the form of a warning that England would be found at the side of France and Russia should the conflict escalate. Grey ignored the advice, which he regarded as 'premature'. Whatever the excuses put forward then or later for this hesitation, London cannot be absolved from a degree of responsibility – as opposed to outright guilt – for the catastrophe which followed. Just as Francis Joseph thought that the crisis could be dealt with through more audiences, so Sir Edward Grey deluded himself that it could be warded off with more conferences. To do him justice, he was to brood over his attitude right down to his death in 1933.

That Berchtold and Conrad were now hell-bent on war with Serbia (and, if need be, with Russia) is shown by the way they now propelled events forward, regardless of the alarm their ultimatum had caused abroad. Giesl had already been instructed by Berchtold that there could be no discussion over the note, no reservations entertained, and no extension of the time limit. The Serbian Prime Minister, Nicholas Pašić, arrived in person at the Austrian Legation, somewhat breathless, and deposited his government's reply at 5.55 p.m. on the twenty-fifth – only five minutes before the ultimatum was due to expire. The Serbian note came to be widely regarded as a masterpiece of diplomatic and emollient draughtsmanship, which accepted almost everything. But, as Berchtold had calculated, there was one point on which Belgrade could not yield: the demand for official Austrian participation in the investigation.*

One misplaced comma would have been enough for Baron Giesl, who knew how to obey orders (he was also a general in the Austrian army). He had in fact written his official note of rejection in advance; he now signed it and despatched it to Pašić, who had barely regained his office. It was a speed record for the rupture of diplomatic relations. Giesl then burnt the code books, boarded the car waiting outside, with the luggage already packed and loaded, and was at Belgrade station with his wife and the legation staff in time to catch the 6.30 p.m. sleeper train for Budapest. Even this timetable had been prescribed for him by Berchtold, as had the procedure when the train rolled across the nearby Hungarian border at Semlin only ten minutes later. Giesl telegraphed confirmation of the rupture *en clair* to Vienna and phoned Tisza in Budapest. Not unnaturally in view of all his attempts at moderation, the

---

* This was the infamous Clause Six. Of the other nine detailed demands, Pašić had accepted five and had been evasive, though without rejection, on the remaining four.

Hungarian Prime Minister did not jump for joy. Indeed, his immediate question in German was: *'Musste es denn sein?'* ('Did it have to be?')

There was a similar reaction at Bad Ischl, where Berchtold was again already in attendance, waiting for the ultimatum to expire. *'Also doch'* ('So, after all'), the Emperor was said to have muttered when the news from Belgrade came through. The tone of weary resignation was understandable, coming from an aged monarch who would surely have preferred to have ended his massive reign in peace. He underlined this by commenting separately, first to Berchtold and then to Giesl, that the breaking off of relations did not necessarily mean war. This was an imperial version of that Austrian habit of looking both ways at once – a stance that could only work in heraldry. The Emperor had approved demands on Belgrade which were savage rather than severe. He had reckoned with war against Serbia and even – thanks to that fatal guarantee from Berlin – with war against Russia. Yet, having conjured up the conflict, both Francis Joseph and Berchtold winced as they saw the sword actually being drawn. Only Conrad, whose business was war and whose slogan was war, rubbed his hands. The Emperor was persuaded to sign the order for Austrian mobilisation on the evening of the twenty-fifth. Conrad immediately ordered that it should take effect on the twenty-eighth.*

The most remarkable – and unexpected – reaction to the happenings in Belgrade came, however, not from the Austrian monarch but from his fellow-emperor and ally. The exact timing of events, at a stage in the crisis where one hour, let alone a whole day, could be vital, becomes crucial at this point. William II, having broken off his cruise in a mood of alarmed frustration at being so isolated, got back to his capital on the morning of 27 July. According to the account of one eye-witness (Count August Eulenberg), his first question to his Chancellor on the station platform was to demand how the whole mess had arisen. A flustered Bethmann-Hollweg offered his resignation on the spot, only to be told: 'You have cooked this broth and now you are going to eat it!'

Though Bethmann-Hollweg had begun to panic in the face of the mounting storm, he did nothing at first to ward it off. The official text of the Serbian reply was already on his table when he returned from

---

* Paradoxically, it was Count Tisza who was largely responsible for the speedy decision. He had telegraphed direct to the Emperor from Budapest on 25 July, arguing that any delay in mobilisation now could only damage the Monarchy's standing.

the station, and should have been put before the Emperor immediately. Instead, he hung on to it overnight so that William did not read it until the morning of the twenty-eighth, when it was too late to prevent Austria sending off her declaration of war.* Bethmann-Hollweg and the German Foreign Office had been clamouring for this with increasing urgency in Vienna and assumed they would still have the backing of their Emperor and Supreme War Lord. They were in for a shock.

William annotated on the Serbian reply: 'A great moral success for Vienna; but with it every reason for war drops away.' Moreover, he immediately wrote out a long memorandum to Jagow at the Foreign Office, sketching out the road for a negotiated settlement which he now saw open: Austria's honour should be met by the temporary military occupation of part of Serbia (later dubbed the 'Halt in Belgrade' idea), while he would personally mediate for peace on his ally's behalf. It has been widely assumed ever since that the Emperor's spectacular *volte-face* was inspired by sudden fears that Britain might not remain neutral in any wider conflict. Yet the facts, if examined closely, do not support this. So far Grey, while stressing the gravity of the situation to every ambassador he received, had put his faith in negotiation and given no hint of British involvement, except in the diplomatic field.

His main initiative was launched on 26 July, after the rupture of Austro–Serbian relations.** It had called for another London Ambassadors' Conference, but this time only of the four powers not directly involved in the current conflict: Germany and Italy, who would speak for their Austrian ally, and England and France, who would represent the interests of their Russian partner. Germany rejected this for a variety of reasons, not the least of which was the suspicion that Italy would prove a very uncertain voice around the table, and might well end up supporting the Entente powers. Germany, the Kaiser had minuted, would not countenance her Austrian ally being arraigned before an 'areopagus'. But still, both he and his Foreign Office clung

---

* On orders from Berlin, the German Legation in Belgrade had declined to hand this over on her ally's behalf so that, in the end, it was sent by ordinary telegram. Berchtold's original draft included a reference to a Serbian attack allegedly carried out already at Temes Kubin along the Danube borders. He suppressed this, on his own initiative, when the report proved false.

** It was typical of the countryman's lifestyle Grey was so reluctant to abandon that his authorisation of the plan submitted by his officials had come from his beloved trout-fishing retreat at Itchen Abbas, where he had snatched a weekend.

to the belief that they had little to fear from England. The only warning signals to come from London so far had been the gloomy personal assessments of Prince Lichnowsky, a dedicated Anglophile, whose views were constantly being derided by the Kaiser.

Though Grey was becoming steadily less ambiguous in his comments, it was not until late in the evening of 29 July that the first unequivocal warning of British involvement to come from his own lips reached Berlin. Lichnowsky reported that the Foreign Secretary had summoned him once again that afternoon to make it clear that Britain could only stand aside if the issue remained confined to Austria and Serbia. If the conflict spread further, such detachment would 'not be practicable' and the British government would 'find itself forced to make up its mind quickly'. Grey did not consult the Cabinet, which he knew to be divided over British policy, on this. He did not need to. He stressed that what he had to say was 'a friendly and private communication'. It was no less effective for that. The Kaiser fairly plastered Lichnowsky's despatch with his explosive comments, ending up by describing Grey as 'a common cur' who was threatening Germany instead of restraining Russia. His conclusion was revealing: 'England *alone* bears the responsibility for peace and war, not *we* any longer.'

Two things need noting about the episode. The first is that the Kaiser had launched his own peace initiative some thirty-six hours *before* having seen the red light flashed at him from across the Channel. He therefore deserves such credit as can be given for trying to stop the Austrians cashing in full the 'blank cheque' he had rashly sent them three weeks ago. The second, of course, is that Grey's solemn personal warning came several days too late, a delay that was to be rendered even more fateful by the prevarication in which the German Chancellor now indulged. Imperial commands, as at the beginning of the month, still dictated the course of German policy, and Bethmann-Hollweg had no option but to follow the Emperor's latest course. But he waited the whole day before, at 10.15 on the evening of the twenty-eighth, some six hours after Austria had declared war on Serbia, transmitting new instructions to Tschirschky in Vienna – who did not receive them decoded in his hands until breakfast on the twenty-ninth.

Even then, what the envoy read was a carefully watered-down version of the instructions the Kaiser had issued from Potsdam nearly twenty-four hours before. The statement that 'every reason for war has dropped away' was not even mentioned, as war had anyway been declared that afternoon. Nor – an even more staggering omission – was the Kaiser's offer to mediate in person. Instead, Bethmann-Hollweg merely urged the Austrians to restrict themselves to a 'temporary occupation of Belgrade and certain other Serbian localities', and to do everything in the meantime to ensure that 'responsibility for the eventual extension of the war . . . should, under all circumstances, fall on Russia'. This became Bethmann-Hollweg's obsession from now on. What he was shivering about was not the impending catastrophe so much as his own place in history.

By now, that catastrophe was anyway rapidly becoming unavoidable as mobilisation followed mobilisation and the generals took over from the politicians. Desperate attempts at a diplomatic settlement swirled around like dust devils during these last days of peace, only to be blown away by the gathering military storm. The Kaiser himself backed out in a huff once he learnt from the Tsar on 29 July that Russia had already ordered partial mobilisation measures along the Austrian border five days previously. 'My work is at an end,' he wrote under his cousin's telegram.* And it was the Tsar's anguished decision to reorder general mobilisation on the afternoon of the thirtieth (after cancelling his earlier order overnight) which mustered the armies of the other great powers one by one, and drew their governments successively into the conflict.

The Austro–German relationship during these last days of peace is particularly fascinating. Bethmann-Hollweg, who failed in a very clumsy attempt to bribe Britain into neutrality, suddenly panicked and threw all restraint with Austria to the wind. On 29 and 30 July, he pounded Vienna with telegram after telegram, urging Berchtold to accept the 'Halt in Belgrade' formula which had been taken up as a last resort by Grey. Berchtold listened, 'pale and silent' (in Tschirschky's words), to the German appeal. He was neither pale nor silent when, on the morning of 31 July, he presided over a joint Austro-Hungarian Council which rejected outright his ally's advice. A mere occupation of Belgrade was of no use; the war against Serbia must continue unabated; no negotiations could be entertained unless Russia cancelled her mobilisation. This last condition he well knew to be fanciful, for the 'iron dice of war' had started to roll. The next day, both France and Germany mobilised, to follow the Russian example. Successive declarations of war followed,

---

* Part of the final exchanges in the famous 'Willy–Nicky' series of telegrams which had started in the previous century.

culminating in that of Britain against Germany on 4 August, after German troops had invaded Belgium.*

So Austria, for forty years the junior partner in the Germanic alliance, defied her powerful ally in the worst crisis the alliance had faced. The Monarchy, which Berlin had begun to despair of as a weak and vacillating liability, proved as stubborn as a mule in plodding steadily forward over the cliff's edge, dragging all Europe after her into the abyss. The Kaiser, who had started her out on the journey and then failed to rein her back, blamed everybody around him, allies and antagonists alike, for the 'frivolity and weakness' which were plunging the world into war. Even his genial but politically astute uncle, King Edward VII, dead for four years past, was singled out for abuse, as having triumphed from the grave with his 'encirclement' policy against Germany.

The Kaiser never thought, of course, of blaming himself, nor his General Staff, whose modified 'Schlieffen Plan' for fighting the war nullified even the faintest chance of a last-minute settlement. All the other great powers could mobilise and wait behind their borders. Only Germany was pre-programmed under that plan to mobilise and attack her prime adversary, France, in one simultaneous movement, which engulfed both Luxembourg and Belgium as mere staging-posts on the march.

If, in this final phase, Austria had pulled Germany politically towards Armageddon, it was Germany who immediately set its military dimensions. As far as the Dual Monarchy was concerned, this dominance was to reach strangulation point during the long struggle ahead.

---

* For a variety of reasons, sentimental as well as strategic, France and Britain did not declare war on Austria until eight days later. Both King George and Sir Edward Grey arranged for Mensdorff to make personal calls of farewell. The fact that the Monarchy had been largely responsible for the conflict was totally overlooked.

PART FOUR

THE ROAD
TO DESTRUCTION

I

The End of Illusion

EACH NATION HAD ITS special impulse behind that general mid-summer madness of joy which greeted the outbreak of war. The Germans saw in it their call to arms as the predestined masters of Europe; the French, revenge for the humiliations of 1870; the Russians, the fulfilment of their duty as protector of all the Slavs; even the British, who were more astonished and unprepared than anyone else, could draw on jingoistic memories of their great naval rivalry with Germany. The people of the Dual Monarchy were neither astonished nor unprepared. Next to the Italians (still *the* enemy in the popular mind, despite the fact that Italy had been an ally since 1882), the Serbs, with their dream of 'Greater Serbia', were perceived as the greatest menace on their borders. With the annexation of Bosnia-Herzegovina in 1908, the Monarchy had driven a thorn into its own heel, a thorn which had flared up painfully in the Balkan Wars of 1912–13. Now the moment had come to draw it.

But there were also psychological reasons which went both wider and deeper, to explain the frenzy of the Habsburg peoples. War had come as a catharsis for that gloomy preoccupation with decay and decline which marked their entry into the twentieth century. They felt, rather like old Francis Joseph, that, if the empire were to die, it should at least die decently. There was even, in August 1914, an unfamiliar sensation that perhaps the Monarchy was not going to die after all, but was instead experiencing a strange rebirth. The war brought with it a surge of pride in being a subject of the multi-national empire, and all its nations, as well as all classes, professions and creeds initially shared in the feelings. At the highest level, the rivalry between Schönbrunn and the 'Belvedere Clique' of Francis Ferdinand had been buried with him.

So, it seemed, had the rivalry between the political parties. For Dr Friedrich Funder, one of the murdered Archduke's advisers, and editor of the Catholic monarchist *Reichspost*, the war had given the empire the chance to fulfil its mission in protecting the freedom of its mixed nations and in preserving the political balance of Europe. He had watched – elated and amazed in equal measure – as the crowds cheered and marched, not just in the prosperous bourgeois parts of the capital, but in pure workers' districts like Ottakring, bastions of the Socialist left. Even the Czechs, who formed a good part of the population of these dreary suburbs, sang the praises of dynasty and empire, and flocked to the colours. (Among the enthusiastic Socialist recruits was none other than Otto Bauer, later to emerge as the high priest of 'Austro-Marxism'.*) The organ of the Social Democrats, *Arbeiterzeitung*, under its editor, Friedrich Austerlitz, was just as enthusiastic for war as Dr Funder's *Reichspost*, though with a difference. For the Catholic right wing, the fight was to realise the old dream of 'Greater Austria', to the glory of the dynasty. For the Socialist left, it was all about preserving the 'German nation', perhaps through the instrument of the international proletariat. We shall see this contrast widening into an ideological chasm for Austria in the years ahead. For the time being however, the Emperor's subjects – who like all the other combatants were confidently expecting to be home in triumph 'by Christmas' – were united. Loyalty to the supra-national dynasty, one of two key factors we have noted as shaping the Austrian character down the centuries, thus experienced a sudden uplift in the summer of 1914. The hunger, suffering, mass casualties, defeats and sheer weariness which were to eat away at that loyalty were not imagined at the time. Like the rest of Europe, the peoples of the Dual Monarchy had simply no idea of what world war meant. Understandable: there had never been one.

As for that other factor which had always pressed down hard on any Austrian identity, the Germanic tie, this now came into its element. After thirty-five years, the Austro–German alliance had moved out from the archives and on to the battlefields, on the precise terms which had been laid down in 1879.** During the final days of the crisis, the

---

* Another to serve in the imperial army was a Croat corporal called Josip Broz. He was to achieve greater fame as Marshal Tito of Yugoslavia.
** The key clause had been that if either power were to be attacked by Russia, its partner would come to its assistance with all its strength. The same would apply if Russia joined forces with another power (i.e. France).

two Chiefs of Staff, Moltke and Conrad, had been telephoning and telegraphing each other directly, without previously consulting their monarchs or their ministers. The military had taken over from the civilians and, unfortunately for the Austrians, this was the sphere of action where the Germans now steadily took over from them. In the context of the Austro–German relationship, the Great War resembled a slow-motion replay of Königgrätz; instead of the Germans crushing the Austrians as enemies within hours, they now gradually ground them into submission as allies over the space of four years.

It was an uneven match from the start. The German army of 1914 was the finest military machine of its day, perhaps of modern times. In its commanders, its arms and equipment, its training, its supply services and communications, its cadres of long-serving officers and NCOs, in the quality of its General Staff and the planning they produced – in short, in everything which went to make up a fighting force – it was generally superior to its ally. On top of this came its vast superiority in self-confidence and morale. The Austrian army had a chequered history of success and failure behind it. The German army had known only victory for longer than anyone could remember. It regarded war as the apotheosis of its existence, not as some baleful interruption to the pleasures of peaceful garrison life. Above all, like the German people themselves, it had the unity and sense of common purpose which sprang from belonging to one race and one nation. The ethnic patchwork of the Habsburg empire, stitched together mainly by loyalty to the ancient dynasty, had nothing comparable to drive it forward once the suffering and sacrifice began to mount.

Indeed, it was the dynasty, with its plethora of uniformed archdukes, which actually created problems for the army. At the age of eighty-four, the Emperor was far too old to take command on the field of battle, where he had not exactly distinguished himself even when young. Francis Ferdinand, who had been groomed to take his place, now lay in the Artstetten crypt, and the new heir, Archduke Charles, could not possibly fill the breach.* He was just short of only his twenty-seventh birthday; had no military experience, beyond the obligatory spells of garrison duty; and though certainly no coward, was of a gentle and almost pacifist frame of mind. Nor had he ever stood out as a personality

* Charles was the grandson of the Emperor's second eldest brother, Charles Louis, and had come to the steps of the throne through a long chain of suicide, premature deaths and, finally, his uncle's assassination.

in the Habsburg ranks. Indeed, the only mark he had so far made on the public imagination was his marriage, on 21 October 1911, to a beautiful and strong-willed French princess, Zita of Bourbon-Parma. This unusual choice for a Habsburg heir had caused something of a stir among his future subjects. They were not to imagine the sensations it would one day bring.

An archduke had to be found, however, to serve as Commander-in-Chief, especially as the Supreme War Lord, William II, was exercising that role in Germany. Two brothers, of ripe but not excessive years, were in the running: the Archdukes Eugene and Frederick, both grandsons of the great Archduke Charles, who had bested Napoleon on the field of Aspern. The Emperor picked Frederick, the richest of all the Habsburgs, whose wife was the ambitious Isabella who had sought to catch Francis Ferdinand as her son-in-law, back in what now seemed a remotely vanished world. He was first named as Commander-in-Chief for the Balkans and then, when it was clear that the Austro–Serb conflict would widen, was given command over all imperial forces on land, sea and in the air. (The Monarchy already possessed a fledgling air arm, thanks partly to Francis Ferdinand's patronage.) The command was nominal, particularly as regards the land forces. The mild-mannered Frederick was given the inescapable Conrad as his Chief of Staff, and it was Conrad who ran the war in his name. The Archduke's place in the Balkans was eventually filled by General Oskar Potiorek, the vain numbskull who had made such a hash of the security arrangements at Sarajevo in June.

Potiorek now proceeded to make an even greater hash of things on the battlefield. Indeed, the costly fiasco of his 1914 Balkans campaign was the first of many question marks to be placed against the Monarchy's credentials as a fighting partner. He was not helped by a conflict of purpose within his own High Command, and another between them and the Germans as to how the first stages of the war should be fought. Moltke wanted the Monarchy's forces to be concentrated in an offensive in Galicia, thus pinning down the Russian army on the Eastern Front while the Germans disposed of France in the west. (Their optimistic timetable for this, dating from 1909, reckoned on a mere six weeks.) Then, so the vague understanding went, the two allied armies would combine to crush the Tsar's forces into submission. The question of how, when, and with what resources the Serbs were to be vanquished in the Balkans fell awkwardly in the middle of this grand concept. It had muddled even Austria's mobilisation, with divisions being earmarked for service first against Serbia, then against Russia, and shuttled between the two concentration areas as fast as an overloaded and antiquated rail network could carry them.

But the arguments and muddle over planning were nothing compared with the costly chaos which ensued when operations began. For the Germans, the Balkans were a military sideshow. For the Austrians, and above all for General Potiorek personally, they were the prime target, the seat of that 'Greater Serbia' menace which had just taken the life of their heir-apparent. Conrad had supported this idea in principle, but a debilitating squabble broke out as to how it should be carried out in practice. Potiorek, who on 21 August persuaded the Emperor to make him an independent commander in the Balkans, wanted all the three armies – the Second, Fifth and Sixth – mobilised on the Southern Front to march with their full strength against the Serbs. Conrad, realising he had blundered by allowing too much of his strength to be concentrated in the south, demanded that the Second Army be transferred north to the Galician front. Intrigue piled upon intrigue in an embarrassing spectacle as Potiorek tried to persuade not only the Emperor but the empire's political leaders (Tisza in Budapest and Berchtold in Vienna*) to support his cause.

Though he partly won his argument over the Second Army, his cause turned out to be not worth supporting. At the end of four months of confused fighting, with Potiorek being hailed as the hero of the Monarchy after initial successes, only to be damned as a manic blunderer when he failed, the imperial forces finally retreated from Belgrade on 15 December. It was the fourth time since the summer that they had captured and then yielded the Serbian capital. Now, at the end of the year, they were back where they had started when the war began. The cost of the defeat, which had been brought about largely by their commander's insistence on a series of all-out midwinter offensives regardless of terrain, weather or the human toll, was horrendous. There had been over 270,000 casualties, including some 100,000 dead or captured. This was well over half of the total forces which the Monarchy had committed to the battle; it was also more than twice the losses inflicted on the three exhausted and indifferently equipped Serbian armies which had opposed them. Potiorek resigned, just before being dismissed, one week

* Berchtold was replaced as Foreign Minister on 1 January the following year by a solid, hard-working official, Baron Stefan Burian; the very opposite of his predecessor.

after the fall of Belgrade. He retired on full pension to the pleasant Carinthian lakeside town of Klagenfurt, grumbling that he had been denied the chance of final victory.

However poorly his rival had performed, Conrad was in no position to throw stones. In command on the Russian front, he had led a campaign which, after similar swings between advance and retreat, and similar exhortations to the troops to go forward at all costs, had ended in a far more comprehensive disaster. To make matters worse, this coincided with the great German triumph over the Russians at Tannenberg, at the far end of the line in East Prussia.

If Belgrade was the military and psychological key to the Balkans, across the Carpathians in Galicia it was the fortified town of Przemyśl, which lay astride the River San, fifty miles due west of Lemberg (Lwów), the capital of the Monarchy's most northerly province. The fortress was the strongest to be built anywhere on the soil of the Dual Monarchy. Ringed by thirty miles of defence works, manned by a thousand guns, and with vast fields of barbed wire strung out ahead, it was considered impregnable. Not that Conrad imagined that it would even be assaulted when, on 15 August 1914, he advanced against the Russians along a 250-mile front which had Lemberg at its centre. Yet, one month later, after a muddled see-sawing running battle against four Russian armies, Conrad's forces had been driven back, not just to Lemberg but then to the line of the River San, and finally right out of the whole Galician province. By the end, he had retreated some 150 miles, losing more than a third of the 900,000-man force he had launched in the attack.

A cry of help (the first of many) had gone out to the Germans, who responded by regrouping their victorious forces at Tannenberg into a new Ninth Army which moved south to relieve pressure on their ally by engaging the 'Russian steamroller' in the rear. But a single German army could not save Galicia, and now Przemyśl lay isolated on the wrong side of the Carpathians, a huge Austrian hedgehog surrounded on all sides by enemy forces.

To relieve the siege of Przemyśl became for the Austrian empire what relieving the siege of Mafeking had been for the British empire in the Boer War at the turn of the century: it was not just a target of military strategy but a symbol of national honour. Conrad knew he would not even attempt it without German help. The Germans had already come to the sober (but, for them, not surprising) conclusion that their

Austrian allies were unlikely to register a major victory on this or any other front, if left to their own devices. Their leadership, in the German view, was too erratic and indecisive; their planning too muddled, erring either on the side of over-caution or over-ambition; and the fighting quality of the troops just was not up to the exacting Prussian mark.

Nonetheless, the Germans were willing to consider a new joint thrust on the Eastern Front, if only because their own great offensive in the west had foundered. (Conrad's order to retreat to the River San coincided almost exactly with Moltke's withdrawal of his right wing in France.) So, a week before Christmas, Conrad left Teschen, the Silesian town where the Austrians had set up their supreme headquarters,* for talks with the Chief of German Army Staff, General Erich von Falken-hayn. These were held in the unlikely setting of the railway station at Oppeln, in Upper Silesia, and at first produced only deadlock. Only after some high-level squabbling in Berlin (with both Hindenburg and Bethmann offering the Kaiser their resignations over the issue) was it agreed to form a new combined force, the so-called 'Army of the South', to advance in midwinter on the besieged Przemyśl. This relief army was not so much combined as mixed up together like a shuffled pack of cards, with German and Austro-Hungarian troops serving alongside one another even at divisional level.

The experiment – never to be repeated on this scale – proved a depressing one. Three separate Carpathian offensives, running from January through to March, failed to reach the beleaguered fortress, despite heavy losses, including thousands of men who simply froze to death. After one desperate attempt by its garrison to break free had been crushed, a starved-out Przemyśl surrendered to the Russians on 22 March 1915. The siege had not matched the 217 days of Mafeking's resistance; nor, in the end, had it been relieved. On the contrary, another 120,000 Austrians now joined the 200,000 of their comrades who were already in Russian prisoner-of-war camps.

The collapse of these combined offensives left two ugly traces behind. The first was a permanent worsening of relations between the two allies, each of whom blamed the other for the costly failure. The German High Command moved from its attitude of military condescension towards its partners to one of suspicion and contempt. This spread into the

---

* They could not have made a more appropriate choice for a multi-racial empire. The town was divided in half by the river Olsa. Of its 25,000 inhabitants, 15,000 were Poles, living on the right bank, and 10,000 were Czechs, living on the left.

political and diplomatic fields, thus poisoning Austro–German relations at a time when they should have drawn closer. The omens for the dynasty were even darker. The freezing hell of those Carpathian winter campaigns quickly smothered that glow of loyal enthusiasm with which all the peoples of the Emperor had greeted the war six months before. Mass desertions, first noted in the autumn, steadily increased in scale until whole companies were running over to the Russians. Ominously, they were mostly Czechs, openly seeking refuge with their big Slav brothers. The ethnic seams of the Monarchy's army had already started to fray.

The lower the opinion the Germans had of their allies, the more resigned they became to stiffening their performance, though in campaigns which, wherever possible, the Germans would themselves plan and control. This became a regular feature of the fighting which followed. When the allies returned to the attack on the Eastern Front in May 1915, for example, General August von Mackensen was placed in overall command, and it was another Prussian, his Chief of Staff, General Hans von Seeckt, who had devised the operational plan. In contrast to the winter débâcle, this offensive proved a spectacular success, but only for so long as it was led by German brains and brawn. Four Austro-Hungarian and three German armies (including Mackensen's newly-formed Eleventh at the centre of the line) rolled forward on 1 May along a 180-mile line which stretched south of Warsaw all the way down to Bukovina. The Russian forces, outnumbered and caught napping, were routed.

Within a fortnight, the advance had cleared the whole eighty-mile stretch from the Carpathian foothills back to the fateful River San. On 3–4 June, Przemyśl itself was retaken. For the Austrians, there were two bitter tastes to these fruits of victory. The first was another crop of mass desertions – this time in summer weather – from the Seventh Army fighting in the extreme south. The second was that the recapture of Przemyśl, though duly celebrated throughout the Monarchy as a triumph of its heroic soldiers, had been mainly the work of Mackensen's men. The Germans tactfully allowed their allies the public laurels; but a greater Austrian embarrassment, and one which could not be dismissed, lay ahead.

After the retaking of Lemberg and the forcing of the River Bug defence line, Mackensen's onslaught finally ran out of steam, and of supplies, in mid-August. At the end of the month, Conrad began a follow-up attack all on his own, the so-called 'Black Yellow' offensive, to prove that the Monarchy did not need German help to defeat their common enemy. Despite having almost twice the strength of the Russians who opposed him, the thrust ended in dismal failure. Again, it was Austria's General Muddle which served the enemy best. Back at Teschen, there were constant squabbles and intrigues over the chain of command and the strategy to be followed. In the field, there were failures of leadership and, all too often, of fighting morale. Within a month, the Eighth Russian Army of General Brusilov (a name the Austrians were to hear much more of the following year) were counter-attacking with skill and grit. Conrad continued to flail out in defiance, but only worsened his predicament. By mid-October, when he accepted defeat, he had sacrificed for his vainglorious dream more than 230,000 men, nearly two-thirds of his striking force. Of these, about 100,000 had been taken prisoner. The numbers of German soldiers captured or missing during these Eastern Front campaigns was but a small fraction of such percentages. The contrast said everything.

It was the same story that autumn in the Balkans, where the Central Powers, now strengthened in that region by the recruitment of Bulgaria to their alliance, launched their fourth offensive against Serbia. Mackensen, despatched south to conduct this campaign, set up his headquarters at Temesvár in Transylvania, from where he proceeded to issue orders to his Austrian and Bulgarian allies. Conrad's attempts to gain command himself of operations in this backyard of the Dual Monarchy were brusquely rejected. It was perhaps just as well, for nothing would have bettered Mackensen's onslaught. He began the attack on 6 October; five days later Belgrade was again in allied hands; by the end of the month, the bedraggled and half-starving Serbian army had been driven right back into Montenegro, leaving tens of thousands of prisoners behind. There were as good as no Serbian deserters.

These crushing victories in Russia and the Balkans, combined with the deadlock on the Western Front, meant that as 1916 dawned, the Central Powers did not envisage defeat, and could even hope for victory. It is one of those phases in the Great War which are so easy to ignore when looking back from the perspective of November 1918. Yet this was a moment when the balance of advantage between the warring camps was so finely poised that a compromise peace between them would have been feasible. That, in turn, would have meant the survival, in some form, and at least in the short term, of all three continental empires. It was not to be: the only serious peace moves were to come too late.

The only loss suffered by the Central Powers which affected the overall balance of the alliances had been the defection of Italy from their ranks. It was not unexpected. Her loyalty from the start of the war had been blatantly up for sale, and the massive territorial bribes offered to her by the secret 'Treaty of London' swung the scales in the Entente's favour.* In May 1915, she declared war on her partners and promptly unleashed a pre-prepared offensive on the Trentino and Isonzo River fronts. For psychological reasons already explained, it was here that the Austrians fought well enough without their allies to hold their own, at least in this first phase of the campaigns. The Italian commander Cadorna opened his main attack on 23 June. When that petered out, he renewed the offensive in the autumn, only to be held again by stubborn Austrian resistance. By the time he finally called a halt in December, his losses had risen to over 275,000 men, almost twice those suffered by his opponents.

Single-handed Austrian success in Italy was, however, the exception to the general military pattern which was emerging. 1915 had seen the Germans laying the foundations of their dominance in the alliance. Throughout 1916, the Austrians helped them to complete the process. The key battleground in this respect was again Russia, though in the spring and summer of 1916 all the war fronts were interacting on one another. In the west, the great German onslaught against Verdun had finally been checked, but the Austrians took the opportunity to launch an offensive of their own in the Trentino. Italy appealed to Russia (her ally since 1915) to put renewed pressure on the Austrian forces in Galicia so as to prevent them sending any reinforcements to the Southern Front. After arguments with his Supreme Command, General Alexei Brusilov, who had given the Austrians plenty to think about the year before, was allowed to launch an offensive by himself. His first blow, struck on 4 June, fell on the Fourth Austro-Hungarian Army at Luck, on the north of the 150-mile battle line. It crumpled like tinfoil. Brusilov took some 40,000 prisoners on the first day, and by the sixth had driven fifty miles

---

* As well as twelve Dodecanese islands from Turkey and a few colonial pickings in Africa, Italy was promised – all at Austria's expense – the whole of the Trentino up to the Brenner Pass, with some 250,000 German-Austrian inhabitants, plus the great port of Trieste, most of Istria and about half of Dalmatia, with strings of Adriatic islands attached.

westwards, rolling up the entire Fourth Army front. Its commander, the ineffective Archduke Joseph Ferdinand, was replaced on the spot by a career general. This unprecedented step gave some idea of the panic which had broken out at Teschen, souring the easy-going atmosphere of concerts, hunting expeditions and family gatherings which characterised social life at Austrian headquarters.

Worse was to come. On the tenth, another Austrian army, the Seventh, which was defending the extreme south of the line in front of Czernowitz, also collapsed. This second disaster produced the result the Italians had been hoping for. The Austrian offensive in the South Tyrol was broken off as reinforcements were rushed up to Galicia. There was another ominous result: the Prussian General von Seeckt was summoned once more to the rescue, this time installed as a 'supervisory' Chief of Staff to the decimated Seventh Army. Conrad again protested at this imposition of German control, but again in vain. The plain fact was that in 1916, as in 1915, it was the Austrian armies which had been routed while German forces had held firm.* The conclusions were inescapable, as was their effect on the chain of command.

Two other by-products of the Brusilov campaign – the last major military contribution which Russia made to the war – need noting. The first was the opportunist defection of Romania to the Entente camp, a decision she was rapidly to regret. The second was the surprise appointment of the young heir-apparent, Archduke Charles, to command an entire new Army Group of combined Austrian and German forces in Galicia. His Chief of Staff was the omnipresent von Seeckt. The Archduke's close day-to-day experience of the Prussian ethos in action was an instructive memory he was to carry with him as emperor.

For the rest of the year, the German army carried all before it. In July and August, the so-called 'Hindenburg Front' finally broke the challenge of Brusilov's offensive, and there were even more spectacular results when the Germans turned their attention to the foolhardy Romanians. Just before they launched their Balkan campaign, the Germans had achieved their goal of supreme command over all the forces of the Central Powers. The proclamation to this effect, finalised on 7 September, placed that command formally in the hands of the German Emperor. In reality, of course, it was now Hindenburg and Ludendorff

---

* By the time Brusilov's advance came to a halt before the Carpathian mountain barrier, he had taken some 350,000 Austrian prisoners who, once again, included Czech deserters.

who exercised military control over the Dual Monarchy. Despite various face-saving formulae designed to soften the blow for Francis Joseph (the integrity of whose empire was guaranteed as a pillar of German policy), this was a twentieth-century political triumph of 'Greater Germany', as well as a dynastic triumph of Hohenzollern over Habsburg.

The old Austrian Emperor, still to his dying day also 'a German prince', did not take it nearly so badly as Conrad, who had fought to the end for independent command. What the Germans could achieve when they both planned and controlled an operation was now demonstrated against Romania. By the end of September, they had thrown back the Romanians advancing in Transylvania; by mid-November, they had broken through the mountain passes just before these were closed by snow; and on 6 December, General Mackensen's forces, after a brilliant pincer movement, entered Bucharest. The hopeful new entrant to the Entente camp had been disposed of in less than four months.

A fortnight before that final triumph in the Balkans, however, all eyes in the Dual Monarchy had turned from the battlefields to Vienna. At five minutes past nine on the evening of 21 November 1916, Francis Joseph died in his plainly furnished bedroom in Schönbrunn. He had struggled on, signing his daily mound of documents, right into the final hours. Now the old heart, which for sixty-eight years had also set the heartbeat of his empire, stopped at last. With his death, a brief but astounding new chapter in the saga of Austro–German relations opened up.

II

Pot of Iron and Pot of Clay

THERE WERE MIXED FEELINGS among the silent crowd which, on 30 November 1916, watched the funeral procession wind through the streets of Vienna to the Capuchin Church where the dead Emperor would be laid to rest alongside his ancestors. For many, it felt as though the most powerful force in that cortège lay in the coffin. Life without Francis Joseph seemed unimaginable, as did an Austrian empire without him on its throne. The grief would have been greater in peacetime: two years of war had brought enough grief of their own to deaden the shock. Nonetheless, for all those mourners rooted in the past, the war itself now took on a more desperate look. The old Emperor had acquired an air of immortality, and that signified invincibility. Without him, the spectres of defeat and destruction loomed larger.

But, to judge by private diaries and other contemporary accounts, not all the onlookers felt like that. Many fixed their eyes on the trio following immediately behind the hearse: the twenty-nine-year-old new Emperor Charles, little known, but at least unblemished by the catastrophe of 1914; his twenty-four-year-old French-born Empress, a moving column of black, draped from head to toe in veils; and, between them, the four-year-old Crown Prince Otto, a speck of white with his blond hair and light tunic. Might they not represent a new and brighter future, an escape route from the war, and survival after it? Charles's great-uncle may have been the bedrock of empire, but perhaps that dynastic rock had become so fossilised that only now could something new and green grow out of it.

The proclamation which Charles issued the day after his accession gave some hope of fresh life. The domestic scene was dealt with only in benign platitudes about 'promoting moral and spiritual welfare', 'preserving the equality of all before the law', 'protecting freedom' and so on. But the cry which followed for an end to the fighting was unexpected in its force to his subjects, his allies and his enemies alike: 'I will do everything to banish in the shortest possible time the horrors and sacrifices of war, to win back for my peoples the sorely-missed blessings of peace.' This was strong language for a ruler whose empire was committed to military victory, and for a soldier recently returned from commanding three imperial armies in search of that victory on the Russian front.

Subjects, allies and enemies would all have been far more surprised had they known the ideas which were already taking shape behind that pledge. Charles was not only resolved to end the war. He was also determined to end with it that subjugation of Habsburg to Hohenzollern which he had just witnessed in the field. It must be stressed that his thoughts on Germany had not first sprung up on the battlefield. They had been born in peacetime, and shaped largely by his marriage which, in itself, had foreshadowed much that was to come.

Austria's archdukes were restricted, by the iron laws of their faith, to Catholic brides; they sought these most readily among German royal families, with the women of Bavaria and Saxony cropping up time and again in the family tree. The doleful marriage of Crown Prince Rudolph to Princess Stephanie of Belgium did not break the blood tie. Her father, the odious Leopold II, was a Saxe-Coburg, from that miniature German house dubbed 'the stud farm of Europe' by Bismarck because of the marriage web it had spun across the continent, embracing even Queen Victoria of England. Moreover, Stephanie's mother, Queen Marie Henriette, was herself born an Archduchess of Austria.

Nothing could have been further from all this than the wedding, on 21 October 1911, of the young Archduke Charles to Princess Zita of Bourbon-Parma. She was one of the twenty-four children of Duke Robert of Parma,* who had been deprived of his kingdom, but not his virility, by the Italian Risorgimento. The ceremony was held at Schwarzau, a castle in the so-called Steinfeld, south of Vienna, which the Duke used as his summer residence, and where the bride and groom had played together as children. This was one solid and much-cherished

---

* He had produced twelve children by his first marriage to Maria Pia of Sicily and then – after her death from childbed exhaustion and his remarriage – another twelve, including Zita, by Princess Maria Antonia of Portugal.

Austrian link between the two families. They were also distantly tied in blood, for there were two Austrian archduchesses among Duke Robert's eighteenth-century ancestors. Yet he was first and foremost a Bourbon, and that meant first and foremost a Frenchman. 'We are French princes who reigned in Italy,' was his reply to Zita's question when, as a curious child, she had asked him to explain what her family really was.

The significance of Schwarzau and the wedding celebrated there in 1911 cannot be overestimated in the final chapter now opening in the saga of Habsburgs versus Hohenzollerns. The marriage had been a true love match between complementary opposites. Charles was of a pleasing but mild and unremarkable appearance, whereas Zita's face, which just missed dark-haired classical beauty, radiated intelligence and vitality. The contrast was reflected in their characters. Had he not been royal, the modest, decent and fair-minded qualities Charles was born with would have suited the requirements of some colonial governor in an honourable but undemanding career. Zita was born to be an empress, and no mere consort at that. She was the stronger personality and had the quicker mind of the two with, on top of this, a willpower of tempered steel. Yet though her influence over Charles was considerable, it was not, as many have portrayed it, dominant. His passion for peace owed nothing to her persuasion, for example, and could not have been deflected, had she opposed it, by any of her arguments. The same applied to his resolve, even as a young archduke, to modernise the empire which would one day be his.

The figure who was to prove of decisive influence on both their lives was that of Prince Sixtus, the oldest of Duke Robert's sons by his second marriage. Sixtus was one of the most remarkable behind-the-scenes operators of his time, and his significance for our story is that he strove throughout not merely to weaken German power but, if possible, to destroy it. The marriage of 1911, which gave him a brother-in-law who stood near the Habsburg throne, opened up great prospects even if, at the time, they seemed far removed. Long before the wedding, Sixtus and his less energetic younger brother Xavier had often debated with Charles and his circle how the Austrians could replace their rigid alliance with Germany by a looser and more congenial relationship with France and England. This was not just a matter of geographically shifting the Habsburg axis in Europe from the vertical to the horizontal, but of transforming it politically from the conservative to the democratic mould.* Many of these talks between the young royals had taken place on the broad balcony of Schwarzau castle where, at Charles and Zita's wedding, an exceptionally jovial Francis Joseph had marshalled the guests for the marriage photographs.

When the outbreak of war came to split up the families, the Bourbon princes gathered, for the last time, on that same balcony.** But war and separation only intensified the Sixtus campaign to attack Germany through its Austrian ally. His brother-in-law, heir-apparent after the Sarajevo murders, now appeared as the heaven-sent ally, and it mattered not one jot to Sixtus that Charles stood in the opposing camp. The enemy of France could surely be turned by dynastic diplomacy into the instrument of French interests. Indeed, with the war only five weeks old, Sixtus transmitted, via Luxembourg, his first secret letter to his sister in Vienna. It urged her without ceremony to start working for a complete rupture in Austro–German relations. How that was to be achieved with the armies of the two allies advancing side by side in their first joint offensive against Russia was not spelt out. No one, in these early days, realised how shifting fortunes on the battlefields were to overshadow all parallel moves to end the fighting. Sixtus was, in any case, only laying the foundations for a long-term strategy: March of the following year saw him at the Vatican, trying to persuade Pope Benedict XV to work for a separate peace between Austria and the Entente powers.

In the months that followed, he cultivated the interest of the French authorities who came to realise that he was the perfect tool to drive a royal wedge into the enemy camp. He was a Bourbon prince, a fanatical Frenchman, and a rampant political animal; yet he held no official post and could therefore be disavowed if necessary. On the other hand, the future Emperor of Austria was his brother-in-law and a man over whom he clearly had personal influence. The idea of using him as an emissary gradually gathered strength in Paris. The former Foreign Minister, War

* According to accounts of these family discussions given later by the Empress Zita to the author, a federation or confederation of nations was envisaged under the Habsburg crown which might include even republics – a feat of political juggling which only the British Commonwealth was to achieve.
** Sixtus and Xavier returned, not without difficulty, to Paris and the Entente camp. Thanks to the intervention of the old Emperor, they were allowed to leave Austria on 22 August, having spent a fortnight on enemy soil. Three other brothers, the Princes Elias, René and Felix, who had been brought up in Austria, stayed behind and soon joined the imperial army.

Minister and Premier, Charles de Freycinet, became his chief sponsor, and by the autumn of 1916 the Sixtus campaign was in full swing.

In November, the Prince finally got down to discussing the detailed framework of his mission with Jules Cambon, the pre-war ambassador to Berlin who was about to be appointed General Secretary at the Quai d'Orsay.* They quickly agreed on the imperatives. France must at all costs regain Alsace-Lorraine and thus wipe out the shame of 1870. On the other hand, Austria must accept the loss of those southern territories promised by the Entente powers to Italy by the secret bribe of 1915. Perhaps the Habsburg empire could be compensated with the acquisition of Serbia after Germany's defeat? More important than the substance of all this exalted talk was the date. The discussion took place on 23 November 1916. Francis Joseph had died two days before. The Prince's brother-in-law was now Emperor of Austria-Hungary and had just issued from Vienna his loud cry for peace.

That was not the only encouraging signal from the young ruler, for Charles had promptly set about removing the hawks of 1914 from their perches and replacing them with untainted figures after his own heart. Thus, Berchtold had lasted only a month into the new reign.** On 22 December he was replaced as Foreign Minister by Count Ottokar Czernin, whom Charles took for a man of peace and also a loyal servant of the crown. He was to prove partially correct in the first belief but hopelessly wrong in the second. Czernin was to become the most controversial and scandal-ridden of any minister in living memory who had served the Habsburg crown. He was a human and political enigma to everyone around him – perhaps even to himself. There were only two constants in his erratic temperament. The first was a fierce pride in the honour and standing of his ancient Bohemian lineage, a pride which was obsessive even by the neurotic standards of his caste.*** Stemming from this came a sublime over-estimation of his political talents. When put to the test of high office, his brilliance lacked depth and his energy lacked stamina. He was another of Austria's would-be Bismarcks, yet

* Cambon was one of a brilliant family duo who shaped French diplomacy of the day. His brother Paul was the long-serving ambassador in London.

** He was offered, and accepted, the purely ceremonial post of Chamberlain at Charles's court. Though his social graces were better than his political qualities, it was a ludicrous comedown for the man who had helped to launch the Great War.

*** An ancestor headed the court of King Przemyśl in the year 1200, well before the Habsburgs began to play any role on the European scene.

without either the statesmanship of the Iron Chancellor or his unshakeable devotion to his monarch.

Czernin thus becomes another key example of the conflicting tendencies at work in the Austrian character. He had been a prominent member of Francis Ferdinand's 'Belvedere Circle'. Like the murdered Archduke, he wanted to cut the Hungarians down to size and could be classed as a 'Greater Austrian' whose aims could best be realised in peacetime. That is, if they could be realised at all, for there were times when Czernin privately despaired at whether anything could save the wobbly Habsburg edifice from collapse – in which case, like Francis Joseph, he could only advocate 'an end with dignity'. There were other ways in which Czernin reflected the contrasting images in the Austrian mirror. He admired Germany and did not seek her destruction. Indeed, he was always in two minds about any step which might be construed as a renouncing of the alliance. As Foreign Minister he worked closely with his German colleagues and, as we shall see, fell drastically under their spell towards the end. This produced more than ambivalence towards his own sovereign; it resulted finally in betrayal. Nonetheless, at the time of his appointment it seemed as though Austrian diplomacy was entering a more confident, as well as a more flexible, phase.

All that remained for the young Emperor wielding his new broom was to make similar changes in the military field. This took more time, for General Conrad, the other supreme hawk of 1914, was a more formidable figure to sweep aside than the obliging Berchtold. The first tussle between Charles and his solidly entrenched Chief of Staff had come over the Emperor's decision to transfer the Monarchy's military headquarters from Teschen in Silesia all the way down to Baden, the cosy little spa town in the wine hills just south of Vienna. Though overall control of the Central Powers' strategy and operations still remained in German hands, the move was designed to put some distance, psychologically as well as geographically, between the two imperial armies. Charles's assumption of supreme personal command over all the armed forces of his empire (promulgated less than a fortnight after his accession) had served the same end.

Conrad's resistance to the move was brushed aside and it duly took place on 3 January 1917, with Charles installing himself and his personal staff in a modest yellow-washed villa off the main square of the town.*

---

* These quarters, though cramped, had an atmosphere which appealed to the imperial couple. And Laxenburg, their favourite castle, lay nearby, enabling Charles to 'commute'.

That left only Conrad himself to be displaced. It was a prospect which petrified many of his fellow generals who nourished the legend of his military genius, despite there being so little real evidence of it in action. Charles remained adamant and, after a long tussle, Conrad was finally dragged kicking into resignation on 27 February 1917. He was consoled somewhat by the award of the Grand Cross of the Maria Theresa order and the appointment to command the Monarchy's forces in Italy, a front where great things were being planned. His replacement was the Infantry General Arz von Straussenberg, whom Charles had known as a capable Corps Commander in Galicia. If uninspiring, von Straussenberg was solid and dependable. The young Emperor had had enough of military geniuses, just as he had had enough of military hawks.

These developments were all of import for the immediate future of the Dual Monarchy, as well as for its relationship with its German senior partner. But they paled into near-insignificance before other happenings in the first months of the new year, which transformed the entire character of the war. On 1 February, Germany launched her unrestricted U-boat offensive against all neutral as well as enemy shipping, in the hope not merely of breaking the economically crippling British naval blockade of Germany, but of bringing Britain herself to her knees with starvation. Six weeks later, on 15 March (February in the Russian calendar), Tsar Nicholas II abdicated before a tidal wave of hunger strikes at home and mass desertions on the battlefield. Though the first Provisional Government, headed by Prince Georgi Lvov, proclaimed continued loyalty to the Entente, the revolutionary soldiers and sailors who had done so much to spark off the explosion were already turning Russia's back on the war. Moreover, it was soon clear that the well-intentioned Prince would not last long against the radical workers' and soldiers' councils, the so-called Soviets, who were snatching power in garrison after garrison, factory after factory, and town after town throughout this crumpled giant of a realm.

Yet, as one huge door was swinging shut for the Entente, another, even greater one, was opening. On 6 April the United States, incensed, among other provocations, by the sinkings of its own commercial shipping, declared war on Germany.* Though nothing tilted immediately on the military scales, the Entente had gained a potential increase in

---

* America's declaration of war against Austria-Hungary did not come until eight months later, on 17 December 1917.

strength from the west which far outweighed the Russian support drain-
ing away in the east. All of these events produced, behind the scenes,
their impact on Austro–German relations and, in particular, on the
fraying ties of solidarity between the two emperors.

Czernin had been told of the proposed U-boat offensive when paying
his first official visit to Germany on 5–7 January, and had brought the
news back to Vienna. Whatever deadly gaps were to open up later
between the Emperor and his Foreign Minister, the two men were at
one on this. Charles, in particular, was horrified, on both moral and
practical grounds. He was dubious about German boasts that even their
new fleet of 102 modern submarines (compared with the nineteen old
units available in 1914) would starve England into submission within
three months.* On the other hand, he was convinced that all-out German warfare in the Atlantic would inevitably drag America into the war.
For Charles, the mere presence in Vienna of an accredited Minister from
the mightiest neutral left in the world was a beacon of hope, and he
had been at pains to cultivate the American envoy, Charles Penfield,
accordingly.

On 20 January, a powerful German delegation descended on Vienna,
headed by the Foreign Office Under-Secretary, Arthur Zimmermann,
and the Naval Chief of Staff, Admiral Henning von Holtzendorff, to
win their allies over to the new strategy. Charles himself presided over
one of the joint conferences; Czernin over the other. It was a case of
Cassandras shouting themselves hoarse into stopped-up ears. But
though the Austrians could not be convinced, they could be overruled,
for supreme control of the alliance rested with their partners. A week
later, on 26 January, Czernin travelled with his royal master to the new
German headquarters at Pless to convey acceptance of the U-boat plan.
If their consent was grudging, the timing at least was gracious. The
next day was the Kaiser's fifty-eighth birthday.

Much talk of peace had swirled around these changes in global strategy, if only because at the end of 1916 the balance of advantage between
the warring camps was again finely poised. On the major fronts, the
days of envelopment and seemingly all-conquering advances were over.
The Schlieffen Plan had failed, and fighting in the west was literally
bogged down in trench-war struggles for a few miles, or even a few

---

* They came dangerously close: by April 1917, Britain was down to a few weeks' grain
stocks due to the sinkings. New anti-submarine techniques eventually turned the tide.

yards, of Flanders mud. Both in Russia and in Italy, rival armies surged forward, and then back, across the same familiar river lines. Only in the Balkans, where small countries like Serbia and Romania were their quarry, could German-led campaigns sweep up all before them in heroic Prussian style. It was on 12 December 1916, a week after Mackensen had entered Bucharest, that the Central Powers thought the moment ripe to publish from Berlin their long-debated peace appeal to the Western democracies. The note was brief, somewhat haughty in tone, and without a single concrete proposal. It was promptly rejected with equal haughtiness by the Entente powers as being simply a 'war manoeuvre'.

Then, a week after the abortive German approach, America's President Wilson entered the political stage he was ultimately to dominate with an enquiry to both warring armies about the terms on which they might be prepared to settle. The Entente powers replied on 11 January with a long list of preconditions which ranged from the restoration of Belgium, Serbia and Montenegro to the evacuation of all invaded territories and the total expulsion of the Ottoman empire from Europe. Reparations and indemnities were demanded all round. If the Germans had said too little in their note, the Entente had perhaps said too much. But what killed Wilson's first mediation move stone-dead was the tone in which it was rejected in Paris. 'The only basis for future peace,' the French Prime Minister Aristide Briand declared, 'is the capitulation of the Central Powers.' Language like that meant that only total exhaustion in one of the warring camps would force them to lay down their arms.

The return of Alsace-Lorraine to France had not been listed among the territorial requirements of the Entente, though it was known to be a *sine qua non* of French demands. However, the two provinces were now about to be entered by name in the exchanges between the two sides, and the man who, more than anyone else, got them written in was the indefatigable Prince Sixtus. On the night of 23 March 1917, accompanied by Xavier, he arrived in a snowstorm at Laxenburg Castle on his semi-official secret peace mission to his imperial brother-in-law. After a long series of Byzantine contacts with French officials in Switzerland, the two princes had been smuggled in civilian disguise across the frontier into Austria and so, via an overnight hiding-place in Vienna, to this extraordinary rendezvous.*

* They were now serving as lieutenants in the Belgian Army. As Bourbons they were forbidden by a Republican law of 1889 to serve in the French Army, and had tried in vain to be enrolled as interpreters in the British Army.

Sixtus brought with him a number of preconditions, such as the restoration of Belgium and Serbia, already put forward by the Entente. To these he added the demand for a pledge of personal support from his brother-in-law for the return of Alsace-Lorraine. Much more: he insisted that Charles should put down this pledge in writing, as Emperor of Austria. Verbal promises, he assured him, were not enough to satisfy Paris; indeed, Sixtus had already been at work preparing documents in draft. While this was being debated, Czernin arrived to join the talks. The Foreign Minister (and he alone in the government) had been kept informed about the Sixtus contacts. He had reacted from the start with a classic display of Austro–German ambivalence.

On the one hand, he expressed enthusiasm for the venture, even penning a private letter to the Empress on 17 February urging her to pursue the family approaches with all speed. This note was, of course, signed. On the other hand, the guidance memorandum he wrote for the Emperor's contact group in Switzerland emphasised the 'indissoluble character' of the Central Powers' alliance and stressed that none of the partners could ever conclude a separate peace. To muddle up further this contradiction of his sovereign's thinking, he refused to put his name under this, or any other of his comments. Czernin was equally enigmatic now at Laxenburg. He remained reserved and vague, so much so that, the next day, when all but the royal couple were back in Vienna, the princes pressed Czernin for an assurance that he stood behind the Emperor's initiative. The assurance was eventually given, though it was hedged about with some very significant caution. 'Be very careful,' the Minister urged them. 'Remember the might of Germany and my own responsibility.'

Charles, in the meantime, had taken the plunge. The result was the famous Laxenburg letter of 24 March 1917 which he spent most of that day composing. He was aided, as regards the French text, by his wife, while Czernin was consulted by telephone over certain diplomatic niceties. When Sixtus returned to give a further hand with the drafting, he ended up with a veritable prize for France. At the heart of the letter, which was addressed to him as intermediary, was the sentence: 'I beg you to convey, secretly and unofficially, to M. Poincaré, President of the French Republic, that I will support the just claims of France to Alsace-Lorraine with all means at my disposal and exert all my personal influence with my allies to this end.'

This was a bold pledge to give, even verbally. Though Charles was

Duke of Alsace-Lorraine through the marriage of his great ancestress Maria Theresa to its ruler, the provinces had been for almost half a century part of the German empire. He was thus disposing of property which no longer belonged to him. To put the promise in his own handwriting was to advance from boldness to rashness. Both he and his empire were to pay a crippling price for a venture which had been as amateurish in style as it was over-ambitious in substance. When Sixtus departed for Paris, carrying off his copy of the letter, it was decided to hide all evidence of his visit, not in a safe, but stuffed into a heavy cupboard in Zita's bedroom. The papers consisted of numerous jottings about the talks and several drafts, all jumbled together without any record regarding the final version. This 'Sixtus Affair' was the last exercise in old-world dynastic diplomacy. It was hardly a brilliant advertisement for the art.

It was, in any case, dogged with bad luck from the start. By the time Sixtus got back to Paris with his precious autograph letter, the government of Aristide Briand, who had sponsored the venture (and who was to remain, even after the war, a champion of Austria and its royal house), had fallen. Alexandre Ribot was the new Prime Minister, an unimaginative figure who shared little of Briand's enthusiasm for these royal intrigues. It is true that his passivity was more than made up for by the blazing enthusiasm with which Britain's war leader had greeted the separate peace idea. Lloyd George had long been sickened and frustrated by the blood-soaked deadlock on the Western Front, and he leapt at the chance of aiming a blow at the German giant through her weaker partner in the south.*

But Italy, the third Entente partner involved, still had to be won over, and the venture foundered on 19 April in a railway carriage at the little French alpine resort of Saint-Jean-de-Maurienne. This was the odd setting for a tripartite meeting at which Lloyd George and Ribot, without revealing the secret of the Laxenburg letter, pressed the Italian Foreign Minister, Baron Sidney Sonnino, to consider in principle the idea of a separate peace with Austria. Sonnino responded with an absolute veto, even threatening to quit the alliance if the project were pursued. His reasons were no less clear for being unstated. Those huge territorial bribes proffered to Italy by the London pact of 1915 (which

---

* A forerunner of the similar strategy propounded by Churchill in the Second World War of striking at 'the soft underbelly of the Axis'.

Sonnino himself had negotiated) could only be cashed in if the war were pursued to the point of Austria's total military defeat. It was vital for Italy to have her traditional enemy knocked out in battle, not lured out, still undefeated, by bargaining. The Italian veto, which might have been anticipated from the start, buried the Sixtus mission as a diplomatic venture, though it lay for a year, still ticking under the ground, as a political time-bomb.

Meanwhile, Charles, like the Entente leaders, had been sounding out his crucial ally. First, Czernin went to Berlin for a general discussion about joint war aims with Bethmann-Hollweg. He met with a terse rejection from the German Chancellor when he gingerly suggested that perhaps part of Alsace might be returned to France in exchange for the French mining area of Briey-Longwy. Next, at Charles's suggestion, Czernin and the new Chief of Staff, General Arz, accompanied him to the little German spa of Homburg vor der Höhe for a 'summit talk' on 3–4 April with William II and that mighty duo, Hindenburg and Ludendorff.

At Homburg, as at Berlin, not a word was said about the Sixtus mission, let alone the Laxenburg letter. All that the Germans knew for certain was that Austrian and French spokesmen had been in contact in Switzerland, discussing, among other things, the future of Alsace-Lorraine. But they became a little suspicious, as well as puzzled, when a possible handover of the two provinces to France was again raised by the Austrian side, this time with a much grander inducement. The two allies had long been in dispute as to which of them should control the Polish kingdom they proposed to recreate after the war. Austria, who had wanted the new Poland ruled by one of their archdukes, or even by Charles himself, now raised the possibility of it passing under German control, with the Habsburg crownland of Galicia added on. All this for the return of Alsace-Lorraine to France. In the end, Charles achieved nothing because he had revealed nothing. The meeting ended in vapid platitudes.

The day after Charles regained his capital, the bad news he had long predicted was announced: America's declaration of war against Germany, a move which was bound to be followed eventually by a similar step against Austria-Hungary. Charles and Czernin – fully in agreement on this occasion – now despatched to the German leaders the blunt warning they should have issued face-to-face at Homburg. Czernin composed a dramatically pessimistic memorandum for his sovereign, who forwarded it with a personal note to William II. The fighting must be ended, Czernin wrote, because the Monarchy was almost at the end of its military strength. Moreover, though the Russian Revolution threatened the entire monarchical structure of Europe, Austria-Hungary was uniquely vulnerable because of its millions of Slav subjects. Another winter of hostilities could not be contemplated, especially as the vaunted U-boat offensive had failed to bring England down.

The dialogue of the deaf between the two allies continued on paper. William's reply was another German war chant of 'final victory': his submarines were winning the food battle against England (it had indeed been a record month of sinkings); North America had little grain to spare for her new allies; finally, in Russia, the extremists were in effect working for the Central Powers. It was in that same April of 1917 that the Germans acted to ensure that those extremists on whom they placed such hopes became even more extreme. The revolutionary leader Vladimir Ilich Lenin was smuggled out of his Swiss exile and conveyed in a sealed German train to St Petersburg, to hasten the destruction of Russia as a factor in the war. Here again, the allied monarchs saw different horizons through different spectacles. The eyes of the German Kaiser and his generals were fixed solely on the forty divisions of their army which could be transferred to the Western Front once the fighting in the east had stopped. For Charles, to insert Lenin into the war equation was to inject a fatal bacillus into the old European order, which it would surely end up by killing. His warnings to this effect were dismissed in Berlin as typical Viennese gloom-mongering.

There was indeed no shortage of gloom in Vienna, and throughout 1917 – the only complete year of his reign – the young Emperor tried to lighten it by any means he could on the domestic front. An answer had to be found to the overthrow of the Tsar and the establishment of what appeared at first to be a democratic regime in Russia. This exposed Vienna as the only warring capital in either camp to be ruled without even the outward shell of democracy. Parliament had not met once since 1914, its powers supplanted by the notorious Paragraph Fourteen of the 1867 constitution which amounted to rule by imperial edict. Charles and his advisers duly decided to reconvene it.

The great day arrived on 31 May 1917, and was surrounded by high expectations. However, the chance to herald a new political dawn by proclaiming, at least as a peacetime aim, national autonomy for all his peoples was allowed to slip away.* The Emperor's address to the Assembly confined itself to those same generalities about 'guaranteeing free national and cultural development' which had been issued from the throne for more than half a century. What the Slav deputies (and the Czechs, above all) wanted to hear about was not the development of autonomy but a pledge of its actual establishment. Yet it is worth noting that, despite a clarion call for 'Czech rights' issued from Prague in the so-called 'Authors' Manifesto', virtually everyone sitting in that reconvened Parliament envisaged national self-government as existing only within the framework of a multi-national empire.** Thus, among the Czechs, only the tiny Progressive Party, which had two seats, and the so-called Realist Party of the exiled Thomas Masaryk, which had no deputies at all apart from him, opposed the dynasty. In the spring of 1917, they could still be regarded as the lunatic fringe; not for another year were they to be moved, largely by outside hands, to centre stage.

If Charles had failed to proclaim the freedom of nations to Parliament, he at least acted, that same summer, to secure the freedom of nationalist agitators. Again, the Czechs were at the heart of the problem. In Francis Joseph's reign, their radical leader, Dr Karl Kramář, and three of his chief associates had all been sentenced to death by military tribunals, accused, among other delicts, of 'promoting the dismemberment of the empire'. The sentences, which had been suspended, were promptly commuted by the new Emperor to prison terms. Now Charles pushed his royal prerogative not only to its legal limit but to its political extreme. In the face of stiff opposition from his own political and military advisers at home, and the stern disapproval of his German allies abroad, he promulgated on 2 July 1917 a general amnesty for all persons 'sentenced by military or civil courts on charges of high treason, insults to the Royal Family, disturbance of the public peace, rebellion and agitation'. The only exceptions to the measure were military deserters or those, like Masaryk, who had turned their backs on the Monarchy by fleeing abroad. Otherwise, the pardon was complete and sweeping, and before

---

* This course had been pressed on the Emperor by his influential private secretary, Arthur von Polzer-Holditz, but was opposed by most of his ministers and, needless to say, by both the Austro–German and the Magyar magnates.
** In Budapest, where Magyars filled all but a handful of the 413 seats in the Parliament, all that was envisaged was the perpetuation *ad infinitum* of this racial dominance. Charles tried in vain to force the Hungarians into some form of universal suffrage as introduced in 1905 in the Austrian lands. On 15 May 1917, the great Tisza resigned over the issue.

the month was out 2593 political prisoners had walked out of jail.

This was a personal challenge by the Emperor to the conservative forces which surrounded his crown; he had not informed either Count Czernin or General Arz of his intentions in advance, knowing that both would try to argue him out of it. Even the Empress needed talking round to the idea. The amnesty was as far as Charles could go off his own bat towards appeasing nationalist agitation. Indeed, the tumultuous welcome given to the liberated Kramář when, on 15 October, he re-entered Prague like some victorious Roman general, suggested that the Emperor had gone too far for the Monarchy's comfort. But its immedi-ate comfort had not been in Charles's mind; rather its long-term chances of survival. Over in America, Masaryk himself had recognised the poten-tial importance of the amnesty, commenting that another step along those lines could well finish him off.

These midsummer glimpses of hope on the domestic front were matched in the autumn by the most spectacular triumph ever recorded by Austrian armies on the battlefield. The fact that it was scored at the expense of the Italians, Austria's most detested enemy, only sweetened the victory of Caporetto further. More sobering was another indisput-able fact, namely that it was planned and directed by German generals and executed largely by German troops. It was Ludendorff himself who had decided that if the Monarchy's dire warnings of its imminent col-lapse were to be countered, there would have to be a morale-raising offensive against Italy. Accordingly, General Krafft von Dellmensingen, a mountain warfare specialist who had played a leading role in the rout of the Roumanians, was despatched to the scene of action to discuss possibilities with the Austrian commanders there, above all the chastened Conrad. A small bridgehead which the Austrians still held on the west bank of the Isonzo between the towns of Flitsch and Tolmino was soon selected as the jump-off point.

Ludendorff's next problem was to find men for the joint attack. In the east, Russian pressure was still flickering under the Provisional Government of Kerensky. In the west, the German Army was under much stronger pressure from the new British offensive in the Ypres salient, a scandalously costly campaign which culminated in the grim and useless slaughter of Passchendaele. There was nothing for it but to call on the six divisions of the German general reserve for this temporary crash assignment. They were duly transferred to the Isonzo front where they formed up, along with nine Austrian divisions, in the newly created

Fourteenth Army commanded by a German, General Otto von Below, with Krafft as his Chief of Staff. This was the strike force which, on 24 October 1917, delivered the decisive breakthrough.

Its success was overwhelming. By the end of the month, a mere week later, the Austro–German forces had swept past Udine and were on the line of the River Tagliamento, an advance of some thirty miles. Twelve days later, they had covered another thirty and were across the next key river line of the Piave, where supply problems and Entente reinforcements eventually brought them to a halt. The attackers would have moved even faster had they not paused to gorge their rumbling stomachs with the undreamt-of quantities of good Italian food and wine. As it was, in this victory of Caporetto they achieved more than even the planners had hoped for. The Second Italian Army fleeing before them was as good as wiped out. The Italians had lost some 10,000 dead, with three times that number wounded and – the most significant statistic – nearly thirty times as many taken prisoner.

The Austrian people got their morale booster as the victory bells pealed out the length and breadth of the Dual Monarchy. Yet, ironically, the victory only heightened the friction between the military leadership of the two allies. The Austrian forces had played very much the second-ary role in the advance and had been sidelined in the planning. Conrad, predictably, had fumed. The Germans, predictably, had been enraged by what they saw as further evidence of Austrian flabbiness and muddle, especially in the faltering supply lines. Ludendorff's six crack divisions returned to their base convinced, more than ever, that the fortunes of war for the Central Powers rested firmly on German shoulders. The Quartermaster General himself had long been of that conviction.

And therein lay the political dangers of this unequal military partner-ship. Many years later the Empress Zita recalled a long walk with her husband near Schönbrunn Palace in August 1914 just before the young Archduke left to join his regiment at the front. He was worried, now that war had come, about the alliance between the two German empires, comparing it to La Fontaine's fable about the pot of iron and the pot of clay who set out walking amicably together. 'The Germans are the pot of iron, and if we go too far and too fast hand in hand with them, we will bang together, as in the story, and it will be our Austrian pot of clay that will be shattered.'*

---

* Anecdote told to the author by the Empress Zita at Zizers, 28 March 1985.

III

A Fatal Scandal

THE LAST TERRIBLE YEAR of the Monarchy's life began at a furious pace on all fronts. At home, the New Year's reduction of the basic bread ration to a scanty 165 grammes of flour per day touched off the most violent and widespread wave of food rioting which the long war had seen. It began on 14 January in the industrial centre of Wiener Neustadt, where the men of the Daimler engineering plant downed tools and besieged the town hall. Within the next five days, more than half a million Austrian workers had joined them in striking, and a ripple of sympathy protests ran all the way down from Galicia to Trieste. Nor by now did the anger concern only empty bellies and the prolongation of the war. Ideological appetites had been sharpened as well and, for the first time, Bolshevik slogans were shouted down the Danube's banks. The Lenin bacillus of which Charles had warned had indeed begun to infect the Monarchy. Its carriers were the deserters and released prisoners arriving from the Russian front; its exploiters were the political and racial extremists, with Czech radicals again to the fore. For them, the famous Communist call on proletarians of all lands to unite against the capitalist order became a summons to all Slavs to unite against the crown.

These outright revolutionaries were still in a small minority and, as always in the story of Austrian protesters, their lungs proved far stronger than their will. Nonetheless, the government and the court were sufficiently alarmed to prepare for suppression by military force. It was thanks largely to the calming influence of the Social Democratic Party that the violence ebbed away. Its own Workers' Councils neutralised the strike committees by absorbing them. Its organ, the *Arbeiter-Zeitung*, which had continued printing throughout the tumult, carried appeals from the leadership for a return to work. Perhaps these leaders, who included the veteran founder of the 1882 Linz Programme, Viktor Adler, as well as Karl Seitz and Karl Renner, sensed that their day would come (as it did) without blood being spilled in the streets. In the meantime, these pragmatic pillars of the left stood by the throne. Adler had pledged his support personally to Charles at a private talk with the Emperor; Renner, one of the Emperor's civil servants, conceived of reform only in the imperial context. Time and opportunism were to change much.

While these convulsions were shaking the home front, this first month of 1918 brought political developments abroad which were to shape the empire's whole future, along with that of the rest of Europe. On 8 January, President Wilson moved to the centre stage of diplomacy with the launching of his Fourteen Points as the platform both for peace and for a new world order. Our concern here is only with those two of the Fourteen which bore directly on the Dual Monarchy. Point Nine seemed to guarantee the post-war status of the quarter of a million Austrian Germans of the South Tyrol. Any readjustment to the frontiers of Italy, it stated, 'should be effected along clearly recognisable lines of nationality'. Point Ten referred directly to Austria-Hungary, saying merely that its peoples 'should be accorded the freest opportunity for autonomous development'.

This mild formula echoed precisely the pledge which Charles had himself made to the reconvened Parliament little more than six months before. That it accurately reflected current thinking in the Entente camp – namely that the Dual Monarchy remained, in some reconstituted form, part of the national order of things – was shown by flat statements to that effect issued by Western leaders. It was barely a month ago, after all, that America had finally declared war on Austria-Hungary, and the main motive behind that move had been to stiffen Italy. Wilson's support for the Monarchy, reaffirmed on 8 January, was thus hardly surprising. Even less so was a parallel statement issued three days earlier by Lloyd George which had even hinted at a strengthening of Austria-Hungary being in the Entente's interest.* So, of course, it was, provided that this went hand-in-hand with a weakening of Germany. This was the prime aim of everyone in the Western camp, and the British war leader had never abandoned the hope – first glimpsed by him during

* His speech to the Trades Union Congress on 5 January included the words (which had been cleared the day before by his Cabinet): 'We consider the existence of a strong Austria to be desirable.'

the Sixtus mission – of achieving it through a separate agreement with
Austria.

Indeed, when he spoke in favour of the Monarchy on 5 January,
Lloyd George was still digesting the first reports of the most remarkable
of all the secret peace moves ever staged between Vienna and the
Western democracies. These were the talks, held in Geneva on 18–19
December 1917, between Count Albert Mensdorff, the pre-war
ambassador to London, speaking for Austria, and no less a figure than
General Jan Smuts, the South African leader who was now a member
of the Imperial War Cabinet, representing Britain. It was Lloyd George
who had sponsored his mission so, unlike the unrealistic French feelers
put out the previous August,* this was a serious attempt, made with
the full authority of the British government, to get Austria out of the
war. Along with various suggestions for post-war territorial exchanges,
Smuts proposed nothing less than a programme of special assistance
from the British empire if Austria could free herself from German domination. 'If Austria were prepared to play that role and break with Germany,' he declared to an astonished Mensdorff, 'she would not only
have our sympathy but our active support and we would do everything
in our power to uphold and strengthen her and assist her economic
reconstruction.' Smuts went on to draw a seductive parallel between
the historic role of the two imperial powers. Provided Austria could
embrace liberal reforms, 'she would become for Central Europe very
much what the British empire had become for the rest of the world . . .
and she would have a mission in the future even greater than her mission
in the past'.

In Vienna, it was Czernin who directed proceedings (as he had done
during the earlier French–Austrian exchanges), and Czernin remained
at first doggedly loyal to the German alliance.** Indeed, he had
despatched Mensdorff to Geneva with orders to reject any suggestion
of a separate peace and to discuss only a general settlement which would
include Germany. As this was the exact opposite of the brief given to

* After an initiative from the French military, a French Army Major, Count Abel
Armand, had met the Austrian diplomat, Count Nicholas Revertera di Salandra at Frei-
burg, in Switzerland. The two counts exchanged various ideas as to how Austria might
gain compensation, at German expense, for ceding the Trentino to Italy. It was a *ballon
d'essai*, launched at low altitude, which never gained height.
** The Emperor, though informed of what was going on, left these formal diplomatic
contacts to his Foreign Minister.

General Smuts, it was hardly surprising that the talks became amicably deadlocked. The final face-to-face session began, again in Switzerland, on 9 March 1918. The General's negotiating partner on this occasion was the highly capable counsellor of the Austrian Legation who rejoiced in what must have been for Smuts a well-nigh unpronounceable name: Ladislaw von Skrzynno-Skrzynski. To begin with, there seemed to have been a complete change of heart on the Austrian side: yes, a separate peace could be discussed. But total evasiveness set in when Smuts tried to fix dates and details. After nearly a week of getting nowhere, the General departed empty-handed on 14 March and the contacts just melted away, like a will-o'-the-wisp, into thin air.

Certainly, Austria's need for peace had been growing no less urgent all this time. If January had been the month of food riots, February was the month of mutiny. On 1 February, sailors at the great Adriatic naval base of Kotor (Catarro) seized control of the entire Fifth Fleet of the Monarchy, which was lying at anchor there. The action was signalled by a shot fired from the *Saint Georg*, flagship of Admiral Hansa, whose officers were flabbergasted to hear their lunchtime band suddenly switch from Viennese waltzes to '*La Marseillaise*'. Soon red flags were fluttering, not only from the *Saint Georg*, but from almost every other of the forty-odd cruisers, destroyers and torpedo boats in the harbour. However, in all their meticulous preparations, the mutineers had forgotten one thing: to seize the fleet's communications system. The Austro-Hungarian Third Fleet was summoned up from Pola, and when it steamed in on 3 February, the rebellion collapsed. As ever, Austria's great ally also came to the rescue. Indeed, it was the sight of German submarines appearing in the harbour which finally overawed the mutineers.

The events at Kotor were, in military terms, puny compared with, say, the great French army mutiny of 1917. Yet their political significance for the Monarchy's fortunes was far graver, for it had also been a racial revolt. Of the four ringleaders eventually executed, one was a Czech and three were South Slavs. It had also been an ideological rebellion. The material demands of the mutineers largely concerned extra cigarette rations and longer shore leave. Their political demands were more substantial: immediate peace with Russia; acceptance of Wilson's Fourteen Points; and a democratic reform of the Monarchy. To emphasise the link with the Russian Revolution, Frantisek Ras, the Czech Social Democrat who was among those later to be executed, had set up his own 'Soviet' on board the flagship, a 'Central Council of Sailors' to which mutineers from all the captured vessels sent their representatives. The 'Soviet' on the flagship was short-lived; not so its revolutionary message, which sent a shudder through more than the officer complement – predominantly Austrian and Hungarian – of the Fifth Fleet.

On one thing at least the two allied Emperors and their advisers, military and civilian, could agree with the mutineers of Kotor: the need for a speedy peace with Russia. The Bolsheviks, who had duly seized power in November 1917, also came out with an immediate peace programme of their own, partly in the belief (which was to prove sadly misplaced) that this would spark off sympathy uprisings of the proletariat in Berlin and Vienna. But the Monarchy was in the direst need of all for a settlement, primarily to get its hands on grain supplies to ease the winter food crisis which was shaking the Austrian half of the empire. There was a mood of near-panic in Vienna lest the negotiations, which began in December 1917 at Brest-Litovsk,* should fail. Indeed, Czernin, who led the Austro-Hungarian delegation, had been instructed by his Emperor that if any breakdown were threatened by Germany's excessive territorial demands, the Dual Monarchy should conclude its own separate peace with the Bolsheviks.

The Austrian Foreign Minister was thus dealt a poor hand from the start. His game was not helped by the personal dominance of other players round the table: Leon Trotsky, the formidable revolutionary leader for Russia and, even more overpowering, Major-General Max Hoffmann, the bullheaded spokesman for the German High Command. After much brinkmanship, on 3 March 1918, Hoffmann secured a treaty which cut away from the new Bolshevik state a swathe of territory stretching from the Baltic down to the Black Sea. Czernin was powerless to prevent this annexationist programme of his ally, which was ominous for Austria-Hungary in that it demonstrated how a multi-national power could be split up into nationalist pieces by force. On the other hand, this same nationalism had enabled him to score his one success. The Ukraine, which had declared its independence from Russia on 22 January, proceeded to sign its own treaty with the Monarchy on 9 February: a separate peace at last. What Austria hoped to get from this was a million tons of grain (in fact, far less was to be delivered). The political

---

* The town on the River Bug, seventy miles east of Warsaw, which was then the seat of German Army headquarters on the Eastern Front.

price she had to pay was a heavy one. The Ukrainians demanded, and got, the Polish town of Cholm for their new republic. The result was a backlash of fury from the Poles in the Monarchy. Hitherto loyal to the crown, they now became restless and resentful. The 'Austro–Polish' formula as a solution to their future was as good as buried.

All such concerns were swamped under the wave of hysterical delight that Austrian stomachs would now be filled without begging for more grain from their reluctant German allies or from their tightfisted Hungarian partners. The treaty with the Ukraine was hailed, over-optimistically, as the 'bread peace'. The Emperor declared this to be the happiest day of his life and offered to make Czernin a prince (the Foreign Minister, proud enough to be Count Ottokar Czernin von und zu Chudenitz, declined). But, prince or not, when he returned to Vienna he was the popular hero of the day. Loyal addresses flooded in and a great service of thanksgiving was held in St Stephen's. The adulation mounted disastrously to his head.

It was, in more ways than one, a time for over-confidence. On 21 March 1918, the German Army, strengthened by the forty extra divisions transferred from the now silent Russian front, launched what was to prove their last great onslaught on the Western Front. Czernin had been told by Hoffmann that this so-called 'Kaiser's battle' was in the offing and that it would dispose of the Western Allies once and for all. It is significant that only a week before this offensive, of which so much was promised, Czernin had allowed the Mensdorff–Smuts talks to die away: there would surely be no need to negotiate peace if it could soon be imposed. To begin with, it seemed as though the headiest German predictions of victory were coming true. Within a fortnight, their forces had driven a salient forty miles deep – a colossal advance on the trench-warfare scale – into the front before Amiens held by the British Third and Fifth Armies. The line of the River Marne, and beyond that Paris, seemed in their sights.

It was in this heady atmosphere that, on 2 April, Czernin delivered what would these days be called a 'keynote speech' in Vienna. His immediate audience was a delegation of city councillors, headed by the Mayor, Dr Weisskirchner, who had called to thank him, in the capital's name, for the 'bread peace' with Ukraine. But Czernin's real target was the camp of the Entente and, in particular, Georges Clemenceau, the dynamic ex-journalist who had taken over as French Premier the previous November. Clemenceau was the personification of French revanchism and, in Czernin's eyes, now represented the greatest political obstacle to victory. Having settled with the Ukrainians and helped, however modestly, to dispose of the Russian Bolsheviks, the would-be Bohemian Bismarck turned his rhetorical guns on 'The Tiger' in Paris. Referring to the great German offensive which was already rolling up the Western defence lines in France, Czernin claimed that some while before it began, Clemenceau had put out a personal peace feeler to him. It had failed because the French leader had ruled out any compromise over the return of Alsace-Lorraine. Clemenceau, who had had no contact whatever with the Austrian Foreign Minister, was perfectly justified in issuing a flat denial.* However, the form in which he issued that denial went beyond the bound of diplomatic usage, even in wartime. Havas, the official French news agency, published on 4 April one terse sentence which the Premier had barked down the telephone at them: 'Count Czernin has lied.'

Throughout the following weeks the two men, both tinged with megalomania, bombarded each other in public with telegram and counter-telegram, whereby the communiqués from Paris edged steadily closer to the matter of Charles's written pledge to Sixtus.** Czernin was too flushed with conceit and fury to see the danger. Instead, he fired off more propaganda missiles at Paris, revealing in the process details of all and sundry secret contacts between the two camps, including the very recent Smuts–Mensdorff talks. Finally, Clemenceau lost patience and replied with a salvo which blew Czernin's case to smithereens. On 12 April, the French news agency published, for all the world to see, the full text of the Laxenburg letter of 24 March 1917, with its categorical promise that the Austrian Emperor would support, by all means in his power, 'the just claims of France regarding Alsace-Lorraine'.

The drama which now unfolded was preceded by twenty-four hours of black comedy which would have been hilarious in anything but such a tragic context. For when Charles and Zita hurried to the hiding-place in her bedroom at Laxenburg where the Sixtus documents had been

---

* Presumably, what Czernin had in mind were the Armand–Revertera talks in Switzerland; yet these had taken place, and fizzled out, in August 1917, three months before Clemenceau came to power.
** Already on 4 April the Quai d'Orsay had revealed, to a delighted Clemenceau, the Sixtus dossier, including the autograph letters of the Austrian Emperor. A solemn promise given by Sixtus that the letters would be shown to French leaders, but never let out of his sight, had been broken, or circumvented.

stowed away, draft after draft of the fateful letter tumbled out and they had no idea which was the definitive one. Indeed, another later version surfaced, dated 9 May 1917, which flatly contradicted the Sixtus letter by declaring that France's claim on the disputed provinces was, alas, *not* justified. Their memory alone told them that these were not the words Sixtus had carried away. The hapless imperial couple had made a truly imperial muddle of things and, from that muddle, terrible consequences were to flow.

The damage was universal. To the Western powers (and above all to President Wilson, whom Charles was striving so hard to impress with his sincerity*) the Emperor of Austria-Hungary appeared as a well-meaning but confused and somewhat devious bungler. This was embarrassing and unfortunate; but no more than that, for the Entente was still the enemy camp. It was with his German ally that the deadliest harm had been done. The anti-Habsburg camp headed by Ludendorff had long denounced the Monarchy as a feeble supporting arm in battle and a dubious partner in diplomacy. But now their Emperor stood revealed as somewhere between a double-dealer and an outright traitor to the alliance.

Charles had only made matters worse for himself by a personal message to the German Kaiser, despatched when the exchange of telegraphs with Clemenceau was approaching its climax, in which he assured his fellow-sovereign that the French Premier was lying and that 'I would fight for your provinces . . . as though I were defending lands of my own.' This woeful pretence was not made any more credible by an accompanying reference to 'Austro-Hungarian guns thundering alongside German ones along the Western Front'. The puny contribution which the Monarchy had always made to the German battle in the west had long been a sore point in Berlin. Now the Austrian Emperor seemed to have added false heroics to false dealings. But whatever he suspected about the goings-on in Vienna, William II sent back a supportive reply: of course, their enemies, having failed in a fair fight, were simply resorting to dirty tricks and, of course, the solidarity between their two empires would only be strengthened as a result. That heartening message

* In February 1918, for example, Charles had sent a personal appeal (via his kinsman Alfonso XIII of Spain) to the American President, asking for direct talks based on the Fourteen Points. Wilson replied that there was no use in a meeting until and unless certain concrete assurances were given in advance. These included 'the national aspirations of the Slav peoples' and, even more ominously, 'definite concessions to Italy'.

was received in Baden the day before Clemenceau played his 'dirtiest trick' of all, the publication of the Laxenburg letter.

In fact, whether William II was aware of them or not, some very sinister undercurrents in the Austro–German relationship had been swirling about weeks before the great wave of the Sixtus scandal broke. Early in March 1918, Austrian intelligence had reported to Charles that a *coup d'état* was being mounted to displace him temporarily, through a pro-German Regency, if not to dethrone him altogether. The conspiracy was said to have had its origins in the German High Command and its principal tool in Vienna was claimed to be none other than Count Czernin.

Those intelligence reports have not survived, nor has any other documentary reference to this alleged conspiracy, beyond a diary which, for the one and only time during her reign, the Empress kept of these sinister Ides of March. The mere fact that she had departed from her iron rule never to put on record anything about political events is, however, sufficient proof that the alarm had been raised. The diary, which covers the frenetic days from 2 to 14 April 1918, has an undated preface, written in staccato phrases as though the Empress herself could scarcely grasp what she was putting on paper:

> Warning of a conspiracy. Burnt all papers. Count Cz. becomes ever more intolerable: impulsive, superficial, nervous. Tried his hardest in January to persuade the Emperor to move [from Baden and Laxenburg] to Vienna ... Brest-Litovsk, great friendship with the German General Hoffmann. The plot was hatched there. Austrian and Hungarian generals, governors or senior provincial officials involved. Conspiracy among the aristocracy, archdukes ...*

Whether the plot really existed in these dimensions, and on the ground as opposed to in the air, will probably never be known. What is clear, again according to the first-hand account given in the diary, is that Czernin behaved like a conspirator – albeit a deranged one – throughout the crisis of the April 'war of communiqués'. Twice, on 12 and 13 April, he descended on Baden, trying to persuade his Emperor

* The diary was found by the author in the Habsburg private archives put together by the family over the years in Switzerland. Its reference in the extensive catalogue is Kassette 22, File 128.

into certifying that the real letter he had given to Sixtus was the discarded draft version which, among other things, had questioned France's right to Alsace-Lorraine. When hectoring failed, he tried bullying, and when that failed, blackmail. In a long session with the Emperor on the twelfth, he threatened that unless Charles gave him a written statement declaring the false letter to be the true one, he would 'immediately telephone Berlin to carry out the invasion'. Then the Emperor would have it on his own conscience to answer for the 'heap of ruins which would arise from the march-in and from revolution'. Charles, not deranged but sick and at the end of his tether, foolishly signed the declaration, which both men knew to be bogus, just to get rid of his exhausting visitor. The condition was the Minister's promise never to reveal its contents to a soul. He needed it, he said, 'just for the honour of his family'; it would never leave his locked desk. That same day, on his return to Vienna, Czernin showed how little regard he had either for his own honour or that of his sovereign. He published the declaration in full as part of another of his futile communiqués for Paris.

The final confrontation between Czernin and the imperial couple came when he descended on Baden again the following morning. As the Emperor was in bed with severe chest pains, the Empress had the tearful and overwrought Czernin to herself from 10 a.m. until 11.45 a.m. Her diary, which has added immediacy at this point, records a series of outbursts from the Foreign Minister which put even his behaviour of the previous day into the shade. He first threatened his own suicide. Alternatively, he suggested that all three of them should end their lives together. (This proposal was met by the Empress with the icy rejoinder: 'If ever I am to descend into Hell, I would prefer to go there in better company than yours.') Czernin then threatened the safety of her brothers who (as he had already claimed at breakfast time over the telephone) 'were in great danger of being shot'.

Finally, he came out with his solution to the quandary into which Clemenceau had plunged the Monarchy. Charles should admit to suffering from 'mental lapses', and state that it had been during one of these that he had penned the Laxenburg letter, which could no longer be denied. Accordingly, the Emperor should temporarily renounce power on health grounds and hand over to the popular Field Marshal Eugene, an archduke of the cadet Teschen line, as Regent. Real power, however, would rest with him, Czernin, who as 'Iron Chancellor' would negotiate a proper union with Germany. When that was accomplished, the

Emperor could return to his throne. Charles arose from his bed to join his wife in dismissing the idea as ludicrous: 'Where shall we end up,' he demanded, 'once we start declaring monarchs to be lunatics?' Only one thing stood out clearly in this tangle of confusion, blackmail and hysterics: Count Czernin would have to go. Resign he did, in a tearful fit of remorse during another brief session with the Emperor the following day. That reliable old packhorse, Baron Burian, was summoned by Charles back to office again as his successor.

Apart from the historic interest of the Empress's diary, the drama is worth recounting in some detail for two reasons. The first is the personal example it provides of that tug-of-war between an Austrian and a Germanic identity which had already wreaked such havoc in the Monarchy, and was to do even more damage to its successor. Czernin was a Monarchist who remained intensely proud, for example, of his Order of the Golden Fleece. This was an order that only the Habsburg Emperor could bestow on illustrious Catholic recipients, and which Charles had invested him with shortly before their ways had parted.* At that parting Czernin was happy to accept, as a figleaf to cover up embarrassment all round, the Monarchy's next highest honour, the Grand Cross of the Order of St Stephen with Diamonds. Yet the fact that the German Emperor also chipped in for the occasion with his own Iron Cross, First Class, showed the other side of the coin. If Czernin was really guilty of treachery, he was a traitor in the German cause.

But there is another and far more important reason for recounting the Sixtus scandal of April 1918. It led, swiftly and directly, to nothing less than the burial of the Habsburg empire as an independent force in world politics and so, ultimately, to its own burial as a state. This is the crowning irony of Charles's reign: the bungled peace initiative by which he had hoped to rescue his realm ended up by destroying it.

His private explanation to the German Emperor that a bilateral understanding with France would only have served as a preliminary to a general agreement between the two camps was brushed aside by Hindenburg and Ludendorff. By now, the Supreme War Lord had been reduced to a mere puppet who danced on the stage to their strings.

* After the war, when the widowed Zita was living in exile with her children in Spain, Czernin pleaded in letter after letter not to be expelled from the order because of his behaviour in 1918. One such letter, dated 14 December 1923, contained the admission that, in those troubled times, 'I committed the most serious mistakes which I deeply regret' (Habsburg Archives, K 22, File 84).

Apologies and protestations of good faith from the Austrian side were of no use to the German High Command. What they wanted were guarantees that the sinner could never stray again from the path of loyalty, and these could only be achieved by binding him hand and foot to the German war chariot. The clamour from Berlin for steps to 'clear the air' was matched, during the last fortnight of April, by pressure on Charles from both Burian and General Arz to reassure their ally.

The outcome was another top-level gathering in occupied Belgium at the Germany Army headquarters at Spa, but this time it was for Charles a journey to Canossa. The agreement, which was signed there on 12 May 1918 and embellished with the seals of the two emperors, followed the outlines of a text already drawn up in Berlin. It bound the allies to the conclusion of 'a close and long-term political treaty between the two empires'; to the creation of a 'military union'; and to the achievement of 'maximum possible economic coordination', with the ultimate aim of establishing a single tariff-free unit. This threefold German penetration was annexation in disguise, and closely resembled the '*Zusammenschluss*' or fusion policy which Adolf Hitler originally had in mind for his old homeland twenty years later.

To leave no doubts over the Monarchy's future status in the partnership, Field Marshal Hindenburg and General Arz signed a separate Directive (also virtually identical with the German draft) for strengthened military ties. These included provisions for uniform, training and organisation; for standardised equipment, arms and ammunition; for a coordinated railway construction programme and even for an exchange of officers.* All this, it was blandly stated, would be essential 'for future wars'. Again, it was to be left to Hitler to fulfil that part of the programme. What mattered for the current war was that Austria had gone to Spa as a junior partner and had returned as a satellite.

There was much criticism in both Vienna and Budapest of the humiliation which the Dual Monarchy had suffered at German hands. But this was of little significance compared with the deadly impact it produced in the enemy camp. In January 1918, both the American President and the British Prime Minister had publicly declared their support for the Dual Monarchy, albeit in a reformed and democratised condition. In

---

* The only clause which the Austrians managed to reject was the proposal to switch troop contingents between the two armies. They did not need to argue for very long. Even Ludendorff soon realised that there would be little point in having Croat or Slovene regiments in a German 'fight to the finish against the Slavs'.

March, speaking through General Smuts, Lloyd George had offered the Monarchy full support as a continental mirror-image of the British empire, provided that it cut loose from Germany. Now the German knots had been pulled so tight that Austria, it was clear to everyone, could never wriggle free. They would both therefore have to be destroyed, roped together as they stood.

On 30 May, little more than a fortnight after the Spa Treaty became known, the American Secretary of State, Robert Lansing, wrote in a memorandum to the White House: 'The Habsburg Monarchy has clearly now become a satellite of Germany. It must be blotted out as an empire.' Wilson returned the memorandum with the two-word endorsement: 'I agree.'

Britain had reached much the same conclusion. A Foreign Office memorandum presented to the Cabinet that same day stressed that the Treaty of Spa had converted a military alliance into 'a permanent community of interests'. Lloyd George could not dissent from the verdict. The policy he had doggedly pursued for more than a year, designed to split the two Central Powers apart, would have to be abandoned. That meant abandoning the Habsburg Monarchy to its fate.

It was now, and only now, that the cause of radical nationalism began to triumph, steered by the North and South Slav leaders from abroad. Politicians in exile are usually more extreme than their fellow-spirits at home, if only because they have no need to compromise with the realities of everyday life. The exiled opponents of the Monarchy during World War One were no exception. Thus, as far back as July 1917, the former Serbian Prime Minister Nicholas Pašić and the Croat leader Ante Trumbić had proclaimed, from their comfortable asylum in Corfu, the merging of the South Slav peoples into a post-war union of Serbs, Croats and Slovenes (conceived of as a kingdom under the Serbian Karageorgević dynasty). Yet the three peoples concerned had never been consulted as to their wishes, and the Croats, in particular, were uneasy in case they would only be exchanging submission to Budapest for subordination to Belgrade.* Indeed, until the summer of 1918, three rival concepts of the south Slavs' future – the Yugoslav federal solution of the exiles; the 'Greater Serbia' dream of rule from Belgrade; and some version of

---

* A justifiable fear, as events proved. Very soon after the creation of the post-war Yugoslavia, Croat nationalists were up in arms. Their Peasant Party leader, Stepan Radić, was thrown in jail, and eventually murdered, for demanding greater autonomy within the Triune State.

the old 'Trialism' within a reformed Habsburg Monarchy – had swirled indecisively around one another. That last alternative rose and fell with the empire's changes of fortune in battle, but it was only after the great turning-point of Spa that it was abandoned altogether. As Trumbić declared, in leaflets dropped soon afterwards by Italian planes over the South Slav lands: 'The [Western] Allies are now all convinced that Austria can no longer exist after the war. Now we can achieve our freedom, and our union.'

It was a similar story in the case of the Czechs who now, more than ever, became a prime factor in determining the Monarchy's future. A special factor was in play: the Czech Legion, formed in Russia by Masaryk from prisoners-of-war released after the peace treaties of Brest-Litovsk. This extraordinary fighting force had both monarchist and Bolshevik splinter groups in its ranks, thus epitomising the general confusion about the future shape of things. Yet, by the summer of 1918 it had settled down as a disciplined anti-Bolshevik army, some 50,000 strong, which had seized and held control of the vital Trans-Siberian railway on behalf of the Western Allies, then engaged in a muddling battle against the Soviet revolution. The Legion was formally under French command and took its directions from the Paris-based Czech 'National Council'. Thus whatever ambivalent feelings the Czech leaders at home still harboured about the Habsburg Monarchy,* the exiles abroad had become co-belligerents in the Entente's fight against that Monarchy. When, therefore, on 29 June 1918, France became the first of the Western Allies to recognise the Czech National Council as the 'prime basis of future government', it was with an eye on the Russian battlefields as well as on the transformed political picture in Central Europe. One way or the other, the French decision (followed by Britain on 14 August and by the United States on 3 September) converted the exiles from pressure groups into the acknowledged heirs of the Habsburg throne. Internationally, the empire had been written off.

---

* In the so-called 'Epiphany Declaration' of 6 January 1918, the Czech parliamentary delegates assembled in Prague had demanded the right 'to a free national life and self-determination', but avoided saying whether this should or should not be under the Habsburg sceptre.

IV

An Empire Shatters

THESE NEAR-MORTAL BLOWS to the Dual Monarchy on the political front could only have been overcome by victory, or at least a negotiable stalemate, on the military front. But the tide of battle, which had seemed to be running so well for the Central Powers in the spring of 1918, now turned, rapidly and remorselessly, against them. The great 'Emperor's Battle' in the west, on which all hopes had been placed in the spring, had run out of breath by midsummer. The Flanders offensive had already been blocked by the British Second Army at the end of April. In July, the German drive for Paris was halted at the historic battle of the Marne, the last natural defence line before the French capital. Then, the Allied counter-attack began and the huge over-strained hinge of the German onslaught was pushed steadily backwards. It nearly snapped off altogether on 8 August. In a surprise dawn attack east of Amiens, led by a battering ram of over 450 British tanks, the German Second Army was simply overrun. The scale of the victory was measured not only in distance – an advance, by nightfall, of between six and eight miles along a fourteen-mile front – but by the almost unprecedented collapse of the enemy forces. More than 20,000 German prisoners were counted at the end of the day. For the first time, the juggernaut had been toppled over backwards.

The controller of that juggernaut, General Ludendorff, overreacted somewhat when, after calling that 8 August 'the black day of the German Army', he went on to declare, almost in the next breath: 'The war must be ended.' As things stood, the Entente armies, without adequate reserves, were unable to follow up their breakthrough on the spot, while the Central Powers still possessed great potential for resistance, provided the line in the west were shortened and everything concentrated on holding it. This was one theme at a crisis meeting held at Spa on

14–15 August between the two emperors and their military and civilian chiefs. The Austrians got little sense out of Ludendorff, who had now changed from being despairing to being delphic about the prospects of victory; however, they went some way towards meeting his demands by postponing their planned offensive in Italy and transferring more troops to the Western Front.

On political decisions, the two allies remained totally at odds. Charles had come to Spa hoping to get German agreement for an unqualified peace appeal to be issued publicly to the Entente. The Germans refused, arguing that 'the moment was not yet favourable'. This was the last time Charles was ever to see his fellow-Emperor, and as his train pulled out of Spa station with William II saluting from the platform, the last hope of a joint move to end the war steamed away with it. Eventually, on 14 September, Charles published his 'cry to the world' alone from Vienna. It proved pathetically ineffective: too vague and philosophical in style and, above all, too late in the timing. Just forty-eight hours later, the Entente armies launched their decisive battle which was to break the German grip on France, the offensive at St Mihiel, a salient between Verdun and Metz. For the first time, American troops, who were now streaming across the Atlantic at the rate of a quarter of a million a month, fought in powerful battle formation (seven divisions grouped into two armies) alongside their allies.* Theirs was a tidal wave of fresh manpower, raw but exuberant, which simply rolled over an exhausted opponent. Though two months of fighting still lay ahead, the issue in the west was decided.

As far as the Habsburg Monarchy was concerned, September 1918 brought an even graver blow in the south. On the fifteenth, just as the St Mihiel offensive was reaching its climax in France, the mixed Allied Army of the Orient (it contained Italian, Serbian, French and British divisions) struck northwards from its Salonika base at Bulgaria. The Bulgarians, and the German Eleventh Army fighting with them, were driven back on a broad front. On the twenty-sixth, Bulgaria capitulated

---

* On the other side, a handful of Austrian infantry divisions were now fighting with their German allies on the Western Front. This was part of the military price exacted by the Germans out of the Spa pact (thus far, only Austrian artillery units had served in the west), and it had been enforced by threats to withhold deliveries of German flour. The 35th Austrian Infantry Division suffered heavy losses in the St Mihiel fighting. It fought tolerably well but without its commander, General von Podhoransky, who was absent for a whole six weeks – on leave!

without warning and sued for a separate peace with the French Commander-in-Chief, General Franchet d'Espérey. The psychological blow to the Central Powers' alliance was even heavier than the military loss. At his headquarters in faraway Spa, Ludendorff was already reeling from fresh blows struck at him in the Meuse-Argonne sector of the French front. He was literally toppled over by the news of Bulgaria's defection: on the day she signed her surrender, he fell to the ground in his map room, foam coming out of his mouth. In Vienna, at an emergency meeting of the Crown Council, the Foreign Minister Baron Burian bluntly warned his Emperor: 'In jumping clear from us, Bulgaria has knocked the bottom out of the barrel.'

This overpowering sensation that the Great War had suddenly been decided in the remote Balkan theatre was not confined to the generals and the ministers of the Central Powers. A British cavalry officer fighting with his regiment east of Rheims wrote at the time in his diary: 'Towns and prisoners and guns and ships had been captured by both sides for four years without any apparent effect on the War . . . But when whole nations began to capitulate without conditions, then indeed there seemed ground for hope . . . If one fell away, others would surely follow.'

Turkey, the other minor member of the four-power camp, looked as though it would be the next one to follow Bulgaria's example. In that same fateful September, British and Commonwealth troops under General Allenby had advanced from Palestine all the way up to Damascus, driving the Turkish army* some five hundred miles before them and opening up the path towards Constantinople. In the space of a fortnight, the Quadruple Alliance had been effectively cut back again to that basic forty-year-old partnership between the Habsburg and Hohenzollern empires. They, in turn, were now the defenders of a beleaguered fortress whose outer bastions were all either crumbling or under threat. How were their rulers to save their crowns, and even their own skins?

At the end of his Crown Council meeting on 26 September, Charles had sanctioned an emergency rescue policy on two fronts. At home, there would have to be a crash programme for restructuring the empire. Despite the virtual impossibility of achieving political reform in wartime, the attempt would have to be made if the Slav nations inside the

---

* Commanded by the formidable German General Liman von Sanders, who had only handfuls of German and Austrian units to shore up his ragged and demoralised Turkish divisions.

Monarchy were not to opt out and go their own way, as the Bulgarians
had done. On the international front, pressure would have to be increased
on Germany to sue for an immediate peace. In fact, pressure was no longer
needed. At last the German High Command agreed, for Bulgaria's defection had knocked some sense into their heads as well as knocking the
bottom out of the military and political barrel. On 29 September, two
days after the decisions taken in Vienna, Hindenburg and Ludendorff
went to their Emperor of their own accord and admitted the hitherto
unmentionable: the German Army was facing total defeat. Three days
later, they sent a formal demand to Germany's new 'Peace Chancellor',
Prince Max of Baden, to sue for an armistice. Two days after that, on
4 October, the Central Powers despatched parallel notes to President
Wilson, calling for peace talks on the basis of his Fourteen Points. So,
by the autumn of 1918, those shouts of 'final victory' which had
resounded in Berlin in the spring had turned into cries of surrender.

Charles did not need to consult his German ally to implement the
second part of this eleventh-hour rescue package – constitutional reform
at home. But in this he found himself shouting at the ears of the Magyar
nationalists, which were even more tightly blocked than those of the
Prussian Junkers had been. After a fortnight of trying, in vain, to persuade the Hungarians of the need to accord autonomy also to their own
subject peoples (a need that was being increasingly emphasised in every
message which came out of Washington), Charles went ahead on his
own. On 16 October 1918 he signed his famous 'People's Manifesto'
which was published two days later. The vital passage read:

> Following the will of its peoples, Austria shall become a federal
> state in which each racial component shall form its own state
> organisation in its territory of settlement . . .
> To those peoples on whose rights of self-determination the
> new empire will be built my call goes out to implement the great
> work through National Councils – made up of the parliamentary
> deputies of each nation – which shall represent the interests
> of the peoples with each other, and in contact with my
> government.

A doleful sentence in the middle of the text made it clear that the
proposed reconstruction 'shall in no way affect the integrity of the lands
of the sacred Hungarian crown'. In other words, this was a programme

for Cisleithania only. It was addressed primarily to the Austrians themselves and to that great swathe of Slavs – from Galicia down through
Bohemia and Moravia to Slovenia and Bosnia – over whom they had
ruled in the western half of the Dual Monarchy. Even within this restricted radius, a commitment to such federalism might have served some
purpose, abroad as well as at home, had it been announced by the
Emperor as a fundamental peacetime aim at his accession two years
earlier. Coming in the autumn of 1918, after the lethal Spa Treaty and
the victory this had handed to the radical exiles, and with the disintegration of the Monarchy looming ever larger on the battlefields, the
Manifesto was limping painfully behind the march of history.

This was rubbed in by President Wilson's eagerly-awaited response
to Austria's message in the joint appeal of 4 October, which had added
its own gloss in reminding Washington of Vienna's previous attempts
to secure peace and justice. Already on 9 October, Germany had received
her reply, which Prince Max and the generals had accepted as a basis
for negotiations. But Charles had still not obtained his response when
the 'People's Manifesto' was rushed out. Wilson took another two days
to digest this new development, but then, on the twentieth, sent Austria
a crushing answer. Things had changed, he pointed out, since he had
affirmed the general principle of self-determination as the tenth of his
Fourteen Points. The Czecho-Slovak National Council was now a '*de
facto* belligerent government clothed with proper authority'. Therefore,
to proclaim the 'mere autonomy of these peoples as a basis for peace'
would no longer suffice. They must now be the judges of 'what action
on the part of the Austro-Hungarian government will satisfy their aspirations'. This was ironic, for Charles had, in fact, just delivered that
action.* Throughout his realm, the National Councils he had enjoined
his peoples to form took shape – sometimes with different names, sometimes building on the foundations of existing bodies. None, however,
followed the second injunction in his Manifesto, namely that they should
henceforth collaborate with the imperial government as members of
'a new empire'. One by one, the nations of the Monarchy took the
independence which the crown had formally blessed yet turned their
backs on the crown.

* Charles was to make one final vain approach to Wilson a week later. On 27 October
he telegraphed to Washington seeking an immediate armistice and the opening of negotiations with Austria-Hungary only. The famous 'separate peace', without Germany, had
been launched at last, when Austria had not a card left to play.

Nothing could be further from the truth than the impression given by many republican leaders at the time (and cherished by Europe's left-wing ideologues ever since) that, in the autumn of 1918, the Habsburg empire imploded from within, destroyed by the mass rebellion of its peoples. In fact, it was only in Budapest, in a manner entirely true to Hungarian history and the Magyar temperament, that a change of regime was actually achieved by violence.

Until the last week of October, the old phalanx of the conservative Magyar magnates, still dominated by the giant figure of the ex-Premier Count Stephen Tisza, remained in precarious control. But their power was fast ebbing away and flowing towards the reformist parties of the left, notably to the so-called Independents, headed by the maverick aristocrat Count Michael Károlyi. This misguided idealist, whose fate it was to be both the traitor of the old order and the victim of the new,* was the hero of the frenzied hour. Inside the Parliament, where his party held some twenty seats, there was much exchange of invective between him and his conservative opponents, each accusing the other of betrayal. But it was street mobs, not parliamentary oratory, which swept him to power. On the evening of 24 October, after Budapest University students and disaffected army officers had clashed, sabre to sabre, with police, Károlyi felt strong enough to declare a National Council of Liberal and Socialist factions under his leadership as President. Charles, who was in Hungary himself at the time in an attempt to make some sense out of the chaos, still hesitated to name this disturbing harelipped eccentric as his constitutional Prime Minister. Instead, he chose a stopgap nonentity, Count John Hadik.

At that, the pro-Károlyi agitators erupted in a fresh surge of street disorders, and on 30 October three were shot dead in clashes with the police. The Budapest army garrison sat on its hands in its barracks, despite a direct telephoned command from Charles to its commander, General Géza von Lucacics, to use whatever force was necessary to quell the gathering mayhem.** With the police cowed and the garrison finally declaring itself for the National Committee, there were no forces of

---

* He was eventually elected, on 16 November 1918, as the first President of Hungary's first so-called 'People's Republic'. Within three months, the Hungarian Bolshevik demagogue Béla Kun had brushed him aside and inaugurated a Communist regime of terror.
** Ironically, Charles had personally selected the highly-decorated Lucacics (who was known as the 'Iron General') as Military Commander in Budapest, in order to have a loyal and resolute officer in charge for any emergencies.

order left in Budapest, only the forces of disorder. The Károlyi political bandwagon was now unstoppable. On the thirty-first, he was formally appointed Prime Minister of Hungary in the name of the King-Emperor, now back in his Austrian capital to cope with other and even graver emergencies facing him there. That same day in Budapest, another mob of soldiers and civilians closed in on the villa of Count Tisza whom – in crass ignorance of how he had really behaved in the summer of 1914 – they accused of starting the war. Tisza had laid aside his own pistols to save his family being caught in any crossfire, and was shot down in front of them. It was the first of many bloodstains that were to come in Budapest.

This display of sustained violence and sporadic savagery marked the only true uprising which the Dual Monarchy endured during its rapid dissolution. When compared with events in Hungary, the transfer of power from imperial into republican hands in the other crown lands of the empire was as decorous and disciplined as a minuet.

In Prague, for example, the National Committee, formed on the sanction of the Emperor's Manifesto, waited quietly until the last days of October before making any attempt to seize the reins. Until the end, there were those like the very influential leader of the Young Czechs, Karl Kramář, who clung to a monarchist solution and doubted whether a new Czech state could ever survive as a republic. Men of his persuasion had always believed that, with all its faults, the multi-national Dual Monarchy afforded the best protection against the rampant anti-Slavism of Germany. Together with a group of other elder statesmen, Kramář had left for Geneva in mid-October to debate the future with Beneš and his radical exiles.* In their absence, the younger and more nationalistic members of the Committee, who had been left in charge in Prague, decided to wait no longer.

On 28 October, the day the discussion in Geneva began, they passed a resolution calling for the establishment of 'an independent Czech state'. Though this did not proclaim any outright breach with the Monarchy, it amounted to implicit rejection of the federal concept which Charles had put forward. More to the point, the Czech nationalists proceeded to make that rejection quite explicit on the ground. The President of the Council, Antonín Švelha, announced that henceforth he was assuming

* They stopped off in Vienna *en route* for an imperial audience with Charles, and talks with the ministers in his last Cabinet. No one seems to have tried to strengthen the pro-monarchism in their ranks.

responsibility for feeding the people of Prague, and moved into the Corn Distribution Office without even a word of protest from its officials. From there, his delegates went to the palace of the imperial Governor of Bohemia, Count Max Coudenhove, declaring that, in the interests of public order, they would now take over the entire administration of the country. Again, there was no resistance as power was snatched from listless hands. By nightfall on 28 October the National Council was, in effect, functioning as the provisional government of Prague. The stars and stripes were hoisted at some points in the capital alongside the red and white colours of the new state. The Czech republicans knew who their real saviour had been.

It took them another two days to bring the other provinces into their fold. Both the Sudeten Germans and the Slovaks, reluctant to be absorbed by the Czechs without at least a popular vote on the subject, had set up National Councils of their own. These were portents of far graver conflicts to arise later in the century. But in October 1918 they proved to be mayfly administrations. By the thirtieth they were already spent, and both Moravia and Slovakia declared themselves part of the republic. That same day, one Vlastimil Tusar presented himself in Vienna as the diplomatic representative of the new republic. His oft-quoted exchange of compliments with Dr Heinrich Lammasch, the last Prime Minister of imperial Austria, encapsulates the sedate atmosphere of this momentous transition: 'I take pleasure in welcoming you as ambassador of the Czech-Slovak state,' Dr Lammasch declared. 'The pleasure,' Tusar replied, 'is all mine.'

By this time, the Croats had followed the Czech lead with the proclamation, on 29 October, of a 'common sovereign state of the Serbs, Croats and Slovenes'. Their territories, plus Dalmatia and Fiume, were declared independent of both Austria and Hungary. The Poles took up day-to-day administration of the old crown land of Galicia,* and their rivals, the Ukrainians, proclaimed their own republic with its capital at Przemyśl. When, on 1 November, the Ruthenes followed suit, the great Slav crescent of Cisleithania had broken away, in its entirety, from Vienna. What of the Austrians, now left isolated, though still imperial, at the centre?

They, who for centuries had been the privileged subjects of a great

---

* The Poles had set up their so-called 'Liquidation Commission' in Cracow, but this was not recognised by the Entente as it stood in immediate conflict with the new state of Poland, resurrected as a republic.

multi-national empire, now transformed themselves within the space of three weeks into the citizens of a tiny 'German-Austrian Republic'. In this process of transformation, all those psychological traits we have seen developing down the generations blossomed in historic style. What came out again was the same old Austrian reluctance to grasp any nettle firmly; the same tendency to face both ways at once; the same pragmatism and opportunism which sprang from that ambivalence; the same tussle between the opposing loyalties towards dynasty and 'Germandom'. It was no wonder that the constitutional freak which emerged was dubbed, even by its creators, as 'a nation without a state'.

The Austrians had been the first people of the Monarchy to translate the imperial Manifesto into practice. On 21 October, five days after it was signed, the so-called 'Provisional National Assembly of Independent German-Austria' was formed in Vienna, as a direct response to the Emperor's invitation to all his subjects in Cisleithania to set up National Committees within their own territories of racial settlement. Accordingly, all the deputies returned to the 1911 Parliament from closed German-speaking areas of the Monarchy were in attendance, and all parties were therefore represented. Yet it was already clear that the Social Democrats would take the lead. They, after all, were the party of reform, even if they were far from clear in their own minds what this reform should be. Karl Renner clung to his old concept of a federation of nations within a democratised monarchical framework and was still backed in this by Viktor Adler. But the party's grand old man, now in the last days of his life, coupled his final appeal for a federation between Austrians and Slavs with an alternative call for union with Germany. The Monarchy was not supported but neither was it explicitly denounced in his declaration. Ambivalence could not go further.

At this stage in the proceedings, the leaders of the main right-wing parties sounded far more positive in their convictions. Both the spokesmen for the Christian-Socials, the Tyrolean Provincial Governor Josef Schraffl and his German-Nationalist colleague Dr Otto Steinwender, came out clearly for a constitutional monarchy. The outright republicans of Otto Bauer's stamp were still in a small minority. On one thing, however, all were agreed: the need to establish some formal body to represent the growing authority of what the resolution called 'the German people in Austria'. Nomenclature remained a problem. The 'Provisional National Assembly' appointed twenty of its members to represent it. At first, this body called itself merely an

'Executive Committee' ('Vollzugsausschuss'), and only later ventured to style itself 'Council of State' ('Staatsrat'). As such, it claimed both authority over 'the entire territory of German settlement' and the right to speak for Austria in any peace negotiations.

An element of Viennese farce thus entered the death-throes of this once-mighty empire. For when, ten days later, the Assembly convened again to proclaim a republican constitution (though still without declaring a republic!), it also appointed twenty State Secretaries who were supposed to take charge of each government department. It could not appoint ministers because it possessed no head of state. That prerogative still rested with the Emperor, and on 27 October Charles had nominated the Prime Minister of his last imperial administration – Dr Heinrich Lammasch. Those last days of transition thus passed in a dual vacuum. The State Secretaries of the emerging republic sat in the heart of the capital (the building of the Lower Austrian Provincial Government in the Herrengasse), claiming power but not yet exercising it. In Schönbrunn Palace, in the western suburbs, the Emperor still ruled, losing power almost by the hour, but not yet renouncing it. It was a tandem of impotence, steered only by the tug of momentous events.

Of these, there had been enough in those ten days which lay between the two October meetings of the National Assembly. In the last week of that month came the military débâcle which set the final seal on the dynasty's fate and turned the political crumbling of the empire into disintegration.

On 24 October, the anniversary of the start of the Caporetto offensive which had brought the Austrians such triumph the year before, the Italians, supported by French and British troops, launched the last Allied campaign of the war. Fifty-seven Austrian divisions, numbering some 400,000 men, stood against them along the long line stretching up from the Piave River to the mountains of the Grappa Massiv. It looked, on paper, a powerful force, and indeed represented more than two-thirds of the Monarchy's nominal strength in fighting formations. But the figures had little real meaning. Nineteen of those divisions were down to half or even quarter strength; nine were riddled with malaria; and another seven were being reformed after transfer from the east. Moreover, most men were lucky to get one solid meal a day, if the diet of dried fruit, cheese and cabbage served up by the field kitchens met that description. The position with uniforms and equipment was even worse. Proper underclothing was almost non-existent, and one regiment (the

16th Infantry) resorted to cutting up its snow capes to make just one set for each man. The corpses were often laid as they had fallen in rough coffins. No linen could be spared for shrouds.

Yet, when the attackers struck, this army of hungry scarecrows – including Czechs, Poles, Croats, Slovaks, Ruthenes and Magyars, whose spokesmen at home were already detaching themselves from the Monarchy – fought back for three days as though the Habsburg empire which they still represented were in its prime. It was a battlefield mirage as deceptive as the true note which a violin string can give out even when frayed to its last strands. On 26 October, the string snapped. Desertions and mutinies, which had begun even before the Italian attack, swept across the whole line, which was anyway buckling. Not surprisingly, in view of events in their homeland, the Hungarians now led the way. The first act of Béla Linder, the Defence Minister in Károlyi's new government in Budapest, was to order all his soldiers to return from the front. Even before that order went out, Hungarian division after division, including troops who had distinguished themselves in battle, simply downed their arms and demanded transport home. Though the Austrian formations held relatively firm, the rot spread throughout the Slav regiments. By the end of the month, General Arz, whom Charles had put in command of the Italian campaign, signalled in desperation to Hindenburg that more than thirty divisions under his command were paralysed by mutiny and that the only course now left was to sue for armistice. By now, the Entente armies were across the Piave; Arz had nothing left to throw against their bridgeheads.

This was the grim situation which awaited Charles when he returned to Schönbrunn from his fruitless visit to Budapest. The first contacts with the Italians showed that they were after something much more than an armistice. Their demands amounted to a total Austrian capitulation: withdrawal right back to the Brenner (thus securing for Italy the 1915 bribe of the Trentino province); the complete demobilisation of the imperial army and its reduction in peacetime to a maximum of twenty divisions; and, in the meantime, the right of the Entente armies to 'move freely inside Austria-Hungary and occupy strategic points'.

As the last two conditions affected the future of the Austrian state – whatever form it might take – Charles decided to ask the shadow government lurking in the Herrengasse for its views. It was an admission that such power as still remained in the capital was now shared. At 4 p.m. on 2 November, the two sides, representing Austria's past and future, came face-to-face in the exquisite setting of Schönbrunn's Blue Chinese Salon. For the monarch, it was a depressing encounter. The five-man delegation of the State Council* agreed that the fighting should be stopped at once, but had no ideas as to how this should be done and no proposals to put forward. Instead, the mortally ill Socialist leader Viktor Adler (who had actually collapsed while mounting the grand staircase) recovered sufficient strength to launch a tirade on responsibility for the outbreak of the war, as opposed to any suggestion as to how it might be ended. The delegation departed after two hours, still refusing to share in any decision. Clearly, they were determined to let the exhausted imperial eagle fly on until its wings dropped off, and to stir only after it had crashed. Charles consulted his own ministers, who agreed there was no choice but to accept the Italian terms almost as they stood.

The disaster now became compounded by fiasco. The armistice talks at the Villa Guisti in Padua left the exact timing of the ceasefire dangerously imprecise. The Austrian representative, General von Weber,** whose muddle-headedness seems to have been primarily responsible for the confusion, took it to be 3 p.m. on 3 November. The Italian commander, General Badoglio,*** on the other hand, remained icily convinced that the time agreed was twenty-four hours later. The argument was to rage for years as to whether Austrian stupidity or Italian duplicity was to blame for the misunderstanding, but its immediate effects on the ground were beyond dispute. The territory which, in twelve successive campaigns since 1915, the Italians had failed to take by force they now rode over, unopposed, by default. Some 350,000 Austrian soldiers, who had duly stacked their arms on the afternoon of 3 November, found themselves taken as prisoners-of-war by the afternoon of the fourth. And all this on the one battlefront which, for the Austrians, had always been held sacred above all others.

The Italians, who had many wartime complexes to smother, dubbed this military procession of theirs the triumph of Vittorio Veneto, and later erected in Rome the most pompous of all victory monuments in its honour. But it was in the Austrian capital that, on the day, the

---

* The Parliamentary Presidents of the three main parties plus two of the recently appointed 'State Secretaries'.

** Major General Viktor Weber von Webenau had been President of the Austrian Armistice Commission since 4 October, when it had been formed on the eve of the peace appeal to President Wilson.

*** Later to earn dubious laurels in Mussolini's Abyssinian campaign.

heaviest impact was felt. We have seen how even Francis Joseph, during the zenith years of his empire, had had to endure the hisses and boos of his Viennese subjects when he returned, a defeated commander, from the Italian battlefields. And here, in November 1918, his young successor, barely two years on a throne that was already shaking, and in a war that was already lost, had to face the humiliation of a far greater military rout, greater because its massive scale had been avoidable. The honour and standing of the dynasty itself had been fatally weakened. It was not surprising that it was on the night of the Italian disaster that the first mutterings about abdication were heard in Schönbrunn.

It was also the first time that the question of the safety of the royal family had been raised. Dr Johann Schober, the capital's much respected Police Chief (both the Staatsrat and the imperial Chancellor had confirmed him in office), was a monarchist to his bones. In the middle of the Emperor's frantic discussions over the Italian armistice, Schober rang Schönbrunn to say he could no longer guarantee the security of the palace (whose garrison and lifeguard units were gradually melting away*), and that the Emperor should move elsewhere for safety. Charles had given short shrift to the idea of abdication, but the warning of the Police President had to be taken more seriously. His wife later recounted how suggestions for emergency refuges had rained in from all sides, 'all different, all emphatic'. What was significant, however, was that the destinations proposed lay, without exception, within the empire: Innsbruck, the traditional haven of Habsburgs threatened in their capital; Brandeis on the Elbe, where Charles, when a young Archduke, had once served as a garrison officer; the abbey of Kremsmünster, where the church would surely give protection; the castle of Prince Starhemberg in Upper Austria; or the town of Pressburg on the Danube, where the royal couple had been given a rapturous popular reception only a few months before at the Harvest Festival of 16 July.** Flight abroad was not even contemplated. Even the idea of fleeing the palace was dropped for the time being when, at 4.30 a.m. on 3 November, Schober rang

* Military cadets from the Wiener Neustadt and Traiskirchen Academies suddenly appeared, without being summoned, to replace them. Various offers of help were sent to Vienna from commanders in the field, only to be held up in pending trays at the War Office.
** Pressburg, or Bratislava, was the principal city of the Slovak people, who regarded the dynasty as a protective shield against encroachment from their Czech or Hungarian neighbours.

again to say that the danger 'had somewhat receded' and that the royal family might as well stay where they were.

This is perhaps the point to ask just how violent popular agitation against the Monarchy had become in the capital during these autumn weeks (it had not existed as a political factor before). In other words, was there ever an uprising in Vienna in November 1918, as much literature, especially of the left wing, later maintained? The answer must be that revolution, in any accepted sense of that word, simply did not occur. There were anti-monarchist street gestures, such as the ripping-off of imperial insignia from officers' uniforms (sometimes the officers themselves prudently forestalled the protesters). There were looting and mob demonstrations which both became uglier when soldiers returning from the collapsed Italian front swelled the bands of marauding *soldateska* which were swarming all over the empire.* But not a single government ministry or building was stormed. Indeed, not as much as a brick was hurled through any imperial window. Nobody was murdered in their home, as Tisza had been in Budapest. Nobody was shot on the streets. There were no barricades. The 'revolution' was a popular mood, not a popular movement. Its components were the indifference or dithering of the military garrisons, who stayed in their barracks; the upsurge of hostility among a civilian population half-starved by the war and now sickened by the defeats and humiliations it had suddenly produced; the inroads of extremist agitators, especially those returned from the Russian front, with Bolshevik ideas – and nothing much else – in their knapsacks. Above all, there was the vacuum at the centre of things which all these elements rushed in to fill and the feeling that this centre itself, in the shape of the beleaguered Habsburg dynasty, had been written off by the outside world.

The paradoxes continued to the end. 4 November was the Emperor's name day, and on 4 November 1918, as in previous years, Cardinal Archbishop Piffl conducted a High Mass in St Stephen's Cathedral in his honour. Vienna's greatest church was crowded and most of the ministers and other imperial notabilities were in their usual places in the front pews (even though they had appeared out of uniform through side doors). The imperial anthem, *'Gott Erhalte'*, was duly sung with fervour – and a few sobs – at the end. It was the last time it was to be

---

* The Socialist State Council performed a valuable exercise of stability by incorporating the radical 'Soldiers' Councils' in their own *'Volkswehr'* security battalions, formed largely out of unemployed factory workers.

heard from such a company. This Mass was the dynasty's memorial service.

As throughout the final phase of disintegration, the decisive blows came from outside. On 8 November, President Wilson sent a greetings telegram to Dr Karl Seitz, Chairman of the State Council in Vienna, expressing pleasure that 'the constituent peoples had now thrown off the yoke of the Austro-Hungarian empire'. Ten days before, the State Council had reported its formation directly to the former Princeton professor in the White House, 4000 miles away. He had responded as though he were the formal, as well as the *de facto*, controller of Austria's fate. With that telegram, Wilson had as good as proclaimed the Austrian Republic dead – four days before its own republicans got round to it. Hard on this, on 9 November, came the news from Berlin that the Kaiser had abdicated and been bundled off by his generals into exile in Holland, with as little ceremony as the despatch of an unwanted piece of furniture into storage. Hohenzollern and Habsburg became intertwined again, this time in their death-throes. The senior partner and Supreme War Lord of the imperial alliance had been toppled from his throne. The future of the junior partner was an issue which could no longer be dodged. Somehow, the indecision and unreality which had hung over Schönbrunn palace for weeks would have to be dissipated. So, in the end, it was the 'pot of iron' which had indeed smashed the 'pot of clay'.

Few things illuminated the gulf between the two Germanic dynasties – the one in Berlin a militaristic upstart, the other in Vienna woven into the historical tapestry of Europe for six and a half centuries – than the contrasting manner of their departure. The Habsburg eagle still inspired a certain awe, though its strength was spent, and nobody stretched out a hand to knock it bodily from its perch. Indeed, had Francis Joseph lived another two years and still been residing in Schönbrunn, it is questionable whether his subjects would have dared suggest that he quit the palace after what would, by then, have been seventy years on the throne. This, at any rate, is the speculation prompted by all the head-scratching and soul-searching which preceded the honourable compromise now produced for his successor – the decent but uncharismatic Charles, who had reigned for just under two years.

It was the young Emperor who outlined a solution to his dynasty just as, a month before, he had outlined a solution for his empire. He would not abdicate and he would not flee the country, he told his advisers at a midnight meeting on the ninth, but it was up to the parliamentary parties to declare their hand on the political front. Emissaries were sent out in the small hours to the party spokesmen and to Cardinal Archbishop Piffl, to whom Charles wrote a personal appeal. The voice of the Church was all-important. Johann Hauser, leader of the right-wing Christian Socialist Party – by tradition the political pillar of the Monarchy – was himself a prelate, while Ignaz Seipel, the brightest of the younger stars in the movement, was also a Catholic priest.*

It was Seipel who was largely credited with producing the magic formula which would preserve the dignity, and even the nominal existence, of the dynasty, while at the same time allowing the Austrian Republic to emerge from under its folded wings. The sovereign would formally renounce power but not his throne. This was the compromise hammered out on the tenth, after all-day discussions between Lammasch and his ministers for the crown and Seitz and Renner for the Socialists.

So, at eleven o'clock on the following morning, the swell of republicanism finally reached Schönbrunn. It was not borne down the Mariahilferstrasse by any tidal wave of mob protest or violence, but arrived decorously by motor-car with a declaration to be presented to the Emperor by two members of his own Cabinet, his Chancellor and his last Minister of Interior, Edmund Gayer. Both men were bordering on nervous collapse. They pursued the Emperor from salon to salon, urging him to sign immediately the document they had only just pressed into his hands, for it was due to be printed and published in Vienna by three o'clock that same afternoon.

Charles shook them off for one last session alone, in the so-called Porcelain Room, with his advisers and his wife. Zita needed convincing that the document did not represent outright abdication. Charles's counsellors all agreed there was no other – or at least no better – way forward. The Emperor returned to the Blue Chinese Salon next door and, with the metallic pencil he always carried with him, put his brief signature, 'Karl', to the instrument which wound up his ancient dynasty in anything but name.** The essential passages read:

> I recognise in advance whatever decision that German-Austria
> may make about its future political form.

* Only four years later Seipel was to become Chancellor of the infant Austrian Republic, and was to remain for a decade the dominant right-wing leader in the state.
** Even the Second Austrian Republic preserved the memory of this historic event. In the summer of 1992, when the author was filming a TV documentary, with scenes in

The people, through its representatives, has taken over the government. I renounce all participation in the affairs of state.

May the people of German-Austria, in unity and tolerance, create and strengthen the new order ... Only an inner peace can heal the wounds of war.

It was a fitting way for the man whom history was to call 'the Peace Emperor' to bow out of power. However, he had not yet bowed out of the limelight, much less from his own realm. Both the Swiss and the Dutch envoys to his court had offered him safe passage to asylum in their countries. But it was to Eckartsau, his shooting lodge north-east of Vienna, that the royal party drove that evening, their car convoy slipping out unopposed through the eastern side-gate of the palace. Maria Theresa's great building was left empty and unguarded.* It remained quite unmolested, except for one midnight burglar who reached the bedroom of the Empress and sat down on the *sonnette* hidden under the coverlet. The bells of the call buttons started shrilling at once, all over the palace. There was no one to answer them.

The next morning, 12 November 1918, the 'democratic German-Austria' was formally proclaimed in Vienna, 'as part of the German Republic'. Karl Renner pronounced a litany to the ethnic bond of the hour: 'Hail to our German people and Hail to German-Austria!' The Christian Socialists, who had still declared for the Monarchy only two days before, now abandoned it almost to a man. Even in these times of agonising self-doubt, confusion and opportunism, this was a spectacular about-face. Among the tiny loyalist band of three who refused to turn their coats was the forty-six-year-old Deputy Wilhelm Miklas. Twenty years later, as Austrian President, he was to show the same rare courage of convictions to Adolf Hitler.

One anecdote among many lights up the decorous nature of this transition from Monarchy to republic. In the first hours of the new republic, Prince Francis Liechtenstein, one of the pillars of the fallen order, strode into his Vienna haberdashers to buy a new pair of gloves. He was politely ushered to the door by the assistant. 'No, Your Highness, please call again tomorrow. Today is revolution day!'

Schönbrunn, on the collapse of the Monarchy, the palace administrators proudly produced the table on which the Manifesto was signed.

* Eckartsau was in the Marchfeld, close to that battlefield where in 1278 Charles's remote ancestor Rudolf of Habsburg had launched the dynasty into history.

PART FIVE

THE ROAD TO HITLER

I

'What's Left is Austria'

THE HABERDASHERS' COUNTER at which prince and shop assistant had held their polite exchange was not the only place in Vienna where the transition from ancient Monarchy to raw republic seemed to be going with amazing smoothness on that 12 November. Karl Renner, as Secretary of the State Council, became the *de facto* head of the new government, in advance of the first elections.* Dr Lammasch had retired from the scene the previous day, gratefully, and laden with honours. (During the final hours in Schönbrunn, the Emperor had found time to invest him with the Grand Cross of the Order of St Stephen and – a very Austrian touch – to award him a handsome pension.) But the officials who had served under his last imperial regime had nearly all turned up again at their desks, to work under the State Secretaries of the republic, and thus ensure continuity of administration. Schober, a key figure for stability, now and in the years to come, stayed on, trusted by all, as Police President.

This peaceful scene looked too good to be true, and it was. During the very ceremony when the red-white-red flag of the republic was being hoisted outside Parliament in place of the Habsburg black and yellow, a group of Communist demonstrators managed to grab it, tear the middle strip out and run up a red banner instead. Shortly afterwards, a band of their fellow extremists in uniform from the so-called 'Red Guard' stormed the building itself.** In the ensuing mêlée, shots were

---

* Viktor Adler, the grand old man of the Socialist Party, had died on the eve of its greatest triumph, the proclamation of the republic.
** The Red Guard had been formed at the beginning of the month under the leadership of an army lieutenant and peacetime journalist, Egon Erwin Kisch. Its active membership never exceeded a few hundreds, but it produced a ferment out of all proportion to its size.

exchanged, leaving two dead and some forty-five wounded. This was partly the result of good old Viennese muddle. The soldiers were supposed to have left their weapons behind in the barracks that day, while the Parliament itself was supposed to be properly guarded. Both arrangements failed to materialise. But the clash pointed to something else: the unresolved tension between a minority of Bolshevik-style extremists of the left and the majority of their more moderate Socialist comrades. This was to flare up in more violent though equally ineffective fashion in the months ahead. 'Revolution' was against 'revolution', not against the dynasty. Vienna had been marked with the first stain of blood twenty-four hours *after* the Monarchy had tiptoed from the scene. Ominously for the future, this blood had been spilled in an ideological, rather than a political, clash. Renner was quick to fudge the issue: he pardoned the extremists' ringleaders on the grounds that they were merely actors on a mighty transition stage of history. Viewed from this perspective, the scuffle of 12 November was indeed a loud squeak of protest rather than a *putsch*.

For the moment Renner and his colleagues were, in any case, faced with two much more formidable problems. The first was how to keep the citizens of the new state alive. The second was how to defend their borders from invasion. The people of German Austria, especially the urban population, had been steadily tightening their belts down to the last notch throughout the four years of war. Now, in the autumn of 1918, just when a good harvest was needed, the output from the reduced areas still under cultivation fell to less than 50 per cent in both wheat and rye compared with pre-war yields. This covered less than a quarter of the need for flour, even based on the draconian ration system in force. The shortfall in meat, potatoes and, above all, fats, was even greater. Without the modest supplies of food distributed through the Allied Famine Relief programme (directed by the future American President Herbert Hoover) the Viennese would have faced starvation in this first winter of their republican existence. As it was, a medical survey carried out among 186,000 schoolchildren of the capital registered more than 150,000 as undernourished, the majority severely so.

The physical isolation of this famished dwarf of a republic added to its sufferings. As the dominant people of the old Cisleithania, they could always look to the Bohemian and Moravian crown lands to provide them with the coal for their hearths and factory ovens (as well as for the sugar in their coffee). Now the newly established state of

Czechoslovakia cut off virtually all supplies. In November 1918, five successive diplomatic protests in Prague were needed to secure the transit along Czech railways of one single coal train bound for Austria. The blast furnaces went out, as well as the home fireplaces; even the Vienna trams ground to a halt for lack of coal-fed electricity. Again, it was the ex-enemy, in the shape of the Allied Relief Programme, which supplied such emergency help as was deemed feasible.

On top of the Slav economic blockade came the military challenge of their armies to the ethnic borders of 'German-Austria'. Without waiting for the verdict of the victors at the Peace Conference (which, in Austria's case, was still six months away), Czech troops occupied the territories of the three million Sudeten Germans whom the Austrians claimed as their blood brothers in the north.

In the far south, along the historic fault line of Carinthia's racial borders, came a more immediate threat from the new Slav state of Yugoslavia. The first intruders were Slovenes, one of the component peoples of that state whose sprinklings of fellow Slovenes inside Carinthia had, for generations past, formed one of the Monarchy's most troublesome ethnic irritants. Within a fortnight of the Austrian Republic's formation, Slovene units who only weeks before had been fighting for the Monarchy seized the town of Ferlach and pushed north to the line of the River Drau. There things were to rest until the spring when more powerful units, this time from the combined armed forces of Yugoslavia, launched a new offensive aimed at Klagenfurt, the Carinthian capital itself. But if the Vienna government had been both unable and unwilling to go to the help of the Sudetens, the Carinthians proved quite determined to defend themselves, whatever nervousness Vienna displayed about their struggle.

Arms and ammunition were available in abundance, for the whole area had served throughout the war as the main supply zone for the Italian front. Soldiers were there too in their tens of thousands, an untidy mass of military flotsam pushed across the border by the final waves of the Italian advance. Many became marauding freebooters, joining the ranks of the undisciplined *soldateska* who were plaguing the whole country. Many made straight for their villages, casting their uniforms as they went. But enough were left, especially among those who had served in Carinthian units with the Sixth Army in Italy, who were now prepared to fight against a new enemy to defend their homeland. A force of irregulars was raised under the command of one Lieutenant-

Colonel Ludwig Hülgerth, in which the party politics of Vienna played little part. These were Carinthians, not Social Democrats or Christian Socialists, and they fought out of local patriotism. There were many traditionalists in their ranks, fighting in their hearts for an old crown land of the Monarchy rather than for a new province of the republic.*

In the short term, they were to serve that republic well, for even the mighty peacemakers in Paris came to recognise their case and to make special provision for it. For the longer term, Colonel Hülgerth's soldiers had a more dubious significance. They had shown that it was not only the left wing with their *Volkswehr* who could raise an emergency army in the name of socialism. Austria's conservatives could raise one as well, and in the name of patriotism. Thus in the first weeks of the republic's life the outlines were emerging of that confrontation which was to tear it apart.

The fact that Carinthia had acted off its own bat in response to danger reflected one of the most far-reaching decisions of the State Council in Vienna, which was to confirm the integrity and semi-autonomy of the old Habsburg Länder within the new republic.** It could not have been otherwise, for these ancient provinces had always been, and would remain, the pillars of any Austrian state, whether imperial or republican. They had stood, virtually unshaken, throughout all the turmoil of the dynasty's expansion; through the great Christian wars of religion; through the Monarchy's struggles against Islam, Napoleon and Prussia; finally, they had breasted all of Francis Joseph's reform schemes, even the introduction of Dualism and the emergence of Parliaments. As we shall see, they were also to survive the attempts of Nazism to impose its standard mould on them all and, by surviving, they preserved the basic elements of an Austrian identity.

That lay twenty years ahead; in 1918, their fierce individualism gave the new state some of its worst constitutional headaches. The Tyroleans north of the Brenner, for example, looked to Berlin, rather than Vienna,

---

* 'Carinthia for the Carinthians' was their slogan, and they made it clear that, if need be, the wishes of Vienna, as well as those of the Slovenes and Serbs, would have to be defied.

** One of the republic's first laws, passed on 22 November 1918, had entrusted each President ('*Landeshauptmann*') of the Provincial Diets with executive powers of administration in his province. In the republic's constitution of 1 October 1920, the provinces 'surrendered' control of basic common affairs, such as defence and foreign policy, to the central government, while remaining sovereign over all else.

as their best champion in the struggle to keep their fellow-Tyroleans south of the mountain pass out of Italian hands. 'Only when the black-red-gold flag flies alongside our red eagle in Innsbruck will the first dawn of deliverance come for our land in the south,' declared their spokesman, Dr Richard Steidle. There was no mention of the red-white-red colours of Austria fluttering anywhere among these banners of Germany and the Tyrol. Fortunately for the republic, this surge of separatism soon fizzled out, mainly because Steidle was rebuffed by the Germans themselves when he went to Berlin, Weimar and Munich to plead his cause.

Much more sustained was the breakaway threat which came from the Vorarlberg, the most westerly and also the most self-absorbed of all Austrian provinces. In this case, Switzerland was the magnet. The history of the Vorarlbergers had often become entangled with that of the Swiss cantons, and their thick, guttural speech was closer to the '*Schwyzerdutsch*' of Zurich than to the dialect of Vienna. Moreover, they had long resented their capital, Bregenz, being under the control of Innsbruck. It came as no surprise, therefore, that, the day after the republic was proclaimed, they launched their official campaign for all-out union with Switzerland. Vienna played for time and declined to let the province go, and the Swiss hedged their bets over letting the province in. But after the Vorarlbergers came out 80 per cent for the union (in a plebiscite held on 11 May 1919), it was clear that a long constitutional and diplomatic tussle still lay ahead. Indeed, two more years were to pass until the province grudgingly accepted its place within the republic. That was not before both Georges Clemenceau and the Peace Conference in Paris, as well as the newly-founded League of Nations, had been pestered with this Lilliputian Alpine problem.

These two individual challenges from Innsbruck and Bregenz to the authority of Vienna struck at the very marrow-bones of the infant republic: should its structure be centralised or federal? Like so much else, it was a question which only arose in this stark form now that the Austro-Hungarian empire had dissolved. Though the ancient '*Länder*' had also been the pillars of that empire, the Habsburg Monarchy was such a vast and sprawling edifice that they had never looked out of proportion under its roof. Now they dominated the scene and, with common loyalty to the crown and a tradition of common service to the dynasty both swept away, the Austrian sense of identity was splintered once again, this time from inside.

In the event, the federal concept won hands down, but not before the issue had become, for the first time, an ideological one. There are always contrasts and tensions between the capital city and the country-side of any state. Under the Monarchy, these had been primarily social and functional, and relatively easy to contain. Even towards the end of the nineteenth century, when the voice of the expanding industrial workforce in the towns grew almost as loud as that of the peasantry in the fields, they could still sing much the same tune. What greater boon could any emperor enjoy than to have Karl Lueger, an ardent right-wing Catholic and Monarchist, emerge as the unchallenged spokesman for Vienna's 'little men'? These were the very artisans, small shopkeepers and factory workers who, elsewhere, were flocking to join hands with the emerging Socialist parties of industrialised Europe.

Now, in 1918, that link-up was cemented also in Austria, and even institutionalised. 'Red Vienna', despite becoming a *'Land'* in its own right, pressed for centralised control, if only because that was part of the essential dogma of Socialism. The countryside became not just a rival, but a class enemy. Everything that was conservative, right wing and 'counter-revolutionary' (as though there had even been a revolution!) flourished here: the nobleman in his castle, the peasant in his cottage, the priest in his parish church. The Socialists of Vienna – and especially those of Bauer's 'Austro-Marxist' stamp – looked forward to a Utopia of universal proletarian brotherhood which was never to materialise. The conservatives of the countryside looked back to a past which could never be resurrected. This was a new variant of that familiar Austrian pose of gazing to no purpose in opposite directions. It was to underlie much of the tragedy which lay ahead.

For the time being, however, both town and countryside (with the exception of those recalcitrant Vorarlbergers) were broadly behind the demand for 'German-Austria', the union of all the German-speaking areas of the old Cisleithania with the new republic of Germany. That nearly every Austrian flocked to these ethnic colours in the autumn of 1918 was not surprising. With the multi-national empire dissolved and the call of race sanctified by Wilson's gospel of 'self-determination', what other rallying cry was there? Yet there was both irony and self-deception in all this. The irony was that for centuries the Slavs of the Monarchy had looked to Vienna to protect them from Berlin; now, the Austrians of that vanished Monarchy were looking to Berlin to protect them from the Slavs.

The self-deception was that the German Republic, no more than the German empire, wanted the troublesome burden of Austria to be added to its own problems. It was a paradox, as well as a personal tragedy, that it should have been Otto Bauer, the most passionate advocate of this original 'Anschluss' concept, who was the first to learn the bitter truth. Bauer had been captured during the early campaigns on the Eastern Front and, after three years behind barbed wire, had returned to Vienna full of the blinkered and fanatical extremism so often bred in those Russian prison camps. He became the high priest of the doctrine that Anschluss with Germany was vital because it was 'Anschluss with Socialism'. Only by union with the German Republic, he argued, could the menaces of 'Entente imperialism', 'Czech imperialism', and even old-fashioned Habsburg imperialism, be kept at bay.

This doctrine was to prove as destructive for the future as it was unrealistic at the time, for it made what was already a complex racial issue into an ideological one as well. Moreover, it converted what was essentially a question of national identity (ignored and probably despised in Bauer's thinking) into one of party politics. For if the Socialists made the Anschluss the central plank of their policy, what should their opponents do? The outcome of the republic's first elections,* held on 16 February 1919, had been to return seventy-two Social Democrat deputies to the National Assembly, closely followed by sixty-nine Christian Socials and twenty-six representatives of the German-National groups. A working coalition was formed between the two main parties, with the smallest of them holding aloof, to try and hold the crucial balance. (This, incidentally, established a political mould which was to be broken and reset at intervals in Vienna throughout the century.) The German-Nationals, by their very name and tradition, stood closest to the Anschluss concept, but it was a very different story with the Christian Socials. What support they gave initially to the idea of union with Germany was born out of a sense of despair and disorientation. When the storm subsided, they followed again what were their natural compass points of tradition, of pride in what Austria had once achieved and might yet achieve again – perhaps through a Danubian Federation. A great divide was opening up between the two major political forces in

---

* These were, of course, incomplete, in terms of all the German-speaking areas represented in the old Parliament. Parts of Carinthia and Southern Styria as well as the Sudetenland and the South Tyrol were under foreign occupation and could not vote.

the republic, not only as to how Austria was to be ruled but as to where it belonged in Europe.

In that first government Dr Renner became, as expected, the Chancellor, with the Christian Social Tyrolean leader Jodok Fink as Vice-Chancellor. Otto Bauer took over foreign affairs and, almost immediately, set off for Germany with the object of concluding an immediate *Anschluss*, at least in the vital field of currency. The fiscal scene was in turmoil as both the Yugoslavs and the Czechs had invalidated the old crown notes of the Monarchy, thus threatening their existence as a medium of exchange. With Renner's approval, Bauer went to Berlin in early March to try to secure from the Reichsbank a huge loan in paper notes to prop up the Austrian currency and thus convert the crown, in all but name, into the German mark. The Germans refused, pointing out that such commitments were impracticable before the financial implications of the forthcoming peace treaties were known. Bauer managed to secure the personal pledge of the German Foreign Minister, Count Brockdorff-Rantzau (soon to head his country's delegation at the Paris talks), that German-Austria would be given favourable financial treatment by Berlin if the victors were to sanction an *Anschluss*; but everything depended upon that. The conditional promise was an easy one to make, for it was already looking unlikely from the tone of French pronouncements that Germany would ever be allowed to honour it. The *Anschluss* was, in reality, stillborn before the Allied powers pronounced it dead. Nonetheless, it remained a central part of the dossier which, throughout the spring of 1919, Renner and his colleagues were drawing up to present to the peace conference.

Before he appeared at that conference as the spokesman for the republic, one very awkward manifestation of the Monarchy had to be removed from within its borders. The Emperor Charles, together with his wife and family and a small suite of aides, was still in residence at the Eckartsau shooting lodge north of Vienna where he had driven on the night of 11 November 1918. On an impulse, Renner had gone there himself early in the New Year, intending to make a personal appeal to the ex-ruler that, in the interests of the new state which Charles had promised to respect, he should both leave the country and declare his formal abdication as he went. The visitor never as much as saw the man whose empire he had once served and supported. Though ravaged with Spanish 'flu, short of food, cut off entirely from the world and occasionally menaced by unruly marauders rattling at the park gates, Eckartsau regarded itself as being very much a court in miniature.

Dr Renner, one-time imperial bureaucrat as Director of the Library of Parliament, had not sought, nor been granted, an audience. He could not, therefore, be received. But protocol did not rule out courtesy. So, while the royal family remained in their rooms on the first floor of the exquisite baroque building, the visitor was entertained by an aide downstairs to as good a lunch as could be scratched up. Politics were not even discussed, let alone abdication. There was some mention, dismissed by the aide, of the Danube water-meadows being bad for the health. It must have been a bemused and frustrated Republican Chancellor who drove back to Vienna that January afternoon: how on earth could the monarch who had stepped down from the throne be persuaded to step away from it altogether?

The solution came out of the blue for Charles, Dr Renner and everyone else involved, and it originated in the most unlikely setting of Buckingham Palace. Yet again, the prime mover in the destiny of the Austrian royal family was Prince Sixtus, who at the beginning of February had launched a private rescue mission on their behalf. He first approached President Poincaré, pleading for French help to bring Charles and his family into the safety of Swiss asylum. When Poincaré declined, Sixtus tackled King George V in London, pointedly recalling the assassination of the Russian imperial family at Bolshevik hands the previous July. Surely another Ekaterinburg must be avoided at all costs, even if it was an ex-enemy monarch with no blood tie, and not an ex-allied sovereign and first cousin who was involved? Sixtus could not have guessed at the time how much the parallel had stung; only in later years was it revealed that it had been King George – fearful of mass public protests in Britain – who had decided to abandon the Tsar to his fate.

The pang of conscience now stirred that unenterprising King, who normally did everything by the rulebook, into very unconventional activity. The final result was that on 21 February 1919 one Lieutenant-Colonel Edward Lisle Strutt had his lunch disturbed at the Hotel Danieli in Venice with a telegram ordering him to report at once for special duty to the British Military Mission in Vienna. The task he took over from it was 'to endeavour by every means in his power to ameliorate the living conditions of the Emperor and Empress and give them the moral support of the British Government'.* The vaguely worded message failed to indicate what 'moral support' was to consist of, but Strutt proved quite capable of both writing and directing the script himself from the moment, on 27 February, he drove through the gates of Eckartsau. He was travelling, appropriately, in a large Austro-Daimler he had requisitioned from the royal garage in Vienna, with the coat of arms painted out.

Though King George had had no hand in selecting his special escort (indeed, having launched the undertaking, he kept his hands off everything from then on), no better choice could have been found anywhere in the British Army. Strutt was a Catholic aristocrat (of the Belper family); skilled in languages, including fluent German; a fighting officer with a chestful of British and foreign gallantry medals; and, last but not least, a member of that royal European social scene which had now vanished for good.** Yet with all these assets, it took him a whole month to persuade Charles to exchange his 'exile at home' for a less precarious residence abroad. It was not only the worsening security situation around the shooting lodge which, for Strutt, dictated this step. On 15 March, the day Renner's coalition government was formally constituted, the British War Office stepped up the pressure for action with a crisp order to Vienna to take 'all possible steps to expedite the Emperor's departure'. The single-headed eagle of the republic being now formally in place, there could be no room anywhere on the same perch for its old double-headed rival.

Working through the Empress, whom he regarded as 'the real head of the family', Colonel Strutt finally persuaded a reluctant Charles to accept the Swiss government's offer of asylum. Sunday 25 March was fixed as the day of departure. Strutt, who had given his word that the Emperor would not be smuggled out 'like a thief in the night', assembled for the journey the royal train in all its splendour, including the imperial coats of arms on the carriage panels and the Habsburg flag (alongside the Union Jack) flying from the engine. The timidity (cowardice would hardly be too strong a word) of the Austrian aristocracy on this occasion did the former ruling class little credit. Though they owed their titles and, in many cases, their estates, to the dynasty, not a single man-jack

* The Mission had already been alerted over the matter a week before, but the War Office had decided, for political reasons, to avoid it being officially involved.
** The first thing to greet him in his bedroom at Eckartsau was a photograph of himself and Archduke Francis Ferdinand wintering at St Moritz.

among them is recorded as having turned up at any station along the long journey to bid the last wearer of that imperial crown farewell, even with the faintest of 'Hurrahs'.* Only on the platform at the Tyrolean village of Imst was a royal salute staged by a file of soldiers who presented arms in faultless drill as the train rolled past. But these were men of the Honourable Artillery Company, a part of the local British garrison who were living up to their regimental name.

The Allied powers must have been almost as relieved as Dr Renner to see Charles quit the republic (even if, before crossing the Swiss border, the ex-monarch had issued a manifesto of defiance against its legitimacy**). All that the Chancellor now needed to demonstrate was that as well as being in office, he was also in control of his people. A sudden challenge to his authority had flared up on the Thursday before Easter 1919, when the Vienna apostles of world revolution (stirred up and financed by the Bolshevik regime of Béla Kun in neighbouring Budapest) took to the streets again. Once more, Parliament was stormed; the deputies fled, and this time the rowdies succeeded in starting fires. Once more, shots were exchanged between police and demonstrators, with a few casualties on both sides. But yet again, and in true Austrian style, nothing was pushed to a conclusion.

The government held back from giving full rein to the forces of order and refused to declare martial law. The demonstrators, having let off steam and presented their demands to the Chancellor (mainly concerning more bread and more jobs, with not a word about any New Jerusalem), simply melted away into the evening air, to leave the capital in total calm. Typical of a very muddling day was the fact that elements of the extremist 'Red Guard' had been identified fighting both alongside the police and against them. The Austrian revolutionary spirit had shown itself, as ever, to be made up of very damp dynamite. The Allies, who were withholding any conference invitation to Hungary in view of the Bolshevik mayhem in Budapest, now decided that Austria was

---

* Throughout the entire crisis of the renouncing of power, only one aristocrat seems to have volunteered his services for the protection of his sovereign. He was Count Franz Karl Walderdorff, a regimental comrade of Charles's from their days in the peacetime Seventh Dragoons. In November 1918 he left his hospital bed in Bohemia and made his way to Schönbrunn Palace with a hunting rifle under his shooting cape.
** The so-called Feldkirch Declaration, by which Charles repudiated the legitimacy of the republic as being 'null and void'. This somersault had been prepared in advance to justify future attempts to regain his crown.

stable enough and respectable enough to hear its fate. On 14 May 1919 Dr Renner arrived in Paris at the head of his delegation. They were quartered in comfort at the Villa Reinach near the castle of St Germain-en-Laye, where, on 2 June, after a frustrating wait of over a fortnight, the peace terms were presented to them.*

St Germain is a gloomy castle, and the 'Stone Age Hall', so named after its ceiling frescoes, is one of its more forbidding rooms. The ceremony matched the setting. Renner and his colleagues (who, as the vanquished, had been admitted through the narrow spiral staircase of the servants' entrance) stood, like the accused in a court of law, before the horseshoe bench of their judges. The principals, who all remained seated, were the Allied 'Big Four': Georges Clemenceau for France, President Wilson for the United States, Lloyd George for Britain and Vittorio Orlando for Italy. This was the expected setting, though it was in fact to be the only occasion when the four leaders all assembled together to decide the Austrian case. What Renner had not expected was to see a military uniform among the black coats on the bench. It belonged to the French Marshal Ferdinand Foch, who, in the desperate spring of 1918, had been appointed General-in-Chief of the Allied Armies. He now took his place, not just as Supreme Commander in war, but as the spokesman for France's supreme demand in peace: the reduction of Germany's military, political and economic power to a level from which she could never again rise to threaten the continent.

It was the message of that uniform, and the steely will of the slight sixty-eight-year-old man inside it, which dominated the proceedings. Foch had been thwarted, in the parallel but separate negotiations with the Germans at nearby Versailles, in his wish to seize the far bank of the Rhine as a permanent buffer against any future aggression from the east. At St Germain he was therefore doubly determined to build up as large a Slav buffer as could be constructed around the Teuton bloc in the south, and to reduce the size of that bloc in the process. His political master, 'The Tiger', had needed no persuading over this priority. It came out now, in the first minutes of the proceedings. As Clemenceau's formal words of introduction were translated into German, the interpreter referred to Dr Renner and his colleagues as the 'plenipotenti-

---

* The delay had been damaging for the Austrian cause. Whereas Renner and his team were left isolated from all direct contact with the Allied powers, the 'co-belligerents' – and notably the Czechs – used their privileged access to lobby the Allied delegations for concession after concession.

aries of the German-Austrian Republic'. The French leader raised his hand to call a halt and, after some whispered exchanges, the interpreter dropped the word 'German'. From the end of May onwards, in every verbal and written exchange at Paris and in every official document which ensued, reference was made solely to 'the Austrian Republic'.*

Clemenceau's intervention has sometimes been presented, for dramatic effect, as the moment when the Austrian delegation first learned of the *Anschluss* ban. The suggestion is fanciful. Throughout April and May the French diplomatic representative in Vienna, Henri Allizé, had made it quite clear what stand France would take. During the fortnight they had spent kicking their heels in the Villa Reinach, Renner's team had gathered ample proof that, on this matter, French policy would prevail among the Allies.** It came, nonetheless, as something of a shock for the Austrians to hear the actual name of the state they represented being altered so swiftly and so abruptly. The First Republic had had a hard enough time getting into this world alive. Now the birth certificate issued by its parents had been torn up.

In this brief opening ceremony, which lasted little more than an hour, Renner was handed a hefty document some three hundred pages long. It contained what Clemenceau described as 'the essential parts' of the draft treaty. More was to come. In the meantime, the Austrians were told, they had just fourteen days to prepare any comments on what they already had.

When the Austrian delegates got back to their villa and turned over the three hundred pages, the gaps in the draft soon emerged. There was no provision as yet, for example, to fix the future strength of the republic's armed forces;*** nor were there any details about reparations. But the new frontiers of the republic were as good as set in cement by Clemenceau's 'essential clauses'. They dashed every Austrian hope of

---

* Even Clemenceau had to admit that the inhabitants of that republic could not be prevented from describing themselves as 'German-Austrian' if they chose; but the state itself had to be named otherwise.

** Austria's only hope of limited support had rested, ironically, with her traditional enemy, the Italians. Italy's prime aim was to prevent the emergence of a possible alternative to the Anschluss – a Danubian Federation which might threaten her own ambitions in the Adriatic. Britain and the United States, after some initial hesitation, had fallen in behind the French stand.

*** Characteristically, Foch was proposing a drastic ceiling of 15,000 men, whereas Lloyd George was prepared to allow a much more generous figure of 40,000. The Allies were finally to compromise on 30,000.

keeping Vienna as the centre of a large and solid German-speaking bloc. Border areas of Lower Austria were to go to the new Czechoslovak state, and similar strips were to be shaved off for the Yugoslavs in southern Styria. By far the greatest loss, calculated both in square miles and in population, was the Sudetenland, whose 3½ million German-speaking inhabitants were also allotted to the Czechoslovak Republic.

The Austrians could, and did, protest against this as a denial of Wilson's 'sacred doctrine' of self-determination. Yet they were forced to accept the practical reality: once 'German-Austria' had been killed off, the Sudetenland was lost with it. In isolation, the Austrian Republic would have had no direct communication lines with the Sudeten fringe of Bohemia, while even the ethnic line was broken at several points. The new Austria would often be likened to a tadpole, with the huge head of Vienna in the east, tapering to the narrow, wriggling tail of Vorarlberg in the far west. It would have defied the logic of everything except ethnicity to superimpose the Sudetenland, like some unmanageable quiff of hair on to this hydrocephalic capital. Unmanageable it remained: Masaryk and Beneš had won at Paris a political prize which they, and the Western democracies, were to pay for dearly at Munich twenty years later.

The loss of the South Tyrol was a much bitterer pill to swallow, despite being much smaller in size than the Sudetenland. The quarter of a million inhabitants of the province had been solidly German in race, language, culture and tradition for centuries past, and much blood had been spilled in protecting them from French and Italian armies. Yet, here again, the battle in Paris was lost before it was engaged. Renner could not have known in advance the full details of that fateful territorial bribe by which, in 1915, France and Britain had lured Italy into the war on their side. Yet he did know that large areas of the old Monarchy, both in the Adriatic and in northern Italy, were at stake, if only because, in the spring of 1915, Vienna had itself been competing with the Western powers in making territorial offers of its own to Rome. Yet now, in 1919, even if the partly Italian-speaking province of Trentino had to go, surely that solid quarter of a million German block further north could be held? Otherwise, where was the logic and where was the justice in the whole Wilsonian doctrine on which the Paris Conference was supposedly based?

The same contradiction had struck the President's advisers, the more forcibly since the ninth of his Fourteen Points had gone out of its way to specify that the post-war frontiers of Italy should be drawn up 'along clearly recognisable lines of nationality'. Even before he embarked for Europe on 4 December 1918 on board the liner *George Washington*, Wilson's 'Argonauts' (as he dubbed the two hundred-odd historians, scientists, geographers, ethnologists, economists and lawyers who set sail with him) had been scratching their heads over this, and the many other racial puzzles, which would have to be unravelled. As he had assured them, when cruising past the Azores on the tenth, that he would always back their judgement at the peace talks ('Tell me what's right and I'll fight for it!'), it was with some assurance that, once in Paris, they put forward their chosen compromise on the problem of South Tyrol. This proposed that the new Austro–Italian border should be drawn midway between 'the linguistic line' and the Brenner frontier promised to Italy in 1915. This would still have left some 160,000 German-speaking inhabitants of the area under Italian rule; but it at least made a modest obeisance towards the self-determination doctrine. A team of British experts had gone even further, arguing that the linguistic line should itself form the frontier, with one or two adjustments to meet Italy's security needs.

The President, whose country had never signed nor seen the 1915 London Pact, and whose voice in Paris was always potentially decisive, turned them all down and sanctioned the '*fino al Brennero*' so coveted by Italy. The reasoning which this self-anointed philosopher-king gave for abandoning his Point Nine was geographical: the Alps formed a natural boundary which overrode all ethnic principles and could not be denied. In fact, he had simply been worsted, here as on several other issues, by the very secret diplomacy of the old European order which he had sworn to destroy. Orlando and Sonnino, who had both ingratiated themselves with him, secured his support by a subtle combination of blackmail and fair words.

The most effective blackmail consisted of demanding the key port of Fiume, in addition to all the Adriatic territorial booty promised to Italy in 1915. The most effective of the fair words was the pledge to give the President Italy's unconditional support for his League of Nations project, designed to safeguard the post-war peace of the world. This was Wilson's principal concern, amounting almost to an outright obsession, throughout his six months in Paris. It constantly deflected his attention from the detailed peacemaking issues, of which he anyway had a

woefully uncertain grasp.* Moreover, he was being faced with strong
opposition from Britain and France over certain articles of his proposed
League Covenant. The backing of the smallest of the 'Big Four' for the
Wilsonian dream, coupled with Italy's agreement to 'renounce' the
Fiume claim, proved enough to secure her the Brenner frontier, and
with it the quarter of a million South Tyroleans who had lived for
centuries in its south-facing valleys.

Renner did his best for them, proposing, for example, that to meet
Italy's demand for security, both North and South Tyrol should form
one demilitarised zone, to be occupied, in case of war, by Swiss troops.
But this, admittedly bizarre, proposal was rejected. The great powers,
he wrote bitterly to his wife, were simply marching over Austria's head,
'dwarf-state as we are'. The general legal case, which he cogently presented to the Conference, had argued that the war had been fought just
as much by the Hungarians, Czechs, Poles, Croats and Slovenes of the
old multi-national empire as by its Austrian subjects and that, in any
case, the Austrian Republic was a *de novo* creation, like the other new
states. Why, therefore, should it now be singled out for punishment?

The allied experts were forced, in private, to admit the force of this
argument, though little recognition of it was allowed to emerge in
public. Austria, Wilson decided, was both a new state *and* an enemy
state. The second concept prevailed, and the final treaty text which
Renner was obliged to recommend to the Vienna Parliament at the
beginning of September 1919 was the dictated peace of victors to the
vanquished. Concessions had been made over post-war military ceilings
and the levels of reparations, but the central political clauses as presented
in June remained intact. On 6 September Parliament, under protest,
formally accepted the terms by ninety-seven votes to twenty-three. Four
days later, Renner entered the 'Stone Age Salon' of St Germain once
again to sign the treaty. As before, he had gone in by the servants'
staircase, escorted by French police. But once his signature was on the
document, he was no longer the representative of an enemy power. For
the first and last time, he left the castle by the main stairway, now saluted
by French gendarmes.

Woodrow Wilson, the architect of Austria's fate, was not there to
witness its execution. He had left for home immediately after the signing

* When the question of the German-speaking South Tyroleans was first discussed, for
example, he had naïvely enquired whether they would prefer to belong to Austria or to
Italy.

at Versailles on 28 June of the main peace treaty with Germany.*
His mood on the return crossing was very different from the buoyant
optimism he and his 'Argonauts' had displayed aboard the *George
Washington* six months before. He was, anyway, by now a sick man. A
sense of failure over aims that had been both ambitious and simplistic
added to his dejection. 'What was expected of me,' he remarked, 'only
God could perform.' For many of the peoples of Europe, this outburst
of Presbyterian humility had come rather late in the day.

The price which the Austrian Republic had paid for Allied recognition was enormous. It was Clemenceau who had summed it up by
pointing to the transformed map of Central Europe with the words,
'*Ce qui reste, c'est l'Autriche.*' The remainder was modest indeed. Compared with the old 'Austrian half' of the Dual Monarchy, it had been
reduced from thirty million to some 6½ million in population, and from
180,000 square miles to barely 50,000. Vienna had been transformed
from one of the great seats of European power, whose size and make-up
matched its status as the capital of a multi-national empire, into the
over-heavy and badly positioned centre of a small republic. The mis-
match was never to be remedied; the nostalgia took decades to fade.

There was some consolation to come, in square miles as well as in
poetic justice, for the new republic. Long after its peace treaty had been
concluded, it was able to secure both its Yugoslav and its Hungarian
frontiers by those very principles of ethnic identity which had been
denied to it elsewhere. The first of these settlements, the plebiscite held
in Carinthia, had been provided for by the victors. The treaty-makers
had been forced to take note of the border conflict by the fierce fighting
which had erupted there between Yugoslav troops and Austrian paramilitary forces at intervals throughout the winter and spring of 1918–19.
The fact that Italy, fearful of any expansion of Yugoslav power, worked
in this instance for the Austrian cause was one of the many ironies of
the Paris scene. The outcome was that an American mission, under a
certain Lieutenant-Colonel Miles, toured southern Carinthia from top
to bottom in January 1919 and reported on ethnic grounds against any
division of the Klagenfurt Basin which would make the River Drau the
new national boundary, as demanded by Yugoslavia. On 10 October
1920 this judgement was confirmed by the Carinthians themselves. In

---

* Article 80 of this had obliged Germany to recognise and respect the independence of
the Austrian Republic, thus formalising the *Anschluss* ban.

an exemplary plebiscite conducted under Allied supervision, 59 per cent of the inhabitants of the disputed areas voted to stay inside Austria, and only 41 per cent opted for Yugoslavia. The ethnic irritant never disappeared; indeed, Marshal Tito was to inflame it in alarming style at the end of the world war to come. However, for the First Austrian Republic, the problem had been put politically to rest.

The struggle to secure the eastern frontier was more complex and protracted. The area of the so-called Burgenland lay across the Leitha River and, under the Monarchy, had therefore formed part of Hungary. But as the mass of its peasant inhabitants was made up of some quarter of a million German-speaking Austrians, the Paris Peace Conference had little moral or legal option but to award the territory to the republic. This issue was not complicated by any secret pledges between the Allies, and such outside diplomatic calculations as did arise – between the strategic aims of Italy, Yugoslavia and Czechoslovakia – tended to cancel each other out.

What did stand in the way was that same Magyar fanaticism which had made Austria's life in the Dual Monarchy so arduous. In one way, it was like the old days: the Hungarians applied the same pressure they had always exerted against Vienna – the threat to withhold food. Their mood was understandable. They had suffered even more grievously than the Austrians at the hands of the victors, and were reluctant to give up another single square metre of 'St Stephen's Lands' – even to their former partner in the empire and fellow-sufferer in the peacemaking.* In the end, after much military skirmishing and diplomatic intrigue, they were obliged to yield up almost the whole of the 15,000 square miles at issue. The only consolation prize for St Stephen was the town of Sopron (Ödenburg) which, after a controversial plebiscite staged there on 14 December 1921, was fenced off from the rest of the Burgenland and allotted to Hungary. This artificial arrangement demonstrated that even self-determination could become a nonsense when carried to extremes.

The winning of the Burgenland represented the republic's only territorial gain. Though welcome because it was based on ethnic arguments, it was dwarfed into insignificance by the loss of the South Tyrol and, above all, by the failure to secure union with the new German Republic.

---

* The Treaty of Trianon, signed by Hungary on 4 June 1920, left her with only one-third of her pre-war territory and only 7½ million of her twenty million multi-racial inhabitants.

In 1866, Bismarck had thrown the Austrians out of the German Federation and forced them to ask themselves who they were and for what they existed. There was much muddled thinking about the riddle, but no clear conclusion. In 1919, Clemenceau had again separated the Austrians from the Germans, presenting the former with similar questions about their identity and their purpose in life. The muddled thinking started up all over again, in republican guise. However, this time the riddle was to find a brutal solution.

II

Suicide by Ideology

CLEMENCEAU WAS NOT THE ONLY ONE to speak dismissively of the rump that was Austria. Renner himself had dubbed it 'a republic without republicans'. For others, it was 'a nation without a state', 'a land without a name', 'a country which had no right to exist' or 'the state nobody wanted'. What all this added up to was that a body politic had been born without a heart. Vienna was still there, with its great palaces and ministries still intact. Yet their very presence was a mockery: there was no longer a centre around which either government or people could revolve.

A president duly took up office in the Hofburg. However, thanks to the Socialists – still the dominant political force when the 1920 Constitution was being framed – he was made a purely representational figure, unlike his counterpart in Germany. Nobody on the left in Vienna, moderates and extremists alike, wanted to risk some populist Caesar raised to the empty throne of the Habsburgs. So, instead of the head of state being elected by the voice of the people, as was the common practice for republics, the President of Austria was nominated by both chambers of the National Assembly. The Christian Socialists, speaking mainly through Ignaz Seipel, the Secretary of the Drafting Committee, argued in vain that direct elections would be a guarantee of popular freedom rather than an invitation to autocracy. But Socialist ears remained stopped up and the republic had to wait nearly ten years before the dangerously lopsided scales of power were adjusted. By then, it was almost too late to reach a balance.

Throughout that first decade, therefore, Parliament held almost unchallenged sway. This was the first wound which the new Austria inflicted upon itself, for neither the Vienna Parliament nor the parties who filled its benches were even remotely capable of responsible rule. As we have seen, they had only begun life as quasi-representative legislative bodies in 1908. In the six years before their suspension at the outbreak of war, they had given no sign that they realised what a modern parliament was all about. There was the same mayhem, the same ravenous pursuit of nationalist issues, the same contempt for procedure as the old National Assemblies of the Monarchies had always displayed, and these unlovely qualities promptly surfaced again when the Emperor Charles reconvened the delegates in 1917.

Had a country like Britain lost both its dynasty and its empire in one sudden blow at the war's end, then its ancient and well-proven Parliament (which had beheaded its monarch and installed a republic back in the mid-seventeenth century) could have stepped into the breach. The building on the Ringstrasse had always been an angry dwarf when measured on this scale of power and responsibility, though, in the old days, the blame lay as much with the despotic structure of the Monarchy as with the quality of its delegates. But when the farce now resumed, those delegates had become a collective despotism in their own right. The same inkwells were soon flying again and the chamber again echoed to personal abuse. This time, however, the target was changed. The old racial invective was gone. Despite bursts of pan-Germanism in the chamber, in reality the lost war had put both the Slavs and the Germans out of the Austrians' reach. The confrontation now was ideological, and so a new battle began to capture the Austrian mind and soul: the partisan and largely sterile battle between political parties. These now moved from the wings of power to centre-stage and, with no emperor and no effective head of state to stand above and between them, they simply slogged it out unchecked, until they eventually destroyed themselves.

Other tensions clamped on to this ideological conflict, intensifying it in the process. 'Red Vienna', the bastion of the Socialists, developed more and more into the fixed anti-pole of the 'Black' conservative countryside. Class warfare also sharpened the political battle, once the extremists of the left wing unfurled the flags of the 'international proletarian revolution'. These banners were gradually to wither away where they hung. Nonetheless, throughout those first crucial years of the republic's life they served as yet another distraction to erode the common loyalty of its citizens. It was now a case of the bourgeoisie against the workers, as well as the capital against the provinces.

The left wing's grip on parliamentary power lasted just under two years for, in the elections of October 1920, the Christian Socialists emerged as the clear winners.* From then until its obliteration eighteen years later, the republic was governed continuously by its right wing, operating through a series of shifting coalition pacts and drifting all the time steadily closer to authoritarianism. Such was the abysmal level of parliamentary life that once they had lost control, the Social Democrats never thought of functioning as a responsible opposition. Instead, under Bauer's inspiration, they resorted to systematic obstruction tactics inside the Assembly while building in the city outside their own Socialist 'New Jerusalem'. This they achieved with obsessive and justifiable pride, yet it was almost as though the rest of the country did not exist.

As a result, 'Red Vienna' became more and more a model for a cradle-to-grave welfare system, yet less and less a centre for the nation as a whole. The society they sought to create was based on party membership, not on citizenship in the broader sense. For men like Friedrich Austerlitz, 'Austria' remained simply the name of a hated and banished dynasty. Even the more moderate and pragmatic Renner continued to deny the validity of an independent Austria a decade after it had come into being. 'The Austrians were never a nation by themselves and never could be,' he declared in December 1928.

Two years before, his own Social Democrats had passed what amounted to the same despairing verdict on its own prospects as a party of government. Meeting again at Linz (where the famous programme of 1882 had been launched), the convention accepted the plain fact that the bourgeoisie had consolidated their hold over power in the republic. The question therefore arose as to how this hold could be shaken. Could these bourgeois rulers be talked into accepting a working-class republic? Probably not, in which case, should they be forced into acceptance, and if so, how? Bauer, for all his ardent Marxism, had never been a champion of violence, and he warned of its perils now. Yet the 1926 formula which he was largely responsible for drafting was dangerously vague on this score. There was mention of 'counter-revolution' (fascist or monarchist) from the right which might force on the left a solution through civil war (there was unconscious prophecy here). Like Laocoön of old, Bauer was hopelessly caught up in the coils of his own semantics.

His ambivalence – the willingness to wound but the reluctance to

* The distribution of seats was seventy-nine Christian Socialists; sixty-two Social Democrats; and two groups of pan-Germans totalling twenty-four mandates between them.

kill – was a very Austrian trait. That was a description which would have made him wince, indicating as it did that he too could display the distinctive characteristics of his own people.* For here lay the real significance of the so-called 'Linz Programme': the talk was all of class, of party, of left and right and ideology, as though the debate were taking place in some areopagus on the moon. There was no thought of Austria, of the Austrians as a people, and even less of that unmentionable word, 'fatherland'. This sums up the party's role in the life of the republic: they gave it a social consciousness but denied it a national consciousness.

For that, we have to turn to the party leaders and Federal Chancellors produced by the right wing, which was never displaced from power after 1920. A dozen of them came and went before the republic was snuffed out, but only three were of historic significance. They happen to be the same three who, in these turbulent years, tried to convince the Austrian people that their republic was a valid entity which could stand on its own. They were, in short, the flagbearers of a new Austrian patriotism. The trio was strangely assorted: the son of a Viennese horse-cab driver (and thus the archetypal 'little man' of Lueger) who rose to be a Catholic prelate and philosopher; the illegitimate child of a Lower Austrian peasant girl, whose first ambition, when he grew up, was also to enter the Catholic Church; and finally a minor Tyrolean nobleman (though of Slovene origins) who had been educated, and indoctrinated for life, by the Jesuits. Their names were Ignaz Seipel, Engelbert Dollfuss and Kurt von Schuschnigg.

The first was a high intellectual of little passion or charm; the second a somewhat naive peasant leader with enormous passion and charm; the third a worthy but colourless figure more suited to a lawyer's office or a professor's study than to the hustings of any political world – let alone the brutal one of Adolf Hitler. Despite the differences between them, they had two things in common which underpinned their Austrian consciousness. The first was their deep Catholic faith; the second was their reverence for the past. There was thus a contrast in orientation, as well as ideology, between them and their political rivals. The Socialists, tired of scanning those global horizons which never seemed to

* He was the son of Philipp Bauer, a Jewish textile merchant of Vienna. The family came from Northern Bohemia and the father brought with him all the pan-German fervour of that racial fringe. The son embraced this, but translated it into the cause of all-German Socialism.

come any nearer, looked instead at the horizon immediately around them and constructed that welfare world of 'Red Vienna', a self-contained Disneyland with its huge tenement dwellings, kindergartens, sports clubs and even death clubs – to pay for the comrades' burial fees. The right wing let them get on with it and looked instead for their inspiration upwards at the heavens and backwards at history.

Ignaz Seipel, the first Christian Social leader in this mould, started the first of his two spells as Chancellor in May 1922. This was only a month after the death, in banishment on Madeira, of the luckless Emperor Charles. Seipel was a monarchist through and through, and in August 1920 had visited the former ruler in Switzerland, his first scene of foreign exile. Seipel never ruled out the possibility of a restoration, which indeed was to come under serious consideration in the decade ahead. Yet he certainly could not entertain the idea during his first spell in office, particularly in view of the hair-raising adventures which Charles had launched himself upon during the year before his death.*

The prelate could well do without any immediate worries over the dynasty, for he had inherited problems enough with the republic. The new state had survived starvation in its first four years of existence. Now it was stricken with the fever of galloping inflation. To fill her weekly food basket, the working man's wife had already needed over 75,000 crowns at the beginning of 1922 (ten times the figure of the previous summer). By the time Seipel took office, she needed nearly 300,000 crowns, and the price of a single loaf of bread soared during the summer months from 1230 to 5670 crowns. Wages were being adjusted accordingly (including the 20,000-crown annual pension which Seipel, as a junior member of the Lammasch Cabinet, had himself received from the Emperor Charles), but this reprinting and overprinting of the bank-

---

* Hungary had emerged from the peace treaties with its name and its status as a kingdom unaltered. Admiral Horthy, once an aide-de-camp at Charles's wedding, had seized power in 1919 and become Regent a year later in the King-Emperor's name. At Easter 1921 Charles smuggled himself back into Hungary from his Swiss exile in a futile attempt to talk Horthy into handing over power. He returned in October and raised a miniature royalist army in western Hungary (in the midst of the Burgenland referendum turmoil). This moved by train on Budapest, only to be defeated in the suburbs by a combination of treachery and indecisiveness in Charles's camp, and tough improvisation by his opponents. The international outcry raised by the neighbouring 'succession states' persuaded the Western powers to deport the royal family to Madeira, where Charles died, aged only thirty-five, on 1 April 1922.

notes was the economics of the madhouse. Somehow, someone would have to restore order.

The prelate-politician scarcely looked the part for the task. Seipel preferred being photographed from the side, and the official camera studies highlight the domed forehead, long beaked nose and slightly sunken cheeks reminiscent of some ascetic philosopher. There is little in this patrician profile of the Vienna cab-driver's son, and even less to suggest the down-to-earth operator in international banking. Yet Seipel turned out to be just what was needed: the republic's carpetbagger in the world of high finance. A London conference on foreign aid failed to produce the answer. A personal appeal to King George V predictably had even less effect. Undismayed, Seipel set out on a one-man mission to lobby first his neighbours (Czechoslovakia, Germany and Italy) and finally the League of Nations which was holding its Third Assembly in Switzerland.*

The speech he delivered to that gathering on 6 September not only rescued his country's finances. It placed republican Vienna for the first time as a player, albeit a minor one, in European diplomacy. The key-words came at the beginning. He had appeared before the Council, he said, to plead the cause of 'my fatherland, Austria'. His appeal was not that of a supplicant holding out a begging-bowl. He stressed rather that as the republic had been the creation of the war victors, it was up to them to make it viable. Only thus could the stability, not simply of Austria, but of Central Europe as a whole be assured; only thus could the dangers of a power vacuum be avoided, and the peaceful ideals of the League be realised.

The speech from this black-robed figure was delivered with the quiet authority of a preacher addressing his congregation and had an enormous impact. The final upshot was the so-called Geneva Protocols, signed on 4 October 1922 by the governments of Great Britain, France, Italy, Czechoslovakia and Austria. The key provisions gave Austria a supervised loan of 650 million gold crowns to put her house in order. In return, at Anglo–French bidding, she promised that the house would not have a German roof: the Peace Treaty Clause 88, which effectively banned the *Anschluss*, was renewed – somewhat strangely – for a fixed period of twenty years. This was old history; but the

* Austria had joined the League on 15 December 1920, but was not given full-member status until 16 August 1927.

affirmation of the republic's international status was new. No less a
figure than Lord Balfour, speaking for Britain, declared that the agreements, while designed to bring Austria 'prosperity, solvency and self-
respect', would also enable her 'to become once again a great factor in
European civilisation'.

It cost the spokesman of 'his fatherland, Austria' nothing to pay
formal homage once more to its independence and sovereignty, which
was the form in which the veto on union with Germany was phrased.
He had long argued that peoples who shared a common language did
not automatically belong to the same nation,* and that the true Austrian
mission was, in its essence, a supra-national one. He had once written
that it was by no means certain 'where God wants us German-Austrians',
but that their place was almost certainly within a Danubian Confeder-.
ation of the future. He knew that his pan-German partners in the right-
wing coalition would swallow hard to accept the renewed *Anschluss* ban,
but the virulent abuse hurled at him over the issue by the Socialists
exceeded his worst fears.

In the eyes of the left wing, moderates and extremists alike, he was
not the saviour of the state but its traitor. For them, his was a threefold
betrayal. He had placed the control of Austria's destiny in foreign hands
(by which was meant he had prevented that control passing into German
Socialist hands); in doing so, he had dared proclaim the heresy that the
republic was viable as an entity separate from Germany; and finally, he
had embraced capitalism, the Satan of the Marxist universe. Only after
a campaign of left-wing invective and obstruction** had fizzled out
were the Geneva Protocols sanctioned by Parliament; even then, the
critical voting was passed on to a special committee rather than being
taken in plenary session. This particular device was attributed to the
Machiavellian cunning of 'the prelate in the Jesuit's cowl', as Seipel was
described in one Socialist epithet. Another attack accused him of trying
to make himself 'the Emperor of Austria'.

It was all a sad demonstration of the fact that the Socialists, the party
of democracy, had ceased to be the party of Parliament once that
body had passed from its control. Nor did the overall results of Seipel's
reconstruction programme do anything to narrow this breach. By the

* For example in his *Nation and State*, the study published in 1916 which first established his name.
** In October, for example, Renner travelled to Prague in an attempt to whip up attacks
from the Czech capital on the Austrian Chancellor's policy.

following autumn, well ahead of schedule, the budget had been balanced and the Austrian crown was even being described (somewhat optimistically) as 'the alpine dollar'. But, as agreed at Geneva, the financial reform had gone hand in hand with a programme of severe retrenchment. Unemployment soared and taxation increased. Both burdens fell mainly on the workers, though the sacking of more than 80,000 public employees struck also at the middle class.

Yet the Socialists were unable to translate this discontent into votes. Seipel was comfortably re-elected in October 1923, as much for his anti-Marxism as out of pride for his performance on the world stage. Austria was on the map again abroad, and her financial accounts were now balanced at home. What remained dangerously out of balance was the party political equation and the growing strength of forces which stood outside those parties. All this toppled over and nearly brought the state down with it during Seipel's final term in office.* This began on 16 October 1926, and the two and a half years it lasted were to mark a watershed in the republic's history. By the time Seipel stepped down again, the confrontation between left and right had moved from Parliament to the streets. The rival paramilitary forces had drawn up their battle lines, and violence had succeeded invective. The rioting and bloodshed on 'Black Friday', 15 July 1927, was a tragedy long waiting to happen. Despite this, as is often the case with the seemingly inevitable, it seemed to erupt out of the blue. On the fourteenth, the Vienna High Court had pronounced its verdict over two deaths resulting from a clash between right-wing paramilitaries and the Socialist 'Schutzbund' in the Burgenland village of Schattendorf six months before. The victims on this so-called 'Bloody Sunday' of 30 January 1927, a war veteran and a worker's seven-year-old son, had unquestionably fallen to bullets from right-wing guns, fired from the windows of the village inn at the Socialist street demonstrations below. The question which then had to be decided was whether the three men in the dock had shot in self-defence. After an eleven-day trial, the jury found that they had, and accordingly acquitted them of the charge of 'public violence'.**

---

* He had withdrawn from the Chancellorship in November 1924, primarily because of disputes over competence between Vienna and some of the provincial governments. But his successor, Dr Rudolf Ramek, continued both with his coalition and his policies, and Seipel remained the dominant right-wing figure.

** This mild charge was itself significant. Street clashes between Austria's rival factions had become such an established feature of the political scene that the accusation of murder or wilful manslaughter was not even raised.

Though the verdict had been handed down by a properly constituted jury and not pronounced by some arbitrary court martial, 'Red Vienna' became nonetheless the scene of mass protest. What happened in the next twenty-four hours was not only a classic case of Austrian muddle in general, but of the weakness of the left-wing command structure in particular. Without consulting anyone, the capital's electricity workers decided to issue a strike call. To secure some sort of authorisation, they then called, in the small hours, not on their party headquarters but at the offices of the *Arbeiterzeitung*. There they found its messianic editor, the same Friedrich Austerlitz of old, composing his leading article on the affair. When this appeared the next morning, it served not merely as a blessing on protest but almost as an invitation to violence. No Socialist could attack the jury system as such, for it was a pillar of democracy. Instead, he denounced these particular jurors for having 'broken their oath' and warned of the disaster which might spring from these 'seeds of injustice'.

The disaster duly came. From all directions, demonstrators streamed from the tenements of the workers' suburbs towards the Inner City. For some hours, there was a vacuum of control from all sides. The party leadership had failed to put its own Schutzbund on alert to contain any violence. When the demonstrators turned to stone-throwing mobs, the police could only charge them on horseback, with drawn swords. They had no rifles from which sobering warning salvoes might have been fired. By the time a few Schutzbund units appeared on the streets, it was too late. Soon after midday, the mob stormed the Palace of Justice in the Schmerlingplatz and set it ablaze. For them, it had become a citadel of right-wing injustice which had to fall.

Lunacy piled upon lunacy. For nearly two hours the mob prevented the Vienna firefighting machines from reaching the burning Ministry by barricading all the approach roads. When the firemen finally got there, it was too late to save either the building or the situation. Police reinforcements, this time carrying army rifles with full authority to use them, had also arrived on the scene.* Salvo after salvo was fired to clear the square and there were other bloody clashes, mostly at police stations in workers' districts, throughout the capital. By the end of that 'Bloody Friday', when the fighting died down as quickly as it had erupted, there

---

* Dr Schober, again Police President of Vienna, had taken the necessary measures to restore order in what was fast becoming a rebellion. Like Austerlitz, he was a survivor in the same post from the first days of the republic.

were eighty-four dead, nearly all of them demonstrators, and some five hundred wounded. As Seipel commented later, it was violence on a scale which Vienna had not witnessed since the revolution of 1848. The republic had taken over from the Monarchy without a life being lost. Now it had begun to bleed itself to death.

What stood out most of all was the helplessness of the Socialist leadership in the face of the mayhem unleashed by their own propaganda slogans. Few spectacles that day were more pathetic than the sight of the great ideologue Otto Bauer and the venerable Socialist Mayor of Vienna, Karl Seitz, trying to pacify the mob from the rostrum of a fire-engine. Their enraged comrades simply drove them back with stones. The same pair met with an equally firm, if more decorous, rebuttal when they called at the Chancellery to try to persuade Seipel to make concessions, or even resign, to calm the workers' fury. Law and order measures, the Chancellor pointed out, were a matter for the Minister of Interior, Karl Hartleb, whom he would be happy to summon for them. As for his resignation, the prelate replied with stinging irony, this would of course have been simple under the Monarchy, but would now require a vote of no confidence against him in Parliament.

Seipel thus showed himself as masterful in a political emergency as he had been in the financial crisis five years earlier. His own personal position was impregnable, but the street violence had taught him a vital lesson. If his recently-formed 'Unity Front'* were to be protected, all the disparate right-wing paramilitary units which were scattered throughout the country would have to be organised into a single fighting arm. Thus the Austrian 'Heimwehr' was reconstructed as a centralised force as the answer to the Socialist Schutzbund. The clash of ideologies was reflected in their very names. The left wing had possessed for nearly a decade its 'League of Protection', and what it existed to protect was the Socialist party and its ideology. What the right wing had elected to defend was the concept of 'Home', a synonym for 'Homeland'.

Though the Heimwehr eventually exceeded in numbers the strength of the Austrian Federal Army (restricted by the Peace Treaty to 30,000 men), its effectiveness was always limited by the rival loyalties of the

---

* The fact that a 'Unity List' or 'Unity Front' had been formed by Seipel to bring together all the non-Socialist factions in the country, including the pan-Germans, under one movement, only accentuated the division between left and right. In the elections of April 1927, Seipel's new 'Front' was returned with eighty-five seats to the Socialists' seventy-one.

local and provincial groups on which it was founded. Despite its social cohesion as a 'bourgeois bloc', it was also a political jumble. Within that bloc were pan-Germans who sought to base Austria's future on her racial links to the north* (the same direction in which the Socialists were looking, though for ideological motives); but also traditionalists or outright monarchists who wanted the republic to turn east towards the old links in the Danube Basin. Within its ranks marched both virulent anti-Semites and Jews seeking protection from them. The mixture could only be shaken together by a common rallying-cry, and that could only be the cry of anti-Marxism. Thus a tragic paradox arose in the last year of Seipel's reign. At the very time when the Socialists, sobered by their defeat on 'Black Friday', began to seek an accommodation with the right wing, an increasingly authoritarian Chancellor, egged on by an increasingly strident Heimwehr, ruled out any prospect of political compromise.

Seipel stepped down, again without warning, in April 1929. A diabetic, he had long been a sick man physically, and he now felt politically exhausted as well. In foreign affairs, his attempts to increase Austria's influence in Central Europe had stalled, while Mussolini had contemptuously spurned his bid to secure concessions for the quarter of a million South Tyroleans who had been living under Italian rule since 1918. Seipel was also depressed by the domestic outlook, seeing no resolution either of the tensions within his own 'Unity List' or of the frictions between the capital and the provinces. This had led him, at the end of his long reign in power, towards an increasingly authoritarian philosophy. It was also becoming an increasingly confusing one. He saw the Church as the true guardian of democracy, but only in the guise of a Catholic autarchy, which might even embrace the Germans. As a politician, he was now clearly at a loss as to how the Austrian 'Fatherland' should be run.

He had also been sickened as a priest by the success of the revenge campaign launched by the Socialists to persuade the Catholic faithful to desert his Church. They claimed to have secured 13,000 such defections in the two months following 'Black Friday'. Seipel had always declared that God had placed him in political office. He must now have

* Seipel's attitude to this, and to the *Anschluss* question in general, was shrewdly balanced. Though always holding firm on the republic's sovereignty, he also proclaimed that Austria 'could do nothing without Germany', and that vague formula satisfied his pan-German partners.

felt that it was in God's interest that he should leave it. Whatever his motives, his sudden withdrawal from the Chancellorship left the Austrian right wing stunned. For the best part of a decade, they had got used to having this totally incorruptible father-figure to do their thinking for them. He had also given to the republic the only European profile it had ever possessed. Now that had gone as well, and Seipel's three-month spell during the autumn of 1930 as Foreign Minister in a minority coalition government was too brief to restore it.

The end of the Seipel era ushered in a time of governmental chaos. No fewer than five chancellors of varying right-wing flavours followed him in the space of four years. Financial turmoil spilled over onto the political scene in June 1931 when the Creditanstalt, the last of the old-established banks to have survived the Monarchy, collapsed with huge debts.* The same year saw a diplomatic crisis for the republic when its plan for a customs union with Germany was blocked, primarily through French pressure, as contravening Austria's Geneva pledges of independence. The republic seemed to be drifting around the rim of a whirlpool. The drift only stopped in May 1932, when the firm hand of the prelate-politician Seipel was replaced by the even firmer hand of the peasant-politician Dollfuss. Unhappily, the course he steered, once he got hold of the tiller, was to lead Austria onto the rocks.

Engelbert Dollfuss was the most remarkable of all the political figures in the history of the republic. He had the most obscure of starts in life and the most dramatic of exits. His Chancellorship lasted only twenty-six months, yet within that brief spell he not only gave his people a new sense of identity but turned their country into a new and unique type of state. Finally, his death, as Hitler's first foreign victim, marked the beginning of Europe's ten-year struggle against Nazi domination.

The infant who was born on 4 October 1892 at a thatched farmhouse in the Lower Austrian village of Texing never knew his father. According to gossip, this was a local labourer deemed quite unworthy to marry into the mother's family, whose name the child was given. It was a proud name. There had been a Dollfuss working these lands as an independent peasant farmer back in the late sixteenth century, and the line had never been broken since. This upbringing in the serene and

---

* This prompted Seipel's last political intervention, which came from behind the scenes. He floated the idea of a grand coalition with his traditional rivals, the Social Democrats, who had emerged again as the largest single party in the elections of November 1930. Not surprisingly, the Socialists declined to pull his chestnuts out of the fire.

conservative heartland of the old Monarchy was to stamp both the man and the politician for life. Here, an Austrian, whether imperial or republican, could feel roots which went deep down into native soil.*

If the peasant farmhouse was the main formative influence in the boy's life, the village church did not lag far behind. His first ambition was to swing the incense-burner at Sunday Mass. He succeeded only after he had persuaded the sacristan to cut six inches off the prescribed children's vestments (he was a diminutive child, and even the fully-grown man was to stand an inch under five feet tall). His second ambition, also achieved, thanks to a free place, was to study at the archiepiscopal boys' school at Oberhollabrunn on the other side of the Danube. He spent eight years of his life there, preparing for the priest-hood; and that was still his aim when, in 1913, he moved to the Theo-logical Faculty of Vienna University to complete his studies. But a few months in the *Kaiserstadt*, with all the glittering new perspectives it opened up, were enough to change his mind. In January 1914 he threw it all in, telling his friends that he 'would rather be a good Christian than a bad priest'. The real reason was that he had now glimpsed a world far wider than the arc of an incense-burner, and he wanted to be part of it.

There was now less than half a year to go before Princip's pistol shots at Sarajevo put Dollfuss, alongside millions of his countrymen, into the Emperor's uniform. Yet the three steps he took during those six months all pointed the direction he was taking. He took up law, which was an even broader gateway to public office than the Church. He became a member of that powerful sworn Catholic brotherhood the 'Cartell Verband', and as a 'CV' man entered the innermost closed world of Austria's 'Blacks'. At the same time, he threw himself into the social welfare work of the Christian student societies, spending many a free evening teaching stenography in the workers' hostel of Vienna's Third District. All the elements of Dollfuss the statesman were there: the down-to-earth ambition as well as the spiritual faith; the political rigidity as well as the private compassion.

Dollfuss returned from the war four years later, a first lieutenant of the crack Kaiserschuetzen, with eight medals across his small chest and

---

* When he was barely a year old, Dollfuss's mother made an entirely suitable marriage to a peasant farming some thirty acres at Kirnberg, only three miles from her own home. The infant thus acquired a stepfather in the Dollfuss family mould and, eventually, a family of stepbrothers and sisters.

an even greater appetite to achieve something in civilian life.* The ladder which led him into politics was public service. By 1922 his foot was on a congenial first rung, as Secretary of the Peasants' Union whose imposing Vienna headquarters on the Löwelstrasse lay only three hundred yards away from the Chancellery building itself. Five years later he was promoted to Director, and promptly set about transforming Austria's agricultural economy.

His agrarian reforms, whose impact was to be felt down the century, went along a twin track: technical and social. New machinery, fertilisers, seed cultures and cattle-breeding methods were introduced; even more revolutionary, new insurance legislation was launched to cover sickness, accidents and even pensions for the 'proletariat' of the countryside – the hired labourers in the fields and the domestic hands in the farmhouses. By the end of the twenties, the name of Dollfuss had become one to conjure with in the capital. It thus came as no surprise when, on 18 March 1931, he was made Minister for Agriculture and Forestries in an emergency government cobbled together under the leadership of Dr Otto Ender, the Christian Socialist Governor of Vorarlberg.

Dollfuss was not the only newcomer to Vienna's political scene. The year before, the Heimwehr had assumed a new identity and elected a new leader. The new identity was its emergence as a parliamentary party. In view of the ideology it had proclaimed for the movement as recently as 18 May 1930 in the notorious 'Korneuburg Oath' ('We repudiate Western parliamentary democracy and the party state'), this was a somewhat confusing venture. But then, almost everything about the Heimwehr was confusing, to itself and everyone else, and this applied above all to the man it had now chosen to lead it. Prince Ernst Rüdiger Starhemberg had previously commanded the Heimwehr's forces in his native province of Upper Austria, where the ancestral castle of Eferding and several other of his vast estates were situated. As the direct descendant of the eponymous warrior who had marched down from the Kahlenberg against the Turks in the historic battle of 1683, the young prince was almost bound to have an Austrian consciousness in his genes, whatever else was there.

It was that 'whatever else' which was to cause his countrymen so many headaches in the critical decade which had now opened for them.

* He had only managed to join up in 1914 by standing on tiptoe to reach the minimum height required on the corporal's measuring-stick.

As we have seen, ambivalence had long been a feature of the Austrian character, largely imposed upon them by geography and history; it usually consisted of trying to look in two opposite directions. But this erratic young political adventurer, in seeking a place for himself within the Austrian maze, had tried in his time to look in at least three directions for inspiration. The first of those inspirations had been Adolf Hitler, in whose volunteer ranks he had actually fought during the street battles which culminated in the Munich *putsch* attempt of 1923. For the next ten years Hitler tried to court his prince, even offering him, in 1931, the leadership of a new movement which would combine the forces of the Heimwehr with those of the burgeoning Austrian Nazis. But by then Starhemberg was looking to another star, Benito Mussolini, and to another ideological model, that of Italian Fascism.

Finally, in addition to the swings in his political affections, Starhemberg had another permanent distraction – that of the social playboy with the wealth and standing which enabled him to pursue private pleasures with the same energy he devoted to chasing the public limelight. He was the only leader of the First Republic who had both the temperament and the means to opt out of front-line politics altogether for months on end when the mood struck him – as in the second half of 1931, much of which he spent at his hunting lodge in the Mühlviertel hills. He was technically on 'extended leave' to sort out his financial affairs, having handed over the acting leadership of the Heimwehr to Dr Walther Pfriemer, head of the Styrian branch. Pfriemer, whose instability bordered on political insanity, used his new authority to launch a Heimwehr *putsch* against the government over the weekend of 12–13 September, proclaiming himself the 'Führer' of Austria. Badly organised – as ever – it fizzled out within hours and Starhemberg promptly declared against it from his rustic retreat. The contrast between the playboy prince and tireless, single-minded politicians like Bauer and Renner on the left or Seipel and Dollfuss on the right could not be more fundamental. All of them found it impossible to read the true face of Starhemberg behind the ever-changing masks it wore.

Dollfuss was the one who had to live with the enigma when on 10 May 1932 he was unexpectedly nominated as Chancellor by the Austrian President,* to end yet another political deadlock. Like Seipel before

* Dr Wilhelm Miklas, who, as a Christian Socialist Deputy had taken an almost isolated stand against the proclamation of the republic in November 1918. Thanks to long-overdue constitutional reforms introduced in 1929, the presidency had been invested

him, Dollfuss needed the right-wing ranks of the Heimwehr to balance the paramilitary Schutzbund on the left (their basic strengths by now were roughly equal, with some 30,000 armed men in each camp). He also needed the eight elected deputies of its so-called 'Heimatbloc' to give him a parliamentary mandate, though it was only with the greatest reluctance that he joined hands with this motley and unpredictable band. Even with their crucial backing, it took him ten days to cobble together a right-wing majority, and then it amounted to a razor-thin margin of only one vote: eighty-three to eighty-two.

Such was the Parliament whose sanction Dollfuss had to seek when he returned from Lausanne in July with another life-giving League of Nations loan for Austria. It had been extended, like the one Seipel had secured ten years before, with provisions for international control and a pledge to renew the Anschluss ban. On both grounds the Socialists now united with the pan-Germans, their partners in the opposition camp, to try and block it. Again, party ideology and party intrigue were ranged against the evident needs of the country.

Dollfuss managed to squeeze his motion through only after a struggle that was both exhausting and macabre, and it left him incurably disenchanted with what passed for parliamentary democracy in Vienna.* It had also placed him more and more in the Heimwehr's debt, and thus increasingly at their political mercy. He had already accepted two relatively minor Heimwehr figures into his first Cabinet. Now, in a government reshuffle carried out in the autumn of 1932, Major Emil Fey, Starhemberg's deputy, moved into the key post of State Secretary for the Interior, a Ministry he was soon to head. Even Starhemberg later admitted that his promotion of Fey within the Heimwehr was a grievous error for the movement. Fey's arrival in government was to prove an even greater menace to the country. This much-decorated wartime major had turned in peacetime into a ruthless political freebooter, consumed with a manic hatred for Marxists, Socialists, democrats and parliaments alike – all of which he lumped together as a deadly red peril which he was predestined to destroy. His opponents were well aware of his views and of his ruthless ambitions. Indeed, one immediate result of his

---

with some real authority. The head of state, now elected by the people, had the power to summon and dissolve parliaments.

* At one point, the death of Seipel had threatened the wafer-thin right-wing majority; soon afterwards, the death of Schober presented a similar threat to the opposition. It was as though the undertaker had become the Speaker of the House.

appointment was to poison the exploratory talks which Dollfuss was holding with Socialist spokesmen in the hope of reaching, if not a political peace treaty, then at least a ceasefire. Despite the invective exchanged over the Lausanne loan debate (with Bauer being branded as a 'Bolshevik' and Dollfuss as a 'Fascist'), the left-wing moderates, for their part, were prepared to negotiate with a Chancellor who still seemed prepared to slog it out with them inside the constitutional arena. With the likes of Fey, no talk was possible, for the vitriolic Major had sworn to bring down the entire parliamentary structure in ruins.

For all concerned, the problem was soon to be settled by the structure destroying itself, in the most clownish parliamentary suicide of the century. On 4 March, the House had assembled to debate disciplinary action against striking railway workers and the division had, predictably, ended in deadlock, with eighty-one for and eighty-one against. Tumult broke out when irregularities were revealed in the votes cast by the Socialist camp, and a fresh division was called for. It was now that Otto Bauer, who had stood at the cradle of the parliamentary democracy in the republic, started unwittingly to dig its grave. He persuaded Renner, the First Speaker of the Assembly, to leave the rostrum and sit with his party colleagues on the floor. The calculation was that the Second Speaker, the Christian Socialist Rudolf Ramek, would follow suit, and that somehow the government would end up with one critical vote less.

Lenin had once called Bauer 'an educated idiot', which might be translated in political terms as a man with more cunning than commonsense.* If ever that verdict was justified, it was now. What Bauer had failed to foresee was that in a parliament as hysterical and irrational as this one, the whole roof was likely to fall in once you started tampering with the only pillars which held it up. As Bauer had predicted, Ramek duly followed Renner's example. This still, however, left a third and final Speaker, the Greater German Party spokesman, Sepp Straffner, in place, who was expected to carry on with business. Yet to everyone's surprise and consternation (not least that of Otto Bauer), Straffner also leapt up and resigned, acting on nothing more than a Pavlovian reflex. Parliament had rendered itself incapable of functioning and slid into a limbo of its own making. In some ways it was a fitting climax to a depressing chronicle of feckless mayhem.

* This was promotion of sorts in Lenin's sarcastic lexicography. It was the 'useful idiots' he scorned the most: Western idealists who had duped themselves into supporting the Bolshevik system.

Dollfuss was no dictator at heart, otherwise he would have spontaneously entered the doorway to power which had suddenly swung wide open in front of him. Two things propelled him through it. The first was the pressure of the activists around him, above all the Heimwehr, to seize this heaven-sent opportunity of setting Parliament aside without the need to stage a violent *coup d'état*. But for the devout little Chancellor, the truly heaven-sent impulse (indeed, he called it 'the finger of God') was what happened in Germany over that critical weekend. On Sunday 5 March, the day after Parliament had abdicated its responsibilities in Vienna, Adolf Hitler staked out his own parliamentary mandate for power in Berlin.

Hitler had already been appointed German Chancellor on 30 January 1933, the nominee of the industrial barons who saw in this ex-Austrian corporal turned German firebrand their best instrument for suppressing Communism, Socialism, trade unionism and anything else which threatened their profits.* That, however, had been the Hitler of the black frock-coat. He had cut a grotesquely decorous figure, compared with the transformation which lay ahead, when accepting office from that living legend Field Marshal Hindenburg, just reappointed for the second time President of the German Republic. But the vote of 5 March enabled Hitler both to change his wardrobe and to show his real face. His National Socialists won 288 of the 648 seats in the German Parliament and, together with their allies, commanded the absolute majority. Hitler was no longer the appointee of an industrial camarilla looking for a political hatchet man to do their bidding. He was the choice of his adopted people, expressed in free elections. The frock-coat could now be replaced by the brown tunic and all that it came to symbolise.

So, yet again, the course of Austrian history was shaped by events in Germany. Earlier in the year, local elections had already shown spectacular gains by Austria's National Socialists.** In both the capital and the provinces, Nazi victories had been largely at the expense of the Chancellor's own party. Impelled by the German example, might not the same brown tide engulf the Vienna Parliament itself, if the dikes were opened through fresh general elections? Dollfuss decided not to risk it, and in so deciding was convinced that he had the good Lord on

---

* Alfred Hugenberg, leader of the German Nationalists, who were Hitler's political allies, was also Director-General of the Krupp arms giant in Essen.
** They had polled, for example, more than 200,000 votes in Vienna, compared with a mere 27,000 two years before.

his side. That left only the Federal President, Wilhelm Miklas, to be won over, and all that this stickler for legality required was the observance of proper procedure.

It was found for him in the law books of the vanished Monarchy which this one-time schoolmaster had never ceased to mourn. The Emergency Powers Act of 1917, brought in so that wartime food distribution could be regulated by official decree, was still on the statute books of the republic.* (Indeed, there had been times, in the post-war years of near-starvation, when it might well have been needed.) But whatever the restricted aim of the original law had been, it could feasibly be extended to cover the imposition of direct governmental rule over the entire field of public affairs. This was the expedient at which Dollfuss now grasped. To face a challenge from abroad, the Austrian Republic produced a solution from its past.

On Tuesday 7 March, proclamations were posted up which began in democratic style, by deploring the absence of a national assembly 'to serve the common good'. What followed marched further away from democracy with every sentence:

> The leadership of a state does not, however, reside alone with the legislature, but just as much with the head of state and the government. This government, legally appointed by the President, is still in office. It has not been affected by the parliamentary crisis which it did nothing to bring about. There is therefore no state crisis.

And the state then went on, citing the 1917 law as its authority, to ban all mass meetings and processions and to introduce press censorship.

Taken together with events in Germany, this fateful weekend in Vienna had marked a turning-point in the history of Europe no less than in that of the republic. Austria had indeed shown itself to be 'that small world in which the greater world finds its image'. By that proclamation, the power of the governing state had been set above that of the elected law-makers – as was graphically demonstrated a week later.

When the egregious Third President of Parliament, Dr Straffner, suddenly stirred himself into reconvening it for 15 March, the police were ordered in to disperse the gathering, expel the opposition deputies

---

* Under the Monarchy, it had applied only to Cisleithania.

present, and lock the doors behind them.* As one final touch of farce, a nervous Dr Straffner had already declared the session ended ten minutes before the first gendarmes entered the chamber. So, in true muddle-headed Viennese style, nobody was at first certain whether Austria's Parliament had suspended itself by the rules or been broken up by outside force.

Two things were, however, crystal-clear. The first was that Austria's left wing – in 1932, as in 1927 and as in 1919 – had again failed to match its fiery words with even a glimmer of fiery action. On 8 March, the day after his state-of-emergency proclamation, Dollfuss had made one final bid to reach a peaceful compromise with the Socialists by offering the Party Secretary Robert Danneberg a new form of national assembly to be created along corporate lines. The offer was declined, in the hope that the Chancellor might back down completely if faced by a general strike combined with mass marches of the Schutzbund. In the event, neither was ordered. The leadership dithered for a week and finally funked any confrontation. On the day the police padlocked the Vienna Parliament, not one Socialist punch was thrown inside the building, let alone one Schutzbund rifle being fired outside.

The second result stemmed from the first. With no opposition in sight, Dollfuss could move easily from ordering one mild police action to creating a mild police state. The Ides of March 1932 had brought to an end the First Republic in its original form. At the same time a struggle for survival against Hitler began whose climax was to come in another Ides of March six years later.

---

* The Christian Socialist deputies and their Heimwehr and Landbund allies had absented themselves, on orders from their leaders.

III

Builders and Wreckers

'HE WHO SAYS "A" MUST ALSO SAY "B",' runs an old Austrian dictum. Dollfuss, who had pronounced a loud 'A' with the closing-down of Parliament, now had to follow it up not just with a 'B', but with a 'C' as well. He needed, first, to create a new political framework for a republic which was henceforth to function without either parties or polls. He then had to devise a new political philosophy to give that framework the respectability of a moral purpose. Both choices personified the devout Catholic peasant boy from Kirnberg.

Before launching himself on either front, he made a hurriedly arranged visit to Rome. Its official purpose was to negotiate a new Concordat with the Vatican. Its real aim was to assure himself of Mussolini's support in any trial of strength between Austria and the newly-installed regime of Adolf Hitler in Germany. Dollfuss returned to Vienna a much relieved man. Not only had an instant personal rapport been struck up between the diminutive Chancellor and the bull-like Duce, it was clear that they shared political interests as well. Like the Italian leaders he had displaced, Mussolini had his eye on expansion across the Adriatic. Here, the post-war kingdom of Jugoslavia, Italy's new rival ever since the intrigues at the Paris peacemaking, stood in his way. The Duce's gaze went even further. Italy's old enemy, the great Habsburg Monarchy which had lorded it over most of her territory, was now a weak little republic seeking protection. The entire Danube Basin lay in a power vacuum which the Duce felt well capable of filling. Austria was thus his natural ally against both Serbian ambitions and any expansionist drive which might be launched by the dynamic regime now installed in Berlin. The essential condition was that the republic should be ruled by firm hands and fellow-spirits.

So the fate of Austria again fell prey to forces outside her borders and beyond her control. Just as the destiny of the Second Republic was to be determined by the conflict between two great European power blocs, so the future of the First Republic was, from now on, decided by the balance of strength between two great European dictators. Austria was safe, but only while Mussolini's Italy outweighed Hitler's Germany in military clout and diplomatic influence. In 1932, that balance was tipped clearly in favour of the scales of Rome. Though this balance was to change swiftly, it lasted just long enough for Dollfuss's brief reign.

The Chancellor had not been back in his capital for more than a few weeks before he felt Hitler's hands tightening around his country's windpipe. On 29 May 1932, the Führer seized on an Austrian 'provocation'* (a tactic he was to adopt from now on) and clapped a thousand-deutschmark levy on any German visa for private travel to Austria. This was a savage blow to the country's tourist trade, especially in the Tyrol, which had recorded more than 1.5 million German visitors the year before; but it did not, as Hitler had fondly hoped, trigger an economic collapse and bring Austria sinking to its knees within twelve months. Accordingly, an uglier challenge was mounted during the following summer.

The first cadres of the so-called 'Austrian Legion' were raised in Bavaria, formed out of Austrian Nazis who had fled their country and dreamt of marching back on Vienna in triumph. This dream was to be denied them by their Führer (who preferred, when the showdown came, to rely on his regular army). Nonetheless, the Legion, organised and equipped along Nazi paramilitary lines, eventually grew into a force of some 15,000 men, divided into thirteen commando groups who represented a perpetual source of cross-border skirmishes and sabotage. Even more alarming was the sustained campaign of terrorism unleashed by local Nazi groups inside Austria itself in the midsummer of 1933. Street fights and bomb attacks erupted in what was clearly a coordinated offensive the length and breadth of the country. Its bloody climax came on 19 June when Nazi hand grenades claimed one dead and twenty-nine wounded at Krems in the Wachau wine valley of the Danube. This was provocation indeed, and Dollfuss immediately rose to the challenge.

* In this instance, the expulsion of the Bavarian Justice Dr Hans Frank who, on an unwelcome visit to Austria in the middle of May 1932, had held public speeches calling on the people to disavow Dollfuss and all his works. The 'provocation' was entirely German.

Within hours of the outrage, the Nazi Party in Austria was declared illegal and all its offices closed down. Though both the battlefield and the contestants were very different, the gloves were publicly off between Germans and Austrians for the first time since Königgrätz.

The nation was solidly behind Dollfuss on this issue. Though millions of Austrians had worshipped Bismarck even while he was kicking them in the teeth, veneration for Adolf Hitler in the summer of 1933 was confined to an extremist minority. Indeed, the arrival of his vicious system in power in Berlin had dealt a sobering blow to pan-German sentiment as a whole in Austria. The Socialist Party, for example, now deleted the *Anschluss* from its political programme with a heavy heart, while clinging to the hope that union with Germany might still come about in a new democratic dawn. But to keep this national backing, whether grudging or enthusiastic, Dollfuss had to beat the nationalist drum, and beat it much more loudly than Seipel, who had never had to call out the people to face such a threat. So the first sounds of a blatantly Austrian patriotism echoed around the republic. It called for pride in Austria's present, as a viable sovereign state which was winning an honourable place for itself in post-war Europe. But it also drew strength and inspiration from Austria's past. In this way it marked the first attempt to link in the same human chain the citizens of the tiny republic with the subjects of a once-mighty empire, and so preserve at least some strands of their common history.

The pan-German circle still had to be squared in the minds of these novice-patriots. This Dollfuss tried to do by harking back to the gospel which Prince Felix Schwarzenberg had preached in politics and Franz Grillparzer in literature a century before: the Austrians were the true bearers of the sacred Teutonic grail. He spoke at Dornbirn on 30 June 1933 of Austria as the embodiment of 'a Christian German civilisation' showing herself at a time when the world was 'shrinking before a certain German spirit'. Five months later (speaking at Retz on 15 November) the language had become much blunter and the appeal to the past much louder. It was unthinkable, he declared, that Austria, 'once governed for centuries by the imperial crown, should become a province of Berlin, and that our native people should be denationalised and placed under foreign rule'. Instead, Austria should be left in peace to discharge her 'historical mission in the German and Central European lands'. It was an open declaration of political warfare against Hitler. Moreover, the implication was that if the Goliath in Berlin wanted to fight in earnest, the diminutive David in Vienna was quite ready to take him on.

Dollfuss called his new political forum 'The Fatherland Front'. It was a forerunner of many such fronts to be created in Europe down the century ('Peoples', 'Patriotic', 'National', 'Democratic'), and most of them, like that of Dollfuss, were structures erected over the graves of parliaments. However, the Fatherland Front, unlike its successors, did not mock its name. For Dollfuss, it meant what it said. Its battle-cry was 'Austria, awake!', and the Chancellor did not hesitate to apply the message to those ancient provinces on which the nation rested. Barely had Hitler imposed his 'Thousand-Mark' blockade, for example, than Dollfuss was down in Innsbruck, asking a mass open-air meeting: 'Are we going to sell our freedom for a couple of tourist seasons?' The roar of 'No!' which came back from 40,000 throats showed that he had stirred that defiant Tyrolean pride against which Napoleon's generals had once stubbed their toes.

Unlike the repudiation of Hitler (which, in Dollfuss's day, was shared throughout Austria), his Fatherland Front had little hope of becoming a nationwide movement. He had problems roping in his own Christian Socialists, still reluctant to lose their established image as 'the party of state'. Even after they wound themselves up to clear the decks for Dollfuss, resentments lingered on, especially among those members of the party who had been active in the Christian trades unions or who still hankered after the parliamentary traditions. These were but cracks in the Front. The great divide, of course, was with the Socialists.

Repeated efforts were made to find a formula which would win left-wing acceptance, if not membership. Sometimes, the initiative came from Dollfuss, as when he sent Friedrich Funder, the editorial voice of Austria's right wing ever since the Belvedere days of Francis Ferdinand, to sound out the Socialist Mayor of Vienna, Karl Seitz, political veteran of the left wing. Dollfuss also put out feelers at a provincial level and, given his own birthplace, it was not surprising that the province he chose for this was Lower Austria. Here his spokesmen were often friends and colleagues from his days with the Peasants' Union, and their opposite numbers were men like Oskar Helmer, a moderate Socialist who was to play a major role in the life of the Second Republic. Behind most of the left-wing proposals stood the tireless figure of Karl Renner, Austria's pragmatist *par excellence*, who was racking his inventive brains now to find some sort of dignified accommodation with the new order.

In the event, there was precious little dignity about the Socialists' surrender. On 15 October 1933, at their last party conference, they backed away from any immediate showdown with the government, but named four provocations which would bring them to the barricades: the dissolution of their party; the disbandment of their independent trades unions; the undermining of 'Red Vienna'; and the creation of any new constitution which was not based on parliamentary democracy. As usual, Otto Bauer was behind this brave talk, and the ideologue again showed himself a lion in words but a lamb in action. Every one of the four moves named as a *casus belli* was executed by Dollfuss, in whole or in part, over the months to come. But the barricades never appeared – until, as we shall see, they were suddenly set up quite by accident. It would be unfair to suggest that Dollfuss was playing politics in all his contacts with the Socialist camp. Certainly the anti-Nazi card was, for him, also a very useful anti-Marxist one. But patriotism was the mainspring of his politics, and it had been only tightened by Nazi pressure against him. To face that threat, he would have formed his Front whatever political advantages or disadvantages it brought.

Nothing was more symbolic of the Chancellor's new political order than the date he chose to announce it: 11 September 1933, the 250th anniversary of the defeat of the Turks at the gates of Vienna. 'The memory of that siege,' he said in the opening words of his keynote Trabrennplatz speech, 'recalls for us the great history of our homeland.' Once again, memories of the past were being invoked to inspire faith in the present, with Prince Starhemberg, seated on the podium of the great Vienna square, as the living link between them. Two and a half centuries before, Austria had saved Western civilisation by saving herself. Dollfuss was now calling on his countrymen to repeat that achievement, this time with the Nazis replacing the infidel as the common enemy. 'We believe it is our duty to preserve the true German culture in these Christian lands of Central Europe . . . to fashion this culture into a Christian mould.'

The speech contained the first public pledge to create what became known as the '*Ständestaat*' or corporate state. For his inspiration here, Dollfuss went fondly back to the Middle Ages: 'that period in which the people were formed up according to their calling or occupation; when the worker was not incited against his master; when the economy and social order were both based on the grouping together of all those who earned their bread by the same form of work'.

Only three weeks before delivering his speech, Dollfuss had held his most important meeting with Mussolini, the so-called 'bathing costume conference' of 19–20 August, held at the Adriatic holiday resort of Riccione. The speech was the product of that conference inasmuch as the Duce had urged his guest to launch Austria's new system 'on a Fascist basis' in the month ahead. But the ideological link with Mussolini's Italy can easily be exaggerated. To begin with, the Duce himself had often declared that Fascism was designed for the Italian people, and could not be exported *tel quel*. Moreover, Dollfuss had already decided in principle in the spring, four months before the Riccione meeting, to base his new order on some form of corporate state and, like Mussolini, he had the instincts of his own people in mind. This becomes clear when we examine the dual meaning of the German word *'Stand'*. It signifies not just a profession or calling but also a clearly-defined place on the social ladder. (The union of Francis Ferdinand with Sophie Chotek, for example, had been declared not *standesgemäss* because the Archduke had married beneath his station.)

This reverence for hierarchy lived on after 1918. Indeed, with all aristocratic forms of address forbidden, other titles – whether academic, professional or bureaucratic – took on additional lustre, and there is no nation in Europe more addicted to them than the Austrians.* Just as life under the emperor was said to have begun 'from count upwards', so polite society in the republic started with the dignity of 'Herr Doktor', an appellation which need have nothing to do with medicine. Indeed, it is worth noting that the purely monarchical title of 'Hofrat', or 'Imperial Councillor', has survived in the bureaucracy of both republics despite repeated moves to abolish it. Archaic it may well be; but it *sounds* so nice and, as such, is still coveted by Socialist and right-wing officials alike. Thus, however bizarre the attempt looked to replace the horizontal structure of class with the vertical one of profession and calling (and however doomed it was from the start, in view of the increasing complexity and mobility of modern society), the Ständestaat responded to something deep in the Austrian psyche. It still dances on in the Vienna of today, with the traditional Carnival balls of the lawyers, the dentists, the architects, the actors, the journalists, the policemen, the firemen, and even the electricians, the butchers and the chimney-sweeps.

An overpowering influence had come up from Italy to shape the

---

* The most graphic example the author has ever found is the inscription on a grave in Vienna's central cemetery recording, in one long word, that the interred was the widow of an engine driver on the imperial railways.

philosophy of Dollfuss, but this had originated not in Rome but in the
Vatican and, specifically, in the famous encyclical *Quadragesimo Anno*,*
issued by Pope Pius XI on 15 May 1931. Pope Pius not only sanctified
the Dollfuss vision of '*Austria Instaurare in Christo*'; he provided it
with a ready-made exegisis. The crying need of the day, the encyclical
proclaimed, was to heal the rift between capital and labour opened up
by the Industrial Revolution. Unscrupulous liberalism had become the
doctrine of the possessing class and unscrupulous Marxism the doctrine
of the dispossessed. The conflict between the two was destroying Christian civilisation, and it could be resolved only by building a new structure
for society:

> The revival of a corporate order is the socio-political aim . . .
> effective remedies can hardly be achieved except through
> creating . . . *Stände*, which the individual joins not because he
> belongs to the different labour market camps of the employer
> and employed, but because of his own individual social function.

The idea of the corporate state as the instrument of Catholic social
reform in Austria also had its lay roots. The strongest had been planted
in the late nineteenth century by Baron Karl von Vogelsang, a Catholic
convert from the north who had settled in Vienna to edit the arch-
conservative paper *Vaterland*** (yet another in the long list of Germans
who had come to Vienna to help the Austrians sort out their mental
muddles). Pope Pius had left it to the people 'to have complete liberty
in choosing any form of state they please'. Vogelsang, on the other
hand, was an outright supporter of authoritarianism, and thus, in the
thirties, blew straight into Mussolini's horn.

A more immediate influence on Dollfuss was the ideologue and publi-
cist Ernst Karl Winter, a close friend and wartime brother-officer of the
Chancellor's. Winter was the leading apostle of Catholic Socialist welfare, a creed which made him an acceptable negotiating partner to the
moderate left wing. Indeed, it was primarily Winter to whom Dollfuss
turned to mend the political bridges after these had been shattered by
a brief but bloody civil war. His great slogan was 'Stand on the right
but think on the left'. This was admirably high-minded but proved, in

---

* So-called because it was published on the fortieth anniversary of *Rerum Novarum*,
the encyclical of Pope Leo XIII which had pioneered the theme.
** A Karl von Vogelsang Institute is still active in Vienna today.

the end, to be just another unworkable Austrian contortion. A similar fate awaited Winter's attempts to reconcile past with present by restoring the Habsburg dynasty – a course which Dollfuss never favoured, despite his reverence for the empire and his pride at having worn the emperor's uniform. Winter's significance for Austria was not what he achieved but what, like Francis Ferdinand, he believed.

Yet whatever influence Vogelsang, E.K. Winter and their disciples had had over the Chancellor's thinking, its fountain was *Quadragesimo Anno*. The devout peasant from Kirnberg, who had first headed for the priesthood, had read it and re-read it scores of times. He absorbed its message so completely that many of the key passages of his Trabrennplatz speech echoed it, not just idea for idea, but phrase for phrase. Indeed, by trying to give that encyclical a concrete political shape, Dollfuss had, among other things, launched another Counter-Reformation in Austria, with the Catholic CV taking the role of the Jesuits. The Protestants hit back, and far more effectively than in the eighteenth century, claiming that in 1934 alone more than 25,000 Austrians had moved over to their Church. This was even more damaging politically than ideologically to the embattled Chancellor. More and more, Austria's Protestants became linked with Austria's Nazis, in mutual opposition to the Dollfuss concept of a rampantly Catholic fatherland. It was a small-scale replay of Lutheran Germany versus the Habsburg Monarchy.

Though Pope Pius had avoided general guidance on forms of government, he had uttered one uncompromising political edict: 'It is impossible to be at the same time a good Catholic and a good Socialist.' Dollfuss may have been reluctant to accept this, yet he now had to preside over a tragedy which showed how wide the gap had become between Austria's warring camps of right and left.

If 'Black Friday' of July 1927 had been an outburst waiting to happen, the far greater eruption of February 1934 was years overdue. In any political conflict, extremists are usually men of violence. What made the tensions in the Austrian Republic so lethal was that the men of violence had the means of violence at hand: the rival private armies which stood outside the law and which could be used to overthrow it. From the start, the fanatics on the right were, in this respect, more reprehensible than those on the left. The Red Guards who had tried to storm Parliament in 1918, like the mob which set fire to the Justice Ministry nearly ten years later, were led – when led at all – by agitators who were nonentities with no notion and no hope of seizing office. But the fanatics who struck from the right were driven by personal ambition, and sought to use intrigue or violence as a lever to put themselves in power. So it had been with Pfriemer's farcical *putsch* in 1931; so it was now with the chain of disaster set in motion by Emil Fey.

The Heimwehr leader, who had never settled into civilian life after Great War glory, had been promoted Vice-Chancellor the previous September, in addition to retaining overall control of security. Backdoor contacts between the Heimwehr and the Nazis had never been broken off, and there were those in Berlin (and in Rome*) who saw Fey as the coming leader in Austria. For his part, Fey now sought to project himself as the strong man best suited to hold the new authoritarian republic together. He succeeded instead in almost tearing it apart. On Sunday 11 February, in an inflammatory speech at Langenzersdorf near Vienna, he told his Heimwehr followers: 'Tomorrow we will go to work and we will do the job properly for our Fatherland.' The following morning, the Heimwehr duly went to work by spearheading dawn raids on all suspected Schutzbund arms depots in the Upper Austrian capital of Linz, including the Workers' Home in the Hotel Schiff, which was the main Socialist strongpoint in the city. Fey was probably not expecting much resistance; he was certainly not contemplating civil war. That this was, in fact, the outcome was due solely to the reaction of another maverick in the opposite camp, the commander of the Linz Schutzbund, Richard Bernaschek.

Bernaschek was that *rara avis* in the Austrian aviary, the man who despised half-measures. Not for him the wordiness of Bauer nor the pragmatism of Renner; he wanted action.** The sequence of events which he started up would have been comical had the result not been so tragic. He had sent two couriers overnight to the party leaders in Vienna, warning them that if the new arms raids (already being rumoured) took place, he would first resist and then go over to the attack. 'This decision, and its execution, are unalterable,' his message

---

* Fulvio Suvich, Mussolini's Under-Secretary for Foreign Affairs, had been in Vienna on 18–20 January. He came to urge Dollfuss to implement immediately the anti-Marxist measures discussed with the Duce at Riccione. But Suvich also held private talks with Fey, the anti-Marxist *par excellence*.
** It should be noted that Bernaschek in fact had Bauer's own last-ditch blessing on his side. The Socialist Linz Programme of 1926 had envisaged the use of force by the workers if the government should act outside the law.

ended. The Socialist leadership were thrown into panic, both by the resolute language of their local paladin and, even more, by the prospect of actually having to fight for their convictions. Bauer, who had spent that evening at the cinema with his wife, despatched a telegram to Bernaschek in the small hours, ordering him to 'postpone the operation'. The only reason given in the cryptic message was that 'Ernst and Otto are seriously ill.' Otto, of course, happened to be Bauer's Christian name. If this had been a slip of the pen, it was a very fitting one.

Unfortunately for Bauer, and for Austria, Bernaschek turned out to be the republican equivalent of those pre-war fatalists who felt that, if the Monarchy had to die, it should at least die with honour. He refused to shoulder arms; indeed he was the first to fire his pistol when the police broke in. The shots in the Hotel Schiff started off a three-day running battle between the Schutzbund on the one side and the massed forces of the right-wing paramilitaries, the police, the gendarmerie, and finally the regular Federal Army, on the other. Though the casualty count made on 15 February showed roughly balanced losses,* the issue was never in doubt from the moment, at 11.30 a.m. on the twelfth, that the workers largely ignored the call of the Socialist leadership to come out on a general strike. Post, telephone, telegraph, railways, water and food supplies all went on as usual. The apathy of Bauer's cherished proletariat had exceeded even his most pessimistic calculations, showing once again that the Austrians were not made for the barricades.

If that demonstrated something of the Austrian character from the left wing, the reactions of Dollfuss to the crisis were equally illuminating from the right. Vienna was the key battlefield. Here, the Schutzbund was a force some 17,500 strong. According to the prearranged plan of action, its 'storm units' were supposed to seal off the seat of government in the Inner City, using as their 'tanks' mobile incinerators provided by the Socialist town hall. The fact that this bizarre offensive never took place did not diminish the latent threat. Dollfuss knew he had to quash it immediately, not least to stop it spreading outside his borders. The Czechs could be counted on to give the rebels support in any sustained conflict. Hitler could prove a far greater menace: a 'Bolshevik uprising' in what he regarded as the second German capital would give him the ideal pretext for intervention, and even Mussolini would have found it hard to argue about that.

* 105 dead and 319 wounded on the government's side, compared with 137 dead and 399 wounded suffered by the Schutzbund.

The question for Dollfuss was how resistance should be stamped out, particularly in the huge workers' tenement blocks which the government suspected of harbouring the main Schutzbund arsenals.* Dollfuss did not leap gleefully into ruthless action, as was the image portrayed of him ever afterwards in left-wing demonology. There was, in fact, something of the typical Austrian 'half-and-halfness' about his approach. The largest of the Schutzbund's Vienna strongholds was the 'Karl Marx Hof' in Heiligenstadt, a gigantic concrete complex some 1200 yards in length, with corner towers up to eighteen inches thick, and four courtyards linked with iron communications doors. To storm such a residential fortress with infantry would have cost hundreds of casualties; artillery was the only answer for a government faced with open armed rebellion. Yet four separate eyewitnesses** have testified to the reluctance with which Dollfuss sanctioned the bombardment, and the anguish with which he looked back on it.

His first idea was to subdue the 'garrison' at the Karl Marx Hof with teargas shells. Shortly before midday on the twelfth, he telephoned the army's main arsenal from his flat in the Stallburggasse (where he had returned for a hurried lunch with his wife, whose birthday it happened to be). The reply, when he ordered gas shells for immediate use, caused him to ram the telephone back on its hook with anger. The Austrian army had no teargas. All forms of gas warfare had been forbidden under the military clauses of the St Germain Treaty. That left only normal artillery, as an emergency Cabinet meeting agreed. Yet what followed that evening was far from being an indiscriminate rain of shells poured onto unarmed workers. Four light mountain howitzers fired at intervals a series of single shots of practice ammunition, many of which failed to explode. Calls for surrender followed each salvo, with Dollfuss himself appealing to the workers over the radio at least once an hour. Finally, as nothing in Vienna can happen without music, trumpets were sounded to announce the beginning and the end of each burst of fire. Some

---

* As subsequent police searches showed, their suspicions were well-founded. Substantial caches of arms were found in almost every settlement in the capital. Four separate dumps were found in the 'Rudolfsheim', the biggest containing two heavy machine-guns and 146 Mannlicher rifles, plus steel helmets and gas masks. The great settlement of Floridsdorf concealed 2500 rifles, 250 revolvers, 1500 hand grenades, 100,000 rounds of ammunition and enough dynamite to blow up every Ministry building in the city.
** A family friend, Irmgard Burjau-Domanig; his wife Alwine; Dr Stepan, the leader of the Fatherland Front; and Hofrat Rischanek. All four gave the author sworn statements to this effect when he was writing his biography of Dollfuss.

blood was shed by the action; bloodthirsty it was not. On the fifteenth, the government achieved the desired result without having to storm the complex. The white flag was hoisted at last; out trooped the Schutzbund units and in marched, unopposed, two battalions of infantry.*

Where Dollfuss and his entourage were both foolish and culpable was not so much the way they suppressed the uprising as the government's behaviour afterwards. Isolated excesses committed by regular army troops (for example by the shooting, out of hand, of eight Schutzbund captives at Holzleiten) could not be laid at their door. Nor was the wave of arrests – some 1500 in all – excessive, given the scale of the conflict. What was indefensible, on both moral and commonsense grounds, were the nine death sentences subsequently carried out. The man directly responsible, the then Justice Minister Kurt von Schuschnigg, could argue in defence that the nine represented only a small percentage of the total charged, and that his Chancellor had anyway exempted the ringleaders from the blanket amnesty promised to all rebels who gave up their arms. This was the pedantry of the lawyer who could not look beyond his office desk. As he well knew, death sentences can be passed and then commuted. For even one of the executions to be carried out was one too many, both for public opinion abroad and for reconciliation at home. As Schuschnigg discovered for himself when he succeeded Dollfuss, that hangman's rope was to stretch like a barrier between all subsequent attempts to bring Austria's left and right wings together to face the Nazi menace in unison.

The outcome of the civil war had removed the Socialist Schutzbund as a threat to the regime's security, but it had increased the tensions within its own fold. The Heimwehr, together with the quaintly named 'Ostmärkische Sturmscharen', or 'Storm Bands of the East Mark',** had been at the forefront of the fighting and had taken disproportionately high casualties. As a result, Fey presented himself as the true hero of the hour, and though Starhemberg's wounded vanity prompted him to indulge in a rival show of force, the Vice-Chancellor's stock had risen

---

* Bauer and Deutsch were in another Vienna tenement complex, the Ahornhof, from where they tried to coordinate operations during the first twenty-four hours of the uprising. As soon as he saw the game was up, Bauer slipped away, and by the afternoon of 13 February was already across the Czech border in safety. Deutsch followed forty-eight hours later. There was understandable bitterness among those left behind to face the music.

** A paramilitary force raised by Schuschnigg and based in the Tyrol.

even higher in Berlin. At the same time, more dark threads were being spun between Theo Habicht, Hitler's Special Commissioner for Austrian Affairs, and potential traitors inside the Dollfuss camp. The most dangerous of these was Major Fey himself. The most unscrupulous was Dr Anton Rintelen, the Provincial Governor of Styria whom Dollfuss had got out of the way by despatching him as Austrian envoy to Mussolini. Both were prime examples of that deadly band of opportunists who, without even becoming Nazis, were prepared to sell their Austrian souls to Hitler to reach power under the Swastika.

There were two moments for Dollfuss to cherish in the ten weeks left to him after the ending of the civil war. Paradoxically, both had given him cause to hope that his new order would survive. The first was the signing in the Italian capital on 17 March 1934 of the so-called Rome Protocols between Italy, Austria and Hungary. As the Hungary of Regent Horthy was also authoritarian, he made a suitable ideological bedfellow for Dollfuss and Mussolini. But the agreement they now concluded for a coordination of foreign policy between the three countries also seemed to make political sense all round. Mussolini secured another foothold on the Danube Basin. Hungary acquired backing against the French-sponsored 'Little Entente' (Czechoslovakia, Romania and Yugoslavia) which surrounded her borders.* Above all, Dollfuss got as much diplomatic protection against German aggression as he could hope for (given the prevailing balance of power in Europe). The agreement between the three signatories 'to consult together' whenever any one of them thought this necessary did not amount to a great deal; but it was far better than nothing at a time when Mussolini was still the continent's most powerful dictator.

The measure of the Austrian success was the anger it aroused in Berlin, where the Rome Protocols were regarded as a serious diplomatic setback as well as, inevitably, a 'provocation' by the Austrian leader. But it was Dollfuss's second moment of glory – this time on the domestic front – which aroused the greater Nazi fury. On 1 May 1934, after heated discussions over a series of drafts, his new Constitution for the Corporate State was finally promulgated. Details of its complicated

---

* The previous summer, Dollfuss had tried to bring the Little Entente into a new Austro–Hungarian association, thus linking the Danubian winners and losers of 1918 in a five-power grouping against Germany. But Hungary shied away from any agreement which might imply acceptance of her territorial losses in the peace treaties. The thousand-year-old 'lands of St Stephen' were still sacrosanct.

machinery are of little concern, for this freak of political jurisprudence was never to be fully implemented in its brief four-year span of existence.* Its significance for our purpose is what it said about the Chancellor's vision for his countrymen.

He saw them as the bearers of a sacred mission, for his May Constitution marked the century's first (and last) attempt to erect a Kingdom of God on earth. Its opening words declared that the Austrian people had received their new governance 'In the name of God the Almighty, from whom all Justice flows', and Dollfuss called on them to serve it with the same zeal as the crusaders of old. He invoked Austria's imperial past as well as her Catholic faith against the Nazi demon. The coat of arms adopted by the republic in 1918 had been something of a heraldic abortion. It displayed a single-headed eagle with broken chains dangling from its spurs and a hammer and sickle brandished in its claws: the symbol of Germany clamped on the symbols of Marxism. Dollfuss knocked this unnatural bird off its perch and brought back in its place the double-headed eagle which had flown over Vienna for centuries. Austria's renewed challenge to Nazi Germany would now be hoisted from every official masthead in the land.

Hitler reacted with a new wave of systematic terrorism. The Austrian provinces were picked out one after the other for dynamite attacks on railways, telephone exchanges, pumping stations, power installations and public buildings. In May and early June, the saboteurs concentrated on Salzburg; then came Lower Austria, followed by Styria; by the end of June, the campaign had switched to Tyrol and Vorarlberg, where vital aqueducts were among the targets. Away from the bomb blasts, the Führer also tried personal pressure on Mussolini to withdraw his protective hand over Dollfuss. At a meeting between the two dictators at Venice on 14 June, Hitler, while declaring that the *Anschluss* question 'was of no interest, since it was in no way acute and was anyway . . . not internationally feasible', was emphatic that he could never work with

---

* The final version left executive power firmly in the hands of the government, which was given five new legislative bodies to 'advise' it: a Council of State, Federal Councils for Culture and Economics, a Provincial Council and a Federal Diet with the 'power to reject measures put before it' (as the government could rule by emergency decree if it chose, this power amounted to very little). Seven *Stände*, or occupational groupings, were established to send their delegates, but of these only two – those of the peasants and the civil servants – ever got themselves organised. The squabble between the capital and the provinces as to how the head of state was to be chosen was settled by having him elected by all the town mayors.

the present Austrian Chancellor. Dollfuss, he said, should be replaced by a 'neutral' person (whom he declined to specify), and fresh elections should then be held to clear the political atmosphere.

But the Duce, so far from dropping his protégé, went out of his way to defend him. Dollfuss, he replied, genuinely desired an understanding with the Reich and 'could not be blamed for defending himself by all available means in view of the method of fighting used against him'. So, by the beginning of July, Hitler found himself blocked on two fronts. Inside Austria, his terrorist campaign, for all the damage it had inflicted, had broken neither the government's nerve nor its capacity to survive. Outside Austria, he had failed to have Dollfuss quietly removed from office by peaceful means. Indeed, his tough little opponent was counter-attacking on both fronts, profiting by the Führer's temporary preoccupation with his own domestic problems.* His increasing suspicions about the loyalty of Fey had already caused him to strip the enigmatic Major of the Vice-Chancellorship in May (to be replaced in that office by Starhemberg). On 10 July, Dollfuss carried out a further reshuffle in which Fey was also removed as State Secretary for Security, a key portfolio which the Chancellor now took in his own hands. This gave him direct control of the police and the gendarmerie, as well as over the armed forces. He had prepared his citadel as best he could.

Dollfuss was also aiming, in that fateful July, to consolidate his position abroad by another visit to Mussolini, just to make sure that Hitler had done no damage at Venice. It was to be another private trip to the Adriatic, to join his wife and family who were already staying there as the Duce's guests. He was preparing himself in a special way for the trip. In a family seaside holiday, bathing costumes would have to be donned; the trouble was that Dollfuss had never learnt to swim. So, in order not to let himself and Austria down, he repaired to an isolated villa on the Mattsee, one of Salzburg's quietest lakes, for three days of lessons from a police instructor. Dollfuss never got to show off his breaststroke. That lakeside weekend was to be the last of his life.

How directly Hitler was involved in the abortive Nazi *putsch* launched in Vienna on 25 July 1934 has never been established. It is clear, given the reception he had just had from Mussolini in Venice, the turmoil he was still subduing at home and his novice status in the Europe of the

---

* Notably the elimination of the SA (*Sturm Abteilungen*) wing of his party after an alleged *putsch* attempt by its leader Ernst Roehm, backed by some army leaders.

day, that he would not have sanctioned open German backing for any violent action in Austria. Accordingly, no intimidating military moves were staged along Austria's borders during the brief crisis, and even the paramilitary Austrian Legion which stood right against that frontier was never ordered across it. Government spokesmen and German diplomats kept up a correct and non-provocative tone, and went on, throughout the summer, preaching the doctrine of peaceful penetration. This was probably as much the product of ignorance as of deliberate deception.

What is equally clear, however, is that the *putsch* attempt could not have gone ahead without at least the tacit approval of the Führer, handed down to his chief henchman for Austrian affairs, Theo Habicht. Hitler had repeatedly made it clear to his ministers that all final decisions about Austria's future would be taken by him personally, and Habicht was constantly travelling from his Munich base to Berlin both to report and be briefed. Indeed, the most likely scenario is that he managed to convince Hitler that support for the Nazi movement in Austria had reached such nationwide proportions that once the Dollfuss regime was displaced, the country would flock to the Swastika. To this, Hitler could readily give the nod of assent. If anything resembling such a massive spontaneous reaction could be expected, then the deadlock would be broken and all his problems solved. Any Austrian military resistance would collapse, leaving Mussolini to face a *fait accompli*.

The reality turned out to be very different. It would be unduly flattering to the Austrian image to pretend that the plot was foiled by a united front of resistance on the part of the doomed Chancellor's countrymen. Ambivalence and hesitation hung over Vienna that day like a mist on the Danube water-meadows. The whole disaster revealed the nation's 'half-and-halfness' at its dithering worst. At the same time, it showed how Nazism was now starting to join all the other forces which were eroding Austria's new sense of identity. The only resolute actors in the drama were the leaders of the plot, their intended 'front man', and the victim with his immediate entourage. Almost everywhere else the treachery, as well as the loyalty, was shifting and dubious.

The *putsch* plan itself was more than a year old, though the first top-level conference of Dollfuss's assassins had been held at Zurich only a month before the action was launched. Two of the four plotters at that meeting were Germans: Habicht and his Chief of Staff, the industrialist Dr Rudolf Weydenhammer,* and another of Habicht's advisers. The remaining members of the quartet were Austrian 'illegal Nazis': Dr von Wächter, an intelligent young lawyer who became the chief organiser, and Fridolin Glass, head of the so-called 'SS Standarte 89'. This was a small commando unit assembled underground in Austria and made up largely of soldiers dismissed from the army for their blatant Nazi sympathies. Like their German sponsors, Glass and Wächter never wavered in their purpose.

The equally ruthless figure in the middle of the picture was that pathological Heimwehr conspirator Dr Anton Rintelen, who would have sold his soul to Genghis Khan for the prospect of high office. He was the man chosen by the plotters to succeed Dollfuss in a Nazi-run government, and he had taken up comfortable quarters in Vienna's Hotel Imperial to await the call of destiny. (The ostensible reason for his presence in the capital was to report, as Austrian Minister to Rome, on Mussolini's intentions in advance of the planned meeting with Doll-fuss.) There could be no doubt of his undiluted treachery. Weyden-hammer later disclosed that he had paid no fewer than fourteen clandestine visits to Rome during the first six months of the year to discuss the details of the plot with Rintelen, who had been clamouring for action 'before the end of July'.

The plot itself had been efficiently worked out, at least on paper. Glass and his 'Standarte 89' were to strike on 24 July, when Dollfuss was due to hold his last Cabinet meeting before everyone dispersed for the long summer holidays. The Chancellor and all his ministers were to be kidnapped in the main action at the Ballhausplatz (there was no mention of any killings). The Federal President, Dr Miklas, was to be secured in a simultaneous raid on his offices which were in the same complex of buildings. Other SS teams were to storm the Austrian radio transmitter Ravag, and the main Vienna telephone exchange. In this way the entire government, the head of state and the key communication channels would all fall to the rebels; Rintelen, nominated by the captive President, would move in as Chancellor of a new and pliable adminis-tration; and his German puppet masters across the border would hold Austria in their hands.

Weydenhammer and Wächter had met up in Vienna to pull the

---

* It is his 'Report on the Uprising of the National Socialists on 25 July in Vienna', submitted afterwards to Hitler, which contains most of the details of the affair from the Nazi side.

strings on the spot (the former travelling as 'Mr Williams', a British businessman). Their organisational skills were soon tested. First, it was discovered that the President had already left for his summer villa on the shores of the Wörthersee in Carinthia, and a special task force had to be sent by overnight train to hold him fast there. An even more awkward complication arose when, at the last minute, the Cabinet meeting scheduled for the twenty-fourth was suddenly postponed for one day. Though all buttons for the action had been pressed, and some of the armed lorries were actually rolling towards their targets, Wächter and his team, operating from a café house, managed to call everyone back to their bases without showing their hand. The plotters were up all night rejigging their plans in what was a significant change of venue. They were now meeting in the flat of Herr von Altenburg, a member of the German Legation staff.

There had been one leak from the rebel camp to the police about the conspiracy on the twenty-fourth, though, ominously, it never reached the Chancellor, nor were any extra precautions ordered for his safety.* This was treachery by default, but it was nothing compared with the series of betrayals and semi-betrayals which spattered the Vienna scene on the twenty-fifth, the day the *putsch* was launched. Taken together, they present a vivid picture of the schizophrenia which had seized the Austrian mind.

The first example, and a prime specimen of the species, was Johann Doppler, a district inspector of the Vienna police force. He had only joined in the plot two days before, and then not out of conviction but out of respect for his superiors; he had been assured that Dr Steinhäusl, the Police President designate, was on the rebel side. By the morning of the *putsch*, however, Doppler's Austrian conscience had got the upper hand and he decided to betray the conspiracy: the only question was, to whom? Distrusting, with reason, his own police force, and fearful that government departments might also have been penetrated, he turned to the one person he felt he could trust, Dr Karl Maria Stepan, leader of Dollfuss's Fatherland Front.

The action now moved again, in true Viennese style, to the coffee houses of the capital. Doppler, having failed to reach Stepan by

---

* Smelling a rat somewhere in the Vienna sewers, Dollfuss had, however, ordered extra security measures himself, targeting the principal suspects. He ordered a special police guard to watch Rintelen's activities at the Hotel Imperial, and assigned three detectives to shadow Fey night and day.

telephone, simply left a message asking him to come for 'an important communication', to the Café Weghuber. There, while twiddling his thumbs in frustration, the police inspector recognised, at a nearby table, a cashier of Fey's Vienna Heimwehr office and poured out his heart to him. Doppler's message was passed on and up, through the correct Heimwehr channels, which nobody ventured to short-cut. Via the Chief Cashier and the Head of Accounts, it finally reached Fey's adjutant, Major Wrabel, who telephoned his chief in his Vienna apartment. It was now just after ten o'clock, and the Cabinet was due to meet at eleven. Major Wrabel was soon rung up and received a second warning signal, this time from the commander of one of his own Vienna Heimwehr regiments, Captain Ernst Mayer. The Captain, like the cashier, had been taking breakfast at the Café Weghuber, and the panic-stricken Doppler had ended a busy morning's work by also pouring out to him the news of the imminent coup.*

And so to the most impenetrable and probably the most turbulent of all Austrian minds on the day, that of Major Emil Fey himself. The Major was still fuming over the double demotion he had suffered at the Chancellor's hands, and knew that Dollfuss was now his sworn enemy. But he had been allowed to remain in the government with the face-saving role of Minister without Portfolio, and so was due to attend the Cabinet meeting. He arrived soon after 11 a.m., when the Cabinet was already in session upstairs. He made no move to alert them, and took no immediate action even when final proof of the conspiracy was brought to him by Major Wrabel: Doppler's own written orders, under the code sign '89', to report for action. What Fey did do in all that fatally lost time was to mobilise reinforcements from his own Vienna Heimwehr: one of his regiments, on manoeuvres in the Prater, was ordered to march immediately to the Chancellery.** Fey's motives at this stage seem clear. As in 1932, but this time to far greater effect and far greater personal glory, his Heimwehr would rescue the country from Nazism just as, before, it had rescued Austria from Marxism. Only after he had set this in train did Fey slip into the Cabinet room, excuse his lateness, call

* Doppler seems to have been reduced to a nervous wreck after the experience of betraying both Dollfuss and Hitler within the space of forty-eight hours. He committed suicide shortly afterwards.
** Starhemberg later claimed that, anticipating trouble, Fey had ordered these manoeuvres as a precaution before the twenty-fifth, issuing the men with live ammunition. The claim, like so much in Starhemberg's unreliable memoirs, is unproven.

Dollfuss over to a corner, and whisper the first words of warning.

It was now noon, and though Fey was unaware of the exact timing, the armed rebels were due to burst in below in less than an hour's time. Fey's alert came just in time to save the government, and so doom the *putsch*, even if, unwittingly, it had sealed the fate of Dollfuss. Fey's whispered message (the exact words are unknown) amounted only to a vague warning that something ugly was afoot, with the Chancellery as its target. But this was enough for Dollfuss, who had been sniffing danger in the air for some days. Suspending the meeting, he kept only three of his Ministers with him: Fey, Baron Karl Karwinsky, Fey's successor as Secretary for State Security, and General Wilhelm Zehner, the newly-appointed Minister of Defence. All the remainder, and notably Schuschnigg, were ordered to return immediately to their offices. That total vacuum in government on which the plotters had counted was thus avoided, though with less than an hour to spare.

The fifty minutes between the dispersal of the Cabinet and the storming of the building brought further signs of what was at best muddle, and at worst prevarication, in the bureaucracy. No attempt was made to call in the army, perhaps because its loyalty could not be entirely guaranteed. (At least one of its senior officers, Lieutenant-Colonel Sinzinger, Chief of Staff of the Vienna Headquarters, was a member of the conspiracy; indeed, the original plan was for the rebels to assemble inside the main garrison building.) Even more extraordinary (to put it at its mildest) was the fact that, during those fifty minutes, no police riot squads reached the Chancellery in time to do any good. It was not until 12.35, when the rebels were mounting their lorries, that the police squads left their barracks. Even then, a journey which should have taken less than five minutes lasted for more than fifteen. The armed police arrived just after the rebels had stormed the building.

Unlike everyone else, they were dead on time, and for a very good reason. They knew that at 12.50 precisely the military guard on the Chancellery was changed. As the relief detachment marched in, the lorries of the SS Standarte 89 simply roared in behind them through the open doors. They had made their way unchallenged through the streets from their hiding-place (a gymnasium in the Siebensterngasse) despite the fact that many of the 154 'soldiers' in the convoy were standing up and dressed like bandits, whereas some of the old civilian lorries still had the names of business firms painted on their sides. But the bluff had worked, and once inside the courtyard the band of desperadoes found luck – in the shape of good old Viennese witlessness – on their side. For when the bogus soldiers set about disarming the genuine ones, they found there was no need. The Chancellery guard was classified as 'ceremonial'. That meant it had no ammunition in its rifles.

The meticulous planning of the assault very probably did not call for the murder, as opposed to the capture, of the Chancellor, though Nazi documents found later included among their code signals a message to announce Dollfuss's death. 'Old cutlery samples arrived' was the distinctly unflattering text. When the rebels broke in, Dollfuss was alone with Karwinsky and Fey in his first-floor office. His last known order had been to despatch General Zehner back to the Defence Ministry to make sure the army could be counted upon. With this step, Dollfuss helped to save the life of the republic, though he was now nearing the end of his own. After some confusion as to which escape route he should take, the Chancellor found himself locked inside the so-called *Eckzimmer* or Corner Room, which adjoined his office. As Dollfuss and Karwinsky were turning on their heels, a group of ten rebels, led by one Otto Planetta, broke in from the guard staircase. Without uttering a word, Planetta advanced on the Chancellor and fired two shots at him from close range.* They entered his neck and armpit and he fell, bleeding heavily, to the floor. It was shortly after one o'clock, little over ten minutes after the *putsch*ists had stormed through the gateway.

The mortally wounded man took over two and a half hours to bleed to death, and went through a multiplicity of agonies in the process. On top of the physical suffering came spiritual torment, in that his assailants had denied him a priest as well as a doctor. There was also sharp political grief, for he died believing that the rebels had succeeded and that the arch-traitor Rintelen was preparing to step into his shoes.** In fact, by the time (about 3.45 in the afternoon) that death put an end to his sufferings, it was the rebel cause which was lost, and the Austria of his Fatherland Front which had survived.

Of the other two main operations planned in the *putsch*, the attack on the Vienna radio had brought only temporary success. A small team

---

* Planetta was later to claim that he had fired 'in self-defence' to ward off a blow the Chancellor had aimed at him. This version is made to seem all the more specious in view of the second shot fired.
** Dollfuss was spared one other pang of sorrow. He died without knowing that his murderer had once fought with him in Italy, as a soldier in his own cherished regiment of 'Kaiserschuetzen'.

of rebels managed to storm the building at about 1 p.m., forcing the announcer to broadcast that Dollfuss had 'resigned' and that Dr Anton Rintelen had taken his place. They got no further. The police shut down the main transmitter station at Bisamberg (which the rebels had overlooked), and by 2.45, after a lively exchange of fire, the Ravag building was itself under government control again.

The third operation, the capture of President Miklas in Carinthia, never got off the ground. The local police, tipped off by an anonymous informer, broke up Wächter's kidnap squad before they could go into action. The President, who alone had the constitutional power to appoint a new Chancellor, got through to the Defence Ministry in Vienna, where the bulk of the Cabinet were assembled. Technically, the Vice-Chancellor (now Starhemberg) would have been the natural replacement, but   fortunately for Miklas, and for Austria – the playboy-prince was again sunning himself in Italy. With relief, the President could turn to Schuschnigg,* who was sworn in over the telephone as the Chancellor *ad interim* and ordered to use all force necessary to suppress the uprising and free the captives in the Chancellery. As it was only 2.30 p.m., the true Chancellor of Austria was still alive, though helpless and slowly dying.

Though the rebellion was, by now, well and truly broken, it took an incredible five and a half hours before, at 8 p.m., the seat of government was again in Austrian hands. One reason for the delay was the increasingly dubious behaviour of Fey inside the building. Even if he had played no part in mounting the rebellion, he now seemed resolved to extract from it any advantage he could gain. Twice he appeared on the balcony to dissuade the army and Heimwehr forces now massed below from storming the building; instead, they were invited in for a time-wasting parley. Next, Fey was persuaded by his Nazi captors to sign messages, for distribution outside, that Rintelen was now Chancellor and that his orders should be obeyed. To claim he only did this at gunpoint is not to say much for the bravery of one of the most highly decorated Austrian officers of the Great War. And he was certainly under no coercion when (as was later established) he accepted the rebel commander's offer of the Security portfolio in Rintelen's non-existent

---

* Schuschnigg, though only Minister of Education at the time, was the most respected figure in the Cabinet, and it had been the hope of the dying Dollfuss that he should succeed him. Moreover, with his 'Storm Bands of the East Mark' he possessed his own private army which, for Miklas, was infinitely preferable to the Heimwehr.

'government'. Fey had become a collaborator after the event, a new variant of the Austrian malaise.

In fact the Chancellery was never stormed, even after it became known that Dollfuss was dead. It was the Germans who had sent the rebels in, and it was the Germans who got them out. At around 7.30 p.m. the rebel leader, Captain Holzweber, rang the German Minister in Vienna, Dr Kurt Rieth, and pleaded with him to come to the Chancellery in person. He was to act as a guarantor of the government's offer of safe conduct to the German border for the rebels, once they had surrendered. Very foolishly (for it gave the stamp of official backing to the uprising), the envoy agreed. He turned up 'in a private capacity' at the Ballhaus-platz, complete with Homburg hat and walking stick, as though paying a formal call, and whispered through a crack in the door that he had indeed received the necessary assurances from Schuschnigg's Minister. He then shot away like a frightened rabbit to return to his diplomatic burrow.

The rebels, believing their necks were safe, now opened the gates, and the besiegers – a force of soldiers, police and Heimwehr men several thousand strong – streamed in unopposed. At any point from the late afternoon onwards they could have simply pushed those gates open themselves. The only thing that was clear-cut about the end of this sorry episode was the government's broken promise. Instead of being escorted to the German border, the men of SS Standarte 89 were taken straight to prison, and the ringleaders were executed only a week later. Justifications were, of course, presented by Schuschnigg for this breach. But it was a depressing omen for the future that he only acted ruthlessly once all danger had vanished.

Had he been the man directing operations from outside, Dollfuss would have acted very differently. This is the real significance of the day. Just as Francis Joseph had been the heartbeat of the Monarchy, so Engelbert Dollfuss had become the heartbeat of the republic, of Austria *tout court*, and not the German-Austria as envisaged in different guises by both the Nazis and the Socialists of the nation. That beat was never to be heard so strongly and constantly again.

IV

Rape by Consent

AUSTRIA HAD ONLY FOUR YEARS to live herself after the murder of her stoutest champion. It was a remorseless countdown to extinction which, given the changing power balance in Europe, was seemingly unstoppable. Hitler had never left any doubts about his ultimate intentions. The second sentence on page one of his *Mein Kampf,* written in prison in the early twenties,* stated unequivocally: 'German-Austria must come back again to the great German motherland.' But the crude and premature attempt to wrench Austria back by an internal *putsch* had failed, and he dared not resort to military force against his native country so long as Mussolini's arm was stronger than his own. It had reached out during the July crisis by the despatch of Italian divisions to the Brenner, and was still stretched protectively over Vienna. Indeed, barely six months after the removal of Dollfuss from the scene, that protection was even broadened in a way which would have gladdened the little martyr's heart. In January and February 1935, alarmed by Hitler's mounting provocations, France and Britain had signed separate Protocols undertaking 'to hold joint consultations' in the event of any threat to Austria's independence; the following April, the arrangement was consolidated by the three-power agreement with Italy concluded at Stresa.

The so-called 'Stresa Front' was made of paper, or at best stiff cardboard, in that it promised only diplomatic action in any Austro–German crisis. This pledge would always mark the limit of any intervention by Britain. Now, as in the days of the Habsburg Monarchy, she regarded the Danube Basin as a complicated trouble-zone of little

---

* After the failure of his 1923 Munich *putsch*, Hitler was sentenced to five years' imprisonment in Landsberg jail, but was amnestied and soon released.

strategic concern to a British empire which had problems enough ruling, with ever-weakening resources, over a quarter of the globe. France had a far greater interest in the region; indeed, as the political, economic and military patron of the Little Entente, she had been the strongest and most prominent European power along the banks of the Danube until the end of the twenties. Yet the Third Republic was never geared to mounting any firm defence of those interests. Its spirit was passive and fatalistic. Its politics were a chronicle of constant turmoil. There were some forty successive governments in Paris in the twenty-five-year span between the World Wars; the Chautemps Ministry, one of them, was to choose the very hours of Austria's final agony in which to collapse.

But it was, of course, in the sands of the east African deserts that the Stresa Front – and much else besides – was finally buried. By the end of the thirties, Nazi Germany would anyway have overtaken, and then eclipsed, Fascist Italy in military and economic strength. Mussolini's embarking, in October 1935, on his disastrous Abyssinian campaign only accelerated the process. On the one hand, he had blown his political bridges to the Western democracies, who led the righteous if ineffective campaign of sanctions against Italy. That had driven him, on the other hand, into the arms of his fellow-dictator, a partnership that was soon sealed by their joint intervention in the Spanish Civil War. The Berlin–Rome axis was like a stake driven straight through the heart of Austria.

Dollfuss's successor therefore had little realistic hope of saving his country from falling one day into Hitler's hands. What Schuschnigg might have done was to delay the blow for a while. What he could have done was to parry it, diplomatically and even physically, with more imagination and courage. In some respects, Austria's last two chancellors came the wrong way round. The lawyer-like calm of Schuschnigg might have proven a better foil against Nazism at the beginning. The passion of Dollfuss would almost certainly have served the Austrian cause better at the end. If there is a simple summing-up of the difference between these two close friends and colleagues of the patriotic right wing, it lies in the call of race. For Dollfuss, there was such a thing as Austrian blood. For Schuschnigg it did not exist. For him, there was only German blood, and this he could not bring himself to spill, even if his own country were to bleed to death as a result.

The reasons for this lay largely in his upbringing, but they went back beyond his birth to a family history rooted deep in the Monarchy. On his father's side, the Schuschniggs were third-generation Tyrolese,* but their eighteenth-century roots were in Kamnik in Slovenia, where the family name was spelt 'Susnik'. They were, in fact, Germanised Slavs, and though Schuschnigg always sought to play down the connection, it was probably not without its influence on his character. Protestants who convert to Catholicism often become 'more papal than the Pope', and a Slovene converted to Tyrolean can easily become more pan-German than the pure native, precisely because he is seeking to obliterate his Slav roots. (Schuschnigg was obliged to examine them when, as a captive of Hitler's, he was required to prove his Aryan ancestry and had to cite the parish records of Kamnik as distant proof.)

The second and more immediate formative element in his background was the family's tradition of military service. A year after his own birth, on 14 December 1897, his grandfather Alois was ennobled by Francis Joseph for his services as a major-general in the imperial army. The title was the very minor one of 'Ritter von' but, being hereditary, it can be compared with the British rank of baronet. The arms which the General chose were symbolic: they included, apart from the imperial double-headed eagle, the blue and white of Bavaria, representing family links across the border on the maternal side. Kurt carried in his genes both of those rival elements we have been tracing down the years – the pure German as well as the multi-racial Austrian. He thus personifies both the dilemma and the tragedy of the First Republic.

All four sons of Alois followed the famous General, nicknamed 'The Thunderer', into the imperial army. Kurt's early years thus took him, with his father Artur Viktor von Schuschnigg, from garrison to garrison of the Monarchy. Again, something Germanic, as well as imperial, must have left its mark on the boy. Whenever the postings sent them to any of those Slav lands which predominated in Cisleithania, he would be made conscious, by the self-contained nature of garrison life, of the gulf between the privileged German-speakers and the rest of the Emperor's subjects in the 'Austrian half' of his Monarchy. Without ever becoming a racialist as a man, Kurt grew up as a boy well knowing what German stood for in language, blood and culture.

Foggy these concepts may have been, when glimpsed across the

---

* Barely long enough, by the ultra-conservative standards of that province, to classify him as 'ein echter Tiroler', a true son of Tyrol.

parade ground of some Polish or Slovak garrison town. However, they were to be sharpened, and then set in concrete, by the next phase of his upbringing, the years he spent as a boarder at the Jesuit college of the Stella Matutina at Feldkirch in the Vorarlberg. He entered it in 1907, not yet ten years old, and stayed until he was nearly seventeen and a half, when the empire was already at war. Those years fixed his character for life. It was not simply that the austere and semi-monastic regime of the college turned the shy boy into a withdrawn young man with little of the charm, zest for life and talent for human relations which the Austrian traditionally possesses. Much more important for his countrymen, and for his own place in history, this particular band of Jesuits turned him into a convert to the Germanic creed as well as a son of God.

The priests who taught at the Stella Matutina were not Austrians by birth, but exiles from Hohenzollern Germany whom Francis Joseph had allowed to settle in Vorarlberg forty years before. Spiritually and intellectually, they clung to their old fatherland with all the frenzy of the émigré. On all festive occasions, the black eagle of the German Reich was hoisted above the college building, alongside the Habsburg banners of Austria. Though classical studies were the priority, music and literature were strong features of the curriculum, and here Bach and Beethoven would come before Mozart and Schubert, while Schiller and Goethe would positively eclipse Grillparzer. It was a short step of mental association from preaching that the Germans were the bearers of European culture to suggesting that they were the natural leaders of Europe itself. The seventeen-year-old student left the Stella Matutina with an inferiority complex towards all things German. Unhappily for himself and his countrymen, he was never to shake it off, not even when Hitler put on his brown Nazi shirt over the white mantle of the Teutonic knights.

In less than twenty years, the pupil of the Jesuits became the Chancellor of Austria. His footsteps in those two decades followed exactly the path of the Monarchy to extinction and the painful progress of the republic which replaced it. He had quit the college (against the wishes of his teachers, who saw in him a promising recruit for their own ranks) and volunteered, in July 1915, for the imperial army in which his own father had now risen, like his grandfather, to become a general. As a Tyrolean with such an imposing military pedigree, he was commissioned into one of the 'Kaiserjaeger' regiments – if anything even more prestigious than the 'Kaiserschuetzen' which Dollfuss had joined. Like Dollfuss, he saw long and arduous service on the Italian front, ending with a similar chestful of medals as testimony to his bravery.

Schuschnigg's three war years as an artillery observation officer did nothing to lessen his respect, almost amounting to awe, for the Germans. As we have seen, Germany at war became an even more overpowering partner for the Monarchy than Germany in peacetime. Lieutenant Schuschnigg saw for himself what the discipline and self-confidence of the Germans could achieve when they both planned and spearheaded the great Isonzo offensive of 1917. He also saw enough evidence of muddle and uneven leadership on the Austrian side, including the most costly muddle of all, over the timing of the 1918 armistice. He saw the disintegration of the Monarchy in uniform as regiment after regiment of its multi-racial army mutinied or deserted during that terrible November. He joined his own father as a prisoner-of-war of the Italians, finally returning with him to Innsbruck in the autumn of 1919. Here he experienced for himself the bitterness of this strange new Red Republic which had replaced the imperial city he had enlisted in four years before. Like many another ex-officer walking the streets in his field-grey uniform (because, like them, he had no money to buy civilian clothes), he had to hide his medals and remove his badges of rank to avoid the hisses of passers-by. For the Catholic monarchist, it was a first impression of mindless Marxism which never quite faded.

His path up and out of the ruins closely followed that of the man to whose place at the Ballhausplatz he would one day succeed. Like Dollfuss, he entered the world of public affairs after qualifying, as a 'Herr Doktor', in law. Like Dollfuss, he fell under the spell of the great prelate-statesman Ignaz Seipel and, like Dollfuss, he gravitated naturally towards Seipel's right-wing 'party of state', the Christian Socialists. In Schuschnigg's case, Seipel himself personally sponsored his entry into politics as a Christian Social representative for the Tyrol. It was the summer of 1927 when the new twenty-nine-year-old Deputy arrived to take his seat in Parliament. His first impressions of republican Vienna were as sobering as had been those first impressions of republican Innsbruck. It was the summer of 'Black Friday' and the burning of the Justice Ministry by a left-wing mob beyond the control even of their party leaders. Schuschnigg was able to watch the mayhem himself. The experience brought the final conviction that his country had to find a new way of government and a new faith to replace this senseless clash of party slogans and street brawls which, for nearly ten years, had passed for parliamentary democracy in Austria.

Only five years later, Schuschnigg, whose advance up his party's ranks had been meteoric, was himself seated in that restored building on the Schmerlingplatz, as Minister of Justice in the restructured Christian Socialist government of Dr Buresch. One of his Cabinet colleagues was another young newcomer to office, the Agriculture Minister Engelbert Dollfuss. There was an immediate rapport between the two men. It was the attraction of opposites in temperament and character: Schuschnigg, the reserved and introspective man of intellect; Dollfuss, the outgoing figure of passion and charm. Yet they shared the same religious and political vision, and it was this combination of head and heart which served to launch the Fatherland Front. Such was the personal and political story of the Tyrolean lawyer who, at the age of only thirty-six, now stepped into the shoes of his murdered friend. Over the next four years, this man, who personified so many of the republic's problems, became the catalyst of its self-destruction.

Schuschnigg won, and won decisively, the main purely domestic battle of his Chancellorship, against the continued challenge of the Heimwehr to the authority of the government. This had always been weakened by the Starhemberg—Fey rivalry, and eventually Schuschnigg was able to dispose of both of these ill-assorted mavericks* and absorb the Heimwehr army itself into the newly-formed Militia of the Fatherland Front. (With a heavy heart, he had to apply the same merger process to his own 'Storm Bands of the East Mark'.) But the truly lethal challenge came, of course, from across the border with Nazi Germany. Given the shifts already described in the European power structure over these four years, Schuschnigg could not hope even to stand still for long against this pressure, let alone quell it. Before contemplating capitulation, he simply had to give ground. It was the manner of this retreat which revealed so much about the man, and left such a dubious testimony behind for his country.

* In October 1935 he used Starhemberg (who mobilised his provincial Heimwehr units to counter a possible *putsch* attempt by Fey's Vienna regiments) to help eject the Major from all his political and party posts – consoling him with the lucrative but powerless position of Chairman of the Danube Steam Shipping Company. The following July, Starhemberg signed his own political death warrant by sending a telegram to Mussolini congratulating him on the victory in Abyssinia. One of the ironic consolation prizes given to the fallen playboy-prince was the Presidency of the Aid Association for Austrian Mothers.

The halfway point of the retreat was also the halfway stage of Schuschnigg's Chancellorship. The famous Austro–German agreement of 11 July 1936 was largely the work of the oleaginous Franz von Papen. The former Vice-Chancellor of Germany had paved Hitler's road to constitutional power in the sadly mistaken belief (shared by his friends, the industrial barons) that the demagogue in the raincoat would become their puppet once he was dressed up in a frock-coat. This may have been the miscalculation of the century, but it was a rare lapse of judgement on the part of von Papen, who had helped his career along by reading the ambitions and weaknesses of those around him, and playing one off against the other with a blend of flattery and cunning. These were precisely the qualities Hitler needed to employ in Austria after the embarrassing fiasco of the 1934 *putsch*. As the republic could not be bludgeoned to death at a blow, slow strangulation was to be tried instead.

Accordingly, von Papen had been despatched to Vienna with the special rank of ambassador (which immediately placed him second only to the Papal Nuncio on the diplomatic list*) and the special task of squeezing Schuschnigg, slowly and gently, into submission. This he achieved – ironically, in view of the fact that his target was an Austrian – by possessing far greater charm, in addition to sharper political wits. The path selected was the so-called 'evolutionary way', which meant bringing the two Germanic nations closer and closer together by a spider's cobweb of special links, a cobweb in which Austria was ultimately to play the role of the helpless fly. The fly was to be lured inside by the attractions of the so-called '*Zusammenschluss*'. This was the notion (which we first met with in the century before) that the two countries – their defences, their economies, their foreign policies – could be gradually fused together though each, at the end, would still retain a separate identity.

If this had already been a dim prospect in the age of Bismarck, it was a lunatic's dream in the age of Hitler. There were a few in Schuschnigg's entourage who nonetheless indulged in the dream. The Chancellor himself was probably too realistic, too pessimistic and, when it came down to it, too pan-German to share their belief that salvation could be sought in compromise. The July Pact – which was very Austrian in that, yet

---

* Austria being a minor power, foreign countries were represented in its capital only by Ministers.

again, Vienna tried to look both ways at once – encapsulated the problem. The published text announced that while, on the one hand, Germany recognised Austria's 'full sovereignty', the republic, for its part, pledged henceforth to conduct its policy 'always according to the basic principle that Austria recognises itself to be a German state'. Thus, what was given with the one hand was taken away with the other.

The clauses of a separate 'gentlemen's agreement' showed how much Hitler was clawing back. Under these, Schuschnigg promised to carry out a political amnesty for all but the most culpable of Austrian Nazis (in all over 17,000 were freed). Even more ominously, he agreed that, in the near future, 'representatives of the so-called national opposition in Austria should be given a role of official responsibility'. This was something new in warfare: the commander of the besieged fortress was being called upon to construct his own Trojan horse.

Some of the fighters inside that Trojan horse now took up their places – though with varying ideas as to how to move it forward to serve their own ideas and their own advantage. Schuschnigg had undertaken to appoint two so-called 'prominent nationalists' to his government. One candidate more or less selected himself: General Edmund von Glaise-Horstenau, the Director of Military Archives. The General had served as a wartime liaison officer between the armed forces of the Monarchy and Hindenburg's High Command and now, as a leading light of the 'German Club' in Vienna, he was determined to make Austria and Germany as inextricably intertwined in peacetime as they had been in war. He was given a promising working platform: Minister without Portfolio but with the specific task of supervising the newly-declared domestic truce. The other nominee, much less expected, was the Chancellor's own choice: the young lawyer Guido Schmidt, whom he made State Secretary at the Foreign Office while maintaining overall control of the Ministry himself. Schmidt wanted to keep some daylight between Austria and Germany and so did not belong, like the General, to the camp of the out-and-out nationalists. But he was quite happy to follow the so-called 'German path', especially if it coincided with the Guido Schmidt path, which was what interested this pliable careerist above all else.

A third figure to move out of the shadows, though not yet into office, at the time was the doom-laden Arthur Seyss-Inquart. A lawyer, like Schuschnigg and Schmidt, and like them a former pupil of the Stella Matutina, he had the additional bond with the Chancellor of having served with him on the Italian front. Seyss-Inquart, who moves steadily further forward on the Vienna stage from now on, was the classic apostle of 'Zusammenschluss', the weird belief that fusion with Nazi Germany was somehow possible without total absorption. It was to bring him close to outright treachery; then to brief mayfly glory; and, finally, into the dock at Nuremberg. In 1936, however, he was not even a member of the Nazi Party. Like Schmidt and Glaise-Horstenau, his was just another of the blurred colours within Austria's right-wing spectrum.

When justifying what he regarded as *his* pact a year later to an impatient Führer, Papen pointed out that, apart from isolating Austria, the agreement would halt 'the steadily increasing efforts to secure a Habsburg restoration'. 1937 was the right year to draw Hitler's attention to the problem. By now the heir to the Habsburg claims was no longer an irrelevant and immature exile under the tutelage of his widowed matriarch mother, the Empress Zita. Archduke Otto, now twenty-four years old and a graduate of Belgium's illustrious Louvain University, had grown up to be the nearest thing his dynasty had ever produced to a pure political animal. The family refuge of the thirties, Ham Castle at Steenokkerzeel near Brussels, was both the think-tank and the power centre of Austrian monarchism, and the young head of the banished house was already making his personal mark in Europe.

In Austria itself, the monarchist movement in the thirties was estimated, by the young Pretender himself, to have numbered no more than some 20,000 active supporters. Even as a pressure group (it could not campaign formally as a party) it was weakened by suffering from that same jumble of membership and that same muddle of aims and ideas which afflicted all Austrian thinking at the time. But a chink in the closed political door had appeared in the May 1934 Constitution of Dollfuss, which had dropped some of the draconian anti-Habsburg laws of the republic. On 13 July of the following year, Schuschnigg opened the door much wider by ending the banishment of the royal house. All its members were now given the unconditional right to return, with the sole exceptions of Otto himself and his mother. They undertook, however, not to cross the border without the express permission of the Chancellor – which was never forthcoming. Only a lawyer's mind could have devised such a classic exercise in 'half-and-halfness'.

Yet Otto and his cause were looming larger and larger in Schuschnigg's mind. As Mussolini's hand grew weaker and Hitler's grew stronger, and as all belated efforts to bring the Socialists back into the political game were falling through, the Legitimist card was literally the only one left to play. Moreover, in 1936–7 it was enjoying an upsurge in popular support, especially in the conservative countryside, where more than 1500 villages and municipalities had bestowed honorary citizenship on the young Pretender. Indeed, he had been treated by Schuschnigg almost like an extra-mural member of his entourage over the launching of the July Pact. Just before it was signed, the Chancellor despatched his Press Chief, Edmund Weber, as a special envoy to Steenokkerzeel to sound Otto out over the agreement and to ask whether, in any case, he would help to allay French government fears after it was announced. The request for help Otto agreed to. The pact itself he denounced as a sell-out. Schuschnigg did not prevent the Legitimists, in due course, from issuing their public rejection of it in Vienna.

Hitler did not need Papen to remind him that the one pure and constant source of opposition which he faced in Austria – undiluted either by opportunism or by the Germanic complex – flowed from the Legitimist camp. The Swastika and the black-yellow banner could never fly side by side. Not for nothing had the German General Staff plan for eventual military action against Austria been given the code-name 'Operation Otto'. Indeed, its initial purpose was to forestall any restoration bid by invasion. The Führer would have been sorely tempted to march without further ado had he ever learnt what took place at the remote convent of Einsiedeln near Zurich on 7 January 1937. On that day, under conditions of the most stringent secrecy, Chancellor Schuschnigg, accompanied by Guido Schmidt, met with the Pretender and his advisers to discuss how and when a restoration could be carried out. The only account of this discussion which has survived are the notes taken on the spot by the Archduke's secretary, and preserved in the Habsburg family archives.* Guido Schmidt said nothing about the affair during his exhaustive trial for treason before a Vienna court of the Second Austrian Republic in 1947, and Schuschnigg makes no mention of this key meeting in the various volumes of political apologia which he published after the war. This is not surprising, in view of the pledges

---

* HFA Kassette No. 33, File 805, from which all the following quotes are taken. Otto Habsburg told the author he had already had two exploratory secret sessions with Schuschnigg at a 'safe house', the Hôtel du Parc in Mulhouse, placed at his disposal by the French Secret Service. This Einsiedeln meeting was, however, the decisive one.

which he made that day and broke over the following months. He was probably counting on the secret never coming out.

The Einsiedeln Protocol begins, under the unequivocal heading 'Preparations for the Restoration':

> There is agreement that this should now be set energetically in motion. Schu. intends to carry out the restoration as soon as possible in the current year . . . even if this should lead eventually to a serious European conflagration.

There followed much discussion over the Chancellor's proposal that Hitler ('the only possible active opponent') should be informed of the plan and German agreement, or at least acquiescence, secured in advance. Otto, whom Schuschnigg addressed throughout as *'Eure Majestät'*, or 'Your Majesty', turned this suggestion down flat. The Chancellor accordingly agreed to put it on ice and to take no further steps in that direction without royal approval. 'In the meantime,' the record continues, 'Schu. will sort out his ideas and communicate them to H.M. in the course of this month.' The two sides then discussed the current political situation in Austria and what the likely reaction would be from Hungary and Yugoslavia to a restoration in Vienna. (Czech hostility was taken for granted.)

Finally, before parting, Schuschnigg was recorded as having promised: 'Any form of aggressive action on Germany's part against the independence of Austria will be resisted by Schu. with force of arms.' That pledge, above all, was to have a hollow and miserable ring about it when the Chancellor was put to the test fourteen months later.*

Though the Einsiedeln meeting remained simply an historical curiosity, it is important for our purpose for the light it sheds on the utter confusion in Schuschnigg's thinking. Of all the scenarios which could be devised to solve Austria's plight, the most fantastical was a restoration which would be actually sanctioned by Hitler. The idea could only come from a mind split into two conflicting allegiances – one towards Austria's Germanic past, and the other towards her imperial glory.

Yet Schuschnigg really hoped that, somehow, he could reconcile the

---

* Fortunately for its own peace of mind, the 'court in exile' never believed in Schuschnigg's tough words. The Empress Zita once commented to the author: 'Schuschnigg certainly showed he had goodwill. The question was whether he also possessed the necessary willpower. This we always doubted.'

two. Indeed, at a meeting which, thanks to the German archives, is recorded,* he pressed Hitler's Foreign Minister Baron von Neurath earnestly on the subject when he visited Vienna on 23 February 1937. According to the mystified visitor's report, Schuschnigg had argued that 'there was great affection in Austria for the old ruling house and that the return to monarchy was the best way of quieting domestic political conditions'. Von Neurath retorted bluntly that a Habsburg restoration 'would be the best way for Austria to commit suicide'. Despite this rejection, the Chancellor refused to be put off. He pressed his visitor again, even telling him that though he would prefer to consult Germany on the matter, he could give no guarantee that Austria might not act on her own. Whatever was to happen a year later, Schuschnigg was doing his best for the moment to square the Legitimist circle he had drawn at Einsiedeln.

It was, of course, hopeless to expect that Hitler would honour any agreement which put Austria out of his reach. For him, the whole purpose of the 1936 pact was to get his foot in the Vienna door. His only thought in the months that followed was how to wrench it open. No ornate bolt, mounted with the double eagle, could have held it shut. The oft-quoted Hossbach Protocol** of the strategic planning 'summit' which Hitler convened in Berlin on 10 November 1937 shows the Führer pencilling in the year 1938 as a propitious time for a lightning invasion of both Austria and Czechoslovakia, in order to shorten and strengthen Germany's defence lines.

Nor were his satraps idle in Vienna. On 25 January 1938, Austrian security forces, alerted by cypher codes they had broken, raided the home and the office of the Gauleiter-designate for Vienna, Dr Leopold Tavs, and discovered detailed plans to topple the republic from inside. The Austrian Nazis, who had been given much greater liberty of action under the July Pact, were to launch a terrorist campaign of such ferocity in the spring that Schuschnigg would be forced to call in his army. The Germans could then march in to save their 'persecuted brethren'. In the event, Hitler was to need neither a military offensive nor a domestic uprising to bring Austria into the 'German motherland'. Papen delivered

---

* *Documents on German Foreign Policy*, Series D, Vol. I, No. 215.
** Colonel Hossbach acted as 'rapporteur' at a gathering which brought together all the commanders of Germany's armed forces, including Göring, who was soon to play the leading role in executing the *Anschluss* itself.

her up for him by finally persuading Schuschnigg to visit the Führer in Berchtesgaden.

Papen had started to press for this over Christmas, and had returned from Berlin early in the New Year with Hitler's private invitation in his pocket. Schuschnigg had accepted this in principle on 8 January, but then sat on his hands in silence. He had sensed what Papen was counting on: that as a shy gentleman from the Tyrol with a hatred of theatrical publicity, he would prove no match in a face-to-face encounter with the toughest political bruiser and greatest showman of the century. Schuschnigg had his own misgivings about the encounter, but when Hitler's formal telegram of invitation arrived on 26 January, he had little option but to commit himself. The visit was after all being presented, in the most convivial way, as 'a meeting between the two German Chancellors'. (The sinister aspect of that phrase probably never entered Schuschnigg's head.)

The preparations which he now put in hand for the event were bizarre but very revealing, both of his own character and of the Austrian temperament as it was reflected in that character. So far from mounting a resolute defence (let alone an attack), Schuschnigg plotted out, in detail, a retreat. This conformed perfectly with that pessimistic Austrian view of life expressed in the verdict: '*Es wird schon schief gehen*,' or 'It's bound to go wrong.' Thus it was that Seyss-Inquart, who was already taking his instructions from Göring, suddenly got his so-called 'Little Programme' accepted by the Chancellor. This was a packet of further concessions to the Austrian Nazis, including the prospect of their admission to a restructured Cabinet, which Schuschnigg had been resisting for months, despite the personal trust he still placed in his right-wing Catholic friend and wartime comrade.

More disastrously, as things turned out, he set about defining Austria's detailed fall-back position (an advance line seems never to have been traced out) for the meeting itself. This was set out in ten points (the so-called '*Punktationen*') prepared by the Secretary of the Fatherland Front, Guido Zernatto, and presented by him to the Chancellor on 11 February, the eve of his departure. Seyss-Inquart was also at the meeting and duly arranged in secret for a Nazi courier to leave by overnight train for Berchtesgaden with an outline of the Austrian position. It was an outright betrayal for Schuschnigg, and a precious boon for Hitler.*

---

* In an earlier work, *The Last Empress* (London, 1991), the author mistakenly ascribed this vital leak to Baron Viktor von Frölichstal, the chancellor's secretary.

The ten points went beyond the 'Little Programme' and marked further concessions all along the line – even on the military and ideological fronts – to Nazi Germany. The Führer thus knew, a few hours before Schuschnigg (accompanied by Schmidt) arrived at the border, that his visitor would be an easy prey.*

Hitler's tirades at Berchtesgaden (like the presence at the Berghof of three of his top generals who had been summoned solely to act as stage-props) were typical of those calculated exercises in bluster and blackmail he was to employ later with so many of his political quarries. The only first-hand account of them to survive is the oft-quoted one, reconstructed from memory and first published in Schuschnigg's memoirs. As he was recording his own place in history, one can be certain that – without attempting any falsification – he tried to present himself in as favourable a light as the facts would allow. This is what makes his nervous defensiveness and the almost total lack of resolution which he describes throughout all the more lamentable. Hitler accused *him* of flouting the 1936 Pact; denounced Austria for committing 'racial treachery' against Germany throughout her history; and declared that he was now resolved to end this 'betrayal', if need be by force: 'Who knows – perhaps you will find me one day in Vienna, like a spring storm. Then you will go through something . . . nobody will be able to stop the acts of vengeance, not even I!'

It was a naked threat to invade the country whose sovereignty he had pledged himself to honour less than two years before. Schuschnigg did not as much as point this out, let alone (as Dollfuss might well have done) throw the broken promise back in the Führer's face. Nor did he even contest the grotesque charge of 'racial treachery' down the centuries. Instead he pleaded that Austria had, after all, made her contribution to 'overall German culture', and went on to cite Beethoven (as opposed to, say, Mozart) as an example. The Führer retorted, acidly and accurately, that Beethoven happened to be a German. The gaffe did not faze Schuschnigg in the slightest, because he did not see it as a mistake. Metternich, he replied, had also come to Vienna from Germany, 'but it would never occur to anyone to think of him as a

---

* Schuschnigg's journey had been camouflaged in suitably Austrian fashion. It was the height of Austria's carnival season, and he had duly turned up at the ball of his Fatherland Front – destined to be the last festive parade of Dollfuss's corporate state. For the first part of the train journey itself, Schuschnigg donned sporting garb as though he were leaving for a weekend's skiing in the Tyrol.

Rhinelander'. Certainly not this former pupil of the Stella Matutina.

When Hitler moved on to rant about Austria's border defence works (erected primarily against marauders from the Austrian Legion), Schuschnigg at first pretended he knew nothing about them; he then undertook to suspend construction. Like the '*Punktationen*', it was retreat all the way. Hitler well knew how, in the case of this visitor, he could help it along. 'I am giving you, Herr Schuschnigg,* the unique opportunity to have your name entered in the roll of the great Germans.' (And, in a snide reference to Schuschnigg's remote Slav ancestry, Hitler pointed out that, if anything, *he* had the greater right of the two to call himself an Austrian.) The price that Schuschnigg was asked to pay for being enrolled in the Germanic pantheon was presented after a politely conducted luncheon. The Chancellor was handed a two-page list of ten concessions to sign which amounted to the total abandonment of his country's independence. The key demands were for Seyss-Inquart immediately to be made Minister of Interior 'with unrestricted powers over the police'; the Nazi party to be accorded complete political equality in Austria and all its remaining prisoners – including the leaders of the 1934 *putsch* – to be released; and an exchange of one hundred officers to be promptly carried out between the German and Austrian armies. In an almost farcical touch, Hitler, for his part, repeated his promise to respect the independence of the country he had just sentenced to death. Schuschnigg signed the sentence, almost as it stood, extracting the sole 'concession' that he would be allowed three days in which to carry out its provisions. Papen accompanied the Austrian party back to the frontier. Feeling he was obliged to say something, he assured the traumatised Schuschnigg that Hitler did not always behave like that.** On the contrary, the Führer could sometimes be 'really charming', as the departing visitor would doubtless discover for himself at their next encounter. The two 'German Chancellors' were never to meet

* The Führer used this dismissively plain style of address throughout, with one significant exception. When Schuschnigg mentioned the events of July 1934 – though without denouncing the Nazi *putsch* – Hitler addressed his visitor as '*Herr Bundeskanzler*', and claimed he had had nothing to do with the murder of Dollfuss.
** Papen was himself in something of a traumatised state. Less than a week before, he had been abruptly recalled to Berlin, along with other German ambassadors in key posts, in connection with the political upheaval in Germany. This, among other things, had made Joachim von Ribbentrop, hitherto ambassador in London, the new Foreign Secretary. The moment Papen told the Führer that Schuschnigg had agreed to the meeting, he was sent back to Vienna.

again. Hitler's next visiting card came, by proxy, from the Gestapo.

Schuschnigg had trouble enough getting his government colleagues and President Miklas to agree to his new Cabinet, with Seyss-Inquart in the key post designated by Hitler. A wider problem was how to present the Berchtesgaden nightmare to the outside world. Again, the natural shyness of the man and his ambivalent stance over all things German got the upper hand. The bare truth — even if conveyed only through diplomatic channels — should have proved enough to prod Britain and France into at least seeking 'consultation' with Italy, as laid down in the 1935 Stresa Pact. Instead, London and Paris, where disquiet and sympathy were growing,* were told only part of the truth, and that by instalments. Austria's envoys throughout Europe were first informed only of 'difficulties' which had arisen at Berchtesgaden. They were then ordered even to play these down in all official discussion in order to meet 'the general need for a reduction of tension'. Austria's relations with the Reich, they were instructed to stress, 'had now been cleared up by the Berchtesgaden discussions'.

Falsehoods that serve a good cause are acceptable in international relations. The Chancellor was, however, lying in a disastrous cause, hoping the crisis would go away if he pretended it did not exist. Schuschnigg now compounded the folly. What had dominated his thinking all along was to avoid, at all costs, provoking the Führer; yet the course he finally adopted amounted to the greatest provocation of all. At Berchtesgaden, Hitler had issued one sober challenge amid all the threats: 'Hold a free plebiscite in Austria, in which you and I stand against one another. Then you will see!' This was precisely what Schuschnigg decided to do.

The quiet and almost predictable temperament of the Chancellor now underwent some wild oscillations of mood. He later interpreted them as being partly emotional upsurges, probably due to stress, but which he could not fully explain, even to himself; and partly the product of a calculated strategy.** In a speech to Parliament on 24 February the

* In London, the then Socialist opposition leader, Clement Attlee, launched a campaign in Parliament to try to force the government into more positive action over Austria. In Paris, the French Foreign Minister, M. Delbos, was also trying to prod the British into making a joint *démarche* in Berlin.
** This account of Schuschnigg's behaviour in the critical weeks after Berchtesgaden is based largely on his letters to the author, and several conversations with the author, held in Salzburg and New York during the 1960s.

lamb of Berchtesgaden suddenly became the lion of Vienna. Patriotism, not Nazism, was the order of the day, he declared. As for the recent agreement with Germany, this was a case of 'Thus far but no further.' He ended with the almost frenzied cry 'Until death! Red-white-red! Austria!' For the first time, something which he had never known was in him had broken the surface: passion and a power of oratory which could sway the masses. The immediate reaction went far beyond the Ringstrasse crowds who broke out into the old imperial anthem on reading his speech. In Paris the next day, the National Assembly was enthused by Schuschnigg's defiance, and one deputy went so far as to declare that 'France's fate would now be decided on the banks of the Danube.' It all showed what a display of bravura could achieve.

Years afterwards Schuschnigg also put a practical gloss on his speech. It was intended, he said, as a final test of Hitler's will. If there was a strong reaction from the Führer, then there could no longer be any doubt about his violent intentions. It was a strange line of reasoning, and Hitler's minions promptly put paid to it. Local Nazi groups staged mass protests throughout the provinces. They were at their most violent in Graz, where the demonstrators managed to get the swastika flying briefly over the town hall. Schuschnigg quelled the riot with a show of armed force but felt obliged to remove his staunchest political supporter, Dr Karl Maria Stepan, from the post of Provincial Governor as a sop to the rioters. Meanwhile, his new Security Minister, Seyss-Inquart, was touring the country proclaiming in speech after speech that 'Austria is German and German only'. Hitler's nominee for power was behaving as though he were already Chancellor, although even he had to admit that the rioters were beyond his control.

Hemmed in like this, Schuschnigg lunged in four directions at once. Far too late in the day, he put out serious feelers to the Socialist leadership, bruised and driven underground ever since the civil war four years before. The one concrete result was a pledge from the trades unions, reluctantly confirmed by the Socialist leadership, that the workers would support him in any struggle against Hitler. At the same time, he closed out the Legitimist option as being too risky to attempt. Otto Habsburg had written to him on 17 February a long and moving letter ('From a foreign land') urging him to stand firm against German pressure and even offering to take over as Chancellor – 'for when Austria is in peril, the heir to the House of Austria must stand or fall with that country'. Schuschnigg the monarchist, who had been so full of pledges the year before, took a full fortnight to mull over this novel* proposition and then replied, putting the double-headed eagle firmly back on its perch of exile. Echoing almost exactly the warning spoken in the Ballhausplatz by Baron von Neurath, he told the Pretender that 'any attempt at a restoration . . . as far ahead as one can see, must assuredly, with 100 per cent certainty, mean the death of Austria'.

Having opened a slender path to the Socialists and closed an even narrower one to the monarchists, Schuschnigg made a final bid to open again the road to Rome. To Mussolini he revealed the most startling of the initiatives he had in mind, the calling of a national plebiscite, and asked for his advice. The Duce, by now with only a shadow of his former European stature, and as anxious as Schuschnigg had hitherto been not to provoke the Führer, counselled emphatically against it. Whatever the outcome of such a vote, the Duce replied, it would be 'a bomb which would burst in the Chancellor's hands'. Better by far to trust in Göring's good faith. The invitation to stroke the man-eating tiger was the last personal message Schuschnigg was to receive from Austria's one-time protector.

Of the outcome of the plebiscite, which the Chancellor finally decided upon on 6 March, there could be little doubt. The formula he announced in another bravura performance at Innsbruck three days later ran: 'Are you in favour of a free and German, independent and social, a Christian and united Austria?' This covered everything, except democracy and the corporate state. It was noticeable that the call for freedom, which matched the mood of the hour, was followed immediately by the call of common race which had echoed down the centuries. Nobody could object to the other premises, and with the support of the industrial workers now assured, Schuschnigg could look forward to a majority of around 70 per cent.** His closing words, 'Say "Yes" to Austria,' had a ring of confidence about them.*** The only condition was that this glowing iron of patriotic fervour was not given a chance to cool. With

* And, frankly, impracticable, as Archduke Otto admitted to the author after the war when making with him a German television documentary for his eightieth birthday. The project had originated with his indomitable mother, who even urged him to ignore the rebuttal and just land in Vienna by private plane.

** It must be said that Schuschnigg had done his best to 'massage' the outcome. The eligible voting age, for example, had been raised to twenty-four in order to exclude a youthful population who had been heavily infiltrated with Nazi ideology.

*** To the delight of his Innsbruck audience, he added Andreas Hofer's famous call to arms against Napoleon: 'Mander, 's isch Zeit.'

this in mind, Schuschnigg fixed his polling date for the coming Sunday, 13 March. That was only four days away, but it still gave Hitler time enough to trample the plebiscite, and Austria with it, into the dust.

Hitler knew, as soon as he heard the live broadcast speech on the Wednesday evening, that he was facing not simply a political challenge, but a personal humiliation. At best, a third of the Austrian voters, grouped around the Nazis and extreme pan-Germans, might be counted on to vote 'No'. The outcome would be a public rebuttal for the Reich and its Führer, and delivered in the form which would have the greatest impact on the Western democracies, a nationwide public verdict as expressed in a free vote.* Hitler broke into a rage against Schuschnigg which was now genuine, not simulated, and by the early hours of Thursday morning he had already begun the preparations for his destruction. The prestige of 'the greatest of all the Germans' was now at stake.**

Before dawn on 10 March he had summoned to Berlin the two generals who would have a key role in any operations against Austria: General Schober, in command of the Seventh Army Corps at Munich, and General von Reichenau, Commander-in-Chief of the Fourth Army Group at Leipzig (the latter was pulled back from Cairo, where he was attending a meeting of the Olympic Games Committee). The two top generals of the Wehrmacht, Keitel, Head of the Army Supreme Command and Beck, the Chief of Staff, were called in during the morning to report on their plans for an invasion. When Beck confessed that nothing existed on paper in any detail ('Operation Otto' had been drawn up only on broad lines as a contingency plan), Hitler ordered him to produce one within hours and gave him a verbal outline.

The result was the Führer's 'Instruction No. 1', which designated the 8th Army as the attacking force and laid down its first objectives: the occupation of Upper and Lower Austria, Salzburg and the Tyrol, the prompt seizure of Vienna and the securing of the Austro–Czech border. As for the Austrian Army, any resistance was to be 'mercilessly

* 'It seems a tall order to say that a head of government cannot have a plebiscite if he wants to.' Thus Lord Halifax, who had just succeeded Anthony Eden as British Foreign Secretary, to Ribbentrop, who was back in London paying his farewell calls as the former ambassador. The conversation took place at the Foreign Office on 10 March. Stern words were exchanged, but nothing more.

** Hitler had, in fact, been given a few hours' advance warning of the plebiscite project, thanks to a leak from a woman secretary in Zernatto's office. But the Führer could not believe that Schuschnigg had such defiance in him, until hearing it for himself over the radio.

crushed'. On the other hand, the invaders should try to create the impression 'that we do not wish to start a war against our Austrian brothers'. Stick and carrot were being extended at the same time. As things turned out, even the waving of the stick proved enough, while the Austrians provided the carrots themselves.

Hitler had also been in touch with Göring in the small hours of 10 March, and it was his Field Marshal and Supreme Air Force Commander who now took over in the Führer's name. Göring was to declare proudly at his Nuremberg trial eight years later that 'I went my own way over Austria and that way was clear.' Clear enough indeed for the Field Marshal to have had painted on the wall of his Karinhall shooting lodge a fresco map of Germany and Central Europe which showed no frontier at all with Austria; and clear enough for him to show this off to his visitors, who included Mussolini and, in November 1937, Guido Schmidt. 'I must say, Your Excellency, you have gone pretty far ahead of events,' was the most that Schuschnigg's State Secretary could muster by way of protest. The Duce merely admired the artist's work. There was a lot of symbolism surrounding that Karinhall fresco.

Göring did not, of course, 'go his own way' independently on 10–11 March. Though it was he who issued the invasion order on the tenth, this was 'obviously in the Führer's name', as he later testified. What he did do the following day was to adopt his own method of conquest. On 11 March, the First Austrian Republic became the first – and so far the only – country in history to be taken over almost entirely by telephone.

Admittedly, the Führer had laid the groundwork. Schuschnigg's 'pronounced nationalist' Minister without Portfolio, Glaise-Horstenau, happened to be in Berlin at the time and he was bundled back to Vienna early on the morning of 11 March, carrying the Führer's personal letter for Seyss-Inquart, his principal henchman. The Minister of Interior was ordered to call on the Chancellor immediately to demand a two weeks' postponement of the plebiscite. Both of Hitler's appointees in the Cabinet would resign if Schuschnigg refused, and the ultimatum (noon on the eleventh was the original time set) was framed with thinly veiled threats of Nazi violence and even German invasion.

An extraordinary transformation in Schuschnigg's mood took place over the next three hours. At midday, he had seemed to be spitting defiance, as though he were still standing on the rostrum at Innsbruck. He had issued a string of emergency security orders to the Vienna Police

President, Dr Michael Skubl, on whose loyalty (unlike that of many in the lower echelons) he could rely. The 1915 class of army reservists were called up, ostensibly 'to keep order on the day of the plebiscite', extra petrol supplies were ordered for motorised troop movements, and the guards patrolling the federal railways were issued with arms and live ammunition. The Nazis had their spies everywhere, and within the hour of these measures being ordered, the German Legation had reported them to Berlin. Hitler knew therefore that he was facing either real defiance or a show of it, but he did not know which. It is arguable that even if Schuschnigg had only been bluffing, by persisting with it, and at the same time making a public appeal to world opinion, Hitler might have stayed his hand. This, at all events, was one of the options Schuschnigg put to a group of his closest advisers who gathered in his office at around 2 p.m. But only half an hour later, after a further brief confrontation with Seyss-Inquart and an even briefer discussion with President Miklas, he suddenly caved in and decided to call off the fateful plebiscite.

Even his colleagues were taken aback by this abrupt surrender over an issue on which he had staked his own future and that of his country, and on which he had been showing such tenacity all morning. The only depressing factor to have emerged over lunchtime was that in Rome the Duce was declaring himself 'not available' to take any of his attempted telephone calls. Yet this was only confirmation of what the Chancellor already knew to be an established fact: that in 1938, unlike in 1934, Mussolini would not lift a finger against Hitler. His reply to Dollfuss's widow Alwine, who sent him a personal appeal to repeat the help given four years before, was eloquent: she was advised to leave for Switzerland with her children. One theory to gain widespread credence, then and later, for Schuschnigg's backward somersault was that his nerve had simply given way. This would have been a credible, and not dishonourable, explanation for the Chancellor to have adopted for himself. In fact, he rejected it. He wrote long afterwards* that, despite the strain, his nerves remained under control throughout that terrible day. There had indeed been a nervous collapse, but this had come as a delayed reaction weeks later, when he was in a Nazi prison cell.

The real explanation lay not in Schuschnigg's nervous system, but in his character and his split personality. Quite the opposite of his

* In a letter to the author, 16 February 1962.

fellow-Austrian Adolf Hitler, he was neither a bluffer nor a lover of the limelight. This shy and essentially undemonstrative man seems to have recoiled before the very blaze of publicity he had just lit for himself. As for the split personality, this was the old struggle between loyalty to the Austrian state and loyalty to the German race, emerging for one last fatal time in the republic's history. He was to write in his memoirs that his resolve deep down had always been: 'Never again a war against Germany, as in 1866.' It was in some ways an odd parallel to draw from the past; yet, in another way, it was history come full circle. At Königgrätz, the Germans had gone to war to expel the Austrians from their Reich. Now Hitler was trying to pull them back into it, and from 2.30 p.m. onwards on Austria's longest day, the road to Vienna had been opened up for him.

Göring's telephone *Blitzkrieg** started only fifteen minutes after Schuschnigg's abandonment of the plebiscite. When he heard from Seyss-Inquart that Schuschnigg had abandoned the plebiscite, the Field Marshal commented grimly that this was 'in no way sufficient', but he could say no more for the moment. An hour later, having consulted Hitler on the matter, Göring was back on the phone to his Vienna henchman, and this time he had plenty to say. Schuschnigg had 'broken faith' over the Berchtesgaden agreement. Therefore he must resign himself, and within the hour President Miklas must appoint the man on the earphone, Arthur Seyss-Inquart, as his successor. If there were any delay, Hitler's Chancellor-in-waiting should send a prearranged telegram to Berlin asking for military support.

Just as, an hour and a half before, Schuschnigg's advisers had been taken aback by his retreat over the plebiscite, so now the entire entourage was thrown into confusion by the brutal suddenness of the German advance. Seyss himself could only shrug his shoulders when pressed by his fellow-Ministers for an explanation. 'Don't ask me,' he replied, 'I'm only an historic telephone girl.' The reaction to the news of Hitler's other Cabinet spokesman was even more revealing of the muddled naïveté which was paralysing much of Austrian thinking. 'I really don't know whether, under these circumstances, one can continue and remain a gentleman,' was the pained comment of that one-time imperial officer General Edmund von Glaise-Horstenau. It almost beggars belief that

* The complete transcripts were recorded by his telephone operators at the Air Ministry in Berlin, and came into the hands of the Allied powers in 1945.

he and his like ever expected the Führer to go to work with white kid gloves.

Schuschnigg now knew better, but after yielding to the first punch, he had no fight left in him to resist the knockout blow. By four o'clock, he was already with the President to hand in his resignation.* Miklas, as he had demonstrated in 1918, was made of sterner stuff, and it was only due to his stubborn resistance and delaying tactics that Austria's formal surrender was delayed until after midnight. To Göring's demand that he should appoint Seyss-Inquart as the new Chancellor, he bluntly retorted that it was no business of Germany's to decide who governed Austria. This was the language of Wednesday and Thursday, though it was already sounding disturbingly out of date on Friday. Yet Miklas had a point, and one of which Hitler was very conscious. Like all political brigands (the Soviet Communists followed him in this respect), he wanted to throw the cloak of legality over his deeds, and the signature of the Austrian head of state was needed to confer that legality.**

For more than ten hours – an eternity on the lightning scale of happenings that day – Miklas refused to sign. He first tried to persuade Schuschnigg to remain in office, but had to be satisfied with his grudging agreement to carry on purely as a caretaker while a replacement was found.*** Miklas searched everywhere for that replacement, but met with at least three outright refusals. Skubl pointed out that he was already on Hitler's blacklist; the former Christian Social Chancellor Dr Ender said that he had had 'more than enough' of that office; General Sigismund Schilhawsky, the Inspector-General of the Armed Forces, replied that he was a soldier, not a politician, and that he was anyway 'not feeling too well'. Göring had meanwhile brought a general of his own into play, the Military Attaché in Vienna, Wolfgang Muff. This worthy was despatched at around six o'clock to the President's office to

* It is worth noting for the record that the oft-quoted message from Lord Halifax in London stating that Britain was not able 'to guarantee any protection' did not reach the British Legation in Vienna until half an hour later. In other words, Schuschnigg's surrender came before confirmation of his abandonment, however much this was anticipated.

** The other legal pretext had been prepared by the Führer in advance: a telegram from Seyss-Inquart appealing for German help to 'restore order'. The text was duly published in Berlin, though Seyss denied ever having sent the message.

*** In his memoirs, Schuschnigg makes a revealing comment on his behaviour at this juncture: 'My task was finished . . . I refused to be instrumental in the preparation of Cain to slay his brother Abel.' (By Cain, he presumably meant Austria!)

deliver the ultimatum that unless Seyss-Inquart were appointed Chancellor by 7.30 that evening, the German Army would march in. Miklas saw the intruder to the door, with the equivalent of a Presidential flea in his ear.

But though Miklas was the keeper of Austria's constitution, Schuschnigg was still in charge of what was left of Austria's government and executive authority. A report that German troops had carried out Göring's orders and were now marching across the border reached Vienna soon after the expiry of the ultimatum. Though the message turned out to be quite false, even the rumour was enough to push Schuschnigg from retreat into total surrender. At ten minutes to eight, in a radio transmission from the Ballhausplatz, he declared in the President's name that Austria was 'yielding to force' before threats of German invasion. The Austrian Army had been ordered to offer no resistance because 'we are resolved that, on no account, and not even at this grave hour, shall German blood be spilled'. The racial muddle was echoed in the very last words he addressed to his countrymen: 'I end with a German word and a heartfelt wish – God protect Austria.' The microphone had been set up in the Corner Room next to his office, only a few feet from where Dollfuss had been struck down by Nazi bullets in the abortive *putsch* four years before. Now the whole country was about to be struck down, and without a shot being fired.

This was capitulation, but it was not yet a solution. Though Schuschnigg had bowed out, Seyss-Inquart had not been ushered in, for Miklas refused to accept the original Cabinet list he had drawn up. Hitler's Chancellor-in-waiting tried again, and produced another mixture of Austrian Nazidom tempered with pan-German Catholicism. The indestructible Glaise-Horstenau was the principal spokesman as Vice-Chancellor of the latter camp. Göring's own brother-in-law, Dr Franz Hueber, and the sinister figure of Ernst Kaltenbrunner represented Austria's Nazis as Minister of Justice and State Secretary for Security respectively. This was the list to which Miklas, well after midnight, finally put his signature. For Hitler, it was the cloak of legality; for Austria, the shroud over the republic's corpse.

For Seyss-Inquart, however, it represented something else again: the illusion that the double-headed eagle (now restored as the Austrian emblem) and the German Swastika could fly side by side from the same flagpole. To chase this dream he even had Hitler woken up at 2.30 that same morning with a plea that the invasion should be called off. This was the very peak of ambivalence, the idea that there could still exist a frontier between Nazi Germany on the one side and, on the other, Austria as some sort of separate satellite.

Hitler, of course, gave the suggestion short shrift. His 'Operation Order No. 1' he declared before returning to bed, was to be launched as planned at dawn. Seyss had forgotten, if he ever knew, about that fresco map in the Karinhall.

PART SIX

THE SWASTIKA YEARS

I

Brief Honeymoon

THE GERMAN MARCH-IN (it could not be called an invasion) hardly lived up to those *Blitzkrieg* threats which Hitler had uttered at Berchtesgaden and which Göring had just been bellowing into the telephone. Quite the reverse: after the Germans moved in at dawn on 12 March 1938, the road to Linz and, beyond that, to Vienna, became strewn with stranded lorries and half-track vehicles, all of them broken down.* There were also serious deficiencies in communications and, all in all, the Eighth Army of General Schober was not an impressive military sight. It surged ahead so effortlessly only because the Austrians were themselves sweeping it along. At many crossing points the barriers had already been removed long before the German soldiers came into view; at the remainder, the Austrian customs guards willingly lent a hand with the dismantling. The key frontier areas of Passau, Salzburg and Kiefersfelden – where Austrian Army engineers had prepared the Inn Valley flood scheme as their first line of frontier defence – were all in German hands by breakfast time. This result could certainly have been denied to them had the Austrian Staff plan for resistance been put into operation. The plan, which had been approved in detail by Schuschnigg in late 1937, called for two days of all-out fighting against the Germans in the fortified border zone, followed by armed withdrawal along the mountain valleys. On the code signal 'Secure the frontiers' the Austrian Army was to activate the land mines and shoot on sight any and all armed invaders.**

* The German General Staff estimated afterwards that nearly a third of their tanks had come to grief on the roads, and some 70 per cent of all vehicles involved had become stranded – either because of mechanical failure or because of their untrained drivers.
** The plan envisaged a force of 5000 men being in position within six hours of the preceding alarm signal 'Watch the frontiers'. Within two days, the main force of 25,000

After the war, Schuschnigg repeated again and again (thus inviting attention to the French maxim of '*Qui s'excuse, s'accuse*') his reasons for never issuing that order. In purely pragmatic terms, they made good sense. From the Western democracies he could have hoped for nothing beyond diplomatic protests in an emergency. From Italy (and this was the crippling blow) he could not even expect that. By 1938, the Duce was very much the junior member in Europe's partnership of dictators and, as things turned out, he proved anxious not even to offend the Führer, let alone threaten him. In military terms, an Austria left to her own devices could not put up more than a very short-lived defence; a twentieth-century battle between the two German nations would have lasted longer than Königgrätz, but not by much.

Though not overwhelming, there was also a case for resisting. Hitler, it was argued, could not be certain that Mussolini would simply sit on his hands and watch Germany march right down to his Brenner frontier.* On top of this uncertainty came the Führer's domestic political crisis, which might have made him vulnerable to a continued show of Austrian defiance even if, in reality, that were nothing more than bluff. Moreover, the Austrian Army could have been relied upon to fight, had the order been given. Its officer corps had been carefully pruned and was thought to contain no more than 5 per cent of Nazi sympathisers. Indeed, there were those among the loyal majority who were resolutely getting ready for a conflict. The commander of the Wiener Neustadt Military Academy, Major-General Towarek, had, for example, issued live ammunition to his cadets, as though he were preparing them to come to the defence of the republic in 1938 just as their predecessors had rallied round the Emperor at Schönbrunn twenty years before.

Finally, there was the disturbing Czech factor to be entered in the German equation of risk. Göring's gloomiest scenario for his swoop on Austria was not so much a hostile reaction from Rome (which he, unlike Hitler, seems to have written off from the start) as an intervention from

---

men, supported by 350 artillery units, would be fully mobilised in the western provinces and along the line of the Traun River. This would have doubled in five days.

* This speculation proved later to have been well-founded. Hitler had despatched a special personal envoy, Prince Philip of Hesse, to Rome, charged with persuading the Duce to accept a *fait accompli* in Austria. When Mussolini obliged, Hitler sent ecstatic messages of thanks and pledged his help in any future crisis. It is worth adding that as late as 1936 the Duce was helping to arm Austria to fight Hitler. In that year he handed back 150 Austrian guns, with ammunition, which had been stored in Italy since their capture during the 1914–18 war.

Prague, capital of a Slav nation which for centuries had resisted Teutonic aggression in any uniform and under any guise. Had President Beneš (who had succeeded Masaryk in 1935) simply massed his troops demonstratively along the German border, Russia, the old pan-Slav protector, might well have backed him up, and even France might have bestirred herself as the patron of the Little Entente. The fate of Vienna would then have become overnight what it was ultimately recognised for, but far too late: a European issue and not just an Austro–German one. It took all Göring's efforts (backed up by the German Foreign Office) to persuade the Czech Minister in Berlin, Mastny, that Hitler intended Czechoslovakia no harm. By the evening of 12 March, the envoy had in turn succeeded in reassuring Beneš, who then distanced himself from the whole affair.

Thus, in reality, a case could be argued for defiance, but Schuschnigg did not balance the arguments so much as follow the call of blood. Had the roles of the Axis dictators been reversed in 1938, with a powerful and aggressive Mussolini crossing the Brenner to seize the north Tyrol, then the Austrians with one accord would have fought him like alley-cats. Hitler's Germans, however, were not the traditional enemies of another race, but the old allies of the same race. The *Anschluss* could thus be seen as the climax, and the resolution, of a long family quarrel. This helps to explain the most remarkable thing about the military aspect of that 12 March, which was not that Schuschnigg issued the order to his soldiers to capitulate, but that every single man-jack of them obeyed that order. No matter in what rank or regiment or province, not an Austrian shot was fired that day, even into thin air as a gesture of defiance or despair. Nor, however many officers were later purged, did a single one resign on the spot in protest. Austria's darkest hour was not her finest.

The pattern was repeated on the civilian front when, at ten minutes to four on the afternoon of the march-in, Hitler himself crossed the Austrian border at his birthplace, Braunau-am-Inn. It was a curious homecoming. In a message he had broadcast to the world before leaving Berlin by air that morning, Hitler had concentrated on the 'fraud' of Schuschnigg's proposed plebiscite. This, he alleged, was the culmination of a long campaign of injustice 'against which the German people in Austria have finally risen'. (An extravagant claim for the intrigues of a handful of pan-German hopefuls whipped into action by Göring.) Because of this 'uprising', the broadcast continued, it had been decided 'to place the assistance of the Reich at the disposal of the millions of Germans in Austria'. The aim was to give them the opportunity 'to decide their future and their destiny by means of a genuine plebiscite'. Hitler concluded: 'I, myself, as Führer and Chancellor of the German people shall be happy, as a German and a free citizen, once more to enter the country which is my homeland.'

But how was he to enter? No war had been declared, so he could hardly appear as a victorious Commander-in-Chief. The Austrian Nazis were still technically illegal, so he could not be attending a party rally. It could not be put down as an official governmental call, as he had not been invited by an Austrian President who was still in office. So the explanation given on behalf of 'the free citizen' was that he had crossed the border 'to visit his mother's grave'.* The entire charade symbolised several things: the eternal confusion between the concepts of 'German' and Austrian; the lengths to which the Nazi propaganda machine was already prepared to go to stand the truth on its head; and the evident contempt held in Berlin for the opinions of the Western democracies.

Judging by the reception that Hitler was now given on his triumphal progress to Vienna, those Western leaders might well have believed that he was indeed coming as the saviour of an oppressed nation. Just as no single shot had been fired by Austria's soldiers, so no single stone was thrown by her civilians, and not a clenched fist was to be seen among the forests of arms, either waving or raised in the Nazi salute, which lined the route through Ried and Wels to the provincial capital of Linz. Here it was estimated that almost five-sixths of the entire population of the town turned out that evening to greet him. Seyss-Inquart had flown to Linz to lead the reception committee and Hitler, the 'free citizen', acknowledged that the head of what was still an Austrian government was present. 'Germans, German racial comrades, Herr Bundeskanzler,' the Führer's speech began. More calculated muddle: the existence of an Austrian government was, for the moment, accepted, but there was no longer any mention of Austrians.

The muddle was soon to be cleared up, at least from the German end, and the entire charade brought to a speedy halt, thanks to the tumultuous reception which Hitler had just experienced. Self-

* The 'explanation' was given by Göring to the British Ambassador in Berlin, Sir Nevile Henderson, who had (somewhat reluctantly in view of his notoriously pro-German views) delivered a formal note of protest about the Austrian crisis. Göring was acting as head of government in Hitler's absence.

destruction runs like a twisting thread through the Austrian saga, yet rarely did it emerge more strongly than on that night of 12 March at Linz. The ecstatic crowds assembled in one provincial capital literally cheered their entire country into extinction. Hitler had crossed the border that morning with nothing more drastic in mind than the *Zusammenschluss* or fusion of the governments of the two countries with himself as their joint head of state. This was the solution – leaving Austria with a nominally separate existence – for which the pan-Germans of the Seyss-Inquart camp had been hoping and for which a draft law had actually been drawn up in Berlin. Hitler now found himself forced to the conclusion that more was expected of him – from his own native countrymen, as well as from destiny.

As always when he took an instinctive decision, he acted with breath-taking speed. State Secretary Stuckart of the Interior Ministry, who had drawn up the legislation for the 'Personal Union' of the two countries, was summoned by air to Linz and ordered to get to work straight away on new laws proclaiming an outright *Anschluss*.* By the morning of 13 March they were ready, and by the same afternoon were being presented in Vienna to Seyss-Inquart and his Cabinet. Austria's last Chancellor, whose lifelong dream of the two German states lay suddenly in ruins, accepted the new 'Reunification Law' without protest. He could argue neither with Hitler nor with the cheering multitudes. Once again President Miklas made a gesture for himself, and for the history books, by declining to sign the document. But as he agreed to hand over all his functions to the Chancellor of the day, it remained merely an ineffective act of disassociation. Seyss-Inquart returned once more to Linz to formalise the extinction of his country. The only favour he asked of a Führer now weeping tears of joy was for a better exchange rate for the Austrian schilling against the German mark. Hitler agreed; it was a small price to pay for so painlessly declaring Austria 'a province of the German Reich'.

The way was now open for him to enter the capital. Of his reception there, it can only be said that if the citizens of Linz had not persuaded him to change his annexation plans, the Viennese would certainly have obliged. There are embarrassing, even shaming, episodes in the lives of all nations. One such, for any Austrian with a glimmer of patriotic

---

* In Berlin, Göring had drawn the same conclusion from the rapturous welcome at Linz, which he had listened to on the radio. It seems that his courier to Linz suggesting the *Anschluss* had crossed in the air with Hitler's messenger ordering it.

conscience, was the spectacle of the huge crowd which filled Vienna's Heldenplatz on the morning of 15 March. Hitler had entered the capital the previous afternoon, a sombre figure in the brown overcoat of the Storm Troopers, standing upright in his open car, the right hand locked stiffly in the Nazi salute. The journey from Linz had taken more than six hours. This snail's pace had been brought about partly by the succession of loyal addresses and floral bombardments delivered *en route*, but partly by the need to clear away all the broken-down vehicles of his Eighth Army which littered the roadside. The sight of them may have had something to do with his unsmiling demeanour.

But now, after a night spent at the Hotel Metropole, he was back to ebullient form. From the balcony of the Hofburg, he made what was not so much the address of a conqueror as a speech of acceptance for a gift delivered into his hands. Again, there was scarcely a mention by name of Austria in what was, in fact, its funeral oration: 'I proclaim for this land its new mission. The oldest eastern province of the German nation shall from now on be the youngest bulwark of the German nation.' There was an echo in Hitler's closing words of the pledge he had written down in Landsberg prison fifteen years before: 'I can in this hour report before history the fulfilment of the greatest aim of my life – the entry of my homeland into the German Reich.'

The spectacle of those 250,000 citizens of that 'youngest bulwark' cheering and waving below has troubled the Austrian conscience ever since. That crowd alone represented, after all, about one-seventh of Vienna's population, and over the years various attempts have been made to explain the phenomenon away. Vienna, and not Linz, is indeed the place to put the general euphoria into some sort of balance. It is not good enough to suggest that the Heldenplatz audience had been simply 'packed' by Austrian Nazi cohorts shipped in from outside by the SS Chief Heinrich Himmler, who had arrived in Vienna three days before the Führer. Several thousand Hitler Youth groups had been drafted in (all schools were closed), but the crowd was basically Viennese, even if it did include a good helping of the city's traditional '*Adabeis*', who could be relied upon to turn out on any colourful occasion.* The fact that all shops and factories had been closed

* Forty-four years later, for example, crowds poured into the Inner City when, on 13 November 1982, the former Empress Zita was first allowed to revisit the Vienna she had left in November 1918. There were loud cheers then, but many had just turned up to gawk at this unique survivor from the past.

IV: First Republic to *Anschluss*

RIGHT: Cheers, and drizzle, outside the Vienna Parliament as the First Austrian Republic is proclaimed, 12 November 1918.

BELOW: Karl Renner, the Socialist Chancellor of the post-war Republic, signs the dictated peace of St Germain, 10 September 1919. Under the treaty the old Austrian lands of the Monarchy were reduced by more than two-thirds in size and three-quarters in population.

15 July 1927: left-wing mobs beyond the control of their political leaders set fire to the Ministry of Justice in Vienna.

BELOW: February 1934: a victim of the Austrian civil war almost inevitable in a country where 'the democrats were not patriots and the patriots were not democrats'.

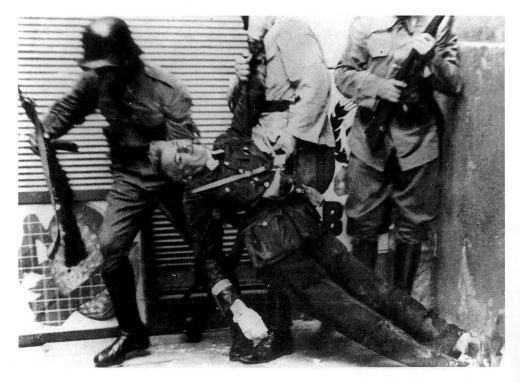

Ignaz Seipel (1876–1932), the prelate-statesman who dominated the Republic's right-wing rule in the 1920s. He also put Vienna back on the political map of Europe.

Engelbert Dollfuss (1892–1934), the heartbeat of a new Austrian patriotism which Hitler silenced.

ABOVE: Wilhelm Miklas, the right-wing Austrian President who held out against Hitler to the bitter end.

LEFT: Kurt Schuschnigg (1897–1977), the Austrian Chancellor who yielded to Hitler because he 'could not shed German blood'.

14 March 1938: Hitler enters a half-passive, half-enthusiastic Vienna after the bloodless *Anschluss*.

12 March 1938: the mayfly Austrian pro-Nazi Cabinet of Seyss-Inquart (5th from left). It lasted less than three days.

RIGHT: Rampant anti-Semitism moves in at Hitler's heels: in Vienna, a portly Austrian Nazi supervises the daubing of 'Jew' on one of the capital's many closed-down Jewish shops.

BELOW: The grim entrance gates to Mauthausen concentration camp, near the confluence of the Danube and the Enns. It was the first and most infamous of the thirty-one such camps eventually constructed in Hitler's 'Ostmark'. More than 35,000 prisoners perished here.

April 1945. Red Army troops storm the outskirts of Vienna.

Vienna, spring 1945. A start is made on clearing the mounds of rubble. In the last months of the war, Allied bombing raids and the final battles between the Wehrmacht and the Red Army had laid waste great tracts of the capital.

1945: the symbol of the Allied presence in Vienna. Military police of the four occupying powers on their daily joint patrols.

Four-power occupation: the agreeable side. A 'British soldiers only' swimming bath in Vienna.

2 July 1948: Vice Chancellor Schärf (centre) signs the Marshall Plan accord. Six months later, food rationing could be partly abolished.

London, 8 May 1952: Leopold Figl, the tough little right-wing Chancellor of the Second Republic, meets the great war leader who had returned to power as British Prime Minister the year before.

15 May 1955: Foreign Minister Figl holds up the freedom treaty just signed in the Belvedere Palace to the cheering masses below. On his immediate right the French Foreign Minister M. Pinay and the American Secretary of State John Foster Dulles. On his left, Vice-Chancellor Schärf, Soviet Foreign Minister Molotov and Chancellor Raab.

Spontaneous jubilation from a lesser Viennese balcony on the day the treaty was signed.

October 1955: after ten years the occupation ends. The last Russian soldier boards his train, clutching his final acquisition.

The Cold War, and the Iron Curtain closes in around Austria. Frontier gendarmes mark out their border before the Czech watchtowers near Bratislava.

Neutral Austria playing the role it sought as bridge between East and West. Vice-Chancellor Schärf sits between President Kennedy and Soviet leader Nikita Khrushchev at the 1961 Summit Meeting in Vienna.

RIGHT: Bruno Kreisky, the longest-serving and normally ebullient Socialist Chancellor of the Second Republic, seen here with something on his mind.

BELOW: Kurt Waldheim, Austria's pariah President, 1986–1993. Throughout his term of office he was shunned by nearly all the world states after controversy over his wartime military record. Nonetheless his plight obliged all his fellow-countrymen to face up to the role they had played under the Hitler regime.

12 June 1994: a happy end to their odyssey. The Austrians vote to join the European Union by a massive two-thirds majority. Right-wing Vice-Chancellor Erhard Busek greets the results in triumphant style.

and that there was brilliant spring weather on the day only swelled their number.

Much more to the point in balancing the books was the lightning operation which Himmler had set in motion the moment he got to the capital. On the night of 12–13 March, every prominent Austrian anti-Nazi on the Gestapo's lists was seized and imprisoned, many of them destined for onward shipment to the Dachau concentration camp. The figure of more than 70,000 victims falling to this first wave of arrests (as given in the official Austrian 'Red-White-Red Book' of 1946) was to prove heavily exaggerated. Many – perhaps the bulk – of those immediately seized were released over the next weeks and months. Indeed, one Gestapo report recorded that by the end of the year fewer than 1500 Austrians were still 'under protective arrest', out of a total of just under 21,000 cases which had been handled in all. The true calculation is difficult, if not impossible, to make, as the Germans themselves gave contradictory statistics. But even if the lower limit of some 20,000 arrests is accepted for the spring of 1938, Himmler had removed from the scene, at one blow, everyone in the political, bureaucratic or military framework of the First Republic who might in the Nazis' eyes constitute a threat to the 'New Order'.*

Moreover, apart from those who cheered Hitler on 15 March and those who were already behind bars, there were hundreds of thousands of other Viennese who just sat in their homes on that day, either numbed by what was going on, or actually dreading the future. Foremost in the latter category were the city's 175,000 Jews, who knew that with the last hope extinguished of even nominal independence for an Austrian state, their turn would surely come. Yet, where there was not enthusiasm for Hitler, there was passivity over his presence. A rare exception was a Tyrolean gentleman of impeccable anti-Nazi credentials (a monarchist as well as a liberal conservative Catholic), Dr Fred Payrleithner, who set out on the morning of 15 March with a loaded pistol in his pocket whose bullets were intended for Adolf Hitler. Only when he had been walking for an hour through streets seemingly thronged with nothing but joyful citizens did he return dejectedly to his apartment, the mission

---

* His victims included Schuschnigg himself, who had rejected the idea of fleeing the country (unlike several leaders of both left and right). The first stage of an incarceration which was to last until 1945 was spent at the Hotel Bristol. His first guard was the same Austrian Nazi who had saluted him as sentry at Berchtesgaden the month before.

abandoned. Even if it had been possible to take a shot at the Führer, assassination seemed that day to be totally out of place.*

Not only on that day: the general climate of welcome seemed to deepen further in the weeks ahead. In the next breath after proclaiming Austria to be a province of the German Reich, Hitler had announced that on Sunday 10 April 1938, 'a free and secret plebiscite of the German men and women of Austria over twenty years old' would be held over the issue. Though the Austrian people would be voting on a *fait accompli*, a mere majority would not suffice for the Führer. That may have been enough for democracies, but in true dictatorial style, he was after universal sanction, or as close to it as the polling-booths could get. With the Fatherland Front eliminated from the scene, and the Socialists long suppressed, it was not necessary to fight any political opposition to achieve that result, but merely to lobby the camps of potential waverers. These were now clustered around the Catholic Church on the right and what remained of the Socialist leadership on the left. Both proved easy targets.

The Vienna Archbishop, Cardinal Innitzer, had shown from the very beginning that he was prepared to bend before the prevailing wind. On his instructions, the Führer's progression to the capital had been greeted with chimes of welcome from the churches and swastikas unfurled from their towers. So much for the man who had been the spiritual leader of the Christian corporate state. But it was Papen who completed the conversion. The German Catholic gravedigger of the republic now finished the burial work by persuading Hitler, during the Heldenplatz celebrations, to receive the Cardinal immediately afterwards. The result of their private talk at the Hotel Imperial probably surprised even the expectations of Papen, who was present at the occasion. Innitzer (himself of Sudeten origin) pronounced his delight at the realisation of 'the old dream of German unity'. Austria's Catholics, he promised, would become 'the truest sons of the great empire into whose arms they had been brought on this momentous day'. Hitler, in turn, pledged 'a good working relationship'. By this, the Archbishop hoped for a free rein, or at least a loose rein, over religious education and training throughout the enlarged Reich.

It was the familiar bargain which the Catholic Church had struck

* His son, another Fred Payrleithner, and a distinguished executive of Austria's state television, kindly placed his father's diary at the author's disposal. This was a personal chronicle never intended for publication, which lends extra weight to its authenticity.

down the centuries with the powers that be: rendering up the body politic to Caesar as long as he left the soul alone. In Austria, in the spring of 1938, it was the Führer who got the better part of the bargain. On 27 March, a solemn proclamation which the Austrian bishops had signed ten days before was read out from all the pulpits of the country. After hailing the National Socialist Party for its work among the poor and its battle against Bolshevism, the message ended: 'On the day of the plebiscite, it is an obvious national duty for we bishops to declare ourselves, as Germans for the German empire, and we expect that all faithful Christians will also know what they owe to their people.'*

Two of the prelates summoned by Innitzer to Vienna to sign the proclamation had already had a foretaste of how 'national duty' was to be enforced under the new regime. Archbishop Waitz of Salzburg had been placed under Nazi police guard for two days, while his colleague from Graz, Bishop Pawlikowski, had actually been jailed for twenty-four hours. As another ominous sign of the times, Innitzer had been obliged to sign his covering letter to the proclamation with the words 'Heil Hitler'. Only a week before, on 11 March, Innitzer's diocese had declared: 'As Austrian citizens, we stand and fight for a free and independent Austria!'

When the bishops' proclamation was read out, the plebiscite was only a fortnight away. It took the Nazis another week to nail down their second quarry. The Socialists had shown more misgivings than the Church over speaking up for Hitler, and they had much more difficulty in finding the spokesman. A crash programme of job creation and children's welfare projects softened their hostility. Finally, on 3 April, seven days before the poll, their surrender was announced by that perpetual pragmatist and political survivor, Karl Renner. It took the form of an interview in the Vienna *Tagblatt* in which the ex-Chancellor harked back to his own vain efforts to have Austria fused with Germany twenty years before. The 'stray wandering of the Austrian people' which had followed was now ended. It was a measured and dignified acceptance which even ventured disapproval for the methods by which the *Anschluss* had been brought about. But its final pledge was all that mattered, and this supplied the banner headline: 'I will vote Yes!'**

* Austria's Protestant Church leaders followed suit on 1 April with a declaration in even more ringing terms, recalling their historic yearning for a 'return to the German empire'.
** By this time Renner's colleague Dr Robert Danneberg, a former Secretary-General of the party, was already in a Vienna prison cell after a vain attempt to join Otto

When the urns were emptied and counted, the official returns showed both a huge turn-out and a massive approval for the *Anschluss*. 4,453,000 of the eligible electorate of 4,484,000 had voted 'Yes'. Only 11,929 'No' votes were returned and – almost equally defiant – another 5776 had spoiled their ballot papers in protest. That worked out at a majority of 99.73 per cent in Hitler's favour, and though such figures may have been startling in their novelty they were not really surprising, given the unseen pressures exerted on the day, the mood of the moment, and all the traumas which had preceded it.

The main factors at work were not political, and not even ideological (if one excepts the fanatical Nazis). They were psychological, with a sense of isolation combined with a feeling of helplessness uppermost. The little state which had leant so heavily on Italy for protection and looked so hopefully to the Western democracies for support had been as good as written off in Rome, Paris and London. The Austrians who, apart from Dollfuss and a few stalwarts of his Fatherland Front, had never had much faith in their republic, had now also written it off, and themselves with it. On top of this came a wealth of other factors: griev-ances over the St Germain Peace Treaty, for example, which Hitler had sworn to put right; the hope that his dynamic economic programmes could solve Austria's problems and, in particular, reduce the high level of 400,000 unemployed.

That huge majority would certainly have been reduced had any oppo-sition party been in existence to argue the case for a 'No' vote without fear of intimidation. Even without such a free debate, the 'Yes' figures would certainly have been trimmed had not over 350,000 voters, an estimated 8 per cent of Austrians over twenty, been declared ineligible to take part from the start. The main contingent of those excluded were the Jews – some 170,000 in Vienna alone – with an assortment of other undesirables, including, of course, the thousands of political prisoners already behind bars. This aspect was overlooked by the posse of foreign journalists who, after touring the election booths on polling day, reported that they had witnessed no irregularities and seen no violations of secret voting procedures. Nor did they seem to have inhaled the acrid breath of the police state which was already in the air. It was a fine line between urging the Austrians to support Hitler and hinting that they

---

Bauer and company in Prague. Danneberg was a Jew, and one motive behind Renner's declaration may well have been the hope of securing his release and that of other captives.

would be unwise to oppose him. All the time, the Nazi propaganda machine, unopposed, was working at full blast in a campaign which culminated in a Vienna visit from the Führer himself on the eve of the poll.

But when all these factors have been taken into account, and all theoretical adjustments made to the result, it seems likely that, even in a free vote, the majority on 10 April 1938 would have been behind Hitler just as, on 13 March, it would have been behind Schuschnigg had he been able to hold his plebiscite. The transformation in this span was, nonetheless, an amazing phenomenon: from a chorus of 'Red-white-red until death' to shouts of '*Sieg Heil*' for the undertaker; from crowds chanting the old imperial anthem of '*Gott Erhalte*' to many of the same throats echoing the '*Horst Wessel Lied*' of the Nazis. To some extent, the violent swing of events had carried with it this violent swing of moods. Fear, weariness, opportunism and hope certainly outweighed fanaticism. But there was also something very Austrian about the sudden switch which applied particularly to the Viennese. They had been born with the 'one eye laughing, the other weeping' which came out in Schubert's music. The capital of waltzes and operettas was also the city of *Angst* and record suicide rates. There is a pendulum built into the Austrian psyche.

And, finally, we must look once more at that anti-symbiosis of race which had dogged the Austrians down the centuries, and which in these weeks had reached its turbulent climax. Schuschnigg refused to spill 'German blood'; Seyss-Inquart worshipped at the shrine of the 'German cultural heritage'; Renner revived the 1918 dream of 'German Austria'; both Hitler and Innitzer resurrected the 'German Ostmark', a concept which went back a thousand years to the Babenbergers. By the spring of 1938, the word 'German' stood for almost everything, and therefore meant practically nothing.

However, the pendulum now started to swing again, more slowly, but this time more decisively. In what was perhaps the greatest of all the paradoxes in their story, the Austrians began to find their identity from the moment they lost it.

II

Unhappy Marriage

THE AUSTRIANS NOW had to struggle with something even more arduous than looking two ways at once: namely living a life in two dimensions – that of the Austrian and that of the all-German identity which had absorbed them. Their experience under the swastika was unique among all the peoples of continental Europe who were to fall, one by one, into the Nazi Reich. All these countries produced their quota of Quisling leaders and rank-and-file collaborators. But, precisely because the nations concerned were Slav or Gallic or Nordic, these groups were minorities, regarded as self-seekers or traitors by the population at large.

The case of Hitler's Austrians, a Germanic people who had done so much to welcome him in, was very different. For the next seven years, they were the agents of terror as well as its victims; they became the torturers as well as the tortured; they were the props of an evil regime as well as those who tried to knock those props away. The emphasis was to shift between these two roles as disillusionment replaced hope and rapture, and the process speeded up once it became clear that the Führer was not merely a harsh taskmaster but a military loser. But, to some degree or other, the duality lasted for seven years and it ran throughout the nation. This needs bearing in mind from the start, more especially because, after it was all over, the Austrians laid stress on the respectable role and tried to play down or cover up the disreputable one. No apologist could, of course, go so far as to deny its existence.

The disillusionment began very early, even among those who had cheered themselves hoarse in mid-March. It was set off by the realisation of what it actually meant for Austria to be degraded, thanks to that cheering, into a mere province of Germany. The so-called Cabinet of

Seyss-Inquart lasted barely three days as his dream of '*Zusammenschluss*' and Hitler's matching concept of a 'Personal Union' were dissolved. On 15 March, the mayfly Federal Chancellor became instead Governor (Reichsstatthalter) of the Austrian Provincial Government. Any lingering hopes he might still have entertained of using this post to preserve some fragments of a separate identity were rapidly dashed. The very next day, Hitler appointed Wilhelm Keppler, his principal Austrian Nazi henchman in the pre-*Anschluss* era, to be Special Commissioner for the reunion of Austria with the German Reich. This clipped Seyss-Inquart's already ragged wings. The feathers were torn out altogether on 23 April, when Keppler was replaced by a German Nazi, Hitler's former Gauleiter for the Saarland, Josef Bürckel. Bürckel had operated with great success three years earlier in absorbing the Saarland into Germany and was now to fulfil the same task, on a far greater scale, with Austria. From now on, the days of Seyss and his fellow dreamers were numbered. The new Ostmark province was still administered by governmental officials who were technically under their control. But the real power had passed to a Nazi Party network controlled from Berlin and kept in place by the apparatus of terror.

Its arrival was signalled by a memorandum which Bürckel sent to Seyss-Inquart a week after taking over from Keppler. In it, Hitler's new Reich Commissioner instructed the Provincial Governor to submit to him, for prior approval, any pending changes in the laws and legal system of the old Austria. All new measures were to be implemented through his office only. The party police state had been formally installed.

It had already mopped up the Austrian police force. One of Himmler's first acts on arrival in Vienna had been to sack Dr Michael Skubl, the State Secretary for Security who had remained loyal to Schuschnigg. He was replaced as Minister by Ernst Kaltenbrunner, who had helped reorganise the Austrian SS during the years when the Fatherland Front had driven the party underground. Kaltenbrunner was one of that insalubrious band of top-level Austrian Nazis who were to rival in their fanaticism and misdeeds any villains to be found anywhere in Hitler's Reich. As we shall see, he continued to believe in that Reich, and to struggle for it, right down to the end.

Himmler did not have to look far to find a replacement for Skubl in his capacity as Chief of Vienna police. The new man there was none other than Otto Steinhäusl, a leading member of the abortive *putsch* against Dollfuss four years before. There was little problem with the rank-and-file of the force. Many of them had turned out on the morning of that critical 11 March with swastika bands tucked away in their pockets; by nightfall, these were already around their arms. Nonetheless, Himmler thought it prudent to reinforce these instant local recruits to Nazism with his own well-proven men. More than 6000 ordinary German police moved in behind the German Army, followed by greater contingents of German SS and Gestapo.

Though deprived of power, Seyss-Inquart launched one last battle to preserve some separate role for Austria and for himself inside the New Order, and he fought it on the only field remaining to him, the cultural one. He had already been promised by Hitler (in a personal letter dated 23 April 1938) an unspecified ministerial appointment within the Reich once his post in Austria had been formally wound up. Throughout the summer and autumn of 1938 he pleaded with the Führer that this appointment should be to a specially created Ostmark Ministry whose task would be to spread Austrian-German culture throughout the Danube Basin. This concept of the 'Austrian Mission' had its long pedigree rooted in the Habsburg Monarchy, and had run down the Austrian Republic from Seipel to Dollfuss.* But Seyss was never to see it realised, for Austria's cultural autonomy became swallowed up for the time being, together with the last remnants of her political identity. In June 1939, the name 'Ostmark' was indeed officially substituted for 'Austria', but only nine months later, in April 1940, this was replaced by the more nebulous term 'The Reichsgaue of the Ostmark'.**

The creation of these *Gaue* may have obliterated, on paper, all traces of Austria as a separate country, denying the nation its long history in the process. In fact, in yet another paradoxical twist to the *Anschluss* tale, by splitting his Ostmark up into party fiefdoms, Hitler had unintentionally nourished the ground roots of Austrian identity. The seven *Gaue* which he finally nominated on 23 May were based on the historic provinces of the Monarchy, as transposed into the republic.*** All

---

* It was, in fact, to surface again in Vienna with even greater vigour towards the end of the century.

** On 19 January 1942, Hitler forbade the use of the name 'Ostmark' altogether. Henceforth, only the *Gaue* were to be mentioned.

*** They were Vienna, Lower Danube, Upper Danube, Salzburg, Styria, Carinthia with East Tyrol and Tyrol with Vorarlberg.

the seven Gauleiters he appointed were Austrians, who thus became native-born princelings not unlike the republican governors they had replaced and enjoyed similar wide-ranging administrative powers. This may have been a purely party structure, answerable to Bürckel in Vienna (who in turn was answerable to Göring in Berlin). Yet the old provincial loyalties and traditions were not extinguished underneath it; they merely went into hibernation and would awaken once the long winter of the swastika was over.

With the Nazi regime firmly established in the Ostmark, it is time to look at those Austrians who were its instruments – willing or involuntary – over the next seven years; at the opposite camp of its victims and opponents; and finally at the broadest group of the general population, who floated restlessly and, for the most part, passively, in between. For the instruments of the regime we must take, first and foremost, those who served Hitler in uniform, either in that of the Wehrmacht, or that of the SS.

Along with the Austrian foreign exchange reserves and stocks of unminted gold (valued by the Germans at 230 million and 148 million Reichmarks respectively), the entire supply of military manpower represented for Hitler the most valuable material dividend of the *Anschluss*. The German Army of March 1938 numbered only some forty divisions, so that the Austrian Bundesheer – which at that time comprised seven infantry divisions plus one light mobile formation and over a hundred assorted regiments, battalions and technical companies – came as a welcome reinforcement. In a conscious bid to revive memories of the long-standing alliance between the two armies in imperial times, selected Bundesheer units had marched along the Ringstrasse only three days after the *Anschluss* in a massive 'shoulder-to-shoulder' parade with their German comrades.

The reality behind this propaganda façade of total solidarity was very different. On that same 15 March, sixty-seven Austrian officers, including twelve generals, nine colonels and twenty-nine staff officers were dismissed. By the time the process was completed a year later, some 55 per cent of all generals and 40 per cent of all colonels who had served in the Bundesheer had been excluded from service in the Wehrmacht. Some had been removed for practical operational reasons: older officers being pensioned off, for example, to make room for young blood. But it was also a purge of the politically unreliable. A defiant hard core, including some who refused to take the oath of allegiance to

Hitler, were very harshly dealt with. Some thirty officers of the Bundesheer were sent to prison or concentration camps, and six actually died in captivity.

The most prominent victim of the purge was General Wilhelm Zehner himself, Schuschnigg's resolute Secretary of State for Defence, who would certainly have shot back at Hitler's Eighth Army had he been ordered to do so.* At the same time, the fifty-odd Austrian officers who had been dismissed by Schuschnigg because of their Nazi sympathies returned to the new Wehrmacht in triumph, and it was now their turn to help identify the candidates for expulsion.**

Like their German comrades, all the new Ostmark officers of the Führer's Wehrmacht had to swear their solemn and public mass oath of personal allegiance to him. Despite the hideous and ultimately disastrous course which Hitler's war was to take, this oath retained, to the very end, a hypnotic hold over many who had sworn it, Austrian and German alike. Indeed, for many young Bundesheer recruits who swore it in 1938, it symbolised the beginning of a military career whose prospects were far more dazzling than anything they could have expected in the small republic. One such Austrian officer who had just been commissioned at the time summed up the feeling many years later in one sentence: 'After all, a posting to Dresden was much more exciting than garrison duty at Pinkafeld.'*** The fact that the man who spoke those words was to become one of the leaders of the July 1944 plot against Hitler gives them extra weight.

That lay far in the future, when Hitler's cause was shown to be militarily hopeless as well as morally odious. Yet at no time during the war (contrary to popular gossip) did Hitler have cause to distrust the divisions raised in his two Austrian military districts† on grounds of ideological unreliability. Nor did he have any cause to question either the professional ambition or the personal bravery of his 'Ostmärker' in uniform. Over two hundred Austrians rose to the rank of general in

---

* He was found dead in his apartment soon after being discharged. Officially, he committed suicide, but strong rumours had it that he was killed by the Gestapo.

** As a bizarre concession to sentiment, these were allowed to wear their old Austrian uniform on suitable occasions, though forbidden to don that of the Wehrmacht.

*** Major Carl Szokoll, in conversation with the author in Vienna, 11 October 1994.

† Numbered XVII and XVIII. There were no divisions in the Wehrmacht made up exclusively of Austrians, though this was due to administrative and operational reasons.

Hitler's armed forces,* and forty-nine of these were to die on active service. (As will be seen later, five more were to be executed after the German defeat as war criminals.) Moreover, by the war's end there were 326 Austrians among the holders of Germany's highest military decoration, the Knight's Cross. In fact the first soldier in the German Army ever to receive that award was an Austrian: Lieutenant Josef Stolz, who won his medal fighting in Poland in September 1939. Nearly one-third of the 325 who were to join him in this elite company were either killed in action or died of their wounds, with the Air Force and the Navy ahead of the Army in this particular count. In August 1940 Hitler paid special tribute to the bravery of his Austrian soldiers in a speech read out for him in Vienna by his deputy, Rudolf Hess. After the war, one Austrian military historian praised these Austrian Knight's Cross heroes in even more ringing tones: 'They covered themselves with the same immortal glory as did their fathers and forefathers in their tireless defence of the West.'** The eulogy was doubtless sincerely meant, and the laurels were certainly earned. Precisely because of this, they remain hard to reconcile with the familiar post-war Austrian approach to their losses under Hitler. This ingenuously lumped all their battlefield dead together with the Jews and other helpless sufferers of the regime into the one category of 'Nazi victims'.

Nor, when the order of battle in the various campaigns is analysed, does the belief hold good that Hitler 'sacrificed' his Austrian troops in order, presumably, to preserve his more reliable Germans. This accusation went the rounds in Vienna, especially in the wake of the Wehrmacht's disastrous defeat at Stalingrad. That great battle – whose climax, between 10 January and 2 February 1943, brought about the liquidation of the entire Sixth German Army – transformed the Austrian perception of Hitler as well as being a turning-point in the war itself. Austrian losses in the disaster (more than 40,000 Ostmärker were killed or died in Russian captivity) were undeniably high in proportion to German casualties. But this was due to bad luck rather than deliberate policy: many of the recruits for the Sixth Army happened to have come in the

* Over a quarter had non-German names, those of Czech origin being the most prominent, alongside South Slavs, Ruthenes and Magyars. The old multi-national Monarchy still marched on under Hitler.
** Professor Nikolaus von Preradovich, in the Austrian military journal *Feldgrau*, 1961.

first place from the two Austrian military districts who had raised three of the twenty Wehrmacht divisions wiped out in the battle.* (According to Soviet figures published after the war, a total of thirty-five divisions were formed on Austrian soil, containing up to 80 per cent Austrian personnel.)

The overall population framework of the Reich needs considering to put this, and other comparisons, in context. Hitler's Germans totalled around seventy million at the time of the *Anschluss*. The Austrian Republic he had swallowed up numbered nearly seven million. A ratio of one in ten could therefore be taken as the future norm. On this basis, Hitler's German soldiers came off overall rather worse than his Ostmärker when the grim tallies were put together long after the war.** Some eighteen million men were called up in all into the Wehrmacht and the Waffen SS between 1939 and 1945. Of these, 1.2 million came from Austria, or rather less than the population balance. German losses were finally put at a minimum of 3.5 million, or one in five; Austrian losses at around 250,000, or one in six.

This was no longer a 'shoulder-to-shoulder' propaganda march along Vienna's Ringstrasse. It was a story of the two German peoples fighting side by side for five years in actions which were often gruesome but also often heroic. Inevitably, the spirit of comradeship-in-arms which had been fired in the First World War was rekindled. But for Austrians of the old school this could be dampened by the realisation that Hitler's war was something very different. That same ex-imperial officer, Dr Fred Payrleitner, who had taken out his pistol on *Anschluss* day found himself commissioned again in 1941 and posted, as a man well into his middle age, as adjutant to a transport unit on the home front. Then, in the autumn of 1942, when the Sixth Army of General Paulus was massing before Stalingrad, came the order that officers in his category should be transferred to battlefield duty. He recorded his misgivings when the possibility arose of being given command of an armoured unit. They were not those of a coward:

* I am indebted to Dr Manfried Rauchensteiner, Director of the Military History Institute at the War Museum in Vienna, for elucidation on this and several other statistical aspects of Austrian participation in the war. The three Austrian divisions in the Sixth Army were 44 and 297 Infantry and the 100th Light. Two Roumanian divisions also fought and fell at Stalingrad.
** The figures which follow are based on the latest calculations (made in September 1993) of the Vienna War Museum.

I would have thrown myself totally into it to defend my own fatherland proper, as in the World War. But for a war of conquest, on the other hand, I had no inclination. Greater Germany and National Socialism are now the same. As I was never a National Socialist, and will never become one, I cannot fight an offensive for Greater Germany because that would make me a fighter for National Socialism. To take up this command would therefore plunge me into a conflict of conscience.*

In the event, he was spared the dilemma. The war dice fell kindly for him and he found himself posted to an ambulance transport company in Tunisia. In this relatively humane setting, he was spared exposure to rampant Nazism. But there was plenty of the (to him offensive and counter-productive) Prussian ethos about his German fellow-officers, and he did his best to combat it:

> We old-time officers had very different concepts implanted in us about the fulfilment of one's duty, about taking care of our soldiers, and the pleasure that came with a sense of responsibility. They are concepts which today still seem preferable to those principles of obedience and discipline which prevail in the German Army. This sort of robot obedience will always be incomprehensible to any Austrian officer of the imperial school . . . That a soldier has to carry out his orders is obvious. But it is our belief that the soldier must know why I gave that order . . . He must feel that his officer shares both joy and suffering with him and has understanding for all his little worries.**

These are more than the thoughts of one middle-aged Austrian officer serving in the African desert in 1943. They encapsulate the contrast – and the conflict – between what was most appealing about the Austrian philosophy of life and what was most disagreeable about that of the Germans.

Thus far, we have looked only at Austrians serving in Hitler's army. The picture is more varied, but also more sombre, when we take those wearing the uniform of his fanatics and executioners. The least disreputable of this group (though that is a very relative expression) were the Waffen SS, elite fighting formations who fought with great bravery at

* Private diary of Fred Payrleitner, p.6.
** Private diary of Fred Payrleitner, p.218.

the front but committed some of the worst atrocities against civilians behind the lines. The total strength of the Waffen SS by the spring of 1945 was put at some one million men and, according to estimates compiled by the War Museum's Military Institute in Vienna, up to one-tenth of those were Austrians, reflecting the overall population balance. In theory, all of these were volunteers. In practice, the Austrian contingents also contained many ethnic Germans from the Balkans who were classed at the bottom of the Aryan scale and were given the blunt choice of either joining the Waffen SS or going to concentration camps. What is quite clear is that the genuine volunteers lived up fully to what was expected of them. More than forty of those 326 Austrians to be awarded the Knight's Cross had fought in the Waffen SS. Fifteen fell in battle, four of them generals, including the renowned Obergruppen-führer Arthur Phelps. At one point he had commanded the crack all-volunteer SS mountain division 'Prinz Eugen', a glorious name in the chronicles of the Habsburg Monarchy now dragged in the mire of Hitler's war. All in all, Heinrich Himmler, the Reichsführer of the SS, had little to complain about over the ardour of the Ostmärker in his military ranks.

He had even less reason to grumble over their contribution to the supreme evil he created in his other capacity as Hitler's police and Gestapo chief – his devil's web of concentration camps. The Austrians bore no initial blame or responsibility for the setting up of these camps on their soil. They eventually totalled more than thirty-one, but the first to be established, at Mauthausen, near the confluence of the Danube and the River Enns, remained the largest and became the most infamous. Its creation was the personal decision of Himmler, who surveyed the site soon after he arrived in Austria in March 1938. Mauthausen was an early example of what emerged as perhaps the most chilling aspect of the concentration camp programme: the enlistment of human suffering into the Nazi production effort on a scientifically planned basis. The new camp was to serve a special firm which had been set up by the SS itself for the exploitation of granite deposits throughout the Reich. This firm, the Deutsche Erd und Steinwerke GmbH (German Earth and Stoneworks Company), saw the Mauthausen quarries as a chief source of raw material to refurbish the great cities of the Reich and rebuild a new one at Linz, which Hitler dreamt of turning into a second Ostmark capital along the Danube.

The double irony of the situation was that not only was Vienna one of the cities singled out for improvement, but that the quarries themselves actually belonged to the municipality. Throughout April and May 1938, the SS in Berlin had therefore to negotiate with the town hall in Vienna over the terms of the takeover. The city authorities do not come out too well in the exchange. Their archives show that, despite being informed from the start that the intention was 'to create a state concentration camp at Mauthausen for between 3000 and 5000 inmates', their reactions were coldly bureaucratic. They made sure that, as a condition of the agreement, those inmates would deliver the traditional cobblestones needed for Vienna's streets. The only other reservation expressed was over the quality of the product. Would these 'newly installed untrained workers' be able to turn out the high-grade cobbles which had taken 'long years of improvement to create'? The answer to that question is not known.

A special SS 'Death's Head' unit was raised to guard Mauthausen in 1938. Named the 'Ostmark', it was only the fourth such unit to be created in the Reich; the other three bore the names 'Oberbayern', 'Brandenburg' and 'Thüringen'. The camp was to rank high in suffering, and the casualty figures came to match this regime of special harshness. From 1938 to 1945 Mauthausen took in more than 197,000 prisoners, of whom 35,318 were officially entered in the books as having died, more even than at Buchenwald. One wonders whether the Vienna City Fathers had any inkling of this, or ever learnt that the very first batch of inmates to arrive, on 8 August 1938, were three hundred Austrian political prisoners transferred from Dachau.

The majority of victims, at Mauthausen as at other concentration camps, were of course Jews. While the Austrians cannot in any way be held responsible for the launching of Hitler's ferocious campaign of persecution against these unfortunates, they certainly did their share in carrying it out. A claim was made long after the war by an established if controversial authority to the effect that, in one way or another, Austrians were responsible for the deaths of up to half of the six million Jews who perished in the Holocaust.* Such a broad calculation is impossible to prove or disprove. What is clear is that from the first day of the *Anschluss* the traditional anti-Semitism of the Austrian people, and above all of the Viennese, was given full rein.

---

* Dr Simon Wiesenthal, Head of the Vienna 'Documentation Centre', in conversation with the author, 23 September 1993.

The initial outburst, concentrated in the capital, was unsavoury rather than brutal, and it did not only concern the city's Jews. Immediately after the German march-in, Austrian Nazis, many in SS or SA police uniform, raided and plundered shops and offices at will and seized, as their personal property, offices and apartments which had belonged to Jews or members of the Fatherland Front. These uncontrolled excesses got so out of hand that the Gauleiter's office had to issue an edict forbidding all property evictions and seizures which were not officially authorised. But these 'personal initiatives' persisted until the middle of May, when Reich Commissioner Bürckel issued another and much sharper order threatening all future culprits, and their immediate supervisors, with expulsion from the party.

The second wave of centrally controlled pressure against the Jews now set in. This phase of so-called 'legalised anti-Semitism' concentrated on the 175,000-strong Jewish community in Vienna (the overwhelming majority of the total in the country as a whole). They were ejected from schools, forbidden to practise as lawyers and chemists, and hounded out of the artistic and cultural life of the capital which they had dominated for decades past. This was accompanied by an organised drive to persuade them to leave the country. To administer the programme, on 22 August 1938, Bürckel set up in Vienna's former Rothschild Palace a special bureau, the Central Office for Jewish Emigration.* Its deputy chief was an SS officer who was to go down in history as the Satan's apostle of the Holocaust, Adolf Eichmann, a native of Hitler's favourite Austrian city of Linz. Eichmann displayed his talents for efficiency from the very beginning. By the end of the year, a total of 79,000 Austrian Jews had left the country, most of them legally, via the Central Office. By the autumn of 1939, the figure had shot up to over 126,000. There had been various ominous reminders that only abroad could safety be found. Some were deliberate exercises in persuasion, as when, in May 1938, Bürckel ordered the mass arrest of 2000 Viennese Jews, to concentrate their minds on the merits of an exit permit. A far greater scare was the wave of plundering and arrests which struck the Jewish community on 9 November 1938. This, the so-called 'Crystal Night' (a reference to the thousands of smashed windows of Jewish properties), was part of the notorious reprisal action ordered throughout the Reich

---

* Danegeld was paid for their exit permits by Jewish Aid offices abroad. In all, the Austrian operation brought in more than US$1.6 million.

in the wake of the murder, by a young Jew, of Ernst von Rath, a Counsellor of the German Embassy in Paris. By the time the operation was broken off, on 16 November, 6547 Jews had been arrested, of whom 3700 were packed off to Dachau. More than half of these unfortunates were however 'provisionally returned' to Vienna as being medically unfit to work.

Such scruples were later, of course, dropped, as totally new directives came from Himmler. By the end of 1942, only 8102 Jews remained in Austria, of whom more than half were in mixed marriages. The reason for this further drastic drop was simple: extermination had succeeded emigration as the ruling policy for the Ostmark, as elsewhere in the Reich. Eichmann, now based in Berlin, had embarked on his last and most ambitious mission: the 'Final Solution'.

In more ways than one, Eichmann came to symbolise the Austrians' share of guilt and responsibility for the horror of the Holocaust. The fact that they had provided more than their 10 per cent population ratio of concentration camp guards was due in part to their special qualifications: multi-racialism was, quite literally, in their blood. Accordingly, Himmler deemed them more suitable than his pure German Aryans to handle the ethnic mix of the '*Untermensch*' collected behind the barbed wire and destined eventually for the gas chambers. The same special qualifications rooted in history were reflected in Himmler's choices for higher-ranking posts. Most of the top SS and police chiefs throughout the Balkans were Austrians, now serving the swastika and not the double eagle in the old crown lands. Indeed, some of the worst apparitions to appear on the whole of the nightmare landscape were Austrians.

A typical example was the one-time Gauleiter for Vienna, Odilo Globocnik, a Carinthian whose Slav ancestry resounds in his name. Transferred in 1940 to the so-called 'General Government' of occupied Poland, he supervised the slaughter of some two million Jews in the camps of Treblinka, Sobibor and Belzec. Ninety fellow Austrians worked on his staff, and the commandant of Treblinka, the most notorious of the camps, was another countryman, one Franz Stangl, born, like Eichmann, in Linz. Another Austrian camp commandant, the Vienna-born Amon Goeth, achieved worldwide notoriety long after his death through a famous book turned into an equally famous film.*

* Steven Spielberg's *Schindler's List*, based on Thomas Keneally's exhaustively researched *Schindler's Ark*.

Ernst Kaltenbrunner was to tower over them all in rank, for the illegal Austrian Nazi installed in March 1938 as the police and security supremo of the Ostmark rose to the second-highest SS post in the whole of the German Reich. In 1942 he succeeded Reinhard Heydrich (murdered by a Czech death squad trained in Britain) as head of the Central Office for Reich Security.

Yet, though not approaching Kaltenbrunner in rank, and not equalling a Stangl or a Goeth in psychopathic fury, Eichmann remains the most chilling Austrian Nazi of them all. Unlike the others, he was a pure robot. Right down to his trial and hanging in Israel in 1962,* he maintained that the extermination of millions of Jews organised by him had nothing to do with good or evil. He had simply been obeying orders, and for him that was the beginning and the end of the matter. To be fair to the Austrian people, it must be added that this most infamous of their countrymen was the reverse of typical. The Austrians, like all nations, are a mixture of good, bad and indifferent; they are, however, anything but robots.

There has been much reference to the ambivalence of the Austrians, torn between Germandom and imperialism, in the days of the Monarchy, and to their opportunism when confronted with so many sudden changes of political futures in the republic. But we now come to a chapter in their saga which shows neither ambivalence nor opportunism: the story of their resistance to the Nazi regime. It is, as always in these cases, the story of a minority. The most realistic post-war estimates put the total number of Austrians engaged in some form of active resistance against the Nazi regime between 1938 and 1945 at around 100,000.** At one in seventy of the population over the whole seven-year period, that does not look impressive compared with the percentages produced by almost every other German-occupied country of Europe. The figures look much more respectable, however, when two major factors, each of them unique to Austria, are borne in mind.

The first is that, unlike the conquered countries to the west – and notably Norway, Holland and France – there was no open seaboard or direct geographical link of any sort between the landlocked Ostmark

---

* He succeeded in fleeing after the war to Argentina, where he was tracked down and kidnapped by an Israeli commando unit in 1960.
** The estimate concerns activity inside the country. To it can be added the 20,000 exiles who joined the Allied armies and some 5000 who fought with partisan forces operating outside Austria.

and the Allied armies. Moreover, the resistance movements in countries like those had stemmed directly from military campaigns fought against the Germans, while the Austrians formed part of the Wehrmacht. Of even greater weight was the second factor, the familiar one of Austria's basically Germanic character. For the French, Dutch, Belgians, Danes and Norwegians, and even more so the Poles and Yugoslavs, Germany was a foreign invader, of another tongue, race and culture. For many Austrians, the Germans had arrived in 1938 as the Teutonic big brother, who had won a drawn-out family quarrel.

Any active Austrian resistance fighter had therefore to overturn in his mind the dictum of March 1938 that German blood must not be shed, and risk his life heavily in the process. (The fact that the Germanic pull always existed, and that German was the language on both sides of the struggle, made all Austrian resistance efforts uniquely vulnerable to penetration and betrayal.) This fundamental psychological contrast with the rest of occupied Europe was expressed, quite unintentionally, by some of the principal works written by Austrians themselves about their resistance efforts. One such was entitled *The Call of Conscience*; another, *The Lonely Conscience.** A Frenchman writing such a book would not have bothered with the moral concept of conscience. For him, it was a simple matter of defending France against a familiar enemy.

The first public demonstration against the regime was also to be both the largest and the last of its kind. This was the mass anti-Nazi protest of some 10,000 Catholics in Vienna's Cathedral Square on 7 October 1938. The day, the Feast of the Rosary, did have a patriotic association, though, in true Austrian style, this went back centuries: it was first ordered by Pope Gregory XIII in 1573 as thanksgiving for the great Austrian naval victory over the Turks two years earlier, and was extended by Pope Clement XI in 1716 to mark Prince Eugen's triumph over the same infidel in the battle of Peterwardein. The demonstrators, largely from the Catholic youth movement, were however concerned less with the distant glories of the Monarchy than with the bands of Hitler Youth rowdies who were trying to break up the meeting. Scuffles broke out; Nazi slogans were countered with Dollfuss songs, imperial anthems and cries of 'Austria! Austria!'; and, belatedly, the police arrived to restore

---

* *Der Ruf des Gewissens* by Otto Molden, Vienna, 1958; *Das Einsame Gewissen* by Ludwig Jedlicka, Vienna, 1965. (Both men were friends of the author's.)

order and hand the Catholic youth leaders over to the Gestapo. Dozens of them ended up in Mauthausen and Dachau.*

It was a Catholic priest who headed one of the three distinct resistance movements which flickered into life, bravely but briefly, in Austria's first years under the swastika. Karl Roman Scholz was a twenty-six-year-old priest at the great abbey of Klosterneuburg in the Vienna hills. Born in the Sudetenland, he had come to Vienna with all the pan-German and pro-Nazi fervour which blossomed in that border region, but the bloom soon perished when he saw the reality of Hitler's police state. Working from the abbey, he founded his 'Austrian Resistance Movement' in the year of the *Anschluss* and eventually gathered together between three and four hundred followers, each of whom was issued with a miniature membership card.**

Scholz soon learnt of the existence of two other resistance groups, also based in Vienna and with similar or even identical names. One was the 'Greater Austrian Freedom Movement', founded by a lawyer friend and colleague of Schuschnigg's, Jakob Kastelic, which dreamt the old Catholic dream of a union with Bavaria and a Danubian mission. Kastelic had managed to join hands nonetheless with Social Democrat sympathisers and, through that indomitable Jewish Monarchist, Lieutenant-Colonel Johann Blumenthal, had set up links with Austrian traditionalists in the Wehrmacht. The third group, which had chosen the same name for its network as Scholz, was led by a Viennese finance official, Karl Lederer, who managed to produce and distribute a regular stream of anti-Nazi leaflets. It was Lederer who, in April 1940, persuaded all three groups to band together, with a total strength of over a thousand active members.

Given the essentially amateurish nature of the organisation, the number was dangerously high for safety, and so it proved. In 1939, the Gestapo had planted their own man in the Scholz group, one Otto Hartmann, a second-rate actor who, like so many of the professionally frustrated, turned to the Nazi Party for fulfilment. On 22 July 1940,

---

* Fritz Molden, who was present as a lad on the square, described how the police asked him, and all his young friends, how old they were. If the answer was under fourteen, they were simply sent home. If over fourteen, they were sent to Gestapo headquarters in the Hotel Metropole. (Conversation with the author, Vienna, 27 September 1993.)
** This somewhat bizarre arrangement was to ensure that members of the separate cells could identify themselves to one another and also, in the event of war, to the Allied armies. The movement did not last long enough for that.

after Hartmann had betrayed the movement's plans to raid an ammunition dump and blow up a gasometer in the Vienna area, the Gestapo decided it was time to pounce. Over the following weeks, 143 members of all three groups were jailed and more than twice as many held for questioning. Torture no doubt helped the investigations along. By the time the last cases were heard, 127 of the accused had been imprisoned, some for life, and eleven death sentences had been passed. Those on the ringleaders were not handed down by the courts until February and March 1944; the nine sentences confirmed (including those of Scholz, Kastelic and Lederer) were carried out during that summer. As Karl Roman Scholz was brought to the guillotine in Vienna's central prison he cried out: 'For Christ and Austria.' The priest and the patriot were fused into one.

The efforts of these early Austrian resistance groups had no impact whatsoever on the course of the war. The outside world never heard about them and could, in any case, have done nothing at the time to help them. But it is precisely this which gives a truly heroic quality to the fate of these first victims. They were not part of any recognised underground movement supplied and partly controlled by wartime asylum governments in Britain. Thanks partly to ceaseless bickering between the various factions abroad, Austria never possessed an exile government and was regarded, in these first war years, as an integral part of Hitler's Reich: 'There is every evidence that Austria has now accepted German domination. It is not considered that the Austrians are ready or able to rise against Germany.' So ran the verdict of a British Chief of Staff's report prepared on 4 September 1940 to review, country by country, the prospects of anti-Hitler resistance in occupied Europe.* That paper was presented barely a month after the last of Kastelic's group had been seized in Vienna. These men had fought alone and were to die alone, without real hope of success or rescue.

The Communist resistance movement in Austria, which was to prove by far the largest and most stubborn of them all, belongs to a rather different category. Its motivation was ideological rather than national and, from first to last, it was supported and, at times, totally controlled by Moscow. It could never feel alone or abandoned. It proved, however, to be just as vulnerable as the conservative groups to betrayal. The first Gestapo swoop early in 1941 (which resulted in 536 arrests and no

---

* Appendix to Chiefs of Staff 'Review of Future Strategy', COS (40) No. 683.

fewer than three hundred executions) was due to the capture of a courier travelling to Prague. But from then on, nearly all the damage was done thanks to the presence of two Gestapo stool-pigeons in their Central Committee, a Communist Jew and his Jewish mistress who had been threatened with the concentration camp if they did not cooperate. As a result, the movement's leadership was repeatedly wiped out, replaced by Moscow, only to be wiped out again, thanks to this pair of informers who remained undetected because of their impeccable party record (the man, Kurt Koppel, was a veteran of the Spanish Civil War).

The Communists spread more leaflets, threw more bombs, blew up more railway lines and damaged more military installations than the rest of Austria's resistance groups put together, and they paid a correspond-ing price. It was estimated after the war (by non-Communist sources) that, out of their 20,000 active members or supporters, more than half had seen the inside of a Gestapo prison at one time or another, and some 2500 had been executed.* The Soviet Communist leadership, it should be added, had not been unaware of the political dividend which this record of sacrifice might bring them after the war.

The last phase of Austrian resistance can be taken together with the final collapse of Germany. In the meantime, we need to look at the behaviour of the Austrian people as a whole in the post-*Anschluss* years – that majority, impossible to quantify, but probably anywhere between 70 and 80 per cent, who were neither fanatical Nazis nor active anti-Nazis but who simply wanted to make the best of things, get the most out of life under the swastika and, above all, survive. Hitler was heard to remark, as early as 1 April 1938, that he hoped his Austrians would not exchange their '*Anschluss* joy' for 'Reichsweariness'. The transition did, in fact, take place, though it took much longer than the bare fort-night the Führer had in mind. Indeed, the steady surge in Ostmark Nazi Party membership for four years after the German march-in shows the Austrians flocking to get aboard the Nazi bandwagon – whatever increasing misgivings they may have felt about the people holding the reins.

By November 1938, over 207,000 Austrians were registered members of the party, with many more applications still to be entered on the books. By 1942 (the peak year, after which membership generally

---

* After the outbreak of war with Russia, orders were issued from Berlin for the indis-criminate execution of Communist troublemakers anywhere in the Reich.

started to fall away) the total, including those members serving in army or auxiliary units, was nearly 850,000, more than two-thirds of whom had joined up since 1938. It was calculated that, if the families of these registered Nazis were included, more than a quarter of the Ostmark's population would have been in the party's embrace. Membership was predominantly masculine and middle class. In many cases – for example, officials serving in the legal system or in central and local governments – the party badge went persuasively with the post.* But these professionals still remained a minority. The bulk had signed up out of natural motives of self-interest and well-being.

This is to some extent reflected in the wide discrepancies of the figures between the seven '*Reichsgaue*' which Austria had become. The increase in membership had been most marked in *Gaue* like the Upper Danube, Salzburg and the Tyrol, areas where the standard of living had broadly increased since the *Anschluss* and where the planners in Berlin had concentrated their development programmes. Membership was lowest (under 45,000) in Carinthia, a backward economic region which had remained relatively neglected.

Yet whatever material benefits Hitler's New Order brought with it in the short term, there was grumbling and disenchantment which set in early on as well – especially in the cosmopolitan, ethnically mixed capital, which was always the Führer's greatest headache. The new regime could boast of rapid and drastic reductions in the unemployment figures, from 400,000 in March 1938 to only 250,000 two years later (partly by shipping thousands of Ostmärker to work on construction projects elsewhere in the Reich). However, the introduction of lower wage scales and higher taxes hit the pay packets of all those in work and even led, within a year of the *Anschluss*, to protest strikes at factories in and around Vienna.

That disenchantment which Hitler had feared started even sooner and went far deeper. This was not, in its early stages, resistance, so much as the nation's not untypical desire to have its cake and eat it. Even those, like the ambitious newly-commissioned Bundesheer officer quoted above, who relished their professional prospects of belonging to a great Reich, were reluctant to see old Austria swallowed up, its very name alongside its traditional habits and customs. Thus the Gestapo

* More than 90 per cent of Vienna's town hall and municipal officers (mostly ardent Social Democrats by their background) swore allegiance to Hitler and joined the party or one of its associated groups in order to keep their jobs.

reported that the prescribed 'German greeting' was being widely side-stepped, especially in the government ministries of Vienna.* Instead of *'Heil Hitler'*, the bureaucrats would begin their office day with the old-style *'Grüss Gott'* or *'Guten Tag'*, depending on their old-style ideological roots.** There are even cases of the Hitler greeting being scoffed at, a heinous offence often very lightly dealt with by Austrian judges.

The many dissimilarities of language were also an irritant in the post-*Anschluss* months. It had been one thing to hear Germans saying *'Tomaten'* instead of *'Paradeiser'* and *'Kartoffeln'* instead of *'Erdäpfel'* when they passed through Austria as tourists. It was quite another thing when these, and hundreds of other differences, had to compete with each other in everyday speech. To adopt that well-known aphorism applied to the British and the Americans, the Austrians and the Germans found themselves divided by a common language. All this was symbolic of the wider struggle between rival cultures, a struggle which went on in the mind of the Führer himself, with Vienna as its focus.

Though Adolf Hitler was very uncharacteristic of his fellow-countrymen in his demonic energy and in the ruthless speed with which he carried out his decisions, some very Austrian ambivalence always hung over his attitude to the ancient imperial capital. On the one hand, he despised it for its large population of Slavs and Jews; on the other, he respected it for the cultural pre-eminence it had always enjoyed in the Germanic world – partly because of those creative non-Aryan layers in its make-up. Nor could he deny its unchallengeable position as the gateway to Central and south-east Europe. Indeed, before the outbreak of war put a stop to such grandiose projects, he planned to convert the city into a sort of Hamburg on the Danube, a great trading entrepot, equipped with new canal systems and port facilities, which would link up the Reich with the whole of the Balkans.

He could never get Vienna out of his mind, personally intervening to change the names of some of its streets and reserving for himself the

* This, and all following extracts from Gestapo reports in Austria, is taken from the illuminating work *Österreich 1938–45, im Spiegel der NS Akten*, by Carl Stadler (Vienna, 1966).
** A further way to avoid invoking the Führer, at least at lunchtime, was provided by the Germanic one-word greeting of *'Mahlzeit'*, or 'Have a good meal', to which the same word could be used in reply.

final say on all top appointments to the State Opera. At the same time, he was resolved to destroy its dangerous memories of imperial grandeur. On 6 September 1938, for example, he had the Habsburg insignia and crown jewels removed from the Hofburg *Schatzkammer* (where they had been deposited since 1796) to Nuremberg, the medieval free city of the old German Reich and now the temple of the new Nazi faith. Humiliations like this rubbed home the unpalatable reality that Vienna was being demoted from a capital founded on imperial splendour to a provincial centre of the New Order. As we shall see, after the outbreak of war, Hitler decided to smooth Vienna's ruffled feathers by allowing her something close to autonomy in the cultural field; this, he shrewdly calculated, was the best way to stifle political opposition from mounting in wartime in this bastion of his south-eastern front.

But all that still lay ahead as, on 13 March 1939, the first anniversary of the *Anschluss* came round. The Gestapo glumly admitted in their reports that, as regards the capital, popular jubilation on the day left very much to be desired; even the official orders to hang swastika flags from house windows in celebration had been in many cases ignored. In that same month, Hitler delivered a further blow to the enthusiasm of his Viennese subjects by his invasion of Czechoslovakia. After all, 30 per cent of the city's population were by origin Slav, and predominantly Czech. For them, the sight on the propaganda newsreels of German soldiers marching triumphantly into Prague could only revive those racial resentments which went back for centuries.

When, after the Danzig crisis and the German invasion of Poland, Hitler's war with the Western democracies finally broke out in September 1939, the Austrians reacted in very different style to their predecessors in August 1914. There was acceptance mixed with a certain excitement, but none of those spontaneous mass rejoicings which had led the Habsburg Monarchy into the great conflict which was ultimately to destroy it. Indeed, that parallel of catastrophic defeat was immediately to be drawn by at least one humble son of the Austrian people. The Gestapo reported this piece of home wisdom from a carpenter's apprentice in rural Herzogenburg: 'The English have never lost a war, and they are going to win this one as well.'

This was a far cry from the fighting spirit his Führer was looking for. Nonetheless, over the coming years, as first Russia and then the United States joined Britain in the conflict, that verdict of the carpenter's apprentice gradually became the verdict of the nation. It led, at the war's climax, to the nearest thing the Austrians ever produced to an organised resistance which could pose a threat to Hitler and offer some crumbs of armed aid to the victors.

III

Violent Divorce

ANY EARLY ADMIRATION felt in the Ostmark for Hitler's military successes seems to have been more than outweighed by something to which the Austrians had always attached more importance than battle-field glory, namely enjoying life and filling their stomachs. Apart from a steady increase in taxation, it was the steady decrease in rations which caused the most grumbling, thus providing a background of growing disenchantment against which active resistance could develop. The first winter of the war saw shortages of potatoes, fruit, vegetables, rice and cooking fat. Those old enough to remember made unfavourable com-parisons with the food situation in 1914, and there were widespread suspicions that Germany was now being favoured with supplies at the expense of its Ostmark. This led to some extraordinary outbursts. On 27 January 1940, for example, the police reported a furious anti-Nazi demonstration of housewives at the Vienna Meisel Market. One went so far as to shout: 'The Führer is responsible for this war, but what does it matter to us – we get nothing out of it! Under Schuschnigg this would never have happened!' Her audience was evidently behind her, for when one elderly woman tried to speak up for the Führer she was chased off the market square.

These grumbles over food even led directly to mild acts of sabotage. Thus, in that same month, a section of the ammunition factory at Enzersfeld just south of the capital had to be temporarily closed down because a woman worker had poured canteen tea into the cases of the hand grenades. It tasted so awful that it was fit for nothing else, she declared in her defence. Much more serious were the cases reported of sabotage acts carried out by skilled industrial workers who knew pre-cisely where and how to cause the most damage at key plants: screws dropped into the metal boring machines; sand poured into oil tanks and thrown into machinery; wires tampered with in pumping installations; clumps of old iron fed into steel presses; the cutting of railway brake cables, and so on.

That the banned Socialist movement was behind at least some of these incidents was indicated by one of their underground leaflets seized by the police in April 1940. It read:

> Comrades, Friends!
> What practical steps can we take to put an end to the Hitler dictatorship? One thing above all – Sabotage! . . .
> Don't carry out large-scale actions which might put your own lives and those of your comrades in danger. But every worker can do his bit to bring the Hitler regime down by slowing down work, by damaging machines through rough handling . . . It's your duty to get together in twos and threes and discuss how to act . . .
> Help will come to you from at home and abroad but you must at least show some sign of activity so that your friends know where you are.
> Long live true Socialism!
> Down with the Nazi bosses!*

Despite the repeated betrayals and purges in their ranks, it was the Communist saboteurs who posed the greatest threat to the regime, especially after Hitler launched his war on Russia in June 1941. From that point on, the Communist underground became, as everywhere in the factories of occupied Europe, like the partisans fighting in the mountains and forests, part of the Red Army's struggle. Apart from producing some 90 per cent of all anti-Nazi leaflets, they led the field in sabotage. One of the most serious cases uncovered in 1942 concerned a group of miners at the big Styrian iron ore complex at Erzberg, where the harsh working conditions helped to build up the local Communist cell. Fourteen of them were arrested and accused, 'in the name of the German people', of treasonable acts ranging from the use of explosive for 'Communist sabotage' to listening to forbidden foreign radio transmissions.** (The prosecution admitted that after the outbreak of war

---

* Quoted in Stadler, op. cit., pp.178–9. The Gestapo may have exaggerated the importance of such incidents, but they did not invent them.
** Seven of the accused were sentenced to death by a Berlin war tribunal headed by Hitler's principal legal henchman, the notorious President of the People's Court, Dr Freisler.

with Russia, the enemy had succeeded, through its propaganda broad-casts, in stimulating sabotage activity in plants which were vital to the Reich's war effort.)

Resistance, both active and passive, hardened in 1943, not merely due to the German disaster at Stalingrad which ushered in this year of sea-change. As throughout the Reich, Stalingrad was perceived in the Ostmark as the beginning of the end for Hitler's Wehrmacht. But for many Austrians a less momentous Allied victory at the opposite end of the huge battlefield had an even greater impact: the final rout of Rommel's forces in North Africa, completed in Tunis in May, and the Allied landings which followed on Sicily and then on the Italian main-land. One young Austrian patriot who was now about to play a leading part in a resurrected resistance movement described his reaction many years later: 'This was for us really more important than Stalingrad. The Eastern Front was still hundreds of miles away and, in some ways, remote. But to have the Allies sweeping along the Mediterranean and actually moving up Italy towards us brought Austria, for the first time in the war, inside the circle of the fighting and made it possible for us at least to make contact with the action.'*

Meanwhile, throughout the Ostmark, public hostility to the Germans was growing, and increasingly it was directed towards them as Germans rather than as Nazis. This was not only due to the privations of war and the feeling that the Austrians were now on the losing side of the war. It came from the sobering realisation, after actually living for five years with their Teutonic partners above and around them, that the Germans were not natural blood-brothers after all. Whatever family feeling was left among the non-Nazi majority now classed them as, at best, first cousins. Increasingly, the old appellation of *'Piefke'*, which had come down from the Monarchy as a supercilious term for the Germans, began to replace the word 'Nazi' whenever Austrians grumbled. The Swedish journalist Arvid Fredborg reported to his paper, *Svenska Dag-bladet*, after a long visit to Austria in the spring of 1943, that many ordi-nary people were asking themselves: 'Are we really the same people as the Germans?'

It is a pity that this perceptive neutral observer did not include the

* Fritz Molden, talking to the author, Vienna, 22 September 1993. In the following months, Molden established the first such contact himself by making his way through the German lines in Italy to Allied Forces Headquarters at Caserta. The author, then serving at Caserta, always regretted not meeting him at the time.

tiny Lower Austrian village of Schleinbach in his tour. There he would have found the villagers up in arms about one of their peasant girls who was expecting an illegitimate child. This was a very familiar happening, but what they were incensed about was the fact that, in this case, the father was a *German* soldier. It did not seem to worry them that at least a dozen other girls in the neighbourhood were also expecting babies out of wedlock, but all from love affairs with French, Polish and other amorous foreign workers assigned to local factories. The villagers of Schleinbach deserve an honourable mention in Austria's slow march towards her own identity.

The most decisive event for Austria in 1943 did not come from any battlefield but from a political decision of the 'Grand Alliance', as the wartime partnership between the United States, Britain and the Soviet Union became known. After lengthy deliberations and much redrafting, the three powers published, in Moscow on 1 November 1943, the declaration which was to decide Austria's future in the post-war era – yet another example of the Austrians having their fate determined for them from beyond their borders. On this occasion, however, they were to have every reason to congratulate themselves on the decision taken above their heads. Except for one clause, they could hardly have put things better themselves.

After describing Austria as 'the first free country to fall victim to Hitlerite aggression', the three powers recorded their wish to see it re-established as 'a free and independent' state. In view of the enthusiasm with which so many Austrians had welcomed Hitler across their frontiers, without so much as throwing a brick at any of his tanks, this was indeed a flattering verdict. It put Austria on the same broad level as those later victims who had fought furiously, if briefly, against the German invader with their regular armies and then, almost from the moment these were crushed, with their nationwide underground movements. Austria's luck, in this regard, was that a country cannot be classed as a semi-victim any more than a woman can be described as semi-pregnant. The nation was, therefore, given the benefit of the doubt, and the events of March 1938 (which the Western democracies had, after all, accepted at the time as a *fait accompli*) were put aside.

What could not be forgotten was the part which the Austrians had then played, willingly or reluctantly, in manning Hitler's huge machine of military aggression and police state terror. Account was taken of this in the last paragraph of the declaration: 'Austria is reminded, however, that she has a responsibility for participation in the war on the side of Hitlerite Germany and that in the final settlement, account will inevitably be taken of her contribution to her liberation.'

That contribution to the 'final settlement' will be examined below. What needs to be set out here is the series of lucky strokes which had helped the Austrians, without them even knowing about it, to benefit from the rest of the declaration. There has been much ignorance on the subject ever since. It is, in fact, Joseph Stalin who emerges as the founding father among the Big Three of Austria's post-war independence. Anthony Eden, then Churchill's Foreign Secretary, describes in his memoirs how the subject cropped up when he went to Moscow in December 1941 for his first meeting with the Soviet dictator since the Grand Alliance had come into being. When the talk turned to the shape of Europe after Hitler's defeat, Eden writes, Stalin had proposed that Poland should expand westwards at Germany's expense. All the other occupied countries, he added, should return to their old frontiers, 'Austria being restored'. Eden concurred: 'We are certainly in favour of an independent Austria.'

In fact, that was a long way from being the preference of the Western governments, Britain included. When Anglo–American planners started the following year to study the problem of Austria in earnest, the consensus which was to persist for the next two years was that independence was far from being the best answer. The country, it was argued, might once again fall, passively or willingly, under German domination. Perhaps, some experts argued, it should be absorbed straight away into a new federal Germany. The ideological bickerings of Austria's exiled factions in both London and Washington, which had prevented the formation of any government-in-waiting, were seen as a poor advertisement for her political maturity. These squabbling refugees, like the Bourbons of old, seemed to have learnt nothing and forgotten nothing.

Accordingly, the general view in the West was that Austria could only flourish and perform a useful service for the stability of Europe if she reverted to her old role as the centre of a confederation of Danubian peoples. Churchill wondered whether this might be extended northwards, to include Bavaria in an enlarged Catholic bloc. Though he was probably unaware of the parallel, Sumner Welles, the American Under-Secretary of State, even toyed at one point with that radical change of course first attempted by the young Emperor Charles:

dragging Austria out of Germany's magnetic field altogether by linking her with France.

It was the thought of such alternative functions for Austria, and especially that of the Danubian Federation, which had prompted Stalin, as far back as 1941, to propose her independence. He wanted Austria to be stood up alone on her own feet after the war because he was already planning to knock her down, as far as possible like the other Danubian countries which were to be taken one at a time by the Red Army. Prominent Austrian Communists who had fled to the Soviet Union in the 1930s were sitting the war out comfortably in Moscow hotels, as were some of their ideological brethren from Poland, Hungary, Czechoslovakia and the Balkan states. In Stalin's programme, these were the men who were to form the nucleus of pro-Soviet regimes throughout Eastern Europe when the war was ended. Once these regimes had been set up, they would inevitably be linked together; but the centre of that grouping was to be Moscow, not some imperialist-dominated Vienna.

The 'imperialists' meanwhile continued with their own plans, and by the summer of 1943 these had been brought together at ministerial levels. A British Foreign Office paper of 11 July 1943 called 'The Future of Austria' had been approved by the War Cabinet and, when presented in Washington, it was found to accord with State Department's views. The regional solution was confirmed and the establishment of Austria as the linchpin of a post-war democratic Danubian Federation seemed to have become official Anglo–American policy. Not for long, however: less than three months later came the Moscow Declaration with its totally different emphasis. Austrian independence was now adopted as a specific Allied aim, with no mention at all of similar free statehood for all the other German-occupied countries of Eastern Europe. Indeed, the only faint echo of the original Anglo–American federation concept was the hope, expressed in the declaration, that the Austrian people might find 'political and economic security' together with their neighbouring countries. Why this apparent *volte-face* in the Western approach?

One factor was the change, at the highest level, which was coming over President Roosevelt's thinking. Despite the proposals of his State Department experts, the President was now inclining to the view that his priority was to keep 'Uncle Joe' on his side for joint operations against Japan once the war against Hitler had been won. If this involved allowing Stalin to obtain a political foothold along the Danube's banks in the wake of the Red Army's advance, then the price would have to be paid, as a temporary measure.* This indeed was what emerged at the Big Three's Teheran Conference, held only a month after the Foreign Ministers' meeting in Moscow. At that summit, Churchill suddenly found himself alone in arguing the concept of a Danubian regional grouping to offset the influence of Germany. Stalin left his partners under no illusions that he regarded the countries of Eastern Europe as falling within the Soviet sphere of influence and insisted that Hungary, as well as Austria, should remain as a separate state. Roosevelt concurred and came out with a bizarre new plan to split post-war Germany into seven separate zones.

But there was another factor, operating from a lower but still important rung on the ladder of power, which had shaped the Moscow Declaration. This was the growing influence in the Anglo–American camp of the so-called Political Warfare Executive. Britain's propaganda warriors looked back to a distinguished pedigree from operations in the First World War and had scored considerable successes in the Second (operating both on the open front and on the so-called 'Black Front' of covert deception campaigns). When the Americans entered the war, their passion for mass-media and popular persuasion joined hands with British expertise to form a formidable lobby, and it was this lobby which, in 1943, selected Austria as its prime propaganda target. Once Italy had been disposed of, the next prop in the structure to be knocked away was Austria. The best way to undermine that prop, the political warfare warriors argued, was to stimulate anti-German resistance among the Austrian people, and that could best be achieved by a combination of promises and warnings.

Throughout the late summer and early autumn of 1943, discussions went on in the Anglo–American camp to agree on the precise mixture, with the propagandists in both capitals often at odds with the diplomats.** Draft after draft was drawn up and then revised. Should a reference be made to the 'Atlantic Charter' for free nations? No, it was finally decided, because Austria was, after all, enemy territory and she

* Roosevelt naïvely believed that America's economic supremacy would be so overwhelming after global peace had been secured that it could impose on Moscow any adjustments thought necessary to the European scene.
** The author was serving at this time on the General Staff at the War Office in London and working in close cooperation with the Political Intelligence Department (PID) of the Foreign Office. As such, he was familiar with the whole process described.

had contributed to her own loss of independence. Should that loss be described as 'annexation' or merely 'occupation'? And, most tricky of all, how should the war guilt clause be phrased?

What is important to be clear about is that this clause, together with the rest of the declaration, was part of the agreed Anglo–American text presented in Moscow. It was not, as has been commonly supposed, a Soviet proposal in origin, but part of the Western plan to stir the sluggish Austrian resistance into life. All that the Russians did was to tighten the Western draft at several points to suit their own political interests as well as to reflect the terrible losses which Austrian divisions had helped Hitler to inflict upon them. Thus, the Austrians were not 'asked to remember' their part in Hitler's war but bluntly 'reminded' of it. At another point a reference to 'the Austrian people' was altered, at Soviet insistence, to 'Austria', thus identifying the future state as being liable for reparations.

There was no serious East–West argument, however, and the three Foreign Ministers simply issued the declaration without comment, and without even signing it. For the Austrians, this document was the birth certificate of their new state. For the Big Three at the time it was basically an invitation to the Austrians to start up some serious and organised resistance, coupled with a warning about the consequences of failing to do so. The main question at issue for those who framed the document was whether the invitation would be followed up. It had been included in the Moscow agenda as one of several elements in the approaching defeat of Germany on the battlefield and was to be judged, therefore, by its military dividends. Taken in this strategic context, the Allies were to be sadly disappointed. Months went by after the declaration was published and there was no outward sign that Austria was making any significant 'contribution to her liberation'. Individual acts of sabotage were taking place in armaments factories and power plants, yet they seemed to be quite uncoordinated, and there was certainly nothing brewing in the Ostmark which might affect the final phases of the war.

The resulting disenchantment in the Allied camp was largely of their own making. They had taken at face value earlier reports – eagerly embroidered and disseminated by the exile groups – that the Austrians were simmering so furiously with anti-Nazi discontent that a national uprising could result. They too had to learn that the Austrians were very good at simmering but not so good at boiling over. Moreover, from first to last, both the political warriors and the diplomats under-estimated the practical difficulties which any Austrian resistance faced, as well as the unique psychological problems it had to overcome. Perhaps because of their own misjudgements, there was a note of bitterness as well as disappointment in the Allied camp. By the summer of 1944, the Western planners had concluded that all their hopes of open revolt by the Austrians had been in vain: too few of them, it was now clear, were prepared to risk their necks. Oliver Harvey, Head of the Foreign Office Central Department, which ran German and Austrian affairs, was much less charitable. On 4 July 1944 he minuted: 'If it were not for the strategic importance of keeping Austria separate from Germany, we would let this flabby country stew.'

This, of course, was in the aftermath of the Allied invasion of Nor-mandy the month before, a momentous event which, ideally, should have been backed up by simultaneous resistance uprisings throughout occupied Europe. Austria had certainly done nothing to match those expectations. However, less than three weeks after that dismissive verdict was written, the 'flabby country' concerned showed that it was not without resolute resistance fighters even among those who were wearing Hitler's uniform. What was by Austrian standards much more remark-able, their efficiency fully matched their bravery.

The ill-fated plot of 20 July 1944, designed to kill Hitler and over-throw his regime by a *coup d'état* of the Home Army, cannot of course be classified as an Austrian resistance campaign. It was conceived, planned and launched entirely by German – and above all Prussian – anti-Nazis led, on the military front, by that archetypal hero Count Claus Schenk von Stauffenberg. But nowhere in Europe, except perhaps in Paris, did its branch-lines operate so swiftly and so smoothly as in Vienna. Within a few hours of the code-word for action, '*Walküre*', being received, every Wehrmacht headquarters in and around the capital had been seized by Austrian Home Army units, as had the airports, radio and communication centres and railway stations. Moreover, almost without exception, the Nazi Party leaders, SS and police chiefs preselected as targets had been taken into custody. After the plan had collapsed and the Hitler regime had taken its revenge, some six hundred Austrians on the Gestapo's watch list were behind bars. Dozens of Austrian Army officers suspected of involvement in the plot were also arrested, and two of the three ringleaders – Colonel Rudolf Marogna-Redwitz and Lieutenant-Colonel Robert Bernardis – were among those executed the following month in Berlin's Plötzensee prison.

The third man of the top trio escaped, thanks to his own personal security precautions. This was none other than that young officer, newly commissioned in 1938, who had welcomed a career in Hitler's great Wehrmacht as being professionally more enticing than garrison duty in the Austrian Bundesheer. Carl Szokoll, now a captain serving on the staff of the Austrian Military District XVII, had insisted on one condition when agreeing to join in the German conspiracy: 'I told Stauffenberg that I wanted my own channel of communication with him, to be separate from the rest and made absolutely watertight. He agreed and I was given a special direct line of my own to his office. It was this Berlin number which I called on that hectic 20 July to ask whether the Führer was still alive and, if so, what was to be done. Even that conversation did not seem to have been monitored. At all events, I was not troubled afterwards by the Gestapo.'*

Tragic and bloody failure though it turned out to be, in Vienna as elsewhere, 'Operation Walküre' had shown that Austrian resistance could function, and function effectively, provided it could operate within the sort of properly coordinated framework which Stauffenberg's master-plan had provided. There were Austrians who had realised this from the start, notably Dr Hans Sidonius Becker, another of those outstandingly brave anti-Nazis who remained an unsung hero to the outside world because he was forced to operate for years as an individual. Becker, a highly decorated officer from the Great War, became propaganda chief of the Fatherland Front and, with the danger of an *Anschluss* in mind, was already working before 1938 on resistance plans for an Austria under German occupation. He was duly arrested by the Gestapo and sent to the Mauthausen concentration camp which had been one of Himmler's first bequests to the Ostmark. He was released in the spring of 1941 and, despite being under police surveillance, immediately threw himself into setting up a resistance network which would cover all the provinces and all the political factions of the vanished republic as well as opening up contacts with anti-Nazi officers serving in the Wehrmacht.

This task was to take him three years. Not until the spring of 1944 did a broadly but loosely based organisation emerge. This was the 'Austrian Freedom Movement' which was soon operating under the code-name

* Carl Szokoll to the author, Vienna, 11 October 1994.

'O5' (representing the first and fifth letters of 'Oesterreich'). It was an ideal symbol for scratching or daubing on walls, and as this is the easiest of all resistance activities, the mysterious emblem was soon appearing all over the Ostmark. Few people knew at the time what it meant, but it was clear that it was some signal of protest, and this was later made clear in leaflets. It was not until the autumn of 1944 – a full year after the Moscow Declaration – that Becker succeeded in forming a joint leadership council, the so-called 'Committee of Seven', under his chairmanship. By now, his natural support group of monarchists and Catholic conservatives had established a common front with resistance cells among the old Socialist cadres and their trades unions. He thus achieved more in the way of reconciliation than was ever reached by Austria's politicians in exile. This was not surprising: the exiles never went through the sobering experience of living month after month and year after year in a police state. They could therefore concentrate on fighting one another.

With the Allied victory almost in sight, Austria's small and struggling resistance movement had to achieve two things. The first was to establish direct contact with the Western powers, if only to present a sort of visiting card to record the fact of their own existence. This was done, thanks largely to the efforts of 'O5' activists such as Major Alfons Stillfried and the young Fritz Molden who, after repeated arrests, had been given the blunt choice in 1942 between joining the Wehrmacht or being sent to a concentration camp. He naturally chose the field-grey uniform in preference to the broad-striped garment of a 'KZler' (camp inmate). It was a good choice for the movement as well as for himself. As a soldier, he could move around the battlefronts – albeit with forged papers and facing certain execution as a deserter if discovered.

By the autumn of 1944, regular courier contact had been made not only with the Allied Forces Headquarters in Italy but also with the representatives of all three Western powers in Switzerland, and especially with the American Office of Strategic Services in Berne. As a result, half a dozen French and American underground liaison officers were smuggled into Austria, to be distributed as far as possible among the different provinces, and some vital equipment, notably radio transmitters, was brought in. The first parachute drops were also carried out, albeit with very mixed success, as 'O5' did not, to put it mildly, possess the long experience of the French resistance in coordinating such operations. All this activity was on a modest scale, matching the modest contribution in military terms which was all that could be envisaged from the Austrian underground. Yet, even as a token, it went some way towards fulfilling for Austria the obligation laid down twelve months before in the Moscow Declaration.

The second vital need which the Austrian resistance faced in this final phase of the war was to convince the Allies that they represented a national movement. The sterile squabbles of the exiles and their failure to raise even a single Austrian fighting battalion abroad, let alone a shadow Austrian government, had left a damaging vacuum. Otto Habsburg was the only well-known figure among the exiles and, thanks to his pre-war international contacts and his close wartime friendship with President Roosevelt, the only one among the entire menagerie with any political influence. He and his family had indeed been working incessantly on both sides of the Atlantic to bring some representative Austrian body into being. Yet there were always too many among his fellow-exiles who, quite understandably from their ideological viewpoint, could never follow the lead of an archduke, and a royal Pretender at that. As even the most ultra-conservatives of the resistance had themselves realised, monarchism was far too narrow a basis for unity.

Thus, if only to fill the vacuum left by the exiles abroad, the patriots inside Austria tried, in the last months of the war, to set up a body which would supersede the 'O5' leadership and represent the nation as a whole. It was a brave but, sadly, a very brief venture. The decision to establish the so-called 'Provisional Austrian National Committee' (or POEN after the initials of its German name) was taken on 12 December 1944. But it took six more critical weeks before, on 25 February 1945, the list of its members could be finalised. They included, apart from resistance veterans such as Hans Becker and Major Stillfried, the father of the young Molden brothers and publisher of the pre-war *Neue Freie Presse*, Ernst Molden, and the Socialist leader Adolf Schärf, who would one day become President of the post-war republic.* Communists and

---

* In a passage in his memoirs, Schaerf describes how, at a meeting in Vienna in the summer of 1943 with one of the leaders of the planned German uprising, Wilhelm Leuschner, his visitor had enthused about the *Anschluss* being maintained after the defeat of Hitler. After three hours of this, Schaerf suddenly underwent a Damascene conversion, declaring that the *Anschluss* was dead because the Austrians' 'love of the German Reich had been driven out of them'. The passage was often to be quoted by Austrians. What none of them paused to marvel at was that it took an honourable and intelligent man like Schaerf five years of living under Nazis and *'Piefkes'* to abandon his old Socialist dream – and even then only because a German was trying to keep it alive.

liberals were also recruited into what was, at least on paper, a unified national front.

Except in the Tyrol, which we shall come to later, such a broad-based resistance movement was to remain on paper, and even that for less than a week. On 2 March, the Gestapo, who had been on the prowl from the day the Committee was finally set up, pounced on its members and captured most of them. Whether because of loose talk or betrayal, the POEN had been wiped out before it could even start on the main task for which it had been formed, namely liaison with the Allied powers. That left only the titanic battlefield itself, now about to engulf Austrian soil, as the one remaining arena in which the resistance could show its mettle. This final chance was also, potentially, the greatest of all, seen in the context of the Moscow Declaration. That was certainly how the American Secretary of State, Cordell Hull, had viewed it. He had been quoted as early as September 1944 as warning the Austrians that they would have to rise up immediately against the Germans if they wanted to earn their post-war freedom. Yet the call was never answered. At least as far as the main battlefield was concerned, Austrian military resistance was to become another abject tale of failure, redeemed only by the heroic exploits of individuals.

The most notable of those was also woefully late in the day. On 2 April, the indefatigable Szokoll, now a major, who was coordinating what was left of active underground resistance in Vienna, despatched one of his stalwarts, Sergeant-Major Ferdinand Kaes, through the main German battle line along the Semmering Pass in an eleventh-hour attempt to establish direct contact with the Red Army High Command. (Attempts at communication by radio had all failed.) Equipped with false papers, Kaes succeeded the next day in reaching the Headquarters of the Third Ukrainian Army Front which was now set up as far forward as Hochwolkersdorf, less than ten miles north-east of Vienna. It was perhaps fortunate that his mission had taken him to the Russians, now the obvious liberators of the capital. Had the British been in that position, as they had once contemplated,* a mere sergeant-major would

---

* On 17 June 1944, General Wilson, the British Supreme Commander in the Mediterranean, had put forward a plan for an immediate allied landing in the Northern Adriatic. Five divisions, two of them airborne, were to seize Trieste and advance up the Ljubljana to liberate both Vienna and Budapest. (At this point the Red Army was still three hundred miles away to the east.) Despite energetic support from Churchill, the plan was vetoed by the Americans.

have had problems in establishing himself as a full negotiating partner. But the Red Army had fewer inhibitions on this score and, in any case, it was part of a police state in which low rank often served to camouflage high influence.

At all events, Kaes succeeded in convincing the Russian staff officers of his *bona fides* and of pressing home to them the advantages of encircling Vienna by a broad sweep from the west, where German troops were thin on the ground. He returned to Szokoll on 5 May, complete with agreed plans for exchange of rocket signals between the advancing Russians and Vienna's resistance units. Upon this exchange, the latter would don white armbands and sally forth to fight alongside the Red Army by occupying all public buildings, communication centres and railway stations, and seizing key bridges to prevent them from being blown up. The plan was feasible, for Szokoll could count on several resistance units inside the Wehrmacht, including a battery of four field howitzers taken from the Croats. But the plot was betrayed even while it was being hatched. A certain Lieutenant Walter Hanslik of the Vienna Military Police happened to listen in to Szokoll's telephone call to one of his chief collaborators, Major Karl Biedermann, and alerted the Gauleiter's office. Biedermann was immediately arrested and, under severe torture, disclosed the plotters' password 'Radetzky', which opened up to the Gestapo the other cells of the conspiracy.

Once again, Szokoll himself made a Houdini-like escape and even managed in the last days of the battle for Vienna to conjure up some armed activity from what was left of the resistance network. But it was a scrappy substitute for what might have been; the spectacle of a mass uprising in their capital of patriotic Austrians against German Nazis, as envisaged by the Western propaganda machine in November 1943 and conjured up again by Western leaders a year later. Even the claim that the Red Army's almost bloodless envelopment of Vienna from the rear was due to the Kaes mission has been – perhaps understandably – overstated by the chroniclers of the resistance. The battle reports of Marshal Tolbukhin's Third Ukrainian Army Front later showed that his Sixth Tank Army, which was already at Baden, south-west of the capital, on 3 April, had embarked on a great circular sweep through Heiligenkreuz and Pressbaum before the good Sergeant-Major had even arrived at Red Army headquarters. Tolbukhin was determined from the start to avoid another costly frontal attack as had been employed against Budapest, where the Wehrmacht had held out for more than six weeks.

(The Russians would have been, nonetheless, grateful for the information Kaes provided and for the pilot services which the resistance were able to give in the final days of the battle.)

But for the patriots, the most depressing thing, in retrospect, about the failure of the Kaes mission was the motivation of the man who betrayed it. Lieutenant Hanslik was an Austrian yet, as Kaes himself wrote in his memoirs, this was a fellow-countryman to whom 'Hitler's mad orders meant more than his own native city and the people in it'.

By April 1945, there were not very many Hansliks left in field-grey uniform; yet there were no mass desertions or mutinies among the ranks of the tens of thousands of Austrians fighting the advance of the Third Ukrainian Front. Resistance within the Wehrmacht, even when it became clear that Hitler was about to be toppled, was never a spontaneous mass reaction, but remained centred on the handful of anti-Nazi officers who had been cultivated by that trio of stalwart majors: Szokoll, Stillfried and Biedermann. With the exception of such 'traitors', the Führer could not complain about the performance of his Austrian soldiers in this last phase of the war. One reason was, of course, that they were not now engaged in far-flung campaigns of conquest but were defending their own homeland. Another was the fear of capture by an unforgiving enemy many had already encountered in the east.

Hitler's tactics also played a part. Predictably, as early as the autumn of 1944, he had ordered Vienna to be defended to the last man and any rebels to be ruthlessly dealt with. But, as an Austrian himself, he was dubious about the tenacity of his 'half-Slav Viennese', and had taken special measures to coax as well as threaten them into standing firm. Thus the German Army Group South, which faced Tolbukhin's forces, had been renamed the 'Ostmark', and even given an Austrian Commander-in-Chief in the very last days of the struggle for the capital. This luckless officer was Colonel-General Lothar Rendulic who, as late as 4 April 1945, had been commanding the Army Group in Latvia at the opposite end of the huge fighting front. Here, he had won for himself a considerable reputation for defensive campaigning, and he was to serve the Wehrmacht just as well now.

He did not reach his new headquarters (at Sankt Leonard in Lower Austria) until the night of 8 April, which was only five days before the final surrender of Vienna to what was, for him, yet another invader from the east.* He knew, despite the forced optimism of his Führer (who had received him in the Berlin bunker on the way through), that the capital was about to fall and that the war itself was lost. Nonetheless, it was largely due to the skill of Rendulic and the stubborn rearguard fight put up by his army commanders that the bulk of the 600,000 men in his 'Ostmark' command managed to escape westwards towards the advancing Americans. Hitler's 'second city on the Danube' fought for its Führer unto the last gasp. A fortnight after the fall of Vienna, and with the end of the war only ten days away, Rendulic received sixty-five brand new Tiger and Panther tanks which had just rolled off the Linz production lines.

So the other armies of the Grand Alliance now joined the Russians on Austrian soil. Rather, they tumbled in, somewhat incoherently, as if to match, on the ground, the muddling debates which had been going on for months around the negotiating table about Western occupation plans and the future of Austria in general. President Roosevelt and his top advisers had originally opposed any American military participation, and were prepared to see Austria divided into only two zones, between the British and the Russians. This reflected Roosevelt's policy of not stepping on Stalin's toes anywhere in the Danubian region, combined with his reluctance to get involved in the historic tangle of 'Balkan intrigues', of which he considered Austria to be a part. His military advisers had, at first, concurred. They argued that American military might should be concentrated on north-west Europe, thus securing, among other things, the great Baltic ports needed to ship their divisions out to the Pacific Front.

The change of emphasis did not come on the political front until the middle of 1944, when the President yielded to the steady pressure of John Winant, his able representative on the European Advisory Commission, to agree to an American occupation zone in Austria.** The military arguments for shifting some of America's strength southwards were largely fuelled by the propaganda machine of Josef Goebbels. He

* The German commander in the capital, General von Bünau, fought to the end, not least because he feared that his wife and children would be seized at home if he capitulated too soon. This fate had overtaken the family of General Lasch, who had surrendered the Königsberg garrison on 4 April.
** One of the arguments Winant put forward was not exactly flattering: Austria's beautiful landscape, he suggested, would make an ideal 'R&R' (rest and recreation) centre for American forces in Germany.

had helped to convince the Western powers that even if Berlin fell, the Germans, with Hitler at their head, could fight on from the so-called 'Alpine Fortress', a great swathe of easily defendable mountain country centred on the Austrian Alps. The project was hardly credible in the military context of 1945 and was never even seriously attempted. Yet the threat was enough to persuade General Eisenhower, the Supreme Allied Commander, to call off his advance on Berlin at the end of March and divert two American armies, the Third and the Seventh, to turn south. De Gaulle's French forces, who were by now taking on a higher profile, were called on to attack from the west.

In the event, after the so-called 'Fortress' had crumpled like an empty eggshell, it was the Americans who reached Innsbruck first. Here, a pleasing and unusual spectacle met their eyes as the 103rd US Infantry Division arrived on the evening of 3 May 1945. The town had already been liberated by the local resistance groups and the American soldiers marched in along streets lined with Austrian banners instead of the white flags of surrender which had greeted them in Germany. Even the German soldiers standing, still armed, among the cheering crowds had prudently put on armbands carrying the words 'Free Austria'.

The Tyrolean resistance movement had always had a momentum of its own, helped by the mountainous terrain of the province and the fiercely independent tradition of its people.* Moreover, Tyrol faced the south and the Brenner Pass, across which lived the 250,000 of their kinsmen who were lost to them in 1918 and whom Hitler had failed to restore. It was also the front up which the Allied armies were slowly advancing and so, from 1944 onwards, that vital contact with the real battlefield had been established as small Allied commando units were parachuted or smuggled in to help the local resistance groups. In mid-April these had been brought together under the leadership of the future Austrian Foreign Minister Karl Gruber, and it was this united force which, with a loss of forty-one lives, had virtually seized control of Innsbruck over the heads of the German garrison. The action showed what Austrian resistance might have achieved on a broader scale had mouths been kept shut, betrayals avoided, and direct encouragement and support been provided from the outside.

It had always been intended that the main point of entry for the

* Unlike the voluble Viennese, they kept their thoughts very much to themselves ('Three Tyroleans, four tables' was how one saying summed up their reserve). This made for much greater security.

Allied armies should be from Italy in the south. In fact, the British were the last of the four occupying powers to enter Austria: the advance guard of their Eighth Army did not cross the border into Carinthia until 8 May. Here too, there were unexpected complications. To begin with, the age-old ethnic tensions in the frontier zone sprang into life again with a vengeance as Tito's partisan forces – espousing the cause of the Slovene minority for the greater glory of the new Yugoslavia – swarmed all over the area and even laid claim to Klagenfurt, the provincial capital. The situation became so tense that the British 78th Infantry division was actually preparing to about-face and expel the partisans by force* until Tito was persuaded, not least by Moscow, to change his mind and pull back.

If the Russians were helpful on this issue, they were to demonstrate ominous obstruction when the Eighth Army tried to push north and occupy the adjoining province of Styria which had been allotted to it. One reason why the British were so anxious to get their hands on the province, which bordered on Hungary, went back to that Anglo–American vision – still not blown away by events – of building a western bridgehead between Austria and the Danubian peoples to the east. That was precisely the reason why the Russians sought to block it, and it was not until the summer that the Eighth Army was able to cross the River Mur and occupy Graz.

Similar friction over territory developed between the Americans and the Russians in the north, and it was months before the demarcation lines of the four occupation zones were finally established. This gave the Tyrol and Vorarlberg to the French; Salzburg and Upper Austria south of the Danube and west of the Enns to the Americans; Carinthia, with East Tyrol and Styria, to the British; and the Burgenland, Lower Austria and Upper Austria north of the Danube and east of the Enns to the Russians. Though a four-power zonal scheme was agreed for Vienna, the occupation process as a whole had revealed a dangerous imbalance within an already crumbling Grand Alliance. The Western powers were still not clear what they were after in Austria, with the Danube Federation concept still outweighing the notion of a restored

---

* An operation hastily planned under the code-name 'Bee-Sting'. The desperate need to clear the brigade areas of the tens of thousands of prisoners who were totally clogging up communications was one reason for the tragic episode of the handover to the Russians of the captured Cossacks. The author at this point was himself in Carinthia with the British Intelligence Organisation formed for Austria.

republic trying to stand by itself. Stalin, on the other hand, was quite clear what he wanted: as much of Austria as he could grab by force of arms, and eventually, if the cards fell right, to draw Vienna into the new Danubian empire he planned to carve out for himself.

Thus, as Hitler's war ended in the spring of 1945, the East–West Cold War was already taking its place, with Austria at the centre of a giant tug-of-war.

PART SEVEN

THE ROAD HOME

I

The Wait for Freedom

THE TUG-OF-WAR between the great powers over Austria's future began by proxy, long before they met up themselves in Vienna. Pulling at the Russian end of the rope was a powerful quartet of Austrian Communist Party leaders who had spent most of the war in comfortable exile in Moscow: Ernst Fischer, Johann Koplenig, Franz Honner* and Friedl Fuernberg. In April they arrived in Soviet-occupied Vienna to start repaying Stalin's hospitality. Pulling at the opposite end, though not in such unison, was a mixed team of right-wing Austrians. Some of these had just been released from prison or the concentration camps; some had fought as leaders of the resistance; some were simply emerging from the cautious obscurity which they had adopted during the Hitler years. At the centre of the rope stood Austria's master of compromise and supreme survivor, the Socialist architect and Chancellor of the First Republic, Karl Renner.

One of the enduring legends about the creation of the Second Republic was that Stalin and Renner had, so to say, found each other by accident. Nothing could be further from the truth. The Red Army had barely crossed into eastern Austria before, on Stalin's orders, the headquarters of the Third Ukrainian Army Front had been told to search out the veteran Socialist leader. He was to be informed that, once he had shown himself to be trustworthy, the Red Army Command would assist him in 're-establishing a democratic order'. That was on 3 April; by coincidence, it was the very day on which Renner (who had passed the war quietly in the Lower Austrian village of Gloggnitz) revealed his presence by protesting to the local Russian commander about the

---

* In June 1944, however, Honner had left his colleagues behind in Moscow's Hotel Lux and was flown to Yugoslavia, where he raised the first of two Austrian 'Freedom Battalions' which fought with the partisan army of Tito.

behaviour of his troops. But Renner was also seeking Stalin in the sense that he was already groping for the political power which only that great liberator could provide. He had accordingly combined his formal protest with an offer to place all his services at the Red Army's disposal for the re-establishment of the Austrian Republic. It is not unreasonable to suppose that that was the underlying purpose of his call.

If Renner was after power (and wished to serve his people, which all politicians assume to be the same thing), Stalin was after a venerable and respected figure who might one day lead a combined left-wing front for him in Vienna. Events which were soon to unfold in neighbouring Hungary revealed the pattern. There, the pre-war Socialist leader Arpad Szakasits was used by Stalin to fuse his party with the Hungarian Communists into the so-called 'United Workers' Party', of which he was made the nominal Chairman. He was then rewarded with the even more nominal post of President of the new 'People's Republic' before being purged a year later, his work for the Kremlin done. Karl Renner was an altogether tougher figure than Szakasits. Moreover, Austria under four-power administration was a far harder penetration target than post-war Hungary which, though independent to start with, was always under the prick of Soviet bayonets. For all that, Renner's behaviour in the spring of 1945 was enough to raise the worst fears and suspicions in the Western camp.

Though promptly entrusted by the Soviet High Command with the task of relaunching the new republic, and transferred with his family to a spacious new residence at Eichbüchl Castle near Wiener Neustadt for the purpose, Renner still felt insecure about Stalin's support. In Moscow's eyes he was, after all, the cowardly opportunist who had helped to wave Hitler's troops into Austria seven springtimes before. Moreover, he had continued to canvass the *Anschluss* idea after 1938. So, on 15 April, a week after moving into Eichbüchl, Renner composed a long letter to Stalin which, later, he would probably have liked to have forgotten. This *Apologia pro vita sua* was written in tones of servility which may have reflected both self-interest and an uneasy conscience, but which were totally unnecessary in the circumstances. The writer recalled with pride his pre-war meetings with Lenin and Trotsky;* listed his unique qualifications for the task in hand; and called on the Soviet dictator to take Austria 'under his mighty protection'.

---

* An unfortunate reference in any case, given Trotsky's deep rift with Stalin, and eventual murder at his bidding.

To cap it all came this pledge: 'The Social Democrats will work fraternally with the Communist Party to refound the Republic step by step together.' That was precisely the formula for the creation of Kremlin-dominated 'Popular Fronts'. Stalin must have thought that he had indeed found his man. The provisional government formed on 26 April by Renner also corresponded exactly with Soviet needs (not surprisingly, for their High Command had approved the list). Though the newly reconstituted Austrian right wing had its representatives, Renner's Cabinet was dominated by moderate Socialists like himself and Adolf Schärf, and by Moscow's Communist nominees. The two key portfolios from which minds and bodies could respectively be controlled were both in Communist hands. Fischer was put in charge of 'Popular Enlightenment, Education and Culture', while Honner was made Minister of Interior and, as such, in charge of the police. This set the take-over formula in motion, however hard it would have been to complete the process.

But Karl Renner, now Austrian Federal Chancellor again, had not for nothing spent decades in a political juggling act which went back to the time of empire. He sprinkled his Cabinet with a carefully selected mixture of Under-Secretaries of State (as in February 1919) who could act as a check on their respective ministers. The most important of these special monitors were the two appointed to keep an eye on Comrade Honner at the Interior Ministry: the moderate Socialist leader from Lower Austria, Oskar Helmer, and Raoul Bumballa, the only representative of the Austrian resistance movement in this first post-Hitler administration.

The right wing was still under-represented, partly due to its shortage of acceptable leaders with any experience of office, but also because of the problems of its own political relaunch. This had been far more radical than anything undertaken on the non-Communist left. The Social Democrats of old had merely restyled themselves the Socialist Party of Austria, and the moderates, as personified by Renner and Schärf, were now in undisputed control of what was left of Otto Bauer's radicals.* But the pre-*Anschluss* Christian-Social Party was well and truly buried in the spring of 1945, and a new spirit, as well as a new name and new

* The fiery wordsmith of the movement had died in Paris in 1939. A small group headed by the Party Secretary Erwin Scharf tried in 1945 to carry the radical banner by advocating close partnership with the Communists, but the attempt was easily overridden.

leadership, erected in its place. It was not difficult to abandon the word
'Social', which had anyway always been the hallmark of the opposition.
But to drop 'Christian' as well from the party label marked a clean break
with the Catholic-dominated 'Ständesstaat' of Dollfuss and Schuschnigg
and all the political incubus of authoritarianism which went with it.
Instead, the old Christian Socialists renamed themselves simply the 'Austrian People's Party' when the representatives of the right wing gathered
in Vienna in April to plan their future.

There was no political equivalent of Karl Renner to tower over their
ranks. The only one among them to have held even junior government
office was Julius Raab from Lower Austria, but that had been only in
the mayfly administration of Seyss-Inquart in March 1938, which was
scarcely a qualification. Even less acceptable was Raab's history as a
provincial Heimwehr leader. His time was to come; but, in the spring
and summer of 1945, attention turned increasingly towards another
Lower Austrian of the younger generation, the Peasant Union leader,
Leopold Figl. Though Kunschak (another Leopold) was presented as
the Chairman of the new party, this seventy-four-year-old Catholic
Socialist veteran had neither the energy nor the ambition to be its
leader. It came as no surprise, therefore, that when Renner expanded
and reshaped his government on 24 September, Kunschak dropped
thankfully out, and with him the last of the Christian Socialist old guard.
Figl now stepped in to join Schärf and Koplenig in the top triumvirate
of the so-called 'Political Cabinet'.*

The peasant boy turned qualified engineer from the Tullnerfeld had
impeccable personal and political qualifications. His patriotism, which
was to carry his people through the arduous years ahead, was beyond
question. The name of Leopold Figl had been high on the Gestapo's
list at the *Anschluss*, and he was among the first batch of Austrians to
be shipped off to Dachau a few hours after the German march-in. There
he had remained, enduring the worst treatment which a Nazi concentration camp could mete out, for more than five years. Even his release,
in May 1943, brought only temporary freedom. In October of the
following year he was re-arrested on suspicion of underground activities
and despatched, first to Mauthausen and then to Vienna's central prison,

---

* The leader of the Tyrolean resistance movement, Karl Gruber, was brought in on the
People's Party ticket as *de facto* Foreign Minister, and was to be confirmed in this post
for the next eight years.

the dreaded 'Grey House', where only the Russian liberation saved him from the death chamber.

It has often been claimed that Austria's pre-war ideological rifts were healed in Hitler's concentration camps, where the common suffering brought about a common understanding between old rivals which was the foundation of post-war politics. This is true only up to a point. Dachau housed behind its barbed wire inmates from the old right like Walter Adam, press chief of the Schuschnigg regime; stalwarts of the Fatherland Front like Alfons Gorbach, Karl Maria Stepan and the resistance hero Hans Becker; but also inmates from the old left such as the Republican Schutzband leader Alexander Eifler and other prominent Socialists like Robert Danneberg and the former Mayor of Vienna Richard Schmitz. Now, for the first time, they were thrown together as Austrians, and started to think as such. The present being unbearable, they talked about the future, and that meant burying the past.

Yet they were not the only human pillars on which the new Austria would be built. There were also those like Julius Raab on the right and Karl Renner on the left who, without selling their souls to Hitler, had steered clear of trouble and had never seen the inside of a concentration camp. And there were provincial-based ties, like that key relationship which Figl had built up in 1945 with the moderate Socialist leader of Lower Austria, Oskar Helmer, another who kept himself out of harm's way during the Hitler years. Underpinning everything was that slow but eventually massive swing against Nazis and 'Piefkes' which, as already described, had built up among the Austrian people at large. After seven years under the swastika, they would simply not have tolerated a return to the old pre-war party bickering and strife. Without this determined popular mood, no amount of concentration camp reconciliation could have prevailed.

Renner's Cabinet reshuffle may have improved the standing of his government at home, but it did little to dispel the suspicion and hostility felt towards it by the Western powers, with Britain in the vanguard. From the first, they had refused to recognise a regime which had (in their eyes) a suspected fellow-traveller as Chancellor and dedicated Moscow nominees in two key ministries underneath him. This was not the Austria they had visualised, keystone to an anti-Communist federation; it looked more like another brick being shaped by the Kremlin to fit into its own Danubian archway. Soviet obstruction tactics on the ground, which had delayed the Western allies in occupying their allotted zones and in taking up position in Vienna, only increased Western disquiet.

As a result, when the disintegrating Grand Alliance met for the last time at Potsdam between 17 July and 2 August 1945, Britain and America still dug their toes in over the Renner regime. Precious little space was allotted for the exercise. The conference devoted itself almost entirely to 'The principles to govern the treatment of Germany'. These were discussed in all their aspects, ranging from the arrest and trial of war criminals to the sinking of the U-boat fleet, from the enlargement of German coal production to a common policy for forestry and fishing. In the final protocol, even the brief passage settling the future of the city of Königsberg was twice as long as Section VII, which dealt with Austria. This recorded, in two sentences, that whereas the Soviet government had proposed the extension of the Provisional Government's authority to all of Austria, it was subsequently agreed that this question would only be examined 'after the entry of British and American forces into the city of Vienna'. The third and final sentence was to be of greater long-term importance. It recorded agreement that no reparations should be exacted from Austria. This was of political significance in that it underlined Austria's happy status as a liberated rather than a conquered country. It also removed a potentially crippling economic burden, though the Russians were to find their own ways of making Austria pay for her share in Hitler's war.

Renner had to wait another two and a half months to receive joint East–West blessing. It was not until 11 September 1945, after the long-delayed entry of Western forces into the capital, that the four-power Allied Council held its first meeting in the 'House of Industry' on the Schwarzenbergplatz. Its proclamation declared, in ringing tones, that it had assumed supreme control over all Austrian affairs. It repeated the formula of the Moscow Declaration and defined its most urgent task as the 'elimination . . . of Hitlerite misrule and of German influence throughout the whole of Austrian life'. Democratic parties were to be allowed free rein to propagate their policies, with the object of holding free elections as soon as conditions permitted. But there was still no mention of the Provisional Government which had been administering the country for five months.

Only after Renner had widened his Cabinet to strengthen representation from western Austria; held the first meeting in the capital, on 24–26 September, of spokesmen from all the provinces; and announced a firm date, 25 November, for the holding of general elections, did the

Western powers declare him, to use the Jewish word, to be 'kosher'. On 20 October, after last-ditch resistance by Britain had been overcome, Renner was informed that the authority of his Provisional Government was now accepted as extending, under the Council's control, throughout Austria. The first confrontation between East and West in Vienna was over, but it was clear that the competition between them would continue. On that same 20 October, Marshal Koniev, the Soviet Commander-in-Chief, jumped the gun by announcing, in a friendly letter to Renner, that his government would now open diplomatic relations with Austria through an exchange of envoys. It took the Western powers three weeks to catch up with three tersely-worded statements of their own.

The Russians could hardly have opposed the holding of free elections. The fact that they agreed so readily probably reflected their belief that Austria's Communists could easily do well enough at the polls to hold the balance between the two larger parties.* When the urns were emptied and counted, they showed the People's Party, with 1,602,277 votes, to have claimed almost 50 per cent support; the Socialists, with 1,434,898, had 44.6 per cent; and the Communists trailing a miserable third with a mere 174,255 votes, representing less than 5.5 per cent of the entire electorate. The Austrians had lived through some dingy hours in history, notably in March 1938. This was one of their finest. Even in the Soviet-occupied zone, where there was pressure through the mere presence of Russian troops, the rejection of Communism was overwhelming. Translated into parliamentary seats, the nation's verdict read eighty-five for the People's Party, seventy-six for the Socialists, and a derisory four for the Communists.

Various special factors could be cited to explain the débâcle. The orgies of rape and plunder committed by Red Army troops (those belonging to the second wave of lines of communication units rather than the first wave of fighting forces) had struck at women, who accounted, in the autumn of 1945, for 64 per cent of the electorate. The Communists had also blundered in their election campaign by running, even more vehemently than the Socialists, as the sworn enemies

* They were not the only ones to make this prediction. The author was then serving in the Intelligence Organisation of the British High Commission in Schönbrunn Palace, and was, among other things, Secretary of the top-secret Joint Intelligence Committee (JIC). Its estimate was that the Communists might win anywhere between twenty and twenty-five of the 165 seats in the new parliament. Figl reckoned on even more.

of Austria's Nazis. As there were some 670,000 of these (all excluded from the vote), this also aroused hostility among another million of the family and friends of the rank-and-file ex-Brownshirts (an early sign of the key party political problem which the Nazi question was to pose). But after these, and all other factors, had been taken into account, there could be nothing but praise and relief in the Western democracies for Austria's commitment to their values.

Leopold Figl, who now became the first Chancellor of an elected post-war government, was the ideal man to steer his country through the unique problems it faced. A small and weak Austria which did not even possess sovereignty over its own affairs offered no stage for a European statesman of Seipel's stature. Another Dollfuss, though resolute enough, would have been too fiery, as well as too ideological, for the pragmatic down-to-earth needs of the day. Another intellectual, like Schuschnigg, would have been too remote. The people would never have dreamt of calling that austere lawyer 'Kurtl'. But Figl was 'Poidl', even outside the close-knit farming community of his native Lower Austria. He had all the strength and natural dignity of the true peasant but none of his parochialism or taciturnity. Figl, with his twinkling sense of humour and zest for human company, could outshine the Viennese for charm, and this he exerted, in subtly different ways, on each of the four contrasting Allied commanders who succeeded one another as his political masters. A love of wine (though not vodka), a sense of humour, with a fund of anecdotes, and a true Austrian's passion for hunting endeared him to most of them.

Even those to whom he never got close respected him for his integrity and fearlessness. More than once, he stopped an overbearing Russian general in his tracks by telling him to change his tone of voice when talking to the Federal Chancellor of Austria. Some of these confrontations at the sumptuous Hotel Imperial (where the Russians had set up their Vienna headquarters) lasted for so many hours that his family began to fear that he had been whisked away to yet another prison, this time garnished with Soviet barbed wire. But at the end Figl always walked out smiling on to the Ringstrasse, though often with a swimming head.

Neither he nor his People's Party could, however, be expected to govern alone, whatever the parliamentary balance. Two months before the elections, Renner had indicated to the Western powers that some form of coalition would have to be set up after the poll, between the two democratic contestants. Only this would ensure that responsibility in what was an emergency situation would be shared in the eyes of the nation, and that policy would not be shredded by party squabbles. Figl's coalition was duly set up and its list of members approved by the Allied Council on 19 December. The key appointments were those of Adolf Schärf as Vice-Chancellor; Oskar Helmer, the Lower Austrian Socialist leader, at the Ministry of Interior; and Karl Gruber as Foreign Minister, thus giving both the Tyrol and the resistance movement an established place in the central government.*

It was expected that the coalition would not be needed for more than a year at the most for, in the autumn of 1945, that was the over-optimistic life-span given – at least by Western powers – for four-power rule itself. In fact, the occupation, and with it the compulsory coalition, lasted for ten long years, and during that decade one negative aspect of coalition politics became set in concrete in Austrian life: 'Proporz', or the dividing up of all posts in the public sector between nominees of right and left. As we have seen, it was nothing new in the First Republic for Austrians to look primarily to their political parties for protection and advancement. The Socialists of that era had set up, especially in Vienna, a cradle-to-grave framework to govern the lives of their members. The Christian Socialists and, even more, the authoritarian Fatherland Front, had looked after its own flock with almost equal dedication, and the Nazis had, of course, followed suit.

But post-war 'Proporz' was something different: the sharing-out between 'Blacks' and 'Reds' of the entire gamut of bureaucratic, financial, academic, mass media and industrial posts which were in the government's power to appoint – and all this voluntarily organised in a free society and to the evident gratification of both main camps involved. It was not surprising that even in those post-occupation years when one-party rule was, at intervals, restored, 'Proporz' was unaffected. If an ambassador to one of the normally 'Black' diplomatic postings such as London or Rome remained a People's Party protégé, then his deputy would normally continue to come from the ranks of the Socialists. It was the same with banking, the nationalised industries and everything else outside the purely private sector. The result was something which the mass of Austrians scarcely noticed and hardly bothered about, once

* Renner, his task done, moved out of party politics to become Federal President of the Republic.

life had begun to treat them well: the dilution of their refound national identity by loyalty to, and dependence upon, a party rather than the state.

Nonetheless, the coalition provided that united and relatively stable front which the government required to master all the challenges of the occupation years. Four of these can be singled out. The most urgent was to clear away the carnage of war and to fill the nation's stomachs. Parallel with that went the need to win back some measure of independence from the all-powerful Allied Council now installed in Vienna. In the longer term came the two main domestic political problems: how to dispose, on the one hand, of the old Nazi legacy, while at the same time warding off the new threat posed by Communism and its powerful patron, the Red Army.

Figl summed up the immediate emergency in a memorable message to the nation as it tried to celebrate its first post-war Christmas: 'For your Christmas tree, even if you have one, I can give you no candles, no crust of bread, no coal for heating and no glass for your windows. We have nothing. I can only beg of you one thing: believe in this Austria of ours!' The blunt and sombre language was not unlike that used by Winston Churchill on becoming Prime Minister of an embattled Britain five years before. There was one big difference. It would never have occurred to Churchill to ask his people to believe in their own country. He took that faith for granted; Figl knew it would have to be won.

Providing the 'crust of bread' was, to begin with, a slow and harrowing process. At its worst, the official food ration in Vienna was a bare 600 calories a day, less than many a concentration camp level. Thanks mainly to emergency deliveries of flour and other supplies from American army reserves, it rose, during the winter of 1945–46, to a more sustaining 1550 calories a day, only to be cut back again in the spring to 1200. Those were the months when the black market and the barter exchange had their heyday, as Persian carpets were traded for cooking fat in Vienna's Resselpark, and cigarettes became a currency on their own. From 1947 onwards, as regular Marshall Plan deliveries took over from emergency aid, the scramble for food steadily slackened and normality returned to the economy. By the autumn of 1948, the basic food ration had risen to 2100 calories a day; by the beginning of 1949, flour and bread rationing were done away with altogether. By now, the currency had been steadied, if not yet fully stabilised, while industrial production was actually exceeding pre-war levels. Ironically, at this point, the living standards of Hitler's former 'Ostmärker' were already higher in several respects than those prevailing in post-war Britain, which had exhausted and bankrupted herself in the struggle to defeat Hitler. Even more ironically, the victorious British were never to close that gap. Indeed, it was to widen steadily as the century progressed.

The Austrian economy would have expanded even more rapidly in the first years of the occupation had it not been for a damaging blow inflicted by the Russians on 27 June 1946. On that day, Colonel-General Kurasov, who had just assumed the Russian Supreme Command, announced the take-over, with immediate effect, of all the so-called 'German external assets' in the Soviet zone. Already in February the Russians had seized control of one major 'German asset', the Danube Shipping Company, whose headquarters was in Vienna. 'Austria fought with Germany' was their blunt answer to Western objections. Now, frustrated in separate attempts to force joint-stock companies on the Austrians, the Russians had resorted to blanket acquisition. Kurasov had the letter of the law on his side. Almost in the last hours of the Potsdam Conference, the Western powers had agreed that Third Reich properties and investments in its former Ostmark should be divided up on a zonal basis once the Allied occupation of Austria was in force. By this formula, the Western powers had spared Austria, as a 'liberated country', the burden of war reparations. It never occurred to them until now that the burden of Soviet exploitation would be even greater, for they had never defined what a 'German asset' was.

General Kurasov now spelt it out precisely: 252 factories employing over 50,000 people; the great Danube Shipping Company, already in Russian hands; the important oilfields of Zistersdorf just outside the capital; and some 600,000 acres of farming land and forestry. Any Austrian damaging this property, or hindering its transfer into Soviet hands, would be 'brought to justice', a phrase which, in those days, meant summary arrest by the Red Army, with the threat of imprisonment or even execution as a 'saboteur'. Though the Western powers hastened to lessen the effect of this bombshell by formally renouncing any such claims in their own zones, the damage was to prove considerable. The Soviet state-within-a-state had been created inside Austria, paying no taxes and siphoning all profits into the specially created Military Bank in Vienna's Trattnerhof. Over the ten years which the occupation was to last, the total loss to the Austrian state in production and revenue was conservatively estimated at over a billion dollars, an enormous sum in the money values of the day.

By an irony, it was in that same month, June 1946, that the Russians unexpectedly yielded just as much ground to the Austrians on the political front as they had snatched away in the economic field. In a revised version of the Control Agreement (signed the day after the Soviet 'General Order No. 17' for the seizure of German assets) the Austrian government gained in one great leap control over the bulk of its legislation. In future, all the laws it submitted to the Council, with the exception of constitutional measures, would go into effect unless, within thirty-one days, the four Council members (now called High Commissioners) registered their *unanimous* objection.

This abolition of the Soviet veto was no momentary lapse on the part of General Kurasov. His political and legal advisers had been chewing over the revised Control Agreement, which was based on a British draft, ever since February, and various Russian amendments had been adopted.* This makes Soviet agreement to the final text even more surprising, and no satisfactory explanation has ever emerged. At a time when the Kremlin still hoped to draw Austria into its zone of influence (and had just established itself as a sovereign power at the heart of the Austrian economy), Figl's coalition government was being handed virtual autonomy over its law-making.

The Chancellor wasted no time in trying to solve the riddle behind this miscalculation; he concentrated instead on profiting from it. The most important legislation the government now had to deal with concerned the treatment of Austria's Nazis. In the first months of the occupation, this had been in the hands of the four powers, each of which had acted with different emphasis in its zone. The Americans continued to act as they had done in their intelligence-gathering activities throughout the war; they amassed huge amounts of information which they were then unable either properly to interpret or coordinate. The 80,000 questionnaires, each seven pages thick, which they presented to former party members under their jurisdiction were often of dubious validity, as the individual was left to confess, deny or prevaricate as he chose. Above all, the mountain of paperwork was too high to climb, and it was calculated that barely a quarter of the replies were ever processed.

* The four powers had, among other things, agreed on precisely what an Austrian constitutional measure was. This invalidates the argument, sometimes advanced afterwards, that the Russians were unaware of the legal implications of their action.

The British also distributed questionnaires on the American model but, with characteristic pragmatism, expected far less from the exercise and concentrated instead on getting a democratic system working again in the two provinces of their zone.* The French were altogether less assiduous. To begin with, they had appeared late on the scene and had done little preparation. Moreover, unlike the Anglo-Saxons, they faced the problem of Nazi collaborators in their own country, and were thus reluctant to make too much of a fuss in Tyrol and Vorarlberg. The Russian approach had been different again. As we have seen, they had their trusted Communist agents at the heart of the Austrian government (notably Honner as Minister of Interior), and left it to them to guide the detailed work of de-Nazification on the ground through Austrian official channels. Again unlike the Anglo-Saxons, the Russians always kept in reserve the weapon of kidnapping to deal with anyone whom they particularly disliked or mistrusted, and that weapon was in frequent use.

It was only a natural development therefore when, in February 1946, the four powers handed over basic responsibility for the entire de-Nazification process to the Austrian government. The Austrians, after all, were the only ones who could know the truth behind the answers in all those questionnaires. As the Western powers, working from their own inadequate 'black lists' soon realised, the Austrians were also the only ones who could identify the miscreants who had operated in their midst without even wearing the Nazi Party badge. 'Nazism was not so much a question of armbands as a question of character,' was the shrewd verdict of one victim of the regime.**

A total of some 536,000 registered Nazis had been recorded in 1946, of whom roughly 100,000 were the so-called 'Illegals' who had operated underground against the republic in the last four years of its life. These had been placed in 1945 among a 'heavily compromised' class of their own. The implication was that those 'lesser compromised' who had

* There had been special factors, especially in Styria, which affected the Nazi problem. The Styrians were doubly susceptible to Hitler's racial propaganda because they lived on the ethnic fringes of the old empire and the new republic. For them, the River Drau was like the Memel in East Prussia, the frontier line of Germanic race and culture against the Slavs.
** The distinguished Jewish music conductor, Josef Krips, in conversation with the author at a private piano performance given at the latter's Vienna apartment in the winter of 1945–46.

flocked into the Nazi Party ranks after the *Anschluss* might well have been prompted by fear, opportunism or simply mass hysteria – all factors which, as has been described, were in fact in operation after the spring of 1938.

The 'heavily compromised' represented, at least to begin with, a relatively simple group to target under the 1945 'Prohibition Act' which, apart from withdrawing all their political rights and levying special taxes, imposed penalties of the type which later came to be known as 'community service'. The extension of this, Austria's 'War Crimes Act', had a smaller and blacker target, as its name implied. The Act was enforced by special 'People's Courts' against whose judgements no appeal was possible. In the ten years of their existence, these courts returned 13,600 verdicts of guilty, passing ten death sentences and thirty-four terms of life imprisonment at the top end of the penalty scale. Though some Austrian war criminals, notably Eichmann himself, slipped through all the nets at the time, justice was, on the whole, seen to be done, and vengeance seen to be exacted.

When it came to de-Nazifying the Civil Service, the results were more patchy. Austrian bureaucrats, like their colleagues in every country of the world, have a leech-like attachment to their office desks and pension rights. This quality was very much in evidence in Vienna – and even more so in some of the provincial capitals – after 1945. Some of the older officials called upon to swear oaths of loyalty to the Second Republic had already, during their careers, made successive pledges to the Habsburg Emperor, the First Socialist Republic, its Fatherland Front successor and, finally, to Hitler. Though many fell at this fifth hurdle of the Second Republic, a goodly number managed to negotiate their way over, either through friends in high places or on the grounds of their 'indispensability'. The official head count taken on 1 January 1948 showed that over 100,000 officials had been suspended or dismissed from their posts because of their Nazi past. This statistic became widely quoted by a government understandably anxious to establish its democratic credentials. Less advertised was the fact that, of the total strength of 315,200 state employees at that date, more than 40,000 were 'less compromised' ex-Nazis who had managed to survive. In Tyrol and Vorarlberg they represented over 30 per cent of the provincial bureaucracy.*

* One who did not survive in office was a policeman who had been brazen enough to write a personal letter of appeal to the Chancellor. Figl recognised him as the very man who had arrested him on 13 March 1938, during the first wave of Gestapo purges.

Successive amnesties were soon to wind up the entire de-Nazification process, but the real problem in these immediate post-war years was how to handle the large shoals of 'small fish' caught up in the anti-Nazi nets. Before the amnesties of 1948, Austria had some half a million disenfranchised voters who, with their families, represented a quarter of the nation's population. More to the point for the politicians, the numbers of these disenfranchised exceeded the membership strength of either of the two main parties. Once they were given back the vote, therefore, the struggle began (and has never ceased) to persuade them to put that vote in the right ballot box. The outcome of this somewhat unseemly scramble was to be crucial for the politics of the Second Republic.

Not surprisingly, it was the right-wing People's Party which tried the hardest, and came the closest, to luring Austria's former Nazis into its ranks; but, in the end, they went their own way. Throughout 1948, a new strongly nationalist group, led by two Salzburg-based journalists, Herbert Kraus and Viktor Reimann, had been gathering strength under American protection in western Austria. In the early summer of 1949, with the October general elections on the horizon, they founded their own party, the League of Independents (VdU, in the initials of its German name). Their original aim was to cast out a net wide enough to catch those mixed streams of voters who were swimming without direction between the main political camps. These ranged from trade union members with no party obligation on the left, to the standard-bearers of Schönerer's pan-Germans (indomitable survivors of imperial days) on the right.

It was, however, the small fry of the recently amnestied Nazis whom they mainly scooped up, and on a massive scale. Their vote above all established the VdU in the autumn poll as the third largest power in post-war Austrian politics. With mathematical precision, they took eight mandates each from People's Party and Socialists, and the sixteen seats which resulted made them the potential king-makers of future coalitions. It would be wrong to regard the VdU, even in its early years, as being simply a neo-Nazi party.* But it was the natural home of ex-Nazis and marked their re-integration, by a fully democratic process, into the life of the Second Republic. This seemed, at the time, a surprising

---

* Reimann's own career symbolised the mixed origins of his movement. He had started off as an 'illegal' Nazi before 1938, only to join the Catholic resistance group of Roman Scholz in 1941 and to be sentenced to ten years' imprisonment in 1943.

phenomenon. Yet, in essence, the structure of the Second Republic had only returned to the political model of the First: two large mainstream parties of the right and left with a nationalist liberal independent group holding the precarious balance between them.

The Austrians had, once again, demonstrated their instinctively conservative character. They had also started to display another of their traditional traits: the tendency to brush unpleasantness of any kind under the carpet, under the hallowed motto of '*Schwamm darüber!*', or 'Sponge it off!' Indeed, the rehabilitation of the Nazis had not been purely a parliamentary affair. It was also taking place within the psyche of the nation as a whole. The first evidence of this came up in a revealing series of public-opinion surveys carried out in Austria by the Langzeit poll organisation between September 1946 and February 1948. Those interviewed at regular intervals during the period were asked the same questions about National-Socialism, as viewed in retrospect: was it a bad idea, or was it a good idea badly carried out? (There was a section also for the 'Don't knows'.)

In September 1946, 45 per cent said yes to the first question, compared with an already substantial 33 per cent who agreed with the second version and 22 per cent voicing no opinion. But by August 1947, those who thought Nazism was a good idea which had merely been badly executed actually exceeded (at 38.7 per cent) the 31.6 per cent who still thought it had been bad all along. By the spring of 1948, with the Amnesty Act in the offing, opinion was equally divided, with roughly 40 per cent in each of the two main response groups.* Ten years after the *Anschluss*, and less than three after the end of the Hitler terror, the Austrians had already begun to wipe their memories clean, and with them their consciences. It was to mark the start of a unique exercise in mass amnesia.

The resolution of the Nazi problem still left the Figl government with the Communists to tame, and here they had to deal not with the past but with the present, in the shape of the Soviet occupation force and the even more powerful shadow of the Kremlin which stood behind it. Already, in June 1947, Figl had been drawn into injudicious direct talks with Ernst Fischer over the conditions under which the Russians might relax their extortionate economic policy in Austria. The answer

---

* The number thinking Nazism had been a good thing in principle leapt to an abnormal 51 per cent in December 1947, doubtless due to unrest caused by the currency reforms of that month. Economic factors anyway predominated in the popular mind.

could only have come directly from Moscow. The price demanded was that pro-Western ministers like Helmer, Schärf, Gruber and the Chancellor himself would have to go, in Figl's case to be replaced by a more 'neutral' leader like Julius Raab, with stronger Communist representation in the new Cabinet. This would have corresponded almost exactly to the political upheaval which Moscow's henchmen had stage-managed in neighbouring Hungary. There, the resolutely pro-Western Prime Minister, the peasant leader Ferenc Nagy, had just been forced into resigning as a preparatory step towards the total Soviet take-over of the country. For the Kremlin, Figl was the Nagy of Vienna; but in Austria, unlike Hungary, the Western powers were present in force, and the so-called 'Figl-Fisching' collapsed the moment it was made public.

The Communists had one weapon left to try and topple, or at least weaken, the Figl government: strikes and mass unrest backed by street violence. They had tried this on a relatively modest scale in 1948; they returned to the charge with a vengeance in September and October 1950, exploiting genuine industrial discontent over a new wages–prices agreement which had been bungled by the government.* There were days in this autumn of crisis when Austria resembled a country plunged again into civil war, with factories, railway stations and post offices being stormed and then retaken by rival political gangs. But, in contrast to 1934, this was not an armed showdown between right and left, but was mainly a struggle between Communists and Socialists, wielding wooden clubs, for the support of the workers. To their lasting credit, the Socialists held firm; organised themselves into strong-arm squads through trade union leaders like Franz Olah; and finally prevailed. On 6 October, the Communist action committee called off their strike and the last serious challenge to democracy in the Second Republic was over.

That the Russians had stood behind this challenge was indisputable. Though they had lost their one top-level survivor in the Ministry of Interior three years before (when Helmer had courageously sacked the Communist State Police President of Vienna, Heinrich Dürmayer), the police chiefs in all the Soviet-occupied districts of the capital were the same Communist stalwarts who had been installed there in 1945.

---

* There was also a global aspect to the affair. The outbreak of the Korean War in June 1950 had brought a new and dangerous dimension to the East–West conflict. It had also had a damaging effect on Austria's economic recovery at the very time when Marshall Plan aid was coming to an end.

Needless to say, they had cooperated with the strikers, and the Soviet military authorities helped them along by paralysing normal police activity in these districts, ordering the gendarmerie off the streets and forbidding the movement of security reinforcements into the capital. But it was equally plain that, pragmatic as ever, the Russians were ready to back down once resistance became too strong and a gamble had failed. They made no attempt to save their henchmen when, on 20 October, the government conducted a massive purge of Communist police officials in and around the capital, including the commissioners in the four Soviet districts of Vienna where the plot had been hatched.

The autumn crisis of 1950 showed how firmly Austria was now caught up in the Cold War which had followed the crumbling away of the Grand Alliance. The Soviet Union was doing all in its power to draw the capital – and, if possible, the whole country – into its new Danubian empire. The Austrian government was equally determined to hold on to the Western powers for support. This needs stressing, in view of all the propaganda, launched after Austria had achieved her freedom through a bargain with Moscow, that the government had always wanted to stand neutral between East and West. Nothing could be further from the truth, at least during the seven years of Figl's leadership.

During the whole of this period, Austria's commitment to the West was not confined to the open ties of economics and ideology. They also extended, though in secret, to the military and strategic field. As early as 22 November 1945, the Special Operations Executive (SOE) of the Western powers had formulated, in conjunction with British Intelligence, a plan for undercover activity in the British zone of Austria to be implemented in the event of war with the Soviet Union. The target area was even given priority as belonging to 'one of those countries which are likely to be overrun in the earliest stages of conflict with Russia but which are not, at present, under Russian domination'.* The objective of the small clandestine nucleus put in place was to bring about 'rapid expansion into a reliable resistance movement in case of war'. A small and select band of Austrian officials was brought into the scheme after the formation of the Figl–Schärf Coalition.

An even more select body of Austrian military and security officers

* A British archive reference may be of interest. It is COS (45) 671 (o) of the Cabinet papers 80/98 in the Public Record Office.

started, soon afterwards, on a top-secret project planned jointly with the Western powers to 'exfiltrate' their forces from Vienna. This was to be put into operation in the event either of full-scale war breaking out with the Soviet Union, or of some lesser emergency such as an attempt to seal off the Austrian capital on lines similar to the total blockade which the Russians tried in vain to impose on Berlin in 1948. For either eventuality, some rather sketchy contingency plans were also made for the defence of western Austria along the strategic line of the River Enns.*

Finally, it is worth remembering that once Allied permission was in sight for the re-establishment of an Austrian army, the first question on the subject which Foreign Minister Gruber put to his British counterpart, Ernest Bevin, in the spring of 1949 was whether this force could not be linked in some way with the North Atlantic Treaty Organisation. This went ahead of anything in Western thinking at the time, and was anyway an unnecessary embellishment. It was tacitly accepted on all sides (including the Soviet Union) that if a third world war should break out, the Austrian Tyrol, with its vital communications link between the German and Italian fronts, would inevitably be part of NATO's field of operations.

Occupied Austria was thus, from first to last, a small but significant element locked into the strategic East–West equation. It was only because of a sudden shift in the balance of that equation that the four-power occupation itself came finally to an end.

---

* One of the Austrian officials actively engaged in these plans was the Jewish Catholic resistance leader Lieutenant-Colonel Johann ('Hans') Blumenthal, who became a lifelong friend of the author's.

II

The Swiss Solution

WHEN THE GERMAN PHILOSOPHICAL poet Friedrich Hebbel described Austria as 'the small world in which the great world holds rehearsal' Vienna was the capital of a great empire which still far outweighed Prussia. But Hebbel's oft-quoted words were never truer than when, nearly a century later, the rivalries of the superpowers were reflected, like rays through a prism, on to the seemingly minor problem of a small post-war Austrian Republic.

The four powers, represented by special deputies of their Foreign Ministers, first sat round a table to discuss the problem in London on Thursday, 16 January 1947. All of them, except perhaps the Soviet member, would have been astonished to have known that, over the next six years, they and their successors would be sitting down another 259 times to debate the same issue, and that even when their own labours came to an end, over two more years would pass before a solution was reached. For the Austrians there were some pleasing contrasts, but also some disturbing parallels, with the pilgrimage to the Paris Peace Conference which the spokesmen for the First Republic had made a generation before. Chancellor Figl, who headed their delegation, was not obliged, like his predecessor Renner in 1919, to enter the conference building through a side door, to symbolise his status as the spokesman of an ex-enemy power. He and his team* came in through the main entrance as the representatives of a 'liberated state' which, as such, was admitted from the start to so-called 'hearings' of the proceedings. The humiliating isolation of Saint-Germain was not repeated.

On the other hand, the demands put forward by the delegation for

---

* Vice-Chancellor Schärf and Foreign Minister Gruber were the other principal members.

the 'Federal People's Republic of Yugoslavia', which had also been admitted to the 'hearings', seemed like a Communist rerun of the hostility which the newly created Yugoslav kingdom had displayed towards Vienna after the First World War. Its leader, Joze Vilfan, immediately slapped down a claim against Austria for $150 million in reparations. Even this was modest compared with the territorial demands: 2470 square kilometres of Carinthia (including the provincial capital, Klagenfurt, and part of the town of Villach) plus a small pocket of 130 square kilometres of Styria. The age-old problem of the ethnic fringes and the German—Slav confrontation along these racial fault-lines had surfaced once more, as the Austrians had indeed feared. What made the renewal of the struggle doubly ominous was that in 1947 the mightiest of the war victors, the Soviet Union, stood behind the claim of its fellow-Communists in Belgrade.

Fortunately for Austria, this support was to be considerably watered down after the spectacular breach between Stalin and Tito in 1948. But by then in any case the issue which was to make or break Austria's prospects of freedom overshadowed everything else surrounding the talks: yet again in her history, Austria's fate was to depend on a resolution of the German problem.

Stalin had now taken over for Russia the part which Clemenceau had played for France at the peace settlements after the First World War: the hobbling of German power by any shackles at hand – economic, military, strategic or political. As in 1918–19, the extension of Slav territory at German expense was one such restraint (though now it had to be Slav territory under Communist control). As in 1918–19, German post-war expansion in any direction had to be blocked at all costs, and this meant, above all, a renewal of the *Anschluss* ban on Austria. At the Paris Conference, Austria had to pay the price for defeat after fighting, at her choice, alongside her imperial ally. Now she was paying the same price for a lost war which she had been forced to fight as an integral part of Hitler's short-lived Third Reich. The setting was very different, as were the main protagonists, but the reasoning was the same.

Nonetheless, there were shifts in emphasis in both the Western and the Soviet approach to the Austrian question as the balance of the Cold War was itself altered by events which had nothing to do with Austria. To begin with, the Russians appeared to be giving ground: quite apart from persuading the Yugoslavs to tone down their territorial demands on Austria, the Kremlin seemed prepared to make concessions of its own in the economic field. Then the confrontation between East and West sharpened on a global scale, trapping the Austrian problem inside it. As early as March 1947, President Truman had proclaimed his historic doctrine of the 'containment' of Soviet expansionism as the basis of American policy. A year later, the Communist *putsch* in Prague, which overturned the democracy installed there with American blessing a generation before, made 'containment' seem even more relevant.

Fresh urgency was given by events in Berlin that same year: the Soviet walk-out from the Allied Control Commission and the attempted Soviet blockade of the city which was only surmounted by the famous Western 'air-bridge'. The following year saw the freezing of the entire German problem within the Cold War conflict. The creation of the Federal German Republic in September 1949 provided the West with a new power-base which would extend, almost inevitably, into a military alliance. The creation of the German Democratic Republic in a knee-jerk reaction a month later prepared the way for the Soviet-occupied zone to be formally incorporated as a state into the Kremlin's new East European empire. To the West, it seemed that the Communist menace was now gathering strength against them wherever they looked. That included upwards at the skies, for in August 1949 America's monopoly in nuclear power had been broken when Russia exploded her first atom bomb. It included also the darkening Asian horizon where, in October, Mao Tse-tung, victor in the Chinese civil war, had proclaimed the Communist People's Republic. When the armed conflict between East and West broke out in Korea in June of the following year, the Cold War was turned temporarily into a hot one. Would the Asian pattern now be repeated in Europe?

One thing was clear: this was no time for either side to evacuate Austria except under terms and conditions which would favour it – or at least place it at no disadvantage – in the overall balance of power. The Second Republic had become a bridge which both armed camps wanted to have a foot on, thus denying total control to their opponents. This strategic stand-off rendered any progress made at the negotiating table to be illusory. The Foreign Ministers' meeting in Paris in May and June 1949 may have brought agreement at last on the Yugoslav case against Austria (Russia having by now abandoned its support for all Tito's territorial claims). There was even some agreement in principle (though not in the all-important detail) over the vexed issue of 'German assets'. But the talks shrivelled up in the hostile climate of East–West confrontation described above. Austria could now only be evacuated, the Russians declared, if Western troops quit Trieste.

September 1949, the date by which the Foreign Ministers' deputies were supposed to finalise the economic aspects of the Austrian settlement, was the very month when, with Western blessing and Western orientation, the German Federal Republic came into being. The North Atlantic Treaty Alliance, the apotheosis of 'containment', had already been founded in the spring. The East–West confrontation in Europe, though destined to be held in check by the new nuclear 'balance of terror', had now become militarised. In this context, Austria's prospects of securing early freedom from the Kremlin had not been helped by a declaration by the People's Party State Secretary Ferdinand Graf that, once she had secured her independence, Austria should herself join NATO. Unlike those secret feelers on precisely the same theme which Foreign Minister Gruber had already put out to his British counterpart, Ernest Bevin, Graf's intervention was highly public, made in an interview given to a Swiss journalist in July 1949. Though his government tried to play it down, Communist propaganda lost no time in playing it up. Graf's remarks may well have been an unauthorised 'solo act'. But they only confirmed what the Kremlin already knew: there were influential Austrian ministers, officials and industrialists, especially on the traditionalist right wing, who were convinced that their country should look to the West for its military protection as well as its economic salvation.

It was hardly surprising, therefore, that during the next few years of unabated East–West tension the Russians blocked every attempt to produce a solution to the Austrian conundrum.* In 1953, the year which brought the end of the Korean War, that tension did abate somewhat, but even more important for the saga of the Austrian treaty were two unconnected changes of leadership which took place within weeks of each other in Moscow and Vienna. On 5 March 1953 came the death of Josef Stalin, for twenty-four years the supreme dictator of the Soviet Union. On 2 April, after a carefully-orchestrated party conspiracy, Julius Raab succeeded Figl as Austrian Chancellor. His inaugural address to Parliament contained a passionate appeal to the four powers to give

---

* The most imaginative idea was the concept of the so-called 'Short Treaty', put forward by the Western powers on 13 March 1952. This draft contained only eight simple clauses and was greeted by Figl as being, in effect, a 'protocol for evacuation'.

Austria her freedom, 'so that only one flag should wave over her land, the red-white-red'. There was nothing unusual about language of this sort. What was new was that, unlike his predecessor, Raab was convinced from the start that the key to independence was an Austrian pledge of neutrality. This matter-of-fact construction engineer had no head for jurisprudence, and was eventually obliged to get the legal experts at the Ballhausplatz to spell out for him precisely what neutrality signified in international law. He had approached it by a more homely route. His brother Heinrich was married to a Swiss woman and had gone to live in Switzerland in 1938. After the war, he constantly held it up as a model for the Second Republic, though Julius Raab was initially sceptical.

But if the arrival of Raab on the top-level political scene was to help move the Austrian problem steadily nearer to a solution, it was the departure of Stalin from that scene which was to give the decisive push. So long as the dictator, and the system named after him, remained in place, no Red Army soldier was ever likely to move back one yard from ground he had occupied if the Kremlin could prevent it. That was the sober appreciation made by Western intelligence at the time, and subsequent evidence was to confirm it. But with Stalin gone, certain options were opened up. That rumbustious extrovert Nikita Khrushchev, who soon emerged as First Party Secretary and therefore victor in the succession struggle, was the man to seize them. What was not known to the West at the time was how rapidly he was changing course. Only many years later did evidence emerge that already in the summer of 1953, during the first months of the Khrushchev era, the Russians were making contingency plans for a withdrawal from Austria. The Republic's neutrality, in some as-yet undefined form, had also been chosen as the political formula which would accompany and justify that withdrawal. Among the first to be told and to make their dispositions accordingly were the all-powerful KGB. It was from their ranks that the evidence about this early shift in Soviet policy was eventually to emerge.

On 25 September 1953, Peter Sergeivich Deriabin, a major in the KGB, arrived in Vienna to take up the key security post as head of the 'Sovetskaia Koloniia', or 'SK', intelligence section in the Russian zone. His task was the surveillance of all Soviet citizens stationed in Austria, with the supreme priority of preventing any defections. There was a rich irony in this appointment. Deriabin had been intriguing for months to get the Vienna posting, in order to defect to the Americans himself.

This he finally succeeded in doing nearly five months later, on 14 February 1954, causing a panic in the Soviet camp, for he had behind him eight years of varied experience at KGB headquarters, the 'Moscow Centre'. What concerns us here are not the many secrets he revealed to his Western hosts about Soviet intelligence but simply the situation which he found awaiting him at his sumptuous new headquarters, the Hotel Imperial in Vienna. He described it to a visitor who was allowed access to him in his American asylum:

> The talk in the Soviet Mission when I arrived was all of the neutral Austria which Khrushchev was now ready to accept. This meant large-scale changes in our field of work, and my new boss, Lieutenant-General Ivan Ivanovich Ilyichev, who had taken on the dual role of Ambassador to the Austrian Republic, was already busy preparing them. He was the right person for the job. Though his title in Vienna may have changed, he remained a top officer in the Soviet Military Intelligence organisation, the GRU, who were in many ways our rivals. I doubt whether the Austrians knew anything about this secret identity of his, and even less about the changes which he was making. On Moscow's orders, our entire KGB and GRU organisations in Austria were being revamped.
>
> This meant, for example, that contact with our so-called 'illegal agents' was being stepped up, since these would form the main espionage network to be left behind after the evacuation. On the other hand, as the time was approaching when the Soviet High Commission would melt away entirely, leaving only a Soviet embassy in its place, our regular intelligence officers were being given formal diplomatic slots, where they would be accredited to the Austrian government, just as though Vienna were already like any other Western capital where we adopted this procedure as a matter of course.*

When Deriabin was asked for the reasons behind this change in policy over Austria he replied:

* Deriabin to the author, Washington, 4 April 1987. In 1973–74 and again in 1987–88, the author left his normal field of studies to compile a two-volume series, *The Storm Petrels* and *The Storm Birds*, on Soviet defectors from Stalin to Gorbachev. For this purpose, he was given privileged access by several Western intelligence services to material on the cases, and to a dozen of the major defectors themselves. Deriabin was one of those produced for several hours of conversation.

The general assumption was that Khrushchev had decided that the isolation of the Stalin era had to be ended and that an Austrian treaty was the cheapest entry-ticket back into polite society. It might even bring advantages, though that would depend on how the link-up with the main problem of Germany could be made, and nobody yet knew how that would be worked out. Khrushchev's determination to heal the 1948 breach with Yugoslavia was another important factor. Marshal Tito had apparently made it clear to him that, if he wanted a reconciliation with Belgrade, he had better remove the Red Army from Austria first.*

Deriabin's first-hand account of the situation in 1953 has never been challenged and was indeed confirmed by later information reaching the West. It follows therefore that, unbeknown to him, Raab was pushing at an opening door when he launched his softer and more flexible approach towards the Soviet Union immediately after taking office.** He must, at all events, have been gratified, and perhaps surprised, by the rapid succession of Russian conciliatory moves which followed, and in some cases matched, the specific appeals made in his inaugural address. Thus, on 29 May, the Soviet High Commissioner (still at that date Lieutenant-General Sviridov) announced that the important hydro-electric plant in the Russian zone at Ybbs-Persenbeug on the Danube would be handed back to the Austrian government. It was one of Sviridov's last official acts. A few days later, Moscow announced that their military High Commissioner in Vienna was to be 'replaced by a diplomat, Ambassador I.I. Ilyichev'. (That the newcomer was also a Lieutenant-General of the Red Army was not, of course, mentioned, much less his branch of the service.) At the same time, with this establishment of full diplomatic relations, the Austrian representation in Moscow was raised to embassy status. Of the activities of Raab's envoy there, the veteran Austrian diplomatist Norbert Bischoff, mention will be made below.

For the moment, it is worth concentrating on the Kremlin's new man in Vienna, for 'Ambassador Ilyichev' flung himself that summer into a veritable frenzy of conciliatory gestures. The Soviet controls on

---

* Ibid.

** It was summed up by his dictum (dating from June 1953) that the time had come 'to stop tugging at the tail of the Russian bear'. It is unclear whether Raab himself realised that he had for some time been the Russians' preferred successor on the right wing to the doggedly pro-Western Figl.

all movements of persons and vehicles in and out of their occupation zones were lifted, excluding only the transport of arms and explosives; agreement was reached to strengthen the authority of Austrian police and gendarmerie within that zone; and hundreds of official buildings, schools and private dwellings occupied by the Russian authorities were evacuated and handed back. This was all done during Ilyichev's first week in office. At the end of July, he announced that henceforth the Russians would follow the American example and pay for their own occupation costs, instead of placing the burden on Austria. A general reduction in troop strengths accompanied the new financial arrangement.* Britain removed two of her three battalions; France withdrew all but a handful of men; the United States now, in effect, policed the whole of western Austria, but with a force cut down to some 15,000 men. (Though considerably slimmed down, the Red Army garrison in the eastern zone was still more than three times that figure.) Finally, in this eventful summer, the Russians announced on 11 August the lifting of postal censorship in their zone, and three days later agreed in the Allied Council to the ending of all postal, telephone and telegraph controls throughout the country. The Austrians could now talk and write freely, as well as begin to breathe more freely.

During those same busy summer months of 1953, the Austrian government used its new diplomatic relationship with the Soviet Union to launch an equally hectic campaign of its own to discover the terms on which the Kremlin might give consent for Austria's freedom. It proved to be hard going. The Russians used the first flurry of bilateral notes to persuade Vienna to abandon the so-called 'Short Treaty' idea put forward by the Western powers the year before. This, in Moscow's view, was quite simply too short and left too little room for manoeuvre in the all-important context of Germany.

Undismayed, Raab tried to enlist the help of honest brokers. The Indian Prime Minister, Pandit Nehru, was sought out while on summer holidays in Switzerland and asked to probe in Moscow on Austria's behalf. Nehru duly obliged through diplomatic channels, but met only with evasiveness. Then, in October, the Finnish leader Urho Kekkonen was invited to Vienna for talks with Raab and Schärf to establish whether the wary but peaceful relationship between Moscow and

* This caught the British and French (who had not matched the American lead, taken as far back as 1947) off-balance. Not until 1 January 1954 did they too agree to pay their own costs.

Helsinki might provide some sort of precedent for Austria. (It obviously could not: Russia's willingness to leave Finland alone was based on healthy respect for the martial ardour of the Finns, who had fought the Red Army to a standstill in 1939. The Austrians could show nothing to match that feat of heroic patriotism.) It was Norbert Bischoff who had engineered the Kekkonen visit in what was an unorthodox but acceptable initiative. However, the following month, the indefatigable old envoy went one step further, and too far, by addressing a personal, and totally unauthorised, appeal to the Soviet Foreign Minister, Vyacheslav Molotov, pleading for the Finnish model to be adopted. Bischoff seems to have escaped without even a reprimand from Vienna. In any case, his solo effort got nowhere. He had failed to realise that, for the Kremlin, Finland was no part of the German question, whereas Austria lay at the heart of it.

All these soundings and exchanges of notes, and the debates in the Vienna parliament which accompanied them, had however allowed one theme to crystallise in public as official Austrian policy: the concept of standing between the two power-blocs and forming military alliances with neither. This was sometimes spoken of in terms of neutrality, but was conceived basically as a 'pact-free status'. As such, it had a heritage which went back to the early years of the occupation. The idea had a certain built-in logic. If East and West were to move off the Austrian bridge on which they stood, then both sides – and especially the Russians – would insist that that bridge should remain unmanned. This reasoning did not stop opposition to the Raab–Bischoff offensive. It came partly from Vice-Chancellor Schärf, who denounced the blatant courtship of Moscow as a dangerous 'foreign policy escapade'. But there were those on the right wing who also had their reservations about pulling up the anchor of Western support on which the Second Republic had so far rested. Would neutrality mean, in practice, neutralism, and allow Soviet Communism to creep in by stealth? There were echoes here of the age-old argument between the 'Greater Austrians' and the 'Little Austrians'. Neutrality could only mean little with a vengeance.

Everything was put to the test in January and February 1954, when the Foreign Ministers of the one-time 'Grand Alliance' agreed to come together again for the first time since their abortive meeting in Paris five years before. There was something ominously symbolic for the Austrians about the venue chosen: Berlin. Once again, the main theme of the talks was to be the future of Germany, over which the four powers had failed to come any closer. Though deadlocked, the issue was still not lost for the Russians, inasmuch as the Bonn government had not yet entered the NATO fold, despite edging steadily towards it. But the Austrians were at least assured that their case would be studied more fully than it had been at Paris, though it was still last on the agenda. More promising still, this time they had been admitted to the table as full partners in the discussions over their own treaty. Their delegation, headed by Leopold Figl (who had re-entered the Raab government as Foreign Minister the previous autumn), thus arrived in the former German capital on 9 February full of hope.

This hope was dashed with unexpected speed and severity three days later, at the very first session of the Austria talks. After a promising start on 12 February, at which Figl had expressed his confidence at the outcome and Molotov had declared that 'the opportunity to restore Austria as a sovereign, independent and democratic state' now seemed at hand, the Soviet minister set out the Kremlin's terms. It was he, and not Figl, who first put down on the official record what the Austrians had long been talking about in public and had lately been offering Moscow in secret, through intermediaries. A separate article, he declared, should be added to the draft treaty according to which Austria would undertake 'not to join any military pact or coalition directed against any of the countries whose forces had fought against Germany'. In addition, all foreign military bases were to be banned from Austrian soil and no foreign military advisers were to be admitted. Though this formula went further than some factions in Austria wanted to go (and much further than what the Western powers desired), it would, taken by itself, have been acceptable.

The bombshell which shattered everything came in Molotov's second additional clause. This proposed that, 'in order to prevent any attempts towards a new *Anschluss*', the Allied forces, though evacuating Vienna itself, would remain in their occupation zones under a new status 'until the conclusion of a peace treaty with Germany'. The Austrians had had enough trouble in Berlin persuading the American Foreign Minister John Foster Dulles that a 'no-pact pledge' dictated by Moscow was not just a step on the slippery slope to neutralism and isolation. A neutral status, he argued, could only be honourable if freely chosen by the nation concerned. In order to meet Western concern, Molotov subsequently agreed that what amounted to an Austrian promise of neutrality should not be laid down in the treaty itself but should come in an annexe to it, as a separate decision by the Austrian government, taken almost as though it had been plucked out of the air.

But neither this piece of window-dressing nor a welcome Soviet concession on the thorny 'German assets' problem* could make Molotov's demand for an indefinite extension of the occupation – under whatever new name and conditions – acceptable. It was, as Dulles dryly observed on 13 February, the 'poison' in the middle of the 'rather odd sandwich' which Molotov had presented to his colleagues. The outside slices were assurances that the Soviet Union accepted the need to establish a free and independent Austria: in the middle came a wedge of conditions which would ensure that she remained neither free nor independent. Figl's reaction, after repeated appeals to Molotov for a change of heart had failed, was more personal: how would the Soviet Foreign Minister feel if he were expected to propose a humiliation like this to his own people?

It was ironic that it should have been that same minister who, a year later, suddenly flung open the door which he had slammed shut in Berlin. On 8 February 1955, in an address to the Supreme Soviet, Molotov began by again stressing the importance which Russia attached to the speedy restoration of Austria's independence. This was the same introductory note he had struck twelve months before, but what followed was very different. Though the danger of 'German militarisation', and with it the need to guard against a new *Anschluss*, were again paraded, the crucial link between the continued occupation of Austria and the conclusion of a German peace treaty was dropped. The only safeguard Molotov now demanded was that Austria should officially pledge herself to the no-pact formula he had elaborated at Berlin, and that the Western powers should each back this up. They were accordingly invited to 'an immediate four-power conference at which both the German question and the issue of the State Treaty with Austria would be discussed'. This must have sounded almost too good to be true in Vienna when it was monitored on Soviet radio. But on 25 February Molotov put forward his proposals officially to a delighted Ambassador Bischoff who, on 14 March, handed over a note giving his government's acceptance.

What had lain behind the Kremlin's change of tactics (for it was this,

---

* Molotov agreed to take the $150 million which Moscow claimed from Austria under this heading, to be paid in goods rather than hard cash.

rather than a change of heart)? One thing it certainly did not represent was any last-ditch attempt to secure some sort of all-German neutrality on the pattern proposed for Austria. February 1955 was far too late in the day for that, as indeed Molotov had himself made clear when warning the Supreme Soviet that the time was fast approaching when the Bonn government would be joining the Western military structure. What had changed over the past twelve months was that the Kremlin had finalised its own preparations to counter that move. Of all the developments synchronised by Khrushchev which lay ahead, two were of supreme significance.

The first was that the very day before the Austrian Treaty was signed in Vienna, the Russians concluded a treaty of their own in Warsaw. This so-called 'Eastern European Mutual Assistance Treaty', or 'Warsaw Pact' for short, provided for a unified command of the armed forces of the Soviet Union, Hungary, Czechoslovakia, Poland, East Germany, Bulgaria, Romania and Albania. This was linked in general strategy with the approaching enlargement of NATO through the recruitment of West Germany, but specifically with the even more imminent evacuation of Austria. Up to now, Soviet forces had been garrisoned in countries like Romania and Hungary on the grounds that they were ensuring the Red Army's lines of communication with eastern Austria. The end of the occupation would have meant the end of the pretext. Now, a broader and stronger framework was in place, under tight Soviet control, which legally secured Russia's military interests throughout its East European empire.*

The second important move to be synchronised in the Soviet game during this momentous spring of 1955 was the reconciliation visit which Khrushchev paid to Belgrade with his new Prime Minister, Marshal Bulganin. This twentieth-century version of the medieval 'journey to Canossa' had been arranged to take place less than a fortnight after the signing of the State Treaty with Austria and the military evacuation of the country provided for by that agreement. Major Deriabin's testimony that Khrushchev was yielding to Tito's insistence that a Red Army withdrawal from Austria was a precondition to any reconciliation was

* In an earlier move connected with the approaching evacuation of Austria, Imre Nagy, already suspect in Moscow's eyes for having founded the 'Patriotic People's Front', was replaced as Hungarian Prime Minister by Andras Hegedus, who could be relied upon to agree to any Russian military requirements. Nagy was, of course, destined to make a spectacular but ultimately tragic comeback in Budapest eighteen months later.

more than supported by later evidence. Indeed it emerged that, for the Soviet leader, healing the breach with Yugoslavia outweighed by itself the merits of hanging on to a contested foothold in Austria. Khrushchev was a dedicated and ambitious Communist who, unlike Stalin in his final fossilised condition, was keen to play an active role on the global stage. State-to-state relations with the new People's Republic of China were still correct (though these were to snap in five years' time). But the party-to-party relationship was already cool, for the two Marxist giants were clear rivals for the ideological leadership of the Communist world. Khrushchev could only contest that leadership with Asia once he had healed this humiliating rift in Europe.*

Apart from these specific reasons for agreeing at last to an Austrian treaty, the general balance of the arguments for or against the move had swung in favour of evacuation. Austria could never be won over ideologically (the poor showing of her Communists in the 1953 elections had again demonstrated that). Moreover, even economically, she was becoming a liability. The lemon of German assets had been squeezed for all the juice it could produce. Russia's own oil production had now expanded to such an extent that the contribution from Austrian fields was no longer important, while the whole complex of industries in the Soviet zone was on the brink of bankruptcy.

Finally, the Red Army marshals (of whom Prime Minister Bulganin was one) had reluctantly accepted that the strategic arguments also now favoured a four-power evacuation. Soviet forces would merely withdraw across the Czech and Hungarian borders from where – thanks to the new Warsaw Pact – they could remain poised for action indefinitely. For NATO, on the other hand, the withdrawal of the Allied garrisons represented a serious disadvantage, for it severed at one blow the direct north–south link between the alliance's forces in Germany and those south of the Brenner in Italy.** Khrushchev's 'entry ticket into polite society' became a barrier, far stronger than cardboard, erected between the armies of his opponents. Molotov appears to have been the one

---

* The author went down to Belgrade from the State Treaty celebrations in Vienna to witness the great 'B and K' visit, and attended the sumptuous banquet which Tito laid on in the White Palace for his guests. Khrushchev was in euphoric spirits. One of the Yugoslav officials commented: 'Now China's only hope in these parts is Albania, and that's not much of a foothold.'

** Eventually, Austria countenanced the secret passage of NATO ammunition trains across the Brenner, but this was a poor substitute for a continuous land corridor.

Politburo member who always remained at heart opposed to the new policy over Austria, and indeed any increased flexibility in Soviet diplomacy. This was indeed ironic for, as Soviet Foreign Minister, he was the man who had to carry it all out.

The next stage in the process was the visit to Moscow of Chancellor Raab and his party* – following Molotov's direct invitation – to discuss the details of the proposed settlement. This invitation had been formally accepted on 29 March and the meeting duly began on 11 April. In the circumstances, it was almost inconceivable that the Austrians would return home empty-handed. However, it was the Russians who shaped the package they were to carry back with them. For the next forty years, the lesson to be chanted like a Buddhist mantra in all Austria's schools was that neutrality had from first to last been the fixed aim of her policy. In fact, in Moscow, the Austrians had to be forced by their hosts even to mention the delicate word, let alone to define it. It did not figure either in Raab's first verbal discussions with the Soviet leaders or in the declaration which he read out on the second day of the meeting. It was left to Molotov to ask bluntly why the word was missing: surely it was neutrality that they were really talking about?**

The Soviet Foreign Minister even pointed the Austrians in the precise direction he desired them to take: towards the Swiss model. This, he reminded Raab, had been the solution publicly favoured in 1952 by the then Austrian Federal President, Theodor Körner. Much more recently, in fact less than a month previously, on 17 March, it had been the main theme of dinner party discussions which Kreisky had held with the Soviet Minister in Vienna, Kudriatsev, on which the diplomat had duly reported to Moscow. What, demanded Molotov, was wrong with the idea; after all, even his American counterpart, John Foster Dulles, had accepted in Berlin that neutrality was an honourable status provided it was freely adopted.

This reference touched on part of Raab's dilemma. As we have seen,

---

* Accompanying Raab were Vice-Chancellor Schärf, Foreign Minister Figl, his Socialist State Secretary (and future Chancellor) Bruno Kreisky, plus a small group of advisory officials and secretaries.

** The sequence of events which follows is based largely on accounts given to the author by Figl and Kreisky, who both became personal friends. The memoirs of the Austrian interpreter at the talks, Walter Kindermann (*Flug nach Moskau*, Vienna, 1955), and of the well-informed Swedish ambassador in Vienna, Sven Allard (*Diplomat in Wien*, Cologne, 1965) are also important.

he personally favoured both the neutral solution and the Swiss model. Yet he was under no illusions that whatever public agreement the Western powers gave to the idea, their acceptance of it would be grudging and suspicious. Even more important were the unhealed rifts in his own Cabinet over the issue. Vice-Chancellor Schärf, in particular, still feared that Austria might be drawn, through neutrality, into an isolation chamber, sealed off even from European political and economic organisations so dear to all Socialist hearts. The 'pact-free' formula, a voluntary abstention from military alliances on the Swedish pattern, was still Schärf's preference and, at heart, also that of Figl. Incredible though it may seem, the delegation had landed in Moscow with such fundamental differences still unresolved. It was Molotov who had now obliged them to make up their minds and waste no time about it. Raab's delegation accordingly retired to an adjoining room. They re-emerged fifteen minutes later to propose that Austria should declare 'permanent neutrality in the manner practised by Switzerland'. Their suggestion was immediately accepted. The impression sometimes given later was that the Austrian leaders had suddenly discovered this magic 'egg of Columbus' in a corner of the Kremlin. In fact the egg had been laid long ago, but it was the Russians who forced them to produce it.

Whether, with more determination, the Austrian delegation could have held out for the narrower and less binding 'pact-free' formula of a year ago was a question which seemed churlish to raise in public, in view of the understandable euphoria about the settlement. But when it was raised in private with Leopold Figl after his return to Vienna, his reply was unambiguous:

> Had we decided to stay another day or two in Moscow and slog it out with the Russians in the way they were quite used to in all their negotiations, I think we might have got them to accept their old proposal – and ours – of simply no military pacts. I would not have minded staying on at all, even if things did get a bit tense. When you have been through Dachau and Maut-hausen, there is nothing in the atmosphere of the Kremlin which can scare you. But Raab, who had never seen the inside of a concentration camp, was uneasy in these surroundings and long-ing to get home. There was a big party gathering in Lower Austria in a day or two and he wanted to have his first celebra-tion there. Had we stuck at it, we might well have come away

with the Swedish model. But the main thing, after all, was that
we had got our freedom.*

And that, of course, was the main thing, for at the end of the Moscow
talks the Soviet government declared its willingness 'to sign the Austrian
State Treaty immediately'. Four days later, it proposed the convening
of a Foreign Ministers' conference for the purpose. Compared with the
snail's pace at which the negotiations had proceeded for the past decade
– with the Russians erecting one artificial barrier after another in the
snail's path – the speed of events now was startling. The so-called 'Moscow Memorandum', issued on 15 April, was nothing more than an
agreed communiqué of bilateral discussions between Austria and one
of the occupying states. It had no standing in national, let alone international, law, and had to be converted into a formal treaty for all the
powers to sign. The instrument for the conversion, proposed by the
Western powers, was a preparatory ambassadors' conference in Vienna
to smooth out the few rough edges which remained. Some very Austrian
touches now emerged.

The first had come at the airport when the delegation returned home
in their Soviet Ilyushin aircraft, for even in this hour of national triumph,
'Proporz' was observed. Raab and Figl, the two People's Party members,
were greeted on the tarmac with a red-white-red bouquet of flowers,
presented by a band of patriotic young workers. Schärf and Kreisky, on
the other hand, were handed Socialist carnations (red only) by their
party's delegation. An even more typically Austrian note was struck by
Raab in his speech to Parliament on 27 April, the tenth anniversary of
the day on which the restoration of Austria's independence was first
proclaimed. Greeting the prompt summoning of the ambassadors' conference to finalise the treaty, he made a special appeal to them to finish
their work before 5 November 1955. That was the date, he pointed
out, on which Vienna's Opera House, so severely damaged at the war's
end, was to be reopened at last with a performance of Beethoven's
Fidelio. 'It would be a beautiful gift to the Austrian people,' Raab
declared, to tumultuous applause, 'if this immortal hymn to freedom
and humanity by the greatest composer of all time could ring out in a
free and independent Austria.'

In fact, the ambassadors finished well ahead of Fidelio's deadline. All

* Leopold Figl, during one of several conversations in Vienna with the author, June/
July 1955.

but five of the fifty-nine articles in the treaty had already been agreed and it took them only ten days, 2–12 May, to prepare the final text for signature. Such last-minute changes as were made were all in Austria's favour. Thus the clause which set a fixed low ceiling for her reconstituted army and air forces was struck out. (The Western powers had pressed for this, to ensure that the new Austria would not be turned by decree into a military midget; the Russians, who were gaining so much anyway in the military field, graciously agreed.) The old bogey of 'German assets', which had been conjured up by the Kremlin in various guises over the past ten years to haunt the negotiations, was finally laid to rest with a series of compromises and special arrangements over oil-producing rights. Finally, the terms of the forthcoming evacuation of troops were modified. The Russians had set a fixed date in Moscow, 31 December 1955. The Austrians, and behind them the Western powers, wanted more flexibility. In the end a French compromise was accepted, providing for four-power withdrawal within ninety days of the treaty coming into force. With political adroitness, the Austrian parliament waited until the last occupation soldier (as it happened, an American*) had left Austria before proclaiming their country's neutral status. Thus the fact that Austria's neutrality was, in the end, the result of a direct bargain with the Russians, was camouflaged.

In some ways, the most significant concession to Austria came on the very last day, 14 May, of the finalisation talks in the Allied Commission building. Paragraph Three of the Preamble had enshrined for all time Austria's share of responsibility in Hitler's war, 'a responsibility which, because of her participation in that war, she cannot avoid'. At the beginning of the last session, Figl asked whether that passage could be struck from the record. Molotov, the first to respond, said without hesitation that he had no objection. The Western powers naturally followed suit. This has been presented as a dramatic *coup de théâtre*. In fact, it seems clear that Figl had taken satisfactory soundings on the matter beforehand, for the effect of an outright refusal would have been catastrophic. As one of the Gestapo's very first captives in March 1938, and the victim afterwards of much suffering at Nazi hands, he was the ideal Austrian to submit the request, and a difficult petitioner to refuse. Whether pre-arranged or not, this last of all Soviet concessions had expunged from

* The deadline was met with ease by the Russians and, with more delay, by the British. It was the American garrison commander in Salzburg, Major-General Nutter, who left it till the ninetieth day to cross the border into Bavaria.

the record of the Second Republic the crime-sheet of the First. As we shall see, the citizens of free Austria now tried hard, but in vain, to remove it from their own consciousness.

There was another characteristic Figl touch the following day when, after the Treaty had been signed in the Red Marble Chamber of the Belvedere Palace, he emerged with the four Foreign Ministers of the wartime Alliance on the balcony outside. The dense crowds packing Prince Eugen's great sloping park, which stretched all the way down to the Lower Belvedere on the Rennweg, had cheered loudly at the sight of the statesmen, but the shouting eventually began to falter for lack of further inspiration. Then Figl seized the great bound volume containing the Treaty, pulled it open, and brandished it high above his head. At that, the greatest roar of the day went up, and lasted until the balcony was emptied. The Austrians, still somewhat dazed by the feel of their freedom, had now actually glimpsed the evidence for themselves.

III

Neutral Slumberland

THE MILITARY OCCUPATION which ended with the departure of the last Allied soldier on 25 October 1955 might well have posed yet another threat to the emergence of an all-Austrian identity. For more than ten years the nation had, after all, been divided into four separate zones, each governed by a different power with different social and cultural standards. Yet, when it was all over, surprisingly little of these contrasting foreign values had left a lasting impact. That was least surprising as regards the Russian zone. The population there, Catholic peasant descendants of the core duchies of the Habsburg empire, stood deep-rooted in Austrian history. As we have seen, the archetypal patriot leaders of both the First and Second Republics – Engelbert Dollfuss and Leopold Figl – had sprung from this soil. In any case, all but the poorest of its inhabitants had little to learn from an occupying force whose living standards seemed to be so low that its members might have come from some distant and primitive planet.*

Yet even in the Western zones, where occupiers and occupied stood closer to the same levels, when the soldiers departed after a decade they left little special imprint behind them. Nobody thought of playing cricket in Styria, or *boules* in the Tyrol, where the beret never displaced the green felt hat. The American zone had felt the strongest injection of a new lifestyle, and the Austrians there were the first to try on jeans, and to sample the mass diet of hamburger and Coca-Cola. This, however, was only the advance wave of a transatlantic cultural tide which was soon to engulf not just the whole of Austria, but the whole of

---

* The author remembers one good bourgeois Austrian lady in Baden who was more dumbfounded than disgusted by the behaviour of the Red Army soldiers quartered in her villa. Seeing the pool of water in the lavatory pan, they had assumed it was for washing in. They had never before been confronted with flush sanitation.

Europe. What had preserved Austrian identity during these ten years of administrative division was the same thing that had preserved it during the seven years of Hitler's rule which had gone before: the roots and traditions of the ancient provinces. Only in Vienna, where four-power rule had been concentrated in one small area, did some extra element of cultural diversity spill over. Yet, as diversity is the very essence of the Austrian capital, this only made Vienna more Viennese.

The legacy of the occupation was felt more on the political and economic fronts. Ten years without sovereignty meant that responsibility had to be shared between the two main parties. That meant coalition, which, as we have seen, produced '*Proporz*', a job-sharing agreement so congenial to the Austrian temperament that it developed a life of its own, whatever the electoral balance. But on top of this party '*Proporz*' – or, to be more accurate, underneath and all around it – came the proliferation of special chambers, representing different industrial and professional interest groups. These bodies, several of which were founded or developed during the occupation years, had steadily increased in influence as well as multiplying in number, so much so that the Second Republic came to be described as the '*Kammerstaat*', or 'Chamber State'. On the 'capitalist' side came the Chamber of Trade, set up in 1948, the Federal Chamber of Commerce, and the even more powerful Union of Austrian Industrialists. The labour side was represented mainly be the old trades union movement, as reconstituted in 1945, and the Austrian Chamber of Labour. Though set up by law, these were soon operating independently, and negotiations between them set the pattern for Austria's so-called 'Social Partnership'.

Two years after the occupation had ended, this relationship became formally established as the permanent 'Parity Commission for Wages and Prices'. The significance of this body was that it was set up outside the law, simply by agreement between the spokesmen of industry and labour involved. The commission duly established three sub-committees (dealing respectively with industrial questions, social matters and the wage–price relationship), but it also spread upwards into the state bureaucracy, with dozens of advisory and liaison units sprinkled throughout the ministries. If we also take into account the creation of various professional chambers – such as those for the lawyers, doctors and engineers of Austria – something of the structure of Dollfuss's Corporate State re-emerges, and for the same two basic reasons. The first was the yearning for a secure social order which ensured personal standing while reducing to a minimum the need for personal responsibility. The second was the parallel hunger for '*Posten und Pöstchen*', or, in its Anglo-Saxon version, 'jobs for the boys'. This had been behind much of the nationalist agitation in the Habsburg Monarchy. By creating literally tens of thousands of lifetime positions, mostly coming with an official title and all rounded off with inflation-adjusted pensions, the 'Chamber State' satisfied the same appetite for status combined with security in the Second Republic.

The advantage which such a structure provided was, of course, the possibility of maintaining economic stability through the so-called 'Social Charter', as regularly renewed between employers and employed. This meant that the everyday life of the nation could be shaped with a minimum of public ideological debate between the parties. But it also meant that much of the decision-making was taken out of the hands of the legislature. In the First Republic, the power of the political parties had been overshadowed by that of the private armies; in the Second, it had been overtaken by that of the chambers. Austria had, once again, become something of a constitutional freak: a fully-fledged parliamentary democracy over which parliament no longer ruled.

Its citizens were quite happy about this state of affairs, despite its potentially alarming implications, so long as it provided them with trouble-free good living. The same was, of course, true of their general attitude towards their country's new position in the world. Neutrality is a boring concept, especially to those not used to it, for it implies a retreat from the cares of the world into the obscurity of the 'quiet life'. But it can become acceptable, and even welcomed, when it is equated with prosperity. Though, as we shall see, some doubts on the subject remained in the popular mind, this was what widely happened in the first decades following independence. Before these years of well-fed drowsiness set in, however, the Austrians were confronted with one perilous drama which exploded right on their eastern frontier. Their spontaneous reaction marked another of those finest hours which light up, at intervals, a history so full of mists and shadows.

On 23 October 1956, the Hungarians again demonstrated that they were the true revolutionaries of the Danube. The spontaneous popular uprising which started in their capital that day – led by students from Budapest University and workers from the great industrial complex on Csepel Island – was more of a Magyar rebellion against foreign rule than an economic protest or an ideological statement. Indeed, it was from the precedents of their turbulent history that they drew their inspiration. The verses of Sándor Petöfi, poet of the 1848 revolution, were again on all patriotic lips, and one of the rebels' first demands had been for the replacement of the alien Communist insignia with the old Hungarian colours of Kossuth, leader of that great revolt against Vienna. The Austrians may not have been too enamoured of these evocations, but when, after ten days of indecision, Red Army tank replacements were sent in to crush the uprising by brute force, the Austrian people, backed by the Austrian government, did all in their power to help their neighbours flee from Communist persecution and vengeance. Some 150,000 Hungarian refugees were given asylum during that traumatic autumn, many of them guided to safety through the border minefields.* This was greatly to the displeasure of the Soviet Union whose armed forces had only evacuated Austria twelve months before. All in all, it was a resolute ideological gesture, and an early fulfilment of Raab's pledge to the West that political neutrality did not oblige the Austrians to be 'neutral in thought'.**

But at the turn of the year, the excitement in Hungary died down after the installation of the moderate Communist regime of Janos Kádár. As peace had also been established between Moscow and Belgrade, a general air of calm descended over the Danube Basin, and Austria herself seemed to slide into limbo. So long as the occupation lasted, Vienna, the only spot on the map where East and West came together regularly once a month, was a centre of international diplomacy, and all four powers picked their ablest men for the job. That role had gone and the top diplomatists and newspapermen were replaced, one by one, by a level of representation more suitable to the needs of a small Central European republic of seven million people. Vienna blossomed as a major tourist city and, less happily, as the chief European trading post for

* By great luck, the author had already secured a Hungarian entry visa before the revolution broke out, and thus could not be prevented from driving to Budapest on the following morning. After ten eventful days in the capital (and two days in Red Army captivity on the return journey to Vienna) he was able to observe and participate in this remarkable improvised rescue work along the border. Prominent among the British volunteers who turned up were the then Viscount Astor and Major and Mrs Derek Cooper.

** The orders issued to Austrian Army units sent to the border area were unequivocal. All Hungarians fleeing across were to be accepted, disarmed where necessary, and passed on to welfare organisations. Any Red Army units crossing over in pursuit were to be fired on.

espionage and arms deals. But so far as politics was concerned, it slipped away into relative obscurity for the next thirty years.

These were the decades when a major alpine avalanche disaster, especially if it claimed the lives of foreign tourists, would fill as many inches in the world press as a landslide in Austrian elections. These did happen: on a modest scale in 1966 when, for the first time, the People's Party secured an absolute majority and formed its own government under Josef Klaus, driving the Socialists into opposition. It happened with greater effect four years later, when the Socialists returned to power with a clear majority of their own and Bruno Kreisky, now the party leader, became the new Chancellor. He was to hold this post for the next thirteen years, making him, in his day, the longest-serving head of government in the Western world. This accumulated experience, added to his eloquence and intelligence, could have made him one of the world's most influential leaders. Had he been Chancellor in Bonn for such a long uninterrupted spell, that would certainly have been the case. But in the Austrian setting he was, quite simply, a man too big for his country. The national power-base was missing, while Austria's neutrality also denied him any voice in the military and economic councils of the West. Instead, he dissipated much of his talents on the international stage by bizarre (and quite fruitless) courtships of Cuba's Fidel Castro and Libya's Muammar Gadaffi.

The Kreisky phenomenon demonstrated more clearly than anything else that, for the time being, Austria hardly mattered. Her traditional field of activity, the Danube Basin, was closed to her by the Communist Iron Curtain. Her equally traditional links with Western Europe lay smothered under the blanket of neutrality. She was, in fact, very much on her own, and from this enclosed situation developed an enclosed mentality. When Pope Paul VI declared Austria to be 'the Island of the Blessed', this mentality seemed not merely justified but sanctified. The Pontiff doubtless meant well, but it was nonetheless a dangerous verdict to pass on a people so prone to flee reality as the Austrians.

This deepest slumber period of the sixties and seventies was not disturbed by many troubling issues. Two major ones which did arise, causing a flicker of interest even in the world outside, both had their roots in the past, and both told something about the Austrians of the present. The first was the continuing problem of the South Tyrol. The decision at the Paris Peace Conference to hand over to Italy the quarter of a million German speakers settled for centuries south of the Brenner had represented one of Woodrow Wilson's most abject performances in his self-appointed role as arbiter of the post-war world. This flagrant breach of his own doctrine of self-determination was not to be repaired by Hitler, and for the same reason: the difference in size and weight between the two contestants involved. At Paris in 1918–19, Italy had sat as one of the great victorious powers, whereas the infant Austrian Republic, remnant of a vanquished state, was a political feather which could be blown in any direction the victors chose. Italy was still strong enough in 1938 for Hitler practically to fall on his knees in gratitude that she had not intervened on Austria's behalf. This was no time to take away from her that coveted '*fino al Brennero*', and Mussolini was anyway his Axis partner. The Austrians, on the other hand, were now simply the Ostmärker of his Third Reich.*

The same critical imbalance had emerged again after the collapse of that Reich. Karl Gruber, a Tyrolean himself and the hero of the hour in Innsbruck in the spring of 1945, had sworn to get the lost territories back. One of the first demands of the newly-elected Figl coalition government in the autumn of that year had also been for the South Tyrol's return, a demand backed even by the Communists outside the coalition. But when the problem came up before yet another post-war Paris Peace Conference in 1946, the Austrians could register only a marginal advance on the total failure of 1918. True, their relative status had now improved: they ranked among the 'liberated nations' whereas Italy was clearly one of the vanquished. But they remained comparative lightweights in that anti-Communist structure which the victors were seeking to erect in Western Europe. On the other hand, the Christian Democratic government of post-war Italy, which was fighting a powerful Communist Party in its own backyard, appeared to be a key pillar of that structure. The outcome was predictable. After a series of proposals for territorial adjustments, customs unions and rule by condominium had all foundered, the Brenner remained the frontier and Austria was fobbed off with pledges of equal rights and local autonomy for the German-speaking population.

It is conceivable – though far from certain – that more could have been won back had that population erupted into mass protest and violence. Yet this would have been much to ask of either the South Tyroleans

* Almost 90 per cent of the South Tyroleans accepted Hitler's offer to be resettled elsewhere in the Reich. Nearly 60,000 actually left, and some 20,000 of those remaining were drafted into the German army.

or their comrades north of the border in the summer of 1946. The greatest orgy of violence in the continent's history had only ended twelve months before; quite apart from that, the Austrians were not yet sovereign in their own country.

It was a different matter when the South Tyrol issue flared up again in the sixties. By now, activist groups had sprung into being north and south of the border, determined to stem the systematic 'Italianisation' of the disputed region. The activists spawned terrorist cells, convinced that only through violence could Rome and the rest of the world be made to listen to their case. The first of their bombs went off in January 1961 and, after the Italians had predictably responded with police round-ups and prison sentences, the gestures of violence grew into a campaign of armed sabotage as the political extremists took over. The Austrians, now sovereign and independent, stood at something of a psychological crossroads. To back the struggle of their blood-brothers south of the Brenner would have been a display of national pride as well as racial solidarity. On the other hand, it now seemed prudent for the South Tyrol lobby to back down. Those blood-brothers did appear to be getting alarmingly out of hand. Involvement with them might well upset the nice quiet life of the neutral Second Republic.

It was not surprising that the Austrians opted for abstention, for by now that life of theirs was not only nice and quiet but prosperous beyond the wildest dreams of the republic's founding fathers. In the ten years between 1950 and 1960, though half of it had been spent under four-power occupation, the nation's wealth had grown by some 75 per cent. One of many statistics will suffice to show the impact of this on the ordinary citizen: in that same decade, the number of motor-cars in private hands had jumped by 500 per cent. This was altogether too rosy a picture to disturb and so, as regards the South Tyrol, undisturbed it remained. The problems of the region were left to ministers and ambassadors to resolve. Over the years, the diplomats tied together a package, or 'parchetto', of cultural concessions and social guarantees which gave the South Tyroleans the right, for example, to speak German in their own schools and in all government offices. The flood of Latin immigration into the region was also stemmed. But South Tyrol remained Italian, still nurturing a sense of betrayal by Vienna. The fate of Andreas Hofer should have served them as a lesson.

The second issue to trouble the neutral snooze of Austria in the sixties had even deeper roots. Moreover, being a strictly domestic question, it could not be shuffled off on diplomats to settle. It was the old problem of how Republican Austria was to reconcile itself with its imperial past. The challenge could no longer be ducked because the challenger would not step aside and was anyway too influential to ignore. Otto Habsburg had been a young and inexperienced Pretender, barely out of his student days, when Hitler swallowed up the homeland they shared. The Archduke who returned to Europe at the end of Hitler's war was a very different proposition. Thanks to his chain of international connections, including that remarkable friendship with President Roosevelt, he was, quite simply, the only Austrian both widely known and well-respected in the Western world.* Compared with him, the politicians of 1945 appeared as mere cyphers on the scene. Though shrewdly remembered by Stalin, Karl Renner, who had never cut much of a figure on the international scene, had been almost forgotten in the West, outside the narrow bands of exiles. Leopold Figl, who suddenly emerged as Chancellor in November 1945, was completely unknown.

Nonetheless, the politicians had the law on their side. The old Act of 3 April 1919, banning all members of the former reigning house from entering Austria unless they swore allegiance to the new republic, was still in force.** It was the threat to use it (a measure backed by all four occupying powers) which persuaded Otto in the spring of 1945 to leave Innsbruck quietly and begin a second spell of exile. But once he had settled in his new home, close to the Austrian–Bavarian border at Pöcking on Lake Starnberg; found an independent livelihood as a writer and lecturer; and started a family with his attractive and eminently suitable bride, Princess Regina of Sachsen-Meiningen, he began his long campaign to get back across that border. As one would have expected from a qualified lawyer, it was carefully planned from the start.

The first step was to have his Austrian citizenship confirmed, and the Provincial Government of Lower Austria, one of the heartlands of the Monarchy, duly obliged on 8 May 1956. The next move was for 'Doktor Otto Habsburg-Lothringen' (he had failed to have his wartime style 'Otto of Austria' accepted) to make some form of renouncement of his dynastic claims. This he did on 21 February 1958, but the meagre style of the statement, which merely bound him and his family 'to recognise

* So far as the American public was concerned he did have a rival, in Baron von Trapp, whose singing family of exiles had found fame in Hollywood.
** The anti-Habsburg law was to be preserved, as Article Ten, Paragraph Two, of the State Treaty, despite Raab's efforts to have it struck out.

the current laws of Austria and acknowledge myself a loyal citizen of the republic', was not enough to satisfy left-wing appetites in Vienna. The problem was to find another, and stronger, formula.

Unlike his father, the Archduke sat on no throne from which he could be asked to step down; nor did he exercise any 'participation in the affairs of state' (to quote the historic statement of 11 November 1918) which he could waive. But as the eldest son of that last reigning emperor, he was still the heir to any claims which might arise. In dynastic terms, any such claims had by now become totally unrealistic, as the royal exile in Pöcking knew full well himself. In political terms he was still, however, a factor. This was not so much because of the strength of Austria's monarchist movement (which was both modest and fragmented), but because of the sermon which Otto was preaching about the validity of constitutional monarchy itself in societies ridden by party strife and the camarillas of special interests. Something, he argued, ought to be set permanently above all these rival factions, in order that democracy itself should be preserved. It was an uncomfortable message for the Austria of 'Proporz' and 'Kammern'.

Behind all this lay the psychological struggle of Austria's republicans (predominantly, though not exclusively, those on the left wing) to come to terms with vanished imperial glory. The problem, above all in Vienna, was one of sheer scale as well as of historical associations. No chancellor of any party could enter the Ballhausplatz without seeming somewhat small in the seat of Kaunitz and Metternich. Much less could a Socialist president occupy the splendid apartments of the Hofburg (and in some cases use the same furniture) without feeling the shadow of Maria Theresa or Francis Joseph towering over him. When the old imperial plate was laid out for official republican dinners the unease mounted, as some of the diners would frankly admit. These ghosts would have to be exorcised. This, it was decided in Vienna, could only be done by getting Otto to go one further than his father and, following the provisions of the 1919 law, renounce even his family. The formula presented early in 1961 called on him, after repeating his loyalty to the republic, 'to renounce specifically membership of the house of Habsburg-Lothringen and all ruling claims arising therefrom'. This he did with a heavy heart on 31 May of that year.

He later commented: 'The very idea that anyone should be called upon to leave their own family struck me as absolutely infamous, a madness that could only have come out of the head of some indescribable little-minded fanatic. But I said to myself, all right, if I want to do something on the European scene (and I had actually seen this European path in front of me ever since the Second World War) then I ought not to enter that scene in a position of conflict as claimant to one of Europe's thrones. That would have made it impossible for me to do what I was resolved on doing, and therefore I took the step I did with the declaration. It was out of purely practical considerations. But it was not easy for me, that I must admit, and not because I had any illusions about my position but because of the sheer infamy of the document.'*

But even that did not lay the ghost for some of Austria's Socialists, who pointed out that the Archduke still had not forsworn all political activity after his return. A ludicrous episode now began, in which all the native reluctance of the Austrians to take responsibility – or to push that responsibility onto somebody else – came to the fore. When Alfons Gorbach (Raab's successor as People's Party Chancellor) put the signed declaration before his coalition Cabinet, recommending acceptance, the Socialists rejected it 'in the interests of the republic's security'. The battle of the law courts now began. The Court of Administration, to whom Otto turned first, tried in vain to get the government to make up its mind, and then, on 31 May 1963, produced its own ruling – in Otto's favour. Austria's parliament, the arena of so many fiascos, now entered the circus ring again. In a confused debate on the issue, the return of Dr Otto Habsburg to his homeland was finally declared 'undesirable' by a majority vote in which the Socialists actually teamed up with the small opposition faction,** who had proposed the motion to defeat their own coalition partners. Whatever electoral calculations lay behind this expedient (and the two main camps were then standing much too close for the comfort of either at the polls), this was a clear betrayal of everything that government and parliament stood for.

It needed the coming to power in 1970 of a moderate Socialist, Bruno Kreisky, to bring about the reconciliation with the past which

* The author had many meetings with Archduke Otto, spread over some thirty years. Most were private, especially during the delicate situation in the sixties. But the above remarks, and any further quotes below, are taken from the full transcript of a three-hour conversation in Pöcking on 18 September 1992, when making a German-language television documentary to mark his approaching eightieth birthday. By then he was well advanced on his 'European path'. Indeed he was already the senior member (for the Bavarian Christian Socialists) of the Strasbourg Parliament.
** The functional successor to the 'League of Independents', and now called the 'Freedom Party'.

the older generation of radicals in his party had blocked. Kreisky had the advantage of single-party Socialist rule: there was no coalition on hand either to consult or betray. He had the even greater advantage of being sufficiently confident and culturally mature to look back at Austria's great traditions without blinking. He also had a keen sense of history. As a four-year-old child, he had been taken by his father to watch the funeral cortège of Francis Joseph with Otto – then the same age as himself – walking behind. Now, sitting in the Ballhausplatz, Kreisky had come to regard himself as part of the bridge between Austria's past and present. A large brick in that bridge was belatedly put in place when, after a five-hour preliminary excursion to Innsbruck on 31 October 1966, Otto paid his first return visit to Vienna on 5 July of the following year.*

After all the melodrama which had gone before, the climax was not very stirring. For the Viennese (apart from the small band of loyalists, who duly bowed deeply and curtsied) this slightly-built figure in a lounge suit did not at all match the lustrous imperial image they had carried in their imaginations. For a Habsburg, he was far too approachable, far too eloquent and, strangest of all, far too intellectual. The Pretender who had renounced all claims in order to tread these streets he had walked on as an infant crown prince was also puzzled and somewhat disillusioned by the people he could now meet face to face. He found the Austrians intangible in the literal sense of the word, in that they seemed impossible to grasp hold of: 'The Austrians of today are strange people. As one eminent German politician put it to me, they live from the Habsburgs yet they also live by discriminating against them . . . A Red Army officer who had once been stationed in Vienna described them as being like a marsh which opens when you strike it but which closes up again when you take your hand away . . . In any case, I have never had any quarrel with Austria, though Austria has perhaps had one with me.'**

All in all, this long-overdue reconciliation between empire and republic left both sides wondering what, at least in recent years, all the fuss had been about.

But the most significant thing about these early decades of slumber was not what the neutral and sovereign Second Republic was obliged,

* Two of his younger brothers, Felix and Karl Ludwig, refused to renounce their family claims and were not allowed to return.
** Pöcking, 18 September, and Strasbourg, 22 September 1992.

from time to time, to remember. It was rather what her citizens tried all the time to forget: their part in Hitler's war and in Hitler's crimes. After a while the mood became not so much one of admitting or denying complicity but of refusing to believe that the problem had ever existed. Like that awkward clause in the preamble to the State Treaty, the whole issue was quietly dropped.

We have seen how, after an impressive-looking purge of the state services in the immediate post-war years, there had remained some substantial gaps in the de-Nazification process. The most notable concerned the large numbers of the 'less implicated' who had hung on to their jobs for a variety of reasons ranging from claims of indispensability to protection in high places. Such was the situation in 1946 when four-power control was still in place. When that control ended and the votes of former Nazis and their dependants weighed ever heavier in the electoral scales, the gaps in the process not only widened but the official machinery set up by the Austrian government to close them had itself been throttled back. That was the central charge in a detailed thirty-page memorandum of protest submitted twenty years later, on 12 October 1966, to the then People's Party Chancellor Josef Klaus. Its author was Simon Wiesenthal, the former Austrian Jewish inmate of Mauthausen, whose Vienna 'Documentation Centre' had become the focal point for Nazi 'head-hunting' throughout the globe. He had already established for himself a reputation for objectivity, in that his work was driven by the search for justice, and not for vengeance. This sober approach is reflected throughout the memorandum, which was unpublished.*

His central grievance was that the part which Austrians had played in Nazi war crimes (in his view greater than their population percentage within the Third Reich) was still being swept under the carpet, thanks largely to the calculated passivity of the government itself. He presented lists of the principal Austrian miscreants who had served not only under the notorious Eichmann – such as Franz Novak, 'head of transport'; Alois Brunner, Greece and Slovakia; Erich Rajakowic, Holland – but also under the equally infamous Odilo Globocnik in the Polish extermination camps of Belzec, Treblinka and Sobibor. Then came the damaging accusation. No fewer than sixty-five Austrians who had been criminally active in these camps were known to the legal authorities in Vienna. Only one of them was in jail.

---

* Simon Wiesenthal handed the author a copy during a meeting in Vienna on 23 September 1993.

Wiesenthal then listed similar charges under other headings. Hundreds of Austrians in the so-called 'Police Guards', who had worked alongside the SS in the killings of Jews in Polish villages, had been captured by the Red Army and came home only after the State Treaty had been signed. Although classified as 'non-amnestied' because of their wartime activities, with few exceptions all had escaped any punishment or penalties.

A greater mockery of justice had, according to his account, occurred in the case of the Austrian Police Battalions 314, 316 and 322 (plus four reserve and mounted battalions), which had been despatched to Poland to take part in the mass killings of Jews. The captured war records kept by these units showed that they had, indeed, discharged their gruesome task. A hundred and fifty individuals had been identified as being among the killers. Wiesenthal commented: 'some of these 150 were actually reinstated in the Austrian security services while the Austrian police force still contains numerous members from the "heavily compromised" category of former Nazis'. The memorandum continues with parallel examples of unpunished war crimes committed by Austrians in Security Police Commandos, the Secret Field Police, the Gestapo and in the administration of the ghettos.*

Such lists of accused and such litanies of mass murder and suffering had become part of a sadly familiar story. What gives the Wiesenthal memorandum of 1966 its special note is the contrast he draws between the post-war record of the Bonn government in the matter and that of the Austrian Republic. In the former, guilt had been accepted from the start, a large compensation fund set up, a centre for War Crimes Studies established in 1958 at Ludwigsburg, and an adequate legal staff financed for the complex task of investigation. In Austria, he complained, there had been no official admission of guilt,** no compensation fund,*** no governmental war crimes centre, and no provision for an adequate legal apparatus. The result of this last deficiency was that, whereas at

---

* The Warsaw ghetto was under the control of a lawyer turned SS man from Upper Austria called Sammern-Frankenegg, who conducted operations until the uprising brought in military forces. There were so many Austrian officials under Reichcommissioner Seyss-Inquart in the Netherlands (where 150,000 victims, mostly Jews, lost their lives) that the organisation was nicknamed 'The Danube Club'.

** This was not, in fact, to come from the top level in Vienna until the early 1990s.

*** Not until June 1995(!) was an adequate fund set up to compensate Austrian victims of the Nazi era, most of whom were already dead.

the time of his report there were fifty German state attorneys assigned to Ludwigsburg alone, only a handful of officials had been assigned to investigative work in Vienna. In the Justice Ministry, for example, there were only six officials at work in the special unit, Section II, which was responsible; these six men were supposed to be dealing with 1100 cases of alleged crimes already on the files, with new cases piling up almost daily.

What clearly incensed Wiesenthal was that most of these cases, new or old, referring to war crimes allegedly committed by Austrians all over occupied Europe, had been passed to Vienna for action by the Ludwigsburg Centre. Not only had the results been extremely meagre, but the suspects, though accused of murder or being accessories to murder, often continued in their official posts instead of being suspended pending a verdict. Wiesenthal appealed to Chancellor Klaus for redress on all fronts. He ended: 'Only swift and energetic action can restore to Austria her already damaged international standing.' When asked what the response had been to this 1966 memorandum he replied: 'As good as nothing; the standard excuse was lack of money.' None of his allegations was however refuted.

There was, of course, a broad political factor behind this contrast between German and Austrian acceptance of war guilt and atonement for it. Germany had forged the Third Reich and, as a defeated and disgraced nation, needed to work her passage back into the bosom of democratic Western society. The Austrians, though they had fought in that war and shared in that defeat, had emerged with the life-saving status of a 'liberated people'. Apart from electoral considerations, they naturally clung on to that status for all it was worth, especially after the State Treaty had given them back their own independent place in the free world. But what was politically understandable was not morally defensible, as the persistent nagging at the Austrian conscience showed. As we have seen, even wartime resistance had been largely a matter of conscience.

Mention has already been made of those opinion polls in the late 1970s which showed almost 50 per cent of Austrians believing that National-Socialism had brought them 'good as well as bad'. The trend persisted in similar polls taken as late as 1987, though by then the number believing that Nazism had brought Austria nothing but bad had significantly increased. This was of course all bound up, after centuries of confusion and debate, with the question of how much the Austrians now felt themselves to be a nation on their own, as distinct from a race of 'German-Austrians'. Polls taken between 1973 and 1989 show an average of around 85 per cent declaring themselves either 'absolutely' or 'mainly' proud to be called an Austrian (with the remainder either having no views on the subject or showing no pride). On the other hand, those believing, whatever their personal feelings, that the Austrians already were or were becoming a separate nation had risen steadily from less than 50 per cent in 1956 to over 90 per cent by 1992. Even more declared that, if asked abroad whether they were Germans, they would reply that, no, they were Austrians.*

No people that are constantly agonising over their national identity can be said to possess one. Nonetheless, the Austrians' increased confidence in themselves reflected, apart from the prosperity they were basking in, satisfaction both with their neutral status and with their future as a small state – each of which received solid support in all opinion polls. This confidence eventually led them to confront the issue of their Nazi past head-on, though, to begin with, only academically. From 8 to 10 March 1985, the Vienna Institute for Science and Art held the first-ever formal symposium on Austrian de-Nazification. It represented, as the organisers themselves declared, the breaking of what had hitherto been 'almost a taboo' on the subject. The title of the published proceedings pulled no punches. It translated as: 'Suppressed Guilt and Failed Atonement'.

The academics had got in first, but only just. The following year these same issues of guilt and atonement leapt on to the centre of the political stage.

---

* It was interesting that a larger proportion, 10 per cent of Styrians and 15 per cent of Carinthians, declared themselves to be German, showing the persistence of the old purely racial feeling along the ethnic borders.

IV

The Awakening

IN THE VERY LAST YEARS of their millennium, the Austrians were confronted with three successive challenges, each of which was to shape their character and their destiny. The first forced them to face up belatedly to their role as the conscripts of Hitler's Third Reich. The second presented them with a Danube Basin which had suddenly delivered itself from Soviet Communism and was thus open again, without restriction, to all the traditional ties with Vienna. The third obliged them to decide their own future in a free Europe and, with it, the future of that cosy neutrality they had wrapped themselves up in for the past four decades.

What obliged the Austrians to confront their Nazi past was, of course, the famous 'Waldheim Affair'. Kurt Waldheim* was Austrian Foreign Minister for two years between 1968 and 1970, and became Secretary-General of the United Nations, where he had served as Austria's Permanent Representative, in 1972. Almost from the day he was appointed to this most prestigious post in international diplomacy, Waldheim commenced lobbying to get his five-year term renewed. He succeeded, partly due to his own single-minded ruthlessness but partly because of the appealing credentials of his country: small, neutral, harmless, but also civilised and decent.

Ironically, it was the last aspects of that image that Waldheim was himself to shatter when in 1986, four years after his reluctant leave-taking from the United Nations, he was campaigning to become Federal President of Austria. This was to have been the dream ending of a dream career: six years in office as head of state virtually guaranteed, with the prospect of a second term if the tactics applied so successfully in New

---

* The family was of Czech origin, and bore the distinctly unattractive surname of Waclevek before changing to the German version.

York could be repeated in Vienna. The dream was to turn into a nightmare, for himself and for his country

The furore over Waldheim's undisclosed wartime record, which erupted during the 1986 election campaign, was not, at least in its immediate origins, a Jewish conspiracy. It is, however, clear that without the weight of the American east coast Jewish lobby pressing remorselessly from across the Atlantic, the controversy would never have grown into such a major domestic and international scandal. This lobby had in fact shown some early interest in Waldheim's past while he was living among them in New York. His personal staff recall that one day during his first term as Secretary-General, he received out of the blue a detailed questionnaire from a Jewish Congressman, Mr Solarz, concerning his wartime record. Waldheim was both irritated and puzzled by the letter, and replied in an abrupt and perfunctory manner. Such evasiveness was a mistake he was to repeat with far more serious consequences later on. For the time being, however, Mr Solarz appeared to have been silenced and the issue laid to rest.

It started to come to life in somewhat bizarre fashion while Waldheim's presidential campaign, as candidate of the right-wing People's Party, was being prepared. Veterans of the Austrian Army – some of them imperial, some republican, some Hitlerite, and a few who were all three – had erected, on military premises in Vienna, a commemoration tablet for Alexander Loehr, one of the 172 Austrians who had reached general's rank under the Nazi regime. This touched off a trail of research interest into Loehr and all he stood for. The veterans were honouring him as a comrade-in-arms who had fought bravely under all the flags he had been called upon to serve, for his earliest medals dated from the First World War. Those decorations were beyond reproach, but his record in the world war which followed posed severe problems for, as Colonel-General Loehr, he had commanded the German Army Group E in the Balkans, taking over supreme command in that desperate theatre of operations during the final months of the fighting.

Excepting only the Russian campaign, this was the most brutal of all the European battlefields. At the turn of the year 1944–45, Loehr's Army Group had retreated into Yugoslavia from Greece together with the rest of the German forces.* Then, after being driven out of Serbia

---

* For once, Hitler had not ordered his soldiers to stand fast and fight to the last man; the looming threat of the Red Army, moving westwards up the Danube Basin, made it vital to draw all available divisions closer to the Reich.

by a combined offensive led by Tito's partisans (now grouped into four field armies more than 800,000 strong), Loehr made his last Balkan stand in Croatia, the Hitlerite puppet state led by that odious native Fascist Ante Pavelić. Odious or not, Pavelić and his Ustashi forces were the only armed support Loehr could count on. His Army Group ended up with eighteen Croatian divisions alongside the seventeen of his own men.

All partisan warfare has a particularly ruthless streak, and the cruelties intensified during these last months of the fighting. Following the pattern already established in Macedonia and Bosnia during the retreat, the Germans now razed Serbian villages to the ground, sometimes burying the civilian population under the ashes. When partisan forces were overrun, they were more likely to face mass execution than captivity. The partisans, not surprisingly, retorted in kind. Loehr's men had often come across the bodies of their comrades which had been hideously mutilated before being despatched. Compared with the campaigns in North Africa, Italy or Normandy, this resembled a battle of savages, accentuated by that racial ferocity which is endemic in the Balkans. For Loehr, it was all for nothing, as he had known it would be. All he could do at the end was to pilot as many as possible of his own men westwards away from the advancing Russians and into captivity behind the American and British lines. He reached those lines in May 1945, and his behaviour on getting there did not lack nobility. Instead of sharing the comparative safety he had secured for his troops, he decided to go back of his own free will to Yugoslavia in order to supervise an orderly military capitulation to the partisans. When his Chief of Staff asked him in astonishment what on earth he would be returning to, Loehr replied: 'Without any doubt, to my death.' It was an accurate prediction. He was promptly arrested and later arraigned as a war criminal for the widespread execution of partisans carried out by his Army Group according to specific guidelines for reprisals laid down by Hitler on 22 December 1943. He was executed in Yugoslavia on 16 February 1947.*

Loehr's story is not without interest in itself as portraying the fate of one Austrian officer who served Hitler's army conscientiously to the

---

* Loehr's decision to face the music was in stark contrast to the behaviour of Pavelić, who, with his leading Ustashi cronies, fled to Italy early in May 1945, leaving his army and his puppet state to fend for themselves. From Italy, he made his way to the standing Nazi refuge of South America, returning to Europe ten years later to die, unpunished, in Madrid.

bitter end, whatever reservations he may have had about the Nazi political regime. But its main significance is that perched on a lowly rung of his command had been the Austrian presidential candidate of 1986. Apart from bewilderingly frequent spells of home leave,* Kurt Waldheim served in the Balkans with the Army Group E continuously from the spring of 1942 right down to those last months in Croatia three years later. His rank was never higher than first lieutenant, and his duties ranged from mere interpreter with the Italian forces in Greece to low-ranking service with the so-called 'Ic' section of Army Group intelligence. This was a purely headquarters assignment mainly concerned, like all such postings in the German Army, with the preparation of daily situation reports based on incoming information from the battlefronts. As anyone with any knowledge of military matters would know – and anyone who had actually served in such a headquarters of any army could confirm – this was a minor if important desk job which was completely divorced from field-work or operations of any kind.

Some of the wilder accusations made forty years later that Waldheim had actually participated in reprisals against the partisans by pulling the trigger himself could therefore be refuted not by any evidence about his character or behaviour but by the plain facts about his job. It is indeed doubtful whether the Lieutenant ever fired his pistol in anger while in the Balkans. Even the '*Odluka*', or formal charge of war crimes, laid against him by the Yugoslav government on 18 December 1947 did not accuse him of taking part in any reprisals, but of knowing full well that they were taking place because of the relevant paperwork crossing his Ic desk. This charge could hardly be refuted and was indeed brought by the Yugoslavs in '*Odlukas*' issued against German staff officers who had served anywhere and in any capacity in the Balkan campaign. Some of the testimony produced in the Waldheim case turned out, on much later examination, to be distinctly dubious. But, dubious or not, it was of no importance at the time. Waldheim was not even informed of the case, and his file, together with 25,000 others considered not serious or not convincing enough to investigate, eventually landed up in a building on Park Avenue, New York, where they

---

* For 'study leave' at Vienna University, for 'rest leave' at Baden, for thyroid treatment, for marriage, for transferring his wife from Vienna to the mountains, and for several other unspecified absences.

mouldered away for decades.* It is indeed ironic to think that, throughout one of these decades, Secretary-General Waldheim had sat high above them in his forty-second-floor office, seemingly quite oblivious to the '*Odluka*' on First Lieutenant Waldheim buried away close by. At a private talk during his election campaign, he was asked whether he had ever had any inkling about this precarious coincidence. His reaction was unconsciously revealing. 'Well, now, do you think that if I *had* only known . . . ?'** And there the reply tailed off.

Waldheim may have never known about the '*Odluka*'. But what gave impetus to the controversy which now erupted was that, forty years later, nobody in Austria except him (and his wife) had been told anything of the circumstances in which that war crimes charge had been laid. Here, Waldheim personified precisely the general amnesia of his countrymen. Ever since the end of the war, he had behaved as though its unpleasant and potentially embarrassing aspects were not just behind him but had simply never existed. The original German version of his memoirs contains just one sentence about the final years of his military career: 'Shortly before the end of the war I was in the area of Trieste.' It is hard to imagine a more inadequate, indeed deceitful, description of Waldheim's service in Army Group E's final bloody stand against the partisans in Yugoslavia. Even this one reference was omitted from the English-language translation which appeared in 1985 and was used as the basis of all other foreign editions. Exactly forty years before, Waldheim had listed 'The Balkans' (alongside France and Russia) as the campaigns of his military service from 15 August 1939 to 9 May 1945. But that was in the *curriculum vitae* he had been obliged to submit to secure registration as a post-war civil servant, and had been buried away ever since in the records of the District Court at Baden. Forty years later, he was happy for it to be concealed completely from the world. (The story that the excision of that short but significant sentence had been just a space-saving decision of his English-language editors strains credulity to the limit.) One sentence stating baldly that he had ended the war unhappily in a campaign with brutalities committed on both sides might have saved him.

---

* They were held under very restricted conditions, with only seventeen members of the United Nations enjoying the right of access. Even that was granted in full in only a handful of cases, such as the Eichmann prosecution.
** Conversation with the author, Vienna, February 1986. Waldheim's actual words were: '*Na, glauben Sie wenn ich nur gewusst hätte . . . ?*'

As it was, this shrouded background meant that the revelations and accusations suddenly published in February 1986 (simultaneously in the Viennese magazine *Profil* and the *New York Times*) stood out in a startlingly glaring light. Despite the intensive research which had preceded the articles, some of the charges could be dismissed at once. The accusation, for example, that he was a Nazi flew directly in the face of the truth. Gestapo records seized by Western intelligence after the war showed that on 2 August 1940 both the young Waldheim and his father were classed as fierce anti-Nazis 'who had openly demonstrated their hatred for our movement'. It was suggested that, as the son had now been called up for military service, his past might be forgiven 'if he proved himself a good German soldier'. The official who wrote that comment never dreamt that, in another world purged of Hitlerism, it was precisely that military service which was to prove Waldheim's potential ruin.

The second key allegation, that he had been 'involved in war crimes in the Balkans', was also, as has been explained, unlikely, if involvement is taken to mean personal and physical participation in atrocities. It was the third main charge which, though unprovable, was to do Waldheim the greatest damage. This was that he had been 'involved' (again the same slippery word), or at least had knowledge of, the deportation of Greek Jews while he was serving under Army Group E. The facts of these deportations, which started in Salonika in July 1942 and continued until the last transports of Jews from the Greek islands two years later, are well documented. Again, there is no shred of evidence that Lieutenant Waldheim ever drew up the deportation lists, let alone pushed the victims into boats or railway trucks. Indeed, those repeated absences on home leave often coincided with the actual shipment dates. But that he had no knowledge of these happenings is hard to accept, and was never categorically denied by his defendants (though it was by him!). The central question as to how far knowledge of evil constitutes an evil in itself we shall come to later.

True or false, it was these deportation charges which raised the American Jewish lobby up in arms against Waldheim, and an awesome display of its power it proved, especially when linked with the parallel reaction in Israel itself. On the domestic electoral scene, the Austrian Socialists naturally made full play of the campaigning gift which had fallen into their lap.* Ever since 1945, they had come to regard the Presidential

* There is no hard evidence that they had actually manufactured it, though they certainly helped with the wrappings. Independent academic research into the role of Army

Palace in the Hofburg as their natural habitat. They were desperate to cling on to it as a power-base in view of their parliamentary election setbacks, and even went so far as to persuade Bruno Kreisky (now an ex-Chancellor) to make the somewhat shabby pronouncement that he 'no longer regarded Waldheim as his friend'. It was all in vain. They had a colourless candidate who was relatively unknown even in his own country. The People's Party, on the other hand, could present their candidate as the most famous of Austrians, 'The man the world trusts', as one of their key slogans went. In June 1986, at the second round of the polling, Waldheim was duly elected to the Presidency by the fairly comfortable majority of nearly 54 per cent.*

Any hopes that his election would damp down the controversy were soon dashed. Though President Reagan sent the customary message of congratulation to Vienna, Waldheim's success at the polls only stoked the fire. The Israeli ambassador to Vienna was promptly recalled to Jerusalem 'for consultations'. More seriously, the United States ambassador, Ronald Lauder, who came from a wealthy Jewish family, boycotted the swearing-in ceremony on 8 July. The domestic debate over Waldheim now became elevated into an international issue; and there were various reasons why it was the American political establishment which raised the stakes. There had never been much love lost between Washington and the United Nations, which was regarded as an anti-American forum of Third World lobbying. Even less love had been lost between the State Department and Waldheim who, in American eyes, had taken up an unacceptably pro-Arab and anti-Israeli stance as Secretary-General.

Most important of all, the World Jewish Congress, which was determined to emerge as the keeper of the Holocaust flame, had decided to burn Waldheim in it, using the question of the Greek Jews as tinder.** For the Republicans, facing tricky Senate elections in the autumn, the Jewish vote was too significant to risk losing, especially as much of the national press was backing the anti-Waldheim movement. The

---

Group E, prompted by the Loehr commemoration tablet, seems to have started the affair rolling.

* It is worth recalling that Waldheim had campaigned for the Presidency fifteen years before, losing to the Socialist candidate in 1971, a year before his election as United Nations Secretary-General. On this occasion he had been slightly more forthcoming about his wartime activities.

** The Congress President, the splenetic Edgar Bronfman, accused Waldheim outright of being 'part and parcel of the Nazi death machine'.

campaign's greatest success came on 27 April 1987 when Kurt Waldheim, now almost a year into his presidential term of office, was placed
on the 'Watch List' of the American Department of Justice. This decision
virtually banned Waldheim, as an 'undesirable alien', from entering the
United States because of his alleged part in wartime atrocities.

The process had the great convenience that it could be implemented
without the need to produce documentary proof of any misdeeds. Under
the so-called Holtzmann Amendment of 1978 to the Immigration Act,
all that was needed was a *prima facie* case. It was a bizarre interpretation
of justice; the amendment amounted to a charter for denunciation.

But such was the law of the land of the free. The Justice Department,
which had secured access to the *'Odluka'* file, duly repeated its accusations to a horrified Austrian government, but declined to produce any
documentary confirmation. This was declared superfluous on the
grounds that mere membership, in any capacity, of any organisation
which had committed war crimes made each individual guilty. That
Waldheim was, however, a special target was brought home to the
then Austrian ambassador in Washington, Dr Thomas Klestil (later to
succeed as Federal President), when he called at the Ministry of Justice
to protest. The official who received him had, pinned up on the wall
behind his desk, a caricature of the posters once used to hunt down
Wild West bandits. The text read: 'Wanted: Kurt Waldheim'.

Austria could only turn to the judgement of international opinion,
and it was in this looking-glass that the wartime dilemma of the Austrian
nation as a whole was now to be reflected. In May 1987, Waldheim
had himself asked his Socialist Chancellor, Dr Vranitsky, to set up an
international commission of military historians to pronounce on the
case. This was duly established under the chairmanship of a Swiss
academic, Hans Rudolf Kurz.*

The Kurz Commission** started its work in Vienna on 1 September

* The author was sounded out by the Austrian ambassador in London at the time as
to whether he would consider accepting the chair. He was very happy (and, as things
turned out, very fortunate) to decline on the grounds that, though he had served himself
as a General Staff officer in the area, his books included only one on military history.
(See Manfried Rauchensteiner, *Die Historiker Kommission*, Vienna, 1988.)
** Its members, selected by the Chairman, included an American general, James L.
Collins, and academics from West Germany, Belgium and Israel, with a co-opted expert
from Greece. Britain was eventually represented by a lecturer from Surrey University,
Gerald Fleming, who had done much work on Nazism and the Holocaust. Contro-
versially, no Austrian representative was allowed.

1987 and sat for 160 days of deliberations which were sometimes leisurely, sometimes frantic and often heated. The final report, which it presented to the Austrian Chancellor on 8 February 1988, was far from being the political 'whitewash' which the press had been predicting. Indeed, so far as Waldheim's reputation was concerned, it was distinctly grey in colour. On the one hand, he was cleared of committing any personal acts of atrocity or other culpable deeds during his time in the Balkans, and it was accepted that he never even exercised any power of command during his service there. He was also cleared of any espousal of National-Socialist ideology – a belated acknowledgement of the verdict which the Gestapo had itself passed on him and his father back in 1940.

On the negative side, the commission found that Waldheim had been 'instrumental' in the deportation of Greek Jews, though it was not specified how he, or the Wehrmacht in general, had been involved. A similar vagueness enveloped the broader charge levelled against him, that he had incurred 'a certain guilt' simply by his 'proximity to legally incriminating acts and orders'. Austrian jurists tore this concept to pieces on legal grounds. As for the man in the street, he was uncomfortably aware that a similar yardstick might well be applied to him or to any of his fellow-Austrians. That, of course, was precisely the problem: was even passivity during the Nazi era a form of participation?

It was from Britain that some comfort, and perhaps some enlighten-ment, came. A so-called 'International Television Trial' was staged on the Waldheim affair in June 1988, for the preparation of which twenty-five researchers had been at work for several weeks in fifteen countries. An official of the US Department of Justice, which had produced the 'Watch List' decision, led the 'prosecution'. Lord Rawlinson, a former British Attorney-General, led the 'defence', and he won hands down. At least on the small screen, Waldheim was virtually acquitted. The panel of five 'judges', headed by the eminent Sir Frederick Lawton, unanimously declared that the evidence they had heard was 'not enough to make it probable that Lieutenant Waldheim committed any of the war crimes alleged against him in this enquiry'. More significant in the broader context of guilt was the precept, later pronounced by Sir Frederick, that: 'A person does not commit a war crime merely because he knows others have committed some crimes, nor because he worked alongside those who committed them.' The Austrians, and all the men in the street of Hitler's Europe could breathe a little more freely for that.

Important though the 'TV Trial' had been, it remained a media event rather than an official proceeding. Proper authority was, however, lent to its findings in October of the following year. The British Ministry of Defence had by then concluded an exhaustive re-examination of the old Yugoslav charges that Lieutenant Waldheim had been involved in war crimes against British commandos captured in the Balkans.* Its findings, which were formally presented to Parliament after an eighteen-month inquiry, not only declared that 'as a junior staff officer, Dr Waldheim did not have the power either to order or prevent the fate of the commandos or indeed affect the outcome in any way', but added the all-important sentence: 'Knowledge in such circumstances is not itself a crime.'

All this now became part of the official record on the affair. What was never published however was the reaction of the World Jewish Congress and its supporters in the American Justice Department to the British findings. This American anti-Waldheim lobby had thus far been mainly responsible for an international boycott of the Austrian President in all Western and, indeed, neutral capitals.** Even the Communists had joined in, so that he was unable, for example, to visit the Soviet Union, along with the capitals of the former Western occupying powers.

There was alarm among his opponents in Washington that the official British clearance of Waldheim might let him out of his cage. So much so that, on the day after the report was published, Neil Sher, who as Head of the Special Investigations Office in the Justice Department had been primarily responsible for the Watch List decision, arrived hot-foot in London. His mission was to lobby the Ministry of Defence and other Whitehall authorities to make sure that Britain would not now relax its own ban on contacts with Waldheim. He succeeded. The British Foreign Office saw no reason to break ranks in a Western boycott which was being led by its mighty American ally and followed even by Austria's neighbours and natural supporters, the Bonn Republic and Switzerland.

Similar American pressure was exerted on Turkey when it was learnt that that country had invited Waldheim on an official visit, scheduled for November 1988. The State Department was reported to have

---

* A 'Führerbefehl' had ordered that any caught should be executed.
** Throughout his six-year term, Waldheim's state or official visits abroad were confined almost entirely to the Arab countries he had backed as Secretary-General: Pakistan, Jordan, Saudi Arabia, Oman, Kuwait, Syria, Tunisia, Egypt and so on. He also managed to get to Japan for the coronation of the new Emperor, and to Liechtenstein for the funeral of its ruler.

threatened a cut-off in American funds if the Turkish government did not change its mind. This it eventually did, and a private trip to Istanbul was substituted for the official visit to Ankara. Senegal and other African countries which had featured on a proposed regional tour for Waldheim proved even easier to browbeat. In March 1992, only a month before new presidential elections were held in Austria,* the West German Chancellor, Helmut Kohl, was persuaded to come to Munich, where he had lunch with Waldheim after a prize-giving ceremony. Even this fleeting contact with the 'Austrian pariah' set off a wave of protest from America's east coast.

It has been necessary to recount this whole saga in some detail because it marked a turning-point, not just in one man's fortunes, but in the Austrians' perception of themselves and in the perception of Austria by the outside world. The nation had been put in quarantine, alongside its President, for six uncomfortable years. During that time, it had been forced to shed some carefully nurtured delusions and illusions. The Austrians, like Waldheim, had got used to thinking of themselves purely as victims of Nazism, with no regard for the part they had played in its regime of evil, the Holocaust included. Both felt that Hitler's war was safely behind them, shut away in unvisited archives, yellowed newspaper files, and even behind the locked doors of their own memories. Both believed that the outside world felt respect and even affection for them, and it must be said that the outside world had given them every reason for that belief. For four decades after achieving independence, Austria had again become, to most foreign eyes, the sweet land of *The Sound of Music*; of Strauss and Mozart; of Danube steamers and alpine ski-runs.

That outside vision had now been shattered, at least temporarily, and the Austrians themselves had been brought up once more against the challenge which had always threatened their sense of identity – the German complication in race, in allegiance and in ideology. They finally emerged from the Waldheim years not so much transformed as strengthened in some of their less admirable qualities. They tended to be more anti-Semitic than ever and – ironically for a people who flourished on tourism – more enclosed. The world had, after all, angrily fenced them inside their 'Isle of the Blessed', making them, for the time being, more

---

* It speaks volumes for Waldheim's dogged ambition – and thick skin – that he had intended to run again. He was only dissuaded by a loud and unanimous chorus of protest from his advisers.

defiantly insular than ever. Fortunately, as we shall see, history was soon to help them think otherwise.

Before leaving the whole affair, it is worth recording how Waldheim himself looked back on those six disastrous years in office. During his very last days in the Hofburg, he unburdened his feelings to a private visitor* who had known him ever since his time as Foreign Minister. These feelings were all incandescent and mostly unrepentant. His ire against the Watch List and the Holtzmann Amendment was however understandable: 'If they bar people on a *prima facie* basis and just because they were in a certain area in wartime, they could just as easily have barred any of our army cooks.'

His denial of even knowing about the deportation of Greek Jews was emphatic, though less convincing. As for the Western powers, he felt gratitude only towards the British, whom he described as 'the only people who have given me a fair trial'. He added that, soon after the Ministry of Defence verdict had been published, he had made a private approach through an intermediary to the then Prime Minister, Mrs Thatcher, who had entertained him handsomely in London when he was Secretary-General. Had not the time come, she was asked, for some British gesture of reconciliation, perhaps even an invitation? Her reaction, as passed back to him, had not been encouraging. 'A visit? Oh, no, that would be bad news!'

He seemed particularly sensitive about his opposite number in Western Germany, the highly respected Federal President, Dr Weizsäcker: 'I was a Lieutenant and an Italian interpreter. Weizsäcker was a Major in Counter-Intelligence.'**

His visitor pointed out that Dr Weizsäcker had openly avowed his part in the misdeeds of the Nazi era and called upon the German people to acknowledge their own responsibility. Why had he, Waldheim, not 'done a Weizsäcker'?

The reply was characteristic of the man: 'Yes, I admit, I handled my publicity very badly. But how could I, as President, apologise for all Austrians? Some were not even born at the time.'

* The author, who was in Vienna at the end of June 1992, making one of a series of historical documentaries for German-language television. On an impulse, he rang the Hofburg and asked if he might call in. He was promptly invited for a *tête-à-tête* which lasted nearly one and a half hours.
** Waldheim tactfully did not mention that the German President's father, Ernst von Weizsäcker, had been sentenced at Nuremberg to five years in prison for his part in running Hitler's Foreign Office.

The argument was purely legalistic. Even the admission had been a regret expressed over bad tactics, not an apology for devious behaviour. His visitor left the magnificent Hofburg office, where Waldheim sat at the very desk of the great imperial reformer, Joseph II, hoping that the Austrian people had learnt a better lesson than their President in coming to terms with the past.

This seemed to be the case. At least they were to respond well to the two challenges of self-examination which were now to confront them in quick succession. The first of these had presented itself during those six years when Waldheim and the republic had been in quarantine. The crumbling of Soviet Communism throughout what had once been the 'Eastern bloc' had begun when he took office and was complete when he left it. The Danube Basin, with which Austria was so closely linked by geography, history and tradition, now lay open, expectantly, in freedom. How was Vienna to respond?

There never was, and almost certainly never will be, any effort to regain that political hegemony over the region which Vienna exercised for centuries under the Habsburg sceptre. The imperial dream faded away with the hopes of the last of the die-hard monarchists. How indeed could they cling to a concept which had been forsworn in person by the heir to the Habsburg claims? By now, that concept lay beyond the psychological as well as the physical bounds of the republic's strength.

On the other hand, very real possibilities had opened up on the economic front. Geography bestowed most of them: Vienna lay less than fifty miles from the borders of Hungary and both the Slovak and Czech Republics. Apart from the Danube itself, the old communication lines of the Monarchy bound them all naturally together.* The prerequisites were thus in place for Austria to become a sort of turntable for East–West trade and investment. This was a prospect the Austrians now seized with both hands and developed to the best of the limited capacity of a nation only seven millions strong. Building in many cases on existing facilities, foreign firms set up their centres for East–West trade by the hundreds on Austrian soil, encouraged by special tax concessions.

Besides receiving this bounty, the Austrians launched an economic

---

* On early post-war trips by car to Hungary, it always struck the author that, even during the worst Stalinist period of the Cold War, when all the Eastern bloc states were supposed to be orientated towards Moscow, the road between Budapest and Vienna continued to be marked as Route No. 1, in both directions.

drive of their own. By 1993, some 7500 joint-venture agreements had been concluded between Austrian firms and East European partners. Austrian banks expanded their financial networks eastwards; Austrian trade representation was increased in all Eastern capitals; many new regional offices were opened up; and training programmes were established in Austria for East European managerial talent at all levels. Clearly, this effort was overshadowed by the giant industrial takeover and financial investment programmes launched in the region by Germany (which often operated under the nominal cover of an Austrian enterprise). The same imbalance appeared in the new patterns of East–West trade, where Germany again predominated, despite Austria's resolute efforts at expansion. But at least this was more of a partnership than a rivalry, and a partnership, moreover, in which Austria acknowledged her role as being (yet again) the junior member.

It was a very different story in the one field where Austria sought to plough a furrow all her own and, with it, to make the deepest mark. As Dollfuss had so passionately proclaimed, if there were still such a thing as an 'Austrian mission' left for Republican Vienna to discharge in the Danube Basin, that mission was a cultural one, or it was nothing. Indeed, he had added, it was this mission which made the Austrians the 'true Germans'. The traditionalists of the Second Republic had, from the first, echoed his call and tried to put a modest programme into operation even when their eastern neighbours were held fast in the Communist grip.

When that grip was shaken off, the cultural standard-bearers of Vienna saw their chance and took it. In doing so, they found themselves engaged in yet another of those centuries-old tussles with the Germans. There was no question here of a consistently harmonious partnership, or of an Austrian acceptance of inferiority. This was a real battle for the hearts and minds of the old lands of the Monarchy. More significant for our story, it was also a final struggle to preserve and project an Austrian identity.

The uneasy relationship on the cultural front between Vienna and Bonn had begun before Eastern Europe was fully opened up, and it had already led, behind the scenes, to outright confrontation. Thus, on 31 January 1975, the Austrian Foreign Ministry had felt obliged to instruct all its cultural missions abroad that, though contacts with the German Goethe Institutes were to be generally welcomed, there were some distinct exceptions. These applied whenever these German cultural bodies featured Austrian artists, musicians, writers or lecturers in their programmes, thus presenting them as though they were Germans.* On all such occasions, the Austrian Institutes based in the same city were to decline their cooperation and even to consider boycotting any social gatherings involved.

Four years later, on 14 November 1979, after diplomatic discussions between the two governments, these severe guidelines were somewhat relaxed. No objections would henceforth be raised, for example, where Goethe Institutes featured Austrian artists who had their established residence in West Germany. Moreover, as the Bonn government had now instructed all its cultural missions to stress the separate nationality and background of any Austrians appearing in their programmes, cooperation was permissible, provided these instructions were clearly being carried out. Much had to be left, the circular concluded, to the judgement of the Austrian officials on the spot. But it ended on an unambiguous note: 'In all marginal cases, the principle should be followed that both the emphasis on, and the regard for, Austria's separate cultural identity ['*Kulturelle Eigenständigkeit*'] should have absolute priority over any other consideration.'

That principle Austria struggled to preserve after the Iron Curtain had been swept aside, though the main problem now was budgetary. A vastly wealthier Germany launched an ambitious cultural offensive throughout Eastern Europe (partly to reinforce its economic drive), and the Austrians simply lacked the funds to match it. Though they had their own Institutes in major Western centres and in the capitals of most of the Eastern states (which they had also peppered, from 1990 onwards, with libraries of Austrian literature), this operation was dwarfed in size by the worldwide network set up by the Germans. Austria had made a special plea in Bonn to be left to operate alone, at least in the provincial cities of the old Monarchy like Lemberg/Lvov, once the capital of Habsburg Galicia.** Assurances to this effect were given but, as often as

---

* The Austrians complained that even their finest poets, playwrights and novelists were being culturally 'hijacked'. Grillparzer, Rilke, even Kraus and Musil were sometimes being passed off as Germans.
** Already in 1978 the Austrians had launched a special cooperation programme along these traditionalist lines. The so-called Arge Project was designed to promote cultural as well as economic and communication links between Carinthia, Styria, Salzburg and Upper Austria on the one hand, and the South Tyrol, Venice, Lombardy and other old imperial lands on the other.

not, Goethe Institutes nonetheless popped up in these cities as well. This all lent uncomfortable emphasis to talk – heard more loudly after German reunification – of Austria being 'the third Germany'. Vienna's cultural warriors were fighting for much more than Grillparzer.

The Austrian cultural lobby had tackled this task manfully in Eastern Europe. Almost as their millennium came round, the Austrians as a whole then had to turn about and face the challenge of Western Europe. After much head-scratching and soul-searching, their government had finally applied for membership of the European Union – with all that that implied for one of the continent's two official 'permanent neutrals'.* But what would the Austrian people say in the referendum which was ultimately to decide the issue? The omens were not good that they were prepared to leave the shores of their 'Isle of the Blessed' and venture into the open seas; and these early indications had nothing to do with Brussels. There was, for example, the sobering (and in some ways shaming) episode of 'Expo 95', the World Exhibition scheduled to be staged that year jointly in Vienna and Budapest.

The plan to hold the 'twin city' event in the two capitals of the old Monarchy had been launched as far back as October 1986. The following year, Austria's new Socialist Chancellor, Franz Vranitzky, and his Hungarian opposite number Károly Grósz, formally announced the resolve of their two governments to proceed with the plan. National committees and joint committees were formed, and in December 1989 (after Miami, the only surviving challenger in the field, had dropped out) the 1995 venue was officially awarded to the two Danubian cities. The way seemed open for Austria to emerge from its neutral shell and to stamp its positive mark again on 'Mitteleuropa'.

The chance was never taken as, over the next eighteen months, enthusiasm for the project slowly seeped away. Jorg Heider, the telegenic young political freebooter who had assumed control of the 'third force' Freedom Party, glimpsed a publicity opportunity and, abandoning his initial support for the plan, pressed instead for a referendum. The main parties dithered, while the politicians of the Vienna municipality indulged in an orgy of back-stabbing over the issue which was remarkable even by their traditions of intrigue. As a result, when a popular vote was held in the capital on 14–16 May 1991, nearly two-thirds

* The other, Switzerland, did not apply. Sweden, the *de facto* neutral, was admitted along with the other Nordic nations.

(64.85 per cent, to be precise) declared themselves against the exhibition, in what had been a high level of polling. The government accordingly withdrew the candidature of which, five years before, it had been so proud.*

Political in-fighting and budgetary constraints had certainly played their part in the fiasco. But underneath all these surface currents ran a popular swell of parochialism and sheer panic at taking any major decision which would involve exposure to the outside world at large. Above all, it would have involved inescapable responsibility, something which the Austrians had always been reluctant to shoulder and which those decades of neutrality had conveniently absolved them from. All this was expressed in some of the popular objections to the project now being muttered in Vienna. These ranged from fears that a world exhibition would create traffic chaos and worsen parking problems to anxiety that it would lead to an explosion in house prices.

1991 brought other challenges to Austria's island mentality and indeed to that neutral status which enveloped it. As Austria had become a member of the United Nations Security Council at the beginning of the year, she was forced to declare her hand when the Gulf War erupted soon afterwards and the world body sanctioned joint military action against Iraq, the aggressor. In Vienna, however, they hesitated over laying down a single card, let alone a full hand, fearful that any participation in United Nations reprisals against Saddam Hussein might conflict with their 1955 pledge of strict neutrality. The most that the government eventually conceded was to allow over-flights and ground transit facilities for the international force being despatched to rescue Kuwait. Even that concession was late in coming. It was not exactly an inspiring contribution to a cause which had united almost the whole of the world community.

1991 also saw the disintegration of Communist Yugoslavia, with the independence declaration of Slovenia and Croatia and the prompt engagement of Serbian forces against them. This not only produced the spectre of war along Austria's southern frontier;** it also raised up

* For some time, it looked as though Budapest was prepared to stage the event on its own, which would have symbolised the rapid emergence of post-Communist Hungary as the leader of the Danube Basin. However, economic stringencies eventually forced Budapest to back out as well.
** In the first phase of the fighting, shells fell on Austrian soil and there were repeated violations of Austrian air space.

some ghosts of history. France, true to her pro-Serb traditions which had been laid before the First World War, started off by supporting Belgrade. Austria could not fail to back the two nearly-declared republics, each of which had once been a crown land of the old Monarchy. But even here there were divisions at the heart of the coalition government. The Socialist Chancellor Vranitsky began, like the French, by leaning towards the Serbs, in the hope of preserving some sort of Yugoslav federal structure. (He had paid an official visit to Belgrade in April 1990.) His right-wing Foreign Minister, Alois Mock, did not share these illusory hopes. Indeed, he openly opposed them, seeking an even-handed approach, and with his declaration of 6 May 1991 he became the first voice to call for European mediation in the crisis. On the whole, therefore, neither the Austrians nor their leaders seemed to be sure where they were heading, or even where they belonged in this rapidly-changing world when the question of European Union membership loomed up.

Brussels had welcomed their formal application to join. Austria appeared as a prosperous and democratic candidate which would have no problems in fitting in with a prosperous and democratic Community, and which would bring with her unique qualifications as a link with Eastern Europe. The Austrians themselves began with no such confidence. Indeed, in the early stages of the public debate, they seemed hopelessly divided on the issue. Polls in 1992, for example, showed that opponents outnumbered supporters, with a bewildering mixture of reasons being advanced on either side. The supporters argued that, among other things, membership would bring cheaper goods on to the home market, help exports, give Austrian youth better work prospects, modernise Austrian industry and attract more tourists. Two significant advantages were glimpsed away from the economic front. Membership, it was argued, would give Austria added military security and would mean that, as a member of a great community, she would no longer feel like 'an insignificant small state'.

The opponents had an even longer and more varied list of arguments. Joining Europe, they claimed, would impoverish Austrian farmers, spell ruin for many firms which could no longer compete, flood the country with foreign workers,* prevent Austria having any policy of her own

---

* This antipathy had already set in after 'economic refugees' by the tens of thousands had poured in with the fall of the Iron Curtain.

and put her at the mercy of the large powers, block her transit roads solid with traffic, cause her cherished traditions to fade away, diminish her cultural heritage, threaten her generous social system with its near-universal pension provisions,* lead to the mass purchase by foreigners of Austrian land and property, and (a revealing objection) mean that bank accounts could no longer be anonymous.** There was also a reluctance on their part to abandon that now-familiar neutrality which had become so identified with the good life. The coalition government had echoed this feeling by formally declaring that Austria's international status would remain unaffected by membership of the Community. It was a last and somewhat despairing cry of 'Neutrality first'.

Then, as the referendum day, 12 June 1994, loomed up on the horizon, the opposition lobby suddenly began to shrink in size with every day that passed as the waverers made up their minds. Opinion polls taken a fortnight before the great day showed the 'Yes' votes jumping to almost double that of the 'No's', and – despite a certain wary scepticism from the corridors of power – those forecasts proved accurate. When the referendum boxes were emptied and counted, 66.4 per cent had declared themselves in favour of membership, with 33.6 per cent against. There had been no apathy: more than 80 per cent of the electorate had taken part. There was hardly any spoiling protest: less than 1 per cent of the votes cast were invalid.

When the results were analysed in detail – according to provinces, age groups, education, income levels and party affiliations – two sets of reasons emerged behind this resounding pro-European support. The first set was economic, the arguments for added prosperity and broadened opportunity having, in the end, far outweighed the fears. But almost as important were psychological factors: the fear that an Austria which remained outside the Community would not only be politically isolated but vulnerable to security threats like that already being posed

---

* Over 99 per cent of the population had health insurance, and over 1.5 million drew a state pension. This had always been the alpha and omega of Austrian existence. The author recalls being shown a poll, carried out among Styrian schoolchildren in the early post-war years, asking them to name their preferred occupation in life. At the top of the list came 'Pensioner'.

** Jorg Haider and his anti-European fanatics had produced a few farcical objections of their own. Austria's pure Alpine water, they claimed, would be piped direct to Brussels, while Austria could expect in return Spanish yoghurt filled with lice.

along her southern borders. The 'Isle of the Blessed' had become the isle of the nervous, and its inhabitants now wanted to cross this causeway to the Western mainland.

The referendum was a vital event for Europe as a whole, since it laid down a marker for similar polls which were staged later in Scandinavian countries. For Austria it was, of course, a major turning-point in her history. In all but name, the Second Republic had come to an end, since the neutrality which had underpinned it and the isolationism which had stamped it were both now bound to fade. This involved a major exercise in mass re-indoctrination. For forty years, the unfamiliar and unexciting posture of neutrality had been hammered home in all school curricula and all official pronouncements as the natural, almost God-given state for the country. The propaganda was based on a falsehood, or at best a half-truth. We have seen how the Austrian delegation travelled to Moscow for the critical state treaty talks with the coalition split down the middle over the price to be paid for freedom – so much so that it was the Russians who obliged them in the Kremlin to turn their talk of a 'pact-free' status into a formal pledge of permanent neutrality. This vacillation had to be concealed both from the people and from the Western powers at the time. Hence the version – fed by selective quotations – that neutrality on the Swiss model had been the fixed aim of the government all along. Hence the even more dubious phrase incorporated into the text of the Constitutional Law of 26 October which proclaimed the country's neutrality. This declared that the decision had been taken by Austria 'of her own free will'.

Forty years later, when Austria's 'permanent neutrality' had shown itself to be as impermanent as the Soviet Communism which had imposed it, a very different song had to be sung. Without a word of introductory explanation, the government cleared its throat and sang it. Wolfgang Schuessel, the Foreign Minister of the day, declared on 14 May 1995: 'Austria must stop being a passive spectator hiding behind neutrality imposed after the second World War.' That word 'imposed' is worth underlining. The truth about the State Treaty had been admitted at last, after four decades of concealment. The reason, of course, was to prepare the people for the novel and unwelcome prospect of having to pay properly for their own defence. The country had shone in its participation in United Nations peacekeeping operations, but this concealed the fact that, ever since 1955, it had run its armed forces on a shoestring budget, as little as 1.17 per cent of the gross national product, banking on the expectation that if ever a serious military menace loomed up from the east (and from where else would it come?), NATO would intervene in the name of Continental security and do any serious fighting for it.* This was dubbed by critics of the policy 'riding on the running board'.

But full membership of the European Union brought with it the obligation to take a proper share in the common defence of the West, to move from the running board to the back of the driver's cabin. As Foreign Minister Schuessel, who was already under pressure from NATO, went on to warn: 'If we want our say in the international community in the questions that affect us, such as the environment, we must be prepared to take responsibility for our part in security policy.'

Membership had also helped to lay those two bogeys which had plagued the Austrians for so long. They could now once again feel themselves part of a multi-national political structure; not one that they could dominate, as in the days of empire, but one they could serve well, precisely because of the special qualities they had developed under the Monarchy. And, apropos dominance, it was the European Union (to give the Community its new name) which offered the best protection against being totally overshadowed by the giant of a united Germany. Their cultural battle they would have to continue fighting for themselves. But any economic or political challenges posed by this new German colossus would henceforth be met in Brussels.

Above all, the decision of 12 June 1994 was not one which, like so many past turning-points in the Austrians' history, had been imposed on them from above, or dictated from outside. This was no measure laid down under the Habsburg sceptre, no transformation dictated by a Napoleon, a Bismarck, a Hitler or a Khrushchev. For the first time in all their thousand-year saga, the Austrian people had freely determined their own destiny themselves. There could have been no better way to open their second millennium.

---

* One Soviet plot, as revealed by senior Communist defectors, was code-named 'Operation Polavka', and called for the invasion of Tito's Yugoslavia via western Austria by 400,000 Red Army troops.

Perceptions

1684

'Austria above everything, if only she wills it!'

Philipp Wilhelm von Hornigk

1799

'The Austrian has a fatherland, and rightly loves it.'

Friedrich Schiller

1805

'Austria must be preserved. That is absolutely vital for the future good of civilised nations.'

Prince Talleyrand to Napoleon

1831

'Oh Austria, you land of the east! Day will dawn in you as well.'

Anastasius Grün (Count Auersperg)

1848

'Indeed, if this Austria did not exist, then, in the interests of humanity itself, one would have to hasten to create it.'

František Palacký

1849

'Austria must collapse because it is a prison of peoples.'

Moritz Hartmann

c.1850

'That is the curse of our noble house;
To strive irresolute, half way,
With half deeds and half measures.'

Franz Grillparzer, Bruderzwist in Habsburg

1870

'There are a few peoples running around this world of whom one really cannot tell why they exist at all. If I count among those above all the peoples of Austria . . . it is simply in order not to conceal an obvious fact.'

Daniel Spitzer

1871

'Austria must be comprehended as a kind of Asia . . . With this key you may solve all Austrian riddles.'

Ferdinand Kürnberger

1874

'Any German statesman who got the idea of wanting anything in Austria would be ripe for hanging.'

Prince Otto Bismarck

1876

'The fate of Austria is the question of the fate of all Europe and of the whole system of the civilised countries of the earth.'

Karl Vogelsang

1917

'Austria can lead the other countries in the respectful recognition of a supra-national order in the outside world and firm social justice at home; it can do this because its own state concept, its character, and its true being rest on these convictions.'

Hugo von Hofmannstahl

1919

'Language alone does not create a people. The Austrians feel foreign inside themselves to all other Germans.'

Oswald Spengler

1926

'Austria is the face behind the ticket office of the world railway.'

Karl Kraus

1931

'Above all, the Austrian spirit still lives, this age-old and multi-faceted cultural spirit ... It is the antithesis of the Prussian spirit, for its way of life rests on gentleness, not harshness.'

Count Hermann Keyserling

1934

'By his death, Dr Dollfuss has given proof that there really exists a German culture which is worthy of saving.'

THE TIMES

1936

'To be Austrian is not a geographical concept but a spiritual idea, the idea of an ethically enlightened humanity springing from a combination of peoples and classes.'

Oskar Bender

1945

'The polarity between the Austrian nation and a sense of world citizenship is not a contradiction and is the ultimate meaning of our being.'

Edmund Weber

1946

'The Austrian idea can only be understood in terms of space. It was born in space, it is defined by space as is no other concept of nationhood.'

Ludwig Reiter

1981

'The Austrian conceals his soul. He doesn't reveal himself and doesn't say what he *really* thinks, believes, feels about the first and last things concerning God, the state, and his own spirit.'

Friedrich Heer

That selection of sayings about Austrians over the last three hundred years (when Europe began to think of them as a people) was chosen more or less at random. Yet it manages to pick up most of the main threads which have run through their thousand-year story. There is, above all, the tortured symbiosis of the German relationship, which produces some odd contrasts in the verdicts. The earliest praise of Austria comes from two Germans, von Hornigk and Schiller; its earliest condemnation, which was to go down in anti-Habsburg folklore, from an Austrian, Moritz Hartmann. From their greatest poet, Grillparzer, came the oft-quoted lines which sum up the dithering and the evasion of responsibility which were to characterise a nation as well as a dynasty. Their greatest enemy, Bismarck, lays bare the terrible truth which Austria's pan-Germans, down to Otto Bauer on the left and Seyss-Inquart on the right, refused to face: Germany never wanted them – until Hitler came along to accept the offer.

To some extent, all the quotations (and there are many more of these) about the spiritual basis of the Austrian character also reflect the same Teutonic complex. The belief that it was their culture which made them not only the better Germans but also (*pace* Dollfuss and his *Times* obituary) the only true Germans is rooted in the nineteenth century, but has branches which have stretched all along the twentieth century and towards the twenty-first. Yet this particular belief is also nourished from another spring, that of the great multi-national experience handed down from the Habsburg era.

If the Austrians still have a special role to play in the Europe they have joined, it is in that same Danube Basin. If they still have a 'mission' there, it is a cultural one, as well as that of the catalyst, helping to bond together the many races and creeds of the region. As in the days of the Monarchy, this supra-national role will not help them to define their own nationhood more sharply, however far they succeed in distancing themselves from their German cradle.

They have never managed to establish a clear-cut identity for themselves as Austrians (as opposed to Styrians or Tyroleans). Perhaps they never will, and that could be in everyone's interests. They are, after all, like a brew of Germanic tea-leaves on to which, for centuries, Danube water has been poured. And, as all the streams of Central Europe feed into the Danube, there are Magyar and Slav currents which flow incessantly into that great river, and into the Austrian consciousness. There is no pure essence which can be distilled out of this. The mixture is the essence. That is perhaps no bad thing for the Austrians of today, or for the Europe they have joined.

NOTE ON BIBLIOGRAPHY

THIS SHOULD REALLY be entitled 'note about the lack of a bibliography'. Over the years I have grown increasingly impatient with the
acres of valuable paper taken up by lengthy book lists which are of
primary interest only to the scholar or very specialised reader. Their
desire for source material can surely be met by referring them to the
extensive bibliographies appended to any major history of the period.
Thus, C.A. Macartney's *The Habsburg Empire* (London, 1968), which
remains the best study in English of the 1790–1918 period, cites some
700 works in what is described as 'only a highly selective short list'.
A.J.P. Taylor's much overrated *The Habsburg Monarchy* is summed up
in that list with the one-word verdict 'Individual'.

The German scholar will find a list approaching 900 (though again
referred to as 'short and selective') at the end of the late Friedrich Heer's
Der Kampf um die Österreichische Identität (Vienna, 1981). I mention
this work because, so far as I am aware, it is the only book apart from
mine which has concentrated, though in non-narrative style, on the
Austrian struggle for self expression down the centuries. I could certainly add to both bibliographies if I listed all the books in various
languages I have read on Austria, Germany, the Danube Basin and
the Balkans in war, peace and peace-making over the past fifty years.
Moreover, I could fill the best part of a page on my own if I cited all
the articles as well as books, lecture texts and contributions to joint
studies I have written over the same period. That would be a ludicrous
exercise in self-indulgence.

Accordingly, I only intend to mention, apart from the best general
studies, a few works which, because of their highly compressed and
detailed nature, have thrown fresh light, especially on post-Habsburg
Austria. Apart from Brigitte Hamann's book on Archduke Rudolf
(Vienna, 1978), nothing much that is new about the Monarchy has
surfaced in recent years, or is likely to in the future. Memoirs have long

since been exhausted and so, apart from the fascinating Habsburg family papers, have the archives. There is, however, some new military material in Manfried Rauchensteiner's excellent study of Austria-Hungary during the First World War (Graz, 1993). An English translation of this would not come amiss.

It is a different matter as regards source material with the story of the two Austrian Republics and the eras of Nazism, war and four-power occupation sandwiched in between. Otto Bauer's book on *The Austrian Revolution* (Vienna, 1923) remains essential reading for the birth pangs of the First Republic, however misleading the title. (There *was* no revolution in Vienna, as opposed to in Budapest, when the Monarchy broke up and Bauer himself proved a revolutionary only in words.) The best general history of that Republic is the composite work edited by Heinrich Benedikt which appeared in Vienna in 1954, and has not been translated. (Again, hundreds of source books are listed, nearly all in German.) Andic's *Der Staat den keiner wollte* (Vienna, 1962) is well-researched despite its journalistic presentation but also exists only in German.

One of the relatively few special studies translated into English is Kindermann's *Hitler's Defeat in Austria* (London, 1988), dealing with the failure of the Nazi *putsch* attempt of July 1934 which cost Chancellor Dollfuss his life. Ulrich Eichstädt, *Von Dollfuss zu Hitler* (Wiesbaden, 1955), is an exhaustive and objective study of the 1933–38 period, while Gerhard Botz produced (Vienna, 1980) an even more detailed book of over 600 pages concentrating entirely on Austria from 1938 to 1939 (the outbreak of war). So far as I am aware, both of these mammoth products exist only in German. The best source book on confused Austrian attitudes during the *Anschluss* crisis itself remains the 700-page protocol of the Guido Schmidt treason trial (Vienna, 1947).

There is a better language balance as regards special studies on Austria, both under the Third Reich and as a resurrected Republic after 1945. Thus, one of the very best books on Austrian history from 1938 to 1945 is Radomír Luža's *Austro–German Relations in the Anschluss Era* (Princeton, 1975). Its footnotes alone are a gold-mine of statistical information and the thirty-page bibliography cites several non-German books and articles covering this period. Robert Keyserlink's *Austria in World War II* (Montreal, 1988) throws much new light on the development of Anglo–American attitudes towards Austria during the Allied struggle against the Third Reich, of which it was a part. William

Bader's *Austria Between East and West* (Stanford, 1966) describes the significance the country had for both rival camps during the first decade of the Cold War. Karl Stadler's *Austria* (London, 1971) is an excellent general account, though inevitably circumscribed by being part of a set series, 'Nations of the Modern World'.

More important, to return to the German source material, is the study by the same author of Austria between 1938 and 1945 as depicted in Nazi police archives (Vienna, 1966). Like the excellent composite work on the Second Republic published by Erika Wienzierl and Kurt Skalnik in Vienna in 1972, this has no English translation. The same is true of Eva-Marie Csáky's exhaustive selection of Austrian foreign policy documents from 1945–55 (Vienna, 1980) and of the papers read at Austria's very first symposium on the de-Nazification problem, which was not held until March 1985 in Vienna's Institute of Art and Science. The very useful short study by Gerald Stourzh on the diplomatic struggle for an Austrian State Treaty (Vienna, 1975) also falls in the German-only category.

Only one work on the modest but in some ways remarkable efforts at Austrian resistance has been translated into English, but it is probably the most informative: *Fires in the Night* by Fritz Molden (San Francisco and London, 1989). The same cannot be said of the one book in English on the Waldheim affair, *Waldheim and Austria* by Richard Bassett (London, 1988). This is a rather scrappy affair with no new information and no contribution from the principal actor in the saga.

All in all, Austria's history is a difficult area for the non-German scholar to pursue. It is hoped that the present work will fill some of the gaps.

INDEX